Pathways to Complexity

Maya Studies

UNIVERSITY PRESS OF FLORIDA

Florida A&M University, Tallahassee
Florida Atlantic University, Boca Raton
Florida Gulf Coast University, Ft. Myers
Florida International University, Miami
Florida State University, Tallahassee
New College of Florida, Sarasota
University of Central Florida, Orlando
University of Florida, Gainesville
University of North Florida, Jacksonville
University of South Florida, Tampa
University of West Florida, Pensacola

PATHWAYS TO COMPLEXITY

A View from the Maya Lowlands

Edited by M. Kathryn Brown
and George J. Bey III

Foreword by Arlen F. Chase and Diane Z. Chase

To Jay and Julie Lindsey with special thanks for your friendship, support, advice and appreciation of all things Maya !

George

4.26.18

University Press of Florida
Gainesville · Tallahassee · Tampa · Boca Raton
Pensacola · Orlando · Miami · Jacksonville · Ft. Myers · Sarasota

Library of Congress Cataloging-in-Publication Data
Names: Brown, M. Kathryn, 1965– editor. | Bey, George J., editor. | Chase,
    Arlen F. (Arlen Frank), 1953– author of foreword. | Chase, Diane Z.,
    author of foreword.
Title: Pathways to complexity : a view from the Maya lowlands / edited by M.
    Kathryn Brown and George J. Bey III ; foreword by Arlen F. Chase and Diane
    Z. Chase.
Other titles: Maya studies.
Description: Gainesville : University Press of Florida, 2018. | Series: Maya
    studies | Includes bibliographical references and index.
Identifiers: LCCN 2017030477 | ISBN 9780813054841 (cloth : alk. paper)
Subjects: LCSH: Mayas—Antiquities. | Mayas—History. | Indians of
    Mexico—Antiquities.
Classification: LCC F1435 .P376 2018 | DDC 972/.6—dc23
LC record available at https://lccn.loc.gov/2017030477

The University Press of Florida is the scholarly publishing agency for the State University System of Florida, comprising Florida A&M University, Florida Atlantic University, Florida Gulf Coast University, Florida International University, Florida State University, New College of Florida, University of Central Florida, University of Florida, University of North Florida, University of South Florida, and University of West Florida.

University Press of Florida
15 Northwest 15th Street
Gainesville, FL 32611-2079
http://upress.ufl.edu

CONTENTS

FIGURES

TABLES

FOREWORD

Pathways to Complexity brings together a host of original archaeological research on the Preclassic period Maya and on the development of their civilization in both the northern and southern lowlands. As Kathryn Brown and George Bey demonstrate in their opening chapter, it is both a fitting and a needed follow-up to the original consideration of this topic that took place at the School of American Research and resulted in a 1977 volume edited by R. E. W. Adams entitled *Origins of Maya Civilization*. The contributions in *Pathways to Complexity* serve notice as to how far our discipline has advanced in our understanding of the rise of complexity within the Maya archaeological record.

Intrigue surrounding the origin and development of Maya civilization dates back to initial discovery of the massive ruined buildings and temples in the jungles of Central America. Initial concerns focused on where such a people could have come from and on how a civilization could have arisen in a tropical environment. From the onset of research on the ancient Maya, there was speculation over whether or not their civilization was of local origin, derived from other parts of the New World, had been introduced from the Old World, or even was related to mythical Atlantis. Focused research in the Maya lowlands began in the early twentieth century with an initial effort to investigate early remains. In the 1920s Sylvanus G. Morley used the long-count dates on Maya stone monuments to identify Uaxactun, Guatemala as the earliest dated site in the Maya area; an excavation by George Vaillant in 1928 in the E-Group at Uaxactun succeeded in locating the first stratigraphically early artifactual materials that were viewed as underpinning the later spectacular developments attributed to the Classic Maya.

In spite of intense interest on the development of ancient Maya civilization, archaeological data relating to earlier time periods were often elusive. Preclassic remains were often deeply buried beneath subsequent constructions, and sampling strategies rarely recovered significant amounts of early materials. While the expectation was that farming villages led to more hierarchical political forms, when and how such a transition occurred could not be answered. Excavation data from Tikal, Guatemala, suggested that this transition may have started in the later part of the Late Preclassic period (300 B.C.–A.D. 300), but subsequent research has pushed this transition point much earlier in time. Archaeological investigation undertaken in the 1970s, 1980s, and 1990s added substantially to our Preclassic period Maya database, especially in the southern lowlands. Ceramic and architectural remains recovered in both northern and central Belize indicated complex developments that could be dated to between 1050 and 850 B.C. Additionally, the massive Preclassic city of Mirador was identified and investigated in northern Guatemala, suggesting that the Maya had transitioned to more complex forms of political and ritual organization by the beginning of the Late Preclassic period.

The last two decades have seen an explosion of work on the Preclassic Maya with the identification of multiple early ceramic complexes throughout the southern lowlands, the retrieval of similarly early ceramic materials from the northern lowlands, the recognition of widespread Preclassic architectural forms throughout the lowlands, and research designs specifically focused on the excavation of early Maya remains. The amount of investigation undertaken on the Preclassic period in the northern Maya lowlands has been significant and five chapters in this book relate to this geographical area, presenting a needed counterbalance to the previously dominant southern lowland data. Additionally, recovered archaeological data from throughout the lowlands strongly suggest that the Middle Preclassic period (900–600 B.C.) witnessed significant transformations of the Maya into complex entities characterized by sizeable architectural constructions, standardized religious organization, and perhaps even the advent of rulership. The chapters within *Pathways to Complexity* present a cumulative synthesis of new Preclassic data from throughout the Maya lowlands and should become a long-standing reference work for researchers interested in complex societies and development of Maya civilization.

Arlen F. Chase and Diane Z. Chase
Series Editors

1

Introduction

M. KATHRYN BROWN AND GEORGE J. BEY III

The idea for this volume came about through numerous discussions between the two editors about the lack of communication between the archaeologists working in the northern Maya lowlands and archaeologists working in the central and southern Maya lowlands. Organized symposiums focusing on the Preclassic were oftentimes regionally focused as well, and very little "cross-pollination" occurred between archaeologists working in Mexico and archaeologists working in Guatemala and Belize. This was the impetus for the organization of a symposium entitled "Pathways to Complexity in the Maya Lowlands" at the 2004 American Anthropological Association. In this symposium, participants presented new and exciting data that pushed back the established timelines for the rise of complexity in the Maya lowlands. We were both excited and pleased to see the engagement of the participants with the subject matter and conversations related to different trajectories in different regions. This edited volume slowly evolved from this initial interaction as we expanded the list of contributors to include researchers from different regions who were actively collecting new data on the Preclassic time period. In fact, much of the data included in this volume had not been documented at the time of our 2004 symposium. We feel that this volume serves as an important step forward in Maya studies as there has been only one previous collection of edited papers dedicated solely to this subject, R. E. W. Adam's 1977 *Origins of Maya Civilization*. Several edited volumes have addressed the issues of the origins of complexity in Mesoamerica (see Benson 1981; Joyce and Grove 1999; Powis 1995; Sharer and Grove 1989), and many peer-reviewed publications have addressed this topic over the years, however, the lack of edited volumes focusing wholly on the rise of social complexity in the Maya lowlands is striking. We believe the strength of this volume is the presentation of new questions, new data, and new interpretations from across the Maya lowlands in a single edited contribution. We hope that this will be the first of several volumes addressing this important subject matter.

The origin of complexity in the Maya lowlands has been a topic of study and debate since the earliest explorers set foot in the region. Many scholars have contributed to our growing knowledge about this topic. We highlight several important studies across the Maya lowlands as we briefly outline changes in our understanding of the origins of Maya civilization over the past 80 years or so.

The first intensive excavation program focusing on the origins of the ancient Maya was conducted at the site of Uaxactun, Guatemala, by the Carnegie Institution of Washington, D.C., from 1926 to 1937. Sylvanus G. Morley visited the site in 1916 and named it Uaxactun (eight stone) because of the Cycle Eight long count date deciphered on Stela 9, which was the earliest known monument at the time (Morley 1943). This site was selected as part of Morley's large-scale program of research in the Maya lowlands to better understand the origins of Maya civilization. The field program at Uaxactun established a Preclassic ceramic sequence (Mamom and Chicanel phases) based on stratigraphic excavations (Smith 1955) and uncovered Preclassic architecture including the archetype for "E" Groups (Ricketson and Ricketson 1937; Smith 1950). This important work conducted by the Carnegie Institution of Washington at Uaxactun was an essential milestone in early scholarly Preclassic research and provided a much-needed chronological framework for future studies to build upon. This and other early studies of Maya centers provided empirical contributions to our understanding of the ancient Maya. These data, however, were often interpreted within the framework of the traditional model of vacant ceremonial centers ruled by a peaceful priesthood, a model that was largely associated with J. Eric S. Thompson.

These ideas were replaced, starting in the 1960s by models that recognized Maya centers as densely populated stratified societies ruled by kings who clearly practiced warfare. These models to explain the formation of ancient Maya civilization were linked to a large extent with "new archaeology" or processual archaeology, and evolutionary models, leading to consideration of such factors as population pressure, environmental degradation, and conflict in state formation processes. A pioneering volume, *Origins of Maya Civilizations,* edited by R. E. W. Adams, was the first truly comprehensive work dedicated to this important topic. This volume was the first attempt to synthesize the archaeological data from across the lowlands.

Looking back at the 1977 landmark volume *The Origins of Maya Civilization* provides a benchmark for establishing the progress that has been made in addressing questions related to the rise of complexity in the Maya area in the past three to four decades. *The Origins of Maya Civilization*, the published results of a seminar held at the School of American Research in Santa Fe, was dedicated to producing a model to explain the "appearance of Maya civilization" (Adams and Culbert 1977:3). *Origins* provided a survey of the earliest regional expressions of Maya culture while trying to elucidate the processes that resulted in Classic Maya civilization. The introduction by Adams and Culbert and the synthetic final chapter by Willey provide much of the results of the various authors. What stands out is how these Mayanists were straddling the cultural history world of their upbringing with the arrival of processual archaeology. There was a strong interest in defining civilization and when we would know it happened, but at the time, this was still primarily a trait list. Civilization was defined by its architecture, art style, writing and calendrics, burials, and urban centers. Temples used for "kinship unit-ritual centers" and burial sites for "apotheosized ancestors," palaces and ballcourts were primary architectural units thought to mark Maya civilization as were dense urban populations (Adams and Culbert 1977:5). These characteristics were seen to reflect a society that was based on a pyramidal social structure headed by hereditary elites who ruled over both craft and occupational specialists and a large agricultural population.

Two other salient points regarding our understanding of the origins of Maya civilization in the 1970s were a heavy emphasis on the southern lowlands and a focus on the Late Preclassic period (300 B.C.–A.D. 300). Only one chapter in *Origins* was focused on the northern lowlands and it was clear that the Maya archaeologists at that time thought the origins of social complexity in the Maya lowlands were to be found during the Late Preclassic. This geographical bias in the study of the Preclassic in Maya archaeology persists until today. In fact, that is one of the major contributions of the present volume, an attempt to provide for the first time a balanced view of the development of social complexity in the Maya area.

However, as this volume also attests, the last 15 years has witnessed an explosion of new information that pushes back the origins of social complexity into the Middle Preclassic. The same could be said in 1977 for the Late Preclassic since at that time most of the evidence for social complexity had been published within the last twenty years. *Origins* offered an excellent presentation of the data from those discoveries and we can only hope our volume does the same 40 years hence. Whereas in 1977 the Late

Preclassic was thought to provide the basis by which archaeologists could explain the rise and nature of Classic Maya culture, it now appears evident to us that any discussion of the development of social complexity must be focused on the Middle Preclassic. In terms of theory, despite the interest in processual thinking, the participants in the 1977 volume were apparently quite comfortable with Adams and Culbert's (1977:12) statement: "By and large . . . present theories are not new but rather variations on the Carnegie set of themes." Mayanists at that time were looking to the 1920s–1950s for their primary set of ideas, modifying them with their newly found data and approaches. For the most part these early "theories" consisted of determining where the traits composing Maya civilization came from with the underlying assumption that most of them came from somewhere else. In 1977 this had morphed into several new versions such as the "Protoclassic theory" which sought to explain the origins of at least part of Maya civilization as "deriving from non-Maya central America" (Adams and Culbert 1977:13). Although what traits, their origins, and the timing varied among the archaeologists in the new "Multi-institutional Period," the majority still argued that Maya civilization was built upon borrowing versus in situ development.

New processual ideas being considered in 1977 to help explain why social complexity developed in the forests of the Maya lowlands during the Late Preclassic attempted to bring the old ideas and new data in line with ecological, demographic, conflict, exchange, and ideological models of causation. Ideology played a much less central role in 1977 than it does today; as Willey noted it was largely considered epiphenomenal in the development of social complexity in the Maya lowlands (if for no other reason than there was a dearth of ideological data from these early times). External stimuli however remained a central idea for the development of lowland social complexity. Other issues grappled with by the authors were related to social complexity in general and whether the Maya ever made the transition from chiefdom to state as well as to how to fit the emerging new data on Maya settlements into models of urbanism.

At the end of the introduction of *Origins,* Adams and Culbert offer what the School for Advanced Research (SAR) participants agreed were the most significant features and aspects to consider in discussing the rise of Maya civilization. It is interesting to note them and see how far we have come—or have not come—in both answering/readjusting these questions or developing alternative ones. We return to several of these questions in the final chapter of this volume and examine them in light of new data presented in the following chapters. They include:

a. The source and mechanism for the arrival of people into the Maya lowlands
b. What these original populations looked like upon initial arrival
c. How fast these populations grew after their arrival
d. When does social complexity appear and how did growth vary across time and space
e. What do we mean by civilization, particularly as regards elite versus nonelite culture
f. What was the nature of Maya civilization by the Late Preclassic and what was the Protoclassic boundary all about.

Origins essentially set the stage and provided a framework for future studies. Since 1977, scholars have worked to refine the chronology, fill in the data gaps, and address new and in some ways, very different questions about the origins of the ancient Maya. Several great discoveries and focused research projects followed on the heels of *Origins*. Below we present several major discoveries that advanced our knowledge of the Preclassic time period.

One of the most significant research projects related to the rise of complexity in the Maya lowlands was focused on the small farming village of Cuello, Belize. As Norman Hammond aptly noted, "the development from early farming communities into such proto-urban centers needs further study" (Hammond 1999:49). Hammond and his team began investigating the site of Cuello in 1975 as part of the larger Corozal Project in order to examine the antecedents of Classic Maya civilization (Hammond, ed. 1991). Hammond's research at Cuello contributed greatly to this realm and documented the establishment and development of a small Preclassic farming village that shed light on the process of the rise of complexity in the Maya lowlands. Hammond states, "the key to this process lies in the Middle Preclassic, in the centuries before 400 B.C. and after the initial village settlement of the Maya lowlands zone: Cuello is one of the first, but undoubtedly not the last, of the sites of this crucial period to contribute to our understanding of the genesis of Maya civilization" (Hammond, ed. 1991:248). In many respects, the discoveries at Cuello opened the door for new questions about the origins of Maya civilization, pushing back the established time-line for the earliest settled villages with the discovery of the pre-Mamom ceramic phase, Swasey (Kosakowsky 1987; Pring 1979).

The extremely well-documented and fully analyzed data from the site of Cuello remains one of the richest and best understood Preclassic datasets in the lowlands. Also of great importance, investigations at the nearby site of Colha (Shafer and Hester 1983; Valdez 1987), similarly encountered pre-Mamom ceramics, designated the Bolay phase, as well as early lithic workshops, shedding light on Preclassic craft production not previously documented.

Until 1990, the Swasey ceramic phase, first documented at Cuello by Hammond and his team, was thought to be the earliest in the Maya lowlands. It was then that Andrews V (1990) made the case, which is widely recognized now, that the Swasey phase dated to the same time period as the previously established Eb and Xe ceramic complexes. These ceramic complexes were argued to represent the earliest Maya settlers and show that it was not until the Mamom complex that the northern Maya lowland region was first colonized (Andrews V 1990; Ringle 1999). More recent findings of terminal Early Preclassic/early Middle Preclassic occupation have challenged these long-held ideas. Two chapters in this volume (Sullivan et al. and Andrews V et al.) present new data that update our understanding of this early time period in the Maya lowlands.

The research at Cuello extended the established timeline of the ancient Maya back into the Preclassic period, demonstrating that settled villages were indeed present by 1000 B.C. This discovery coupled with the recognition that the very large and impressive archaeological site of El Mirador dated to the Late Preclassic greatly challenged traditional models of the day. Early archaeological investigations at El Mirador demonstrated that the site dated predominately to the Late Preclassic (Dahlin 1984; Demarest 1984; Matheny et al. 1980). The monumentality of the Late Preclassic architecture at El Mirador forced scholars to rethink the timing of the emergence of state level society in the Maya lowlands (Dahlin 1984; Matheny 1987). More recent research by Richard Hansen and his team has added significantly to our understanding of the rise of complexity in the Maya lowlands at El Mirador and neighboring centers, particularly Nakbe (see Hansen et al. Chapter 7 this volume; Hansen et al. 1998).

The first major research project focused on the Preclassic in the northern Maya lowlands was at the site of Komchen. Late Middle–Late Preclassic settlements were recognized at a number of northern lowland sites in the 1940s and '50s (Brainerd 1958; Smith 1971) and in the late 1950s and early '60s three such sites were identified near Dzibilchaltun (Andrews IV 1965 [1975]; Andrews IV and Andrews V 1980:41–58; Andrews

V 1981). It was not until Andrews's project in 1980 however that the scale and history of Preclassic occupation in the north was fully appreciated. Designed primarily as a settlement survey, the project included mapping, test pitting and some major excavation of several large platforms located in Komchen's site center. The site was found to contain significant amounts of late Middle Preclassic ceramics though the architecture, including the main platforms, and was dated primarily to the Late Preclassic. Andrews V suggested that although Komchen had evidence of Middle Preclassic occupation, the site experienced its greatest period of growth between 350 and 150 B.C. The picture that emerged from the Komchen project reinforced the model developed by the participants in the SAR volume, that is, that social complexity in the Maya lowlands was associated with the Late Preclassic. A second major outcome of the project was Andrews's detailed ceramic chronology for the Middle and Late Preclassic through Protoclassic periods: a type-variety chronology that forms the basis for all subsequent ceramic analysis in the northern Maya lowlands.

By the late 1980s, research projects such as the Ek Balam project were exploring the eastern part of the northern Maya lowlands, and here too evidence of Middle Preclassic Early Nabanche ceramics, similar to those from Komchen, were identified. As Bond-Freeman discusses in her chapter, evidence for Middle Preclassic occupations was found in several areas that were to become part of the Classic period settlement of Ek Balam, as well as in a number of sites located in the Ek Balam region.

In the 1980s and '90s with great breakthroughs in deciphering Maya epigraphy and iconography, the role of ideology in state formation became, if not paramount in our thinking, at least co-equal to other factors. The role of epigraphy and iconography is emphasized in the important discoveries by the Cerros Project, directed by David Freidel. The iconographic analysis of the symbols on the well-preserved mask façades on the famous Structure 5c-2nd were the basis for the 1988 groundbreaking article entitled "Kingship in the Late Preclassic Maya Lowlands: The Instruments of Places of Ritual Power" by David Freidel and Linda Schele. Freidel and Schele suggested that the institution of Maya kingship (*ahaw*) originated in the first century B.C. in order to accommodate "contradictions in Maya society between an ethos of egalitarianism and an actual condition of flourishing elitism brought on by successful trade and interaction between the Lowland Maya and their hierarchically organized neighbors over the course of the Preclassic era" (1988a:549). They argued that an "empirical difficulty with investigating the origins of the Late Preclassic institution of *ahaw* is the paucity of antecedent evidence pertaining to ideology because of the simplicity and ambiguity of the material symbol systems prior to the Late Preclassic transformation." They further argued (1988a:549) that as a result of the ideological transformation in Maya society, there was a rapid expansion in monumental architecture throughout the southern lowlands as well as a sudden "elaboration of the material implements of power used by rulers and other elites." Freidel and Schele essentially challenged researchers to focus their attention on the understudied Preclassic time period, to examine issues related to trade and interaction, and to uncover patterns within the material symbol systems to better understand the ideology of the Preclassic Maya and how this ideology supported and legitimized the institution of kingship.

In response to the challenge set forth by Freidel and Schele over the past quarter century or so, Maya archaeologists have made some new and important discoveries that demonstrate the antecedent material symbol systems can indeed be discerned in the archaeological record (see Brown et al. Chapter 5 this volume; Estrada-Belli 2011; Saturno et al. Chapter 13 this volume). While we feel that the broad process they outline for the establishment for the institution of kingship is quite plausible, new data presented in the following chapters allows us to refine their model in three ways: first, the roots of Maya kingship occurred much earlier; second, the development of the institution of kingship was not as rapid as they initially suggested; and third, the accompanying surge of construction was not just limited to the southern lowlands.

Several more recent projects and publications have significantly impacted our understanding of the Preclassic time period. Patricia McAnany's book *Living with the Ancestors* contributed significantly to our understanding of the role of ancestors and the importance of kinship in the rise of complexity in the Maya lowlands. In it she outlines a process by which emergent elites utilize the practice of ancestor veneration in order to both gain and legitimize power. She argues that "emergent elites appropriated the practice of ancestor veneration and converted it to an institution that cemented the transmission of political power rather than agrarian rights" (McAnany 1995:164). Her research at K'axob aided in our understanding of the dynamic Middle Preclassic time period by showing that the roots of Maya kingship began prior to the Late Preclassic.

Today many Mayanists believe that by the Late Preclassic (300 B.C. to A.D. 3000), polities like El Mirador were state level polities. Monumental temple complexes at El Mirador, like the more than 70 m high Danta Complex, show the ability of its rulers to mobilize and direct the labor of thousands of subjects. Although no royal tombs have been found at El Mirador to date, with further investigations, this is highly likely. Causeways extend out to sites that were once likely autonomous, and appear to have come under the authority of El Mirador (see Hansen et al. Chapter 7 this volume).

Warfare and conflict can be inferred for the Preclassic period by defensive features at several sites including Becan (Webster 1976) and possibly El Mirador. Evidence from Blackman Eddy in Belize suggests that warfare in the form of raiding and destruction of ceremonial buildings occured as early as the Middle Preclassic (Brown and Garber 2003). Preclassic carved monuments that seemingly depict early rulers have been found at a number of sites including Nakbe, El Mirador, Cahal Pech, Cival, Actuncan, and Loltun Cave. Additionally, the discovery of the San Bartolo murals, by William Saturno, provides further evidence that the institution of kingship was firmly in place by the Late Preclassic. The painted murals depict a royal inauguration scene accompanied by a hieroglyphic text that includes an early glyph for *ajaw*, the title for king (Saturno et al. 2005; Saturno et al. 2006).

A recent book by Francisco Estrada-Belli entitled *The First Maya Civilization* provides an excellent synthesis of early site-planning patterns and the development of monumental architecture in the Preclassic at the well-documented site of Cival, Guatemala. This scholarly work emphasizes new theoretical trends in Maya archaeology as they are applied to the rise of complexity. Grounded in a historical perspective, he suggests that place-making had an important role in the development of Maya civilization. As Estrada-Belli (2011:142) states, "the narratives of Preclassic ceremonial centers are in most respects echoed by the royal narratives of the Classic period, thereby underscoring both the continuity and transformations of Maya civilization through time." Most recently Takeshi Inomata and his team (Inomata et al. 2013) presented an examination of their work at the site of Ceibal, another site founded in the early Middle Preclassic (ca. 1000 B.C.). In this important article, the authors offer further insight into the social processes associated with early Middle Preclassic place-making. Ceibal's early earthen architecture and ritual deposits link it to the Grivalja Basin in Chiapas, including an E-Group architectural assemblage. The Ceibal data, including a fine-grained ceramic sequence of pre-Mamom pottery, suggest that the site's development was demographically dynamic right from the start. Many of the chapters in this volume echo these new

Preclassic discoveries and emphasize the importance of place-making in the early Middle Preclassic.

Recent Preclassic data from across the lowlands are forcing us to re-examine and update traditional models of Maya state formation. With widespread evidence of large ceremonial architecture beginning in the late Middle Preclassic, established settlement hierarchies, warfare, and the formation of the institution of kingship by the Late Preclassic or possibly earlier, it is time that we take a close look at these developments in different regions across the lowlands in order to understand the pathways to complexity that culminated in the state among the ancient Maya. It is our hope that this edited volume is a step in this direction.

The contributors to this volume represent a diverse mix of scholars at different stages of their careers and from several countries including Belize, Canada, Guatemala, Mexico, and the United States. The participants approach the topic of the rise of complexity from a variety of theoretical perspectives and were asked to emphasize the empirical data from their recent research. This compilation of empirical data forms the basis for new interpretations about the timing and avenues of complexity throughout the Maya lowlands (Figure 1.1). The volume is organized in a manner to emphasize changes through time across the Maya lowlands.

Following this introductory chapter, Andrews and Robles (Chapter 2) present a synthesis of the Paleo-American and Archaic periods throughout the Maya lowlands. This is the most poorly known era of the prehistory of the Maya area, and their chapter provides an important synthesis of the scattered data for this period, highlighting new finds in the northern Maya lowlands. Some of the ecological adaptations and horticultural traditions that began during this era would later serve as building blocks in the agricultural lifeways that allowed for the production of surplus crops, which in turn fueled the development of social inequalities during the Middle Preclassic period. There is an ongoing debate about whether the region's inhabitants during the Archaic period were the ancestors of later Maya peoples. Sullivan, Awe, and Brown (Chapter 3) address this debate through the examination of the earliest pottery and settled villages (Cunil phase ca. 1100 to 900 B.C.) in the Maya lowlands, located in the Belize River valley. Although more data is necessary to fully understand this transitional period in Maya prehistory, they suggest that the Cunil culture likely developed from an earlier local Preceramic tradition with influences that were derived from interaction beyond the regional level. New evidence from the northern Maya lowlands suggests that by the beginning of the early Middle

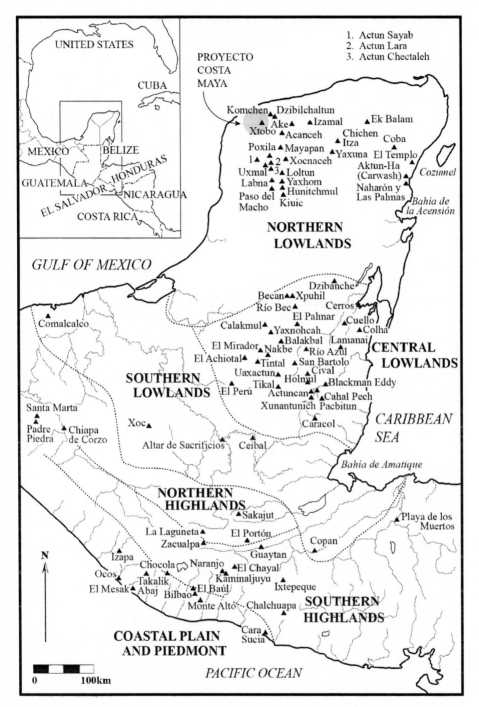

Figure 1.1. Map of the Maya area showing Preclassic sites (after Sharer and Traxler 2006).

Preclassic, there were ceramic-producing populations settled at sites such as Kiuic and Komchen. Andrews, Bey, and Gunn (Chapter 4) present the first evidence in the north for pre-Mamom ceramics and masonry platform construction, possibly dating as early as 900 B.C. Their conclusions are based on a restudy of material from Komchen and recent excavations at the Puuc site of Kiuic. They argue that the pre-Mamom Ek-phase assemblages from these and other northern sites are characterized by a consistent set of post-slipped incised patterns and motifs. Some of the motifs likely possessed symbolic content, and many of them are comparable to early Middle Preclassic motifs in the southern lowlands. Ek-phase masonry platforms at Komchen dated to before 800 B.C. form the first known evidence of a public, administrative, and ritual center in the northern Maya lowlands.

In Chapter 5, Brown, Awe, and Garber examine the role of ritual in the rise of complexity in the Belize River valley. They compare developmental sequences of Preclassic public architecture and associated ritual deposits from the sites of Blackman Eddy, Cahal Pech, and Xunantunich, and identify patterns that reflect the adoption of new ideological concepts to legitimize the role of emerging elites within the Belize River valley. They use a diachronic approach which reveals that emerging elites were using a variety of mediums to transmit ideologically related messages pertaining to the social order. The following chapter by Hohmann, Powis, and Healy (Chapter 6) provides an in-depth examination of craft production in the Middle Preclassic, more specifically, marine shell ornaments. They present new evidence for crafting and argue that emerging elites produced shell ornaments for ritual display and exchange, increasing their power and prestige within the community.

Hansen, Forsyth, Woods, Schreiner, and Titmus examine the rise of complexity in the Mirador region, Guatemala in Chapter 7. The Mirador Basin Project emphasizes multidisciplinary research and examines a number of large Preclassic centers including the massive Late Preclassic site of El Mirador. This chapter presents a thorough synthesis of data collected in the Mirador region and sheds new light on the origins and development of Maya civilization. Hansen and his coauthors highlight the importance of employing experimental archaeological methods in order to better understand the energetics of the Maya.

Anderson, Robles, and Andrews (Chapter 8) present and interpret data from three recent projects in the northwest corner of Yucatan. The Proyecto Costa Maya survey identified 140 new Preclassic sites and the

Proyecto Salvamento Arqueológico Ciudad Caucel found 1500 additional structures, the majority with Preclassic occupation in the area northwest of Mérida. Their analysis identifies a three-tiered settlement hierarchy during the late Middle Preclassic and Late Preclassic with Xtobo and Komchen at the top. These sites include 24 Middle Preclassic ballcourts, most of them associated with nonelite contexts. The new data presented in this chapter as well as the other chapters focusing on the northern Maya lowlands suggest a rethinking of the traditional paradigm for settlement and development in this region.

As the title suggests, the chapter by Robles and Ceballos (Chapter 9) not only provides a synthesis of much of the new data on the Middle Preclassic in the northern Maya lowlands but also argues for the in situ rise of social complexity in the northwestern part of the peninsula. Within the context of a detailed discussion on the early architecture and ceramics of the region they argue that "since the earliest of times the Northwestern region of Yucatan also played a primary and parallel role to that of El Petén's during the gestational period of Maya civilization, moreover, it developed within a set of regionally interacting diverse settlements that for the most part emulated each other and not the southern lowlands."

The contribution by Bond-Freeman (Chapter 10) provides us with an important look at the Middle and Late Preclassic in the northeast part of the Yucatan peninsula. Ek Balam was one of the most important Maya centers in the northern lowlands during the Late and Terminal Classic periods; however, Bond-Freeman shows that this site began its history in the Middle Preclassic. Her work examines ceramic and architectural evidence for Preclassic activity from the 3.3 sq km of the site that has been mapped. Bond-Freeman not only traces the development of Ek Balam from the Middle through the Late Preclassic but also identifies pairs of platforms that may be very early examples of domestic/ceremonial architectural units characterized by variation in ceramic use.

Gallareta's contribution on Xocnaceh (Chapter 11) expands on the chapter by Robles and Ceballos related to the northern Maya lowlands. It focuses on the site of Xocnaceh, one of the largest and most impressive late Middle Preclassic sites yet studied in this region with its main acropolis having a basal platform with a volume of over 100,000 m^3. Gallareta's chapter provides us with a detailed analysis of the evolution of the acropolis based on extensive stratigraphic excavations. It provides evidence of the dynamic change in the nature and scale of northern Maya lowland monumental architecture over the course of the Middle Preclassic. It also helps us understand how soils and water access played major roles in the early development of Xocnaceh and other sites in the Puuc region.

In Chapter 12, Acuña presents new data from the site of El Achiotal, a frontier site located on the western edge of the Mirador region in Guatemala. Although El Achiotal is relatively small, it provides an interesting contrast to other Preclassic sites in the broader Mirador region and in the southern lowlands in general. Recent work at the site revealed that the site was oriented north/south, an unusual site plan for Preclassic Maya centers. Additionally, El Achiotal does not appear to have an E-Group. The architectural arrangement and artistic styles found at the site deviate from other Late Preclassic sites. The new data from this understudied area of the Maya lowlands has great implications for a larger interregional communication network, with possible ties to the Gulf coast.

The lowland Maya site of San Bartolo is famous for the well-preserved and elaborate Preclassic murals that are displayed on architecture. In their chapter, Saturno, Rossi, and Beltrán (Chapter 13) present a developmental sequence of the Preclassic ceremonial architecture from the site emphasizing how ceremonial architecture was used to display ideological concepts that supported and reinforced the institution of kingship. Ballcourts, E-Groups, and triadic complexes are characteristic of Preclassic ceremonial architecture in the Maya lowlands. Saturno et al. examine the establishment and use of these architectural forms at San Bartolo over the last four centuries of the Preclassic.

Barbara Arroyo (Chapter 14) provides us with a comparative view of Preclassic ritual activities from the Maya highlands. She presents current research at the Middle Preclassic site of Naranjo, located on the outskirts of Guatemala City and details the site plan as well as the placement of monuments at the site. She provides a compelling argument that the highland site of Naranjo was a ritual pilgrimage center in the Middle Preclassic that was abandoned around 400 B.C. The abandonment of this ritual center is indicative of political changes in the region. A pattern of Late Classic revisitation and ritual pilgrimage activities was documented at the site and has parallels to patterns of ritual re-use of Preclassic sacred places we see in the Maya lowlands.

In a fitting final chapter before our conclusions, David Freidel (Chapter 15) presents a new synthesis of lowland Maya political history, focusing on what he suggests are three episodes of regional hegemony or empire. His chapter connects many of the ideas discussed in the volume with the subsequent transformations of Maya society in the Late Preclassic and Classic periods. The earliest period of hegemony he discusses emerges in the later part of the Middle Preclassic and is centered at the site of El Mirador. He emphasizes the importance of a commodity-driven economy in the origins of Maya kingship, building on William Rathje's work while also exploring the idea that Preclassic kingship developed more directly out of shamanic orders than lineage patriarchies and matriarchies. This chapter presents new data from the Classic period while emphasizing the deeply rooted ideological concepts and political foundations established in the Preclassic. Freidel challenges scholars to look at Maya history in new and interesting ways.

In the final chapter of the volume, the editors highlight the new data presented in the previous chapters and provide a synthesis that examines the diachronic, social, and political changes that occurred in the Preclassic. This chapter emphasizes the need to look closely at the changes that occurred during the Middle Preclassic period, a period of dynamic change and transition. This chapter brings together the empirical data presented in the volume and recent Preclassic findings from across the Maya lowlands to provide an updated understanding of development of ancient Maya civilization.

Acknowledgments

We are most appreciative of the participants of this volume for their excellent contributions to this book and for their dedication to the field of archaeology. It has been both an honor and pleasure to work with such a professional group of scholars. We are grateful to University Press of Florida and their staff for all their hard work on this volume, most especially Meredith Babb. We also thank our copy editor Helen Myers. We appreciate the insightful reviewer comments by Arthur Demarest and one anonymous reviewer. Additionally, we would like to thank Bernadette Cap, Leah McCurdy, and Thomas Chapman for their assistance with the volume. David Anderson deserves recognition for his help with translations. We are also grateful for the support from the University of Texas at San Antonio. Finally, we would like to thank our families for their support of this book project, Jason and J. C. Yaeger; and Sheryl, Patrick, George IV, and Bridget Bey.

2

The Paleo-American and Archaic Periods in Yucatan

ANTHONY P. ANDREWS AND FERNANDO ROBLES CASTELLANOS

Current data indicate that the arrival of the first humans in Yucatan likely occurred in the late Pleistocene, but the evidence of their presence is limited. Evidence of human activities during the Archaic period is also scarce. In order to place these data in proper context we review the archaeological evidence for an early human presence elsewhere in the Maya area and neighboring regions and examine the investigations of preceramic sites in the northern lowlands conducted to date.

Early travelers of the Ice Age, or Pleistocene, migrated from northeast Asia to northwest America by 13,000 B.C.,[1] or likely even earlier. Some estimates now raise the possibility that they may have arrived in North America as early as 16,000 or even 20,000 B.C. These early migrants, known as Paleo-Americans in the New World, left few traces, but remains of their camps have been found from Alaska to the southern tip of South America. They had clearly passed through the highlands of Central Mexico and Central America by 11,000 B.C., and had reached Monte Verde in Chile by 10,500 B.C., and Tierra del Fuego shortly afterward. There are a number of early sites in Central Mexico, dating between 8000 and 11,000 B.C., and a few that may date even earlier.[2] However, traces of a Paleo-American presence in the Maya area are scarce.

Maya Highlands and Pacific Coast

Evidence of an early human presence has been documented in the highlands of Guatemala, Chiapas, and Honduras, as well as Belize, where a number of sites with Paleo-American occupations have been reported.

These sites are most likely seasonal camps. The bulk of materials recovered from these sites consist of stone tool artifacts, with a variety of simple bifacial and unifacial tools, points, scrapers, cleavers, burins, gravers, blades, cores, and retouched flakes. These tools were manufactured from basalt, chalcedony, quartzite, and obsidian. The collections also include several fluted spear points, used in large game hunting.[3] Many of these are similar to the Clovis points reported from Paleo-American sites from other regions of North America, and a couple resemble the "fish-tail" types more commonly found in South America. The largest concentration of sites in the Maya area have been reported in the Quiche Basin of highland Guatemala; the best documented is that of Los Tapiales, which has been radiocarbon dated to approximately 8700 B.C.[4] Two other sites in highland Chiapas, of similar date, include Los Grifos Cave and Aguacatenango.[5] More recently, another Paleo-American site has been reported at the El Gigante Rock Shelter in the highlands of southern Honduras; it has an early radiocarbon date of approximately 9200 cal B.C. (Scheffler 2001). It is evident that the Paleo-American people of this time period led a transhumant existence, moving on a seasonal basis, hunting and gathering food and foraging for other resources they needed to survive, such as the stone they used to manufacture their tools. At present, there is very little we can say about their lifestyle.

The Archaic period (traditionally dated ca. 8000–2000 B.C.) is better documented at a number of sites in the Maya highlands, as well as at sites on the Pacific coast. Archaic campsites have been reported in the Honduras highlands and the Quiche Basin—where many of the previously mentioned Paleo-American sites continued being used—and in the Chiapas highlands and Pacific coast. At many of these sites we see a continuation of the same lithic industries, but with many new types of tools, and the use of chert becomes more widespread.[6]

Also, during the latter half of this period, the Archaic inhabitants of the Maya area began experimenting with new modes of subsistence, including the intensive exploitation of coastal resources and horticulture. Pollen evidence from Lake Yojoa, in the nearby Honduras highlands, indicates that several species of plants, including maize, were being cultivated by 3000 B.C., probably as a supplement to hunting and gathering activities.[7] In the same vein, a mixed subsistence economy involving the exploitation of maritime resources, hunting, gathering, and incipient agriculture also developed along the coast of Chiapas between 5500 and 1800 B.C., and on the coast of Guatemala by at least 3500 B.C.[8]

Southern Lowlands

Paleo-American remains in the southern lowlands are rare, and for the most part, controversial. The first report of preceramic remains was made at Copan, where John Longyear (1948) encountered an undated preceramic deposit with a small crude lithic assemblage of chert and obsidian flakes, small animal bones, charcoal, and sticks and nuts. A few years later several species of Pleistocene megafauna found along the beaches of the Pasion River in the Guatemalan Peten were reported; these included late Pleistocene camel, mastodon, giant sloth, and giant armadillo. One of the sloth bones exhibited three sharp V-shaped cuts, which were interpreted to be of human origin (Shook 1951). However, this bone was never dated, nor have further studies been made of it.

Many years later, a primitive lithic assemblage was reported at Richmond Hill in northern Belize and proposed as a possible preceramic site, but was later dismissed by other researchers.[9] Still, the evidence of a Paleo-American presence in Belize has been gradually accumulating. The first definitive evidence was a fluted Clovis point from Ladyville, Belize.[10] Since then, several other North American Clovis and South American fishtail fluted points have been reported, though none are associated with absolute dates. Beyond the points, an early primitive tool assemblage has been recovered from Actun Halal, where a discoidal flaked core and a bifacially flaked cobble (a chopper?), as well as some debitage and the bones of three types of extinct fauna (bear, peccary, and horse) were all recovered from the same contexts. Once again, there are no absolute dates, but the tool types and the faunal associations suggest a Pleistocene date.[11]

While the Paleo-American presence in Belize is still poorly documented, there is widespread evidence for an Archaic occupation at a growing number of sites in the northern half of the country. During the early 1980s Richard MacNeish and several colleagues reported several archaic sites in Belize. These sites were identified primarily on the basis of surface remains, and were dated on the basis of tool type comparisons with central Mexico. Subsequent research has shown that several of these sites were not preceramic, and the lithic sequence has not held up to subsequent scrutiny.[12] However, not all of these sites have been dismissed as Archaic, and further research has shown that some do contain evidence of preceramic occupations.

Up until the late 1990s, several Late Archaic sites had been identified in northern Belize, including Colha, Cobweb Swamp, Pulltrouser Swamp, Cob, Ladyville, Lowe Ranch, and the Kelly site, which date from ca. 3500 to 1900 B.C. These sites have large quantities of chert tools, including projectile points, constricted unifaces, macroblades, and bifacial celts.[13] Pollen from Cob has revealed the presence of maize and manioc at ca. 3400–3000 B.C., and widespread evidence of maize cultivation after 2400 B.C., when there is also evidence of extensive forest disturbance (Pohl et al. 1996). At Cobweb Swamp, pollen cores indicate likely human disturbance at 6000 B.C., and evidence of maize cultivation at 2500 B.C. (Jones 1994a, 1994b). Late Archaic materials have been reported from seven additional sites in the Freshwater Creek drainage region; at Caye Coco a pit feature and posthole have been uncovered, indicating a possible residential site (Rosenswig 2001, 2004; Rosenswig and Masson 2001).

In the past decade, the number of sites with Late Archaic materials in Belize has increased dramatically. In recent publications, Jon Lohse, Jaime Awe, Cameron Griffith, Robert Rosenswig, and Fred Valdez, Jr. (2006) and Lohse (2010) have summarized and reviewed the data from a growing number of preceramic sites across northern and central Belize, almost all of them dating to the Late Archaic period. Using the chronological framework developed by Harry Iceland (1997, 2005), they have assigned all of the known Archaic sites to a Late Archaic period, dating between 3400 and 900 B.C. Iceland has further divided the Late Archaic of Belize into Early and Late Preceramic facets. The first facet, dating from 3400 to 1500 B.C., saw the beginnings of horticulture, with maize and manioc cultivation, and a lithic toolkit that included two distinctive artifacts, the Lowe and Sawmill projectile points. The former is a heavy, generalized point that may have been re-used as a knife, whereas the smaller and lighter Sawmill points are characterized by much finer pressure flaking. The second facet, from 1500 to 900 B.C., is clearly a transitional period, with widespread horticulture, increase in the number of sites, early ceramics, and the first settlements. As the appearance of ceramics and part- or full-time settlements is uneven across the region, it would appear that populations with an Archaic lifestyle with a mixed subsistence pattern of hunting and gathering, and some horticulture, accompanied by part-time settlements, may have coexisted with more permanently settled horticulturalists who produced pottery. For a more detailed discussion of the sites, lithics, dating, and other features of the Belize Archaic, the reader is referred to the above works of Iceland (1997, 2005) and Lohse et al. (2006).[14] Jon Lohse (2010) has also written a detailed critique of the radiocarbon dates of this time period, and an assessment of the archaeological visibility of the preceramic to ceramic transition, and of the problems involved in interpreting the transition.

In sum, substantive evidence of permanent settlements and early pottery do not appear until after 1200 B.C. (possibly even later; see Lohse 2010; see also Castellanos and Foias 2017) in the Maya lowlands. However, the appearance of widespread agriculture after 3000 B.C. or 2500 B.C. may indicate the presence of semipermanent or seasonal settlements at that time, or even earlier. On the nearby north coast of Honduras, the presence of permanent settlements and early ceramics has recently been dated to 1600 B.C. (Joyce and Henderson 2001).

The evidence for early agriculture in the lowlands during the Late Archaic is not all that surprising, given its presence elsewhere in Mesoamerica during this time period. In fact, evidence of deforestation around the Peten Lakes region prior to 2000 B.C. has been documented since the 1960s (Leyden 2002; Vaughn et al. 1985).

Research on the coast of Tabasco has supported the notion that full-blown agriculture had emerged in the Maya lowlands at an early date. Fieldwork conducted in the 1980s near La Venta revealed the remains of a possible early settlement (a single house structure) with coarse ceramics and a mixed subsistence economy including the exploitation of aquatic resources—shellfish, fish, and turtle—and of palm nuts, beans, and maize, between 2250 and 1750 B.C.[15] More recently, excavations and coring at San Andrés, near La Venta, have yielded fully domesticated maize dating to 5100 B.C., manioc dating to 4600 B.C., and cotton dating to 2500 B.C. The maize is the earliest reported in the Maya area, and suggests that a farming way of life may have originated in the coastal areas of the Maya lowlands. In addition to the pollen of the plant foods, the remains of fish, shellfish, dog, and manatee were also recovered, indicating that the exploitation of aquatic resources formed an important part of the economy.[16]

Taken together, the data presently available suggests that the earliest travelers entered southeastern Mesoamerica during the Paleo-American period, at some undetermined time before 8000 B.C. These first inhabitants were transhumant foragers, hunting and collecting on a seasonal basis, and all that remains are a few campsites and stone tools. They continued this lifestyle into the Early Archaic period (ca. 8000–5000 B.C.), as their numbers increased and they spread out into all the regions of the highlands and lowlands. Starting around 5000 B.C., they began experimenting with agriculture, especially in the coastal regions, where the foraging of marine resources, coupled with hunting and gathering, allowed them to invest more energy into horticulture.

By the end of the Archaic, around 2500–2000 B.C., agriculture had spread throughout much of the Maya area, possibly accompanied by the first semipermanent settlements. During the Early Preclassic, around 2000–1500 B.C., if not earlier, the first permanent farming settlements appear on the coastal plains of Tabasco, Chiapas, Guatemala, possibly El Salvador, and Honduras. The first ceramics, dating between 1850 and 1400 B.C., also appear in these coastal regions, when the inhabitants of these areas embarked on a new phase of their development.

One pattern that seems to be emerging is that we do not have a clear break between preagricultural, preceramic, nomadic Archaic foragers, and permanently settled, ceramic-producing village farmers, around 2500 B.C., as earlier scenarios suggested. It is now evident that Archaic foragers began experimenting with agriculture as early as 5000 to 2500 cal B.C. in the Maya area,[17] but continued a pattern of mixed subsistence of foraging and horticulture for a long time, in some areas past 2000 B.C. The data from Belize indicates that the late Archaic preceramic settlers of that region had a mixed foraging and incipient agricultural subsistence well past 2000 B.C., and possibly as late as 900 B.C. In sum, the appearance of the earliest permanent settlements and ceramics in the Maya area, definite evidence of the hallmarks of the Early Preclassic period, did not occur until sometime after 2000 B.C., and in the southern Maya lowlands, not until the terminal Early Preclassic or early Middle Preclassic, after 1200 cal B.C. (Cheetham 2005; see also Andrews V 2005; Lohse 2010; Lohse et al. 2006).[18]

Yucatan

In Yucatan, the earliest permanent settlements with ceramics do not appear until the early part of the Middle Preclassic period, ca. 1000–900 B.C., when several settlements with well-developed pottery appear (Andrews V and Bey 2011; Ceballos and Robles 2012; Robles and Ceballos 2003). There is little substantive evidence of a heavy human occupation prior to that time (Figure 2.1).

The search for preceramic sites on the peninsula of Yucatan has not been very successful. The first researcher to attempt to find early sites was Henry Mercer (1896), who excavated ten caves in the Puuc Hills region of Yucatan in 1895. While he was the first investigator to employ stratigraphic methods in Mexico,[19] he did not find any early human remains, but he did recover

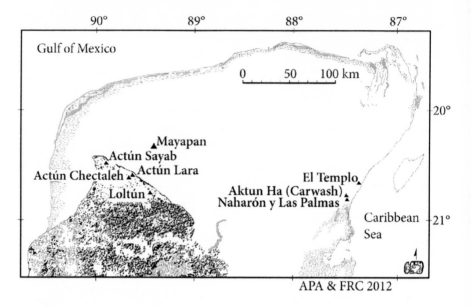

Figure 2.1. Sites in northern Yucatan with remains of the Paleo-American and Archaic periods (ca. 12000 to 1200 B.C.). The exact location of Hoyo Negro has not been published, but it is located in the same region as the caves located in the central east coast of Quintana Roo.

some horse bones and teeth, from three caves, which he classified as modern because they were associated with ceramics. However, given later finds at other caves, discussed below, these might have belonged to an extinct species.

Another potential early site was reported a few years later near Concepción, in southern Campeche. In 1900, Jorge Engerrand, a geologist with an interest in prehistory, found an extensive lithic surface scatter, likely a chert workshop, which he proposed contained "Acheulean" and "Chellean" handaxes (Engerrand 1912; Engerrand and Urbina 1909). In addition, there are a large number of other implements and debitage at the site. His identification of the handaxes as being of ancient manufacture was challenged by Federico Mulleried (1928), who found the tool types to be similar to well-known Classic-period stone tools. Engerrand was correct in identifying this locality as a workshop, for the variety of unfinished tools, retouched flakes, and large volume of debitage clearly indicates that it served such a purpose. Moreover, Mulleried was also correct in his dating, as the ample amounts of Classic-period pottery and low mounds in the vicinity of the workshop would suggest (A. P. Andrews, personal observation, 1971). There are substantial chert-bearing deposits several kilometers to the south of this locality, which would explain its raison d'être. This does not mean that it was not functioning as a workshop in preceramic times; however, there simply is, at present, no evidence to suggest that such was the case.

In 1929 and 1947 Robert T. Hatt excavated 14 caves in the Puuc region in search of faunal remains and related human materials. Like Mercer, he failed to find any evidence of early human remains or materials, though he did recover a variety of faunal remains, including several extinct species, which he considered to be of Late Pleistocene age: these included ground sloth, horse, and two species of rat (Hatt et al. 1953).[20]

The next hint of an early human occupation in northern Yucatan surfaced in the course of the 1961–62 excavation season at the Middle Preclassic Grupo El Mirador or Grupo 600 of Dzibilchaltun, which is located halfway between Mérida and the coast. Charcoal from a hearth in Structure 605 produced an uncalibrated ^{14}C date of 975 B.C.[21] Associated with Early Nabanche–phase ceramics and a group of residential structures, this date has stood as the radiometric benchmark for the earliest known Middle Preclassic occupation of the northern lowlands. However, its 1- and 2-sigma ranges cover the entire Early and Middle Preclassic spectrum, and it is considered to be too erratic to represent the beginning of the Early Nabanche phase, which has been dated to around 1000 to 600 B.C. in the traditional uncalibrated chronology. More recently, another Preclassic site to the east of Mérida, Serapio Rendón, has yielded an uncalibrated ^{14}C date of 910 B.C.,[22] from a piece of charcoal associated with Early Nabanche ceramics, which may be a better indication of the beginning of the Middle Preclassic in northern Yucatan.[23]

As it presently stands, no evidence for an Early Preclassic period has been identified in the northern Maya lowlands.[24]

The first preceramic site with definite evidence of human activity identified on the peninsula to date was found at Loltun Cave, in the Puuc region. Excavations inside the cave in 1977 and 1978, directed by the late Ricardo Velásquez at two different localities in the cave, uncovered a wealth of paleontological and archaeological materials dating from the Pleistocene to the Classic period. The Pleistocene fauna included four extinct species—mammoth (*Mammut americanum*), camel (*Tanupolama* sp.) wolf (*Canis dirus*), and horse (*Equus conversidens*)—and three other species which no longer live in the lowland Maya area: bison (*Bison bison*), wolf (*Canis lupus*) and coyote (*Canis latrans*). The stratigraphy of the excavations was complex, with one unit, "El Toro," containing 16 levels (Figure 2.2), and the other unit, "El Túnel," with 12 levels.

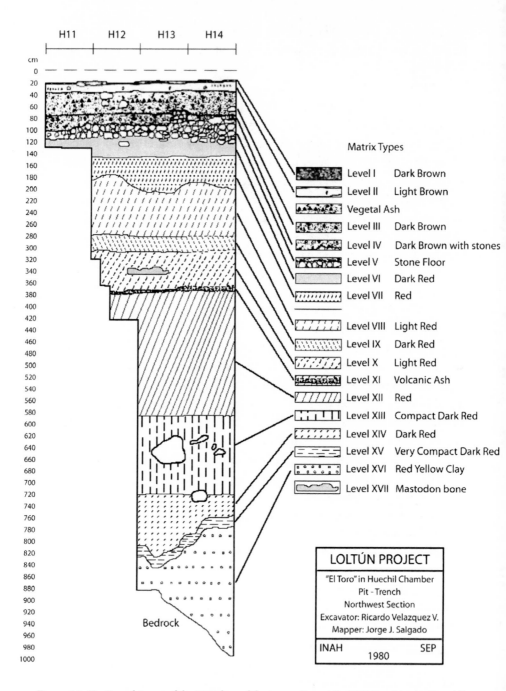

Figure 2.2. Stratigraphic cut of the NW face of the excavation unit of "El Toro" in the Huechil chamber of Loltun Cave, Yucatan. Taken and slightly modified from Alvarez (1983:12).

The critical levels that may show an association between humans and extinct fauna occur in Levels VI, VII, and VIII of El Toro, which may have disturbed stratigraphy. Levels VI and VII have Preclassic ceramics, stone tools, and the remains of extinct horse (the only extinct species associated with human materials). A few pieces of charcoal at the juncture of levels VII and VIII yielded a radiocarbon date of 1840 B.C.[25] Level VIII is the only level without ceramics, but with stone tools and horse remains. The lower levels are rich in faunal remains, but have no human artifacts. Horse remains were the most common species in the cave and were found as high as level II in El Toro. The stone artifacts from level VIII consist of 21 crude flaked tools and two core fragments. The tools, all of local and imported chert, include used and retouched flakes, scrapers, gravers, knife-gravers, denticulated tools, and one point.[26]

While seeming to present a plausible association between human artifacts and extinct Pleistocene fauna, several researchers have commented that the above association may be problematic in several respects. Peter Schmidt (1988) has outlined three of the major problems, and has expanded upon them in personal conversations with the authors, who also visited the excavations on several occasions: (1) there are no clear breaks between the levels in question, and there is a high probability of disturbance, and even of mixing; the presence of extinct horse bones into the upper ceramic-bearing layers is particularly disturbing; (2) the single radiocarbon date is late for preceramic materials, and may also be the result of mixing; and (3) the only animal associated with the preceramic artifacts is the extinct horse, suggesting that this animal survived into the Late Archaic or even Early Preclassic. To conclude, it is quite possible that Loltun may show evidence of Late Archaic human activities, but the current evidence does not endorse a Paleo-American presence, as proposed in several recent texts and surveys of the Mesoamerican Paleo-American and Archaic periods. Verification and clarification of the situation at Loltun will require further excavations and more radiometric dates.

An issue that has not been resolved is the possible association of Archaic populations with Pleistocene fauna. Several hints raise the possibility that the extinct horse may have survived into Holocene times. The most suggestive evidence of this is the association of extinct horse with preceramic lithics and ceramics at Loltun. However, this may be due to mixing. In the three caves (Sayab, Lara, and Chektaleh) where he found horse remains, Mercer assumed that because of their stratigraphic association with pottery, and the lack of fossilization, they were the remains of modern horse. On the other hand, E. D. Cope, a paleontologist who commented on the remains, raised the possibility that they might belong to an extinct species, *Equus oc-cidentalis* (Mercer 1896:172n). Hatt's horse remains were from Actun Lara, one of the caves where Mercer had also uncovered horse remains. These were partially fossilized, and have been identified as extinct horse—either *E. conversidens* or *E. tau*, which may be the same species. These were also associated with pottery, and two foot bones were associated with the bones of modern cattle (Hatt et al. 1953: 71–72; see also Ray 1957). Once again, this may have been a disturbed deposit. Contrary to widely held views, at least two species of large mammals thought to have become extinct at the end of the Pleistocene survived into the Holocene in the Old World (Stuart et al. 2004). Since the horse also survived into post-Pleistocene times in the Old World, the possibility of its survival into Archaic times in the American tropics may also need to be considered.

Since the work at Loltun there have been several reports of Paleo-American sites in underwater caves in Quintana Roo during the last 30 years. The first comes from a cenote cave near Tulum, on the central coast, originally known as "Carwash" and today as Aktun Ha. In the late 1980s divers recovered charcoal from the lower reaches of this cave, at a depth of 27 m. The charcoal, reportedly recovered from a "firepit" on the floor of the cave, yielded a radiocarbon date of 8250 B.P.[27] According to the authors, at the end of the Pleistocene the Caribbean Sea level would have been around 28 m lower than today, and thus, the cave floor might have been just above the water level. However, there are no reported artifacts associated with the charcoal or the "firepit." Thus, the evidence for a human presence is inconclusive, as the charcoal could have been produced by a natural fire.

In 2000 a team of INAH archaeologists led by Arturo González began a survey of underwater caves near the central Quintana Roo coast. This region, located between Chunyaxche (Muyil), Tulum, and Playa del Cármen, has hundreds of caves and cenotes, which have been explored by cave divers since the 1980s; the extensive underwater systems include one of the longest subterranean river caves in the world.[28] Many of these cave systems were dry and above sea level in the late Pleistocene and early Holocene, having been submerged by a eustatic sea level rise that began around 11,000 B.C., and reached current levels around 5600 B.C. (González, Rojas, Terrazas, Benavente, Stinnesbeck, Aviles, de los Ríos, and Acevez 2008; González, Rojas, Acevez, Avilés, Ramírez, Lara, Erreguerena, Morlet, Stinnesbeck, Terrazas, and Benavente 2008). The INAH team has located 11 sites with the remains of late Pleistocene fauna, and seven of these sites

have evidence of human activities, including four possible lithic tools, charcoal deposits and burnt wood in what appear to be hearths, burnt and/or
cut-marked animal bones, and in three caves, human skeletons (González,
Rojas, Terrazas, Benavente, Stinnesbeck, Aviles, de los Ríos, and Acevez
2008; González, Rojas, Acevez, Avilés, Ramírez, Lara, Erreguerena, Morlet,
Stinnesbeck, Terrazas, and Benavente 2008).

The three skeletons, located at depths of 22.6 and 23.5 m below mean
sea level (mbsl), were between 70 and 90 percent complete, and partially or
fully articulated. The first two skeletons came from the caves of Naharon
and Las Palmas, which form part of the Naranjal cave system, which is located about 4.5 km southwest of the modern town of Tulum. Direct dating
of bone from the Naharon skeleton, a 20–30 year-old woman, yielded a [14]C
date of 9720 B.C. (uncalibrated).[29] Two direct bone dates were also obtained
from the skeleton in Las Palmas cave, a 40–50 year-old woman: an AMS
date of 6100 B.C., and a Uranium-Thorium age of 8050–10,050 B.C.[30] Two
additional conventional ^{14}C dates came from charcoal in a nearby hearth,
6991 B.C. and 5790 B.C.[31] A third skeleton, that of a 25–30 year-old man,
was found in the cave of El Templo, 18 km north of Tulum. No dates were
obtained from this skeleton, owing to the poor preservation of the bone
(González, Rojas, Terrazas, Benavente, Stinnesbeck, Aviles, de los Ríos, and
Acevez 2008; González, Rojas, Acevez, Avilés, Ramírez, Lara, Erreguerena,
Morlet, Stinnesbeck, Terrazas, and Benavente 2008). Calibration of these
dates yields a total combined 2-sigma range between 11,660 and 6480 B.C.
(see notes 29–32).

As noted above, the INAH team located at least four other caves with
indirect evidence of a human presence in early contexts, in concentrations
of charcoal at depths in excess of 20 m below the surface. The evidence,
beyond the dense concentrations of charcoal, includes possible hearths, the
aforementioned possible lithic tools, fragments of partially burned wood,
and butchered or cooked extinct animal bones. One of these sites—Aktun
Ha (Carwash)—yielded radiocarbon dates ranging from 7574 to 7230 B.C.
(uncalibrated).[32]

At present, we have only preliminary reports of the material from the
INAH Quintana Roo cave survey, and detailed reports of the contexts, associations, artifacts, and ecofacts have not yet been disseminated.[33] Still, as
the authors cautiously conclude in their 2008 reports, the combined data
from all these cave sites strongly support the evidence for a human presence in Yucatan in late Pleistocene or early Holocene times.

In 2007 cave divers encountered human and faunal remains in a cenote known as Hoyo Negro, also in the Tulum region of the central coast of Quintana Roo. An international team, directed by Pilar Luna and James Chatters, was formed to investigate the site; this effort, known as the Proyecto Arqueológico Subacuático Hoyo Negro, was carried out under the direction of the Instituto Nacional de Antropología e Historia de México, with additional support from the National Geographic Society, the National Science Foundation, and several other organizations in Mexico, the United States, Canada, and Denmark. Beginning in 2014, numerous preliminary reports of the project appeared on the internet and general media (see Hodges 2014, 2015; Instituto Nacional de Antropología e Historia, Mexico 2014). In 2014 the first preliminary report in a professional journal appeared (Chatters et al. 2014). The project divers recovered a complete cranium with full dentition, and most of the post-cranial skeleton of a small gracile 15-to-16-year-old female, now known in the media as "Naia."

The human remains, as well as the remains of numerous species of fauna, were located at the bottom of a pit, at a depth of 40 to 55 meters below modern sea level. As sea level rose after 10 to 9.5 ka years ago, the remains clearly date to Late Pleistocene times. Another indication of the age of the deposits is the presence of several species of late Pleistocene fauna, including sabertooth cat (*Smilodon fatalis*), gomphothere (*Cuvieronius cf. tropicus*), two species of ground sloth (*Nothrotheriops shastensis* and an unnamed species), and bear (*Tremarctos* sp.). Most of these species had become extinct before 10 ka ago (Chatters et al. 2014).

Using a battery of dating techniques, analyzed at different laboratories, the team obtained a wide range of late Pleistocene dates for the fauna and the human remains. The human skeleton was dated to cal 10,910–9,750 B.C. (Chatters et al. 2014:752). The team also extracted a sample of DNA from a molar, and the analysis revealed that the woman belonged to an early lineage with Asiatic origins that probably developed in Beringia after splitting from other Asian groups (Chatters et al. 2014:753).

As is the case with the earlier cave survey, the available data from Hoyo Negro is preliminary, and further analysis of the materials will undoubtedly provide a broader description of these finds. Still, it is clear that the Hoyo Negro finds clearly corroborate the results reported by González and his colleagues, and, taken together, they clearly document the presence of human beings in Yucatan in the late Pleistocene.

Overview of Early Yucatecan Prehistory

The evidence of a human presence in Yucatan during Late Paleo-American and/or Early Archaic times is growing. This is not surprising, as humans had traversed the continent by 10,000 B.C., had established a presence in the Maya highlands and Belize, and would have found ample game and plant resources throughout the lowlands. While the evidence from Loltun cave is far from conclusive, the evidence from the underwater caves of the central coast of Quintana Roo for a human presence in late Pleistocene and/or early Holocene times is much more plausible. When these early foragers arrived, and what their lifestyle was like, will have to await further research.

Another likely locale for early campsites or more permanent settlements is the open coast. The coastal regions offer excellent conditions for settlement and a mixed range of resources within a relatively small area. As in other parts of the world, coastal sites of the Pleistocene, and even of the Early and Mid-Archaic, may be underwater today. The present coastlines may not have stabilized until about 3000–2000 B.C., and because the coastal plain may have extended farther out before 3000 B.C., many earlier sites may be underwater today. However, the likelihood of finding Late Archaic sites near the modern coast, on ancient beach ridges, is also possible, especially given the presence of Late Archaic sites on the coastal plain of nearby Belize.

The development of mixed maritime and foraging economies elsewhere in southern Mesoamerica—along the coasts of Veracruz, Tabasco, Belize, Honduras, and Chiapas—with the eventual early appearance of agriculture in many of those regions, is a widespread pattern that is likely to be duplicated in Yucatan. We think that it is just a matter of time before the evidence comes to light.

It is not possible at present to even attempt to set up a chronological framework for the Preceramic period of Yucatan, given the paucity of materials, sites, and dating. However, the framework proposed for Belize by Iceland (1997, 2005) and Lohse et al. (2006; Lohse 2010) might prove useful for Yucatan.

A major issue that remains unresolved is whether populations persisted from ancient times into the Preclassic period. Were the Paleo-American and Archaic inhabitants of the peninsula the ancestors of later peoples? Were the inhabitants of the Middle Preclassic in northern Yucatan colonizers from the south, or were they the descendants of the earlier Archaic foragers? Harry Iceland (2005) and Jon Lohse (2010) address this issue in light of the data from Belize and discuss the likely possibility of continuity of populations from Late Archaic into Middle Preclassic times (see also Sullivan et al. Chapter 3 this volume). However, in Yucatan, we do not have a well-defined Late Archaic. Given the present evidence, it would seem that the relatively sophisticated village farmers with slipped, decorated ceramics, who began building communities with monumental architecture in the early Middle Preclassic, appeared rather abruptly around 1000 B.C. If these were newcomers, they could have assimilated or displaced the earlier Archaic populations. Or, more likely, they may have lived side-by-side with the Archaic foragers for a period of time before assimilating them. What actually happened during these times is at present totally speculative, as we know next to nothing about the Early Preclassic period in Yucatan, so future research will likely bring major changes to the present scenario.

Acknowledgments

We would like to express our appreciation to several colleagues who provided us with unpublished information and advice: E. Wyllys Andrews V, Jaime Awe, George Bey, Kat Brown, Jon Lohse, Concepción Hernández, Mary Pohl, and Cármen Rojas Sandoval.

Notes

1. Unless indicated, all dates are traditional uncalibrated historic dates (B.C.), or dates as reported by authors (some sources often do not specify whether their dates are calibrated or not). We will attempt, to the extent possible, to present calendric dates based on calibrated ^{14}C dates in the notes. Most recent reported calendric dates are based on calibrated ^{14}C dates. Where possible, uncalibrated radiocarbon dates will be noted as such, and calibrated dates will be indicated following SAA guidelines. Calibrated dates and sigma ranges not attributed to other authors were calculated using the 2005 version of CALIB Radiocarbon Calibration Program (copyright 1986–2005 M. Stuiver and P. J. Reimer, used in conjunction with Stuiver and Reimer 1993).

2. See González et al. 2006 for a review of the evidence for a Paleo-American presence in the Valsequillo Basin, south of the city of Puebla, which includes several sites with dates before 20,000 B.C.

3. There are several reports on fluted points from the Guatemalan highlands, dating back half a century (Bray 1978a, 1980; Brown 1980; Coe 1960; Gruhn and Bryan 1977; Hayden 1980; Rovner 1980).

4. Uncalibrated. For reports on Los Tapiales and other sites in the Quiche Basin, see

Gruhn and Bryan (1976, 1977); Stross et al. (1977), and Brown (1980). Calibration of the earliest dates yields a range of 10,900 to 9300 cal B.C. (Neff et al. 2003:833).

5. The Paleo-American remains from Chiapas have been reported by Joaquín García-Bárcena (1979, 1982; also see García-Bárcena and Santamaría Estevéz 1982). Calibration of the dates from Los Grifos Cave yields an approximate date of 8500 cal B.C. (Neff et al. 2003:833).

6. For information on the Archaic of the Honduran highlands, see Bullen and Plowden (1963a, 1963b), Healy (1984), and Scheffler (2001). For the Guatemalan highlands, see Gruhn and Bryan (1976, 1977), Stross et al. (1977) and Brown (1980). The Archaic sites in highland Chiapas have been reported by Lorenzo (1961, 1977), MacNeish and Peterson (1962), García-Bárcena et al. (1976); García-Bárcena (1982), and García-Bárcena and Santamaría Estevéz (1982).

7. The recent evidence for Late Archaic incipient agriculture in the Lake Yojoa region has been documented by Rue (1989).

8. There has been extensive documentation of the Archaic period exploitation of shellfish at the Islona de Chantuto shell middens of the Chiapas Pacific coast by Drucker (1946), Lorenzo (1955), and Voorhies (1975, 1976). More recent research has revealed several new midden sites, the earliest of which dates to ca. 5500 B.C. (see Voorhies et al. 2002 and Voorhies 2004 for details on dating and subsistence at Cerros de la Conchas), and evidence of the emergence of a more complex mixed economy, involving hunting, fishing, gathering, and agriculture during the Chantuto B period, after 3000 B.C. (Blake, Chisholm, Clark, and Mudar 1992; Blake, Chisholm, Clark, Voorhies, and Love 1992; Blake et al. 1995; Clark 1994b; Michaels and Voorhies 1992; Voorhies et al. 1991; Voorhies 2004). The most recent paleobotanical research has identified *Zea mays* phytoliths dating to 3500 cal B.C. (Jones and Voorhies 2004; see also Kennett et al. 2006), thus bringing the earliest agriculture into line with other areas. For evidence regarding a late Archaic occupation of the Guatemala coast, with evidence of agriculture beginning around 3500 B.C., see Arroyo et al. (2002); Neff et al. (2003); Neff, Pearsall, Jones, Arroyo, Collins, and Freidel (2006); and Neff, Pearsall, Jones, Arroyo, and Freidel (2006).

9. The site was reported by Puleston (1975, 1976). For critiques of its status as a preceramic site, see Miller (1976), Hester (1982), and Schmidt (1988).

10. For discussions of this artifact, see Hester et al. (1981, 1982), MacNeish (1981), Kelly (1993), and Lohse et al. (2006). While there is a consensus that this is a Paleo-American fluted Clovis point, it is from an undated context; Kelly (1993:224) estimates an approximate date of 10,000 B.C.

11. See Lohse et al. (2006) for a more extensive discussion of the Paleo-American material from Belize, including several Clovis and Fishtail points; they also include references to unpublished original reports. They suggest that the Paleo-American period in Belize can be dated to 13,500–10,000 B.P., or 11,500–8000 cal B.C. Until further research indicates otherwise, this seems a reasonable chronological framework for the period in the Maya lowlands in general.

12. For reports of the Belize Archaic Archaeological Reconnaissance (BAAR) project, see MacNeish (1981, 1982), MacNeish et al. (1980), MacNeish and Nelken-Terner (1983), Zeitlin (1984), Nelken-Terner (1987, 1993), and Wilkerson (1985). For a subsequent

discussion of the Projectile typology of Belize, see Kelly (1993); Kelley's study suggests that the entire lithic inventory of the BAAR project dates between 2500 and 1900 B.C.

13. For descriptions and discussions of the dating of these materials, see Kelley (1993), Hester et al. (1996), and Iceland (1997, 2005). Similarities between some of these tools and contemporary assemblages in the Caribbean has led some scholars to posit a possible Middle American origin for the first colonizers of Cuba (Callaghan 2003; Keegan 2000; Wilson et al. 1998). Other authors have also reported possible evidence of connections between Yucatan and the Caribbean (e.g., Callaghan 2003; Coe 1957). However, others have suggested that the evidence of contacts between Middle America and the Caribbean is nonconclusive, and that while sporadic contacts may have occurred, they were likely of little cultural significance (Berlin 1940; Callaghan 2003).

14. M. Kathryn Brown et al. (2011) recently reported a Late Archaic stratigraphic level at Xunantunich with ^{14}C dates falling in the early facet of the Late Archaic.

15. All dates based on uncorrected radiocarbon dates: see Rust and Sharer (1988), Rust (1992), Rust and Leyden (1994), and Pohl et al. (1996). Full reports of this fieldwork have not yet been published, and the results remain tentative and unverified by other research (Grove 1997:73; Von Nagy et al. 2002). The earliest ceramics in the region are currently dated to ca. 1400–1200 cal B.C. (Von Nagy et al. 2002)

16. All dates based on calibrated radiocarbon dates; see Pope at al. (2001) for a detailed discussion of these finds.

17. And as early as 5000 cal B.C. in the nearby Olmec region of the Tabasco coast.

18. Pohl et al. (1996:366) report earlier ceramics in northern Belize dating to 1500–1300 B.C., but these are "rare and undiagnostic." Ceramics appear widely in that region after 900 B.C.

19. His early use of stratigraphic methods has been noted by several archaeologists, including Peter Schmidt (1988), Alfredo Barrera Rubio (1999), and Norberto González (2000).

20. Divers have recovered numerous species of extinct Pleistocene fauna from Yucatecan cenotes over the last few decades, but few have been reported in the professional literature. These include extinct species of gomphotheres, ground sloths, tapirs, horses, camelids, wolves, giant armadillos, and other mammals (see González, Rojas, Terrazas, Benavente, Stinnesbeck, Aviles, de los Ríos, and Acevez 2008; González, Rojas, Acevez, Avilés, Ramírez, Lara, Erreguerena, Morlet, Stinnesbeck, Terrazas, and Benavente 2008; Vesilind 2003). Clayton Ray (1957) reported one upper and three fragments of two lower horse molars from pre-hispanic deposits at Cenote Chen Mul at Mayapan. These were heavily mineralized, which suggests that they were collected in a fossilized state by the Maya and brought to and deposited at Mayapan.

21. 2925 ± 340 B.C. uncalibrated (Andrews IV and Andrews V 1980:282). Calibrated 1-sigma ranges are: 1607–1571 B.C., 1560–1547 B.C., and 1540–773 B.C. Calibrated 2-sigma ranges are: 2012–1999 B.C., 1978–356 B.C., 285–253 B.C., 249–234 B.C.

22. This charcoal, recovered from excavations conducted at the site by Concepción Hernández, has a radiocarbon age of 2860 ± 20 B.P., with a 1-sigma range of 1055 to 975 B.C. (68.2%), and 2-sigma ranges of 1120 to 970 B.C. (90.7%) and 960 to 930 (4.7%) B.C.]. This unpublished date was run in the laboratories of the Instituto Nacional de Antropología

e Historia, in Mexico City (Lab Code: INAH-2412), who supplied the OxCal calibration provided here (Hernandez, personal communication, 2007).

23. For a discussion of new Middle Preclassic dates from Kiuic, in the Puuc region of Yucatan, see the chapter by E. Wyllys Andrews V et al. in this volume.

24. An early ^{14}C date of 3275 ± 80 B.P. (uncalibrated, 1325 ± 80 B.C.), has been reported from Komchen in northern Yucatan. It was from charcoal obtained from preconstruction fill, " . . . a dark humus level underlying the lowest fill of the platform, which contained Ek and Early Nabanché sherds (as well as corn pollen)" (Ringle 1985:154). Given the context, the possibility that the charcoal may have been ambient, and the lack of other comparable dates, it is not presently considered a reliable date.

25. The original date reported by Velásquez (1805 B.C. ± 150; 1980:54) is erroneous. The actual date, uncalibrated, is 3790± 105 B.P., or 1840 ± 105 B.C. Calibrated 1-sigma ranges are: 2434–2421 B.C.; 2403–2379 B.C.; 2349–2123 B.C.; 2093–2042 B.C. Calibrated 2-sigma ranges are: 2549–2538 B.C.; 2490–1936 B.C. (Andrews V 1990:19, note 14).

26. Preliminary reports on the excavations at Loltun Cave were published by Velásquez (1980, 1981). The analysis of the materials was carried out by Ernesto González Licón (1986). Most of the artifacts and ecofacts have been analyzed and reported, including the lithics (Konieczna 1981), mammalian fauna (Alvarez 1983), molluscs (Polaco 1983), and pollen (Xelhuantzi-López 1986). The faunal analysis conducted by Alvarez is the most extensive ever published on early Yucatecan paleontology. Schmidt (1988) has written an extensive summary of the Loltun excavations, along with a cogent critical discussion of the problems involved with the interpretations of the finds.

27. See Coke et al. (1991) for a discussion and dating of this find. For a photograph of the "firepit," see Lockwood (1989:141). The uncalibrated date is 8250 ± 80 B.P. Calibrated 1-sigma ranges are: 7451–7407 B.C.; 7370–7173 B.C.; 7152–7145 B.C. The single calibrated 2-sigma range is 7482–7077 B.C.

28. There is an extensive literature on the exploration of these underwater cave systems. For general accounts, see the books by Michael Ray Taylor (2000) and Alfredo Medina Chemor (2008). The latter has a detailed map showing the location of many of the Quintana Roo caves (120–21).

29. The uncalibrated date is 11,670 ± 60 B.P. The single calibrated 1-sigma range is 13,610–13,430 B.P., and a 2-sigma range is 13,700–13,370 B.P. The authors note that, owing to the almost complete absence of collagen, the date may be too old (González, Rojas, Terrazas, Benavente, Stinnesbeck, Aviles, de los Ríos, and Acevez 2008:12–13, 19).

30. The uncalibrated AMS date is 8050 ± 130 B.P. A calibrated 1-sigma range is 9130–8710 B.P., a calibrated 2-sigma range is 9400–8550 B.P. (González, Rojas, Terrazas, Benavente, Stinnesbeck, Aviles, de los Ríos, and Acevez 2008:19). The Uranium-Thorium date is 10,000 to 12,000 B.P. (González, Rojas, Terrazas, Benavente, Stinnesbeck, Aviles, de los Ríos, and Acevez 2008:15,19).

31. The hearth is an area of dense charcoal concentration 15 m away from the skeleton, separated by a natural wall. The uncalibrated radiocarbon dates are 1) 8941 ± 39 B.P., with a calibrated 1-sigma range of 10,200–9940 B.P., and a 2-sigma range of 10,210–9910 B.P., and 2) 7740 B.P. ± 39, with a calibrated 1-sigma range of 8560–8450 B.P., and a 2-sigma range of 8600–8430 B.P.

32. 9524 to 9180 B.P. (uncalibrated). These dates come from a concentration of carbon that appears to be anthropogenic in origin. The calibrated three 1-sigma ranges span from 11,080 to 10,250 B.P., and the three 2-sigma ranges span from 11,150 to 10,230 B.P. See Table 1 in González, Rojas, Terrazas, Benavente, Stinnesbeck, Aviles, de los Ríos, and Acevez (2008:19) for details.

33. The discoveries of this project have been widely reported in the media and at professional conferences (among others, see Dalton 2005; Elson 2011; González et al. 2003; González and Rojas 2004). In addition, the data have been reported in internal INAH reports, and in at least two professional publications (González, Rojas, Terrazas, Benavente, Stinnesbeck, Aviles, de los Ríos, and Acevez 2008; González, Rojas, Acevez, Avilés, Ramírez, Lara, Erreguerena, Morlet, Stinnesbeck, Terrazas, and Benavente 2008). The information discussed here was taken from these later two reports.

3

The Cunil Complex

Early Villages in Belize

LAUREN A. SULLIVAN, JAIME J. AWE, AND M. KATHRYN BROWN

The adoption and introduction of pottery is one of the most significant aspects of lowland Maya development. The origin of early pottery-producing peoples in the Maya lowlands, however, is still unknown. Scholarly debate between models of indigenous development and immigration has been unresolved due to lack of stratigraphic continuity between the Preceramic period (3500–2000 B.C.) and the end of the Early Preclassic period (1200/1000 B.C). Furthermore, the timing of the transition from the Preceramic to the Preclassic remains unclear and more empirical data are necessary to shed light on this issue. Because of this, we place the end of the Early Preclassic period sometime between 1200 and 1000 B.C. (1200/1000 B.C), and the start of the early Middle Preclassic at around 1000–900 B.C. The latter broadly confirms with temporal frames applied by both previous and current researchers in the Maya lowlands (Adams and Culbert 1977:Figure 1.3; Inomata et al. 2013, 2015; Lohse et al. 2006; Lohse 2010; Sharer and Traxler 2006:155, Table 2.2; Willey et al. 1965). It is our hope that future work on this important transitional period in the Maya lowlands will allow for a more refined chronology. This chapter examines the earliest time periods in Belize, highlighting new data pertaining to the Paleoindian (11,500 to 8000 B.C.) and Archaic periods (8000–2000 B.C.) as well as a more detailed discussion of recent excavations and analysis of Cunil phase (ca. 1200 to 900 B.C.) deposits and ceramics from the Belize River valley (Figure 3.1). These new data, predominately from the site of Cahal Pech, have provided a more detailed picture of this transitional time period and the origins of early villagers in the Belize Valley. Although more data are necessary to fully understand the transitional period, present evidence suggest that late Preceramic occupation in the Belize Valley is followed by

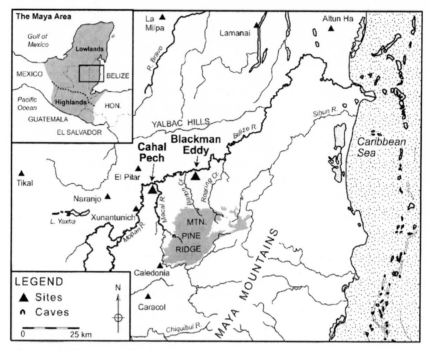

Figure 3.1. Belize River valley map.

the ceramic-producing Cunil culture and that the early ceramic tradition in the Belize Valley was likely the result of in situ development, albeit with influences that were derived from interaction beyond the regional level.

Preceramic Occupation

As recently as the mid-1970s, signs of Preceramic and early Middle Pre-classic occupation in the Maya area were infrequent and not very well understood. New discoveries including several early sites in highland Guatemala (Bray 1978a; Gruhn and Bryan 1977), a fluted point at Ladyville in Belize (Hester et al. 1981), the recovery of stone tools in association with extinct fauna at Loltun Cave in the Yucatan (Alvarez 1983), and at several Archaic sites along the coastal plains of Belize (MacNeish et al. 1980; Zeitlin 1984) all helped to firmly document early habitation of the Maya lowlands prior to 2000 B.C. (see also Andrews and Robles Chapter 2 this volume; Awe 1992). Our understanding of the Preceramic still remains limited as very few projects in Mesoamerica have been primarily focused on this period. The Preceramic sequence is best known from data recovered in the northern and central regions of Belize (Lohse 2007, 2010; Rosenswig et al. 2015), and more recently from southern Belize (Prufer et al. 2017). An intensive effort to document and record Preceramic sites in northern Belize was initiated by the Belize Archaic Archaeological Reconnaissance Project (MacNeish et al. 1980; Zeitlin 1984). Important contributions pertaining to this early time period were made by the Colha Preceramic Project's investigations of Preceramic deposits at Colha and nearby sites (Hester et al. 1996). Data collected from this project allowed researchers to define a lithic tradition (Iceland 1997) for the area that has proved useful as a general sequence for comparison to other regions of Belize (Lohse 2007). Recent work by the Belize Postclassic Project in the Freshwater Creek drainage in northern Belize has added considerably to our knowledge of the Preceramic in this region (Rosenswig 2004; Rosenswig et al. 2015). Regrettably, there are few stratified deposits during these early time periods and much of the remaining data have been compiled from surface collections or finds of single diagnostic artifacts in and out of context (Lohse et al. 2006). Recently, several researchers (Lohse et al. 2006; Lohse 2010; Stemp and Awe 2013; Stemp, Awe, and Helmke 2016; Stemp, Awe, Prufer, and Helmke 2016) have compiled much of the spotty information along with new data to provide a succinct summary of the Paleoindian and Archaic periods (see also Andrews and Robles Chapter 2 this volume).

Several fluted fishtail and lanceolate points recovered as surface finds in northern and southern Belize represent the early Paleoindian hunter-gatherer populations. The only known faunal remains from this time period are found in rockshelters (Prufer et al. 2017) and caves such as Actun Halal (Griffith et al. 2002) and date to the Terminal Pleistocene. Populations at this time were mobile and relied on the now extinct fauna, smaller animals, and plants (Lohse et al. 2006; Prufer et al. 2017; Stemp, Awe, Prufer, and Helmke 2016).

The Archaic begins at 8000 B.C., however, there is still limited evidence for human activity until about 3400 B.C. This period is marked by environmental warming, rapid changes in subsistence strategies such as the introduction and spread of domesticated plants, as well as increasing populations. Pollen data show the appearance of maize and manioc by 3400 B.C. and the widespread adoption of maize ca. 2400 B.C. (Jones 1994a) and therefore, a "continuity in some forms of food production can be seen from Archaic to early Middle Preclassic times" (Lohse 2010:320). Common tool types include Lowe and Sawmill points. The appearance of macroblades, macroblade cores, and large flakes is also noted. A few tool forms associated with the Archaic are also seen in early Preclassic contexts suggesting at least some continuity between these two time periods (Lohse et al. 2006).

Our knowledge of the transitional period in the Belize River valley is unfortunately limited, however, two recent Preceramic sites have been investigated and provide data pertaining to this dynamic time period. Investigations by the Belize Valley Archaeological Reconnaissance (BVAR Project) at Actun Halal, a shallow cave site in Upper Belize River valley, have revealed a Late Archaic stratum indicating the use of this location by Preceramic peoples (Griffith et al. 2002; Lohse 2007, 2010; Lohse et al. 2006). Pollen data recovered from the site provides evidence of Preceramic maize and cotton horticulture. Lohse (2007:2) has documented two possible Late Archaic components, the earlier dating from ca. 2400–1800 B.C. and a possible second occupation from ca. 1440–1210 B.C. It is interesting to note that Middle Preclassic ceramics (as well as later ceramics) were also found at Actun Halal suggesting the knowledge and continued use of this special location.

Recent investigations at Xunantunich by the Mopan Valley Preclassic Project encountered a buried paleosol beneath the Preclassic ceremonial center (Early Xunantunich), just north and east of a Preclassic pyramid (see Brown et al. Chapter 5 this volume). This sticky, black layer, located directly above bedrock, contained highly patinated lithic material, a partial stone dish, and a notable absence of ceramics (Brown et al. 2011). The lithic assemblage in this level appears to date to the Preceramic period and two AMS dates support this interpretation. Carbon samples were dated from the top and bottom of the paleosol at this location. The lower sample (Beta-275307) was collected directly above bedrock and is the earlier of the two, dating to 3320–3230 cal B.C. (NB: all radiocarbon dates list the two-sigma range). The upper sample (Beta-275306) was collected at the top of the level and dates to 1210–970 cal B.C. (Brown et al. 2011). The latter sample corresponds nicely with radiocarbon dates for the Cunil complex at Cahal Pech and Blackman Eddy. It is also interesting to note that at the top of the paleosol several eroded ceramic sherds were encountered and appear to be Cunil types. Although these two carbon samples did not come from primary deposits, they do provide us with a rough chronological framework for future work at this location. Investigations of this potential Preceramic level at Early Xunantunich are preliminary, and this location could prove to be important for understanding the transitional period as it may reflect one of the few locations in the Maya lowlands where deposits from this early time period are found in a stratigraphic sequence directly underlying early Middle Preclassic occupation.

Early Ceramic Occupation

Much like the information on Preceramic occupation, in the 1970s there was considerable controversy regarding the origins (Willey 1977), level of complexity (Ball 1977), and material culture (Awe 1992) of early sedentary pottery-producing society in the Maya lowlands. As late as 1992 our knowledge of this time period is stated by Awe (1992:30) as being "relatively limited, sometimes controversial, and generally obscure." Excavations at sites such as Colha (Hester et al. 1982; Valdez 1987), Cerros (Robertson and Freidel 1986), and Cuello (Hammond et al. 1979) in northern Belize and Altar de Sacrificious (Adams 1971), Yaxha-Sacnab (Rice 1979), Nakbe, and El Mirador (Forsyth 1989) in the Peten were just beginning to recognize and describe Preclassic occupation.

In the Belize River valley, there seems to be a general settlement pattern of early villages located on hilltops overlooking rivers (see Brown et al. Chapter 5 this volume). Investigations at Cahal Pech, Blackman Eddy, and Xunantunich provide the most data pertaining to the first sedentary villages in the region. Excavations at Cahal Pech (Figure 3.2) began in 1988 in part to develop the site for tourism and to halt further destruction of the site. By the end of the first field season, extensive Preclassic deposits had been discovered. The following year the focus of the research shifted to include a detailed investigation of this early occupation (Awe 1992). The majority of early deposits were recovered from Structure B4 in Plaza B, one of the seven plazas that comprise the site core. A 2 × 2 m unit placed into Structure B4 successfully uncovered a stratigraphic sequence documenting the earliest construction levels at the site. Subsequent excavations in 1994 and 1995 (Healy and Awe 1995, 1996) located additional ceramics from Structure B4 and from a series of nine 1 × 1 m test excavations across Plaza B that were analyzed by David Cheetham (Cheetham and Awe 1996, 2002; Clark and Cheetham 2002). These excavations also provided a set of radiocarbon dates that placed the Cunil phase between ca. 1100 and 900 B.C. (Awe 1992; Healy, Cheetham, Powis, and Awe 2004). Awe began a second set of excavations at Cahal Pech in 2002 in order to increase the size of the Cunil ceramic assemblage and to further our understanding of this controversial time period. The three new columns placed into Structure B4 (Columns 7/2002; 8/2006; and 9/2007) substantially increased the

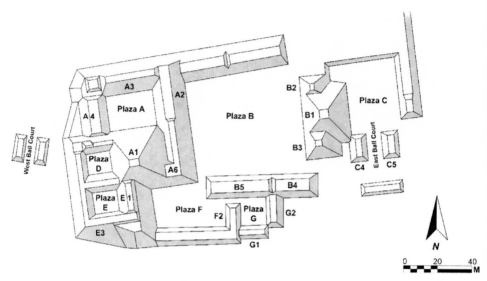

Figure 3.2. Map of Cahal Pech.

size of the ceramic assemblage and established the Cunil phase dating of the lowermost levels of Structure B4. Collaborative investigations by James Garber and Jaime Awe (Garber et al. 2005), and by Awe's BVAR Project (Ebert 2017; Ebert et al. 2017; Ebert et al. n.d.; Peniche May 2016) in Plaza B have also contributed to a more detailed picture of architectural features, activity areas, ritual activity, and community organization. Three calibrated radiocarbon dates from these recent excavations support the original dating and stratigraphic priority of the Cunil Ceramic Complex: 1120–910 B.C. (Structure B4 Unit 8 Level 13), 1280 to 1010 B.C. (Plaza B Op. 1v Level 15) and 1360 to 1350 B.C. and 1310 to 1050 B.C. (Structure B4 Unit 9 Level 12) (Garber, personal communication 2016). Another radiocarbon assay, from charcoal below Floor 13 in Structure B4 and dating to 1205–990 B.C. (Beta-77207), serves to confirm the terminal Early Preclassic date for the initial Cunil settlement of Cahal Pech (Ebert et al. n.d.).

The most common type of early architecture associated with the Cunil phase consists of low platforms. These structures were made from marl, clay, and dirt. At the beginning of the Cunil phase the floors are of crudely tamped marl but by the end of the phase the quality is improved with the use of lime plaster (Awe 1992:205–210; see also Brown et al. Chapter 5 this volume). These low platforms supported simple apsidal super structures of pole and thatch. Many of these structures were surrounded by low walls of coarse or roughly shaped limestone. Red paint noted on daub fragments indicates that even at this early time the structures were decorated. The occurrence of fire pits and other remains suggests these buildings were most likely domestic and/or ancillary structures. Grinding stones and tranchet bit tools suggest that these early settlers were sedentary agriculturalists. Other stone tools recovered include retouched flakes, scrapers, burins, hammerstones, and obsidian flakes (Awe 1992).

Cunil phase pottery, discussed in more detail below, includes decorated serving vessels as well as unslipped utilitarian types. Jadeite objects, marine shell discs, slate plaques, and drilled animal teeth served as jewelry for special individuals and indicate that the community was involved in long distance trade and exchange. Early modified scapulae and pottery figurines are thought to have been associated with early forms of ritual and ancestor worship (Awe 1992). A cache (Cache 1) placed above a floor surface (Floor 10C) in Structure B4 suggests early ritual practices of consecration and may indicate some wealth differences emerging in the community (see Brown et al. Chapter 5 this volume). The cache included a fragmented ceramic vessel, 18 perforated marine shell discs, 27 obsidian flakes, 77 chert flakes, three pieces of greenstone, a perforated peccary scapula, and a perforated canine scapula among other items.

Occupation similar to what is seen in the Cunil phase at Cahal Pech has been identified in the early Middle Preclassic Kanocha phase (ca. 1100/1000–900 B.C.) at the site of Blackman Eddy buried beneath Structure B1 at the northern edge of the site core (Figure 3.3) (Brown 2003; Garber, Brown, Awe, and Hartman 2004). Here, the earliest inhabitants modified bedrock by leveling and filling in low areas. In other cases, bedrock served as a living surface. A series of apsidal and circular patterns of postholes cut into bedrock were encountered through horizontal excavations, which represent several wattle-and-daub construction phases. These early structures were associated with a number of domestic items including *mano* and *metate* fragments, bone implements, and ceramic spindle whorls. Several associated features including a two-chambered chultun, a fire hearth, and several circular depressions cut into bedrock further support a domestic function for these early structures. The chultun contained a number of interesting artifacts including bone needles, stone spheres, lithic debris, a stone *tecomate*, *mano* fragments, marine shell beads and debitage, and

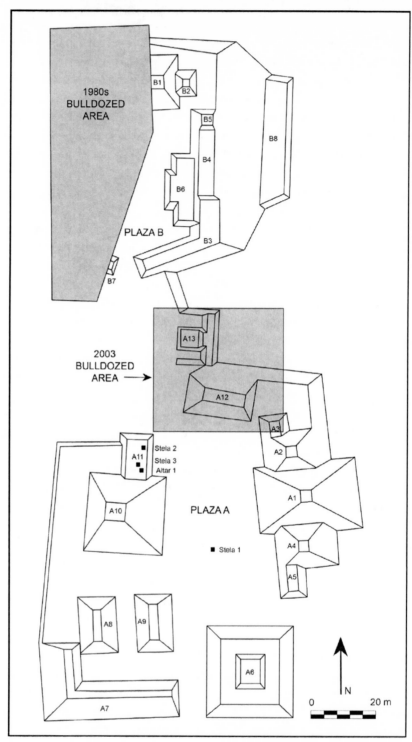

Figure 3.3. Map of Blackman Eddy (courtesy of James F. Garber).

a complete colander vessel (Brown 2003; Garber, Brown, Awe, and Hartman 2004). Two radiocarbon dates from the collapsed chultun support an early date for this feature (Beta 162573 1030–840 cal B.C. and Beta 159142 990–820 cal B.C.). A nearby bedrock feature also yielded an early date (Beta 122281 1395–1015 cal B.C.) further supporting the interpretation that this location was home to an early ceramic-producing village (Garber, Brown, Awe, and Hartman 2004).

The early ceramics of the Kanocha phase at Blackman Eddy are very similar in form and surface decoration to Cunil phase ceramics from Cahal Pech, described below. Surface decoration and treatments include slipping, appliqué filleting, post-slip incising, differential firing techniques, and appendages in the form of wide strap handles. Evidence for early ritual activities can be seen in the presence of a stingray spine, an obsidian flake and blades, as well as numerous clear quartz crystals and quartz flakes. The stingray spine suggests early bloodletting rituals (Garber, Brown, Awe, and Hartman 2004). The high frequency of quartz artifacts associated with the early buildings indicates that these objects may have been part of the household ritual paraphernalia and possibly used as divining stones (Brown 2003). Ethnographic accounts show that crystals were used as divining stones by Yucatec Maya shamans within household contexts (Hanks 1990). The marine shell, stingray spine, and obsidian artifacts indicate that the early occupants of Blackman Eddy were tied into long-distance trade networks and indicate the importance of these exotic items. As we see at Cahal Pech, these exotic items were placed in ritual deposits and indicate that the processes that lead to emerging social inequality began in the Cunil period.

Evidence of early occupation has also been recovered at the hilltop site of Xunantunich. The Xunantunich Archaeological Project directed by Richard Leventhal and Wendy Ashmore conducted tunnel excavations beneath the large acropolis, El Castillo, and discovered Cunil-like ceramics directly above bedrock. This early occupation was designated the Muyal phase (Strelow and LeCount 2001). Recent investigations by the Mopan Valley Preclassic Project within Early Xunantunich, just downslope from the Classic site core, uncovered additional evidence of Muyal phase occupation indicating a more widespread early settlement at the site (Brown et al. 2011).

Across the lowlands, the appearance of pottery at this time is irregular, with Cunil deposits found at Cahal Pech, Xunantunich (Strelow and LeCount 2001), Blackman Eddy (Garber, Brown, Awe, and Hartman 2004), and Holmul (Callaghan 2005; Callaghan and Neivens de Estrada 2016;

Neivens de Estrada 2010). Vilma Fialko has also observed modal, stylistic, and technological (especially paste) differences between the Cunil ceramics and the early pottery from Tikal; however, basic similarities between the assemblages were also noted. More recent INAA analysis of Cunil pottery by Claire Ebert (2017; Ebert et al. n.d.) has confirmed paste differences between Cunil and other early Lowland Maya ceramics, supporting the argument that Cunil pottery is local to the Belize River valley area. Cunil pottery has also been compared to the Swasey Complex established at Cuello (Kosakowsky 1987) and the Bolay Complex at Colha (Valdez 1987). Overall, the Cunil Complex is characterized by: a prevalence of dull slips, the absence of Mars Orange types, an absence of spouted jar forms, few examples of filleting, the presence of incised types and decoration that are not seen in Jenney Creek or in Swasey/Bladen and Bolay assemblages, local varieties that show minor ties to Swasey/Bladen and Bolay from northern Belize (Valdez et al. 2008), and less standardization in ceramic types between Belize Valley, northern Belize, and Peten than during subsequent times (Sullivan et al. 2009). Ceramic materials from the Puerto Escondido site located to southeast in Honduras have affinities to Cunil and Kanocha phase ceramics. The Chotepe phase (1100–900 B.C.) from Puerto Escondido exhibits a coarse paste group and a fine-paste group with volcanic ash temper (Joyce and Henderson 2001). The fine-paste ceramic group is similar to the Cunil (and Kanocha) dull-slipped ware group, in that both have incised and carved motifs on flat-bottom, flaring-wall bowls, and also use differential firing techniques to produce dark fire clouding on cream or white slipped vessels. These assemblages differ from other early ceramic assemblages in Mesoamerica where utilitarian vessels are absent (Clark and Gosser 1995; Lesure 1998). The Barra phase (1550 to 1400 B.C.) pottery of the Chiapas Coast includes vessels decorated with a number of techniques such as slipping, burnishing, grooving, and stamping (Lesure 1998). Clark and Blake (1994) have suggested that this pottery represents a specialized beverage service complex with a limited range of functions where display was important. It was not until the Locona phase (1400 to 1250 B.C.) that a wider range of forms and associated functions are seen. These data support Clark and Gosser's (1995:219) conclusion that "ceramic technology was adopted by various groups in Mesoamerica at different times for different reasons."

In order to facilitate our understanding of these early inhabitants and the comparison of early pottery in other parts of the lowlands we have used the basic type: variety system to classify the Cunil ceramic material (Sullivan and Awe 2013). It is our hope that these descriptions will help others in looking for and recognizing early ceramic deposits. We have defined two basic wares in the assemblage: Belize Valley Dull Ware and Belize Valley Coarse Ware, suggesting that the development of pottery here was both a prestige and practical technology (Awe 1992; Cheetham and Awe 1996; Sullivan et al. 2009). Belize Valley Dull Ware, which forms about 35% of the assemblage, is characterized by a fine paste texture with volcanic ash, calcite, quartzite, and mica and/or hematite inclusions and dull slips associated with serving vessels. Belize Valley Coarse Ware is distinguished by a medium to coarse paste texture with calcite, quartz, quartzite, and small grains of mica and is associated with more utilitarian forms. Belize Valley Dull Ware is comprised of three groups: Uck, Cocoyol, and Chi. This ware is by far the more distinctive and recognized ware associated with Cunil pottery. Dull Ware includes the various incised types that range from grooved geometric shapes to more pan-Mesoamerican or so-called "Olmec style" motifs (Awe 1992). Examples of Uck Group types include: (1) Baki Red Incised: Baki Variety, which consists of a dull red slip with post-slip grooved incised lines that are generally associated with flat bottomed dishes with outsloping walls and wide everted rims (Awe 1992)(Figure 3.4a); and (2) Zotz Zoned Incised: Zotz Variety is similar to Baki Red but is decorated with zones of brown-and-red or brown-and-cream slip (Figure 3.4b). Modally this type is similar to Chanmico Incised from Chalchuapa (Awe 1992; Sharer 1978) and Pico de Oro Incised (Adams 1971; Sabloff 1975).

Another example of decorated pottery is found in Kitam Incised: Kitam Variety. Thin, fine, post-slip incised lines on incurving bowls with a multicolored or mottled slip distinguish this type. As noted by Cheetham and Awe (1996), ceramic designs are variable and include simple incisions encircling the rim, geometric designs, and complex Olmec-style motifs (such as the flame-eyebrow). The second group associated with Belize Valley Dull Ware is the Cocoyol Group. Cocoyol Cream: Cocoyol Variety is the dominant type and consists of a creamy white to brown to grey slip on bowls and shallow dishes. One variety has a light gray to brown resist design over the Cocoyol Cream slip. The third dull ware group is the Chi Ceramic Group, which comprises a very small part of the overall assemblage (less than one percent) and includes Chi Black: Chi Variety and Unnamed Black Punctated-incised.

The appearance of these incised types supports Awe's (1992:366) assertions that the early Cunil cultural assemblage represents a "nascent social complexity" that slowly becomes more pronounced over time. The use of

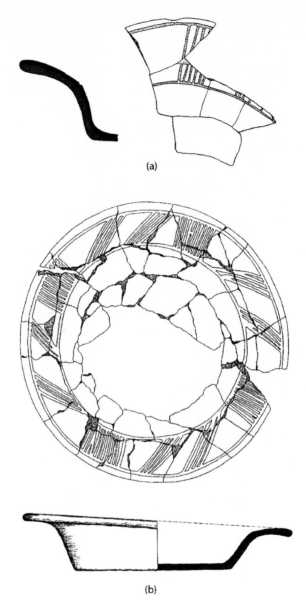

Figure 3.4. Drawings of Cunil ceramics from Cahal Pech: (a) Baki Red-incised, Baki Variety (after Awe 1992:229); (b) Zotz Zoned-incised, Zotz Variety (after Awe 1992:228).

pan-Mesoamerican motifs on many of these serving vessels indicates that the early inhabitants of Cahal Pech were part of a "pan-Mesoamerican ideological interaction sphere" (Garber and Awe 2008, 2009) using a set of shared symbols found in several regions of Mesoamerica including Chiapas, the Gulf Coast, El Salvador, Valley of Mexico, and Oaxaca (Awe 1992; Brown 2007; Cheetham 1998, 2005; Garber, Brown, Awe, and Hartman 2004). As Garber and Awe (2009) have suggested, the symbols associated with Cunil pottery are also uniquely lowland Maya in their expression and execution. Demarest (1989:331,333) also suggests that different groups were not "merely recipients" of Olmec iconography and proposes a "lattice of interregional interaction" model in which "local innovations and contributions" were an important part of the developing pan-Mesoamerican symbol set. As noted in other parts of the world, these early specialized forms of pottery may have been associated with increased competition, overt displays of wealth, personal political advantage, and ritual events (Clark and Blake 1994; Clark and Gosser 1995; Hayden 1995; Rice 1999, 2015). Interestingly, these types of symbols are not typically associated with early facet Jenney Creek pottery (Awe 1992; Brown 2007; Stark 2007). Barbara Stark (2007:55) suggests that by the Middle Preclassic these symbols were so widespread that there was a decline in their exclusivity and "a change in the materialization of ideology."

Belize Valley Coarse Ware has one ceramic group—the Sikiya Group. Jar forms dominate this group although bowls with slightly incurving sides, *tecomates*, and colander fragments are also present. This ware has strong similarities to the Jocote Group of the subsequent Jenney Creek phase. The Sikiya Unslipped sherds are sometimes burnished and have extensive fire clouding and variable color that ranges from tan to brown to black. There is significant variation in sherds of this type in terms of color, paste recipes (e.g., jar forms seem to have a grittier coarser texture than other forms), and firing temperature. The second type in the Sikiya Group is Ardagh Orange-brown, which includes unslipped jars of dark orange, brown, and gray paste with smudging and sometimes a dull orange wash. These types of utilitarian vessels are thought to have been used for food preparation and storage. Lesure (1998:30) suggests that forms like these low-necked jars most likely served as multipurpose vessels used for "cooking, storage, transport, and preparation of food and liquids."

Conclusion

Cunil phase pottery represents the earliest appearance of ceramics in the Maya lowlands known to date, possibly beginning as early as 1200 B.C. Although the Preceramic data are limited, the current data suggests a possible shift in settlement with the beginning of the Preclassic period. The appearance of pottery coincides with a more sedentary society, resource intensification and associated changes in diet, and long-distance interaction and trade. The importation of exotic items including objects of adornment is suggestive of emerging social inequality at this time. Many of these general characteristics are shared with relatively contemporaneous sites in other regions suggesting that these early villagers were full participants in a developing lowland Maya cultural tradition (Awe 1992; see also Andrews V et al. Chapter 4 this volume). However, regional differences during this early time period suggest more or less independent ceramic traditions and an indigenous development (Ebert et al. n.d.; Sullivan and Awe 2013). These early villages probably had intermittent contact with one another perhaps through networks of exchange of raw materials such as shell, jade, and obsidian. By the late Middle Preclassic (600 to 400 B.C.) increasing populations and interregional interaction gradually connected the diverse and independent Preclassic settlements, which lead to a more uniform ceramic tradition (Andrews V 1990; Valdez 1987).

Acknowledgments

The authors would like to thank the Institute of Archaeology and the National Institute of Culture and History of Belize. We want to thank the Social Science Research Council of Canada and the Tilden Family Foundation for their financial support of the research at Cahal Pech. Additionally, we would also like to thank the Foundation for the Advancement of Mesoamerican Studies, Inc. (FAMSI), the National Geographic Society Committee for Research and Exploration, the Brennan Foundation, Texas State University, and the University of Texas at San Antonio for support of research presented in this chapter. We are also grateful to the members of the Belize Valley Archaeological Project, the Belize Valley Archaeological Reconnaissance Project, and the Mopan Valley Preclassic Project. Many thanks to the reviewers of this chapter.

4

The Earliest Ceramics
of the Northern Maya Lowlands

E. WYLLYS ANDREWS V, GEORGE J. BEY III, AND CHRISTOPHER M. GUNN

Ceramics of the early Middle Preclassic (ca. 1000–700 B.C.) were recovered at Barton Ramie, Tikal, Altar de Sacrificios, and Ceibal in the late 1950s and early '60s, usually underlying late Middle Preclassic Mamom structures. In recent years many other southern Maya lowland sites have revealed pottery-using occupations dating to these centuries (Sullivan et al. Chapter 3 this volume). One feature of these earliest Maya ceramic complexes is a set of incised designs including ritual motifs that are widespread in Mesoamerica at the end of the Early Formative. Until recently, however, the northern Maya lowlands have failed to yield comparably early settlements.

Komchen, a large Preclassic community in far northwest Yucatan, is now known to have been the site of a pre-Mamom occupation with substantial masonry platforms and with ceramics that show similarities to contemporaneous pottery of the southern lowlands. Regional variants of the same pottery appear at the base of the stratigraphic sequence at Kiuic, in the Puuc region of Yucatan, where they are dated to 900–800 cal B.C. A few other recent excavations in Yucatan have produced ceramics of this period, and it now appears that pottery manufacture and settled village life was widespread in western Yucatan and Campeche by shortly after 1000 cal B.C., as it was in the southern lowlands.

Inductively coupled plasma mass spectrometry (ICP-MS) analysis of sherds from Kiuic indicate that the pre-Mamom vessels were manufactured locally using clay sources different from those of the following phase (Bey et al. 2012). Analysis of a sherd sample from Komchen likewise suggests that those pre-Mamom sherds were derived from local clay sources that were different from those of the following late Middle Preclassic. The results from both sites support the argument that the earliest pottery in the northern Maya area was of local manufacture, although almost certainly of foreign inspiration, and that it developed into the local Mamom-equivalent ceramic assemblages of the northern lowlands.

The Adoption of Pottery in Mesoamerica and the Maya Lowlands

The beginnings of plant domestication in Mesoamerica go back to about 7000 to 5000 B.C. in some areas of the highlands, and by 5000 B.C. early domesticated maize and probably manioc had reached the Gulf Coast lowlands. Several parts of the Maya lowlands and nearby areas have provided botanical evidence of clearing for domesticated crops by 2500 B.C. or earlier. This gradual addition of horticulture to a foraging subsistence economy must have encouraged many Mesoamericans to adopt more sedentary life styles, but with some exceptions, notably in coastal areas (Voorhies 1976, 2002), we see little evidence of year-round occupations until broken pottery vessels appear with remains of simple dwellings.

Ceramic vessels, replacing gourds, woven baskets and stone vessels, did not appear in the archaeological record until thousands of years after the domestication or introduction of many plants. The earliest known Mesoamerican pottery, at Purron Cave in the Tehuacan Valley, is limited to a few simple forms, including some based on gourds, and lacks surface decoration. The Purron phase dates roughly between 2300 and 1600 B.C., and ceramics probably began early in this span (Flannery and Marcus 1994:375; Johnson and MacNeish 1972:Table 4) (calibrated ranges are used for chronological estimates in this chapter). Similar Espiridión-phase ceramics in the Valley of Oaxaca are contemporary or a bit later (Flannery and Marcus 1994:374–75).

Between about 1900 and 1600 B.C. the Barra-phase inhabitants of Pacific Coast lowland sites in Chiapas began making elaborately incised, slipped, and painted *tecomates* and bowls in a variety of shapes and sizes (Blake et al. 1995; Ceja Tenorio 1985; Clark 1994a; Lowe 1975). At San Lorenzo, the earliest Ojochi ceramics are just slightly younger (Blake et al. 1995; Coe and Diehl 1980:37), as are the earliest vessels around La Venta (Rust and Sharer 1988).

Farther south, at Puerto Escondido, northeast Honduras, the earliest pottery, described as similar to Barra vessels (Joyce and Henderson 2001), may go back to 1700–1500 B.C. In the highlands of Guatemala, El Salvador, and Honduras, the excavated settlements with the first ceramic remains may predate 1200 B.C.

The radiocarbon dates from these sites suggest a spread and increasing elaboration of early ceramics from the highlands of central and southern Mexico south along the Pacific coast and piedmont toward Central America, but the sample of excavated sites that predate 1500 B.C. is small, and we are far from seeing a clear picture.

The manufacture of pottery vessels did not spread into the Maya lowlands until about 1100 or 1000 B.C., one or several centuries after the technology had been adopted in most of the surrounding regions. In the Maya lowlands, as elsewhere, we have so far not been able to find permanent villages until ceramics become part of the archaeological record (Sullivan et al. Chapter 3 and Andrews and Robles Chapter 2 this volume). As Jon Lohse (2010:345) has argued, earlier occupations have been difficult to recognize beneath the earliest pottery-making settlements, because " . . . the processes by which the earliest permanent villages were built eradicated much of the evidence for what cultural continuity may have defined the Archaic-to-Preclassic transition . . ."

Throughout the first half of the twentieth century the earliest Preclassic settlements described in the Maya lowlands were those related in time and cultural content to the Mamom phase at Uaxactun, dating from about 700 to 300 B.C. Then, during the late 1950s, '60s, and early '70s excavations at Barton Ramie (Gifford 1976:61–83), Tikal (Culbert 1993:Figures 116–120, 2003), Altar de Sacrificios (Adams 1971:79–84, 117–120), Ceibal (Sabloff 1975:8–9, 46–60; Willey 1970), Lakes Yaxha and Sacnab (Rice 1976; Rice 1979), and Cuello (Hammond, ed. 1991), brought to light earlier, pre-Mamom ceramic complexes that were the earliest at those sites. The five relevant radiocarbon determinations from Tikal, Altar de Sacrificios, and Ceibal suggested that these pre-Mamom ceramics dated between 1000 or 900 B.C. and 700 B.C. The limited excavations indicated that these early ceramic complexes, in the lowest stratigraphic levels underlying Preclassic structures or plazas, belonged to small farming communities. Archaeologists noted the similarities of these early Middle Preclassic pottery complexes to contemporaneous pottery in the highlands of Chiapas and Guatemala, suggesting the arrival of new or expanding populations from these regions (e.g., Adams 1971:119; Andrews V 1990; Rice 1976; Sharer and Gifford 1970), rather than from a single source. The acquisition of pottery technology by sedentary or semi-sedentary Late Archaic communities long accustomed to deriving much of their food from domesticated plants was always considered likely, but some of us favored migration in the initial spread of ceramics.

About two decades later, the lowest stratigraphic levels at Cahal Pech, at a strategic fork of the Belize River, produced a ceramic complex that underlay and was ancestral to the Middle Preclassic Jenney Creek complex documented by the Harvard excavations at Barton Ramie (Gifford 1976). This assemblage, which Jaime Awe named the Cunil complex (Awe 1992; Awe et al. 1990; Healy et al. 2004; Sullivan and Awe 2013; Sullivan et al. Chapter 3 this volume), was associated with modest domestic structures. Once Cunil had been recognized and described, related complexes soon were discovered at other Belize sites, first at Blackman Eddy, where the earliest complex is called Kanocha (Garber, Brown, Awe, and Hartman 2004; Garber, Brown, Driver, Glassman, Hartman, Reilly, and Sullivan 2004), and then Pacbitun and Xunantunich. Cuello, Colha, and several other sites in northern Belize were home to pre-Mamom ceramic complexes that are distinct from Cunil (Hammond, ed. 1991; Kosakowsky 1987; Kosakowsky and Pring 1998; Valdez 1987). Since 2000, Estrada-Belli and Neiven's excavations at Holmul, about 35 km northwest of Cahal Pech, have recovered large numbers of similar sherds (Estrada-Belli 2011:36–44). John Clark and David Cheetham (2002:Figure 5), in a comprehensive presentation and analysis of these early ceramic assemblages, have divided the villages with pre-Mamom pottery in the southern lowlands into four "tribal territories," called Swasey, Cunil, Eb, and Xe, after the first named pre-Mamom phases in the southern lowlands.

The range of the Peten and Belize radiocarbon ages is from about 1100 to 750 B.C., indicating that although these southern lowland pre-Mamom complexes are roughly the same age, they span two or three centuries. The beginning of Cunil and related complexes is sometimes estimated to be 1100 B.C., in calibrated years (Garber et al. 2004; Garber and Awe 2009; Sullivan et al. Chapter 3 this volume), although Lohse (2010) argues that no lowland site has yet produced reliable evidence for ceramics or sedentism before 1000 B.C.

The introduction of ceramics in the southern lowlands therefore dates to about the end of the Mesoamerican Early Formative,[1] but it was not until the excavations at Cahal Pech (Awe 1992; Cheetham 2005; Cheetham et al. 2003; Garber and Awe 2009; Sullivan and Awe 2013; Sullivan et al. Chapter 3 this volume) that the wider Mesoamerican significance of some of the incised motifs on these early vessels was recognized. These designs, which often decorate the sides of hemispherical bowls and especially the horizontal, everted rims of plates, include lightning, shark tooth or perforator, music bracket, Kan cross, flame eyebrow, cleft forehead, and possible avian motifs (Cheetham 2005:Figures 3.5, 3.6). This is the set of Early Formative

Mesoamerican symbols long known on ceramic and stone artifacts from the Central Mexican highlands, down through the Isthmus and the Olmec Gulf Coast, and into the southern highlands as far as Copan. These motifs have now been documented on vessels from many southern lowland sites with pre-Mamom occupations (Clark and Cheetham 2002; Cheetham 2005; Cheetham et al. 2003; personal observations, 2011).

Pre-Mamom vessels in the Maya lowlands and in surrounding regions of Mesoamerica sometimes lack these complex symbolic designs but share equally complex incised motifs executed in a similar postslip fashion, including opposed and zoned incision to indicate a mat or textile; crosshatching; other opposed sets of vertical and diagonal lines, sometimes below horizontal sub-rim incisions; double or single chevrons; and a range of straight and curved lines. A sample of sites that show such designs are Barton Ramie, early Jenney Creek complex (Gifford 1976:Figure 27a and e); Ceibal, Real Xe complex (Inomata, personal communication, 2011; Willey 1970:Figure 22); Chalchuapa, Tok, and Colos complexes (Sharer 1978:Figures 143b 6, 12, 13, 14, 147; c 11; d 3; e 1, 4; f 1, 2); La Blanca, Conchas B phase (Love 2002:Figure 81e–i); La Venta (Drucker 1952:Figures 25b, 31a, 34c, e, i, 36a, 38e, Plate 20f); and San José Mogote, San José phase (Flannery and Marcus 1994:Figures 12.15a, b, c, 12.142l, 12.143, 12.150).

The early Mesoamerican set of complex symbols dates to the final centuries of the Early Formative period throughout Mesoamerica, and the lowland Maya sites that adopted these motifs, such as Cahal Pech, Holmul, and Tikal, must have been occupied during these years. Maya sites that do not have these diagnostic motifs in pre-Mamom complexes might have started to manufacture pottery vessels slightly later than those that do, but the differences probably also reflect regional variation in the use of these early ideographic symbols.

The Northern Maya Lowlands in the Middle Preclassic

Until recently our knowledge of pre-Mamom ceramic complexes has been limited to the southern lowlands. Late Middle Preclassic, Mamom-equivalent settlements were documented in the 1940s and '50s at many sites in Yucatan (Brainerd 1958; Smith 1971) and in the late 1950s and early '60s at three sites near Dzibilchaltun, in northwest Yucatan (Andrews IV 1965; Andrews IV and Andrews V 1980:41–58; Andrews V 1981; Ball 1977–1979b; Joesink-Mandeville 1970; Rovner and Lewenstein 1997; Shook 1955; Taschek 1994). The associated ceramics were similar to those of the late Middle

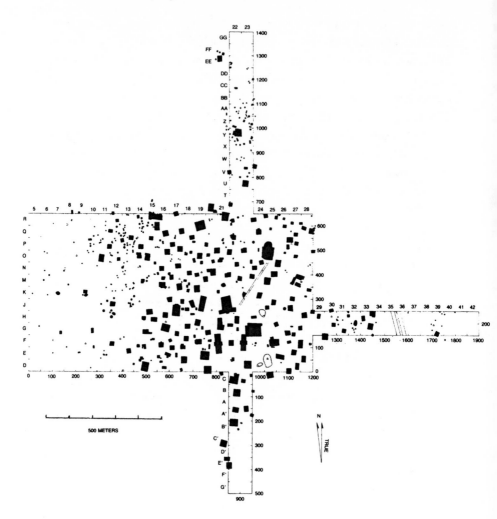

Figure 4.1. The surveyed portion of the ruins of Komchen.

Preclassic and Late Preclassic Mamom and Chicanel complexes at south-ern lowland sites in Guatemala. New Tulane University excavations in 1980 at Komchen (Figure 4.1), one of the largest Preclassic sites on the north-western plains, seemed to Andrews to reaffirm the conclusion of earlier investigators that the earliest ceramics and the first settled villages in the north dated to the late Middle Preclassic, probably no earlier than 700 B.C. (Andrews V 1986, 1988, 1989, 1990; Andrews V et al. 1980; Andrews V and Ringle 1992; Andrews V et al. 1984; Ringle 1985; Ringle and Andrews V

1988, 1990; see also Ball and Taschek 2003, 2007). This interpretation, as we will show below, was wrong.

The 35 years since the Komchen excavations have seen a huge expansion of northern Maya archaeology, including several large projects that have concentrated on Preclassic remains. We now know not only that northern Yucatan was heavily occupied in the late Middle Preclassic but also that some communities during these years were large, with massive constructions at their centers. Investigations at Ek Balam in the 1980s and '90s indicated a substantial community in the late Middle Preclassic (Bey et al. 1998; Bond-Freeman 2007; Bond-Freeman et al. Chapter 10 this volume), and excavations at Yaxuna in the 1990s documented extensive late Middle Preclassic construction (Suhler et al. 1998; Stanton and Ardren 2005). Tomás Gallareta (Chapter 11 this volume) has shown that the enormous rectangular platform at the northern Puuc site of Xocnaceh, with pyramidal structures atop it, dates entirely to the late Middle Preclassic. Recent reconnaissance and surface collections at Xcoch, near Xocnaceh, also suggest extensive Middle Preclassic settlement and construction (Smyth and Ortegón 2008). Fernando Robles's excavations (Robles and Ceballos Chapter 9 this volume) in the pyramidal platform at Poxila, about 20 km southeast of central Mérida, have dated the entire construction to the late Middle Preclassic, and a settlement survey shows the Preclassic site to have been extensive. Anthony Andrews and Fernando Robles's survey of the northwest corner of the peninsula (Andrews and Robles 2004, 2008) turned up a dense Middle Preclassic occupation, with sites scattered everywhere across the inhabited zone, often with small ballcourts. David Anderson investigated Xtobo, the largest of the Preclassic sites found by the survey, reporting hundreds of late Middle Preclassic and Late Preclassic structures, with a core of larger structures linked by causeways to a central plaza (Anderson 2010, 2011; Anderson et al. Chapter 8 this volume).

These northern Maya towns and their public buildings, especially Xocnaceh and Poxila, appear to equal in size the known Middle Preclassic sites in the southern lowlands. The large constructions, geographic extent, and astonishing variety in site layout and architecture of these late Middle Preclassic centers imply that these towns were preceded by a few centuries of smaller communities already characterized by inherited rank and wealth. Despite these indications, no pre-Mamom occupation has been recognized in the north until recently.

The Development of Preclassic Komchen

Komchen was a large Preclassic town about 20 km south of the Gulf Coast and about the same distance north of the center of modern Mérida, 6 km northwest of the Classic city of Dzibilchaltun. At its center lie five large platforms (Figure 4.2) that enclose an irregular north-south plaza about 200 m north-south and 100 m across. The north platform on this plaza is linked to a large structure farther to the north by a 250-m causeway. Surrounding this core of massive architecture was a compact, roughly circular town covering at least 2 km with about 1000 platforms ranging from several hundred square meters down to small structures barely large enough to support a small outbuilding. The density of structures is greater than that of most Classic-period sites in northern Yucatan, comparable to that of Postclassic Mayapan.

The vast majority of the architecture at Komchen dates to the Preclassic, including all the large central and residential platforms. About 15% of the smaller platforms were built during the Late and Terminal Classic reoccupation from about A.D. 600 to 1000, and many other Preclassic structures were reused during this span, although Classic sherds are less than 10% of the total. All of the small, rectangular buildings with masonry foundation braces at Komchen date to the Late and Terminal Classic, except for one or two tiny Late Postclassic shrines on Preclassic platforms. We found no trace of Preclassic masonry buildings atop platforms.

The long Preclassic occupation is divided into four phases defined by four ceramic complexes. Although we placed excavations in about 160 structures throughout the surveyed zone, the most useful ceramic stratigraphy was in the largest platforms bordering the central plaza, where large ceramic samples from sequential construction phases dated from the beginning of the Middle Preclassic to the end of the Late Preclassic. The often-unbroken plaster floors made it possible to document changes in pottery types and vessel forms through many building episodes, and thus to subdivide more than a thousand years of northern Maya prehistory.

The Ek phase, on which we will elaborate below, dates to the early Middle Preclassic. The evidence for this earliest occupation at Komchen appeared at the base of the largest structures around the Central Plaza. Unmixed Ek complex ceramics were sealed at the base of Structure 24G1, a massive platform on the east side of the plaza. These earliest deposits were a 50-cm-thick midden and living surface, and above this a rubble-filled platform, with a remaining height of 120 to 140 cm. Structure 23F1, adjacent

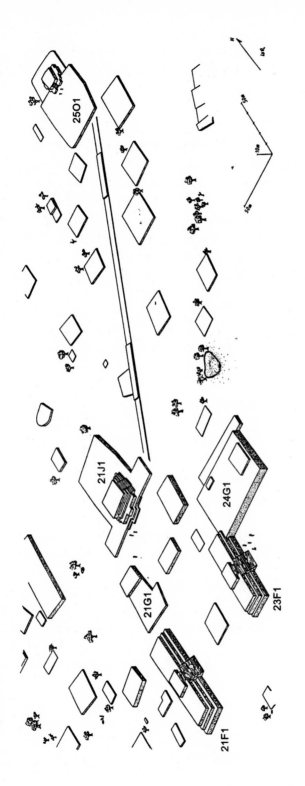

Figure 4.2. The Central Plaza of Preclassic Komchen (reconstruction by Linda Roundhill).

to 24G1, began with a 60-cm-high Ek-phase masonry platform. The limited evidence from the 1980 excavations therefore shows that two of the major structures around the Central Plaza were started in the early Middle Preclassic Ek phase. It is probable that the entire central complex was begun at this time.

The central buildings at Komchen conform to the Middle Formative Chiapas (MFC) pattern described by Clark and Hansen (2001:3–12) that began in the early Middle Formative at La Venta and that appeared at Chiapa de Corzo, Mirador, La Libertad, Tzutzuculi, Finca Acapulco, Vistahermosa, and other Middle Formative sites in Chiapas (Lowe 1977:224–226; McDonald 1983:68). Takeshi Inomata and his colleagues have excavated a deeply buried platform complex at Ceibal that securely dates the origins of the MFC pattern in the Maya area as early as 1000 B.C. (Inomata et al. 2013).

The MFC characteristics at Komchen are a north-south plaza flanked by regularly spaced pyramidal platforms, with the tallest platform to the north (Structure 21J1), smaller platforms near the center of the large plaza, and other platforms delimiting the plaza on the west. On the east side of the Komchen plaza is a broad, high platform (Structure 24G1) analogous to the large platforms constructed in the same position in MFC complexes. 24G1, by volume, was the largest structure at Komchen. Clark and Hansen (2001:4–5) suggest the large eastern platforms were royal compounds or precincts. The only important feature of the early Middle Formative Chiapas pattern perhaps absent at Komchen is an E-Group at the south end of the plaza, unless Structure 21F1, west across the plaza from the long Structure 23F1, was originally a smaller pyramidal structure, and the small platforms inside 23F1 constituted the western E-Group structure. In its initial stages, the northern platform (21J1) may not have been taller than the other structures around the plaza.

The following Nabanche phase, from roughly 700 to 150 B.C., saw the heaviest occupation, to judge from the abundance of its ceramics and from the volume and extent of construction associated with this pottery. The Early Nabanche ceramic complex, estimated to date from 700 to 400 B.C., is typical of the late Middle Preclassic in the Maya lowlands. The slipped pottery types are similar to those of the Mamom complex in the southern lowlands and to ceramics from other northern Maya sites of the late Middle Preclassic, such as Poxila, Xocnaceh, and Ek Balam. These Mamom-related types constitute 30.1% of the Komchen sherd total. Structure 21J1, the most conspicuous structure at Komchen, at the north end of the Central Plaza, dates largely to Early Nabanche, with an extensive platform rising 120 to 170 cm above bedrock. The final pyramidal platform atop this dated to the Late Preclassic Late Nabanche and Xculul phases, but interior constructions may be earlier.

The Late Nabanche phase marked the beginning of the Late Preclassic, from about 400 to 150 B.C. The quantity of construction appears similar to that of Early Nabanche, spread across the site, and the percentage of slipped sherds is similar, at 28.4%. The ceramics developed gradually from those of the preceding Early Nabanche complex. Maintenance of a similar settlement pattern, continued expansion of the community, architecture, and ceramic vessels suggest continuity but steady growth during more than half a millennium.

The Terminal Preclassic Xculul phase, estimated to date from 150 B.C. to A.D.200, shows continuous development from Late Nabanche in both architecture and ceramics. Xculul slipped pottery constitutes 14.8% of the site total, far less than Nabanche slipped ceramics. The latest contexts contain a few Protoclassic sherds, all probable imports, after which Komchen was abandoned. The site appears to have remained unoccupied after the end of the Preclassic until after the founding of the Classic community at nearby Dzibilchaltun in the sixth century. None of the pottery we recovered in 1980 dates to the Early Classic period, but recent salvage excavations 800 m northeast of the Central Plaza have uncovered a few Early Classic sherds under a Late Classic residential group (Echeverría et al. 2011).

The Content and Stratigraphic Context of the Early Middle Preclassic Ek Ceramic Complex at Komchen

In the 1980s Andrews did not recognize the early Middle Preclassic occupation at Komchen. The site was then thought to have been first settled in the late Middle Preclassic, with the rest of the site's history as outlined above. The most problematic part of the sequence throughout the analysis was the temporal placement and the local and external relationships of the Ek phase. Ek was immediately recognized in 1980 as stratigraphically below and typologically different from the rest of the Komchen ceramics, but the radiocarbon evidence for its placement in time created a quandary in which Andrews eventually reached the wrong conclusion.

The Ek pottery complex includes only three ceramic groups. The utilitarian types, Achiotes Unslipped and Chancenote Striated, are visually indistinguishable from those of the following Nabanche complex. These vessels

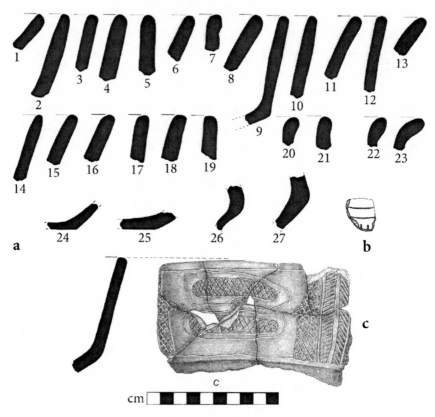

Figure 4.3. Ek Complex ceramics, Komchen: (a) Almeja Burnished Gray; (b, c) Almeja Burnished Gray, Incised Variety. All except three of these sherds came from sealed Ek-phase levels at the base of Structures 23F1 and 24G1.

were nearly all round-sided bowls or wide-mouth jars with flared and usually outcurved necks, globular bodies, and usually rounded bases, probably for storage and food preparation. The finer pottery, probably made for serving food, included a relatively fine-paste, well-smoothed, light gray-to-white ceramic, sometimes with a soft, thin, chalky slip or wash remaining (Almeja Burnished Gray) (Figure 4.3). These seldom bore incised lines (3 of 236), but one large dish (Figure 4.3c) showed a complex geometric and curvilinear postslip design on its exterior wall. Most vessels were large dishes, possibly including some bowls, with gently flared to nearly vertical sides and direct rims, some with flat bases, and some with basal angles and slightly rounded bases.

A more common red-slipped group (Kin Orange-red) was created by adding a bright red slip over the light gray burnished vessels (Figure 4.4).

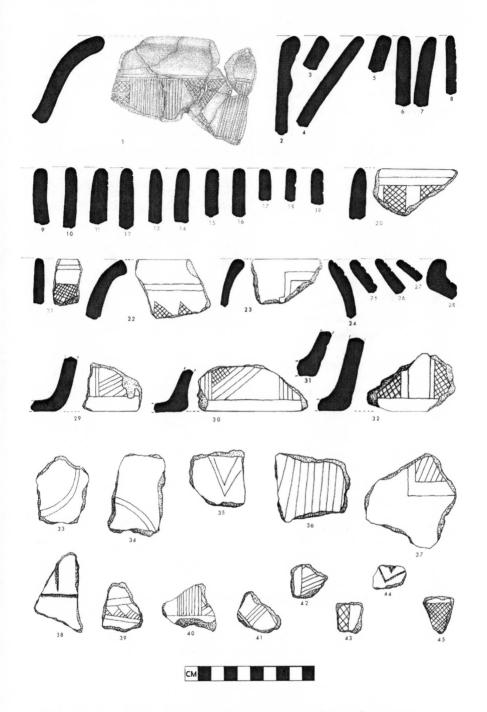

Figure 4.4. Ek Complex ceramics, Komchen: Kin Orange-Red, Incised Variety. One-third of these sherds came from Ek-phase levels at the base of Structures 22N1, 23F1, and 24G1. Most of the rest derived from Early Nabanche levels higher in the same platforms.

In strong contrast to Almeja Burnished Gray, 12% of the red sherds (50 of 418) showed incised motifs. The rough-edged, crosshatched and zoned, vertical, diagonal, and curved incised designs were always postslip, unlike most incisions on late Middle Preclassic Nabanche vessels, which are more frequently preslip, broader, and simpler. Kin vessel forms are similar to Almeja Burnished Gray, with most sherds from the same dish shape, but with a wider variety of dish wall forms and a few jars and *tecomates*.

Most of the Almeja and Kin group sherds came from the lowest layers of construction fill of five platforms, three on the Central Plaza and two nearby. In three of these, Ek complex sherds were mixed with Early Nabanche sherds in our narrow test excavations. In the two others, Structures 23F1 and 24G1, both huge platforms on the Central Plaza, Ek complex sherds were sealed in the fill of the earliest platforms inside the massive constructions or in layers below the fill, without Early Nabanche admixture. The rock fill of the largest platforms around the plaza had been trucked off to a nearby stone crusher for road and construction fill in the 1950s, leaving little more than husks of some of them.

The earliest remains under Structure 24G1, one of the two largest platforms at Komchen, covering about 3500 m^2, consisted of a dark brown soil layer on bedrock, with a thin ashy layer above this, overlain by a compact mottled brown and gray living surface, and finally a 10-cm layer of dark gray midden above this living surface. The basal 50 cm in our test excavation contained 353 sherds of the Almeja and Kin groups and two of the Early Nabanche complex (Table 4.1). Immediately above this rested a platform enlargement of at least 140 cm of massive rock and soil platform fill that contained 246 sherds of the Ek complex and two sherds possibly of the Xculul Xanaba group. The uppermost remaining expansions of the Structure 24G1 platform probably dated later in the Preclassic period, but most of the 24G1 rock fill had been looted, and we do not know how high the Ek platform originally stood. Its 1980 140-cm height may indicate no more than what was left when stone-robbers were finally apprehended by the state police.

Structure 23F1, adjacent to 24G1, began in the Ek phase as a 60-cm high platform. Our sample from this fill contained 94 Ek complex sherds and none later. The subsequent 60-cm increase in platform height may date to Ek as well, but the sherd sample is too small to be sure.

The other huge structures around the Central Plaza at Komchen may also have been started during Ek times, but either they were not tested

Table 4.1. Ceramic Frequencies in the Earliest Building Contexts at Komchen.

	Structure 23F1			Structure 24G1 (Pit 2 an expansion of Pit 1)			
	Test Pit 1			Test Pit1		Test Pit 2	
	M-5201	M-5202	M-5203	M-5208	M-5209	M-5211	M-5212
	20–80 cm	80–140 cm	140–210 cm	90–200 cm	200–225 cm	60–170 cm	170–225 cm
	Platform rubble fill	Platform rubble fill	Dirt floor, earth & midden	Rubble fill & midden	Floor and earth below	Rubble fill	Midden, floor, & soil below
XCULUL PHASE							
Xanaba Group (Red)							
LATE NABANCHE PHASE							
Sierra Group (Red)	4	2		1	2	*1	
EARLY NABANCHE PHASE							
Chunhinta Group (Black)	10	1					
Joventud Group (Red)					1		
Dzudzuquil Group (Cream-to-buff)	1						
Muxanal Group (Red-on-cream)							1
EK PHASE							
Almeja Burnished Gray: Almeja Var.			5	66	5	31	129
Almeja Burnished Gray: Incised Var.				1	1	1	
Kin Orange-red: Kin Var.	2	11	85	90	18	44	166
Kin Orange-red: Incised Var.		3	4	7	2	6	28
Achiotes Group (Unslipped)**		1	31	92	10	52	150
total classified sherds	17	18	125	257	39	134	474
discards	8	6		36		1	27
Total sherds	25	24	125	293	39	135	501

Notes: * possible identification only; ** throughout Preclassic

in our random sample, or our narrow test excavations missed the earliest deposits in these platforms. The four deep test excavations to bedrock in Structure 21J1, at the north end of the plaza, did not encounter early platforms with pure Ek ceramics. Although we may simply have missed such an early construction, most of this platform appears to have been built in the Early Nabanche phase, with additions continuing through the Preclassic. Two other platforms near the center of the site also contained Ek complex materials overlying bedrock and under Early Nabanche deposits, but the samples from these are smaller and less convincing.

Instead of relying on the ceramic stratigraphy, the implications of which are now clear, Andrews dated the Ek complex to 450 to 350 B.C., placing it between Early Nabanche and Late Nabanche, at the end of the Middle Preclassic. He did so because of two nearly identical radiocarbon determinations, one from the midden below the earliest platform inside Structure 23F1 and the other from the midden below the earliest platform in Structure 24G1. The calibrated two-sigma ranges were 752 to 200 B.C. and 750 to 172 B.C., respectively, centered neatly at the end of the Middle Preclassic (Table 4.2).

The first result of this decision was a failure to understand the pre-Mamom stratigraphic position of the Ek complex, below sealed levels with Early Nabanche complex ceramics. The second problematic conclusion, derived from the first, was that the Ek complex had to be interpreted as an intrusive ceramic unit, sandwiched between Early and Late Nabanche, the latter of which without question developed from the former. This seemed highly improbable in the 1980s but had to be accepted if the radiocarbon dates were to be believed. The third consequence of this mistake, a true Catch-22, was that none of the platforms we encountered at Komchen could be dated earlier than the end of the Middle Preclassic, the postulated position of Ek at 450 to 350 B.C., because Ek sherds extended to the base of all of the large structures we tested. This conclusion was especially problematic, because the Mamom-related Early Nabanche ceramics, as noted above, constituted about 30% of the total of slipped sherds at Komchen, and it meant that for about the first two or three centuries of heavy occupation at the site, we could come up with no constructions at all.

Andrews now believes these two dates are too late and that in this instance we should rely on the internal ceramic stratigraphy and ceramic crossties to other sites in the lowlands to assign a pre-Mamom date to the Ek complex (Andrews V and Bey 2011; Andrews V et al. 2008).[2] The Ek complex at Komchen therefore remains undated by radiocarbon, and the best chronometric evidence we have for dating these first pottery vessels comes from the site of Kiuic.

The Development of Preclassic Kiuic

Kiuic is a rank three Maya center located in the Bolonchen District of the southern Puuc region of Yucatan 114 km due south of Komchen. It flourished between approximately 900/800 B.C. and A.D. 900/1000, reaching its apogee in the Terminal Classic. Classic-period Kiuic covers an area of approximately 5 km². Defined by a 1.6 km² central core of occupation, Kiuic is surrounded by a sparsely inhabited agricultural zone that in turn was surrounded by a ring of heavily occupied hills. Together these three zones form the 5 km² area that we consider the "site." Similar in size at its apogee to Labna, Kiuic was founded at least as early as Komchen. Kiuic was the seat of an extensive Early Nabanche occupation represented by the Bah ceramic complex as well as an earlier ceramic complex with marked similarities to the Ek complex of Komchen.

Work began at Kiuic in 2000 with excavations focused on one of the central groups of the site, the Yaxche Group (Figure 4.5). Bey and his colleagues argue that the Yaxche Group was the first major palace at Kiuic. Composed of three plazas and three patios, it served during the Late Classic as the central architectural group of the site. Major features of the group include a 10-m-tall pyramid (or acropolis) on the north side, a 17-m-long, single-room vaulted building (which has been interpreted as a popol nah) and a series of smaller vaulted buildings and single-roomed temple platforms.

Excavations carried out with co-director Arqlga. Rossana May have revealed a long construction history for the Yaxche Group. In Dzunun Plaza a sequence of 6 stucco floors were defined in the civic-ceremonial plaza of the group. The first three are Preclassic and the last three are Classic. Ceramic analysis by Gunn and Bey of the material from the first three floors indicate the first and second construction episodes date to the Middle Preclassic (Early Nabanche), and the third is associated with the Late Preclassic (Late Nabanche) period.

Located just east of a cave, in what was to become the center of Kiuic, a .75-m-high platform was constructed during the late Middle Preclassic. The platform's dry fill is similar to that described for the late Middle Preclassic constructions at Nakbe and Mirador (Hansen 1998). The platform was built directly on the original soil level characterized by reddish brown soil and bedrock. The surface was pounded sascab, and the platform was at least 14.5

Table 4.2. Radiocarbon Ages, Probabilities, and Contexts for the Preclassic Komchen Region and Kiuic.

Lab. No.	Site	Structure, Lot No., Context	Associated Ceramics
I-11,565	Komchen	Str. 28H1, M-3970. Pit in bedrock below platform.	Xculul
LJ-508	Mirador Group	Str. 605, Pd. 1A, platform fill.	Early Nabanche
LJ-279	Komchen	Str. 25O1, Pd. 3A (?). Hearth charcoal.	Xculul
I-11,544	Komchen	Str. 21J1, M-3011. In sealed debris and midden from collapsed platform.	Late Nabanche
I-11,545	Komchen	Str. 21J1, M-3139. In sealed debris from collapsed platform.	Late Nabanche
I-171	Xculul	Str. 226, Pd. 2A. Carbonized beans (Phaseolus).	Xculul
I-11,546	Komchen	Str. 24G1, M-5209, M-5212. In living surface at base of construction fill.	Ek
I-11,566	Komchen	Str. 23F1, M-5203. Under a living surface below base of platform construction fill.	Ek
LJ-505	Mirador Group	Str. 605, Pd. 1D midden, hearth charcoal	Early Nabanche
I-11,564	Komchen	Str. 21J1, M-3145. In humus level below base of platform construction fill.	Early Nabanche
B266394	Kiuic	Plaza Icim, YY-8 basal level, directly above bedrock, beneath sascab floor	Ek
B240469	Kiuic	Plaza Icim, YY-8 basal level, directly above bedrock, beneath sascab floor	Ek

Note: Dates have been calibrated with Radiocarbon Calibration Program Calib Rev 6.0.0 (M Stuiver and PJ Reimer 1986–2010) (http://calib.qub.ac.uk/calib/). The calibration data set is intcal04.14c. Calibrated ranges have been rounded to the nearest 10 years. The Mirador Group (LJ-505 and LJ-508) was a Middle and Late Preclassic site 7.4 km south-southwest of the center of Classic Dzibilchaltun, and the Xculul Group (I-171) was a Late Preclassic site 2.6 km west of the center. All samples are thought to have been wood charcoal except I-171, which was carbonized beans.

adiocarbon ge BP	Calibrated Date Probability Ranges 1 sigma (first line), 2 sigma (second line)
995 ± 180	340–330 B.C. (1.6%), 200 B.C.–A.D. 230 (98.4%)
	400 B.C.–A.D. 420 (100%)
130 ± 200	400 B.C.–A.D. 70 (100%)
	760–680 B.C. (3.0%), 670 B.C.–A.D. 260 (96.5%), A.D. 300–320 (.5%)
200 ± 90	382–174 B.C. (100%)
	410–40 B.C. (98.8%), 30–20 B.C. (.06%), 10–1 B.C. (.06%)
215 ± 80	380–200 B.C. (100%)
	400–80 B.C. (97.4%), 80–50 B.C. (2.6%)
230 ± 80	390–340 B.C. (26.6%), 330–200 B.C. (73.4%)
	410–50 B.C. (100%)
270 ± 80	400–350 B.C. (34.7%), 320–210 B.C. (65.3%)
	710–700 B.C. (.4%), 540–100 B.C. (99.6%)
310 ± 80	510–460 B.C. (14.4%), 450–460 B.C. (4.0%), 420–350 B.C. (38.6%), 320–210 B.C. (43.0%)
	750–690 B.C. (5.7%), 670–640 B.C. (1.8%), 590–170 B.C. (92.4%)
330 ± 80	540–350 B.C. (76.6%), 290–230 B.C. (21.6%), 220–210 B.C. (1.8%)
	750–690 B.C. (8.8%), 670–660 B.C. (3.4%), 630–610 B.C. (.8%), 600–200 B.C. (86.9%)
925 ± 340	1610–1570 B.C. (2.8%), 1560–1550 B.C. (1.0%), 1540–770 B.C. (96.2%)
	2010–2000 B.C. (.2%), 1980–360 B.C. (99.3%), 290–250 B.C. (.4%), 250–230 B.C. (.2%)
275 ± 95	1660–1650 B.C. (5.3%), 1640–1450 B.C. (94.7%)
	1870–1850 B.C. (.9%), 1770–1380 B.C. (98.3%), 1340–1320 B.C. (.8%)
710 ± 40	900–810 B.C.
	900–820 B.C.
580 ± 70	810–760 B.C., 680–670 B.C.
	840–550 B.C.

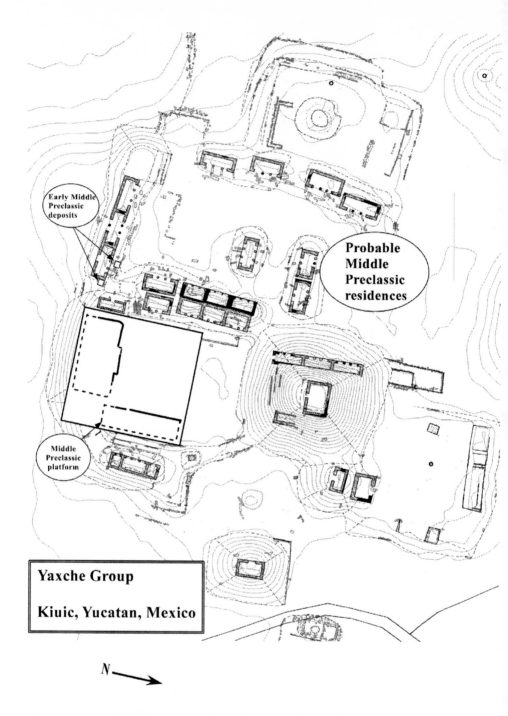

Figure 4.5. The Yaxche Group at Kiuic. Site of the early palace at Kiuic and the location of the Middle Preclassic platform and early Middle Preclassic pre-Mamom deposits.

m north-south × 14 m east-west. No evidence of structures on the platform was found. The ceramic sample from the sealed contexts of three 2 m × 2 m units associated with the first platform include local variants of the major types defined by Andrews as members of the Early Nabanche ceramic complex (Joventud, Chunhinta, and Dzudzuquil groups [Flores Waxy ware]).

Sometime during the late Middle Preclassic the platform was expanded. The floor was raised another 25–30 cm, making the second, larger platform approximately 1–1.10 m high. The areas that have been excavated indicate the construction was composed of small-to-medium stone fill and was topped with a 10-cm-thick stucco floor. Excavations have defined two structures built on the platform, one running north/south on the east side and one running east/west on the south side. Limited excavations show the second Middle Preclassic platform was at least 28 × 28 m.

The east building (N1025E1040-sub) consists of a foundation of roughly cut and shaped stones. Eight meters of the building's west foundation was exposed, and in two places two courses were preserved to a height of approximately 50 cm; otherwise the wall is defined by a single course of stones.

The south building consists of the foundation of a single or in some locations double course of cut faced stones forming a talud and covered with a thick (2–3 cm) coat of stucco. The wall is preserved to a height of roughly 30 cm. The building faced north onto the plaza and is thought to have served as the base of a platform that supported a now-destroyed superstructure. The preserved northwest corner of the platform was covered in stucco and rounded.

This structure, called N1015E1015-sub, was 16 m long. The talud construction of the platform raises the possibility that the structure originally had an apron molding, although the stairway riser in the center of the platform was also inclined. Talud construction, apron molding, and rounded corners are all also associated with late Middle Preclassic construction in the southern lowlands at sites such as Tikal and Nakbe.

Also, like late Middle Preclassic construction in the southern lowlands, the Dzunun Plaza structures at Kiuic indicate that "platform construction and the erection of monumental architecture were planned simultaneous events" (Hansen 1998:63).

Our excavations have revealed no evidence of monumental art, burials, or caches. Early Nabanche ceramics have been recovered throughout the Yaxche Group, indicating that the Middle Preclassic Dzunun platform served as the center for an extensive occupation. Several round and apsidal features underneath the Late Classic palace directly on bedrock appear to be Middle Preclassic. These structures measure roughly 2 × 1.5 m and consist of a sascab floor laid down over a base of small stones and baked mud. The mud along the edges of the structure was baked and fire blackened. Whether this was done at the time of its construction or at the end of its life is unclear. Although no postholes or wattle-and-daub construction were identified, it is possible these foundations supported wooden superstructures. They appear to be perishable constructions surrounding the late Middle and Late Preclassic Dzunun platform, perhaps the remains of cooking or storage buildings. Other Preclassic perishable structures may lie beneath and around the plazas and patios of the Yaxche Group. In addition, several single-course walls resting on bedrock have also been exposed during subfloor operations in the Yaxche Group. Finally, in 2006 a pounded sascab floor was encountered in the Icim Plaza several meters west of the Middle Preclassic platform discussed above. This context provides dated evidence for an occupation with Ek pottery vessels similar to those discovered at Komchen.

We now know that a small community was established at Kiuic in the late Middle Preclassic probably surrounding the original platform defined in Dzunun Plaza. This community continued to grow during the late Middle and Late Preclassic and persisted until a major population explosion and reconfiguration of the area in the early Late Classic when the once public platform and community was covered by a sprawling palace complex. Although there are late Middle Preclassic occupations elsewhere in the southern Puuc, particularly the site of Paso del Macho, which we explored several years ago, evidence for the in situ development of civilization in the Puuc is at the moment most clearly seen at Kiuic. Kiuic proves that Middle Preclassic Maya culture took root in the Puuc and served as the basis for the evolution of complex society in the region. What is equally important is that Kiuic was founded at least as early as Komchen and represents a second example of a pre-Nabanche occupation in the northern Maya lowlands.

Evidence for Early Middle Preclassic Occupation at Kiuic

In 2005 and 2006 excavations in the Icim Plaza of the Yaxche Group indicated an occupation predating the late Middle Preclassic platform defined in Dzunun Plaza. Sherds now recognized as local versions of Almeja

Burnished Gray and Kin Orange-red were found in two nearly adjacent units (C-6 and YY-8) beneath a series of floors in the plaza. Although ICP-MS indicates these ceramics were produced locally and are compositionally distinct from those at Komchen (Bey et al. 2012), the surface treatment and decoration are so similar to Ek complex types that we are comfortable using the same type names. Originally considered an early facet of the Bah complex (Early Nabanche), a reexamination of the small collection based on the comparative study of the collections from Cahal Pech, Tikal, Holmul, and Ceibal now supports placing the material in its own complex completely predating the Early Nabanche complex at Kiuic. We call this complex the Ch'oh Ek ceramic complex. The Almeja Burnished Gray (Figure 4.6a) and Kin Orange-red (Figure 4.6b) at Kiuic show the exact same use of postslip fine-line incisions in geometric patterns creating the same motifs found at Komchen.

The two units where Ch'oh Ek pottery was recovered present the same stratigraphic sequence, although the Ch'oh Ek levels in C-6 were not partially sealed beneath a crushed sascab floor like those in YY-8. Beneath the late Middle Preclassic deposit in YY-8 and the stratigraphically equivalent levels in C-6 was a soil lens containing pre-Mamom pottery. This lens sat directly above bedrock, and in the case of YY-8 directly beneath the remains of the largely intact sascab floor. The pre-Mamom samples recovered in both units were small (15 sherds in YY-8 and 38 in C-6 not including Achiotes and Chancenote sherds), and the soil lens in both units, though defined by Ch'oh Ek pottery, also contain some additional sherds that may be from the Bah complex.

A large piece of burned wood was recovered in YY-8 below the sascab floor sitting directly on bedrock. Two dates were determined from this piece of wood. The first sample was tested in 2008 using traditional radiometric dating and returned a calibrated date with a one-sigma range of 810 to 760 B.C. The second sample run in 2009 used the AMS dating procedure and produced a calibrated date with a one-sigma range of 900–810 B.C. and a two-sigma range of 920–800 B.C. The excavations at Kiuic indicate that the pre-Mamom occupation of the northern Maya lowlands presently can be dated to somewhere roughly between 800 and 900 B.C.

Because of their distinct paste and surfaces combined with decorative motifs that link them to the northern Ek complex types and to southern pre-Mamom pottery, the Kiuic ceramics are without a doubt another example of an early Middle Preclassic ceramic complex in the northern Maya lowlands.

Figure 4.6. Ch'oh Ek Complex ceramics, Kiuic: (a) Almeja Burnished Gray; and (b) Kin Orange-Red from Ek-phase levels in the Icim plaza of the Yaxche Group.

The Relationship of Early Komchen and Kiuic Ceramics to Pre-Mamom Pottery Elsewhere in the Maya Lowlands

Despite the similarity of Ek and Ch'oh Ek incised designs and slips to decoration on pre-Mamom vessels from southern lowland sites, differences between the earliest pottery complexes in the north and south are apparent, just as differences among southern complexes are striking.

One difference between the early ceramic complexes at Komchen and Kiuic and pre-Mamom complexes in Belize and Guatemala is that the earliest southern lowland incised vessels of the Cunil horizon include the pan-Mesoamerican Early Formative symbol set (as illustrated, for example, by Cheetham 2005:Figures 3.5 and 3.6 and Garber and Awe 2009). The Komchen and Kiuic samples so far do not. If this lack results from our limited sample, further excavations may document these Early Formative motifs. An alternative explanation is that the currently known northern assemblages are slightly later than some pre-Mamom complexes in the south and therefore postdate the Early Preclassic motifs. Despite the absence of the Kan cross, music bracket, flame eyebrow, cleft forehead, avian serpent, shark's tooth, and other Mesoamerican Early Formative motifs in the north, the northern Ek-phase postslip incisions form a consistent set of patterns and motifs, some of which likely possessed symbolic significance and many of which are similar to pre-Mamom southern incised motifs. The Ek-phase motifs did not remain in vogue in the late Middle Preclassic Early Nabanche complex.

The most common slip colors in southern lowland pre-Mamom complexes are red and white, the only colors identified at Komchen and Kiuic. In Belize and Guatemala, however, early complexes may include vessels with black slips, orange slips, mottled slips of several colors, red-and-white and red-and-black bichromes, and unslipped burnished orange-brown or buff surfaces (Adams 1971:79–84; Awe et al. 1990; Cheetham 2005:29–30; Cheetham et al. 2003; Estrada-Belli 2011:36–41; Healy, Cheetham, Powis, and Awe 2004; Neivens de Estrada, personal communication, 2005–2011, 2014; Sabloff 1975:46–60; Gifford 1976:61–62; personal observations, 2011). These southern pre-Mamom ceramics, usually bearing what are called dull slips, developed into Mamom-horizon complexes with a similar range of slip colors in waxy or glossy slips. The northern pre-Mamom complexes also appear to have developed directly into Mamom-level assemblages, as indicated at Komchen and Kiuic by the persistence of similar unslipped plain and striated pottery and the similarity of Kin Orange-red to Joventud

Red, especially in slip color. Much of the Early Nabanche pottery is black (Chunhinta group) and variegated or mottled (Dzudzuquil group), and the absence of these slip colors in the earlier Ek and Ch'oh Ek complexes, in contrast to their presence in some southern lowland pre-Mamom assemblages, is a striking difference.

The northern pre-Nabanche (pre-Mamom) ceramics also exhibit a more restricted range of forms than do the southern sites, lacking some of the specialized southern vessel shapes, especially in the white to light gray burnished ware, but also in the red pottery. Komchen and Kiuic ceramics lack the wide, horizontal everted rim so characteristic of pre-Mamom Cunil serving and eating plates in the south (see Sullivan et al. Chapter 3 this volume). Incisions appear on flaring-to-vertical, straight-sided dishes with direct rims, which may have served the same purposes, or on rounded jar walls rather than on horizontal plate rims. The Komchen and Kiuic pre-Mamom ceramics are of high quality. Their forms, slips, and incised decoration attest skilled and sophisticated potters. Nevertheless, the more limited variety of forms, slip colors, and possibly incised motifs in Yucatan at this time suggest the earliest northern potters, geographically more isolated than their southern contemporaries, were in contact with fewer pottery-producing communities, and hence were exposed to a more limited range of ceramic products. Not until the Early Nabanche phase, perhaps about 700 B.C., did the north adopt a ceramic repertoire comparable in variety to that of the southern lowlands.

Recent investigations by Jerald Ek (2013, 2015) at sites on the Río Champoton in Campeche, about 150 and 220 km southwest of Kiuic and Komchen, respectively, have recovered an early Middle Formative ceramic complex (Champoton 1a) that shows similarities to the early pottery of Komchen and Kiuic. These include postslip incision, zoned rectilinear designs, a red-orange slip, a matte white or cream wash or slip similar to the soft white or cream slip that sometimes appears on our Almeja Burnished Gray, and possibly dish forms. As in our earliest complexes, the black slips and mottled orange-buff slips so common in the late Middle Preclassic appear to be absent, as do motifs of the pan-Mesoamerican symbol set.

In late 2011 Andrews and Bey were able to examine four pre-Mamom ceramic collections in Belize and Guatemala, including the Cunil and later sherds excavated by Jaime J. Awe at Cahal Pech, the University of Pennsylvania early Eb type collections and the Proyecto Nacional Mundo Perdido collections at Tikal (the latter reorganized in 2011 by Nina Neivens), the early K'awil ceramics recovered by Francisco Estrada-Belli and Nina

Neivens at Holmul, and the Real Xe lots at Ceibal excavated by Takeshi Inomata, Daniela Triadan, and their colleagues. All of these pottery collections illustrated the gradual change from Cunil horizon ceramics through the early Middle Preclassic to late Middle Preclassic Mamom complexes, but the most useful for demonstrating this two- or three-century development were the Cahal Pech and Ceibal sequences, in which one could follow modal changes through many still-intact lots and stratigraphic levels. In these two collections the gradual development of pre-Mamom ceramics to Mamom were clear. All four pre-Mamom complexes show some modal similarities to the Ek complex ceramics of Yucatan, but the closest ties appeared to be to the Real Xe vessels at Ceibal. Inomata and his colleagues have encountered enough superimposed Real Xe levels, separated by plaster floors and dated by radiocarbon, to subdivide the Real complex into three well-dated facets (Inomata 2011; Inomata et al. 2013). Of these, the sherds of Real 1–2 look to us and to Inomata (personal communication, 2013) to be the closest to the Ek complex ceramics. The span of Real 1–2 is 1000–800 B.C., encompassing the range of the dates Bey obtained from the earliest pottery-bearing levels at Kiuic. The closest similarities appear to be in the vertical, diagonal, and crosshatched, postslip-incised designs on the red- and white-slipped Ceibal vessels. The northern Kin Orange-Red and Kin Orange-Red Incised are very similar in slips and decoration to the Real Xe Abelino Red and Pico de Oro Incised, and Almeja Burnished Gray and its incised variety at Komchen and Kiuic are correspondingly similar to the Ceibal Huetche White and Comistun Incised. Real 1–2 pottery at Ceibal includes straight-walled dishes similar to those in the north but has a greater variety of rim forms.

To judge from these close similarities, which are not equaled at other early southern sites, the closest ceramic ties between northern Yucatan and the southern lowlands in pre-Mamom times were to Ceibal, or to the western Peten generally. Andrews in 1990 suggested that Early Nabanche ceramics of the north were more like those of Ceibal and Altar de Sacrificios than to other southern lowland Mamom complexes. These ceramic links to the western Peten now appear to extend back to the beginning of pottery-making in the lowlands.

The Ek Phase in Northwest Yucatan

We think that the ceramic stratigraphy at Komchen and Kiuic demonstrates the existence of the Ek complex, consisting of the unslipped Achiotes group, the orange-red Kin group, and the burnished gray-to-white Almeja group, and that this earliest assemblage of pottery at Komchen underlies and is not mixed with Early Nabanche/Mamom sherds. The sealed and protected position of the pre-Mamom complex below two of the central constructions at the largest Preclassic civic complex in far northwestern Yucatan is a logical place to expect to encounter remains of the earliest pottery-making settlement. Without these unmixed midden and fill deposits, the Kin and Almeja sherds would not readily have been separated from later Nabanche assemblages. Mixed deposits at the base of all of the largest structures at Komchen would have made it difficult or impossible to recognize and define the Ek complex in the 1980s.

The past decade has witnessed an explosion of archaeological survey and excavations in far northwest Yucatan, generally to the northwest of Mérida, in addition to the investigations at Poxila, Xocnaceh, and Xtobo mentioned above (see Robles and Ceballos Chapter 9; Gallareta Chapter 11; and Anderson et al. Chapter 8 this volume). Chief among these research projects are the Proyecto Costa Maya survey (Andrews and Robles 2004, 2008; Anderson et al. Chapter 8 this volume) and the subsequent salvage excavations near Caucel, just northwest of Mérida (Ceballos et al. 2008), but other sites have provided additional evidence of Preclassic architecture and ceramics, including Tipikal, near Mani (Peraza et al. 2002), Quintas del Mayab and Site 16Qd(4): 49, both bordering Dzibilchaltun (Maldonado and Echeverría 2004; Uriarte and Mier 2004), and Serapio Rendón, in Mérida (Hernández and Ceballos 2006).

A recent article by Teresa Ceballos and Fernando Robles (2012) presents an interpretation of the ceramic sequence for Preclassic northwest Yucatan that is based on the ceramic stratigraphy from the above projects (see also Andrews and Robles 2008; Ceballos and Jiménez 2000; and Robles and Ceballos Chapter 9 this volume). Their focus in this article is on the Middle Preclassic, and one goal of their presentation is to contrast their proposed sequence with the Komchen sequence as it was developed in the 1980s and as it has been revised in the past few years to include the pre-Mamom Ek phase.

Ceballos and Robles divide the northwest Yucatan Preclassic sequence, running from 1000 B.C. or a bit later to A.D. 250, into two stages, or phases. The first corresponds roughly in time to the Ek and Early Nabanche phases, and the second to the Late Nabanche and Xculul phases at Komchen. They place the ceramics of this 1200-year span in one ceramic complex, called Xanilá.

They state that the Ek complex does not exist, arguing that Ek pottery is contemporary with Early Nabanche. The evidence for this, they believe, is that Kin Orange-red is rare outside of Komchen in their excavations, and when sherds do appear at other sites they are in lots that also contain Early Nabanche sherds. Kin Orange-red is not a separate type, they argue, but should rather be classified as Joventud Red or the later Xanaba Red. It is therefore not pre-Nabanche (pre-Mamom). Ceballos and Robles note also that in 20 years of excavations they have not encountered sherds of Almeja Burnished Gray. They believe that this ware is foreign to the northern Maya ceramic tradition and that Almeja Burnished Gray at Komchen must be an intrusion from outside the northern lowlands. They think it is "very probable that Ek ceramics correspond to . . . a ceramic subcomplex with functional rather than chronological implications for Komchen" (Ceballos and Robles 2012:412).

We think that the failure to identify Ek complex deposits in far northwest Yucatan outside of Komchen stems from the extremely shallow soil deposits in this area and the consequent mixing of Ek with later Preclassic pottery. We were fortunate at Komchen in finding Ek middens and a living surface effectively sealed beneath rubble fill of the largest structures at the site. Had these earliest deposits not been quickly sealed, mixing of Ek and Nabanche refuse would surely have occurred, and Andrews might have arrived at conclusions similar to those of Ceballos and Robles. Although Kin Orange-red is distinct from Joventud and later reds in slip characteristics, surface decoration, and vessel forms, it developed into Joventud Red, and without clear stratigraphy it would have been difficult to separate it from the later ceramic group.

The failure to identify Almeja Burnished Gray in the Proyecto Costa Maya, Caucel, and other far northern collections is a key point in Ceballos and Robles's argument against the Ek complex. But the smoothed or lightly burnished surface of Almeja Burnished Gray, with its soft and friable light gray or whitish wash or slip erodes easily, leaving an eroded sherd that looks like Achiotes Unslipped. If eroded, these sherds would indeed be difficult to identify. But often Almeja sherds can be recognized, as the following evidence suggests.

Recent investigations at the site of Tzubil, just north of the Puuc, near Ticul, have identified Ek-complex ceramics in stratified, but mixed, deposits (Boucher and Palomo 2005). Deep trenches in the central plaza penetrated a meter of Classic and Postclassic layers and floors that overlay three meters of Preclassic midden lenses, most dating to Early Nabanche.

Ek-complex sherds constituted about 8% of the entire collection and included Kin Orange-red (141 sherds), Almeja Burnished Gray (12 sherds), and two cream-slipped sherds. Boucher and Palomo (2005:181) note that the Ek sherds could not be differentiated stratigraphically from the other Middle Preclassic sherds (i.e., they did not appear to be later than Early Nabanche, as was still believed in 2005). In fact, their Middle Preclassic lots show slightly higher relative frequencies for Ek types than for Early Nabanche types toward the base of this deposit, indicating that Ek preceded Early Nabanche at Tzubil, as we now know to be the case.

More recent work by Wilberth Cruz (2010) and Ringle and Bey (Ringle et al. 2014) has recovered pre-Mamom pottery from a number of sites running from the northeastern Puuc north toward Mérida. Cruz analyzed ceramics collected from salvage excavations in 16 archaeological sites in this region and identified Kin group sherds in seven of them. Running south to north these sites include Yaxhom, Sac Nicte, Mani, Tipikal, Mama, Tekit, and Acanceh. His total Kin group sample size is 407 sherds with 227 from Tipikal and most of the others from Yaxhom (n=91) and Mani (n=54). Cruz's text provides no discussion of the contexts the ceramics came from, and he places the Kin group material in an unnamed Middle Preclassic ceramic complex (Cruz 2010:34).

Cruz identifies several types within the Kin group, renaming Kin Orange-red Incised Ekmaben Incised. Kin group forms include *ollas* (jars), bottles, *tecomates*, plates, and basins. His Ekmaben Incised is characterized by the same set of postslip decorative motifs found at Komchen and Kiuic as well as some additional motifs not seen at either site (Cruz 2010:Figures 11–19).

In the summer of 2011 Bey and Ringle (Ringle et al. 2014) identified Kin Orange-red Incised ceramics in a surface sample collected from the edge of the Xpotoit aguada located 600–800 m southeast of the Yaxhom Acropolis, providing further evidence of a pre-Mamom occupation in the northeast corner of the Puuc. Even more recently Ringle and Bey have identified significant deposits of Ek material in test excavations at several Preclassic sites in the Eastern Puuc, including the Yaxhom Acropolis (Ringle et al. 2014).

Like other northern Ek samples, the ceramics from these eastern Puuc sites, Yaxhom, Tzubil, and Cruz's sites between the northeast Puuc and Mérida do not display recognizable examples of the pan-Mesoamerican Early Formative symbol set.

The site of Tipikal, 20 km east of Ticul, beside the Mérida-Oxkutzcab highway, included a buried Middle Preclassic apsidal room, now consolidated, with a rich cache of nine complete early vessels on the plaster floor abutting the room (Peraza et al. 2002). The excavators interpreted this as a termination ritual. Six of the vessels are common Early Nabanche types (ca. 700–450 B.C.), two are Kin Orange-red Incised bottles, and one is a Kin Orange-red *tecomate*. This cache provides the only solid evidence to date that Kin Orange-red overlapped with Early Nabanche (Mamom) ceramics.

The Tipikal cache did not contain Joventud Red vessels, signaling that the other two major Early Nabanche decorated groups in the deposit (Chunhinta Black and Dzudzuquil Cream-to-buff) appeared in northern Yucatan before Kin Orange-red had developed everywhere into Joventud Red. Black and variegated cream-to-buff vessels do not appear in the Ek complex, and their appearance by or before 700 B.C. in the north suggests a stimulus from the southwestern lowlands. The matte gray-white slips of the Ek complex disappeared as the hard, glossy, colorful slips of Early Nabanche were introduced.

By 900 to 800 B.C. pre-Mamom settlements extended from Kiuic in the south to Komchen in the northwest, with many sites in between. Cruz's evidence brings Ek settlement to within 40 km of Komchen, leaving little doubt that pre-Mamom occupation was widespread by early Middle Preclassic times, with significant occupations at Komchen and in the eastern and southeastern Puuc region.

Ceballos and Robles (2012:414–417) further argue that Early Nabanche in northwest Yucatan, with the red Joventud, black Chunhinta, and mottled cream-to-buff Dzudzuquil ceramic groups, begins by 1000 B.C. or shortly afterward (Robles and Ceballos Chapter 9 this volume). Their evidence for this is three early radiocarbon determinations from northern sites associated with Early Nabanche (Mamom-equivalent) ceramics and their belief that Mamom pottery appears at Nakbe by about 1000 B.C., early in the Ox phase (Forsyth 1993b), and that Mamom-like ceramics also appear at Cuello and Colha at about this time (Kosakowsky and Pring 1998), so that similar ceramics could be expected in Yucatan near this date. This argument leads finally to their conclusion that Cunil and Mamom were contemporary in the early Middle Preclassic and that they were regionally, not chronologically, distinct.

The argument that the late Middle Preclassic Early Nabanche complex can be dated to 1000 or even 900 B.C. is open to question. We think that two of the early northern lowland radiocarbon dates presented in support of this position (one from Komchen and one from the Preclassic Mirador Group, also several kilometers west of Dzibilchaltun) are not reliable and that the northern dates, as a whole, do not support a beginning of Early Nabanche before 700 or 750 B.C. Likewise, their proposed dates of 1000 B.C. for Mamom-related ceramics at Nakbe and Cuello are not widely accepted. Closer to home, the existence of pre-Mamom settlements at Komchen and Kiuic dating to 900 or 800 B.C. is incompatible with a 1000 or 900 B.C. date for the following Early Nabanche phase.

Preclassic Redwares in Northwest Yucatan

Ceballos and Robles's (2012) Preclassic ceramic sequence for northwest Yucatan from about 1000 B.C. to A.D. 250 contains one ceramic complex (Xanilá) and differs in several other ways from the four-phase sequence Andrews has established for Komchen. Most of these differences, although they are all of interest and merit careful consideration, are beyond the scope of this paper. The most striking difference, however, is in the redwares, and this subject deserves attention here.

Because redwares are common throughout the Preclassic sequence, they are useful in gauging change. At Komchen, Kin Orange-red (Ek complex) developed into Joventud Red (Early Nabanche), followed by Sierra Red (Late Nabanche), and finally Xanaba Red (Xculul). All of these overlap with their closest red neighbor in our ceramic stratigraphy, especially Joventud and Sierra, the latter of which was the most common type at Komchen, with about twice as many sherds as the second-most-frequent type, the Early Nabanche Chunhinta Black. A large part of the Nabanche reds could have been classified as either Joventud or Sierra Red, especially because a peak occupation at Komchen seems to have been about 400–300 B.C., when Joventud was slowly changing into Sierra.

Ceballos and Robles's Preclassic northwest Yucatan sequence includes two main red types, Joventud Red and Xanaba Red. They think Joventud Red was slowly replaced by Xanaba Red toward the end of the Middle Preclassic. Xanaba Red was dominant during the Late Preclassic, but they believe it continued through the Early Classic, disappearing only at the beginning of the Late Classic, a span of about a thousand years (Ceballos and Jiménez 2000). The apparent persistence of Xanaba Red and other Late Preclassic types for a millennium may result, we suggest, from mixing of earlier ceramics with those of later complexes at both ends of this span.

Sierra Red, the traditional marker of the Late Preclassic, is relatively rare in their collections, and they believe it was inspired by the "foreign" southern Chicanel tradition rather than developing from and replacing Joventud Red as it did at Komchen. They note that one standardized dish form is characteristic of their Sierra Red. The red slip of their Sierra is flaky, similar to that of Sierra Red: Late Variety at Komchen, which begins toward the end of Late Nabanche and continues in Xculul. Either their collections do not have the hard, glossy, earlier Sierra Red: Tiho Variety of Komchen, which appears in a large number of vessel forms, or most of this type has been included in their Joventud Red. Andrews's observation of some of their collections leads him to think the first alternative is more likely.[3]

Ceballos and Robles's redware sequence, running from Joventud Red to Xanaba Red without an intervening span characterized by Sierra Red, may be correct for most of northwest Yucatan, but it is not an accurate portrayal of ceramic history at Komchen. Nearby sites sometimes have ceramic sequences and other aspects of material culture that are stylistically or functionally different from each other, for many possible reasons, including different loci of production, modes of distribution, status, identity, intended uses, and simply historical events. Komchen was the largest and probably most powerful Preclassic community in this part of northwest Yucatan from earliest times, and the production and consumption of distinct pottery finishes and other decoration by a central and influential group is a possible interpretation of the different redware sequence.

Summary and Conclusions

The earliest ceramics in Mesoamerica, probably in Puebla and Oaxaca, may precede 2000 B.C. This technology appeared on the Pacific coast of Chiapas between 1900 and 1600 B.C., extending as far south as northeast Honduras. Similar pottery appeared in the Olmec heartland shortly afterward. It was not until about 1200 B.C., however, that ceramics spread into the highlands of Guatemala, and in the Maya lowlands the introduction of pottery lagged still farther behind.

By 1000 B.C. or earlier, semi-sedentary agricultural groups scattered throughout the southern Maya lowlands adopted the use of pottery vessels. Their broken remains are associated with the first small, perishable houses archaeologists have been able to find. The process of changing from stone, gourd, and basket containers and starting to live in permanent structures year-round seems to have lasted about a century throughout the southern lowlands. The earliest complexes in Guatemala and Belize, often referred to as the Cunil horizon, may date to the terminal Early Preclassic, but these ceramic assemblages continued with changes through the early Middle Preclassic until the development of Mamom pottery at about 700 B.C.

Until recently it appeared that the earliest ceramics and sedentary communities in the northern half of the Maya lowlands dated to the late Middle Preclassic Mamom horizon, two or three centuries later than in the south. A restudy of the ceramic stratigraphy at Komchen, in northwest Yucatan, and new excavations at Kiuic, in the Puuc, provide the first evidence in the north for pre-Mamom ceramics and masonry platform construction, possibly as early as 900 B.C. Recent excavations in the Puuc and at sites near the mouth of the Río Champotón have documented similar pre-Mamom ceramics. The identification of pre-Mamom sherds in collections from sites located between the Puuc and present-day Mérida indicate that this early occupation was widespread in the north.

The clearest indication that the first southern lowland pottery of the Cunil horizon dates to the end of the Early Preclassic is that these vessels at many sites exhibit incised designs that belong to a set of motifs widely shared across Mesoamerica in the late Early Formative but that fall out of use afterward. The pre-Mamom assemblages from Komchen, Kiuic, and other northern sites do not appear to share this Early Formative Mesoamerican symbol set, but the Ek-phase incisions do form a consistent and complex set of patterns and motifs from site to site. Some of the motifs likely possessed symbolic content, and many of them are comparable to early Middle Preclassic motifs in the southern lowlands. By the Early Nabanche phase these fine, postslip designs had been replaced by other forms of surface decoration. The absence of Cunil-horizon Early Formative motifs may suggest a northern adoption of pottery-making slightly later than most sites in the southern lowlands. An alternate but perhaps less likely interpretation might be that the inspiration for the first pottery in the north came from a different region in Mesoamerica, but at the same early date. Future excavations and more Ek-phase radiocarbon determinations may answer this question but will also almost certainly raise other complex issues.

The Ek complexes of Yucatan are simpler than the Nabanche/Mamom complexes that follow, although their incised designs are more elaborate. The decorated wares include only a gray, burnished pottery, sometimes with a white slip or wash, and a dull red-orange slip. Vessel forms are severely limited in number. Nabanche/Mamom vessels, with many more forms, bear black, red, and a range of cream, buff, and orange slips that are bright, hard, thick, and glossy or waxy. Although the Nabanche plain and red wares developed from those of the Ek complex, the northern Maya adopted many changes in slips, firing techniques, vessel forms, and surface decoration at this time, and the two complexes are radically different from each other.

Large masonry platforms dating to the Ek phase at Komchen, one of which was at least a meter-and-a-half high, formed the initial stages of the largest constructions around the Central Plaza, indicating that the public, administrative, and ritual center of the Preclassic community was laid out before 800 B.C. The Central Plaza and surrounding large platforms conform to the Middle Formative Chiapas ceremonial and residential pattern described by Clark and Hansen (2001) at La Venta and at several roughly contemporary sites in Chiapas, although, at least in its final form, Komchen lacked the characteristic E-Group at the south end of the plaza. The pre-Mamom hilltop plaza leveling documented in recent years at Cival (Estrada-Belli 2011) and Ceibal (Inomata 2011; Inomata et al. 2013) in the Peten required more preparation than the earliest constructions at Komchen, but the Maya at Komchen started with a level surface. The Ek pre-800 B.C. linear plaza and surrounding platform complex appears to have been the earliest in Yucatan and among the first major ceremonial constructions in the Maya area. Ceibal, however, is the earliest known (Inomata et al. 2013), with a plaza and large platforms conforming to the Middle Formative Chiapas pattern initiated by about 1000 B.C., apparently predating the far more massive arrangement at La Venta. Although not nearly as large as the later Middle Preclassic platforms at Komchen and many other sites, the earlier Komchen civic and elite constructions indicate a level of social and economic complexity far beyond the simple farming villages once envisaged for the ninth and tenth centuries B.C.

An examination of the pre-Mamom ceramic complexes at Cahal Pech, Tikal, Holmul, and Ceibal in 2011 suggests to us that the closest ties to the northwest Yucatan pre-Mamom ceramics in the southern lowlands are at Ceibal, and that these ties are strongest in the pottery of Real 1–2, which is dated to about 1000 to 800 B.C., corresponding closely to the pre-Mamom dates from Kiuic. Takeshi Inomata, after examining the Komchen, Kiuic, and other northern Ek pottery, agrees with this assessment (Inomata, personal communication, 2013). Andrews wrote in 1990 that the closest links to the northern Early Nabanche/Mamom complex were with the western Peten, and it now seems likely that these similarities began at least two centuries earlier.

Although pre-Mamom ceramics are scattered over northwest Yucatan and the Puuc, and will surely be found at the base of many more sites, the population density, community size, and extent of public construction in pre-Mamom Yucatan is dwarfed by the huge platforms of the later Middle Preclassic. The reasons we believe it has taken so long to define this early occupation are not only that it is buried at the bottom of later sites, but also because it is rarer. The change that takes place by the beginning of Nabanche/Mamom following this initial ceramic occupation is striking— a huge expansion of the population in northwest Yucatan, with extensive settlements and massive constructions at Xocnaceh, Poxila, Komchen, Yax-una, and many other towns in the Puuc and on the northern plains. The southern lowlands witnessed the same expansion at this time, from a similarly limited pre-Mamom population base. Some demographic spread from south to north is conceivable in the late Middle Preclassic, but the similar patterns of cultural development in the north and south suggest that local population growth in all parts of the lowlands offers a better explanation for this massive increase in social complexity than does migration.

One goal of this chapter has been to contrast our interpretation of the northern Maya ceramic sequence from about 1000 to 700 B.C. with that proposed by Teresa Ceballos and Fernando Robles (2012). We have argued for the existence of an early Middle Preclassic Ek ceramic complex at Komchen, Kiuic, and many other northern sites. Ek corresponds in time and content, we believe, with Cunil and slightly later complexes throughout the southern lowlands. Ceballos and Robles do not accept the existence of Ek and prefer to extend Nabanche (their Xanilá phase) back to 1000 B.C.

The differences in interpretation, we think, stem from differences among the sites we have excavated. The large platforms at Komchen, despite the devastation by stone-robbing, still preserved some excellent and deep stratigraphy defined, in Structure 21J1, by intact plaster floors. Ek sherds were sealed at the base of and in the lowest fill levels of more than one structure. At most other far northwestern sites Preclassic cultural remains are mixed, making it more difficult to define the Preclassic ceramic sequence.

As more Preclassic sites and adjacent regions are investigated and their earliest remains analyzed and dated, the nature and external relationships of the northern Ek phase should clarify. Understanding the origins of northern Maya civilization will depend on understanding the sequence of the earliest local societies and their interactions with nearby and distant communities.

Acknowledgments

Research at Komchen, co-directed with Norberto González Crespo in 1980, was funded by the National Science Foundation, INAH, and the Middle American Research Institute at Tulane University. Our colleague William Ringle is responsible for much of the research and analysis at Komchen. Research at Kiuic with Tomás Gallareta Negrón and William Ringle was co-directed by Arqlga. Rossana May and was funded by a number of private foundations, Millsaps College, INAH, and the National Science Foundation. We are grateful to our many colleagues in Yucatan for decades of stimulating conversations, help, and friendship. Fernando Robles Castellanos and More Ceballos Gallareta have spent many an hour showing their northwest Yucatan collections to us and engaging us in spirited discussions about how they differ from ours and what that might mean. Tony Andrews has inspired us to be sure our interpretations make sense. A trip to Belize and Guatemala in October 2011 to look at and discuss four important early Maya ceramic collections was made possible by Jaime J. Awe, who laid out the Cahal Pech type collections for us and explained them, level by level; by Erick Ponciano Alvarado, Director General del Patrimonio Cultural y Natural of Guatemala, and Álvaro Jacobo, Director of the Tikal archaeological zone, who allowed us to inspect the Tikal collections; by Takeshi Inomata and Estela Pinto, who permitted us to examine the superb Ceibal collections; and Nina Neivens and Francisco Estrada-Belli, who graciously hosted us in their home in Antigua so that we could see their early ceramic collections from Holmul. To Nina Neivens and Jaime Awe, who accompanied us to Guatemala after we saw his Cahal Pech materials, we owe a huge debt for their help and companionship.

Notes

1. Because the earliest permanent settlements with pottery in the Maya lowlands date back only to 1000 B.C. or a number of decades earlier, they are placed in the early Middle Preclassic. Some of these Maya sites, however, have ceramic vessels with incised motifs and a widespread symbol set that elsewhere in Mesoamerica are dated to the late Early Formative, as this period is usually referred to outside the Maya area, and that disappear in the Middle Formative. Rather than causing confusion, this circumstance and a large number of radiocarbon determinations help place the introduction of both the ceramic technology and the motifs near the juncture of the Early and Middle Preclassic.

2. When Nina Neivens and Francisco Estrada-Belli in 2005 showed Andrews photos of similar postslip-incised motifs on early sherds from new excavations at Holmul,

Guatemala, it was clear that Andrews needed to reexamine what he had considered a shaky chronological and typological interpretation more than 20 years earlier. At about the same time, Bey sent Andrews photos of his earliest ceramics from Kiuic, which, as described below, are strikingly similar to Ek complex sherds from Komchen.

3. In the 1980s, when Andrews first struggled with the placement of the Ek complex, he noted that some of the Kin Orange-red pottery was similar to Joventud Red of Early Nabanche but that the bright orange-red slip was often more like the later Xanaba Red, which reached its peak at Komchen in the Terminal Preclassic Xculul phase. This led Andrews at first to interpret Kin as an early variety of Xanaba Red, until it became clear that it had none of the late diagnostics of Xanaba Red and that its stratigraphic position, and the pottery that did, and did not, accompany it, demanded a separate complex.

In the summer of 2010 Andrews asked More Ceballos to look at the Komchen collection of Ek-phase Kin Orange-red. As noted above, the Ek complex has not been found elsewhere in unmixed contexts in northwest Yucatan, and Ceballos and Robles consider it part of their early Xanilá complex. Ceballos thought that all of the Kin Orange-red collection could be classified as Joventud Red or, more frequently, Xanaba Red, that is, as part of the Xanilá complex.

One conclusion that is supported by the similarity between Kin Orange-red and Joventud Red is that the unslipped pottery and the red pottery of the early Middle Preclassic Ek complex developed into the late Middle Preclassic Nabanche complex. Although new black and buff orange mottled wares are introduced in Nabanche, the unslipped smooth and unslipped striated pottery of these two complexes, Achiotes Unslipped and Chancenote Striated, cannot readily be distinguished, and the change in the redware from a dull finish to a hard, lustrous slip is what happened at many southern lowland sites in the transition from pre-Mamom to Mamom.

5

The Role of Ideology, Religion, and Ritual in the Foundation of Social Complexity in the Belize River Valley

M. KATHRYN BROWN, JAIME J. AWE, AND JAMES F. GARBER

The role of ideology, religion, and ritual was fundamental in the development of ancient Maya civilization and has been the subject of much scholarly discussion. David Freidel (1992:116) characterizes "ancient Maya ideology as the interconnected, fundamental ideas held by elite and commoners alike about the order of the cosmos and everything it contains." Arthur Demarest (1992b:135) emphasizes "ritual, religion, and explicit cosmology" in his use of the term ideology. He suggests that religion was the principal source of power of Classic Maya rulers (Demarest 1992b:147). Ritual practices are guided by ideology in order to achieve certain goals, and thus, Maya ideology "was a collective enterprise involving nobility, craftspeople, peasants, the spectrum of society" (Freidel 1992:116). Our knowledge of ritual and religion in Classic Maya society has expanded greatly over the past several decades due to advances in epigraphy and intensive archaeological research. Yet, until fairly recently, little attention has been directed toward understanding the complex nature of Lowland Maya ritual and religion during the Middle Preclassic period (1000–300 B.C.). This has been in part due to a paucity of relevant data predating the Late Preclassic, as David Freidel and Linda Schele pointed out (1988a). As this volume shows, excavations in the last 25 years have built a large body of Middle Preclassic data (see Brown and Bey Chapter 1 this volume), but even so, extensive data pertaining to early Maya religion and ritual practices remains limited. This is partly due to the difficulty of investigating Preclassic remains because they are often deeply buried, and current excavation methods only allow a sampling of the early architecture and associated features.

Despite these challenges, understanding early rituals is crucial for understanding the rise of complexity, as it served as the point of articulation between religion and the rise of complexity and sheds light on the utilization and manipulation of religious ideology by emerging elites to ensure the acceptance of new social conventions that ultimately support a hierarchical social system. As Marcus and Flannery (2004:18257) state, "we assume that ritual evolved with social complexity, but we need long accurately dated cultural sequences to clarify the steps involved." In this chapter, we trace the evidence of shared religious concepts through ritual change and examine how the early Maya of the Belize River valley used material implements of power, including objects and ceremonial/public architecture, to constitute and reinforce an emerging hierarchical society. Although we will be briefly discussing the development and importance of ceremonial architecture, we focus mostly on the religious rituals associated with these early buildings.

Ritual occupies a key position in the processes that lead to the rise of complexity, particularly the use and manipulation of religious ideology by nascent elites to ensure the acceptance of new social conventions that support a hierarchical social system. We argue that initially, communal rituals were fundamental to this process, notably feasting. The role of feasting in the rise of social complexity has been examined by numerous scholars (e.g., Blitz 1993; Clark and Blake 1994; Dietler 2001; Hayden 2001), and we argue feasting played an important role in these processes in the Maya lowlands as well. Household ritual also seems to be important during the early Middle Preclassic, including dedicatory offerings and the use of figurines, indicating shared religious beliefs. We document the changes in ritual patterns through time in the Belize River valley, which culminated in religious rituals that celebrate and support a newly established hierarchical order.

The Belize River valley is especially well-suited for studying the processes that resulted in the institutionalization of a hierarchical social system and the role ideology, religion and ritual played in those processes (Figure 5.1). It is home to some of the earliest known ceramic-using villages in the Maya lowlands (Awe 1992; Brown 2003; Garber, Brown, Awe, and Hartman 2004; Sullivan et al. Chapter 3 this volume), and it was in a prime location along the main trade corridor between the Caribbean Sea and the Peten region. We present recent empirical data from the sites of Blackman Eddy, Cahal Pech, and Xunantunich in the Belize River valley in order to examine the role of ritual and religion in the rise of complexity, with particular focus on the changes in early symbolic expression as well as the changing physical mediums of that expression and how this relates to transformations in the social/political landscape in the upper Belize River valley. The archaeological evidence for ritual that we present from these three sites comes from different contexts and, therefore, illustrates a wide range of early ritual activity. The data lead us to reconstruct the following stages in the development of social complexity and the institutionalization of hierarchy in the Belize River valley and the role that religion and ritual played in this dynamic process:

1. By the beginning of the early Middle Preclassic (ca. 1000–800 B.C.), or likely as early as 1100 B.C., some of the earliest known ceramic-using villages in the Maya lowlands had been established on strategic hilltops in the Upper Belize River valley, overlooking rivers and rich floodplains. Such sites include Blackman Eddy, Cahal Pech, and Xunantunich. The earliest ceramic assemblages from these sites indicate that ritual feasting was an important communal activity, one that helped establish local communities and reinforced shared beliefs about the community's place in the cosmos through the use of ceramic serving vessels that displayed key cosmological symbols (Brown 2007; Garber and Awe 2008; Sullivan et al. Chapter 3 this volume). Ritual offerings found at Cahal Pech (Awe 1992) demonstrate the importance of early symbolic references to the cosmos. Even from this early period, exotic materials like jade, marine shell (see Hohmann et al. Chapter 6 this volume), and obsidian were important for ritual purposes and as a source of wealth, suggesting that the rivers were important trade corridors.

2. Slightly later in the early Middle Preclassic period (800–600 B.C.), we see evidence for shifts in ritual activities, manifested in three ways. First, the display of actual symbols on ceramic vessels is deemphasized, although Brown (2007) has argued elsewhere that this is because the vessels themselves take on those symbolic meanings. Second, we see an expansion in the types of symbolic ritual offerings to include the dedication of buildings with offerings that reflect cosmological symbolism and burials that suggest the beginning of ancestor veneration. Third, the valley's earliest known E-Group was built by this period at Xunantunich, suggesting that some rituals were tied to annual cycles of the sun. We argue that the introduction of public architecture, including E-Groups, suggests the beginning of a broadening of ritual behavior to incorporate both public and communal activities as well as religious rituals that are celebrated by a

decidedly smaller segment of the population (Brown 2003; Brown and Garber 2008).

3. By the late Middle Preclassic (600–300 B.C.) or slightly earlier, a settlement hierarchy had emerged in the Belize River valley, as the sites of Cahal Pech, Blackman Eddy, and Xunantunich grew in size while several other sites remained relatively small such as Barton Ramie, Nohoch Ek, Chan, and Buenavista del Cayo. Labor is invested in ceremonial architecture, and early site plans emphasize an east/west alignment, reflecting the path of the sun. Evidence for communal rituals such as feasting continues. Feasting activities emphasize the use of public spaces and appear to be related to the consecration and construction of platform buildings (Brown 2003, 2007; Brown and Garber 2005, 2008; Garber, Brown, Awe, and Hartman 2004). Additionally, the first evidence of warfare occurs during this period, suggesting competition between larger sites in the valley.

4. By the Late Preclassic (300 B.C.–A.D. 300), ritual activities in the Belize River valley reflect a fully stratified social structure. Although we see the elaboration of monumental buildings and the first use of carved monuments, such as stelae, during this period, in this chapter we emphasize the evidence for religious rituals related to important ancestors. These include the reentering of burial locations and removal of bones for important reburial events. We argue that the symbolic enshrining of ancestors in special places and in layered offerings reflects aspects of the Maya creation myth that, in turn, legitimates the higher status of their living descendants. Essentially, we see an expansion of ritual through the Middle Preclassic that culminates in the Late Preclassic time period with an emphasis on ritual offerings symbolically related to cosmology, the resurrection of important ancestors, and are tied to the newly established institution of kingship. More importantly, the diachronic shifts that we have documented in ritual practices within the Belize River valley reflect modification, or perhaps manipulation, of shared religious concepts that gradually enhance the power of specific individuals or groups resulting in sanctioned hierarchies.

We address each of these steps in turn after a brief description of the sites from which the data we present are drawn.

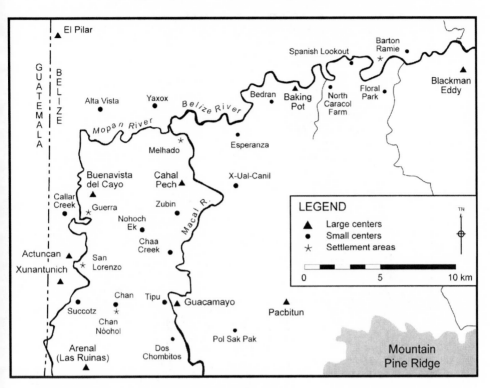

Figure 5.1. Map of the Belize River valley showing sites.

The Upper Belize River Valley

Recent research at Blackman Eddy, Cahal Pech, and Xunantunich has uncovered evidence for early symbolic expression and ritual practices. These
data, albeit different in scope and nature, complement each other nicely
and illustrate certain patterns in early Maya religious ritual behavior, including feasting, symbolic expression through material objects, symbolic
expression through the built environment, and an emphasis on venerating
ancestors.

Blackman Eddy is located on a ridgetop overlooking the Belize River
(Figure 5.2). Excavations at the site were conducted by the Belize Valley Archaeology Project, directed by James F. Garber (Garber, Brown, Awe, and
Hartman 2004). Although a relatively small ceremonial center during the
Classic period, the site had many components of larger centers, including,
stelae, monumental architecture, a ballcourt, and an E-Group. The site was
initially occupied by ca. 1100 B.C. during the Kanocha phase (ca. 1100–900

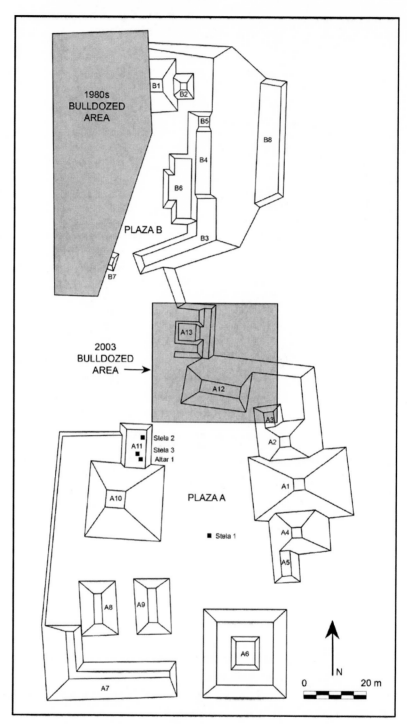

Figure 5.2. Site map of Blackman Eddy.

B.C.), when it was a small village. By the Late Preclassic/Early Classic, the site had expanded to include two formal plazas bounded by ceremonial architecture including an E-Group, a ballcourt, and three stelae (one carved) and an altar. The carved stela (Stela 1), dates to the Early Classic period (Garber, Brown, Awe, and Hartman 2004); however, it is quite possible that the uncarved stelae may date to the Late Preclassic.

The northernmost structure at Blackman Eddy, Structure B1, suffered severe damage from bulldozing in the late 1980s. This unfortunate destruction, however, provided an opportunity to thoroughly investigate the remaining portion of the mound through large horizontal excavations. This led to the discovery and documentation of over 13 construction phases spanning from approximately 1100 B.C. to A.D. 800, along with associated caches and deposits that reflect the activities that occurred on and around those buildings (Brown 2003; Garber, Brown, Awe, and Hartman 2004). The sequence of Structure B1 reveals a history of development from early domestic structures to low communal platforms to restricted-access pyramidal structures (Brown 2003).

Cahal Pech is a medium-sized ceremonial center located on a hill overlooking the Macal River and the modern town of San Ignacio (Figure 5.3) (Awe 1992). Investigations at the site are ongoing, and data presented in this chapter comes from archaeological projects directed by Jaime J. Awe, Paul F. Healy, and James F. Garber. These projects have focused their efforts on locating and excavating the site's extensive Preclassic occupation, which extend back to ca. 1100 B.C., or slightly earlier. The earliest ceramic material, designated the Cunil phase, was first discovered and described by Awe (1992). Radiocarbon analysis places the Cunil phase ca. 1100–900 B.C. (see Sullivan et al. Chapter 3 this volume).

Excavations extending down from the summit of Structure B4 at Cahal Pech encountered deeply stratified architectural remains and an excellent sample of Cunil ceramics in stratigraphic isolation from later deposits. A series of floors represent the remains of at least 13, possibly 14, superimposed platform structures. Although the exposure of these early buildings was limited due to the size of excavation units, the stratified nature of the deposits and the volume of early ceramics that was retrieved from the excavations make this the foremost dataset dating to this early time period. Like Blackman Eddy, the initial occupation at the site was a small village. By the Late Preclassic, the site had grown significantly to include at least four, maybe five, formal plazas bounded by monumental architecture and the center's first ballcourt.

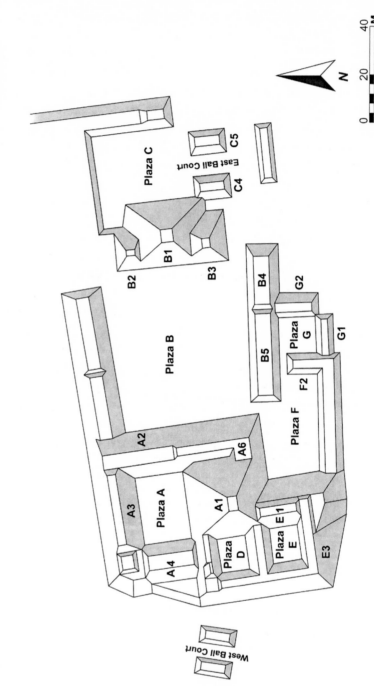

Figure 5.3. Cahal Pech site core.

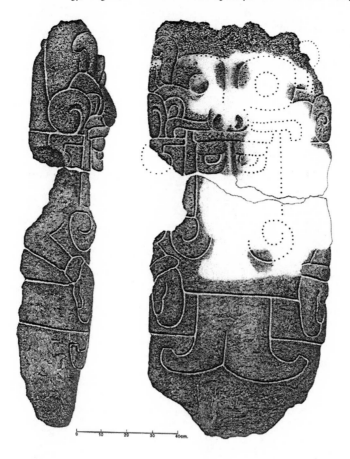

Figure 5.4. Cahal Pech Stela 9.

Stela 9, dated to 300–100 B.C., is the earliest carved monument reported for the country of Belize. This Late Preclassic monument depicts a male figure within the maw of a composite earth creature (Figure 5.4). Awe et al. (2009) argue that the male individual likely represents a deified ancestor or the Preclassic head of the Cahal Pech lineage, which we return to below in more detail. Sometime during the Classic period, the monument was decommissioned and entombed within a large causeway termini pyramid just south of the site core.

By the start of the Christian era, Cahal Pech was certainly one of the major centers of the Belize River valley. Its location near the juncture of the two main branches of the Belize River provided the site a strategic position for participation in trade between the Caribbean coast and sites in the

Peten and the Maya Mountains to the south. The fact that it was continually occupied from the end of the Early Preclassic (ca. 1100 B.C.) to the Terminal Classic (ca. A.D. 800) attests to the long-term success of its inhabitants.

Xunantunich is located south of Cahal Pech, near the modern border of Belize and Guatemala. The Mopan Valley Preclassic Project, directed by M. Kathryn Brown, has been investigating Xunantunich since 2008 and has determined that Xunantunich had two distinct ceremonial cores, a Classic period core and a Preclassic center (Figure 5.5). For the purpose of this paper, we refer to these as Classic Xunantunich and Early Xunantunich. The better known of the two ceremonial centers is focused around Group A. It dates to the Classic period and has a north/south orientation (LeCount and Yaeger 2010). Early Xunantunich lies 800 m to the east and includes Group E. It predominately dates to the Preclassic period and because it was abandoned by the end of the Late Preclassic, it offers a rare opportunity to investigate the formal layout of a Preclassic center without the overburden of later architecture (Brown 2011). The site is oriented east/west and is composed of three formal plazas bounded by ceremonial architecture and large platforms. Brown et al. (2016) have argued elsewhere that Classic Xunantunich and Early Xunantunich were separate centers with different histories. The western plaza group of Early Xunantunich is an E-Group complex,

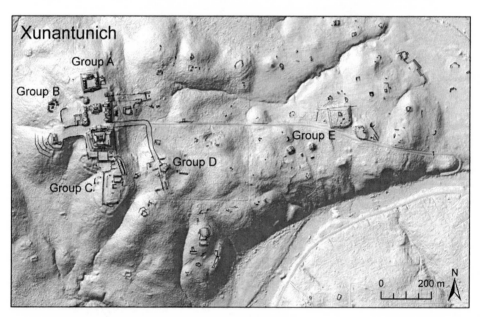

Figure 5.5. LiDAR hillshade of Xunantunich with site map overlaid (structure map courtesy of Angela Keller and Jason Yaeger).

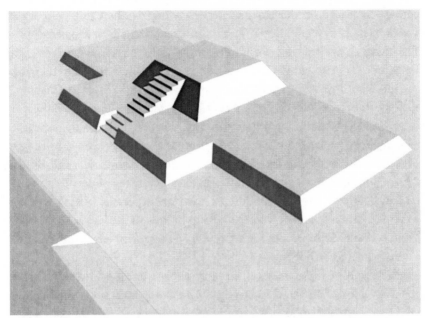

Figure 5.6. Isometric of Early Xunantunich E-Group Eastern Architectural Complex (reconstruction by Leah McCurdy).

and the plaza area itself was heavily modified exhibiting large paved ramps leading to the eastern structure (Figure 5.6). The E-Group, and presumably the other plaza groups at Early Xunantunich, was initially constructed during the early Middle Preclassic (Brown 2017). Two possible uncarved monuments have been found at Early Xunantunich and additional monuments are likely present as only a portion of the site has been investigated to date.

The Early Middle Preclassic: Establishing Community in Early Maya Villages

Although occupation in the Belize River valley extends back to Paleo-American times, it is at the end of the Early Preclassic and into the early Middle Preclassic (ca. 1100–800 B.C.) that we find some of the earliest evidence for settled villages in the Maya lowlands. To date, our research has uncovered evidence of rituals in these earliest villages that include feasting, ritual figurine use, and consecration offerings within the domestic realm.

The use of ideologically charged implements, specifically incised ceramic serving vessels, began by 1100/1000 B.C. when the region's inhabitants lived in small, presumably egalitarian villages (Brown 2007). The earliest ceramic assemblages used in these villages—the Cunil complex at Cahal Pech, Muyal complex at Xunantunich, and the Kanocha complex at Blackman Eddy—consist of both utilitarian wares and serving wares. The latter are tempered with volcanic ash and slipped, and a subset of them are incised with important iconographic motifs (see Sullivan et al. Chapter 3 this volume). The motifs present within the assemblage include the *kan* cross, the cleft, lightning, and a motif that has been interpreted as a stylized avian-serpent. These symbols indicate that the early Maya were part of a pan-Mesoamerican interaction sphere or horizon (Awe 1992; Brown 2007; Cheetham 1998; Garber and Awe 2008). Despite similarities to symbolism in other parts of Mesoamerica, there are aspects of certain symbols displayed on these early ceramics that are unique to the valley, such as the avian serpent motif, which may represent an early symbolic representation of the Principal Bird Deity.

Elsewhere in Mesoamerica, these symbols were used by elites to set themselves apart as special and to legitimize hierarchical social relations. In contrast, in the Belize River valley, there is limited evidence for that degree of social differentiation at this time. For example, elaborate public architecture, another important material implement of power, has not been found dating to this early time period. Ceremonial/public architecture becomes more apparent during the latter part of the early Middle Preclassic. Thus, we argue that these symbols were displayed on ceramic serving vessels that were used in early feasts, possibly hosted by competing lineages, factions, or families. Given the limited evidence for strong inequalities and social hierarchies in these early villages, we assume these feasts were commensal. The host of a particular feast was creating obligations of reciprocity with his or her invitees, obligations that over time could have been developed into more enduring asymmetrical relationships.

Incising these early serving vessels with symbols made them sacred. The *kan* cross, for example, represents the four corners of the universe and the world tree that bridges the underworld, the earth, and the sky. Vessels depicting this iconography are symbolically transformed into portals, and the food served in them is transformed into sacred material, thus sacralizing the feast itself (Brown 2007). It is interesting to note that the symbolism that underlies the *kan* cross—the quadripartite division of the world—is one of the most enduring concepts of Maya civilization, and continued to be a central theme in Maya ritual, continuing into modern Maya rituals today (Brown 2012).

At Cahal Pech, several ritual offerings were encountered that emphasized crocodiles. The earliest entailed the placement of a crocodile lower mandible beneath the earliest Cunil house floor, ca. 1100 B.C. This important offering indicates that the consecration of houses, a Maya ritual act that continues even today, may represent one of the oldest continuing ritual practices of the ancient Maya. The crocodile is a highly charged symbol, representing the earth in Mesoamerican ideology (Reilly 1991; Rust 1992; Stocker et al. 1980). It is possible that the mandible was deposited to petition earth spirits for guardianship of the household, or as part of a ritual offering associated with agricultural fertility. It is also plausible that the mandible was part of a ritual crocodilian mask (also see Flannery 1976:340).

It is interesting to note that the later inhabitants of Cahal Pech may have had a social memory of this important crocodilian mandible offering, as this symbol reoccurs on a slate object placed in an offering associated with a late Middle Preclassic construction phase of the same structure (Structure B4-8th). Moreover, a carved marine shell in the shape of a crocodile was found in an even later Late Preclassic cosmological cache in a subsequent construction phase. The recurring presence of crocodile imagery at Cahal Pech is striking. The crocodile could be a symbol related to the family or lineage who lived in the early house under Structure B4. Marcus and Flannery (1994) have argued that during the San Jose Mogote phase (ca. 1150–850 B.C.) at San Jose Mogote, Oaxaca, ceramic vessels were incised with Sky/Lightning and Earth/Earthquake motifs, and that each of these two spirits were related to competing kin groups (Marcus and Flannery 1996). It is quite plausible that the crocodile was closely associated with a kin group at Cahal Pech that rose to prominence over the course of several centuries.

Additional evidence for household ritual activity comes in the form of consecration offerings of vessels placed under house floors, as seen from excavations at the base of Structure B4 at Cahal Pech. Furthermore, household rituals are suggested by the presence of ceramic figurines, albeit in small quantities during the Cunil/Kanocha phase, in these early Belize River valley villages. These have been interpreted as implements used in domestic rituals.

In summary, the earliest settled villagers of the Belize River valley were conducting household rituals that resulted in the placement of important material symbols, such as the crocodile mandible, into small offerings. They also, presumably, participated in ritual feasts that emphasized cosmology and interaction with important spirits/deities. Such feasts, arguably, would have been part of competitive displays by early aggrandizing kin groups. Both the feasts and the household rituals led to the establishment of sacred space.

The Early Middle Preclassic: Establishing Sacred Place through Consecration Rituals, E-Groups, and Sun Cycles

The latter part of the early Middle Preclassic (ca. 800–600 B.C.) saw an expansion in settlement in the Belize River valley. While hilltop sites like Blackman Eddy, Cahal Pech, and Early Xunantunich that were founded ca. 1100/1000 B.C. continue to grow, we see the establishment of new sites in bottom land areas closer to the rivers such as Barton Ramie, Baking Pot, Buenavista, and San Lorenzo. We also see an expansion into the hills between the rivers with sites such as Nohoch Ek and Chan.

During this same time, the processes of creating sacred space become more materialized, and we see this in both domestic and special function buildings. At Blackman Eddy, an apsidal shaped house structure was consecrated with an offering of the upper half of a Savana Orange chocolate pot placed over thirteen fragments of marine shell. Moreover, we find the earliest demonstrable evidence of ceremonial architecture and special function buildings at Blackman Eddy, Cahal Pech, and Early Xunantunich—the three sites that seem to have had long histories and were established by this time period.

One well-documented example is Structure B4 at Cahal Pech. Awe suggests that the superimposed early Middle Preclassic phase platforms in Structure B4 represent superimposed special function buildings. He bases his argument in the platforms' size and relative complexity, and the high frequency of figurines found within the construction fill. In fact, the approximately 1050 figurine fragments found within this one structure represent approximately 76% of all figurines found at Cahal Pech. Most of these figurines date to between ca. 800–600 B.C. Awe argues that this frequency distribution is the result of purposeful deposition of figurines within the fill of Structure B4. It also suggests that, from quite early, Structure B4 may have served ritual functions that were associated with ancestor worship. It seems likely that this location was initially the house of an important lineage head, possibly from a kin group symbolized by the crocodilian earth motif, and over time, it was transformed into a series of platforms that served ritual functions within the community. This shift of function from domestic to public/ritual is also seen at Blackman Eddy (discussed below), suggesting a broader pattern whereby the earliest public/ritual buildings arose by the sacralization of domestic spaces.

Located to the northwest of Structure B4 and buried beneath Plaza B, a low early Middle Preclassic platform (dating prior to 600 B.C.) was found. Although the platform was poorly preserved, ritual offerings were encountered in several corners. The northwest and northeast offerings represent layered cosmograms (Garber and Awe 2008). Although a crypt burial was encountered in the southeast corner of the platform, Awe suggests that this burial may have been intrusive. A recent AMS date of the burial itself suggests a Late Preclassic date. Moreover, this burial was placed roughly in the center of Plaza B making the association with this early platform difficult to assess. Nevertheless, the layered offerings placed within the other corners of this structure, a possible nondomestic early Middle Preclassic platform, is significant, suggesting that the practice of dedicating structures may have been expanded to include public buildings by this time period. More recent investigations in Plaza B by Nancy Peniche May (2016) has confirmed this early architectural sequence at Cahal Pech.

At Blackman Eddy, we see a shift from apsidal-shaped platforms to plastered rectangular platforms that were low and broad in form. Garber and Brown have argued that these platforms were public in function (Brown 2003; Brown and Garber 2008; Garber, Brown, Awe, and Hartman 2004) and likely served a number of functions including venues for communal feasting that integrated this early community. One of these platforms had a plastered basin constructed into the summit surface that Brown and Garber (2008) have argued may have served as a ritual divining pool. Additionally, numerous quartz crystals found associated with these early platforms may have functioned as ritual divining implements. Ceramic figurines increase in number at this time and include clay bird effigy whistles.

At the Preclassic ceremonial center of Early Xunantunich, excavations have revealed an early Middle Preclassic E-Group. E-Groups have their origin in the early Middle Preclassic in the Maya lowlands and have been suggested to be associated with "large plazas where public rituals were likely performed" (Estrada-Belli 2011:74). The earliest E-Group, ca. 1000 B.C., documented to date in the Maya lowlands is located at the site of Ceibal (Inomata et al. 2013). Within the Belize River valley, it appears that the construction of E-Groups may begin slightly later, ca. 800/700 B.C., which is consistent with the timing of E-Group construction at the site of Cival in Guatemala. It is important to note, however, that this formal arrangement of structures was present early in the region and may represent some of the earliest ritual architecture in the Belize River valley. Investigation of the Early Xunantunich E-Group central eastern structure demonstrates that the E-Group had at least three construction phases, and additional phases are suspected within the core of the mound (Brown 2013, 2017). The earliest version of the E-Group (ca. 800/700 B.C.) had a shaped bedrock platform framing the east side of a plaza and a three-tiered platform on the western edge (see Figure 5.5). Our excavations have revealed that the E-Group complex was significantly rebuilt slightly later during the Middle Preclassic (ca. 700/600 B.C.). The rebuilding event involved shifting the E-Group to the west. The original western structure was re-oriented and converted into the eastern architectural complex and paired with a pyramid on the western edge of a larger sloping plaza (see below). This shift of sacred space to the west is interesting and may reflect social and political shifts within the early community.

These new forms of public architecture are one line of evidence that ritual and religion were important in the development of social and political complexity in the Belize valley. The ceramic assemblages at Blackman Eddy, Cahal Pech, and Early Xunantunich indicate that feasting continued to be important in the early Middle Preclassic period, as well. Elaborate serving bowls and dishes, including new ceramic forms such as chocolate pots and stirrup spouted vessels, indicate an emphasis on the display and serving of desirable food and beverage items.

As noted above, the highly charged incised symbols that marked the early Middle Preclassic Cunil serving vessels are de-emphasized, as the decorative motifs shift to an emphasis on geometric and hatch designs on early facet Jenney Creek vessels. Red slips tend to dominate the assemblages. Elsewhere, Brown (2007) has argued that even plain serving vessels within a ritual context are ideologically charged objects. Ceramic bowls (with or without incised symbols) are employed as receptacles for sacred foods, fluids, and materials which are used as offerings to the gods. Through the ritual use of vessels with displays of symbolic expression the vessel itself takes on the meaning of a portal or "*ol*." This is apparent, as vessels become an important component in most dedicatory caches, especially those that symbolically represent the axis mundi (Brown 2007).

Creating Social Differentiation through Rituals Associated with Sacred Spaces, Ritual Knowledge, and Ancestor Veneration

During the transition from the early to late Middle Preclassic (700–600 B.C.) and into the late Middle Preclassic (600–300 B.C.), we see evidence of a dramatic increase in population, a more established settlement hierarchy, and the emphasis on constructing ceremonial structures that emphasize verticality. We also begin to see evidence of ancestor veneration practices during this time. In this section we highlight empirical data from the Belize River valley that illustrate these general trends.

Although the Belize River valley regional settlement data for the late Middle Preclassic are preliminary, several interesting observations are apparent. First, there is a pattern of re-building on locations that appear to have been established as sacred in the earliest periods of occupation. We have strong evidence for this at both Blackman Eddy (Structure B1) and Cahal Pech (Structure B4). We argue that elites appropriated these sacred places to display their power and authority through ritual acts and new construction efforts on these important structures.

Second, there is variability in size and labor investment of Preclassic public architecture that has implications for site hierarchies and the establishment of early seats of power. Our evidence to date suggests that the Belize valley sites situated in the bottom lands and the hills between rivers do not exhibit large monumental public constructions dating to the late Middle Preclassic, but rather smaller platforms have been encountered. This contrasts with the hilltop valley sites that were established at the end of the Early Preclassic: Blackman Eddy, Cahal Pech, and Early Xunantunich.

Public construction efforts were often accompanied by ritual events. For example, at Blackman Eddy, a deposit of smashed ceramics was uncovered dating to the beginning of the late Middle Preclassic. This deposit has been interpreted as the remains of a ritual feasting event associated with the initial construction of a public building, Structure B1-5th. Although part of this building was destroyed by modern bulldozing activity, evidence suggests that it was an in-line triadic platform (Brown 2003; Garber, Brown, Awe, and Hartman 2004), an architectural form that may reflect the three hearth stones of creation. An in-line triadic form has three structures on a side that face the same direction and differs from triadic architectural groups that become widespread during the Late Preclassic period (see Hansen et al. Chapter 7 this volume and Saturno et al. Chapter 13 this volume).

The smashed deposit was located to the north of this platform complex and slightly downslope, essentially littering the area located on the backside of the building. It consisted of a dense concentration of broken ceramic material associated with faunal remains, charcoal, and exotic materials such as marine shell and obsidian. Ten partial vessels were recovered, all of which were serving vessels. The partial vessels included three Savana Orange bowls, a Savana Orange stirrup spout, a Reforma Incised Mucnal Variety chocolate pot, a volcanic ash tempered Joventud Red bowl, a Jocote Orange-brown jar, and two unusual red slipped volcanic ash tempered bowls, one of which appears to be a new type within the Savana Group, while the other has more affinities to the Joventud Group. It is important to note that numerous refits were also found within the deposit and it is suspected that several other whole or partial vessels may be present within the unexcavated section of the deposit.

The predominance of serving vessels suggests that this deposit is the product of some type of event involving food consumption. Documenting feasting, however, is difficult and necessarily involves a detailed contextual analysis of the deposit including the remains of the foods that may have been consumed as well. Analysis of the 197 fragments of faunal material by Carolyn Freiwald (2008) demonstrated a surprising diversity of animal species with at least 18 (MNI) animals present. Evidence of processing was identified on many of the bone fragments including burning, chop marks, and spiral fracture patterns (Freiwald 2008). The assemblage included many species that were known to be consumed by the ancient Maya including two white tail deer, one brocket deer, one rabbit, one armadillo, one opossum, one agouti, one iguana, one cane toad, one crab, one turtle, three fish, two medium sized mammals, possibly raccoon or weasel, as well as numerous *jute* and freshwater mussels. The wide diversity of animal species present is consistent with a communal gathering in which participants each contributed food items. Freiwald (2008) also identified an interesting pattern of the presence of several immature animals in the assemblage, possibly indicating a preference for younger animals for feasting.

In order to shed light on plant types ritually utilized or consumed, Steven Bozarth analyzed phytolith samples from two vessels, one from the interior of a stirrup spout and the other from charred organic material adhering to the base of a jar. Stirrup spouted vessels are very rare in the Maya lowlands and were most likely used to serve some form of beverage. The sample from this vessel indicated that maize phytoliths were present (Bozarth 2007), suggesting that the beverage served was corn based, quite possibly corn beer or *atole* corn gruel. Additionally, analysis suggested that both maize kernels and chaff were present. This led Bozarth (2007) to suggest that an offering of maize may have been placed above the cluster of ceramic material from which the stirrup spout was recovered. Interestingly, no phytoliths from domesticated plants were found in the second sample of charred organic material, despite a high concentration of phytoliths. Non-domesticated plant material was intentionally burned within this vessel, possibly indicating that it was used as some form of censor (Bozarth 2007). The vessel itself was the lower portion of a large olla, which may have been utilized as on open dish/bowl for burning incense.

Several other lines of evidence are suggestive of ritual activity. First, one of the vessels was placed on top of nine chert flakes, which may symbolically relate to the nine layers of the underworld. Although this is a rather simple cosmological offering, it does have implications related to the ritual nature of the deposit. Second, several of the partial vessels were intentionally halved or quartered. The "broken" edges of three vessels are so regular that they may have been cut with a string saw. The deliberate breaking of vessels into halves and/or quarters may be related to the notion of partitioning the universe, an event that was reenacted with the setting of corner posts in a new building, whether it was a simple house or an elaborate temple structure (Brown 2008).

Third, several exotic items were found within the deposit including marine shell and obsidian. The marine shell included six beads, two tinkler pendants, and 61 pieces of marine shell debitage (Cochran 2009). Jennifer Cochran (2009) has identified a pattern of placing offerings of both finished marine shell artifacts as well as debitage in Middle Preclassic special deposits. The presence of both worked and unworked marine shell clearly indicates the importance of this material category and the symbolic reference to water.

Finally, the presence of certain animal species is suggestive of rituals related to feasting and possible renewal ceremonies. Ethnohistoric and iconographic data suggest that deer were significant in ancient Maya religion (Pohl 1983). Mary Pohl (1983) argues that deer were used in the ritual drama of the Maya ceremonial cycle and were associated with the ritual that marked the New Year. Other animals may have been associated with renewal rites as well including monkey, dog, jaguar, opossum, armadillo, crocodile, turtle, snake, and fish (Pohl 1983). Freiwald (2008) notes that the faunal assemblage from this deposit resembles other faunal assemblages that have been linked to the *cuch* ritual, an agricultural renewal ceremony.

Often these ceremonies utilize both immature and small animals and include fish, all of which are present within this early Middle Preclassic faunal assemblage (Freiwald 2008).

The ritual feasting activity at this location does not appear to have been an isolated event, but rather part of a ritual cycle associated with the termination and construction of public platforms. A second, slightly later, deposit was encountered associated with this structure, and contextual analysis suggests a similar function. This later deposit of smashed ceramics was found above the in-line triadic platform, Structure B1-5th, and likely represents a ritual feasting event associated with the construction of the subsequent platform, Structure B1-4th. As was seen with the first deposit, a variety of faunal material including deer, and other small mammals, as well as whole and partial serving vessels were present. Several of these vessels were intentionally halved, including a stirrup spouted vessel, a Jocote Orange-brown jar, and a Joventud Red plate. A single jade bead was placed upon the halved Joventud Red plate, indicating that it was part of an offering. The presence of two Savana Orange: Rejolla Variety stirrup-spouted vessels suggests a continued emphasis on ritual beverages.

These two Middle Preclassic deposits clearly served a similar function, as both exhibit evidence for ceremonial feasting activities and rituals related to the construction and dedication of public platforms. It is interesting to note that we did not encounter evidence of single vessel offerings or dedicatory caches associated with the earliest public platforms at Blackman Eddy. This early symbolic behavior from Blackman Eddy provides us with a look at communal ritual activities in public spaces. It is interesting to compare this with ritual activities associated with early E-Groups at Early Xunantunich and the celebration of annual cycles of the sun.

As we discussed above, one of the dominant architectural features of the Early Xunantunich's Preclassic ceremonial center is an E-Group. Although we suspect that there are earlier phases yet to be discovered, the earliest phase (as described above) was significantly remodeled in the Middle Preclassic ca. 700–600 B.C. The western structure of the earliest phase was re-oriented and rebuilt to be the new eastern architectural complex. This new phase (Structure E-2-2nd) consisted of a two-tiered pyramid placed on a low platform with wings extending to the north and south. A western pyramid framed the west side of a sloping plaza and together these architectural features form a Cenote-style E-Group. The Cenote-style E-Group type was first documented by Chase and Chase (1995).

Associated with this phase of the E-Group, we encountered a series of postholes in the plaza. These were directly on centerline in front of the steps of the eastern pyramid (Structure E-2-2nd). It appears that a small perishable feature was erected in this location and rebuilt several times. Brown (2013, 2017) has interpreted the posthole feature as the remains of a wooden altar/mesa. An AMS date (UCIAMS 112169) from this feature places the structure at 2435 ± 20 BP, calibrated at the 2-sigma range to 746–407 B.C. (Brown 2013). This date is coeval with an AMS date from a deposit of charcoal and a partial Middle Preclassic vessel that was found ritually smashed on the plaza surface near the corner of the central structure. This sample (UCIAMS 12168) yielded the very same date of 2435 ± 20 BP suggesting that the smashing of this vessel may have occurred at the same time as the burning event associated with the possible wooden altar/mesa. The fact that burned wood from both areas was found above the associated plaza surface suggests that the dates reflect the final use of this phase of the E-Group.

The presence of a wooden altar in the plaza directly in front of the central structure is suggestive of public ritual activities. Moreover, the presence of many postholes suggests that this altar was rebuilt numerous times, which in turn supports the notion of cycles of rituals, quite possibly related to annual solar events like equinoxes and solstices (Brown 2017). When we look at the overall plan of the E-Group, the placement of this altar feature, centerline of the structure, is quite interesting. The plaza associated with the E-Group was heavily modified and included two paved ramps leading to the northern and southern sides of the eastern architectural complex. These ramps limited direct access to the central staircase—and thus the wooden altar—by funneling foot traffic to either side of the altar. Brown (2013, 2017) suggests that the ramps functioned as pathways for ritual processions associated with both solstice and equinox events.

In addition to the postholes, we recovered three fire pits associated with the E-Group. A large circular pit filled with firecracked rock and ash was found in the plaza in front of the western pyramid, directly on the pyramid's central axis. Two smaller circular fire pits were located at the corners of the eastern pyramid. Brown (2017) argues that the fire pits are remains of ritual fires that were lit at night. Nighttime rituals would make sense if the events were held to watch the night sky and the rising sun. We argue that rituals performed at the Early Xunantunich E-Group, although presumably public to a degree, may have been more orchestrated and therefore involved specific ritual specialists that oversaw the events.

When we examine the variability of ritual activities associated with different types of architecture during the late Middle Preclassic, it seems clear that the Belize River valley occupants were experimenting with new ritual venues as well as expanding older traditions. Architecture is used to communicate messages to both the local community and visitors. These messages are often related to cosmology and ideology, but they also transmit information related to social and political relationships, especially as the society becomes more hierarchical. On a broad scale, the east/west site focus and construction of formal plaza spaces bounded by large platforms and pyramids corresponds with evidence of a more hierarchical social system during the late Middle Preclassic. Emphasizing the pathway of the sun, and therefore the special knowledge of annual solar cycles, illustrates this nicely. Additionally, we see that late Middle Preclassic structures begin to emphasize verticality, and therefore, more planning and labor investment. But even smaller construction works, such as the in-line triadic platform at Blackman Eddy, transmit symbolic and ideologically related messages to the community. In this case, it is interesting to note that this was the location of communal feasting activities.

In addition to the symbolic messages that the architecture and site plans transmit, certain ceremonial buildings become a more formal medium for depicting ideologically related iconography during the late Middle Preclassic. We see this first at the site of Blackman Eddy where an early platform was decorated with mask façades. This building, Structure B1-4th, was a low, broad platform with masks flanking the inset staircase. Mask façades become more common and elaborate during the Late Preclassic but they have their humble beginnings in the late Middle Preclassic.

By the end of the late Middle Preclassic, we begin to see an increased emphasis on verticality. For example, a platform (Structure B1-3rd) at Blackman Eddy was rebuilt numerous times, culminating in a two-tiered pyramid form. A single Joventud Red vessel dedicatory offering was placed beneath the plaza surface associated with the earliest version of the pyramidal form (Brown 2003; Garber, Brown, Awe, and Hartman 2004). This fact points to the changing nature and focus of participation in ritual acts. Although the ritual acts performed on the platform at Blackman Eddy can be clearly viewed from the plaza level, the number of actual participants is restricted. The separation of participant and observer is emphasized.

Beyond ritual activities associated with community and ceremonial spaces, we begin to see rituals involving burial rites and veneration practices. The practice of bone manipulation, including placing heads in bowls so that they can be removed for processions and other rituals, has been documented in Classic-period burials and iconography, and it is often associated with ancestor veneration and elaborate reburial rituals (Brown 2013, 2017; McAnany 1995; Robin et al. 2012). The rich diachronic data from the Belize River valley allow us to trace the development of ancestor veneration practices over time and articulate them with broad social processes. Ancestor veneration begins with the placement of honored deceased persons within the heart of the community's ceremonial space in the Middle Preclassic. Important burials were reentered and key skeletal elements, such as the skull, were manipulated and/or removed. By the Late Preclassic, important ancestors were buried in monumental structures of symbolic importance, such as E-Groups and related architectural complexes. These burials included primary interments and the reburial of bones in secondary interments. Certain individuals were interred with their heads placed upon ceramic vessels. This pattern is notable because it allows the skull to be manipulated easily, and it symbolically references the decapitation and resurrection of the Maize God, First Father.

We argue that ancestor veneration was a strategy employed by emerging elites to maintain connection with honored ancestors. It is through certain early burial rituals that connect the living with the dead and, subsequently, the dead with important deities that we begin to see traditions that elevate certain ancestors above other deceased individuals. These practices allow certain conventions to become normalized and thus, the status of the descendants is both elevated and legitimized. We believe that the burial data from the Belize River valley sheds light on the emergence of these conventions.

Buried in the center of the Early Xunantunich E-Group plaza was an adult male individual. This Middle Preclassic burial showed signs of reentry and the head was removed. The presence of two teeth above the vertebrae suggests that the skull was originally present and intentionally removed sometime after burial, presumably for use in ritual activities (Brown 2017). It is important to note that this individual was buried at the center of a community ceremonial space, as opposed to the more widespread pattern of interment beneath domestic houses and courtyards. Although this individual did not have any associated grave goods, the placement within a presumably ceremonial location is unusual and suggestive of special treatment.

This same burial pattern is seen at the nearby site of Chan. Burial 1 at Chan was placed at the center of the Central Plaza in the Middle Preclassic period. The structures around the Central Plaza form an E-Group that was the ceremonial heart of this Maya farming community (Robin et al. 2012). Chan Burial 1 was a simple crypt placed in a pit cut into bedrock (Robin et al. 2012), but it shows signs of reentry at least twice, and "body parts of this ancestor were removed from the grave and in some cases repositioned" (Robin et al. 2012:128). This included the removal of the skull.

The parallel practice at these two sites of burying an important Middle Preclassic individual in the center of the community's E-Group plaza and then manipulating the person's bones is striking, particularly the removal of the skull. We believe that the special funerary treatment of these two individuals represents the earliest evidence of ancestor veneration practices in the Belize River valley. While we believe the skull removal most likely occurred in the Middle Preclassic period, it is possible that it was carried out in later times. Regardless of the timing, the special importance of the skull can be seen in later venerative practices that involved the purposeful placement of the deceased individual's head in a ceramic bowl to facilitate rituals that entailed reentering burials and manipulating bones. We discuss this in more detail in the following section.

The Institutionalization of Social Hierarchies (300 B.C.–A.D. 300)

As we have illustrated above, dramatic changes in architecture and ritual, including ancestor veneration, are evident over the course of the late Middle Preclassic period. We see this further emphasized in the archaeological record of the Late Preclassic. For space constraints, we focus our discussion on four related patterns: the burial of individuals in monumental structures; the reentry of burials and removal of skeletal elements and entire skeletons; the re-interment of those elements elsewhere as secondary burials; and the placement of skulls in ceramic bowls. Taken together, they reflect the elaboration of ancestor veneration and the ways in which it was used to emphasize hierarchical distinctions as the valley's society grew more complex. The practice of placing ancestor skulls in bowls appears to be a Late Preclassic pattern within the Belize River valley and likely represents a continuity in the focus on the skull that is evident in the Middle Preclassic burials discussed above.

A context that shows both continuity and change in burial practices is a Late Preclassic burial at Cahal Pech. The individual was interred in the approximate center of Plaza B, a pattern we described above for important individuals in the Middle Preclassic. The burial shows innovations as well, however, as separate crypts were constructed for the head and body and the skull was placed in a bowl (Garber and Awe 2008). Thus, we suggest that this burial represents the development and elaboration of ancestor venerative practices begun centuries earlier.

The placement of the skull in a bowl and its deposition in a separate crypt allowed the skull to be removed for later rituals without disturbing the other bones. Garber and Awe (2008) argue that the head of this specially treated individual may have symbolically represented the severed head of the Maize God. We believe that funerary rites that included placing heads in bowls were both symbolically and materially powerful, emphasizing the resurrection of a deceased ancestor in a similar fashion to the Maize God, while, at the same time, allowing this important ancestor to be physically present in ritual activities. These associations were further emphasized when skeletal elements of important ancestors—particularly skulls in bowls—were re-interred in new ceremonial locations.

Another important Late Preclassic innovation in the Belize River valley is the placement of burials in important ceremonial architecture. In particular, structures that form parts of E-Groups or related architectural assemblages at sites across the region have early examples of formal burials (Awe 2013; Brown 2017; Chase and Chase 1995; Robin et al. 2012). Below, we discuss examples from Early Xunantunich (Brown 2013, 2017), Chan (Robin et al. 2012), and Cahal Pech (Awe 2013).

Primary burials in these contexts often exhibit evidence of reentry and the manipulation and/or removal of bones, including the placement of skulls in ceramic vessels. For example, Burial 8 at Chan was placed in the central eastern structure of the site's E-Group and contained a young adult male interred with six ceramic vessels, an exotic chert blade, and a jade pendant (Novotny 2012; Robin et al. 2012). The head of this individual was placed in a Sierra Red dish, and the burial showed evidence of reentry and manipulation of the bones (Robin et al. 2012).

Reentry sometimes entailed the complete removal of an individual's remains. In the Late Preclassic construction phase of the eastern pyramid of the Early Xunantunich E-Group, Brown (2013) encountered a cut stone masonry burial chamber, one of the earliest formal burial chambers of this sort found to date in Belize. It was placed in the summit of the pyramid, directly on centerline.

The chamber was reentered at least once in antiquity, as evidenced by the partial dismantling of the northwest corner. The chamber may have been reentered again, as the summit surface above the chamber was not patched. The contents of the chamber were almost entirely removed, but its meager contents suggest it originally held a burial. We found three fragments of bone and one complete Middle Preclassic ceramic vessel, a Savana Orange jar that appears to be an heirloom piece.

After the chamber was reentered, it was filled and an incised slate slab was laid on top. The slab was, unfortunately, eroded, but we could identify the image of a figure in profile. The figure appears to be wearing a headdress and may hold something in front of his body, perhaps a staff.

On the summit of the pyramid near the chamber, two fragments of a *Spondylus* shell ornament, possibly an earflare, were found; these may have been displaced when the chamber was reentered. *Spondylus* shell was highly valued by the ancient Maya and symbolized the watery underworld. This exotic material appears to have been a symbol of power and authority for early Maya kings (Freidel et al. 2002:44). Despite the removal of much of the contents of the burial chamber, the available evidence indicates that this was an important individual, quite possibly an ancestor of the ruling lineage at this early ceremonial center.

In an interesting parallel, a Late Preclassic burial in the eastern structure of the E-Group at Chan (Burial 10) was interred with several artifacts including a *Spondylus* shell ornament as well as an heirloom Middle Preclassic figurine fragment (Novotny 2012).

Although we cannot state with any certainty how the remains removed from the chamber at Early Xunantunich were manipulated, the fact that the bones were retrieved in antiquity highlights the importance of the physical remains of ancestors to their living descendants. The presence of secondary burials of various kinds during the Late Preclassic demonstrates that some ritual manipulation of human remains entailed their subsequent reburial. At Uaxactun, lip-to-lip caches containing human skulls and bones were found within the eastern structures of the E-Group (Ricketson and Ricketson 1937). These secondary interments were most likely the remains of important ancestors whose bones were retrieved and ritually reburied in this sacred location. Similar secondary interments are found in key ceremonial places in the Belize River valley during the Late Preclassic period.

For example, a Late Preclassic offering found within Structure B4 at Cahal Pech provides an intriguing example of a ritual reburial event of bones removed from an earlier interment. This offering also illustrates the role of the bowl as both a reference to the portal and other layers of the cosmos, through the myth of First Father, the decapitated Maize God who emerges from the Underworld reborn, exiting through a crack in the Earth's surface (Awe 2013; n.d.).

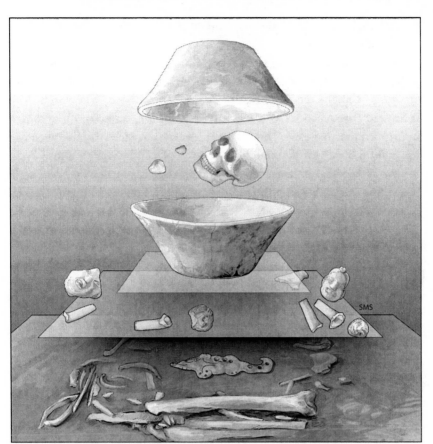

Figure 5.7. Reconstruction drawing of Late Preclassic offering from Structure B4 at Cahal Pech (drawing by Sarah Sage).

The Cahal Pech offering has a quadripartite layout, the central component of which is a secondary burial (Figure 5.7). The head of an individual was placed within a bowl, which was covered with an inverted bowl to form a lip-to-lip cache. This cache was framed with long bones, presumably some of which were from the same individual. The bowl was placed on top of a marine shell pectoral carved in the shape of a crocodile, as briefly mentioned above.

We suggest that the crocodile represents the surface of the earth, the bowl is the portal or *ol*, and the head represents the promise of the resurrected Maize God emerging from this portal. It is interesting to note that this reference to First Father—the Maize God who was also the archetype of Maya kings—was deposited in a pyramidal structure in an architectural context that would have allowed limited participation in the rituals surrounding its placement.

This particular offering and reburied ancestor is especially interesting in light of our earlier discussion of offerings within the architectural sequence at Cahal Pech of Structure B4. We recap these briefly here: Awe recovered three distinct symbolic offerings in Structure B4, all of which referenced the crocodile. The first of these was the early Middle Preclassic (ca. 1000 B.C.) crocodile mandible offering placed beneath a house floor. Several centuries later in the late Middle Preclassic, a carved slate crocodile object was cached beneath the summit surface of a public platform. Finally, beneath the summit of a later construction phase in the Late Preclassic, Awe encountered this elaborate lip-to-lip offering set on the marine shell crocodile ornament.

These offerings span over one thousand years of history and indicate the enduring importance of the crocodilian motif to the people of Cahal Pech. The same motif is referenced on Cahal Pech's first stela, Stela 9, dating also to the Late Preclassic, which shows an early ruler emerging out of the maw of a crocodilian earth creature (see Figure 5.4). Although the crocodile is a universally important symbol in Precolumbian Mesoamerica, its particular emphasis at Cahal Pech suggests that it may have been symbolically related to an important kin group at the site, which may, indeed, have been the lineage of the site's first rulers.

Although we believe that the practice of ancestor veneration served many needs within ancient Maya society including lessening personal distress of the descendants through continued association, ritual reentry and bone manipulation of certain ancestors, likewise, developed into an important strategy for creating and sanctifying hierarchies. As McAnany (1995:162) states, "The practice of ancestor veneration ultimately is not about the dead, but about how the living make use of the dead."

Conclusion

As Marcus and Flannery (2004) argue, long cultural sequences are necessary in order to trace changes in ancient ritual behavior. Our collaborative work in the Belize River valley has documented these kinds of long cultural sequences at Blackman Eddy, Cahal Pech, and Xunantunich. In this chapter, we summarized data related to early ritual behavior and documented how ritual activities and public architecture changed through time in order to both emphasize and reinforce inequalities within the society, and thus reflect transformations in shared religious beliefs. We argue that in the early Middle Preclassic period, Cunil and Kanocha serving vessels incised with powerful symbols were important objects, and that they suggest an emphasis on communal gatherings where these ideologically charged symbols could be displayed. Although serving vessels cease to be decorated in this way later in the Preclassic, new special forms such as chocolate pots and stirrup spouted vessels appear, indicating the continued importance of food and drink in religious rituals and social occasions. We argue that prominent individuals deployed these implements of power in various settings, including feasts, to reinforce their position in society, ultimately leading to the establishment of a hierarchical social structure in the late Middle Preclassic.

This important social transition was accompanied by a transformation in public architecture and rituals, as rulers now had special access to these buildings and the ritual activities that took place there. We also argue that rituals revolving around the veneration of ancestors were a critical component in the processes of both establishing and maintaining social hierarchies. In the Belize River valley, ancestor veneration is present during the Middle Preclassic, and our data indicate that the removal of ancestral bones from graves, their manipulation, and their subsequent ritual reburial were key ritual acts in the establishment and reproduction of a hierarchical social order.

Acknowledgments

We extend our gratitude to the Belize Institute of Archaeology and the National Institute of Culture and History for allowing us to conduct research in the country of Belize. We would like to thank the Foundation for the Advancement of Mesoamerican Studies, Inc. (FAMSI) for their support of research at Blackman Eddy and materials analysis from Cahal Pech. We thank the Social Science Research Council of Canada and the Tilden Family Foundation for their support of research at Cahal Pech. We would also like to thank the Alphawood Foundation, the National Geographic Society Committee for Research and Exploration, the Brennan Foundation, and Ben and Trudy Termini for support of research at Xunantunich. Additionally, we are grateful for the support from Texas State University, the University of Texas at San Antonio, and Northern Arizona University. We would also like to thank the students and staff who participated in the Belize Valley Archaeological Project, the Belize Valley Archaeological Reconnaissance Project, and the Mopan Valley Preclassic Project. We are most grateful to Arthur Demarest and an anonymous reviewer who provided insightful comments and feedback on this chapter.

6

Middle Preclassic Maya Shell Ornament Production

Implications for the Development of Complexity at Pacbitun, Belize

BOBBI HOHMANN, TERRY G. POWIS, AND PAUL F. HEALY

Ethnohistoric, iconographic, and archaeological data provide evidence that shell was of great importance to the prehistoric and historic Maya who inhabited the lowland regions of eastern Mesoamerica. Shell artifacts, particularly items of personal adornment, have been found in archaeological deposits extending from the Preclassic to the Postclassic periods (1500 B.C.–A.D. 1540). Their presence in different contexts (e.g., cache, burial, midden, construction deposit) suggests that they may have served multiple functions in Maya society; however, their predominance in ritual offerings indicates that some were highly valued and imbued with ritual significance.

Although a significant number of marine shell ornaments have been recovered from sites throughout the Maya lowlands, little is known about the industry that produced these items, particularly during the Preclassic period. Knowledge of the Preclassic shell ornament industry has increased significantly with recent finds from the site of Pacbitun, a medium-sized Maya center located in west-central Belize. The presence of complete and broken shell ornaments, ornaments in various stages of production, shell detritus, and chert microdrills and burin spalls indicate that the early Maya inhabitants of the site were involved in the production of marine and freshwater shell ornaments by the Middle Preclassic (900–300 B.C.). This chapter reports on the production, distribution, and consumption of Middle Preclassic shell ornaments at Pacbitun and discusses implications for the development of sociopolitical complexity in the Belize River valley and greater Maya lowlands during the Middle Preclassic period.

Shell Use in Maya Society

Ethnographic and ethnohistoric data confirm that shell objects served many functions in nonstate societies around the world, including use as utilitarian implements, currency or media of exchange, symbols of status, and generalized wealth. Shell items are argued to have served many of these same functions in ancient Maya society. Ethnohistoric accounts reveal that at the time of European contact, shell items were used for a number of different purposes by the Maya who inhabited the lowland regions of the Yucatan Peninsula. In *Relación de las Cosas de Yucatán*, written about 1566, Bishop Diego de Landa noted that shell items were commonly used (1) as a form of currency in market exchanges (Tozzer 1941:95–96), (2) to pay fines or debts (Tozzer 1941:80), (3) as costume decoration or body adornment for priests and other high status individuals (Tozzer 1941:95–96, 148, 231), (4) as ornaments for children during baptism rituals (Tozzer 1941:102), and (5) in a variety of ritual offerings (Tozzer 1941:111). While there is no direct archaeological evidence that shell was being used by the Maya as a form of currency prior to the arrival of the Europeans, there is substantial evidence that it was being used for personal ornamentation and as ritual offerings as early as 900 B.C.

Shell artifacts have been identified in archaeological deposits extending from the Middle Preclassic to the Postclassic period throughout the Maya lowlands. The abundant quantities of shell artifacts and representations of shell in other media and in iconographic representations reinforces the belief that shell was of great political, economic, and social importance in Precolumbian Maya society. The most commonly encountered shell artifacts are items of personal adornment that would have either been sewn onto clothing or worn as jewelry. In representations on carved monuments, painted vessels, and mural paintings, Classic period Maya rulers and other elite personages are frequently depicted wearing shell ornaments (e.g., necklaces, bracelets, ear flares, anklets, and armbands) and/or elaborate costumes adorned with shell items. For instance, Maya rulers often wore shell tinklers suspended from belts or loincloths that were part of their royal regalia (Baudez 1994:Figures 7–9; Jones and Satterthwaite 1982:Figures 29, 33, 72; Spinden 1957:84) (Figure 6.1a). These appear to have been small- to medium-sized gastropods that were perforated and attached to the hem of these costume elements. In some cases, tinklers were suspended beneath a *pop* or *mat* sign, the principal symbol of kingship in Maya hieroglyphic writing (Schele and Freidel 1990:139). Shell items similar to these have been

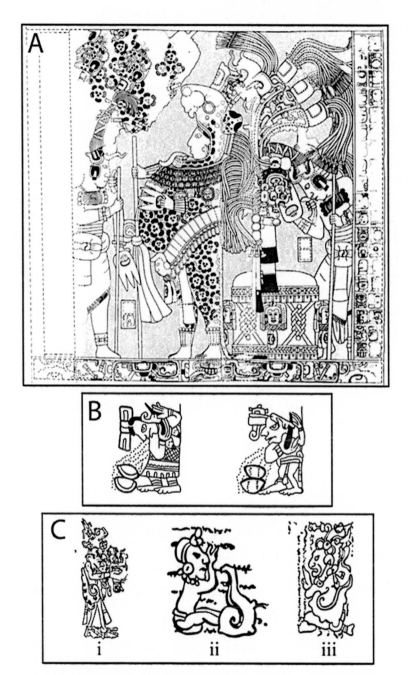

Figure 6.1. (a) Representation of shell tinklers in lintel carving from Tikal (after Jones and Satterthwaite 1982: Figure 73): (b, c) bloodletting rituals depicted in the Madrid Codex (after Sharer and Traxler 2006: Figure 13.9).

found in a variety of archaeological contexts throughout the Maya lowlands from the Preclassic to the Postclassic, a period of approximately two millennia.

Shells were also used as musical instruments and receptacles. Scenes showing individuals blowing conch shell trumpets have been reported on mural paintings (Miller 1986), painted vessels (Coe 1978:30–32, 40–42; Robiscek and Hales 1981:44–45), and in codex representations. Similar shell specimens have been found in archaeological deposits at sites such as Cerros (Garber 1989:70), Chichen Itza (Proskouriakoff 1962:422), Dzibilchaltun (Taschek 1994:60–61), Mayapan (Proskouriakoff 1962:384), Tikal (Moholy-Nagy 1994:190), and Uaxactun (Ricketson and Ricketson 1937:201–202). Halved conch shells are also frequently depicted as receptacles on painted vessels (Coe 1977b; Reents-Budet 1994:36–55), stone sculptures (Fash 1991:118–121; Schele and Miller 1986:151) and in codex representations. On painted vessels, artists or scribes are often depicted using halved conch shells as ink wells or paint containers. On many of these vessels the scribes appear to be supernatural deities, presumably depicting mythological scenes and characters portrayed in the *Popul Vuh*. Similar artifacts appear to have served as receptacles for blood during bloodletting rituals. At least two images from the Madrid Codex show Maya men and women perforating their earlobes while standing over what appears to be a large bivalve shell (Figure 6.1b). Similar finds have been reported from archaeological contexts at the site of Chac Balam, located on Ambergris Caye off the coast of Belize. Researchers have reported burials with associated bloodletting paraphernalia, including obsidian blades placed inside conch shells and intentionally placed near the mouth and pelvic area (Guderjan and Garber 1995:133–135).

There is also evidence that in certain areas marine and freshwater shell was being used to meet some of the more basic, utilitarian needs of the community. In coastal regions, shell was sometimes used to make domestic tools where suitable stone materials were not readily available. For example, in the coastal areas of the northern Maya lowlands, Eaton (1974, 1978) recorded a number of shell tools, including celts and scoops, and production debris associated with their manufacture. Connor (1975:131) also reported carved shell celts, scrapers, scoops and choppers from Cozumel Island. Further south, Dreiss (1994:191) reports four possible utilitarian items from the site of Colha, including two scoop-like artifacts that may have been used as spoons or shallow bowls, one celt fragment, and a possible hammering implement.

Studies in Maya iconography and cosmology have provided evidence that shell was also of great symbolic significance to the lowland Maya. Given its link to the sea, shell has always had a primary association with water. The importance of this connection is no more evident than in the *Popul Vuh,* the highland Quiche Maya creation myth, in which the gods of the sky and sea joined together to create the earth and its many life forms, all of which emerged from this sea (Tedlock 1985:72–75). To the ancient Maya, the earth was the back of a large reptile that swam in the primordial sea (Freidel et al. 1993; Thompson 1950:278). Iconographers have argued that shell and other water-related items symbolize the primordial sea out of which all life began. In these cases shell is believed to represent birth and life, but there is also a connection between shell and the watery underworld or *Xibalba,* a place where the death gods reside. The underworld deity God N is frequently associated with shells in underworld scenes painted on polychrome vessels as well as in the Paris and Madrid codices (Figure 6.1c). He is commonly depicted emerging from a large conch shell or wearing a conch shell on his back (Coe 1978:70–73; Kerr 1992:386; Schellhas 1904:37; Spinden 1957:84). Schele and Freidel (1990:414) note that God N is also thought to represent a *Pauahtun,* one of the beings who held up the four corners of the world in Maya cosmology. *Pauahtuns* are often depicted wearing a cut shell pendant or emerging from a conch shell.

Combined, the ethnohistoric, iconographic, and archaeological data reveal that shell was of great significance to the Maya for a period of more than two millennia, extending from the Middle Preclassic to the Colonial period. Despite the abundant evidence of worked shell in archaeological contexts, the topic of shell working in the Maya area has not been fully explored, particularly during the earliest periods of cultural development. Recent archaeological research at the site of Pacbitun in the southern Maya lowlands has provided significant new data about this important topic and will be explored in detail in the reminder of this chapter.

Archaeological Investigations at Pacbitun

Excavations at the site of Pacbitun have provided new information regarding the Middle Preclassic shell ornament industry in the Belize Valley, and in the southern lowlands in general. Pacbitun is a medium-sized Maya center situated in the foothills of the Maya Mountains of the Cayo District of western Belize, approximately 3 km east of the modern Maya community of San Antonio (Figure 6.2a). The site is located approximately 7.5 km from

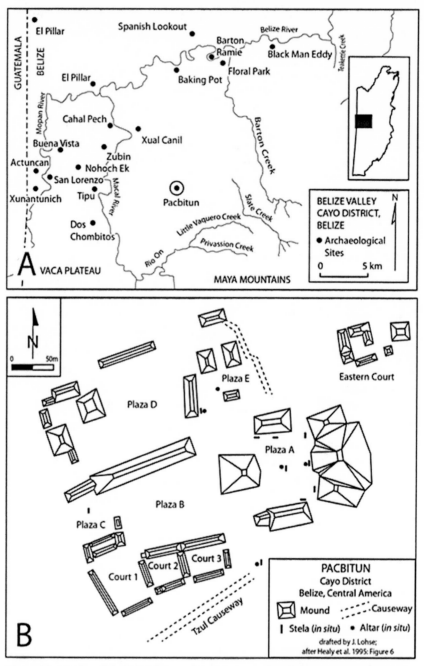

Figure 6.2. (a) Map of the Belize River valley showing archaeological sites mentioned in text; (b) isometric plan of the central precinct at Pacbitun, Belize.

the Macal River, a major branch of the Belize River which empties into the Caribbean Sea approximately 110 km east of the site. There are also several smaller streams within 5–10 km of the site, providing access to waterborne transportation networks and riverine resources throughout much of the year.

The central precinct of Pacbitun consists of at least 40 Classic period masonry structures covering an area of approximately 14.5 ha (145,000 m^2) (Healy 1990a:250; Healy, Hohmann, and Powis 2004) (Figure 6.2b). Initial excavations were conducted at the site during the summers of 1984, 1986, and 1987 (Healy 1988, 1990a, 1990b, 1992; Healy et al. 1990, 1995). During these three seasons many architectural and cultural features within the central precinct were mapped and tested, and a settlement survey and testing project were undertaken in the site's periphery (Healy et al. 2007). These excavations revealed a long, stratigraphic sequence of occupation extending from the Middle Preclassic (900 B.C.) to the Late Terminal Classic (A.D. 900) (Healy 1990a, 1999; Hohmann and Powis 1999). All dates that we present in this chapter are in calibrated radiocarbon years. At Pacbitun, the Middle Preclassic has been subdivided into early (900–600 B.C.) and late (600–300 B.C.) facets, corresponding to the early and late Mai phases in the local ceramic sequence.

Excavations were again conducted at Pacbitun during the summers of 1995, 1996, and 1997 (Healy, Hohmann, and Powis 2004; Hohmann 2002; Hohmann and Powis 1996, 1999; Hohmann et al. 1999) and more recently in 2008 and 2009. Additional research at the site has been ongoing. The purpose of this renewed research was to expose additional Preclassic deposits to gain a more comprehensive understanding of this early period at the site. During these recent efforts, large-scale horizontal excavations were undertaken in Plaza B and test units were placed in Plazas C and D, two smaller plazas located to the west and north of Plaza B (Powis et al. 2009; Hohmann et al. 2009). Excavations in the plaza areas at Pacbitun revealed significant Middle Preclassic architectural and artifactual materials located only 1 m below the present ground surface. Middle Preclassic architecture included portions of five basal platforms (Sub-Structures B1-B5) and a number of stone alignments whose exact dimensions and function are yet to be determined (Figure 6.3). Similar, albeit less substantive, evidence for Preclassic occupation was also found in Plazas C and D. Radiocarbon and ceramic cross-dating indicate that some of the Plaza B platforms date to the early Middle Preclassic, while others date to the late Middle Preclassic

Figure 6.3. Middle Preclassic architecture (Sub-Structure B2) in Plaza B at Pacbitun, Belize (photograph provided by Terry G. Powis).

(Arendt et al. 1996; Healy 1999:69–82; Hohmann and Powis 1996:103, 107; Hohmann et al. 1999).

The Middle Preclassic structures exposed in Plaza B are raised earthen platforms with stone retaining walls that would have supported perishable, wattle-and-daub structures. These structures run parallel to each other and are separated by a 1 m-wide alleyway. The close proximity and common extramural areas suggest that the structures were organized as a small plazuela group with several structures situated around an open patio area, a pattern that continues to this day in most traditional Maya communities (Vogt 1964). The tamped marl and earthen alleyways between these platforms provides additional evidence that these architectural features were associated and contemporaneous. Excavations in the 1990s partially exposed one of the late Middle Preclassic structures (Sub-Structure B2) in the hopes of identifying posthole patterns and possible activity areas within the structure. During the 2009 excavations, Sub-Structure B2 was completely exposed, revealing a platform measuring 9 m × 6 m (54 m^2) (Powis 2009, 2010) (Figure 6.3). To date, this structure represents the largest late Middle Preclassic example of Maya domestic architecture unearthed in the Belize Valley.

Perhaps most significant of the discoveries in Plaza B was the evidence of early and late Middle Preclassic shell ornament production, as interpreted from the co-occurrence of large quantities of shell ornaments in various stages of production, marine shell detritus, and chert microdrills and burin spalls embedded in the tamped floors and alleyways both within and surrounding the early and late Middle Preclassic structures. Additionally, sometime during the late Middle Preclassic a dense, midden-like deposit was laid down over the top of the Preclassic structures and extending further south into Plaza B. The deposit consisted of dark, organic soil densely packed with domestic refuse as well as shell ornaments in various stages of production, marine shell macro-detritus and chert microdrills and burin spalls. The exact nature of this deposit remains unclear and only additional excavations will help confirm its depositional context. It may be a primary midden deposit associated with Sub-Structure 7, a late Middle to Late Preclassic structure located at the base of Structure 8, the large Classic period range structure bordering the north side of Plaza B. Alternatively, the midden may also be a secondary deposit used as construction fill to level the plaza area for future construction. Regardless of the primary or secondary context, the materials recovered from the deposit provide additional supporting evidence that the early residents of Pacbitun were engaged in significant shell-working activities throughout the Middle Preclassic and possibly into the early facet of the Late Preclassic period.

Ethnoarchaeological research has shown that in sedentary communities, little refuse is typically left in primary contexts, making it difficult to identify areas where production activities occurred. Research conducted in highland and lowland Maya communities has demonstrated that living surfaces, including house floors and patio areas, are periodically cleaned to remove potentially hazardous materials and to prevent accumulations of refuse in high use areas (Deal 1985; Hayden and Cannon 1983). The refuse gathered during these sweeping events is most often deposited in the area immediately surrounding structures where they become embedded. Some small materials are also left behind in difficult-to-reach places like corners and along structure walls, where they too become lost and embedded in the floor surfaces over time. Clark (1991) has noted similar deposits among modern Lacandon Maya flint knappers in Chiapas. Particularly rich, but highly fragmented shell deposits were located along the foundation walls both inside and outside the Middle Preclassic structures at Pacbitun, suggesting that their accumulation was likely the result of sweeping and cleaning activities and, more importantly, that shell working activities were at least occasionally undertaken in this area of the site.

In the absence of archaeologically visible, permanent workshop facilities, such as those noted for shell ornament production in the Turks and Caicos Islands (Carlson 1993), these embedded deposits at Pacbitun provide direct evidence of production activities that can be useful in interpreting the organization of craft production. The shell-working evidence here is important for a variety of reasons. First, although shell artifacts are found throughout the southern lowlands by the beginning of the Middle Preclassic, little direct evidence of shell working has been identified to date. This may be the result of sampling bias, as most excavations of Maya sites have not focused on large-scale exposure of Preclassic remains. Additionally, few research projects have attempted to collect and record macro- and micro-remains from Preclassic floor surfaces, allowing for the identification of activity areas in and around structures. Second, to date most of the evidence for shell working in the Maya lowlands has come from secondary contexts, providing challenges to the reconstruction of certain variables related to the organization of production, including scale, intensity, context, and concentration. While some analysis still remains, the Pacbitun data provide a unique opportunity to evaluate shell ornament production activities in the household contexts.

Middle Preclassic Shell Ornament Industry

The Pacbitun shell assemblage (n=8,783) represents the largest Preclassic collection in the Belize Valley, consisting of 5,670 modified shell specimens and 3,113 pieces of marine shell detritus, which is defined as fragmented shell that has not been intentionally shaped or worked. The modified shell assemblage consists of complete and broken shell ornaments as well as ornaments in various stages of production. The unmodified shell assemblage consists of detritus produced during the process of shell reduction and includes macro- and micro-remains, which will be discussed in greater detail below. Combined these data provide valuable information about early Maya resource utilization, procurement practices, artifacts produced, production techniques, and the organization of production activities.

Shell Artifacts

A wide variety of shell artifacts were identified in the Preclassic assemblage from Pacbitun. All the artifacts in this broad category represent items of adornment that would have been attached to various pieces of clothing or worn as jewelry (e.g., necklaces, bracelets, anklets, ear plugs). To date there is no direct evidence that shell was being used in the production of utilitarian tools, but given the durability and sharp edges of fractured shell, it is possible that some unmodified fragments may have been used as expedient tools in everyday tasks such as cutting or scraping.

The worked shell artifacts have been divided into six general types: adornos, beads, blanks, pendants, tinklers, and miscellaneous forms (Figures 6.4a and 6.4b). All the types used in this study are well-defined artifact classes that have been found in deposits dating from the Preclassic to Postclassic periods throughout the Maya lowlands. While the artifacts within most of these types are homogenous in terms of general form and species utilization, there is a great deal of variability within the bead category. For this reason the category has been further subdivided into seven sub-types: barrel, disk, irregular, square/rectangular, perforated gastropod, tubular, and whole shell scaphopods. A detailed technological analysis of the marine detritus and worked shell artifacts has provided important information regarding production techniques and stages in the production process. The techniques used in ornament production varied according to the type of artifact being produced and the species utilized, but drilling, grinding, smoothing, and polishing were the most commonly used techniques at Pacbitun. Ninety-eight percent (n=3,189) of the modified shell artifacts exhibit perforations produced by drilling or puncturing. Small, irregular-shaped holes occur (n=45) on only a small percentage of the artifacts, mostly those belonging to thin-walled freshwater species (*Nephronaias* sp., *Pomacea* sp.). The irregular nature of these perforations suggests that they were made by puncturing or gouging the shell with a sharp instrument, while conical and biconical drill holes would have been made with the chert microdrills found in abundance at the site. Evidence of cutting and incising was also identified, but combined these techniques are found on less than one percent of the total assemblage.

The Middle Preclassic modified shell assemblage is clearly dominated by beads, with disk and irregular forms comprising 89 percent of the total assemblage. As seen in Table 6.1, irregular beads account for 39.7 percent of the total modified shell assemblage and disk beads account for 49.4 percent. Analysis of the data collected in the 1990s reveals that irregular beads dominate the early Middle Preclassic assemblage while disk beads dominate the late Middle Preclassic (Hohmann 2002). This shift may reflect a change in artifact preference as well as increasing standardization of

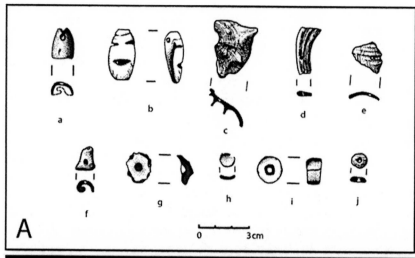

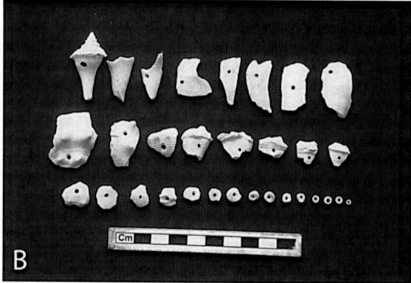

Figure 6.4. A. Representative sample of Middle Preclassic shell ornaments from Plaza B excavations at Pacbitun: (a–b) tinklers; (c–f) irregular beads; (g–h) bead blanks; and (i–j) discoid beads (illustrations drawn by Michael Bletzer and Ruth Dickau). B. Sample of Middle Preclassic irregular and disk beads from Pacbitun (Photograph provided by Bobbi Hohmann and Terry G. Powis).

Table 6.1. Frequency of Middle Preclassic Worked Shell at Pacbitun.

Type	n	%
Adorno	2	0.01
Beads		
Barrel	41	0.7
Discoidal	2800	49.4
Irregular	2249	39.7
Square/Rectangular	275	4.9
Perforated Gastropod	39	0.7
Tubular	6	0.1
Whole Scaphopod	11	0.2
Blank	11	0.2
Pendant	6	0.1
Tinkler	5	0.1
Unidentified	225	3.9
Total	5670	100

artifact form through time. Other forms, such as pendants, tinklers, and adornos occur with much less frequency during this time period. In fact, combined these types account for less than one percent of the total Middle Preclassic assemblage.

Marine shell detritus was also identified in Middle Preclassic deposits, again providing strong evidence for the local production of shell artifacts. The unmodified marine shell assemblage consists of fragmented shell of different sizes and shapes and includes both macro- and micro-detritus. For the purposes of this study, shell micro-detritus consists of fragments smaller than 1 cm and macro-detritus includes everything larger than 1 cm (Figures 6.5a and 6.5b). Abundant quantities of micro-detritus have been identified and collected, but these have not yet been quantified and await further analysis. The detritus counts presented in this chapter represent only macro-detritus. After abundant quantities of micro-remains were identified during the 1995 season, a sample of the Middle Preclassic floor deposits was wet-screened using 1/16" mesh. Based on preliminary observations of the micro-detritus, there are easily thousands of pieces of fragmented shell found in association with the early and late Middle Preclassic structures. Sample analysis of roughly 1,500 shell macro-remains reveals that columella, spire, spine, lip, and body fragments were present in the assemblage, indicating that some whole shells were being imported and further reduced on-site. Large quantities of fragmented freshwater shell,

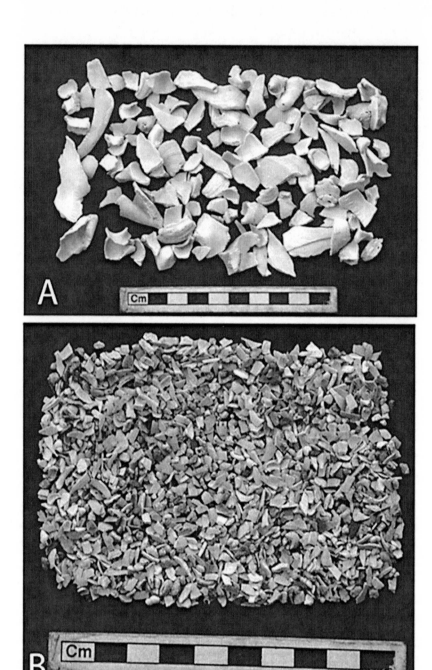

Figure 6.5. (a) Sample of Middle Preclassic shell macro-detritus (photograph provided by Bobbi Hohmann and Terry G. Powis); (b) sample of Middle Preclassic shell micro-detritus (photograph provided by Bobbi Hohmann and Terry G. Powis).

particularly *Pachychilus* sp. and *Nephronaias* sp., were also found in abundance at the site, but these materials were not included in this analysis since it could not be determined whether these pieces represented byproducts from ornament manufacture or refuse from food consumption (Healy et al. 1990; Moholy-Nagy 1978; Powis et al. 1999; Stanchly 1995).

Belize Valley sites reporting Middle and Late Preclassic worked shell artifacts include Barton Ramie (Willey et al. 1965), Blackman Eddy (Cochran 2009), Cahal Pech (Awe 1992; Cheetham 1995, 1996; Ferguson et al. 1996; Healy, Cheetham, Powis, and Awe 2004; Powis 1996), Chan (Keller 2008), Dos Chombitos Cikin (Robin 2000), and Zubin (Ferguson 1995; Iannone 1996; Schwake 1996). Similar shell artifacts have also been identified in Preclassic contexts at other sites in the southern Maya lowlands, including Altun Ha (Pendergast 1979), Blue Creek (Haines 1997), Caracol (Cobos 1994), Chan Chich (Robichaux 1998), Colha (Buttles 1992, 2002; Dreiss 1994), Cerros (Garber 1989), Cuello (Hammond 1991a), and K'axob (Isaza Aizpurua 1997; Isaza Aizpurua and McAnany 1999) in Belize and at Altar de Sacrificios (Willey 1972), Nakbe (Richard Hansen, personal communication, 2000), Ceibal (Willey 1978), Tikal (Moholy-Nagy 1994, 1997), and Uaxactun (Kidder 1947; Ricketson and Ricketson 1937) in Guatemala. These worked shell assemblages are nearly identical to those identified at Pacbitun and other Belize Valley sites. In fact, the Preclassic shell assemblage is remarkably homogeneous throughout the southern Maya lowlands, suggesting a pan-lowland tradition of ornament production similar to that of the Mamom ceramics that have been identified throughout the region.

Shell Resource Utilization

Taxonomic identification reveals that the early inhabitants of Pacbitun used a wide variety of freshwater and marine shell during the Middle Preclassic period. Despite the inland location of Pacbitun, it appears that the Preclassic inhabitants preferred marine shell for the production of shell ornaments. Marine taxa account for roughly 95 percent (n=3,083) of the total modified shell assemblage while freshwater taxa represent only 5 percent (n=170). A list of identified taxa with their biotic community (i.e., freshwater or marine) is presented in Table 6.2. These can be divided into three classes: (1) Gastropoda (univalves), (2) Pelecypoda (bivalves), and (3) Scaphopoda (tusk shells).

Three of the genera identified in the Preclassic assemblage are freshwater varieties, including two gastropods (*Pachychilus* sp., *Pomacea* sp.) and one

Table 6.2. Identified Taxa in Middle Preclassic Deposits at Pacbitun.

Shell Taxa	Habitat
GASTROPODA	
Pomacea flagellata	Freshwater
Pachychilus indiorum	Freshwater
Pachychilus glaphyrus	Freshwater
Prunum sp.	Marine
Melongena sp.	Marine
Oliva sp.	Marine
Strombus sp.	Marine
Strombus gigas	Marine
Strombus pugilis	Marine
Unid. marine gastropod	Marine
PELECYPODA	
Nephronaias ortmani	Freshwater
Ostreidae *Spondylus* sp.	Marine
Unid. marine pelecypod	Marine
SCAPHOPODA	
Dentalium sp.	Marine
UNIDENTIFED	
Unid. riverine	Freshwater
Unidentified	Freshwater/Marine

pelecopod (*Nephronaias* sp.). Each of these species could have been obtained from a number of streams and rivers in close proximity to the site. Varieties of these three genera have been identified in their natural habitats and in archaeological contexts throughout the Maya lowlands (Healy et al. 1990; Moholy-Nagy 1978; Powis 2004). Six marine genera and one family have also been identified, including four gastropods (*Melongena* sp., *Oliva* sp., *Prunum* sp., *Strombus* sp.), two pelecypods (Ostreidae, *Spondylus* sp.), and one scaphopod (*Dentalium* sp.). With the possible exception of two specimens belonging to the *Spondylus* genera, all the marine varieties can be found in the Caribbean Sea, located approximately 110 km east of the confluence of the Macal, Mopan, and Belize Rivers at the heart of the Belize Valley. Determinations regarding more specific points of origin could not be made because the majority of the species have distributions that extend along the entire eastern coast of the Yucatan Peninsula.

While the majority of the modified shell artifacts have been worked to such a degree that their original species and form are now obscured, pieces of the larger marine detritus retain many of the shell's original characteristics and traits, allowing for more accurate taxonomic identifications. Based on the analysis of approximately 1,500 macro-detritus specimens, it is clear that gastropod specimens dominate this assemblage. In particular, *Strombus pugilis* (West Indian Fighting Conch) comprise over 95 percent of the unmodified shell assemblage that has been analyzed. This small marine gastropod is found throughout the western Atlantic, ranging from South Carolina to the Florida Keys and throughout the Caribbean Sea to the northeastern portions of South America (Abbott 1974; Rehder 1981). These gastropods seem to prefer sandy sea grass meadows in shallower water, making them relatively easy to procure without special diving skills or equipment.

Geographic factors such as proximity to major trade centers and access to riverine transportation networks would have played a role in determining access to coastal resources, as would social or political factors. Whether the Pacbitun Maya gathered marine shell themselves or received them through trade is impossible to determine, but the widespread presence of marine shell in Preclassic deposits throughout the southern lowlands indicates that marine resources entered the region on a regular basis.

Shell Working Toolkit

In addition to the modified and unmodified shell remains, a large number of formal lithic tools and debitage was found in direct association with the Middle Preclassic structures. The chipped stone assemblage consists of chert and obsidian artifacts, and the Pacbitun Maya had at their disposal a variety of expedient and formal tools. The formal tool assemblage shows clear evidence of burin spall technology, including both burin spalls and microdrills (n=390) (Figures 6.6a and 6.6b). Burin spalls are triangular in cross section and are relatively thick in relation to their length, with complete spalls measuring from 23.0 to 77.5 mm in length. It does not appear that burins were the desired end product in this process, but rather a by-product of spall production designed to manufacture chert drills. Similar burin spalls have been identified at the site of Colha in northern Belize, but these tools were clearly removed from the large macroblades that are so prominent in the Middle Preclassic lithic assemblage at this site (Thomas Hester and Harry Shafter, personal communication, 2009; Potter 1991; Shafer and Hester 1983). No macroblades exhibiting this pattern have been

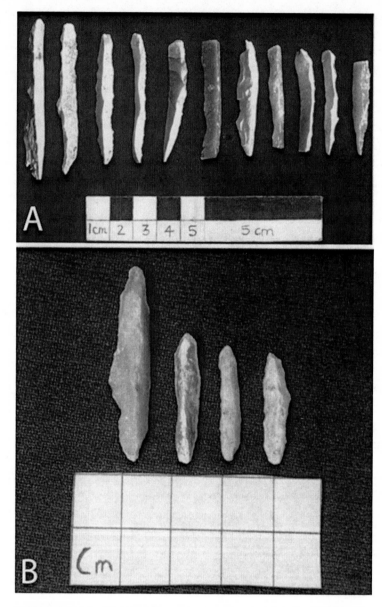

Figure 6.6. (a) Sample of Middle Preclassic burin spalls from Pacbitun, Belize (photograph provided by Bobbi Hohmann and Terry G. Powis); (b) sample of Middle Preclassic shell drills from Pacbitun, Belize (photograph provided by Bobbi Hohmann and Terry Powis).

identified at Pacbitun. The process of spall production at Pacbitun remains unclear since a comprehensive analysis of the lithic assemblage has not yet been undertaken, but a cursory analysis of the lithic debitage reveals that there is some evidence for the removal of spalls from the lateral edges of flakes.

There is abundant evidence that burin spalls were being re-chipped or modified into microdrills at Pacbitun for use in shell working. Microdrills resemble burin spalls in form; however, they are distinguished from the former by the macroscopic evidence of wear on the proximal and/or distal ends. The tip(s) of these specimens exhibit alternate, opposite retouch resulting from rotary motion, indicating that these tools were used for drilling. Most of the microdrills have extensive retouch on one or more lateral edges, suggesting they were chipped to fit a haft, probably of wood or bone. Preliminary observations indicate that the microdrill form remained constant throughout the six centuries of the Middle Preclassic, and the uniformity in tool form and use-wear patterns suggest these tools were standardized.

Similar lithic tools have been found in association with Middle Preclassic shell working debris in both primary and secondary contexts at the sites of Cahal Pech and Blackman Eddy (Cochran 2009), located north of Pacbitun in the Belize Valley proper. Like Pacbitun, lithic analysis undertaken at these sites has not provided much evidence regarding the nature of burin spall production. Given the lack of direct evidence for spall production in these assemblages, it is possible that the spalls were imported from nonlocal specialists and worked into microdrills on site, leaving little evidence other than microdebitage which would be difficult to identify without specialized sampling. Whether the microtools were produced on-site or imported from nonlocal specialists, the evidence strongly suggests that these were specialized lapidary tools made by skilled crafters and used in a specialized industry by the beginning of the Middle Preclassic.

Shell Artifact Consumption

While there is clear evidence of shell working activities at Pacbitun, knowledge regarding how shell was used in the dynamic social system or how the ornaments were consumed is more limited. As already noted, the majority of the modified and unmodified shell artifacts recovered from the site were found embedded in floor deposits as well as later construction fill containing dense, midden-like refuse. Only 52 artifacts have been found in ritual contexts, including a late Middle Preclassic primary burial in Plaza C (n=2) and an early Middle Preclassic cache deposit in Plaza B. The cache consisted of 50 irregular beads stacked together in a posthole along the northern retaining wall of Sub-Structure B1. The form and arrangement of these beads suggests that they may have been strung together at the time they were deposited. Burial, cache and other ritual offerings including shell have also been noted at a variety of Belize Valley sites, including Barton Ramie (Willey et al. 1965:509–110), Blackman Eddy (Cochran 2009), Cahal Pech (Aimers 1992; Awe 1992; Cheetham 1995, 1996; Ferguson et al. 1996; Lee 1996; Lee and Awe 1995; Powis 1996; Sunahara and Awe 1994; Song 1995), Chan (Keller 2008), and Zubin (Iannone 1996; Schwake 1996). The inclusion of modified and unmodified shell artifacts in ritual deposits indicates that shell was already of symbolic significance to the residents of Pacbitun and the greater Belize Valley by the early Middle Preclassic period.

Similar, yet more substantial Preclassic ritual deposits including shell have been reported from northern Belize, including sites like Blue Creek (Haines 1997), Chan Chich (Robichaux 1998), Colha (Buttles 1992, 2002; Dreiss 1982, 1994), Cerros (Garber 1983), Cuello (Hammond 1991a; Robin and Hammond 1991) and K'axob (Isaza Aizpurua 1997; Isaza Aizpurua and McAnany 1999). In the absence of a large dataset from the Belize Valley, an evaluation of these finds provides valuable information that can be useful for determining patterns of more general Preclassic shell ornament consumption and in identifying the various roles shell may have played in early Maya society. Unlike the Belize Valley sites, significant numbers of Preclassic human skeletal remains have been identified in northern Belize, the largest assemblages coming from the sites of Cuello (Hammond 1999; Robin 1989; Robin and Hammond 1991) and K'axob (Isaza Aizpurua 1997; Isaza Aizpurua and McAnany 1999). While some of these individuals were interred with a single shell artifact, multiple shell items accompanied others. The frequent clustering of shell artifacts around different parts of the body indicates that shell items were often strung together as necklaces, bracelets, and armbands or as elements of composite pieces such as headdresses and belts. A variety of different shell artifacts were recovered from the burials at K'axob and Cuello, including beads, pendants, figurines, and tinklers. Disk beads consistently occurred with the greatest frequency during the Middle and Late Preclassic, but after this time there is a decrease in beads and a corresponding increase in the number of shell tinklers and figurines.

While it is clear that at least some of the shell ornaments produced at Pacbitun were for local consumption, others may have been destined for intra- or inter-regional exchange. Given the presence of shell ornament production sites in the westernmost portion of the Belize Valley and the occurrence of marine shell ornaments in Preclassic deposits at sites such as Tikal (Moholy-Nagy 1994, 1997), Uaxactun (Kidder 1947), and Nakbe (Hansen, 1999, personal communication) in the Peten, Guatemala, it is possible that residents of the Belize Valley were exporting finished shell ornaments to these more distant markets. It must be noted, however, that marine shell detritus has also been identified at these sites, which suggests a broader pattern of shell ornament production and consumption that is consistent with that observed elsewhere in the southern Maya lowlands.

Organization of Shell Ornament Production

While a significant number of marine shell ornaments have been recovered from archaeological deposits at sites throughout the Maya lowlands, very little is known about the industry that produced these items, particularly during the Preclassic period. The Pacbitun assemblage provides an excellent opportunity to evaluate elements of shell ornament production and craft specialization during this early period of development. At Pacbitun, shell working areas were recognized by the co-occurrence of (1) broken and incomplete shell ornaments, (2) shell detritus, and (3) chert microdrills and burin spalls within a single context. The presence of these materials in primary floor deposits is viewed as direct evidence that shell working activities were undertaken in and around the Middle Preclassic structures excavated in Plaza B. The identification of shell working areas and associated refuse means that variables like scale, intensity, context, and concentration of production can be evaluated and used to reconstruct the organization of shell ornament production at Pacbitun and inform on the Middle Preclassic economy in the region as a whole.

Based on the nature of the evidence at Pacbitun, only the concentration and scale of production can be adequately addressed, although some preliminary comments about production intensity can be made. The concentration of shell working activities at Pacbitun appears to have been nucleated, with evidence restricted to Plaza B of the central precinct. Although a handful of modified shell ornaments, marine shell detritus, and chert microtools were found in sub-plaza deposits in neighboring Plazas C and D, these materials were recovered from secondary deposits with no clear association to each other. Middle Preclassic artifactual materials were found in test units throughout the central precinct during widespread testing of the epicenter, core and periphery of Pacbitun, but to date no significant evidence of shell working has been identified outside of Plaza B (Campbell-Trithart 1990; Healy 1990a; Richie 1990; Sunahara 1995).

At the regional level, evidence of Preclassic shell-working has been identified at a number of other Middle Preclassic sites in the Belize Valley such as Cahal Pech (Awe 1992; Cheetham 1995, 1996; Powis 1996) and Blackman Eddy (Cochran 2009). In some cases the evidence consists of modified shell artifacts, marine shell detritus, and chert microtools found in the same deposits, while in others it is only modified and unmodified shell. Unfortunately, in some cases the materials are found in secondary contexts, making it impossible to evaluate the production system. Many researchers working in the Maya area have cited the presence of shell working activities and even identified shell workshops and speculated about the intensity, scale, and context of production based only on the presence of a few items in secondary midden deposits and construction fill. Moholy-Nagy (1997:295) argues that "correctly identified debitage, by definition, is always a sign of craft activity somewhere, no matter where it is found." Under this assumption, virtually every Middle Preclassic site in the Belize Valley has evidence of shell working, but the extent and organization of production activities cannot be determined without first identifying shell workshops, or at least workshop debris in primary contexts.

Outside of Pacbitun, the most conclusive evidence for a shell workshop comes from Cas Pek, a settlement located in the periphery of Cahal Pech (Iannone and Lee 1996; Lee 1996; Lee and Awe 1995). Modified shell artifacts (n=43), marine shell detritus (n=1,812), and chert microdrills and burin spalls (n=516) virtually identical to those from Pacbitun were found during excavation of the late Middle Preclassic to early Late Preclassic levels at this site. While this can definitely be interpreted as shell working refuse, the architectural associations remain unclear, so it is difficult to determine whether the deposits are primary or secondary in nature. Small quantities of shell working materials have also been identified in midden deposits at the Tolok peripheral group (Powis 1996), and in recently excavated deposits from the central precinct of Cahal Pech (Garber et al. 2005), suggesting perhaps that Preclassic shell working activities at Cahal Pech were more dispersed than those at Pacbitun.

Research from Oaxaca also provides useful comparative data on shell working during the Preclassic or Formative period. Evidence of shell working (i.e., modified shell artifacts, detritus, tools) has been identified in the Early and Middle Formative villages of San Jose Mogote and Tierras Largas in the Valley of Oaxaca (Flannery and Winter 1976:36–39; Pires-Ferreira 1976, 1978). These deposits were typically concentrated in the corners of structures, but debris was also encountered in general excavations in household clusters (Pires-Ferreira 1976:Table 10.8). The presence of shell working debris at virtually every domestic structure in these two settlements and the virtual absence of this same evidence at other sites in the valley has led Flannery and Winter (1976:39) to argue that shell working may have been a regional specialization, with virtually all households in particular settlements involved in production activities. Given the presence of shell ornaments and marine shell detritus in Middle Preclassic deposits at virtually every site excavated in the Belize Valley, it is possible that a similar scenario existed here.

Regarding the scale of production, the presence of shell working materials in and around the Middle Preclassic domestic structures and the association of shell working debris with domestic refuse suggest that production activities at Pacbitun were undertaken by a small, kin-based group organized at the household level. In many typologies of specialized production, scale and intensity are linked such that small-scale, household-based production is at one end of the continuum and large-scale, factory-based production by unrelated individuals is at the other (Peacock 1982; van der Leeuw 1977). In these typologies, household-based production is typically designed to replenish household goods. Feinman (1999) and Nichols (Feinman and Nichols 2000) have recently challenged the link between scale and intensity using household shell ornament production data from the Valley of Ejutla, Oaxaca. Based on the high density of production debris and lack of finished products, they have suggested that the level of production was greater than that needed by a single household. While production in residential contexts has traditionally been associated with part-time, low-intensity production, Feinman and Nichols argue that this is not an accurate portrayal of some household-based production systems, at least those related to shell ornament production in Ejutla. We believe a similar scenario existed at Pacbitun with household producers manufacturing items for other members of the community or even potentially for export.

The intensity of shell working at Pacbitun is more difficult to discern.

Crafting could have been undertaken full-time during certain times of the year, but it may also have been undertaken on a part-time basis throughout the year as time would permit. Alternatively, it may have been a combination of both depending on the time of year and the number of skilled crafters in the household. From the Peten, Moholy-Nagy (1963, 1978, 1985, 1989, 1994, 1997) has written extensively about the shell artifacts from Tikal, including those dating to the Preclassic and Classic periods. Based on her diachronic study of Tikal shell artifacts, Moholy-Nagy (1994, 1997) argues that during the Classic period nonelite artifacts were being produced by part-time, independent specialists while high status artifacts were produced by full-time, attached specialists possibly living in the same groups. The archaeological signatures associated with different scenarios of production intensity and context are not clearly defined in the Tikal study, nor in most studies of Maya craft production, so this interpretation remains somewhat questionable.

There is a growing body of literature on Classic Maya craft production that reveals a clear association between high status households and craft activities (Ball 1993; Emery and Aoyama 2007; Healy et al. 1995; Inomata 2001, 2007; Reents-Budet 1994; Reents-Budet et al. 2000), but these studies have not spent considerable time addressing the archaeological signatures of part-time and full-time craft production beyond generalizing that large quantities of refuse are associated with full-time specialists while smaller amounts are associated with those engaged in crafting activities on a part-time basis. The problem with this argument is that production refuse may have accumulated rapidly during a few short work sessions staffed by multiple crafters, or it may have accumulated slowly as the result of part-time crafting by only one or two individuals over a much longer period of time. As ceramic cross-dating is typically the first technique employed to date such refuse deposits, it is virtually impossible to capture a snapshot of a particular point in time in an attempt to distinguish between these different production scenarios.

Shell and the Political Economy

In the Maya lowlands, and throughout Mesoamerica in general, marine shell ornaments are typically viewed as high value or wealth items when found at inland sites far removed from their natural range of occurrence. This is especially the case for the more elaborate items with complicated forms or designs. In the anthropological literature, wealth items have been variously referred to as primitive valuables, prestige goods, or luxury and status items, just to mention a few (Brumfiel and Earle 1987; Dalton 1977; Earle 1982; Ekholm 1972; Hirth 1992). Wealth items typically derive their value from the labor invested in their manufacture, technological sophistication, relative scarcity, raw material type, or a combination of these elements. A review of the ethnographic literature also reveals that wealth items often function as visible indicators of an individual's status in society, but they can also serve as generalized wealth that is used in a variety of exchanges at the intra- and inter-community levels.

In many ethnographic studies, "prestige goods" models have been used to describe how control over wealth items has led to the evolution of ranked and/or stratified societies. In particular, this model was initially used to describe the evolution of ranked lineages in African societies (Ekholm 1972, 1977; Meillassoux 1978). In these societies, senior members of the group control prestige goods needed by junior members for marriage exchanges and a wide variety of other social obligations or payments. By controlling access to these items, dyadic relationships are formed between patrons who control access to these social valuables and clients who are reliant upon them for items necessary for social reproduction (e.g., bride price, debt payments). Patrons accumulate surplus wealth by forcing subordinates to make payments of tribute for access to these goods, a process that allows for the differential accumulation of wealth within the community. Alternatively, other ethnographic examples reveal that under the right circumstances, nonegalitarian relationships can form in the absence of control over wealth items. For example, among the Lele of the Democratic Republic of Congo, raffia cloth was historically used in many social exchanges (Douglas 1958). Unlike the prestige goods economy model mentioned above, where an individual or group controls production of items needed in social exchanges, senior Lele males did not have direct control over the production of raffia cloth. In fact, all Lele men were engaged in the weaving of raffia cloth. Since it was impossible for junior males to produce enough cloths needed for all of their social obligations, they would turn to senior men for contributions, thus patron-client relationships were formed between senior men who possessed stores of raffia cloth and junior members who needed these cloths for social reproduction.

Archaeological and iconographic evidence from the Classic period support the theory that the Maya viewed marine shell and products made from these materials as high value items. In iconographic representations, Classic Maya elites are often depicted wearing shell ornaments as jewelry items as well as clothing embellishments such as tinklers stitched to the hems of elaborate garments. And Maya elite were often buried with a variety of different jewelry items created from marine shell as well as whole or fragmented marine shell as accompanying burial offerings. Shell ornaments were clearly designed to be worn, so they may have served as visual symbols or "badges" of authority designed to display an individual's rank or office in society during life as well as in death (Hirth 1992). Freidel and Schele (1988a) have noted the importance of jade bib-head pendants as symbols of Maya royalty or kingship by the Late Preclassic, so it is possible that some shell ornaments also served as badges of office or authority. Alternatively, they may also have served as a form of generalized wealth used by members of society in a number of social, political, and economic transactions, much as they were during the Colonial period as evidenced by the writings of Diego de Landa. The strong evidence for shell working and other craft activities from elite residences at sites like Aguateca (Emery and Aoyama 2007; Inomata 2001) and Copan (Aoyama 1995; Fash 1991; Hendon 1989; Webster 1992) reinforce the belief that Maya elites placed great value on marine shell.

While shell artifacts are a ubiquitous artifact class identified in deposits throughout the Maya lowlands, the role they may have played in the dynamic Middle Preclassic social, political, and economic arenas remains unclear. One suggestion is that shell items were used in exchanges and competitive displays designed to build power and prestige and establish and maintain alliances at the intra- and inter-community levels, a similar scenario to that which has been presented for artifacts like decorated pottery during the Classic period (Lecount 1996, 1999). Using archaeological data, Clark and Blake (1994) and Hayden (1998) argue that new or foreign technologies are often introduced by political aggrandizers as part of their pursuit of prestige. It seems likely that during the Middle Preclassic, politically motivated individuals began acquiring nonlocal marine shell to make ornaments for use in competitive exchanges designed to enhance their position in society.

Given the widespread distribution of marine species along the coast of the Yucatan Peninsula, access to marine shell could not have been restricted like isolated deposits of raw materials like jade or obsidian. Given the great distance between the Belize Valley and the coast, it is possible that access to marine shell was restricted to only those individuals who could sponsor such expeditions or those with extensive trade relationships. For example, in some Pacific maritime societies, access to sophisticated watercraft translated into control over certain coastal resources. Archaeological data from the Channel Islands off the coast of California indicate that the Chumash controlled the production of shell ornaments and their distribution to the mainland (Arnold 1991, 1995; Arnold and Munns 1994). Arnold notes that these goods were controlled by a small number of individuals who owned the only canoes that could make the journey across the channel. Similarly, Nootkan chiefs used sophisticated canoes to harvest *Dentalium* shells from shallow beds off the coast of Vancouver Island (Drucker 1951). These chiefs appear to have had exclusive rights to these sources because they possessed the only watercraft that could withstand the journey. It is quite possible that certain politically motivated individuals from Pacbitun and other sites in the Belize Valley were sponsoring expeditions to the coast with the expressed purpose of procuring marine shell that could then be modified into shell jewelry for use in intra- and inter-community exchanges designed to enhance their prestige. The fact that Pacbitun is an inland site with no immediate access to the Belize River or one of its major tributaries provides some challenges for this particular model, but with the proper connections in the Belize Valley, access to marine shell would not have been a problem.

In her research on Panamanian chiefdoms, Helms (1979, 1992, 1993) argues that rulers or other politically motivated individuals often use symbolically charged items in their attempts to build power and prestige. Several authors have addressed the role symbolic power may have played in the development of social complexity in Mesoamerican cultures (Demarest and Conrad 1992; Drennan 1976; Freidel and Schele 1988a). More recently, Inomata (2001, 2007) has used similar arguments for the Classic Maya elite based on his research at the site of Aguateca, Guatemala. He suggests that elite families were engaged in craft activities that resulted in the production of objects which were imbued with ideological significance, and that by controlling ritual knowledge these elites became indispensable to the community and reinforced their position in society. But was this the case during the Middle Preclassic when the nature and control over craft activities and evidence of social differentiation is more ambiguous? If Middle Preclassic shell ornaments were symbolically charged and tied to the Maya worldview, which appears to be the case, then political upstarts may have tried to exert control over the production and distribution of these items, resulting ultimately in the accumulation of both objective and symbolic power.

Another question to address is whether shell items were needed by all members of Middle Preclassic Maya society to fulfill ritual obligations, such as those associated with burials, caching, or dedication and termination events? If so, then politically motivated individuals may have begun manipulating control over shell items needed by all members of society for important ritual events. By controlling access to these items through production and/or distribution, these individuals would become indispensable to other members of the community, thus enhancing their position in society. Alternatively, given the widespread distribution of Middle Preclassic marine shell artifacts and detritus at sites throughout the southern Maya lowlands, it is possible that a scenario similar to that of the Lele existed in this region. Perhaps every household had access to marine shell or finished ornaments needed for inclusion in ritual deposits, but that senior members of society would be called upon if an individual felt that their stores of shell were not sufficient for the particular ritual or event. Junior members may have been required to pay tribute or otherwise pay for access to these materials, further reinforcing the patron-client relationship and providing a foundation for the development of social stratification within Preclassic Maya society. This could easily explain the disparity in the number and type of shell goods included in Middle Preclassic burial deposits at sites like Cuello and K'axob, where some individuals were buried with much larger quantities of shell than others (Isaza Aizpurua 1997; Isaza Aizpurua and McAnany 1999). In these cases, senior members of society may have been buried with more shell because they simply had more time to accumulate larger quantities of this ritually important material, while junior members of society would include these materials for themselves and their families, but not in quantities rivaling their elders. The same could be said for the inclusion of shell in other ritual offerings such as caches and dedication and termination rituals.

Conclusion

Extensive archaeological investigations at the site of Pacbitun have revealed substantial architectural and artifactual remains dating to the Middle Preclassic period. Most significant of these finds is the large-scale production of shell ornaments that took place in Plaza B of the central precinct. The frequent identification of shell in Middle Preclassic burial, cache, and other ritual deposits indicates that shell played an important role in Maya ritual by the beginning of this early period of cultural development. The fact that this pattern of Middle Preclassic shell use has been identified throughout the southern Maya lowlands indicates that this ritual behavior and associated material culture were a pan-lowland tradition, perhaps with unique regional variations such as in the type of shell artifacts produced or production processes or technologies.

While shell has been a ubiquitous artifact class found in Middle Preclassic deposits throughout the southern Maya lowlands, to date little has been known about the production of these items. The importation of nonlocal marine shell and the restricted nature of its distribution within Pacbitun and other Belize Valley sites suggest that some degree of control may have been exerted over the production and/or distribution of marine shell or the finished shell products. The sheer quantities of shell working debris in the site core of Pacbitun hint at a level of production beyond that needed by a single household, so it is quite likely that these ornaments were intended for intra- or extra-community exchange. In this paper, two different scenarios have been presented to account for the quantity and spatial distribution of Middle Preclassic shell and shell working materials at Pacbitun and in the Belize Valley. Firstly, marine shell and finished ornaments may have been used in competitive displays by members of an emerging elite class to build and maintain alliances at the community and regional levels. In this model, control over the production and/or distribution of shell objects would ultimately translate into more alliances and greater power. The fact that shell was of symbolic or ideological significance adds additional support to this theory. In the second scenario, all households had access to shell resources that were needed by members of society to fulfill a variety of social and/or ritual obligations, but junior members of society could not accumulate enough to satisfy all of these obligations. In this model, power relationships form between junior members who must acquire additional shell from senior members of society as well as pay tribute for access to these materials.

It is still too early to say with any degree of certainty that Middle Preclassic shell working was or was not under the control of a particular individual or group, but the archaeological evidence from Pacbitun and the Belize Valley seem to support this theory. Sociopolitical organization cannot be determined from a single artifact class, but the Pacbitun data has shed new light on the nature of Preclassic economies in this important region and has provided much needed comparative data that may be used to identify patterns of spatial and temporal development throughout Mesoamerica.

Acknowledgments

Investigations at Pacbitun were licensed (#282\3\94) by the government of Belize through the Department of Archaeology to Paul F. Healy. Funding for research was provided by the Social Sciences and Humanities Research Council (SSHRC) of Canada, the Ahau Foundation, and the Latin American Institute at the University of New Mexico. Excavations were made possible by the Tzul family, who graciously granted us access to their private land. We want to express our special appreciation to our local field assistants for their dedication, camaraderie, and good humor: Tarcicio Coc, Rolando Gonzalez, Javier Mai, John Mai, and Eduardo Tesecum. Particular thanks are extended to a number of individuals who provided an exchange of ideas and unpublished data: Jim Aimers, Jaime Awe, David Cheetham, Raphael Cobos, Jennifer Cochran, Jim Garber, Norman Hammond, Tom Hester, Gyles Iannone, Angela Keller, Cynthia Robin, Harry Shafer, Norbert Stanchly, and Sam Wilson. The illustrations were drawn by Ruth Dickau and Michael Bletzer and the computer graphics were produced by Jon Lohse.

7

Developmental Dynamics, Energetics, and
Complex Economic Interactions of the
Early Maya of the Mirador-Calakmul Basin,
Guatemala, and Campeche, Mexico

RICHARD D. HANSEN, DONALD W. FORSYTH, JAMES C. WOODS,
THOMAS P. SCHREINER, AND GENE L. TITMUS

> . . . it should be emphasized that understanding the structure of agricultural labor
> recruitment and control is essential to understanding the rise and fall of any state.
>
> Abrams 1995:210

Introduction

Recent archaeological investigations of a series of monumental sites in
the Mirador-Calakmul Basin of Guatemala and Mexico by the Mirador
Basin Project[1] (University of Utah and the Foundation for Anthropological Research & Environmental Studies [FARES]), and formerly known as
the Regional Archaeological Investigation of the North Peten, Guatemala
(RAINPEG), have focused, in part, on the complex issues surrounding the
origins and development of incipient Maya civilization. The project has
conducted extensive survey, mapping, and specific, problem-oriented excavations at various stratified ancient cities within the basin (n=51). Flannery
(1976:4) pointed out long ago that in studying formative Mesoamerica,
"the methodology most appropriate for the task of isolating and studying processes of cultural change and evolution is one which is regional in
scope, and executed with the aid of research designs based on the principles of probability sampling." To this we would add that interpretations
derived from analytical processes and archaeological data which result in

anthropological conclusions can be enhanced through viable, ethnographically and archaeologically oriented experiments (e.g., Abrams 1984, 1987, 1994; Ascher 1961; Erasmus 1965; Renfrew 1973; Saraydar and Shimada 1971, 1973). Recent attempts to derive sophisticated modeling based on contemporary construction management planning and techniques such as the Critical Path Method (CPM) may also be productive (e.g., Smailes 2011). Such approaches are especially useful in understanding the sociopolitical and economic complexities of the rise of the early complex societies (see Abrams 1994, 1995, 1996; Saraydar and Shimada 1973; Webb 1977). The expenditure of labor in vital industries (defined below) has long been recognized as an important factor to be considered in the development of state-level societies, suggesting that it be considered a dynamic rather than a variable component of society (Bleed 1991; Freidel and Cliff 1978; Hansen 1984, 1990:214–217; Price 1984; Sidrys 1976, 1978; Spencer 1979, 1993; Webster 1990; Wier 1996; Woodbury and Neely 1972).

The identity of the dynamics responsible for the formation (and the demise) of complex societies can be detected partly through study of the energetics of those industries that provided basic subsistence, economic, and political/ideological functions (e.g., Arnold and Ford 1980; Freidel and Cliff 1978). These industries ultimately provided social cohesiveness and organic solidarity on an expanding scale to a point of marginal productivity (see Abrams 1995). Such mechanisms correlate with the equally expanding levels of sociopolitical sophistication. For example, the archaeological appearance of exotic goods and various levels of craft specializations suggest differential consumption, organized technological innovation, economic expansion and surplus, and administrative organization, which are all components of more complex cultural behavior (e.g., Bray 1978b; Brumfiel and Earle 1987; Helms 1993). The dynamics that led to the increased complexity must not only contribute to the generation of political and economic power, but also establish the mechanisms for the maintenance of such power (Abrams 1994, 1995, 1996; Abrams and Bolland 1999; Helms 1993; Kaplan 1963). In this chapter, we shall identify some of these factors in the early cultural evolution of the ancient Maya and illustrate the corresponding relationship to their sociopolitical and economic complexity in the Mirador-Calakmul Basin of northern Guatemala and southern Campeche, Mexico (Figure 7.1). We sought to identify the prime factors that would presumably have led to increased social and economic differentiation that would have allowed progressive cultural complexity among the early Maya.

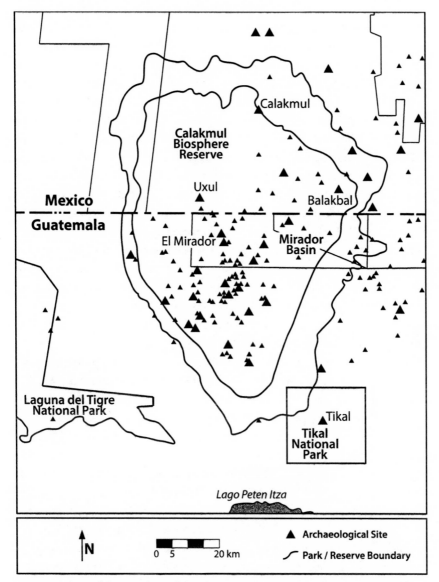

Figure 7.1. Area of the Mirador-Calakmul Basin with some of the sites mapped by the Mirador Basin Project (map by Josephine Thompson, © FARES 2011; used by permission).

We recognize, and indeed, we have evidence to support, the premise that subsistence systems and corresponding labor investments were the fundamental foundations of sociopolitical complexity in the Maya lowlands (and any state-level organization) (see Abrams 1995). The elaboration of subsistence systems in the form of agricultural terraces, irrigation canals, dams, raised fields, and production-oriented agricultural platforms enhanced the sociopolitical and economic vitality of the earliest centers in Mesoamerica, as evident in the case of San Lorenzo Tenochtitlan or highland Oaxaca (Cyphers 1994, 1996; Marcus and Flannery 1996; Price 1984). However, numerous ethnographic examples indicate that subsistence requirements, once having been fulfilled or satisfied, are not necessarily the ingredients that propel societies into more sophisticated sociopolitical behavior (e.g., Carneiro 1973:100–101; Chagnon 1968; Kirch 1984:160; Hoopes 1991; Malinowski 1961[1922]:169). In other words, a society's needs do not necessarily initiate more complex responses. The factors responsible for the next additional leap involve the differential access to—and control of—labor as well as the exploitation and redistribution of natural resources and exchangeable commodities which enhance social prestige and wealth, a step in the development of hereditary status (see Clark and Blake 1994). This implies the ultimate formation of defensive mechanisms to protect and defend acquired wealth, or to otherwise devise the means to plunder or exact tribute in commodities and other forms of wealth. When these ingredients are combined with the intensification of ritual and ideological systems that utilized those resources, they form the most important factors for the generation and maintenance of real political and economic power (Hansen 1992a; Marcus and Flannery 1996).

This paper will present some of the experimental and analytical research to further elucidate the dynamic roles of several of the largest and most labor-intensive ancient industries in the Maya lowlands: ceramics, lithic industries, lime and stucco production systems, architectural constructions, and agricultural intensification in terms of both volumetric and energetic assessments. Our studies, based on archaeological investigations combined with experimental programs in the field as well as laboratory analyses, suggest that previous models for developmental dynamics and energetics of the ancient Maya can be refined. The conjunctive issues involved with the advent of these industries are useful contributions to lower- and middle-range theoretical concerns dealing with the early cultural sophistication and formative interactions of sociopolitical complexity.

Setting

The Mirador-Calakmul Basin is a circumscribed, geographically defined area in northern Guatemala and southern Campeche, Mexico, with a strong Middle and Late Preclassic occupation dating from 1000 B.C. to approximately A.D. 150 (Figures 7.1 and 7.2). Middle Preclassic settlements in various degrees have been identified at the sites of El Mirador, Nakbe, Wakna, Xulnal, El Pesquero, La Florida, and Tintal, Guatemala, and sites such as Yaxnohcah on the Campeche side of the basin, which are among the largest sites within the Mirador-Calakmul Basin (Naachtun has begun to be investigated, and all indications are that the site has a heavy Early and Late Classic occupation with major architecture and numerous stelae (Kathryn Reese-Taylor, personal communication 2008; Philippe Nondedeo, personal communication 2011; Michelet et al. 2013). The precocious nature of the Preclassic development in the basin has resulted in the construction of some of the largest structures in the Maya lowlands by the Late Preclassic period (ca. 300 B.C.–A.D. 150). The density and abundance of such massive architectural assemblages were enhanced by an intricate system of causeways constructed on an intra-site and inter-site level, joining the sites of El Mirador to Nakbe, Tintal, and possibly Calakmul in addition to Xulnal, Wakna, and Paixban (Figure 7.2). Major causeways are also found joining Tintal to other large sites (i.e., La Ceibita) within the confines of the basin, and a major causeway has been recently discovered with new and improved aerial photographs crossing the Laberinto *bajo* to the southwest of Calakmul. A LiDAR study conducted in 2015 of the Mirador Basin has also detected numerous new and important causeways throughout the entirety of the basin.

The developmental sequence for Preclassic architecture has been particularly evident at the sites of Nakbe and El Mirador, where excavations were conducted by the Mirador Basin Project from 1989 to 1998 and were begun again in 2014 (Hansen 1992a, 1992b, 1998, 2001, 2005; Hansen et al. 2002, 2004, 2008). Ceramic analyses and associated ^{14}C data from primary deposits and middens at the site suggest that early sedentary occupation and architectural constructions began between 1000 and 800 B.C., with architecture consisting of perishable superstructures, packed clay floors, postholes, and small platforms. In addition, wattle-and-daub residential structures were constructed with clay floors and retaining walls (Hansen 1992b, 1998). These earliest structures are not yet well understood, however,

Figure 7.2. Contour map of a portion of the Mirador Basin indicating the extensive causeway system in this area that linked major sites with the civic center of El Mirador (map by Josephine Thompson, © FARES 2010; used by permission).

because of the dubious justification and physical difficulty of removing later Middle Preclassic and Late Preclassic architecture from over the buried constructions.

The construction of formal stone platforms appears slightly later, about 800 to 600 B.C. These platforms consistently are composed of vertical walls, up to two meters in height, and made of roughly hewn flat stones approximately 25 cm long × 28 cm wide × 8 cm thick (Figure 7.3). The walls were covered with a rather primitive lime and clay plaster or a chalky stucco while floors consist primarily of packed clay, *sascab* (a decomposed limestone grit or marl), or thin lime plaster.

It is during this period however, that evidence for embryonic leadership and status hierarchy is available, as suggested by the importation and distribution of exotic goods, variations in residence size and structural sophistication, and the introduction of symbols that in later Maya society were representative of rank and status of patron elite. The importation of exotic commodities from long-distance trade networks may have served to demonstrate variations in status, establish political legitimacy, utilize skilled crafting, and display long-distance managerial skills (see Helms 1993). The early Middle Preclassic period at Nakbe and similar chronologically correlated deposits at Uaxactun, Tikal, and the Pasion region are noted by the presence of quantities of Marginelladae shells and, in particular, the exclusive cut fragments of *Strombus* (*Strombus costatus*) shells from the Caribbean (Feldman 2001) (see Hohmann et al. Chapter 6 this volume). These shell fragments are found in primary deposits with a single, frequently biconically drilled perforation and cut to square or rectangular pieces, but otherwise unworked. The spines and natural projections of the shells were left intact. We have yet to identify these shells in burial contexts, and their unique presence in early Middle Preclassic deposits of a ritual and elite character suggests that they represented an important status or economic indicator. These shells were imported possibly via the Belize River valley, where researchers have recovered what appears to be *Strombus* shell workshops in early Middle Preclassic contexts which included shells in various

Figure 7.3. Excavations at the western base of Structure 51 at Nakbe (Op. 51C) showing Middle Preclassic wall (*right*), a Middle Preclassic altar (Nakbe Altar 4), and parallel rows of wall lines in the middle of the image. Nakbe Stela 1 is located to the left of the image, which had been reset in a small Late Classic platform (photograph by F. R. Hillman, FARES).

stages of workmanship, stone awls, and shell workshop debris (Cochran 2009; Hohmann 2002; Hohmann et al. Chapter 6 this volume). It is also significant that the *Strombus* shells do not appear in any of the extensive Late Preclassic contexts in the Mirador-Calakmul Basin, suggesting that the function of the shell may have been specialized and its presence is useful as a period marker.

Obsidian was transported into the site from highland sources (Kunselman 2000). Some of it may have even been imported in raw, nodule form as suggested by the presence of cortex on recovered waste flakes and core shatter, which is evidence of early stage reduction debitage. Chemical analyses by Ray Kunselman (University of Wyoming) of a portion of the Middle Preclassic obsidian blades and flakes (n=85) from sealed, secure contexts show a strong concentration (66%) of Middle Preclassic obsidian from San Martin Jilotepeque (SMJ), with 32% from El Chayal, and 1% from Ixtepeque (Kunselman 2000). Percentages may change with the pending analyses of many more obsidian fragments from Middle Preclassic contexts at Nakbe, but comparisons with other sites suggest that the SMJ percentages are likely to increase, as San Martin appears to be the primary source for Middle Preclassic obsidian exploitation, while El Chayal appears to dominate after about 300 B.C. (Moholy-Nagy and Nelson 1990; Nelson 1985; Rice 1984).

While the appearance of exotic, long-distance trade items used in ritual and/or economic paraphernalia does not, by itself, imply a more complex cultural trajectory since primitive societies throughout the world have employed such tactics, it does place an important contrast between the ordinary citizens of the society and those responsible for the political arrangements for long-distance negotiations, transfer of payment commodities, merchant relations, varied ethnic connections, and skilled artisan development and distribution (Helms 1993:14). Such a process of administrative responsibility usually precedes the development of prestige inherent in the governing elite in societies of increasing sociopolitical and economic complexity (Clark and Blake 1994).

Physical characteristics of elite status, such as skull deformation and inlaid hematite disks in human incisors were also apparent during this time (Mata and Hansen 1992). Figurines depicting the three-pronged Jester image were also recovered from early Middle Preclassic deposits, and the *pop* or woven mat motif, is ubiquitous throughout the Middle Preclassic ceramic repertoire, suggesting that the iconography of rulership, evident in Olmec societies, was also present in the contemporaneous Maya societies prior to 600 B.C. (Hansen 2001:54).

By the late Middle Preclassic period (the late Ox phase between 600 to 400 B.C.), pyramidal structures (up to 28 m high) were constructed at El Mirador, Xulnal, Nakbe, and possibly Wakna. It is also at this time that we see the introduction of a formal consistent architectural form: the E-Group complex (Hansen 1992a, 1992b, 1998:63). The E-Group construction in the Middle Preclassic period at Nakbe correlates well with contemporaneous buildings at Tikal (Mundo Perdido) and Uaxactun (Group D and Group E) (Laporte and Valdés 1993; Laporte and Fialko 1995), Xunantunich (Brown et al. Chapter 5 this volume), as well as those in highland Chiapas such as Chiapa de Corzo, Mirador, and La Libertad (Agrinier 1975:Figure 89; Clark 1988:8; Mason 1960).

It was this period that witnessed the more prominent placement of sculptured stone monuments, increasing lime production and stucco utilization, an increase in agricultural intensification, and major transformations in the size and form of limestone blocks used in architectural constructions. We believe that these changes may possibly represent an inherent instability among rapidly expanding populations founded on lineage organizations that ultimately formed segmentary, incipient city states that quickly coalesced into a unified system (Sanders and Webster 1988). The cultural innovations were fueled by a differential access to wealth, organized exploitation of natural resources, implementation of systematic, intensive agriculture, and an increasing focus on labor intensification and specialist production systems. The result of such radical transformations served to consolidate the economic and political power of an emerging administrative elite.

Ceramics

The earliest and most ubiquitous artifacts indicative of specialist behavior from Middle Preclassic contexts in the Mirador Basin are ceramics and lithics. Detailed studies of the pottery by Mirador Basin Project ceramic analyst Donald W. Forsyth, indicate that the early Middle Preclassic ceramics (Early and Middle Ox Complex) from Nakbe are more similar typologically with the Middle Preclassic materials from Uaxactun than from Tikal, and are more similar to the Xe-Escoba-San Felix Mamom phases of the Pasion and Usumacinta regions than with Belize or Yucatan (Forsyth 1992, 1993a, 1993b:40–41). A similar observation can be made with the early ceramics from the Cascabel and Sacalero groups at El Mirador. The wide variation of surface treatments and forms vary radically from the "mono-systemic" standardized forms and slips of the subsequent late Middle Preclassic and Late Preclassic periods.

A brief overview of the early ceramic complexes in the Mirador Basin demonstrates the presence of specialist production and utilization, beginning by about 1000–800 B.C. and in force by no later than 600 B.C. (Hansen 2005). One of the most common early and middle phase Middle Preclassic types found in the Mirador Basin is Palma Daub, with its characteristic unburnished painting, "daubing," and streaking, often in parallel bands, around restricted-neck *ollas* or jars. Another common type, Achiotes Unslipped, appears to be only lightly brushed, while striated unslipped ceramics (Sapote Striated) do not appear until the latter part of the Middle Preclassic period. Sapote Striated became one of the dominant types of the Late Preclassic period (Hansen and Forsyth 1987). Other wares and types found in the Mirador Basin have close correlations to other early Middle Preclassic sites, but the variety of surface treatments, form, paste, and temper compositions demonstrate specialist license and an area-specific ceramic innovation (Forsyth 1993b).

The slipped, middle, and late Middle Preclassic pottery (Middle, and Late Ox Complex phases, Monos and pre-Monos complexes) at Nakbe, Xulnal, La Florida, Wakna, and El Mirador is dominantly monochrome, with the principal monochrome pottery attributed to the Juventud (Joventud) ceramic group, characterized by an orange-red slip that is, at times, semi-waxy. There are important modal variations of chronological value with particular ceramic types throughout the Middle Preclassic Ox Phases, but for the purposes of this paper, these differences are not discussed. The most common forms are flaring-sided dishes with everted, thickened or direct rims, *tecomates*, and extensive pre-slip and post-slip incising (Figure 7.4). Bases are generally flat. Other forms include cuspidors, near-cuspidors, round-sided bowls, deep bowls, and short-necked jars.

The monochrome ceramics are marked by a high percentage of surface decoration utilizing techniques of incising, fluting, and chamfering (Forsyth 1993b:45–46). Moreover, more than one of these may be applied to the same vessel, and often they grade into, or imitate, one another so that incising may be used to mark off areas that, on other vessels, are commonly chamfered. Incision as a decorative technique occurs in two major forms. One consists of shallow, U-shaped, pre-slipped medium-line grooves which are sometimes so delicate that they are difficult to see without close inspection. They are most common on the bottom of flat bottom plates. Fine-line post-slip incision also occurs, but is not as common as the pre-slip variety.

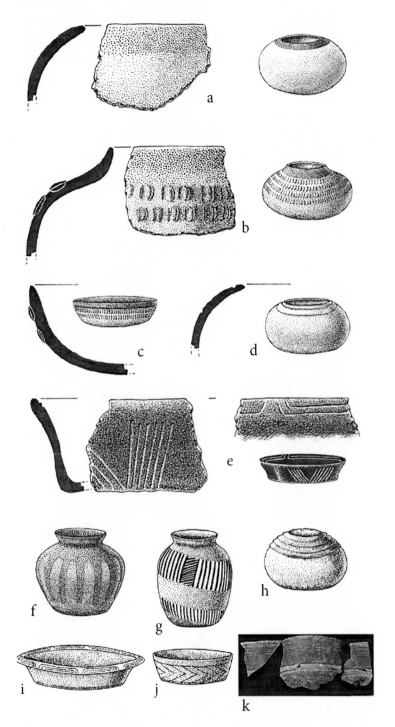

Figure 7.4. Ceramics from sealed Middle Preclassic contexts at Nakbe: (a–e) 1000–700 B.C.; (g–k) 800–600 B.C. (after Hansen 2005).

On deep bowls it is often found as circumferential lines near or on rims, occasionally exhibiting a variant of the "double-line break."

The incidence of chamfering is very high, and serves as a ready marker for the Middle Preclassic period (Forsyth 1993b). Limited to the exteriors of vessels, chamfering exhibits a considerable range of variation in the way it is executed. Sometimes it consists of a single, wide raised band, in other cases as multiple, narrow clapboard bands. The most common vessel forms are dishes or bowls with flat bottoms, flaring sides and direct rims, and cuspidor or near-cuspidor vessels.

Black-slipped pottery of the Chunhinta Group is the next most numerous class of monochrome pottery. It appears to occur in similar vessel forms and decorative modes as in the Juventud Group, except that chamfering is relatively less common. Post-slip, fine-line incising seems to be somewhat more common in this type than in the Juventud Group, but pre-slip, medium-line incision is common also. Fluting and chamfering are also found in this group, either singly or combined with other decorative techniques.

Monochrome cream pottery of the Pital Group is much less common than red- or black-slipped ceramics. But the same decorative modes, including chamfering and incising occur. A bichrome type, Muxanal Red-on-cream consists of areas that are slipped either red or cream in distinct zones. This type often bears raised ridges or abrupt changes in contour on the exterior that mark the borders of the respective colors. In other cases the edges of chamfers serve this function.

Although less common, the Tierra Mojada Group also occurs in this horizon. This pottery is marked by an orange-red slip similar in color to the Juventud Group, but that has resist buff-to-tan splotches or distinct organized patterns on the surface. But this particular resist technique is an excellent horizon marker in the Peten region at interior lowland sites such as Uaxactun, Tikal, Altar de Sacrificios, and Ceibal (Sabloff 1975:73).

The Middle Preclassic pottery recovered to date in the Mirador Basin reflects a relatively sophisticated ceramic technology that suggests a well-integrated process of production, distribution, and consumption. Moreover, the similarity of the Mirador Basin ceramics to other sites across the northern and central Peten suggests that the sites were participating in a consistent complex system of ceramic manufacture that was shared or distributed over a specified region or area.

Monuments

The greater similarity of the early ceramics from the Mirador Basin to those from the Pasion and Usumacinta regions may also have other cultural "footprints" with reference to the importation of a red sandstone monument into the site of Tintal in the Mirador Basin from that area (see Hansen 2005; Schreiner 1992). Excavations conducted by the Mirador Basin Project at Tintal over a series of years (Hansen 1991, 1992a, 1992b; Hansen et al. 2006) located a dense deposit of Late Classic ritual refuse concentrated around Stela 1 (note 2) indicative of the attention Late Classic inhabitants afforded Preclassic monuments in the Mirador Basin. Hansen has argued elsewhere (Hansen 1992a, 1992b, 1994, 1995, 2005) that the size, form, and iconography of Tintal Stela 1,[2] Nakbe Stela 1, and additional large fragments in the Mirador Basin are similar to other examples known in the Gulf and Pacific Coast areas of Mesoamerica in the late Middle Preclassic period, from between 600 to ca. 350 B.C. The analyses of other carved Preclassic monuments now known from the Mirador Basin and stylistic comparisons with other Middle Preclassic sculptures suggest that this chronological assignment has merit.

The ritual veneration of Tintal Stela 1, Nakbe Stela 1, Nakbe Monument 2, and Nakbe Monument 3, as well as the six known monuments at Pedernal (Pedernal Stela 1, Altar 1, Monuments 2–5) included burning of copal in spiked incense burners. It also included the smashing of hundreds of Late Classic vessels consisting of drums, bowls, plates, and restricted orifice vessels of the type Chinja Impressed. In addition, several burials, dating from the Preclassic and Early Classic (A.D. 300–400) were located at the base of the monuments, indicating that ritual veneration of early sculpture had existed for a considerable period of time in the Mirador Basin. Late Classic ritual worship of Middle and Late Preclassic monuments may explain the general absence of sculpture in original contexts in the major sites within the basin.

Chemical analyses of the sandstone and subsequent comparisons of other known red sandstone sources in the Maya area by Tom Schreiner revealed that the source stone for Tintal Stela 1 was from the lower Pasion and upper Usumacinta areas (Hansen 2005; Schreiner 1992) (Figure 7.5). The monument was found at the northwestern base of the massive Pavo Pyramid within the Mano de Leon area of the civic center of Tintal. In particular, it appears that the sandstone slab weighing at least between 7.42 and 9.48 metric tons (at a specific gravity of 2.8 metric tons/cubic meter)

Figure 7.5. Tintal Stela 1; note the unusual carving of the base (or butt) of the stela which predates the carving of the primary iconography of the monument. The badly battered monument depicts a standing ruler, feet in tandem fashion, facing toward the right, with a kneeling individual on the right, facing to the left (photograph by C. D. Bieber, FARES).

(Sidrys 1978:174) came from the region of Altar de Sacrificios, approximately 110 km away, according to the chemical analyses of fragments of the monument processed in the University of California, Berkeley laboratories. When the sculpture was transported is uncertain, but it is most likely that the stone was moved into the Mirador Basin during the Preclassic (probably Middle Preclassic) and subsequently discovered, venerated, and ultimately mutilated during the Late Classic period at Tintal. The monument had been re-carved from an even earlier sculpture, a practice known to exist in Middle Preclassic times throughout Mesoamerica (e.g., Cyphers 1994). Further research in sites with an early occupation in the Pasion and upper Usumacinta may be productive in understanding the relationship with the northern Peten.

Lithics and Architectural Stone

The most ubiquitous artifacts in the Mirador Basin in terms of volume and weight are the quarried stones, used to form walls, terraces, dams, platforms, monuments, fill of structures, and causeways. The neglect of the lithic and architectural stone industry by many scholars reflects the void in our understanding of the scale, dynamics, and importance of this labor-intensive strategy in ancient Maya society. Previous attempts to quantify the nature and effect of lithic production systems and related industries have often been inadequately conceived and executed, primarily due to the use of contemporary or metal tools in experimental replication, while experiments with native materials or replications of ancient implements have a vastly different labor assessment (Saraydar and Shimada 1971, 1973). While we can sympathize with Abram's observation that "Quarrying stone . . . is actually an amazingly straightforward task that requires very little training and skill" and that " . . . the transport of materials required only a strong back and some sense of balance" (Abrams 1994:112), we also suggest that the changes in quarry technology and stone formats through time represent the introduction of more specialized innovations that are archaeologically detectable and empirically testable (see also Erasmus 1965). Our research, noted in more comprehensive formats elsewhere (e.g., Titmus and Woods 1996a, 1996b; Woods and Titmus 1994, 1996), indicates that improvements in stone procurement techniques were the result of skill and familiarity with limestone typology, geological composition, and knapped chert technology. The transformations in the Preclassic lithic and architectural stone technology are reflective of fundamental changes in their society which can be elucidated by archaeological and ethnographic testing.

As discussed above, the earliest walls at Nakbe and El Mirador (ca. 1000–600 B.C.) which utilized quarried limestone were vertical platforms, from two to three meters in height, with flat, roughly hewn stones measuring approximately 25 cm × 28 cm × 8 cm thick (Hansen 1992a, 1998). Platform interiors were constructed by the lineal placement of stones in parallel rows, a pattern known from several other Middle Preclassic sites (Ricketson and Ricketson 1937:110, 112, 136; see also Figure 7.3). These stones weighed up to about 68 kg and were probably carried by one or possibly two individuals as determined through experiments during excavations. Internally, structures were often constructed with a dry fill technique through the incorporation of cell wall constructions (see Hansen 1998:64), although the highest Middle Preclassic structures, such as those in the Cascabel Group at El Mirador, had fill with heavy, wet clay mortar. However, the most visible changes were external. Vertical walls were enhanced by terrace levels.

Between 600 B.C. and 400 B.C., however, stone walls and platforms changed dramatically internally and externally. Stone blocks were quarried with finely finished edges and a much larger size, up to approximately 1.0 to 1.40 m long (average 1.20 m), 45 cm thick, and 50 cm high (Figure 7.6). This formed a surface area of 270,000 cm as opposed to 5600 cm^2, a more than 480% increase in average block size. These stones were placed in the wall with the long axis exposed and often, a slight batter added to the vertical extension of the wall. In spite of the radical change in stone construction, the evidence of the change was ultimately hidden behind a thin layer of lime plaster (Figure 7.7). Apron moldings begin to appear for the first time. The dramatic variations in a prominent industry reflect a change in the social, political, and economic climate that created the need for the change from a previous status quo. What was it that brought about the need for much larger carved blocks, increased labor requirements, and a standardized format for the placement of the stones? Did these changes reflect changes in rank or status of elite individuals? If so, why? What were the methods and procedures of stone cutting in the Middle Preclassic Mirador Basin? Were the larger cut stones indicative of the advent of specialized production systems to quarry, shape, and transport the materials to the specified architectural location? If so, when and in what form did that specialization manifest itself? What insights into sociopolitical and economic organization of the ancient Maya could be obtained by investigating the ancient quarry and transportation systems?

To answer these questions, the Mirador Basin Project began an intensive investigation of the ancient quarries, initially at Nakbe under the supervision of James Woods and the late Gene Titmus (College of Southern Idaho) (Woods and Titmus 1996) (Figure 7.8a). Woods and Titmus conducted near total excavations of six quarries within the site center of Nakbe. Quarries were selected on the basis of their proximity to structures of known age, as well as the preservation of tool marks on quarry walls useful in determining the applied technology (Figure 7.8b). Three quarries which were most likely to be Preclassic and three probable Classic quarries were selected for excavation. Extensive sampling included horizontal exposures

Figure 7.6. Middle Preclassic walls (ca. 600 B.C.) of the south face of Structure 200, in the Cascabel Group at El Mirador, Guatemala. The long axis of the stones are displayed, with the large blocks in the center of the image measuring 1.4 m long (photograph by R. D. Hansen, FARES).

Figure 7.7. Middle Preclassic walls of Structure 34 Sub-1 in the interior of the Jaguar Paw Temple in the Tigre Complex at El Mirador, Guatemala. The long axis of the stone is parallel to the wall line. The massive blocks in the middle of the image measure 1.25 m long, and the quarry marks are still visible on the stone that served to retain and hold the thin lime plaster surface to the stone. The thin plaster is visible in the background which would have originally covered the stones (photograph by R. D. Hansen, FARES).

Figure 7.8. (a) Professor James Woods and the late Gene L. Titmus at quarry excavations at Nakbe indicating a range of quarried blocks, replicating those of the Preclassic and Late Classic periods (photograph by R. D. Hansen, FARES); (b) ancient quarry marks are still visible along the edges of the excavated quarries at Nakbe (Middle and Late Preclassic), showing long, parallel vertical grooves; note the replicated axe on the surface (photograph by J. C. Woods, FARES).

between two and five meters in width and from eight to eleven meters in length, depending on the size of the quarry. In several cases (Op. 206A, 207A), sampled quarries were excavated in their entirety (Woods and Titmus 1996).

Excavations extended several meters beyond the edges of the quarries where broken or worn implements were often discarded. Apparently, those discarded within the quarry had been carried out with fill, since numerous broken implements matching the form, size, use-wear, and fracture patterns of quarry implements have been found in the fill of structures, and relatively few formal tools have been found inside the quarry depressions.

Excavations of the six quarries at Nakbe and examinations of the quarries at El Mirador recovered the original quarry implements, including hammerstones, macro- and micro-waste flakes, rejuvenation flakes, multi-directional flake cores, obsidian blades, and bifacial implements of two types: elongated, thick, pointed implements we have termed "picks," and the ubiquitous axes, or "Standard Maya Bifaces." Marks of the implements on the walls of the quarry and channel remnants of the original stone extractions revealed the size, use, and direction of force of stone tools, the overall quarry strategy, block size, form, and extraction methods of the stones. For example, the channel marks on the edges of the quarries revealed the large sizes and shapes of rectangular blocks in the Preclassic quarries, while in the Late Classic quarries, rectangular cuts of much smaller veneer blocks were defined, as well as angled cuts in the quarry floor which outlined the form of the triangular or trapezoidal vault stones of corbel-vaulted structures.

The patterns of tool discard, the nature of implement use, the breakage patterns of tools, macro- and micro-waste flakes, edge wear and usage striations, and the resultant marks and channels still visible on the walls and floors of ancient quarries indicate the sequence and process of stone block extraction. With these data in place, Woods and Titmus then replicated the chert artifacts recovered archaeologically and began a series of experiments to test hypotheses about stone block extraction processes. Axes were hafted with native materials and formed similarly to those recovered archaeologically, such as the "Puleston axe" and the "Barton Ramie axe" from Belize and the "Rio La Venta–Chiapas axe" from Mexico, as well as those evident in the codices and painted scenes on ceramic vessels (Titmus and Woods 1996a). These implements and associated haftings, shafts, and handles made from native materials (bayal, chico zapote, chicle, pedernal)

Figure 7.9. (a) Workers quarrying large, Preclassic size stones at Nakbe with replicated stone tools; (b) image of a quarry surface indicating the channel grooves required to form and subsequently extract the massive blocks from the quarries (photographs by J. C. Woods, FARES).

were utilized to allow comparison and replicate the ancient marks evident on the quarry walls and floors. In one quarry at El Mirador, the original and last block was left in situ in the quarry before it was permanently abandoned. In addition, the wear patterns, sheen, and fracture patterns from the experimental tools and stump patterns from the quarries were compared with the original ancient tools and quarries (Titmus and Woods 1996b, 2000; Woods and Titmus 1994, 1996).

Quarrying activities by Maya workers using the replicated stone tools, combined with correlative comparisons to minute archaeological detail, provided the first evidence of the most probable process of quarrying procedures and sequences. A total of 33 blocks of various sizes and shapes replicating those from Preclassic and Late Classic architecture were extracted using stone tools during three separate field seasons (Figures 7.9a and b). Stone tools, hafted like the known ancient specimens, left vertical linear scars on quarry walls that were identical to the ancient examples. The process of stone extraction and block isolation also left identical channels, stone "stumps," and marks found in ancient quarries and blocks. Alternate experiments indicated that variations from the methods that were ultimately employed did not leave similar patterns in existing stone. Furthermore, the quarry experiments revealed that chert implements are highly efficient quarry tools which could be used for extended durations without extensive damage. Massive Preclassic-style limestone blocks (approximately 1.4 m to 95 cm × 45 cm × 45 cm) found on the exteriors of monumental Preclassic architecture could be produced by experienced workmen at the rate of two to three blocks per week per person (Titmus and Woods 1998:26, 37), with a refined estimate of 11 person-hours (Titmus and Woods 1998:22) to quarry, remove, trim, and shape each individual block. This is a marked contrast to previous, less energy-consumptive estimates for quarry activity (Abrams 1994; Erasmus 1965).

Transportation experiments of quarried Preclassic-size blocks from a distance of 600 m to the base of the largest structure at Nakbe (Structure 1) and from a quarry near Danta pyramid at El Mirador were also conducted (Figure 7.10). Maya workers chose to construct a litter using native materials (surprisingly similar to ancient palanquins) and then hoisting the litter and stone to the shoulders of eight to ten workers (with an additional two to four workers stabilizing the stone), transported the blocks, weighing an estimated 246 to 300 kg, a distance of 600 m in actual carry times of 17 to 19 minutes. These data suggest to us that transport time is not a limiting factor in block availability, and larger stones could have been transported via a larger labor pool. Erasmus's quarrying and stone transportation experiments at Uxmal arrived at an experimentally derived estimate of 950 kg of stone, transported over a 250 m distance in a five-hour day, which amounts to a carrying weight of 28 kg per trip, or roughly 34 trips per day (Erasmus 1965). The five-hour day was determined because of the harsh environment (heat) and hazardous terrain, but the results seem reasonable for labor estimates for the monumental constructions in lowland Maya sites. These

Figure 7.10. Twelve workers hauling a 900–1000 pound block from the quarry to the base of Structure 1 at Nakbe. Ten workers were required to do the lifting, and two workers were needed to stabilize the block during transport (photograph by R. D. Hansen, FARES).

figures can be extrapolated for more lengthy work day and more favorable environmental conditions to approximately nine hours per cubic meter for a 250 m trip (Smailes 2011:45).

Hansen has previously noted the diachronic forms of masonry in the Mirador Basin and the corresponding volumes of stone needed for architectural constructions (Hansen 1998:97). Known examples of early Middle Preclassic masonry (between 1000–700 B.C.) consists of crudely hewn, small unfinished stones with an average stone size of 25 cm × 28 cm × 8 cm. Thus, 2.5 m³ of stone are required for every 10 m² of wall construction. With 50 m² of wall, approximately 12.5 m³ of quarried stone are used. By the late Middle Preclassic period (ca. 600–400 B.C.), the quarried blocks dramatically change in form and size, with the average blocks reaching approximately 90 cm (to 1.40 m) × 40 cm × 40 cm in size (see Figure 7.6). This indicates a volume increase of 3.8 m³ of stone per 10 m² of wall, or 19 m³ of stone per 50 m² of wall. In addition, the stones of this period are placed parallel with the external wall line so that the total width and height of the stone is displayed with the maximum exposure of stone surface.

By the Late Preclassic period (ca. 300 B.C.–A.D. 150), maximum architectural size, specialized architectural forms, and maximum consumption of stone was incorporated into architecture. Finely cut blocks measuring approximately 90 cm to 1.20 m × 45 cm × 38–40 cm were placed with the axis of the stone extending into the structure, drastically reducing the efficiency of the exposed stone surface, and requiring 8–11.5 m³ of stone for every 10 m² of wall, or 40–57 m³ for every 50 m² of wall (Hansen 1998). The quantity of quarried stone is more than doubled, and in some cases, nearly tripled, from the preceding late

Middle Preclassic period, resulting in what appears to be a conspicuous consumption of quarried stone, since Maya construction techniques using interior cell walls could adequately fortify and contain interior weight pressures, relieving exterior walls of nearly all internal stresses. Furthermore, there appears to be no visible structural engineering advantage, since walls from both periods were subject to the same variable stresses. The labor intensification employed in the masonry of Late Preclassic monumental architecture correlates with the greater settlement density, the expanded ranges of consistent architectural forms (triadic architecture, plaza residence constructions), the proliferation of architectural art, the increased size of architecture, a defensive posture as argued by the construction of a large wall on the southern, eastern, and northern sides of the West Group at El Mirador and an extensive moat system at Tintal and Xulnal (Hansen et al. 2006), and represents what appears to be a zenith of political and economic power in the Mirador Basin.

After what Hansen has determined to be the "Preclassic Collapse" about A.D. 150 (Hansen 2012b), there was a lengthy hiatus during the Early Classic period in the Mirador Basin. However, centuries later, Late Classic architecture was constructed in small settlements among the ruins of the Preclassic centers with less costly use of stone quarry technology. This architectural system employed the use of the ubiquitous "veneer blocks," averaging 40 cm × 40 cm × 18 cm thick, providing a maximum height and width of the exposed stone at a minimum of thickness. This efficient quarrying and construction technique resulted in the quarry extraction of approximately 9 m^3 of stone per 50 m^2 of wall. Such dramatic diachronic changes in the volume and methodology of stone extraction represent significant changes in technology, labor intensification strategies, and consumption patterns of limestone. When examined from a broad range of disciplines, the lithic technology can reflect the sociopolitical, ideological, and economic manifestations of power and state formation processes.

Lime Production

One of the most costly commodities of ancient lowland Maya civilization in terms of labor expenditure and natural resources in transportation and manufacture was the production of lime for plastering walls and platforms, causeways, floors of structures, reservoirs, plazas, and monumental architectural art, as well as minute amounts for food preparation (corn) and insect control (Abrams 1994:73, 116; Erasmus 1965:292; Katz et al. 1974; Morris 1931; Xolocotzi and Tacher 1995). It became apparent that the abundant use of lime, and visible variations of lime use in the Mirador Basin, would require a thorough study of lime production and use from both synchronic and diachronic perspectives to determine the impact economically and environmentally. Previous observations of the importance of this industry, which permeated all levels of Maya society, include Abram's (1988) observation that 1.1 m³ of wood were required to produce 1 m³ of lime. He estimated that the minimal impact at Copan would have been about .13 ha annually to provide the necessary firewood for lime manufacture. However, discussions with Maya informants suggested that such estimates were seriously in error, and it was apparent that additional experiments would have to be conducted to adequately evaluate the consumption of wood and stone, productivity, and relative associated technologies.

Comprehensive surveys and experiments conducted by the Mirador Basin project under the supervision of Thomas Schreiner focused on lime production systems in Mesoamerica, recording the various techniques, procedures, and methodologies, and quantifying production costs and outputs (Schreiner 1998, 2000a, 2000b, 2000c, 2001, 2002 2003, 2007). Schreiner sought the oldest living traditional lime workers (*caleros*) in numerous villages throughout the Maya area and through interviews and actual demonstrations, recorded the techniques employed by lime specialists in their respective areas of the Maya lowlands. Then, with the assistance of lime workers from each area, Schreiner replicated 12 Maya lime kilns incorporating the various techniques from specific lime production areas to determine efficiency (Figure 7.11a and b). This research involved forestry evaluations to determine the production sustainability of the types of trees to be utilized in rigging kilns, the percentages of species, the quantity and types of wood utilized, and the moisture content and combustion properties of fuel wood placed in kilns. Other observations included kiln types; quantity, weight, and type of limestone; burn times; ratios of preburn limestone weight to quantity of lime produced after burning; slaking methods and storage of lime after burning; organic additives (more than 50), particularly water extracts of tree barks (Schreiner 2000a); stucco and plaster recipes (more than 15); ratios, by weight, of quicklime produced per quantity of wood burned; and rituals associated with the lime production process.

Figure 7.11. (a) Replicated lime kilns near Flores which were built by various contemporary Maya lime burners, each according to the particular style of the lime producer; (b) firing of various kilns after quantification of the amounts of wood and stone used (photograph by T. R. Schreiner, FARES).

Schreiner found that traditional Maya lime kilns, which do not require a masonry containment structure, must burn freshly cut, green fuel wood with an average moisture content of 50% by weight, while the colonial type oven kilns which replaced the Maya systems burn dry wood with moisture content nearer to 15%. After mathematical conversion to 0% moisture content (for comparison between different systems) the ratio of 0% moisture wood consumed to quicklime produced in a Maya lime kiln ranged from 3.7:1 to 7.3:1, with a typical average production of about 5:1 or 6:1. Small-scale production of lime in colonial type oven kilns ranges from 2:1 to 1:1. A Maya kiln with a 5:1 efficiency ratio requires 10 loads, by weight, of 50% moisture wood and two loads of limestone or shell to produce one load of quicklime (CaO). For this reason Maya lime kilns are always constructed where the wood is cut to reduce the necessary human labor involved to transport the stone and wood materials. A colonial lime kiln with 1:1 efficiency produces one load of quicklime from 1.2 loads of 15% moisture wood and two loads of limestone. These fixed-structure kilns are located at or near limestone quarries and rely upon wheeled transport of materials. Thus, typical Maya lime kilns, which Schreiner believes have not changed fundamentally since the Preclassic period, produced one weight-measure of lime for 12 of raw materials using stone axes and human transport. For comparison, the colonial oven kiln which replaced the Maya lime-burning system (the least productive of current lime production systems) can yield one weight-measure of lime for 3.2 of raw materials using steel tools and wheeled transport. On average, the Maya kilns burned four to six times as much fuel wood as the lime ovens introduced by the Spanish that replaced the Maya system. Measured ratios of wood weight (corrected to 0% moisture content) to weight of quicklime produced ranged from 4:1 to 8:1, and an average mean of 5:1 and 6:1. This can be compared to the optimal 1:1 ratio of the colonial oven kilns. The vast consumption of wood, which must be green to facilitate proper burning and consistency of temperature, suggests that one of the primary deforestation mechanisms was the process of providing wood for an expanding lime industry. These figures are in line with independent studies, such as those by Barba and Cordova (1999) at Teotihuacan.

Schreiner's research revealed a hitherto unrecorded variety and sophistication of traditional Maya lime kiln designs, some of which correspond well to archaeological examples at Preclassic and Classic Maya sites (i.e., Fauvet-Berthelot 1980). Usually 1.5 to 3 m in diameter, Maya kilns are burned on the surface of the ground or within cylindrical or rectangular pits excavated in the course of quarrying limestone that was to be burned. The kilns, which differ by region, can be classified, not only by the observer, but by the Maya themselves according to the method of wood stacking employed. Kiln classifications such as "vertical round," "radial round," "horizontal rectangular," and a combination round type with "radial-over-vertical" were documented. These are built with a number of variable and interchangeable elements that affect the inflow of combustion air and concentrate heat on the limestone, coral, or shell material being calcined. The kilns were found to function as ovens rather than as simple pyres with limestone heaped on top. Moisture contained in the fuel wood insulates the outer parts of the kiln to prevent radiant heat loss. Packed very tightly, the freshly-cut fuel wood, with a moisture content averaging 50% or higher, burned in a controlled manner at the center of the kiln directing all of its heat upward through the limestone. Thus, while the outer walls of the kiln remain cool to the touch, a sustained 900°C temperature can be reached at the center for the time needed to calcine limestone.

Architectural lime is often burned by Maya *caleros* two to three years before its intended use because of the long open-air slaking time necessary to produce a stable product. Lime production is also frequently seasonal to exploit natural slaking processes in the rainy season, to take advantage of cooler cloudy weather for the hard work, to evade windy days, and, when linked to the agricultural cycle, to take best advantage of wood made available by land clearing. Ancient Maya lime burning systems may have accorded with these observations.

Schreiner also noted that contemporary *caleros* seemed to enjoy recognized status with respect to their hereditary occupation within their communities. Abrams (1994:117) noted that plaster manufacturers in the Copan valley might rank in a socioeconomic position with obsidian workers, woodworkers, groundstone producers, utilitarian ceramic manufacturers, and chert tool producers. It is our contention however, that lime production was a costly activity which resulted in varying levels of specialist production. Schreiner recorded specialized ritual activities associated with lime production in Yucatan, Quintana Roo, Campeche, and Peten (Schreiner 2002, 2003). In addition, ethnohistoric data such as that provided by Ruiz de Alarcon in 1629 noted the Aztec incantations and chants of those who prepare and rig the lime kilns, prepare the axes, and cut the kiln wood (Ruiz de Alarcon 1984). The Aztec rituals serve to indicate the ancient Mesoamerican attention to lime production and the similarity to cyclical metamorphosis and transformation, common ingredients of Mesoamerican religions and shamanic ideology (e.g., Ruiz de Alarcon 1984:87–89).

Analyses of floor thickness levels from over 139 floors with an assigned chronological order in structures of various sizes within the Mirador Basin indicate that floor thickness and lime production seem to have steadily increased from the Middle Preclassic to the Late Preclassic period before

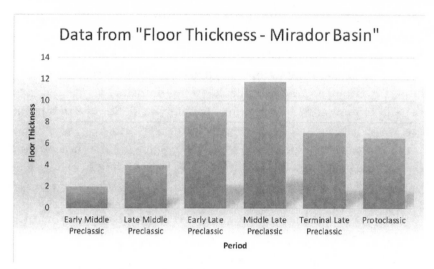

Figure 7.12. Diagram of average floor thicknesses through time, based on 143 floor measurements (after Hansen 1998).

sharply dropping at the close of the Late Preclassic period, and then nearly disappearing altogether before and during the Early Classic period (Hansen 1995, 1998, 2012b) (Figure 7.12). Nearly 600 years later, in the Late Classic period, lime production seems to have resumed on a more modest level, but with an entirely different recipe for lime plaster manufacture and architectural construction (see below) (Hansen et al. 1995; Hansen, Rodriguez-Navarro, and Hansen 1997).

We suggest that the ever-increasing demands on lime production and stone quarry programs, utilized in a variety of formats by rapidly expanding populations during the Middle and Late Preclassic periods, placed a new emphasis on specialist production. In addition, the consumption of wood for lime production in the Preclassic period in particular would have placed a premium on available wood sources, and would have been a prime cause of large-scale deforestation. The effects of such rampant wood consumption, particularly by the end of the Late Preclassic period, apparently had disastrous consequences as part of the multi-causal factors for the major demographic reduction of the Mirador Basin Maya shortly after the time of Christ (Balcarcel et al. 2010; Hansen 1990, 1995, 2012b; Hansen et al. 2002, 2008; Schreiner 2002; Wahl 2005; Wahl et al. 2005, 2006, 2007). Similar stresses may have occurred simultaneously at other Late Preclassic areas in the lowlands (e.g., Dunning et al. 2002). The massive quantities of green-tree deforestation required to adequately meet the requirements for the stucco applications of Late Preclassic plazas, causeways, and architecture probably resulted in large-scale siltation and sediment inundation of the *civales* (*bajos*) in the Mirador Basin, providing an additional stress for the early Maya in view of the extensive use of *bajo* soils in agricultural systems (Hansen 2012b; Schreiner 2002, 2003, 2007).

Data from throughout the Mirador Basin indicate that architectural engineers were utilizing a variety of specialized techniques at least by the Middle Preclassic period in response to construction requirements that must have been stipulated from an administrative, religious, and economic elite (Hansen et al. 1995; Hansen, Rodriguez-Navarro, and Hansen 1997; Hansen, Wallert, and Derrick 1997; Hansen 1992a, 1998, 2001, 2012a, 2012b; Hansen et al. 2002). Analyses of the types and distributions of specialists involved in the Late Preclassic architectural florescence in northern Peten have included excavations of specialist tools, replication of sculpture, quantifications of excavation and transportation of construction materials, and subsequent analyses of stucco, paint, plaster, architectural art, specialized stones and armatures, and standardized architectural patterns.

Stucco, Plaster, and Mortar Analyses

Analyses of ancient burnt-lime products from the Mirador Basin project by Eric Hansen and colleagues (Getty Conservation Institute, Library of Congress, University of New Mexico) have documented diachronic changes in the technological styles of plaster, mortar, and stucco manufacture, and painting practices (Hansen et al. 1995; Hansen, Rodriguez-Navarro, and Hansen 1997; Hansen, Wallert, and Derrick 1997). The diagnostic patterns in technical behavior are indicated by the petrographic, mineralogical, and chemical characteristics of samples of burnt-lime products from the Mirador Basin and other lowland sites (Cerros, Tikal, and Yaxchilan). Optical microscopy, X-ray diffraction, and digital image analyses of petrographic thin-sections were used to determine the composition and texture (the spatial arrangement, morphology, and dimensions of the components in relation to both the cement binder and the added aggregate).

Eric Hansen found distinct textures indicating separate preparation procedures correlating with either the function (floor, wall, or plastic media), location, or chronological period (Hansen, Rodriguez-Navarro, and Hansen 1997; Hansen, Wallert, and Derrick 1997). For example, Middle Preclassic and Late Preclassic floors have a distinctively different texture (chaotic) from the types of textures (sorted) seen in early Late Preclassic painted and sculptural elements. This indicates a marked improvement in both lime-burning skills (lesser quantity of unburned limestone) and plaster formulation (manipulations to obtain uniform aggregate sizes). In addition, Preclassic stucco appears to have more additives in the calcium carbonate and was therefore, more specialized and costly, than that from the Classic period (Hansen et al. 1995; Hansen, Rodriguez-Navarro, and Hansen 1997). Not only can chronological affiliation often be determined in plaster samples, but construction patterns and lime plaster treatment can be defined according to function based upon texture types (at least three).

Another technological innovation utilized by the ancient Maya was demonstrated by the analyses of architectural mortars dating to the early Late Preclassic on Structure 1 at Nakbe. They are superior in hardness and strength in comparison to the more common softer mortars that consist, for the most part, of lime binder and limestone aggregate. This mortar was made with the addition of quartz and clays to burnt lime. Further identification of the clay component suggests that the clays were added after burning (and were not a component of the original limestone), indicating a more complex formulation using inorganic additives (Hansen, Rodriguez-Navarro, and Hansen 1997; Hansen, Wallert, and Derrick 1997).

The Late Preclassic burnt-lime products vary markedly in their textural characteristics (morphology of limestone aggregate) with Late Classic samples from Nakbe (and other Late Classic sites). *Sascab*, a locally available and highly unconsolidated limestone marl, appears to have been used to make plaster in the Late Classic, in contrast to limestone chips used as aggregate in the Late Preclassic. This difference may be related to the quarrying practices and scale of monumental architecture, where more extensive use of large limestone blocks is associated with large amounts of quarrying debris. Woods and Titmus (1996) determined that for every volume of quarried blocks, an additional three volumes of pulverized limestone and rubble were produced that may have been used as aggregate in lime stucco preparation (E. Hansen 2000).

Stucco modeled as architectural art on massive masks and panels flanking the stairways of the largest structures at Nakbe and El Mirador appears to have been formed by the application of a thick stucco (applied as a single layer) over carved stone armatures. The three types of paint present—red, black, and cream—were applied as a single layer. The masks on Structure 1 at Nakbe, for example, appear to have been formed and painted in a single construction episode, although there is evidence that a modification of the panels occurred before being buried under a later (the last) mask and panels that formed the exterior of the building. Extensive instrumental analysis of the "cream" paint via visible light microspectroscopy, FT-IR microspectroscopy, and three-dimensional fluorescence spectroscopy, indicate that a fluorescent organic colorant, similar to those found in organic red dyes from plant sources, was used to make the paint (Hansen, Wallert, and Derrick 1997). The red paint was identified to be red iron oxide (Hematite). Both the red and cream paints were applied to the sculpture in the same thickness, indicating the cream layer is most probably a "paint" and not a bark extract, used as an additive in the preparation of stucco throughout the Maya region (Littman 1960). The cream layer does not appear to be the plaster background, as is the case for later Maya mural paintings (Magaloni 1996).

The Late Preclassic Maya at Nakbe did not restrict themselves to the limited inorganic pigments available, such as iron oxides, but also manufactured paint using an organic material. Landa noted that plaster was treated with a certain juice from the bark of a tree (Tozzer 1941:176), which may have been that of the *chacah* or *chukum* trees (*Bursera simaruba, Pithecollobium albanicans*). Maya informants with the Mirador Basin project reported that the addition of *chacah* tree impedes cracking during drying, which, in a test case, did succeed although there may be other factors responsible. Another observation is that the addition of the *chacah* turned the lime mixture red (although it was not visible when dried), which may have had symbolic connotations for the Maya. This practice of using organic colorants is paralleled with the use of indigo to make Maya Blue in the Classic period. However, the cream colorant was added to a wet-lime mixture and not to clays as in the case of Maya Blue.

These detailed variations, plus the fact that application of stucco on 10 known Late Preclassic masks and panels at Nakbe and three known Middle Preclassic masks at El Mirador and an intact Middle Preclassic structure with a roof comb at the site of El Pesquero was preceded by detailed carving of the stone armatures to replicate the stucco figures of massive proportion, argue for a specialist production and ideological support system of remarkable sophistication (see Hansen 1992a). The fact that architectural art in the form of masks and panels flanking stairways appears in the Middle Preclassic period, and the architectural emphasis of the triadic style format of architecture by the beginning of the Late Preclassic period implies the notion that a state-level impetus was responsible for the wide dispersal and acceptance of the practice and extraordinary labor investment involving specialist production systems.

Architectural Construction

The energetics of architectural construction has been a subject of interest in early economic interactions (e.g., Foster 1942:31ff). When the energetics of quarry production and transportation systems can be reasonably calculated, it is possible to postulate more specific labor investment strategies in architectural constructions in the Maya area. These perspectives can be studied by cumulative investments (diachronic) or single episode efforts (synchronic) as determined by archaeological excavations. For the purposes of this paper, it would be useful to examine the labor investment in two structures: Nakbe Structure 1 and El Mirador's Danta pyramid.

Nakbe Structure 1 is located on a large platform dating to the Middle and Late Preclassic period in the West Group at the site (Figure 7.13). It is the highest structure at Nakbe and is constructed in the triadic architectural form, with three integrated structures located on the 30 m high structural platform. The nature of triadic architecture has been amply discussed elsewhere (e.g., Hansen 1990, 1992a, 1998). The building is situated 48 m above the forest floor on the west side, although the building rises 38 m above the platform upon which it rests. The building measures 104 m wide, north to south, and 95 m east to west, covering a surface area of approximately 10,000 m². The structure is placed on the west end of a 7 m high platform which measures 200 m east-west and 150 m north-south. This entire assemblage is placed on yet another platform which measures between 8 and 9 m high and is 350 m long east-west and 280 m north-south. Extensive excavations were conducted on Structure 1 from 1990 to 1998 (Hansen 1992a, 1992b, 1992c, 1993, 1998; Martinez and Hansen 1993), including a series of tunnels penetrating into the heart of the building both at the summit and at the eastern central base of the building. Such data has revealed a construction sequence dating from the late Middle Preclassic period (ca. 600–400 B.C.). There are at least four stairway construction and two facade construction phases plus a stairway and a facade modification evident at the base of the building and two stairway construction phases in the triadic summit structures at the top of the building. The building is situated over an earlier building (Structure 1 Sub 1), located near the eastern stairway of Structure 1 which measures approximately 21 m east to west. This interior

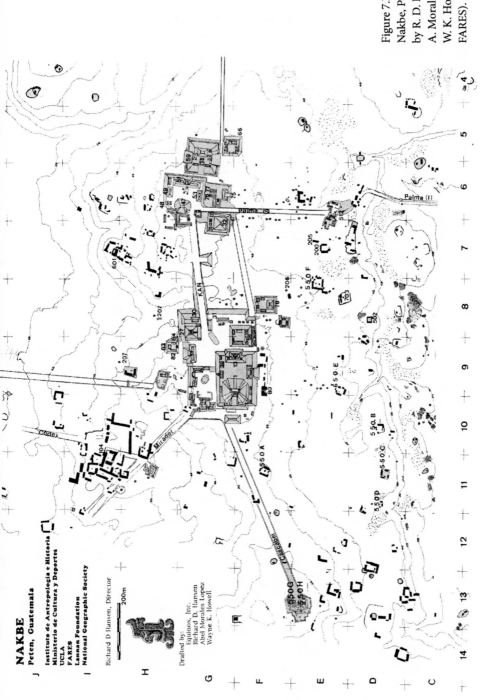

Figure 7.13. Map of Nakbe, Peten (map by R. D. Hansen, A. Morales, and W. K. Howell, FARES).

building has four construction phases (Sub 1-1st to Sub 1-4th). Structures Sub 1-1st and Sub 1-2nd both display apron molding architecture, with ceramics dating to the late Middle Preclassic to early Late Preclassic transition period. Structures Sub 1-3rd (a terrace wall addition) and Sub 1-4th are Middle Preclassic constructions with high (3 m or more) vertical walls, indicating that at least a portion of Structure 1 is a cumulative construction of some antiquity. Tunneling excavations in about 35 m along the side of Sub 1-3rd reveal that much of the volume of Structure 1 was constructed in a single effort.[3]

Excavations of the lower eastern facade of Nakbe Structure 1 revealed the pattern of stone work that formed the last construction phase of the building. The stonework, consisting of cut stone blocks placed end to end parallel with the wall line of the building, is similar to earlier stone walls identified in the late Middle Preclassic period, while stones in the two major terrace levels at the summit were placed with the long axis of the stone tenoned into the building. For purposes of energetics, it must be noted that there is a much greater labor investment implied by tenoned stone blocks because of the dramatically increased volume of stone consumption required to construct the same area of wall (Hansen 1998:97). In addition to the finely cut nature of the blocks, the exterior face of blocks placed in panel facades were carved with a series of J-scroll-and-bracket motifs, ear spools, "droplet" elements, and other iconographic decorations forming the panels, indicating an additional specialist labor investment.

The surface area of Structure 1 at Nakbe was calculated with simplistic geometry to provide a minimum surface area. In reality, the surface area of the structure is greater because of the inset corners, terrace projections, projecting flanks, and outset facades. However, using the flat surface area of the building, we estimate that a minimum 8,270 m² of stone[4] would have been needed to cover the available surface area of the building. At a rate of approximately 12 blocks per each 3.63 m² (actually counted), or between 3.3 and 4.5 blocks per square meter of surface area depending on whether the stone had the long axis parallel or perpendicular to the wall line, as revealed by excavations in Nakbe Op. 01 I, and excavations on Danta pyramid at El Mirador, it appears that at least 37,215 blocks were used in the construction of the outer surface of the building. At the rate of 2.5 blocks per person per week (Titmus and Woods 2000), it would have required 210 specialized workers one year to quarry the necessary facing stone for the final phase of Structure 1 (note that construction fill is not considered here). In addition, since transport of the quarried stones required 12 men (eight to ten men carrying, two to four men stabilizing) to move a single Preclassic block from the quarry to Nakbe Structure 1 for a distance of 600 m in 17 minutes, the transportation requirements of quarried stone anciently ranged between 2.25 and 3.4 person hours to move one block. For the construction of the external wall of Nakbe Structure 1, between 61,513 and 92,953 person hours (7,689 to 11,619 person days at 8 hours per day) were required for the transport of the external stone facing alone, provided that quarries were within the 600 m radius of most monumental architecture. As noted above, the massive amounts of stone and mud fill that comprise the volume of the building are additional factors that can be considered, and tunneling operations are an important tool to determine the location and extent of internal constructions. However, large buildings such as Nakbe Structure 1 (one internal building), Nakbe Structure 27 (no internal buildings), El Mirador La Pava (no internal buildings) and El Mirador Structure 34 (one internal building) show that many, if not most, monumental Late Preclassic buildings were constructed in a single monumental construction effort.

The variation in stone alignment represents an important distinction in the quantity of stone needed for construction, as is evident for example on the summit of Nakbe Structure 1. Under late Middle Preclassic stone alignments (with the axis of the stone parallel to the external wall line), the central summit structure would have used approximately 153 m² of stone to form the facade, or approximately 506 Preclassic blocks. Examples of Middle Preclassic buildings with the long axis parallel to the wall line are Nakbe Structure 32, El Mirador Structure 200 and Structure 204 of the Cascabel Group, and El Mirador Structure 34-Sub 1. However, since the facade of the central summit structure of Nakbe Structure 1 had stones that were placed with the long axis of the stone tenoned into the fill of the building, perpendicular to the external wall line, a total of 20 stones were quarried for 2.25 m² of facade, or 8 blocks per square meter. The number of blocks required to construct the 153 m² of walls would be about 1,224. This represents a 142% increase in the volume of stone required to build the same section of facade. This correlates well with other observations of Late Preclassic stone architectural construction (Hansen 1998:97), and is characteristic of maximum utilization of labor during the Late Preclassic period.

Danta Pyramid, El Mirador

One of the most massive structures in the Maya world was constructed on the eastern side of the civic center at El Mirador. This extremely large building consisted of three successive, truncated platforms to accommodate a triadic architectural arrangement at the summit. Excavations on the western face of the building by Edgar Suyuc-Ley, Sheryl Carcuz, Anaite Ordoñez, Amilcar Alvarez, Paulo Medina, Marcia Chacon, and Francisco Lopez have identified the consistency of massive blocks, 1–1.3 m × 45 cm × 40 cm which were tenoned into the fill of the building perpendicular to the wall line. This practice, which in the case of Danta Pyramid extended from the top to the bottom of the structure, suggests that the building was probably constructed during a relatively short period of time, presumably during the lifetime of the individual who commissioned it. As with Structure 1 at Nakbe, the entire surface of the building was constructed with monumental blocks measuring approximately 1.3–1 m long × 45 cm × 40 cm in size (although in many cases the blocks were much larger). Excavations on all three levels of the primary platforms as well as the summit triadic buildings demonstrate that the entire structure was built in identical fashion, with massive stones extending into the fill of the building, perpendicular to the wall line. Rough estimates for the surface area of one side, the western face, of the building is calculated at 3,100 m² for the first platform, 1,900 m² for the second platform, 3,640 m² for the third platform, and 1,440 m² for the west face of the center summit triad building, and 325 m² for each of the side structures (which face each other) for a total of 10,730 m² for the western face of Danta. At the rate of 4.5 to 4.7 blocks per square meter (2.25 by 2.1), a total of between 43,822 and 48,980 blocks were required for the outer blocks on the primary western facade of the building, which could be approximately doubled to include the eastern side for 87,644 blocks on the eastern and western faces. The stones on the northern and southern sides can be calculated as:

> Lateral sides of Platform 1: 590 × 10 = 5,900 m² × 2 = 11,800 m² × 4.5
> blocks = 53,100 blocks
> Lateral sides of Platform 2: 240 × 10 = 2,400 m² × 2 = 4,800 m² × 4.5
> blocks = 21,600 blocks
> Lateral sides Platform 3: 140 × 26 = 3,640 m² × 2 = 7,280 m² × 4.5
> blocks = 32,760

Lateral sides Center triad building: $40 \times 24 = 960$ m^2 $\times 2 = 1{,}920$ m^2
$\times 4.5$ blocks $= 8{,}460$ blocks
North triad: $25 \times 13 / 3 = 108$ m^2 $\times 2 = 216$ m^2 $\times 4.5$ blocks $= 972$
blocks
South triad: $15 \times 13 / 3 = 108$ m^2 $\times 2 = 216$ m^2 $\times 4.5$ blocks
$= 972$ blocks.

Therefore, a rough estimate of the surface blocks covering Danta pyramid would be 117,864 lateral stones plus 87,644 stones for the east and west facades for a total of 205,508 blocks.

Quarry time, which was experimentally determined, at 11 person hours per block would be 2,260,588 person hours or 282,573 person days of labor, a sum which could be satisfied with 387 workmen quarrying constantly for two years, or 155 workmen working for five years. Transportation costs would be at a minimum of 2.25 person hours per block if the quarries were within 600 m of the structure for a total of 462,393 person hours, or 57,799 person days of labor or 158 workers for one year to transport the stones.

The issue of the volume of Danta pyramid is more complicated, and a more reliable estimate of the volume of Danta can be answered through additional testing. The building is located on a low natural rise, but test excavations in the first platform show a substantial variation of bedrock depth. Howell and Copeland (1989), for example, located bedrock as shallow as 85 cm in a test pit (Op. 60A) in the platform about 30 m to the north of the Pava pyramid (Howell and Copeland 1989:16–17). Ray Matheny placed a pit to the immediate south of Pava pyramid, and located bedrock at a depth of 2.10 m (Howell and Copeland 1989). Yet Op. 60 D, a pit in the platform about 55 m north of Op. 60 A, failed to locate bedrock after penetrating to a depth of 3.70 m. Testing in the plaza at the base of the structure revealed dense layers of *sascab*, which served as the plaza floors, but bedrock was not encountered at depths of 3 m below the surface. Two Late Preclassic plaster floors were found in all excavations on the first and second platforms, although there is a possibility that there was an additional surface floor which is now decomposed. Howell and Copeland's conclusion was that Platform 1 was built in at least two stages over an undulating bedrock surface (Howell and Copeland 1989:19). However, the consistency of the external stone surface of the building suggests that the stages may have occurred within a relatively brief period of time.

Excavations by Edgar Suyuc-Ley in the first platform confirmed Howell and Copeland's suspicions of an undulating bedrock base by placing a pit (Op. 402 D) in the center of the E-Group complex located on the first platform, and found bedrock at a depth of 2 m (Suyuc-Ley et al. 2006:513) and excavations by Anaite Ordoñez and Suyuc-Ley at the base of the 2nd platform (Op. 402 N) located bedrock at a depth of 2.84 m (Ordoñez and Suyuc-Ley 2006). However, rubble and fill from other areas of the platform indicate that the fill extended the full 10 m in depth (SW corner, NW corner, northern side), so the more accurate evaluation of the volume of the first platform will be confirmed by electronic subsurface profiling or additional deep (and perilous) excavations.

Excavations in Platform 2 by Howell and Copeland (1989:54–55) noted bedrock in Op. 38, located at the western base of the primary third platform of Danta at a depth of 3.60 m, and excavations in the southwest corner of the building (Op. 31 A) located bedrock at 4.25 m. Excavations in Op. 30, a structure located on the southern side Danta on Platform 2, located bedrock at 1.10 m. Subsequent excavations by Paulino Morales and Laura Velazquez detected bedrock in the second platform about 20 m west of the stairway of the third platform at 2.20 m (Morales and Velasquez 2006:401, 427, 460). Excavations by Lopez et al. (2007) in the second platform near the base of the original stairs of the building, however, failed to detect bedrock at depths which exceeded 2.80 m.

The original intention of the creator of the Danta pyramid was to portray the construction as the largest ancient structure in the Maya world, with detailed embellishment of the exterior surface from the base to the summit of the building. The basal platform measures 600 m × 320 m × 10 m in height, with modest reductions to account for structural decomposition (590 m × 310 m × 10 m) would have had an appearance of a volume of 1,829,000 m^3 of fill. The second tiered platform measures 200 m × 250 m × 10 m (190 m × 240 m × 10 m used), for an appearance volume of 456,000 m^3. The third platform measured 150 m × 150 m × 26 m (140 m × 140 m × 26 m used) for a real volume of 509,600 m^3. The central dominant triadic structure at the summit measures 60 m × 50 m × 24 m (50 m × 40 m × 24 m used) for a real volume of approximately 16,000 m^3 of rubble. The north triadic structure measures 25 m × 25 m × 13 m for a volume of 2,708 m^3, and the southern triadic structure is the same size for a volume of 2,708 m^3. The total cubic meters of fill, if the structure were entirely artificial, would have been approximately 2,816,016 m^3, making it one of the largest structures in the world, pending verification by additional testing in the lowest platform.

The curious formation of the bedrock surface under the platforms, however, gives reason for caution in the case of Danta. Even if the volume of the first two platforms were reduced in half, the structure still commands a fill exceeding 1,673,674 m³. Furthermore, excavations at the base of the summit structures and at the summit reveal that there are four consecutive floor additions, but a single architectural episode that comprises the primary buildings. Ceramics from sealed contexts below floors demonstrate that the entire structure was constructed early in the Late Preclassic period from the base to the summit of the building.

The labor investment to haul the fill of Preclassic constructions has also been experimentally derived by the Mirador Basin project. During construction of camp facilities by project infrastructure manager, Adelzo Pozuelos, it was noted that transportation of *sascab* was conducted by Maya workers hauling materials a distance of 700 m, with a round trip of between 30 and 40 minutes per person under ideal conditions. During a seven-day experiment, five workers transported 12.48 m³ of *sascab*, averaging 2.08 m³ per day. If the volume of Danta approximates its appearance, then 5,028,600 person days of labor, or 1,000 workers working for 13.7 years could have hauled the fill for the interior of the building, assuming that the source materials were within 700 m of the structure. If the volume of the lower two platforms on Danta are reduced by half, then it still would have required 2,988,703 person days of labor just to haul the fill, which computes to approximately 1,000 workers working 8.2 years. If the quarrying (282,573 person days), and transportation of blocks (57,799 person days) are added to the transportation of fill, then Danta could have been constructed with a minimum of between 3,329,075 and 5,368,972 person days of labor, assuming that the labor force was hauling materials from 600–700 m distant, and that the work day was 9 hours, a factor which did not seem realistic to Erasmus, who calculated a 5-hour work day due to intense heat and other negative conditions which would nearly double the estimates to between a minimum of 6 million and 10 million person days of labor.

By all standards, it is during the Late Preclassic period that the labor conscription, monumental size and scale of buildings, specialist production of stone, lime, and agricultural systems, and extent of settlement size was at a maximum, suggesting a state-level organization as the sociopolitical and economic patron of such dynamic growth (Hansen 1984, 1990, 1992a, 2001, 2005; 2012a; Matheny 1986, 1987).

Agricultural Intensification

Marcus (1983:455) notes that Gann (1925) and Ricketson and Ricketson (1937) were the first to suggest that intensive agriculture, rather than the swidden system, may have been practiced by the ancient Maya. Indeed, extensive archaeological information now suggests that intensive agriculture was practiced throughout the lowlands via construction of dams, dikes, terraces, raised fields, water collection strategies, and varied cropping methodologies (Adams 1980; Bronson 1966; Fedick 1994; Harrison and Turner 1978; Hather and Hammond 1994; Healy et al. 1983; Hopkins 1968; McKillop 1994; Pohl 1990; Puleston 1977, 1978; Ruppert and Denison 1943:13,50; Saxe and Wright 1966; Scarborough et al. 1994; Turner 1974, 1978; Turner and Harrison 1983), and the antiquity of agricultural development has been purported well into the Archaic and Early Preclassic periods (Pohl et al. 1996; Puleston 1977; Turner 1978:113).

The role of agricultural intensification and labor as a dynamic variable in the formation of sociopolitical and economic complexity may be further elucidated by data from the Mirador Basin. Previous models have elaborated the role of a patron elite in the distribution of agricultural commodities (Boserup 1965; Price 1984; Service 1962, 1975). This was done by: (a) combining individual talents and resources with larger community production, and (b) by having a wide diversity ("regional" or "ecological") of specialist residence units (Service 1962:144ff). However, the distribution of commodities implies the antecedent step of the original production and/ or acquisition of such commodities, which provided the economic fuel to consolidate the power of an emergent administrator. This suggests a more delicate interaction of administrating elite and producers especially at the early formation of social complexity, a concept particularly argued by Abrams (1995; see below). While the elite-producer interaction can be found among lower scales of cultural complexity, the scale and extent of production systems can also identify more complex sociopolitical behavior, particularly in the Western Hemisphere where human labor provided the only means of systematic production. The evidence for large-scale primary subsistence production is evident in Late Preclassic contexts (and possibly earlier) at the monumental sites in the Mirador-Calakmul Basin and demonstrates that the recruitment and control of labor were also of prime interest in the initial development of agricultural intensification. The recruitment of such labor, in the absence of evidence for military prowess to acquire slaves or tribute labor, may have been enacted through "internal coercion" or a "theatre state" concept of royal ritual, ceremonies, and public worship (Abrams 1995:209; Demarest 1992b; see also Hansen 1992a:188ff). The fact that it appears early in the formation of complex sites suggests that the development and utilization of intensive agricultural systems in the Mirador-Calakmul Basin and other areas may have been centralized. We suggest that the level of centralization as evident at El Mirador, Tintal, Wakna, Nakbe, and Yaxnohcah indicates a more sophisticated sociopolitical structure than is typical of administrative elite in "middle range" societies (e.g., Earle 1978; Helms 1979). The fabrication of intensive agricultural systems may have served as legitimizing agents for the elite members of society and would have allowed a type of organic solidarity among expanding populations in the Mirador-Calakmul Basin.

Excavations on the southern side of Group 18 at Nakbe, a residential compound to the immediate east of the platform complex of Structure 1 by Juan Luis Velasquez and Gustavo Martinez first identified the presence of terrace constructions consisting of imported clay soils into the civic center of Nakbe (Martinez and Hansen 1993). Subsequent research has identified abundant evidence of a complex system of terraces, fields, dams, and dike constructions with imported muck at Nakbe, El Mirador, Tintal, and Wakna (e.g., Martinez et al. 1999; Pitcavage 2009). Most significantly, the terraces, fields, and agricultural platform constructions were constructed primarily of imported, dark, grayish-brown clay soils found only in the *bajos* surrounding the upland civic center of the site (Figure 7.14). Clear stratigraphic profiles show that the soils are intrusive, and were placed on buried cultural layers, floors, and on natural soil horizon layers, dating to the late Middle Preclassic (600–400 B.C.) and Late Preclassic (300 B.C.–A.D. 150) periods, if not earlier. In one case (Nakbe Op. 18), the fossil surface of an ancient field was uncovered, showing a layer of imported clay of contiguous small depressions, known in Yucatan and Campeche as "*cuyitos*," which provide miniature catchment basins and peaks for planting symbiotic crops (corn and beans) (see Folan and Gallegos 1992, 1996; Martinez et al. 1999). The strata surface had been detected because the ancient Maya had placed a thin layer of lime on the surface of the field. This layer suggested to our workers that the Maya must have been attempting to deter ants and insects since lime is a common remedy in the Peten for insect control, but there is also the possibility that the Maya may have been altering the pH of more acidic *bajo* soils.

Figure 7.14. Excavation showing the surface of the imported mud from the surrounding bajos over the original soil surfaces (photograph by M. White, FARES).

In some cases, the depth of the imported muck was substantial, up to 1.83 m in both the primary platform of the West Group at Nakbe, and in the fields detected below the Danta Causeway at El Mirador.

Phytolith analyses conducted by Steven Bozarth of the soils extracted from the terrace constructions have revealed the presence of corn (*Zea Mays*), squash (*Curcubita*), gourds (*Lagenaria*), and palm (Bozarth and Hansen 1998). In addition, C-13 isotope samples taken from buried soil horizons in the *bajos* surrounding Nakbe that match the terrace constructions in color and texture by John Jacob have demonstrated predominate C4 plant designations (corn, grasses) for the buried level, as opposed to the surface levels which are predominately C3 plants (contemporary forest types) (Hansen et al. 2002:Figure 13; Jacob 1994). On the basis of soil texture, color, stratigraphic contexts, isotope composition, and architectural arrangement, we suggest that the soils of the identified garden terraces throughout the civic center of Nakbe were imported from the adjacent *bajos*, making the factor of agricultural labor and managerial responsibility even more acute in the formation of social complexity at Nakbe. This practice apparently carried on into the Early Classic period at the site of Naachtun, since recent excavations there have also identified imported *bajo* mud that was transported into the city from the surrounding marshlands (Michelet et al. 2013:167).

The use of imported soils has long been observed as a mechanism of intensive agriculture in the Maya lowlands (Hopkins 1968; Turner 1978). In Belize for example, Hopkins noticed that ". . . . soil may have been transported and deposited behind the embankments of the dry-field terraces. Indeed, evidence of aquatic snail shells, taken from terrace fill in the flank lands near Mountain Cow, Belize, suggests that the soil may have originated from inundated zones not native to the terraced slopes" (Hopkins 1968:41).

The presence of a quantity of imported soils in the civic center of Nakbe and Tintal indicates the management of a larger labor system than had previously been supposed on the basis of architecture alone. For example, the terrace construction found adjacent to the elite residential compound at Nakbe, Group 18, had at least two identifiable soil importations throughout the entirety of the single terrace, representing a minimal volume of approximately 2,800 m^3 of *bajo* clays transported from the nearest *bajos*. At Nakbe, the nearest *bajo* is located approximately 800–900 m to the south of the identified clay terraces and platforms in the civic center. Using Erasmus's calculations for earth moving (Erasmus 1965:284–285), a carrier was capable of carrying an approximate weight of 20 kg of soil, and over a 5-hour day, carried 1.76 m^3 of soil in 116 trips (23.2 km). This calculates to approximately .015 m^3 of soil per trip at a speed of 4.64 km/hour. In the case of Nakbe, a distance of 800 m would allow a worker carrying the constant of 20 kg of soil 2.9 trips per hour, which amounts, calculating from Erasmus's figures, to .015 m^3 of soil per trip. In a 5-hour day, as computed by Erasmus, a worker would move .2175 m^3 of soil per day from the *bajo*. The single terrace of Group 18 would therefore have 12,873 person-days of labor in its construction alone, or 35 workers full time for a year. Thus, the intensification of agriculture as evident in Preclassic remains in the Mirador Basin represents a great deal more investment of labor and materials than had been previously assumed, and the importation of soils represents a new consideration of the value of labor in the dynamics of cultural sophistication.

Abrams (1995) has proposed that fluctuating agriculture labor be considered a dynamic in the development of political power through the comparison of total productivity, which could be affected by yield, weather, insects, and numerous other variables, with marginal productivity, which evaluates the measure of efficiency with incremental additions of workers. In this study, Abrams suggests that personal productivity may serve "as a correlate to the rise and expression of political power" (Abrams 1995:203). This is especially applicable at the point of conversion to intensive agriculture when total productivity and marginal productivity would have both been high, and would have been a time of maximum economic and political development for both the laborer and the administrators. As Abrams suggests, "the newly generated power of the king would not have been autocratic or exploitative of such farm families because labor was now associated with both high total product and high marginal product. Conversely the lineage commoners would have been very likely to accept and sanction the position of a powerful agromanagerial elite." (Abrams 1995:208).

Such an arrangement would have allowed the development of a growing economic base required to generate the initial wealth to import exotic commodities, commission large construction projects including causeways, structures, platforms, water collection systems, and imported-soil fields, and develop complex sociopolitical infrastructure that would have been perceived as for the common good of the society, as Abrams suggests. As evident on the panels and masks that began to appear on the facades of structures at the beginning of the Late Preclassic period (ca. 300 B.C.), the ideological concepts, recorded at great expense of specialist labor, materials, and intellectual impetus, were not portraits of rulers or other historical protagonists, but were portraits of deity images that would consolidate the united faith of the masses and give credibility to an emerging governing elite (Hansen 1992a, 2005, 2012a, 2012b). The manipulation of complex ideological subjects would serve to legitimize and justify the growing differential status between the ruler and the ruled. Therefore, the initial appearance of specialized labor in architectural and agricultural intensification projects would have been a period of closer solidarity between the commoner, the specialist, and the administrating elite until the marginal productivity of the individual worker would have declined to the point where the personal value of the laborer was low, creating a greater economic and social discrepancy between the various social levels of the society (Abrams 1995).

Excavations supervised by Beatriz Balcarcel on a Preclassic platform near an extensive terrace system on the southern side of the civic center of Nakbe revealed a possible archaeological correlate for Abrams's model. Excavations in Operation 502 at Nakbe noted a platform measuring 2 m high, 20 m long, and 17 m wide with smaller residential stone structures and structures of a perishable nature placed on the stuccoed surface. The platform had a wide (11 m) stairway located on the western side, and a smaller stairway, 2 m wide, on the northern side. The platform was located precisely on the edge of a large natural escarpment overlooking smaller residential structures that were also excavated (Op. 500, 501) and a system of agricultural terraces constructed with imported soils. Excavations revealed that the building was built in single episodes with two floors, with the earlier one made of packed clay and the second of lime plaster. Both floors had large quantities of chert waste flakes, suggesting areas of tool manufacture and rejuvenation, although it was obvious that such activity was a secondary activity and not a primary activity such as a lithic workshop. Due to the fact that the waste flakes were derived from local chert nodules, with abundant cortex, and the nature and extent of the bifacial implements recovered, we interpret the manufacturing process was the result of forming and sharpening agricultural implements. The earlier phase of Structure 502 was similar to that in Structures 501 and 500, which were simpler constructions near the agricultural terraces. However, by the early Late Preclassic, sufficient status and wealth had accumulated to construct formal platform walls with large, quarried blocks (placed end to end), rounded corners, and broad stairways. The location and nature of the structure and the associated artifacts do not suggest the presence of royal or chiefly officials (as opposed, say, to the Group 18, Group 83 (Grupo Pajaritos) or Group 66 complexes), but rather, the gradual accumulation and developmental wealth of an agricultural producer which had control and administration over terraces and local workers. The fact that the family organization that must have dealt in the Structure 502 construction was allowed to accumulate such evidences of wealth and status (enlarged platform, plaster floors, wide stairways, cut stone blocks) at a time when royal and administrative authorities were exercising maximum architectural construction programs suggests a period of considerable economic success and empowerment of what could be compared to a "middle class" level of society. This phenomenon was also noted by Arlen and Diane Chase at Caracol in the Classic period (Chase and Chase 1992), where a "middle" class seemed to have developed, as evident in mortuary remains and furniture, with the advent of more intensive agricultural methods. Such a model is consistent with the observations by Abrams, and suggests that the cultural dynamics of incipient societies must also be considered from the perspectives of agricultural labor and specialist production.

Conclusion

Specific conclusions regarding explanations for changes in ceramic, stone, lime procurement, stucco technologies, architectural construction programs, and agricultural intensification systems and their correlations with social, economic, and political developments are still undergoing analyses and constant review via a wide range of data acquired from the investigative spectrums of the Mirador Basin Project. We suggest that a refined methodology and an experimental approach based on ethnographic and archaeological data may be the means of identifying varied technological styles, resource allocations, and economic dynamics with the potential for more accurate anthropological and archaeological interpretations that can be established through testable hypotheses and astute data recovery. At this point, however, it appears to us that the development of natural resources and agricultural intensification allowed a rise of status differentiation and variable wealth, factors which fostered the economic foundations of specialist formation and production. The variable marginal productivity proposed by Abrams (1995) may have been increased along with total productivity due to new and innovative technologies and ideologies that fostered an elite-commoner interaction that resulted in a verifiable explosion of labor intensification strategies. The mutually sustaining system that possibly may have emerged between specialists and a governing elite created a favorable climate for innovation and associated justification of specialist production and consumption.

Examination of the indications of specialist technologies and production strategies through ethnographically and archaeologically valid experimental testing and classification programs can have useful insight into the dynamics of early state level societies. In the case of the Mirador-Calakmul Basin of northern Guatemala and southern Campeche, Mexico, the standardized development in specialist production of ceramics, stone tools, quarry technologies, lime manufacture, stucco utilization and consumption, large-scale construction projects, radical innovations in architectural design, ideological content, and structural scale, early settlement densities, causeway constructions, long-distance exchange, social, political, and economic interactions, and intensification of subsistence strategies (terrace systems, reservoirs, garden platforms) by the Middle Preclassic period suggest that a state-level society had begun by no later than 600–400 B.C. in the Mirador-Calakmul Basin with profound and lingering consequences for more than a millennium of subsequent occupation and cultural development.

Acknowledgments

The Mirador Basin Project (aka RAINPEG) wishes to extend appreciation to the Instituto de Antropología e Historia de Guatemala and the Ministerio de Cultura y Deportes of Guatemala for the years of support and collaboration that have made this study possible. The project is under the management of the Foundation for Anthropological Research & Environmental

Studies (FARES), FARES-Guatemala, and the University of Utah. We wish to recognize the economic support of the Global Heritage Fund of Palo Alto, California, which has been a primary partner in this research for nearly a decade. Appreciation is extended to the Foundation for Maya Cultural and Natural Heritage (PACUNAM), the Association of Friends of the Natural and Cultural Heritage of Guatemala (APANAC), the Hitz Foundation, the Rosalinde and Arthur Gilbert Foundation, the Selz Foundation, the Pettit Foundation, the Jay I. Kislak Foundation, Paul Mitchell Systems, and the U.S. Department of the Interior International Affairs Program. Special appreciation is extended to Mel Gibson, John Paul DeJoria, Linda Pierce, Dr. Nancy Furlotti, and Iona Benson, among many other private donors. We could not have done it without you. We would also like to thank the U.S. Department of Education National Graduate Fellows Program, the Jacob Javits Fellows Program, the Fulbright Fellows Program, the National Geographic Society, the Lannan Foundation, the UCLA Distinguished Scholars Program, the Foundation for the Advancement of Mesoamerican Studies, Inc. (FAMSI), the American Mobile Satellite Corporation, the Institute of Geophysics & Planetary Physics of the University of California, Los Angeles, the University of California, Berkeley, the College of Southern Idaho, Brigham Young University, the Getty Conservation Institute, the New World Archaeological Foundation, Texas A & M University, the University of Kansas at Lawrence, the University of Wyoming, Universidad de San Carlos, Equinox, Inc., Burch Manufacturing, and Homelite Division of Textron, Inc. The project is especially appreciative to Steven Graeber and Herbert and the late Elinor Nootbaar who launched the initial funding for this research.

Notes

1. The Mirador Basin project is directed by Richard D. Hansen under the auspices of the Department of Anthropology of the University of Utah and the Foundation for Anthropological Research & Environmental Studies (FARES), based in Idaho.

2. Tintal Stela 1 was first discovered by members of the El Mirador project in 1979 while staff members were briefly exploring the site. The monument was reported to Ian Graham who subsequently went to Tintal and recorded the monument. It was published by Justeson and Mathews in 1983, but excavations were initiated by Hansen in 1990 and again in 2004, 2013, and 2014.

3. Excavations in various areas of the lower platform that comprises the majority of the West Group at Nakbe indicates that an undulating bedrock makes an accurate volume assessment of this platform more difficult. Excavations near the camp for example, located bedrock at a depth of 1.6 m, while excavations near the eastern edge of the platform show a surface depth of 9 m. Furthermore, excavations have revealed that the platform is an

accumulation of remodeling and expansions, since several buried wall surfaces of impressive height were discovered near Structure 31 in the site (Velasquez 1993a, 1993b).

4. Using the simple formula of A=(1/2 bh)2 + hw, the east and west faces of Nakbe Structure 1 total 4,020 m², with an additional 306 m² of surface area on the central summit structure. The sides represent a slightly smaller surface of 3,944 m² with an additional 224 m² on the sides of the central summit structure, for a total of 8,270 m² for the minimal surface area of the building.

8

The Preclassic Settlement of Northwest Yucatan

Recharting the Pathway to Complexity

DAVID S. ANDERSON, FERNANDO ROBLES CASTELLANOS,
AND ANTHONY P. ANDREWS

Traditional models have long held that cultural complexity developed gradually in the northern Maya lowlands (Ball 1977, 2001; Ringle 1999:189). It was thought that the earliest permanent settlements appeared in the region ca. 700 B.C. (Andrews V 1990:14; Andrews V and Andrews 2001:379; Ball 1977:102; Kurjack 1974:4), deriving from a proposed immigration by populations from the southwestern Peten, Guatemala (Andrews V 1990:14). During the remainder of the Middle Preclassic period (ca. 1000 to 400 B.C.), northwest Yucatan's population levels appeared to have remained low with community organization limited to farming hamlets and small villages (e.g., Andrews V 1981:317). Only during the Late Preclassic period (ca. 400 B.C. to A.D. 200) did population levels begin to rise, and a notable sociopolitical center emerged at the site of Komchen (Andrews V and Ringle 1992; Ringle and Andrews V 1990). This longstanding paradigm is now in need of significant revision. Archaeological studies carried out in recent years by the authors of this chapter, as well as several of our colleagues, have documented numerous new sites in northwest Yucatan that date to both the Middle and Late Preclassic periods. These finds demonstrate that the region was home to a much larger Preclassic population than previously expected and that notable examples of cultural complexity, such as regional centers and ballcourt architecture, began to emerge as early as the Middle Preclassic period.

This chapter will focus on presenting data and interpretations resulting from three recent archaeology projects carried out in the northwest corner of Yucatan, Mexcio: Proyecto Costa Maya (PCM), Proyecto Arqueológico de Xtobo (PAX), and Proyecto Salvamento Arqueológico Ciudad Caucel

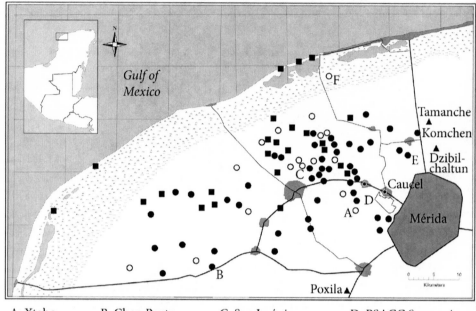

A: Xtobo   B: Chen Panta   C: San Jerónimo   D: PSACC Survey Area
E: Mirador Group of Dzibilchaltun   F: Tzikul

Figure 8.1. Preclassic sites recorded by Proyecto Costa Maya in northwest Yucatán. Triangles represent sites with Middle Preclassic occupations; squares represent sites with Late Preclassic occupations; circles represent sites with both Middle and Late Preclassic occupations. Hollow symbols represent sites with ballcourts.

(PSACC). PCM was a regional survey project directed by Fernando Robles Castellanos and Anthony P. Andrews (2000, 2001, 2003; see also Andrews and Robles 2004) that focused on documenting previously unknown sites within the region. Prior to the project, only eight sites in the survey zone were known to have had Preclassic occupations (Andrews IV and Andrews V 1980:16; Eaton 1978:34–37; Shook 1955:291–292), but by the end of the survey a total of 140 sites with Preclassic occupations had been identified (Figure 8.1). In addition to the sheer quantity of new Preclassic sites encountered, the regional settlement included many notable features indicating a burgeoning degree of cultural complexity. Perhaps the most unexpected feature at these sites was the presence of 23 examples of ballcourt architecture dating to the Middle Preclassic period (Medina Castillo 2003, 2005; Medina Castillo and Lawton 2002). Another unexpected find was a previously undocumented large and complex Preclassic settlement at the site of Xtobo (PCM 166).

Upon the conclusion of PCM, David S. Anderson initiated PAX to further investigations at Xtobo (Anderson 2010, 2011). The apparent lack of Classic or Postclassic resettlement at the site made it an attractive site for studying a complex Preclassic community. Three field seasons were carried out at the site resulting in 67 ha of mapped settlement, the documentation of 387 structures, and the excavation of 32 test pits. Analyses of the resultant data demonstrated that the site included an organized settlement plan, a dense residential occupation, distinct elite residential architecture, a ballcourt, and several triadic groups. The exact period of the site's occupation is still in some doubt, but its florescence appears to have occurred during a transitional period between the late Middle Preclassic and early Late Preclassic.

In 2004, plans for a housing project located outside the town of Caucel were announced by the government of Yucatan. Taking advantage of this opportunity, Robles partnered with Josep Ligorred Perramon, of Mérida's Departamento de Patrimonio Arqueológico y Ecológico Municipal, to form PSACC and carry out an archaeological survey and salvage excavations in advance of the construction (Peniche May 2010; Robles and Ligorred Perramon 2008; Uriarte 2011). PSACC mapped an 8-km^2 expanse, encountering ca. 1500 structures. The majority of these structures were found to have Preclassic construction phases. In addition, three concentrations of Preclassic settlement were noted within the survey zone and were named Nohol Caucel, Xanila, and Xaman Susula. At the Xanila group, an additional Preclassic ballcourt was identified, and at the Xaman Susula group, a large platform with a walled superstructure, a *sacbe*, and a "keyhole"-shaped structure were encountered.

In addition to these new data on the Preclassic occupation of northwest Yucatan, E. Wyllys Andrews V has reanalyzed the original data collected from Komchen (Andrews V et al. Chapter 4 this volume). These new interpretations have a significant impact on the interpretation of our own data, and as a result brief summaries of their revised position will be included below. The key point of these revisions for our purposes is to suggest that Komchen witnessed a much larger occupation during the Middle Preclassic period than was previously proposed. This has a notable impact on our understanding of the growth of populations and sociopolitical complexity in northwest Yucatan.

With this large quantity of new and revised data, the nature of the Preclassic occupation of northwest Yucatan is in need of reexamination. This chapter will synthesize these new data and provide preliminary conclusions.

The first section will present a summary of the results from all three archaeological projects. Next, a new synthesis of the region's chronology and cultural development will be offered. And finally, we will discuss several themes that run throughout our collective data, including the role of the ballgame in Preclassic northwest Yucatan, the elaboration of architecture found in the region's village settlements, interaction with other areas of Mesoamerica, and the relationship between the sites of Xtobo and Komchen. While some of the interpretations presented here are preliminary and may change as work progresses within the region, it is certain that the pathway to complexity among the inhabitants of northwest Yucatan is much older and more complicated than was previously thought.

The Preclassic Archaeological Record of Northwest Yucatan

Analyses of the Preclassic settlements in northwest Yucatan have demonstrated that they were arranged in a three-tiered settlement hierarchy (Anderson 2003, 2005; Peniche May 2010; Ringle and Andrews V 1990; Uriarte 2011). The first tier consists of small settlements covering 2 to 3 ha and including a limited number of residential structures. These sites appear to represent small farming hamlets inhabited by close-knit social groups, likely kin groups. The second tier of settlements included medium-sized sites covering ca. 10 ha and typically including minor examples of public architecture. Almost all of the ballcourt sites documented by PCM fall into this category as do the settlement concentrations identified by PSACC. In comparison to the smaller settlements in the region, these sites can be best described as villages. Finally, the third tier includes the largest sites in the region. These sites cover circa 1 km² or more and include monumental public architecture.

Small Settlements

Small settlements were documented by PCM throughout northwest Yucatan and examples were found to date to both the Middle and Late Preclassic period. The architecture present at these sites most commonly took the form of small house-mound structures, but occasional apsidal structures and platforms were observed. Examples include the sites of Chen Panta (PCM-46), San Jerónimo [1] (PCM-156), and Santa Maria (PCM-240). These small settlements are the most difficult to locate during a large scale regional survey, and the majority of the examples recorded by PCM were encountered due to their proximity to modern roads or footpaths. As

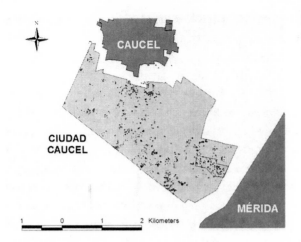

Figure 8.2. Structures recorded by Proyecto Salvamento Arqueológico Ciudad Caucel.

a result, it is likely that these sites were underreported by the survey. The results of the PSACC survey, due to its complete coverage of an 8 km² area, may better reflect the nature of small scale settlement within the region. Many structures were found scattered between the observed settlement clusters (Figure 8.2). These solitary structures and small structure groups are analogous to the occasional hamlets identified by PCM. If the results of this survey better reflect the reality of Preclassic settlement in northwest Yucatan, then many of the smallest sites were not isolated hamlets but rather part of an even dispersal of house groups between villages.

Medium Settlements

Medium-sized settlements were also found distributed throughout the region by PCM. The medium-sized settlements of the region are best known by the excavations carried out in the 1950s at the Mirador Group of Dzibilchaltun (PCM-257) (Andrews IV and Andrews V 1980), and the 2008 excavations by PSACC at the site of Xaman Susula. The work at the Mirador Group has long provided us with our most detailed view of a Middle Preclassic community in the northern lowlands. The site includes a set of six stone platforms arranged around a small plaza, as well as circa 30 additional structures, covering an area of approximately 50 ha. The site was found to date to between 800 and 400 B.C. (Andrews IV and Andrews V 1980:21; Andrews V 1981:315). Of particular interest to us here, excavations alongside one of the structures built on the plaza revealed the stone foundations of a sweat bath (Andrews IV and Andrews V 1980:31). Sweat baths are a relatively common feature of Precolumbian Maya sites (Alcina Franch et al. 1980:104–110; Hammond and Bauer 2001; Ortiz Butrón 2005), but the presence of a sweat bath at the Mirador Group demonstrates that by this early period the site's inhabitants were already experimenting with specialized forms of architecture.

The more recent excavations at Xaman Susula by PSACC investigators have at long last given us a comparative investigation to the Mirador Group. Xaman Susula consists of 105 structures within an area of 6 ha, although the site could have been larger as a modern limestone quarry destroyed at least part of the site (Peniche May 2009, 2010; Peniche May et al. 2009). Excavations at the site demonstrate that it was first occupied in the Middle Preclassic and continuing through to the Early Classic as determined through ceramic typology, architectural stratigraphy, and radiocarbon dating. The site center is composed of a plaza defined on three sides by platforms. From the southern end of the plaza a *sacbe* extends 75 m to the west arriving at a large complex platform (Structure 1714), which included multiple superstructures in its final form (Figure 8.3). Horizontal excavations of Structure 1714 identified three principal construction phases. The first phase occurred entirely during the Middle Preclassic, at which time a platform measuring 23 × 14 m was laid out along with three distinct superstructures. The second and largest construction phase occurred during the transition between the Middle and Late Preclassic periods, with a radiocarbon date of 400 B.C. ± 20 years (Peniche May 2010:61). This construction phase consisted of raising the overall platform level to cover the previous superstructures and the construction of a new superstructure on the west side of the platform (Figure 8.4). This superstructure (Structure 1714-ASub) had walls more than 1 m thick and a well-preserved stucco bench in the center of the room. Nancy Peniche May (2010:12–14, 67) clearly demonstrates that the bench found inside this building is substantially similar to the thrones built by later Classic period Maya rulers, but she notes that the lack of domestic remains in association with the building suggests that the building did not serve as a palace but rather as a public structure. Sometime during the Late Preclassic period this public structure was burned and the interior of the building was filled with stones terminating its role at the site (Peniche May 2010:57–58).

An additional specialized structure was noted at Xaman Susula located to the north of the site's *sacbe* between Structure 1714 and the plaza. Structure 1729, as visible today, is primarily an Early Classic platform, but excavations uncovered an earlier "keyhole"-shaped structure (Structure 1729-Sub) that dates to the Preclassic period. "Keyhole" structures consist of a round platform with an attached rectangular ramp and are commonly found in

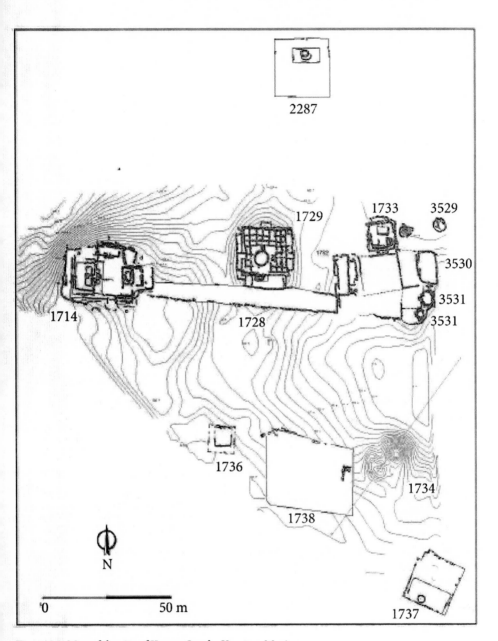

Figure 8.3. Map of the site of Xaman Susula, Yucatan, Mexico.

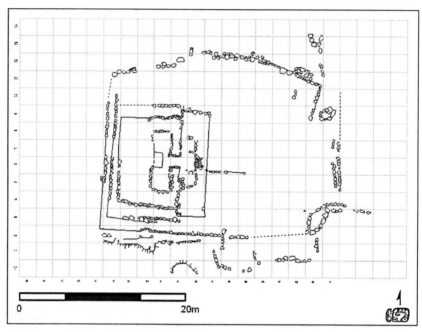

Figure 8.4. Drawing of the Structure 1714-ASub at Xaman Susula, Yucatan, Mexico.

Middle Preclassic contexts at sites in Belize (Hendon 1999:111–113). To our knowledge, no other examples are currently known in Yucatan. Excavations in the remainder of Xaman Susula found both Mamom and Chicanel horizon materials to be widespread throughout the site, thus it is difficult to determine the exact size of the settlement during either the Middle or Late Preclassic period. The excavations at Structure 1714, however, clearly show that there was a permanent settlement at the site during the Middle Preclassic, and that during the transition between the Middle and Late Preclassic period a large public building was built at a site center.

The ballcourt sites identified in the PCM survey make up another readily identifiable category of medium-sized Preclassic sites in northwest Yucatan. Aside from the ballcourt at Xtobo, all of the ballcourts encountered by PCM and PSACC were located at medium or even small-sized settlements. The ballcourts themselves exhibit a fair amount of variation. The playing alleys range in length from 14 to 25 m, and in width from 3 to 10 m. The orientation of the structures is generally north-south, but some structures were found to deviate as much as 25 degrees east of north. The identification of these structures as ballcourts was based on a comparison of their architectural features to the nine features of ballcourt architecture developed by Eric Taladoire (1981; Taladoire and Colsenet 1991:Figure 9.1), including benches, aprons, and upper walls, and so on. At least five of Taladorie's features can be identified at each ballcourt in the region, and if we examine the ballcourts as a group, all nine features were observed.

The ceramics collected by PCM in association with these ballcourts suggest that they were built during the Middle Preclassic. As Middle Preclassic ballcourts are rare in Mesoamerica, particular care was taken in determining the chronological provenience of these buildings. In all, 25 ballcourts were recorded during the survey (Medina Castillo 2003, 2005). Targeted surface collections were made in association with each ballcourt, test pits were excavated in the playing alleys of seven ballcourts, and any looters' trenches and/or tree fall pits were examined for construction details and associated pottery. These efforts resulted in pottery collections from 24 of the 25 sites (Table 8.1). The most commonly encountered pottery groups were Dzudzuquil, Tipikal/Unto, Joventud, and Chunhinta. Each of these groups, with the exception of Tipikal/Unto, are associated with the Mamom horizon and dated to the Middle Preclassic period (see Andrews V 1989; Hernández Hernández 2005; Robles and Ceballos 2003). Tipikal/Unto has traditionally been associated with the Chicanel horizon and the Late Preclassic period (Andrews V 1989; Smith 1971), but Robles and his colleagues have proposed that Tipikal/Unto pottery was first produced during the Middle Preclassic (Ceballos 2005a; Ceballos et al. 2008; Robles Castellanos 1997; Robles and Ceballos 2003). All but one of the 24 pottery collections, the collection from the site of Tzikul (PCM-123), included Mamom horizon pottery. The site of Tzikul produced Mamom horizon pottery, but Early Classic pottery was recovered from beneath a plaster floor in one of the ballcourt's lateral structures that had been exposed by a looter's trench. The summary results are that 22 ballcourts can be associated with the Middle Preclassic period. Without excavations, a direct date of construction cannot be confirmed for each ballcourt, but the general weight of the evidence clearly favors the Middle Preclassic.

The discovery of an additional ballcourt at the site of Xanila by PSACC provided an excellent opportunity to test the conclusions of the PCM survey (Robles and Ligorred Perramon 2008). The Xanila ballcourt is defined by two parallel mounds and a northern closing mound (Figure 8.5). The playing field was oriented to approximately 15 degrees east of north and measured 25 m long and 3 m wide. Excavations of the eastern structure uncovered a low bench defining the structure's edge; proceeding up from the bench was an apron with a 12-degree slope. No upper wall was encountered

Table 8.1. Summary of the Typological Classification of Pottery Sherds Collected by Proyecto Costa Maya from Ballcourt Sites in Northwest Yucatan, Mexico.

Group	Count	Percentage
Colonial	28	0.71
Nabula	6	0.15
Silho	5	0.13
Muna	170	4.29
Ticul	4	0.10
Teabo	12	0.30
Ich Cansiho	10	0.25
Chum	122	3.08
Chuburna	2	0.05
Chablekal	4	0.10
Balancan/Altar	1	0.03
Koxolac	3	0.08
Baca	11	0.28
Batres	41	1.03
Oxil	165	4.16
Maxcanu	142	3.58
Balanza	1	0.03
Aguila	4	0.10
Timucuy	13	0.33
Shangurro	5	0.13
Zotoz	1	0.03
Dzilam	3	0.08
Xanaba	83	2.09
Carolina	3	0.08
Sierra	71	1.79
Polvero	4	0.10
Sapote	26	0.66
Flor	54	1.36
Saban/Achiotes	94	2.37
Tipikal/Unto	668	16.85
Ucu/Chunhinta	205	5.17
Dzudzuquil	925	23.34
Pital	13	0.33
Joventud	389	9.81
Unidentified	16	0.40
Unidentifiable	660	16.65
Total	3964	

at the top of the apron. These details comfortably place the Xanila ballcourt within the range of variation observed by PCM. The excavations at Xanila, however, encountered a feature previously undocumented in the region. At the center of the ballcourt a circular marker was uncovered. The marker was built with multiple pieces of limestone to create a circle 1.15 m in diameter. While Classic period ballcourt markers are typically carved from

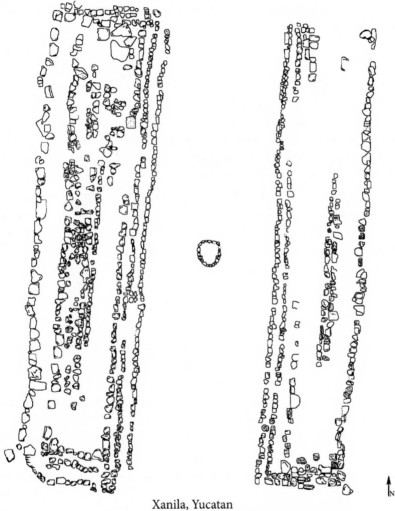

Xanila, Yucatan
Plan of the parallel structures of the Ball Court.
Drawing by: Donato España
Inked by: Edgar Medina
Scale: 1:50

Figure 8.5. Structure drawing of the ballcourt from the site of Xanila, Yucatan, Mexico.

a single piece of limestone, the Xanila marker is otherwise comparable in terms of its size and position to the later tradition. The excavations at Xanila recovered only limited quantities of pottery, but the most common ceramic groups found in association with the ballcourt were Dzudzuquil, Chunhinta, and Joventud, all of which are associated with the Middle Preclassic Mamom horizon. Regrettably, no materials suitable for radiocarbon dating were recovered in association with the ballcourt, but with this addition to our dataset there is little doubt that we are dealing with a Middle Preclassic tradition.

Large Settlements

We now turn to the large Preclassic settlements of northwest Yucatan, which include at a minimum the sites of Xtobo and Komchen. Given the scale and elaboration of these two settlements, it is probable that they both held significant political influence throughout the region. The work by PCM and PAX at the site of Xtobo documented a complex settlement that was once home to a stratified community. The site is arranged in a radial settlement pattern focused on the site's central plaza (Figure 8.6). The north side of the plaza is defined by an 8 m tall pyramid with basal dimensions of ca. 40 × 33 m (Structure 13). On the eastern side of the plaza there is a secondary pyramid of equivalent height, but with smaller basal dimensions (Structure 7). A well-preserved wall has been preserved along the back side of Structure 7, the general disposition of which suggests that the pyramid originally had two tiers with a vertical wall defining the bottom tier and probably the upper tier as well. The south side of the plaza is defined by two small structures, one of which (Structure 4) also serves as the northern closing mound of the ballcourt. The western plaza edge is marked by a medium-sized platform, which was regrettably heavily damaged sometime in the past. The building still retains a well-defined staircase facing the plaza, but very little else can be identified on the structure. The playing alley of the site's ballcourt is defined by Structures 1 and 2, found just to the south of the plaza. Radiating out from the plaza and ballcourt are five *sacbe*, three of which lead to elite residences (Structures 15, 16 and 18), another *sacbe* leads to a pyramid (Structure 14), and the final *sacbe* leads to a double triadic group with an undetermined function (Structure 11). It is interesting to note that the pattern of *sacbeob* radiating out to elite residential complexes has been documented for the Classic period as well (Kurjack 1974). In addition to being connected to the plaza by a *sacbe*, each of these buildings was

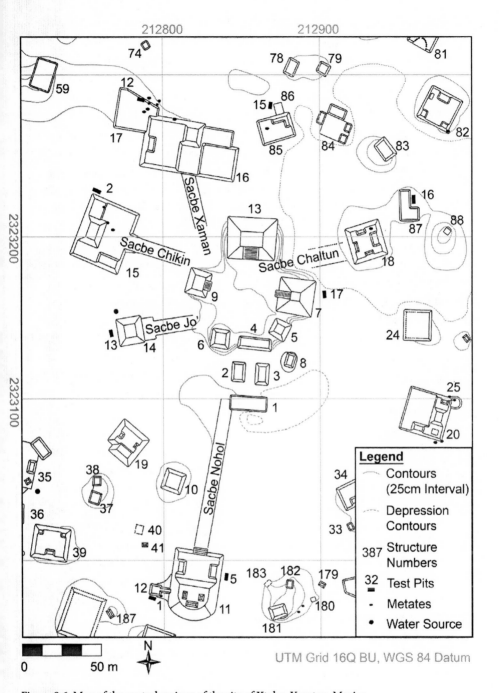

Figure 8.6. Map of the central regions of the site of Xtobo, Yucatan, Mexico.

built to face the plaza. This pattern of orientation continues throughout the site with the majority of large structures built to face the plaza.

The PAX project mapped 67 ha of solid settlement at Xtobo without reaching an identifiable end to the site. A total of 387 structures were recorded, resulting in a structure density of 5.8 structures per ha. This level of structure density exactly matches that observed at Komchen (Ringle and Andrews V 1990:220). The residential architecture at the site took two main forms, simple mounds and rectilinear platforms, both of which are presumed to have served as foundations for perishable structures. Within these architectural types a great deal of variability in the form and size was noted, thereby suggesting that access to labor and resources was variable across the population. An estimate of the site's population found that as many as 1,552 people lived at Xtobo during its florescence (Anderson 2010, 2011). The dating of the community's florescence is still in some doubt as excavations at the site have not encountered stratigraphic contexts or materials suitable for radiometric dating. Using artifact and architecture data, Anderson (2010, 2011) has dated the site's florescence to a period of a few hundred years surrounding the transition between the late Middle Preclassic and early Late Preclassic. It is likely that there was occupation at the site both before and after this period, but it appears to have been minimal. PAX also found evidence for a Classic period reoccupation at the site, but so far only two structures can be associated with this reoccupation.

The presence of a double triadic group at Xtobo is of particular interest to this study. Triadic groups are an iconic form of Preclassic Maya architecture. They have long been known from sites throughout the southern Maya lowlands (Graham 1967; Hansen 1998:77–80; Valdés and Fahsen 1995:199) and now several examples have been reported in the northern lowlands (Hutson 2012; Matheny et al. 1980:Map 8; Mathews 1995:81; Stanton and Ardren 2005:217). Hansen (1998:77–78) defines the triadic group form as composed of "a dominant structure, usually on a platform, flanked by two, inward-facing smaller mounds of equal size." The mapping activities carried out by PAX identified three to four triadic groups (Structures 11, 19, 39, and 82). The simplicity of the triadic group form can regrettably lead to overidentification, but the repetition of the form at Xtobo leaves little doubt that the inhabitants of the site were purposefully constructing a known form. Interpretations of the function and significance of these groups varies, but their presence at Xtobo implies the community was interacting with and influenced by larger Maya cultural spheres.

In contrast to Xtobo, the site of Komchen has a long history of scholarly study and is often cited as representative of the Preclassic northern Maya lowlands (e.g., Hammond 1986:405–406; Henderson 1997:107–108; Sharer and Traxler 2006:277). The site was first recorded by Edwin M. Shook (1955:291)[1] and excavations began shortly thereafter as part of E. Wyllys Andrews IV's Dzibilchaltun project (Andrews IV and Andrews V 1980). The results of the project were preliminary, but the majority of the materials recovered dated to the Late Preclassic period. In 1980, E. Wyllys Andrews V began an expansive mapping and excavation program at Komchen (Andrews V et al. 1980; Andrews V and Ringle 1992; Ringle 1985; Ringle and Andrews V 1988, 1990). This included the mapping of the site center and three transects to investigate the site's extent. A total of 98 ha, including 505 structures, were mapped, and the site's total extent was estimated at 2.4 km². Test pit excavations were carried out in association with 152 of the recorded structures, and horizontal excavations were carried out at ten additional structures. Andrews V (1988, 1989) made a detailed study of the pottery recovered by the project, which has formed the basis of the type: variety sequence of Preclassic pottery used in the region.[2] The initial analyses of these data suggested that Komchen's primary period of occupation occurred during the Late Preclassic (Andrews V and Ringle 1992; Ringle and Andrews V 1988, 1990).

The monumental center of Komchen is defined by a large rectangular plaza. Structure 21J1 sits at the north end of this plaza and consists of a low T-shaped platform with a pyramid positioned on its southern edge. This building has been heavily damaged by stone looting, but the original height of the pyramid is estimated to have been 9 to 10 m, while the platform covers more than 3,500 m². The eastern and western sides of the plaza are defined by Structures 21F1 and 23F1, which are long rectangular platforms that mirror each other in form. The south side of the plaza is open with no defining architecture. A fourth monumental structure, 24G1, is found adjacent to Structure 23F1 on the east side of the plaza. From the northeast corner of the plaza a *sacbe* extends 260 m north-northeast to Structure 25O1. This building consists of a rectangular platform, ca. 2.5m tall, with a 7 m tall pyramid built at its north end.

Surrounding Komchen's plaza is a dense distribution of residential architecture. The structures at Komchen were divided into three types. Type 1 structures were defined as having a surface area "smaller than 40 m²," while Type 2 structures were defined as covering "40 m² or more and usually had retaining walls of dry-laid, roughly cut stone" (Ringle and Andrews V 1990:217). Type 3 structures included the five largest structures at the site.

Overall structure density at the site was observed to be 5.8 structures per ha (Ringle and Andrews V 1990:220). Using this settlement data, it was estimated that the population of Komchen was between 2,500 and 3,000 people during the site's Late Preclassic florescence (Ringle and Andrews V 1990:231). After the recent reanalysis of the site's pottery, Andrews V et al. (Chapter 4 this volume) still holds that the site saw its peak level of occupation during the Late Preclassic, but they now propose that the site had a substantial Middle Preclassic occupation. The exact scale of Komchen during the Middle Preclassic cannot yet be identified, but it appears that the main plaza of Komchen was laid out during this period and that Structures 24G1, 21J1, and 23F1 had all reached substantial sizes. Even without knowing what the remainder of the site looked like during the Middle Preclassic, the existence of a large plaza with monumental structures is a good indication that Middle Preclassic Komchen was the focal point for a large community.

An Outline of Revised Chronology and Preclassic Culture History of Northwest Yucatan

With the current set of data from Preclassic northwest Yucatan we can offer a revised overview of the region's developmental chronology. Based on ceramic analysis by Robles and his colleagues, the earliest permanent settlements in the region have been pushed back to before 700 B.C. Excavations carried out by PSACC suggest that Mamom-horizon pottery began to appear in the region as early as 1000 B.C. (Ceballos and Robles 2012; Ceballos et al. 2008; Robles and Ceballos Chapter 9 this volume). This pushes the arrival of sedentary farmers in northwest Yucatan back by ca. 300 years, but does not necessarily affect the proposed migration from the southwestern Peten as it still involves the same styles of pottery (Andrews V 1990:14).

Andrews V's reanalysis of the Komchen materials suggests a different history of early occupation for the region (Andrews V and Bey 2011; Andrews V et al. 2008; Andrews V et al. Chapter 4 this volume). Andrews V argues that the Ek complex predates the first appearance of Mamom-horizon pottery and suggests that Mamom-horizon materials do not begin to appear at the site until ca. 800 B.C. Andrews V has also proposed that the Kin Orange pottery type, a member of the Ek complex, develops into the Joventud Red type. Placing the Ek complex pottery as the earliest pottery at Komchen disrupts the stylistic argument used to connect the site's earliest population with immigrants from the southwestern Peten. Also, the argument that Kin Orange develops into Joventud Red suggests the Middle Preclassic occupation of northwest Yucatan developed out of the Ek complex population at Komchen.

While it may prove that either Robles's interpretation or Andrews V's interpretation is correct, we can also reconcile the two interpretations if we presume that during the early Middle Preclassic period two distinct populations existed in northwest Yucatan, a Mamom-producing population and an Ek-producing population. In this scenario, the development of Kin Orange pottery into Joventud pottery could instead be understood as a gradual merging of two distinct pottery traditions. It should be said, however, that at this time no materials resembling Ek have been found in the region outside of the excavated materials from Komchen, and a few scattered sherds without good context (see Andrews V et al. Chapter 4 this volume for an expanded regional view including the Puuc region).

During the mid to late Middle Preclassic period, the population of northwest Yucatan underwent a rapid expansion as demonstrated by the large number of Middle Preclassic sites encountered by PCM. The arrangement of these sites in a three-tiered hierarchy further suggests a concurrent growth in sociopolitical complexity. The second-tier communities exhibit a great deal of variability during this period, including the plaza and sweat bath of the Mirador Group, the developing community at Xaman Susula, and the numerous ballcourt sites spread throughout the region. It is probable that before the end of the Middle Preclassic period, the *sacbe* and walled superstructure were built at Xaman Susula and that Xtobo had begun its period of florescence; also it appears that Komchen was experiencing its own rapid growth during this period. By the early Late Preclassic, Xaman Susula, Xtobo, and Komchen all had undeniably reached their periods of florescence, though not necessarily simultaneously. By this time the ballcourt sites appear to have been in decline; seven of the ballcourt sites included no signs of Late Preclassic occupation and no ballcourts were found at Late Preclassic sites that lacked Middle Preclassic occupations. The decline of the ballcourt sites may be related to the decline of Xtobo, but the presence of the double triadic group at Xtobo suggests that large-scale construction at the site continued during the Late Preclassic (see Anderson 2011). Whenever Xtobo and Komchen reached regional center status, they represent the emergence of a three-tiered settlement hierarchy and thus presumably the emergence of a chiefdom-like sociopolitical organization (Carneiro 1981:54; Flannery 1999:4; Wason 1994:131; Wright 1984).

By the mid Late Preclassic period, it appears that the social landscape of northwest Yucatan had fundamentally shifted with Komchen fully consolidating sociopolitical power within the region. Not only have the ballcourt sites been largely abandoned, but also the medium-sized village sites of the region are no longer experimenting with different forms of architecture. The apparently deliberate destruction of Structure 1714-ASub at Xaman Susula at this time may even suggest that this experimentation was forcefully brought to an end. The end of large-scale settlement at Xtobo is difficult to track. As has been said, there clearly was a Late Preclassic settlement at the site, but it is Anderson's opinion that the site was largely abandoned by the middle Late Preclassic. It should also be noted that the number of known settlements within the region, as ascertained by the PCM survey, drops by ca. 20% during the Late Preclassic period. It is likely that some of the people living at these sites were absorbed by the growth of Komchen, but we cannot be sure exactly how the population shifted. Before the Late Preclassic period had ended, Komchen was already in decline. The site's population during the Xculul phase (150 B.C. to A.D. 250) was only half of its Late Preclassic peak population. Looking ahead to the Early Classic period, PCM found the number of sites in the region to increase to 110; it may be that this increase represents the dissolution of Komchen, but our data are not detailed enough to confirm such a speculation.

Discussion

The Mesoamerican Ballgame in Northwest Yucatan

The data collected by Proyecto Costa Maya, Proyecto Arqueológico de Xtobo, and Proyecto Salvamento Arqueológico Ciudad Caucel raise several issues for our understanding of both Maya and Mesoamerican culture. Perhaps the most unexpected result of these projects was the reporting of 24 Middle Preclassic ballcourts, the majority of which were found at small villages rather than sociopolitical centers. Outside of northwest Yucatan, only eight examples of Middle Preclassic ballcourts have been documented in all of Mesoamerica. These ballcourts are found widely dispersed throughout Mesoamerica; in the Maya region examples have been reported at the sites of Paso del Macho in the Puuc hills of Yucatan (Gallareta et al. 2005), Nakbe in northern Guatemala (Velásquez 1993b), and Takalik Abaj on the Guatemalan Pacific coast piedmont (Schieber de Lavarreda 1994). Four more Middle Preclassic ballcourts are found in the state of Chiapas, including the site of La Libertad in southern Chiapas, and the sites of Finca

Acapulco, El Vergel, and San Mateo in the Grijalva River valley (Agrinier 1991). Moving all the way to West Mexico, a probable Middle Preclassic ballcourt has been documented at the site of Campanillo (Weigand 1991).[3] As a precursor to these structures, an Early Preclassic ballcourt has also been reported from the site of Paso de la Amada on the Pacific coast of Chiapas (Hill et al. 1998). The addition of 23 new examples of Middle Preclassic ballcourts more than doubles the number of known early examples in Mesoamerica.

The majority of the scholarly literature on the Mesoamerican ballgame focuses on the elite political and ritual aspects of the game in its Classic and Postclassic forms (e.g., Blom 1932; Scarborough and Wilcox 1991; Taladoire 2003; Uriarte 1992; van Bussel et al. 1991; Whalen and Minnis 1996; Whittington 2001). As a result, on those occasions when Preclassic versions of the game come under discussion, they tend to be interpreted through this preestablished paradigm. For example, in the publication by Warren Hill et al. (1998) announcing the discovery of the Early Preclassic ballcourt at Paso de la Amada, the ballgame is presented as a decidedly elite tradition and the presence of a ballcourt at the site is taken to indicate the development of a complex sociopolitical system. The authors go on to predict that "the earliest ball courts should be located in sites with evidence of status differences among community members" (Hill et al. 1998:878–879). In a more recent article, Hill and John E. Clark (2001:331) further develop a link between the early ballgame and sociopolitical organization by proposing that "the ballgame played a notable role in the origins and perpetuation of the first formal community governments in Mesoamerica."

The ballcourts found in northwest Yucatan decidedly do not fit this model. Almost all of the ballcourts documented within the region were found at relatively small sites belonging to the second-tier of the regional settlement pattern. These are clearly not elite contexts. The ballcourt at Xtobo, however, is found in the center of a large socially stratified community, thereby demonstrating some elite involvement in the game. Following Hill and Clark (2001), it could be suggested that the ballcourt sites were competing among one another for political power and that Xtobo's rise was due to its success in this ballgame competition. Given that some of our ballcourt sites, however, consist of little more than a ballcourt and a few house mounds, it is difficult to conceive that they represent communities striving for regional power. We could also hypothesize that the rulers of Xtobo had ballcourts built throughout the region as markers of their political or ritual power, but this scenario would require that we assume Xtobo held a great deal more control over the region than is warranted from the scale of the site. A simpler hypothesis would be to suggest that the ballgame and the building of ballcourts were activities not controlled by the elites. The Meso-american ballgame is, after all, a game that could be played and enjoyed as a communal sport rather than solely as an act of elite political theater. The raw materials and construction labor required to build a ballcourt would not have been excessive as the structures that make up these ballcourts are scarcely larger than many of the platforms and house mounds found at sites throughout the region. If a family group can be expected to pool labor to build a platform, then it is not difficult to suggest that a community could amass the labor necessary to build a ballcourt. In this situation, the frequency of ballcourts in the region can simply reflect the popularity of the game. There is still, however, the ballcourt at Xtobo to be explained. We would argue that the ballcourt at Xtobo can be seen as an attempt by the site's rulers to develop a bond with a popular commoner tradition, just as politicians today seek to demonstrate that they can relate to the common people they seek to represent (see Anderson 2012).

The Middle Preclassic Villages of Northwest Yucatan

The ballcourt sites form a prominent example of a larger phenomenon within the Middle Preclassic village settlements documented by PCM and PSACC. At many of these sites people were experimenting with multiple architectural forms that are typically interpreted as elite architecture. Classic period Maya rulers sponsored the construction of ballcourts, throne rooms, and even sweat baths to further enhance their prestige and power (e.g., Fash 1998; Harrison 2001). If these buildings were found at Komchen and Xtobo they could easily be interpreted as signs of an emergent elite class, but the presence of these structures at village communities implies they held a different level of significance in the region. The people living at these sites appear to have been free to experiment with different forms of architecture.

The site of Xaman Susula presents the most extreme example of this phenomenon. During the site's peak level of occupation a *sacbe* was built leading directly to a set of stairs, which in turn lead to a throne room set atop an elevated platform. This arrangement of architecture gives every appearance of a high-level elite context, yet it is found at a medium-sized settlement a few kilometers away from the nearest regional center. Peniche May (2010:78) argues that "the architectural traits as well as the arrange-ment of [the throne room] with regard to the other structures suggest that its functions were similar to the later scenic palaces, which are related to administrative, ideological, judicial and diplomatic activities." She goes on to state that we are only "witnessing the beginning of the institutionalization of those activities," and that "the throne room of Xaman Susula must be considered the precursor of the palaces that were built throughout the Maya area during later periods," (Peniche May 2010:80). It is the idea of these architectural forms as "precursors" that can help us understand these settlements. As we addressed while discussing the ballcourts, Preclassic institutions are often approached as if they were nascent versions of their later Classic period counterparts, rather than as institutions in their own right. The structures of Xaman Susula were built by a community that did not yet know what the palace of a royal *ajau* was, and so they could not have conceived of this architectural form as proprietary to an elite class that did not yet exist. During the Middle Preclassic of northwest Yucatan we are witnessing communities that are developing into a complex society and in that process they are experimenting with form and function. On occasions such as this, they created forms that will become well known, but we cannot interpret initial experiments with the full-fledged significance of the later form.

Nevertheless, the presence of public architecture at these village sites suggests that there was limited central control during the late Middle Preclassic period. As a broad generalization, the more centrally organized a political institution is, the more control it exhibits over its constituent populations. For example, in state-level societies, the architecture of secondary centers often reflects that of the primary center (Renfrew 2008:38). In terms of scale, Xaman Susula certainly appears to be a secondary center in comparison to Xtobo and Komchen, and yet it has architecture unlike anything seen at either site. If Xaman Susula had been a political outpost of Xtobo or Komchen, its public architecture is more likely to have taken the form of a replica of the public architecture from one site or the other. The individuality of Xaman Susula instead suggests that it was a politically independent community. The eventual termination of the Xaman Susula throne room during the Late Preclassic period, as well as the abandonment of the ballcourt sites, however, suggests that the independence of these sites did not survive as sociopolitical power matured within the region.

Interactions with Other Regions

Several points of data from Preclassic northwest Yucatan demonstrate contact with other regions of Mesoamerica. The most obvious examples come from the presence of foreign raw materials. The excavations at Xtobo and Komchen, as well as those carried out by PSACC, recovered artifacts made of obsidian, primarily from the El Chayal source in Guatemala (Anderson 2010:205; Peniche May 2008b; Ringle 1985:348). Overall, the quantities recovered were small, but even this small quantity demonstrates a connection with external trade networks. PSACC excavations also encountered over 70 artifacts made from varying forms of igneous and metamorphic rock (Peniche May 2008a). The largest single collection of these artifacts was found in an offering excavated from the ballcourt at Xanila and included four celts made from green basalt. The source of this basalt is uncertain, but it could have come from either the Guatemalan highlands or the Tuxtla Mountains in Veracruz. Seven pieces of jade were recovered by the Komchen project (Ringle 1985:347), but so far Preclassic jade is not well attested for in the rest of northwest Yucatan. We can further speculate that the people of northwest Yucatan were importing either unprocessed rubber plants, or more likely rubber balls, as the varieties of plants that can be used to produce rubber, and thus rubber balls, do not grow in northern Yucatan (Filoy Nadal 2001:Figure 8).

Another set of important data regarding trade contact between the northern Maya lowlands and other areas of Mesoamerica comes to us from the Olmec site of La Venta and its hinterland. In a reexamination of pottery collections from the site, Andrews V (1986) identified examples of the Maya pottery type Joventud Red, which belongs to the Middle Preclassic Mamom horizon. While generally Joventud Red could come from any part of the Maya lowlands, Andrews V identified particular modal similarities with collections of Joventud from the northern lowlands. More recently, Christopher von Nagy (2003:291) identified more examples of Joventud pottery, along with examples of Dzudzuquil pottery from smaller sites within La Venta's hinterland. Dzudzuquil pottery is also associated with the Mamom horizon, but unlike Joventud it is exclusively a product of the northern Maya lowlands. While this data cannot be directly tied to northwest Yucatan, it further establishes the fact that the northern Maya lowlands were broadly interacting with the rest of Mesoamerica.

One more piece of evidence from Xtobo further demonstrates interaction between northwest Yucatan and the southern Maya lowlands; that is the presence of triadic groups. Triadic groups are often thought of as a phenomenon of the southern lowlands in large part because they first came to our notice from work carried out by Ian Graham (1967) in the Mirador basin of Guatemala. While the greatest number of known triadic groups is still found in the southern lowlands, there are an ever-increasing number of known examples in the northern lowlands. Besides the three to four examples from Xtobo, triadic groups are also known at the sites of Yaxuna (Stanton and Ardren 2005:217), Tzacauil (Hutson 2012), Naranjal (Mathews 1995:81), Edzna (Matheny et al. 1980:Map 8; see also Mathews 1995:83), and Ake (Roys and Shook 1966; cited by Mathews 1995:83), likely with more sites to come. With so many examples now known in the northern lowlands we question whether this architectural pattern is properly considered a southern cultural trait appearing in the north, or simply a widespread Lowland Maya cultural trait, but more research will have to be done on this topic.

Komchen and Xtobo

As the two largest and most prominent Preclassic sites in northwest Yucatan, Komchen and Xtobo would have exhibited strong influences on the settlements around them. The revised history of occupation at Komchen indicates that these two sites would also have been occupied contemporaneously, regardless of when either site reached its peak florescence. In this case the two communities would have certainly been aware of one another's existence. With just over 18 km separating the two sites, the communities could have been in almost daily contact. For these reasons we need to look more closely at how the two sites compare and examine what sort of relationship they might have had.

As should be expected, Xtobo and Komchen have many commonalities. The pottery collections from both sites are very similar (Table 8.2). Both are primarily composed of Mamom and Chicanel horizon sherds and include similar groups from the type: variety classification scheme. The presence of these pottery groups demonstrates that the sites had similar periods of occupation and that both sites were associated with a material culture tradition found throughout the Maya lowlands. Both sites were making use of obsidian from similar sources; thus they had access to similar exchange networks. Construction techniques and house forms are also similar at both sites, and all evidence suggests that both communities were primarily supported by maize agriculture. In short, the basics of life appear to have been the same at both sites.

Looking in greater detail, however, there are a number of significant differences between Xtobo and Komchen. While both sites are significantly larger than other contemporaneous sites in the region, the peak Late Preclassic occupation at Komchen was approximately twice the size of Xtobo

Table 8.2. Comparison of the Pottery Groups Recovered from the Sites of Komchen and Xtobo.

Groups	Xtobo		Komchen	
	count	%	count	%
Dzilam			5	0.02
Timucuy	48	2.27	41	0.16
Polvero			183	0.70
Xanaba	199	9.42	2474	9.51
Tipikal	86	4.07	492	1.89
Unto	164	7.76	1083	4.17
Saban	746	35.31	3420	13.15
Caramba	13	0.62		
Tamanche			810	3.12
Joventud/Sierra	467	22.10	9694	37.28
Sierra (only)			*7403	
Joventud (only)			*2291	
Muxanal			54	0.21
Chunhinta	146	6.91	3979	15.30
Dzudzuquil	236	11.17	2560	9.85
Solguna	3	0.14		
Pital	5	0.24		
Almeja			264	1.02
Kin			943	3.63

both in terms of site extent and population. Also, Komchen's monumental architecture was notably larger than the equivalent structures at Xtobo. In contrast, however, structures at Xtobo were on average larger than those at Komchen. The Komchen survey found that ca. 53% of the site's structures had an area of less than 40 m^2 (Type 1 Structures), and 47% had an area greater than 40 m^2 (Type 2 Structures) (Ringle and Andrews V 1988:Table 9.3). If we employ the same schema at Xtobo only 40% of the site's buildings have an area less than 40 m^2 while 60% of the structures have a larger area.

The architecture of Komchen also differs in that it lacks several of the specialized architectural forms found at Xtobo, including a ballcourt and triadic groups. In addition, the site has only one *sacbe* in comparison to the five at Xtobo. Looking at the settlement plans of the two site centers, Komchen's rectangular plaza flanked by two nearly identical long range structures is reminiscent of site plans from sites in the highlands of Chiapas and the Olmec site of La Venta (Andrews V, personal communication, 2010; see Clark and Hansen 2001; Lowe 1977), while the square plaza, radiating *sacbeob*, and triadic groups found at Xtobo is more reminiscent of sites found in the southern Maya lowlands (see Hansen 2001). There are, however, features at each site that show these regional associations are not so simple. Middle Preclassic ballcourts have been found in both the southern Maya and the Chiapas highlands, and the *sacbe* at Komchen is in keeping with southern Lowland Maya architectural traditions. Thus, both sites represent blends of Maya and Mesoamerican traditions.

The differences in architecture between the two sites imply some differences in the cultural practices of these communities. The ballcourt at Xtobo is centrally located amidst the site's public and elite architecture. Regardless of whether the ballgame was an elite or communal tradition, it clearly played a high-profile role within the Xtobo community. In contrast, no ballcourt has been found at Komchen. The lack of a ballcourt does not preclude the possibility that the site's inhabitants played a ballgame, but at the very least, it suggests a different valuation of that game. With the reinterpretation of Komchen's history of occupation to include a significant settlement in the late Middle Preclassic period, the community at Komchen was necessarily contemporaneous with the ballcourt sites of northwest Yucatan. One ballcourt site (Sin Nombre, PCM-275) is located just a few kilometers away from Komchen, and so it is a virtual certainty that the people of Komchen knew of this cultural tradition. We must then ask, why did Komchen not take part in this activity? As has been seen, the ballgame is already a pan-Mesoamerican trait by the Middle Preclassic, thus even if the people of Komchen looked to a cultural background in the Chiapas highlands or the Gulf coast lowlands, they almost certainly would have had a heritage incorporating the ballgame. It would have to be surmised that either the elites of the community or the community as a whole actively chose not to take part in the regional tradition. The rejection of a prominent regional and Mesoamerican tradition is difficult to explain at this time.

The lack of triadic groups at Komchen also raises further questions. Prior to the work of PCM and PAX, the lack of triadic groups at Komchen could be understood simply by the assumption that the tradition of triadic architecture had not reached northwest Yucatan, but such an explanation can no longer stand. Given the prominence of the tradition throughout the northern and southern lowlands, and the presence of examples at Xtobo, it is unusual that a large Late Preclassic center like Komchen would not have a triadic group. Andrews V's comparison of the site's central architecture to sites in highland Chiapas and the site of La Venta could suggest that the elite of Komchen were seeking to identify with other successful culture areas; however, in all other respects Komchen is solidly a Lowland Maya settlement. A better explanation may come not from asking why Komchen does not have a triadic group, but rather why Xtobo does have such a group. If our understanding of the regional chronology is correct, both Xtobo and Komchen would have been emerging as large regional centers during the late Middle Preclassic, and by the mid-Late Preclassic Komchen had become the predominant center of the region. It is possible that during the early Late Preclassic the leaders of Xtobo were looking for ways to keep up with their ever-growing neighbor. Aligning themselves more closely with the successful southern Maya lowlands through the construction of a triadic group may have been their attempt to gain greater prestige within the region.

In the end, there is much that we do not know about the relationship between Xtobo and Komchen. The significant differences between the two sites imply that there is little reason to think that either site had a positive influence over the other; that is to say, neither site was emulating the other. We do not, however, have direct evidence for an antagonistic relationship between Xtobo and Komchen. For example, neither site has defensive features, or any other signs of heightened militaristic activity. We should also keep in mind that similarly sized contemporary settlements may have existed at the nearby sites of Tzeme (PCM-1) and Ch'el (PCM-138), which are currently masked by Classic period occupations. In addition, there are several prominent Preclassic sites in areas neighboring the PCM survey zone, such as Poxila (Robles Castellanos et al. 2006) and Xocnaceh (Gallareta and Ciau 2007). As work continues in the region our understanding of the upper echelons of sociopolitical power in Preclassic northwest Yucatan may continue to shift.

Conclusions

It should now be clear that the traditional paradigm of a gradual development of sociopolitical complexity for far northwest Yucatan, beginning with the arrival of farmers ca. 700 B.C. followed by a slow development eventually culminating in a Late Preclassic cultural center at Komchen, can no longer stand. The studies carried out by Proyecto Costa Maya, Proyecto Arqueológico de Xtobo, and Proyecto Salvamento Arqueológico Ciudad Caucel have documented a complex and nuanced Preclassic cultural landscape throughout the region. We can now demonstrate that the earliest settlers of northwest Yucatan arrived 200 to 300 years earlier than previously thought, and by the Middle Preclassic period well over 100 settlements were found throughout the region comprising a three-tiered regional hierarchy. During this period we also saw the development of, and experimentation with, varying forms of public architecture, most notably in the form of ballcourts and plazas. With the end of the Middle Preclassic period a shift in settlement occurred; many sites were abandoned while several new sites were founded. During the early Late Preclassic period Komchen grew to be the dominant center of the region while Xtobo foundered.

The differences between the region's two sociocultural centers, Xtobo and Komchen, are greater than one might expect, but in the end both sites clearly fit within the cultural norms of the Lowland Maya. Overall, Xtobo shows more variability in its settlement plan. The five *sacbeob* that radiate out from the site's plaza each connect to structures with notably different forms. Even the buildings on the plaza itself each have different forms and dimensions. This variability should reflect greater specialization in structure function, coinciding with greater elaboration in the civic ceremonial behavior associated with those structures. Between the plaza, ballcourt, and excess of *sacbeob*, the rulers of Xtobo do not seem to have ever passed up a setting from which they could carry out public displays. As a result, we can surmise that there was a heavy emphasis on ritual and performance at Xtobo. Komchen, in contrast, has a simple and clean plaza defined by only three structures, two of which are mirror images of one another. These buildings, however, were notably larger than the structures built at Xtobo and thus required greater investments of resources and labor. The overall size of the site and its burgeoning population is further indicative of economic prosperity. It is possible that Komchen's success was tied to a defeat of a rival center at Xtobo, but as was noted above, we have no direct evidence that these two sites were actively competing against one another. Instead, the increased centralization of population witnessed at Komchen may have simply been the result of a leadership more interested in economics then ritual. Marshall Sahlins (1972:41) originally argued that underproduction was inherent to simple societies organized primarily by kinship ties. Thus, production booms resulting in surpluses, and in turn population growth, do not necessarily require developments of technology or improvements in environmental carrying capacity, but rather simply changes in sociopolitical organization (Stanish 2004). If Komchen became the center of a new ideology wherein production was emphasized over ritual, the changes in population density and architectural complexity would be a natural result.

Such an explanation of the changes within the region is certainly speculative, but we would like to think not wildly so. Archaeological work continues in northwest Yucatan, and as more data is gathered, we will be able to further flesh out the region's culture history. We have much yet to unravel in regards to the relationship between Xtobo and Komchen, the role of village settlements during the Middle Preclassic period, and the nature of trade and contact with other regions of Mesoamerica. Thus, as always, we are left with more questions then we began with, and everything we thought we knew may still change tomorrow. What is certain, though, is that the "pathway to complexity" in northwest Yucatan has become longer and much more complicated.

Notes

1. Shook (1955) originally recorded the site of Komchen under the name of Xcanantun.

2. Andrews V's study of the Komchen pottery was substantially influenced by Joseph W. Ball's study of the Preclassic pottery of Dzibilchaltun (Ball 1977–1979).

3. There are several other Middle Preclassic structures that have been proposed as ballcourts but which are questionable for varying reasons. These include structures at the sites of San Lorenzo (Coe and Diehl 1980), La Venta (Wyshak et al. 1971), Chalcatzingo (Grove and Cyphers Guillén 1987:26), Teopantecuanitlan (Martínez Donjuan 1995), and El Macayal, a neighbor of El Manati (Ortiz and Rodríguez 1992; see also Hill and Clark 2001). If any of these structures are demonstrated to be Middle Preclassic ballcourts they would significantly expand the distribution of the tradition.

9

The Genesis of Maya Complexity in the Northwestern Region of the Yucatan Peninsula

FERNANDO ROBLES CASTELLANOS AND TERESA CEBALLOS GALLARETA

From these evidence, scarce though it is, it seems reasonable to conclude that at least the Middle and Late Formative periods in Yucatan saw the erections of massive religious centers by the large, well-organized groups necessary for such tasks. Certainly this part of the Maya culture pattern began long before the stela cult.

George W. Brainerd 1951:76.

Introduction and Background

When examining archaic societies, the construction of public monumental architecture, a tangible symbol of political authority, is considered to be the most significant element used to define the social complexity or civilization. In Mesoamerica, this criterion has been applied when analyzing vast pyramidal foundations, multi-room residencies/palace-type structures, acropolises, and so on. Structures of these sorts constitute the material expression of the presiding elites imposing control within their respective jurisdictions over communal labor forces, environmental resources, and esoteric knowledge.

Thus, sociocultural complexity is associated with the successful process of the *rise* and *consolidation* of a particular form of vertical or hierarchal governmental organization, which in political anthropological theory is known as an archaic state. The last is conceived as an historical process in which a consecutive series of paramount leaders were able to institutionalize a coercive-centralized government. It is assumed that over a relatively prolonged period of time, they imposed a reasonably stable political system among the dispersed leaders that were granted authority within their native regions or states. The prevailing successive leaders forged the efficient means to perennially assert and exercise power over their rivals, utilizing their authority within their respective jurisdictions to unite, control, and organize a given territory's society, and generate resources and defensive means, all to better suit their own welfare. Due to their coercive capacity, as time went on they were not only able to gain general acceptance as legitimate leaders, but also able to conceive a cosmology and official esoteric symbolism that conceptualized ideological references to their "indisputable" prerogative to govern and depute power to their own heir.

The operability of the political centralization process required the implementation of a variety of offices and specialized artisans in numerous occupations outside field production; their existence is primarily based on the needs of the following social sectors: administrative, militaristic, ideological, and the constructive activity of presiding leaders, as well as their overzealous interests to perpetuate not only their own dominant role, but also those of their allies and kin. Although the level of sociocultural complexity attained during the formation of an archaic state (which also includes a generally frustrating process, known as a "chiefdom") is unique in every case, the formation process was dependent on the contingent conjunction of multiple factors, such as: the particular characteristics of the native culture, the weaknesses that developed within the centralized political structure that was established, the system's capacity to generate a greater amount of resources, the ability to adapt innovative technological and ideological aspects, resistance to changes of local sociocultural traditions, the impact of outside pressure, etc. (see Brumfiel 1983, 1994; Claessen and Skalník 1981; Flannery 1972).

The collective evidence at hand appears to indicate that the formation process relevant to the emerging complex societies located in the central and southeastern regions of Mesoamerica crystalized around the second half of the Middle Preclassic period (ca. 800/700–400/300 B.C.); furthermore, this process resulted in the formation of diverse regional cultural-political manifestations. It should be noted however that the material culture of all these regions share the use of the decorative designs and esoteric symbolism of Olmec culture (Clark et al. 2000; González Lauck 2000; Grove 1981, 2000). The word "Olmeca" originates from the Nahuatl language, its meaning can be translated as "those that are from the region of rubber," referring to the historic heterogeneous groups that inhabited the southern coast of Veracruz adjacent to Tabasco at the time of the Spanish arrival (Sholes and Warren 1965). From a retrospective point of view, the term "Olmeca" has been reinterpreted to also include the "high archaeological culture of La Venta," located on the borders of Tabasco contiguous to Veracruz, since this Middle Preclassic cultural manifestation is considered to be the highest form of expression created by the pre-Hispanic groups that occupied the "Olmec territory" (González Lauck 2000:363–364). Therefore, the Olmec iconography and decorative patterns from La Venta found in the material culture of dispersed complex societies that were its contemporaries are considered to be the most significant features when it came to defining the Middle Preclassic Olmec cultural horizon throughout Mesoamerica.

Archaeological and linguistic investigations carried out in the past 30 years have revealed that the ethnic entity of the "archaeological Olmecs" from the Gulf of Mexico was highly likely to correspond to that of the Mixe-Zoquean, who during the Early and Middle Preclassic periods comprised the predominant linguistic group of the entire area of the Isthmus of Tehuantepec (Campbell and Kaufman 1976; Clark et al. 2000; Joesink-Mandeville 1977; Kaufman 1976; Lowe 1977, 1989).

Some scholars have postulated that the late Olmecs from the Isthmus of Tehuantepec began introducing their concepts of power, government, wealth, deities, writing, and so forth, into the Cholan-Maya villages of the southern Maya lowlands adjacent to the east after 800 B.C., which would later characterize Maya civilization (Andrews V 1986; Cheetham 2005; Clark 2001; Clark et al. 2000:452–455). According to this conjecture, the Olmecs were the proverbial spark that ignited the future splendor of the Classic Maya epoch.

Up until the 1980s it was argued that sociocultural complexity emerged in the Maya region during the first centuries A.D., which in turn gave rise to the Classic period (Adams 1977). This point of view would be radically reformed after the works of Ray Matheny and Bruce Dahlin (Matheny et al. 1980), and more recently those of Richard Hansen (1990, 1998, 2000, 2009; Hansen et al. Chapter 7 this volume) at El Mirador, located in the Guatemala-Campeche Peten region, where it has been revealed that during the Late Preclassic (300 B.C.–A.D. 200) this site was a powerful supra-regional capital in which local leaders erected the largest monumental complex that was ever constructed by the pre-Hispanic Maya (e.g., the complex of "El Tigre"). Moreover, recent archaeological evidence suggests that during the Middle Preclassic the site of Nakbe, located 12 km southeast of El Mirador, preceded this site as a regional seat of power in the Mirador region, and that around 500 B.C., during the Late Ox phase (ca. 600–300 B.C., see Forsyth 1993b; Forsyth and Hansen 2007), Nakbe already exhibited elaborate residential complexes, sacbeob, and masonry pyramidal foundations. Regardless, everything seems to indicate that around the second half of the Middle

Preclassic period, the Cholan-Maya communities from the Mirador Basin exhibited the initial stages of sociocultural complexity comparable to the contemporary Zoquean Olmec political entities to the west of them.

With the origins of Maya complexity now established in the Middle Preclassic, doubt is cast on whether or not the Olmecs were actually the principal promoters of Classic Maya sociopolitical complexity. Moreover, it appears that at that time the material culture of the Maya in the Mirador Basin had more differences than similarities to that of the Olmecs (Hansen 2005).

This new "Peten" model used to interpret the origins of Maya civilization appeared to further cement the deep-rooted belief among Maya archaeologists that complex sociocultural transformations in the northern part of Yucatan came later, during the Late Preclassic period, and that these must have been a result of the proceeding influences from developing Cholan-Maya communities located in the southern lowlands (Andrews V 1990; Ball 1977; Rathje 1971). Until recently, our knowledge regarding the Preclassic in northern Yucatan was limited to the site of Komchen, located 12 km north of Mérida, excavated by Andrews V in the early 1980s (Andrews V et al. Chapter 4 this volume). Komchen is a compact medium-sized site, with a 2 km² extension and a dense nucleus, which presumably exemplifies the largest settlements that existed in northern Yucatan during the Late Preclassic (Andrews V and Ringle 1992; Ringle 1985). Although today we seem to have emerging evidence to suggest that at the end of the Middle Preclassic or the early part of Late Preclassic, the neighboring settlement of Xtobo, situated 12 km west of Mérida's center, was a densely populated and monumental regional seat of power (see Anderson 2003; 2009; Anderson et al. Chapter 8 this volume).

Either way, ceramic evidence from an initial occupational phase was recovered within the deepest layers of the test pits excavated at Komchen and dated to the second half of the Middle Preclassic period. This was before they found the stone-cut foundations of a modest oval abode at Komchen, adjacent to the architectural group El Mirador at Dzibilchaltun (Structure 605), whose construction was dated in accordance to the "Nabanche 1" ceramic complex from the first half of the Middle Preclassic period (Andrews IV and Andrews V 1980:25–31). Thus, the accumulating information has been taken as proof that the first Maya settlements in Yucatan emerged during the Middle Preclassic and consisted of small villages (hamlets) of farmers, dispersed throughout the region in a weak state of politico-cultural integration (Andrews V 1981:320, 1986:41; Andrews V et al. Chapter

4 this volume). Recent findings of foundations with stucco flooring in circular huts amongst neighboring sites like El Mameyal, Quintas del Mayab, and Col. Serapio Rendón (southern part of Mérida), which also date back to the Middle Preclassic, appear to reaffirm the notion that the prevailing socio-organizational system in Yucatan during the initial cultural stages of the Maya consisted of villages (Hernández 2004; Maldonado and Echeverría 2004; Uriarte and Mier 2004). However, this has turned out to be a limited part of the cultural reality of the time in question (see below).

In fact, during the early 1950s celebrated ceramicist George W. Brainerd excavated a test pit in one of the most extensive and elevated plazas at Sta. Rosa Xtampak (the so-called Stela Eight plaza). Interred beneath the plaza he found the superior part of an enormous edifice, whose constructive fill exclusively contained Middle Preclassic sherds. In light of the procured material, Brainerd deduced that densely populated Maya communities with an efficient political organization and the unique capacity to erect monuments of this magnitude during ancient times already existed in Yucatan during Middle Preclassic times (Brainerd 1951:76–77; 1958:89). However, this singular finding coupled with the absence of further analogous discoveries lead to the neglect of Brainerd's postulation.

In reference to cultural periodization, Komchen's relative chronology has been utilized to characterize the entire Preclassic period in the northern Maya lowlands, as it was the first early sequence to be established. By association (as well as the lack of better evidence until recently) this implies that in the northern part of the peninsula the transition from a hunter-gatherer lifestyle toward more sedentary ways of life occurred during the end of the first half of the Middle Preclassic period (see Andrews IV 1972:290–291; Joesink-Mandeville 1970; Schmidt 1988; Velásquez 1980). This was only until the Early Classic period, when communities such as Komchen located in the northern part of Yucatan evolved and gave rise to the first complex societies, whose most relevant urban centers were the settlements of Izamal, Ake, Acanceh, Oxkintok, T'ho, and Yaxuna (their political-cultural transformations are explained by various archaeologists based on the supposition that the technical, political, and cultural origins of the southern lowlands impacted northern Yucatan).

Recently, an emerging paradigm in Yucatan has surfaced which drastically differs from the traditional conceptions regarding the origins of Maya civilization in the northern lowlands. This is a result of current archaeological excavations, which have revealed that in the north Maya sub-area, particularly in the northwestern region of the Yucatan peninsula, the formation process of pristine complex societies also dates to the second half of the Middle Preclassic, leading us to now believe that its origin was simultaneous to that of the other regions in Mesoamerica. Thus, the earliest entities in northwestern Yucatan already had seats of power in which their respective leaders wielded the necessary labor forces to erect imposing public constructions of comparable size and skill to those of the architectural monuments in the contemporary capitals of the Zoquean Olmec at La Venta and the Cholan-Maya at Nakbe (Hansen et al. Chapter 7 this volume).

In fact, based on the information compiled over the last ten years, which we shall discuss in the following section, we can now confirm that since the earliest of times the northwestern region of Yucatan also played a primary and parallel role to that of the Peten during the gestational period of Maya civilization. Moreover, it developed within a set of regionally interacting diverse settlements that for the most part emulated each other and not the southern lowlands.

New Evidence Concerning the Origin of Maya Political-Cultural Complexity in the Northern Maya Lowlands

Reevaluating the Middle Preclassic Ceramic Evidence

Recently obtained archaeological evidence tends to substantiate the idea that the earliest sedentary communities in the northern part of the Yucatan Peninsula appeared sometime before 1000 B.C. (see Andrews and Robles Chapter 2 this volume). Archaeologically, these remote groups, which likely spoke an archaic form of Yucatec Maya, are considered to have been creators of a developing Maya ceramic tradition, which can be described as "fancy" monochrome colored pottery with decorative grooves and waxy finish slip. It should also be noted that there appears to be no direct precedent to this ceramic style in the region. This kind of ceramic assemblage, which happens to be the oldest known in northern Yucatan, is categorized as "Early Nabanche" because it is analogous to the distinctive pottery in the complex that was defined by E. W. Andrews V at Komchen, Yucatan. Based on typological arguments, it has been chronologically placed during the second half of the Middle Preclassic period (Andrews V 1986, 1989, 1990; see also Joesink-Mandeville 1970). Recent and more precise calibration of the 16 ^{14}C dates associated with Preclassic material in northwestern Yucatan suggest that Early Nabanche ceramics were originally manufactured some time before 1000 B.C. Additionally, it has been noted that its production carried on without any apparent formal or typological changes until 400 B.C., after which date new ceramic manifestations began to appear and gradually replace the long-standing Early Nabanche tradition (Ceballos and Robles 2012).

Recently, Early Nabanche ceramics were found in isolated contexts while excavating the monumental structures at Poxila (Robles 2004, 2005), Xocnaceh (Gallareta 2004; Gallareta Chapter 11 this volume; Gallareta and Ciau 2007; Stanton and Gallareta 2002), and Tipikal (Peraza et al. 2002). A significant quantity of Early Nabanche materials were recovered within the constructive nuclei of low-lying residential platforms, which were interred beneath the subsequent constructions of sites such as: Serapio Rendón (south of Mérida) (Hernández 2004), Acanceh (Barrales 2002), T'ho (center of Mérida) and its peripheral sites (Ligorred 2007–2008; Maldonado and Echeverría 2004; Robles and Ligorred 2008; Uriarte and Mier 2004), in Yaxuna (Johnstone 2001; Travis and Ardren 2005), as well as Labna (Gallareta 2003), Kiuic (Gallareta et al. 2003, 2005), Oxkintok (Tec 2004) in the Puuc region, and Ek Balam (Bey et al. 1998; Bond-Freeman Chapter 10 this volume; Ceballos 2004) in the western region of Yucatan, among other important areas. Early Nabanche materials have also been retrieved from the deepest layers of the stratigraphic excavations at Yo'okop in the soil that accumulated over the limestone bedrock (Shaw 2002), and various other sites located along the Kantunil-Cancun road (Sierra and Vargas 1995), even the caves in the basin of Yalahau in the northern region of Quintana Roo (Rissolo et al. 2005). They have also been retrieved from various sites excavated along several roads: Muna-Tekax, Kankab-Kantemo, San Diego Buenavista-Pocoboch, and Noh-Bec-El Escondido in the southernmost region in the state of Yucatan (Punto Put) (Ceballos 2005b, 2009a, 2009b), as well as an extensive list of additional sites (Figure 9.1a).

Generally speaking, Early Nabanche ceramics are composed of large bowls with a flat and circular base, thick sides that slightly curve and diverge from one another, as well as pronounced and inclined rounded rims. There are also small jars, jars with spouts, bottles, and *tecomates* or gourd shaped/restricted bowls, although these shapes are less common than bowls. Said materials belong to the following ceramic groups: Joventud (red), Dzudzuquil (mottled "cream-chestnut-red") and Ucu (Chunhinta black). The vessels of the three ceramic groups have a "waxy" surface finish, and frequently exhibit broken or lineal designs whose technique consists of diameter tracings (Andrews V 1986; Ceballos and Robles 2012;

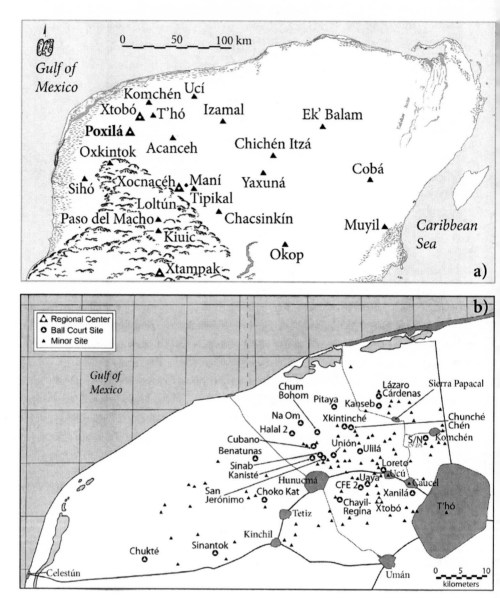

Figure 9.1. (a) Map of the northern Yucatan peninsula indicating the location of sites mentioned in the text whose earliest occupation date to the Middle Preclassic (ca. 800/700–400/300 B.C.); (b) map of the northeast corner of the Yucatan peninsula indicating the spatial distribution of sites that were occupied in the late phase of the Middle Preclassic (ca. 800/700–400/300 B.C.).

Joesink-Mandeville 1970; Robles and Ceballos 2003). "There is nothing primitive in the culture of these people . . . Their pottery was equal, if not superior, to any others that were subsequently produced in northern Yucatan" (Andrews IV 1973:295).

In northwestern Yucatan, the slip on the ceramic sherds of the Joventud group has an inconsistent "reddish-orange" tone with black stains; it's also similar to Joventud Red: Mocho variety from Altar de Sacrificios (however, the shapes of the Joventud vessels from Altar de Sacrificios are different from the Joventud vessels in Yucatan) (see Adams 1971:20, 85; Andrews V 1986:31). Furthermore, bowls and jars from the Dzudzuquil (mottled) group make up a distinctive ceramic style from the Early Nabanche repertoire, whose distribution in the Maya region is restricted to sites on the northwestern Yucatan peninsula. On the other hand, both the black slip color and the surface finishing from the sherds in the Ucu group look like the Chunhinta (black) group from the Peten. It should be noted that it is possible to distinguish the sherds from the Ucu group in Yucatan by their pale red (pink) surface, which on occasion shines through the black slip.

New stratigraphic evidence obtained from various sites in northern Yucatan leaves no doubt that cooking vessels in the Saban (primarily those from the Chancenote brushing type) and Unto-Tipikal (those with brushed decorations coated in a black-to-reddish-brown wash that does not hide striations) groups are also distinctive components of the Early Nabanche ceramic repertoire, and have no comparable types in other parts of the Maya region. Although found in the Middle Preclassic, it is important to mention that archaeological evidence seems to indicate their production increased significantly in the Late Preclassic and Early Classic.

In all the places Early Nabanche ceramics have been unearthed, they exhibit the same consistencies in base color tones and surface finishes, as well as in their use of redundant decorative techniques; additionally they appear to share a comparable repertoire of vessel shapes. However, it is possible to perceive subtle differences within the collections, such as, how the color tones red and chestnut were combined, as well as, the surface finishing consistency and the decorative arrangement. Furthermore, there are regional preferences in the use of certain vessel shapes, which are under current investigation. The presence of "exclusive" ceramic types pertaining to a particular region in Yucatan is also evident, as well as ceramic types of a foreign origin that belong to the contemporary southern Mamom ceramic sphere.

In the eastern part of the state of Yucatan (and the neighboring region of northern Quintana Roo as well) there is a prevalence in sherds that are typologically comparable to those in the Joventud group, although the red-orange slip is homogeneous and adheres better as well, in contrast to the sherds in the Joventud group from the northwestern of Yucatan, whose slip exhibits a gradation of colors from red-orange to yellow, which can be observed in a single sherd.

Another distinctive group of the "Eastern Nabanche" ceramics, which has yet to be specified and whose sherds are still confused with those of the Dzudzuquil group, is characterized by the fact that it exhibits two slip colors: chestnut (yellowish-brown) and red orange; both tones have a homogeneous texture. Said colors alternate on the exterior and interior surface (although they are never found together on the same side); in some cases both sides have been found to manifest only the chestnut color (Ceballos 2004). Either way the two-color chestnut and red unspecified ceramic group is dissimilar to the distinctive Dzudzuquil group mottled "chestnut-red-cream" texture of northwestern Yucatan, which is why the former should be considered a different ceramic group from the latter. Moreover, in the eastern part of the Yucatan state, the mottled sherds from the Dzudzuquil group are scarce, and due to their low frequency, it is likely that they are of a foreign origin.

On the other hand, it is practically impossible to distinguish the sherds from the Ucu group (Chunhinta Black) that are from the eastern and western part of northern Yucatan, since in both regions the sherds manifest the same black translucent matte and the same surface finishes; they also have the same bowl shapes and share similar incised designs.

In the three groups mentioned above, the prevalent vessel shape is that of bowl with flared sides and rounded rims. Usually, in the Eastern Nabanche repertoire, the bowls in the Joventud and unspecified two-color "chestnut and red" ceramic groups exhibit a distinctive ornamentation attained by parallel and horizontal grooves (prior to firing) traced directly over the interior surface of the rim. In some cases the grooves are traced on both sides of the rim (Ceballos 2004).

The Eastern Nabanche repertoire also includes a predominant ceramic group with a homogeneous whitish-cream slip whose surface has a lustrous finishing. The sherds in this group maintain close typological analogies to those in the group El Llanto of Edzna and Yaxuna (see Forsyth 1983; Stanton and Arden 2005; personal observation obtained at the Ceramoteca at

Centro INAH Yucatan). In contrast, ceramics with a cream tone are rare in the Early Nabanche repertoire, not to mention that the scarce sherds that have been found in northwestern Yucatan are basically from the Pital (cream) group and thus of foreign origin.

Lastly, in eastern Yucatan, coarse culinary ceramics are represented by striated pots ("horizontal brushing" pattern) with a narrow bottom and flattened circular base (*monópodos*) that belong to the Chiquila variety from the Chancenote brushing type (Tancah group) (see Brainerd 1958:Figure 65a; Robles 1990:Plate 2a–g; Sanders 1960:252–253, Figure 10d–e). Whereas in the northwest, the use of globular jars from the Chancenote variety ("vertical brushing" pattern) was prevalent (see Andrews V 1988:52, 1989; Smith 1971:31). Furthermore, the Eastern Nabanche repertoire does not include Unto-Tipikal black-red over striation jars, which are common in the contemporary sites of northwestern Yucatan.

Towards the south, within the "Puuc-Chenes" low physiographic hilly region (Bolonchen district) Middle Preclassic ceramics manifest other peculiarities (see Ball and Taschek 2007). Just as in the eastern region of the state of Yucatan, in the Puuc-Chenes hill region a Middle Preclassic ceramic tradition was established, and currently it is comprised of four monochrome ceramic groups: red, chestnut, black, and cream. The distinctive features of the ceramic groups listed above consist of a notable hardness in the paste with which it was made and a glossy rather than waxy finish on the surface of its sherds (Ceballos 2005b, 2008a, 2008b, 2008c, 2009a, 2009b). These characteristics draw similarities between the Puuc-Chenes Preclassic sherds with chestnut and red tones and the Late Classic waxy vessels in the local Muna Slate and Teabo red groups. In fact, if it were not for the notable difference in the shapes of the vessels, in many cases ceramicists would have a hard time separating Preclassic sherds from Late Classic ones.

Either way, within the Puuc-Chenes hill region there is also a prevalence in sherds that are typologically comparable to those in the Joventud group, although the slip is an exception since it exhibits an array of cherry and orange color tones. Sherds can be decorated with straight incised lines that have been traced over the exterior side. Comparatively, both the simplicity in the incised designs as well as the orange color tone at the base associate the materials from the Puuc-Chenes region to those in the Chatel ("orange") group from Edzna, which is the equivalent to the local Joventud (red) group from the Campeche-Guatemala Peten region (personal observation obtained at the Ceramoteca in Centro INAH Yucatan; see Forsyth 1983), therefore differing from the materials found in the red-orange Joventud group from northwestern Yucatan.

Everything seems to indicate that in the Puuc-Chenes hill region, Preclassic ceramics that are of a homogeneous chestnut color are far more numerous than those of a mottled chestnut color from the Dzudzuquil group. In fact, Dzudzuquil sherds are made with a compact paste, this along with the reduced number of finds suggests that these constitute a type of local copy from the traditional mottled Dzudzuquil, which is unique to the northwestern plain in Yucatan (see Ball and Taschek 2007).

In the Puuc-Chenes zone, pottery with a black slip from the Middle Preclassic is predominantly monochrome with a translucent texture, it also strikes a closer resemblance to the pottery from the Peten's Chunhinta group than to that in the Ucu group from northern Yucatan. On occasion, the sherds display decorative traced incised lines on the exterior surface, which contrasts with the bowls from the Ucu black from northern Yucatan, which is not only made with a softer paste, but is also decorated with a wide variety of fluting and incised complex designs (see above).

Lastly, just as in the eastern region of Yucatan State, chestnut colored Preclassic pottery from the Puuc-Chenes hill region is also numerous and comparable to that of the El Llanto (whitish-cream slip) group established by Donald Forsyth at Edzna (Ceballos 2008, 2009; see also Forsyth 1983).

Based on our present understanding we can conclude that if the Early Nabanche regional repertoires from northern Yucatan formed part of the seemingly sudden emergence that gave rise to the traditional Preclassic "waxy" Maya pottery, then all of these constitute cultural manifestations with their own regional distinctiveness, whose production began at the same time the Mamom "twin" tradition from the southern Maya lowlands came about. Thus, Early Nabanche materials should no longer be considered a product that derived as a result of diffused southern Mamom ceramics toward northern Yucatan, but rather as a particular northern ceramic tradition comprising various regional manifestations, which was part of the interactive mosaic of analogous cultural regional expressions that characterized the genesis of the multi-ethnic Maya civilization.

Late Middle Preclassic Monumental Centers: Xocnaceh and Poxila

The evidence at hand seems to indicate that the pioneering Maya communities that established themselves in Yucatan during the Middle Preclassic period densely populated certain regions of Yucatan in a short period of time. This occurred in regions like the northwestern crook of the peninsula, for which we have substantiating findings. Over 116 sites (Figure 9.1b) have been registered in the area as Middle Preclassic establishments. Such a figure was not surpassed until 1,000 years later during the Late/ Terminal Classic (ca. 550–1100 A.D.) (Anderson 2003, 2009; Anderson et al. 2004; Anderson et al. Chapter 8 this volume). Demographic densities of this caliber are particularly intriguing considering the area: not only is this one of the most arid regions in northern Yucatan peninsula, its soils are of notable insalubrious composites. Thus, erroneous suppositions of an underdeveloped agricultural system led to the unfounded conclusions of greatly reduced pre-Hispanic populations. In the fertile northern base of the Ticul low range or Puuc hills region adjacent to the southeast, evidence has been unearthed that dated just prior to the origins of political-cultural complexity among the Maya that inhabited the northern calcareous plains.

Furthermore, along these northern foothills of Ticul's low range or Puuc zone, which extends from Maxcanu in the northwest to Tekax in the southeast, new evidence has been found concerning the emergence of Maya civilization in Yucatan. Over the course of many centuries, the accumulated rainfall that runs down the Puuc hills along this extended region has transported sediments and created an elongated stretch of fertile land that is just under 10 km wide—today known as "Yucatan's Orchard." The archaeological excavations carried out along this region in sites like Xocnaceh (Gallareta 2004; Gallareta and Ciau 2007; Stanton and Gallareta 2002) and Poxila have revealed the existence of two pristine Maya imposing seats of power, which have been dated in correspondence to the second part of the Middle Preclassic period (800/700–400/300 B.C.). These sites not only harbor opulent edifices of monumental stature, but also stay true to the ascribed styles and distinguished features of Maya architecture.

The site of Xocnaceh is situated over the northern foothills of the Puuc region, alongside the road between Pustunich and Yotholin (see Figure 9.1a, Gallareta Chapter 11 this volume). Its center gives rise to an impressive acropolis comprised of a vast foundation whose dimensions reach almost 150 m on each side, while its height extends 8 m above the calcareous surface. At the top of this immense basement rise nine structures surrounding an open plaza. One of these structures, situated at the furthermost point in the north, appears to be a triadic pyramid that stands 20 m above the terrain's natural surface, and 12 m above the vast foundation's surface (Figure 9.2) (Gallareta 2004; Gallareta and Ciau 2007).

The pre-Hispanic settlement of Xocnaceh extends outwardly in every

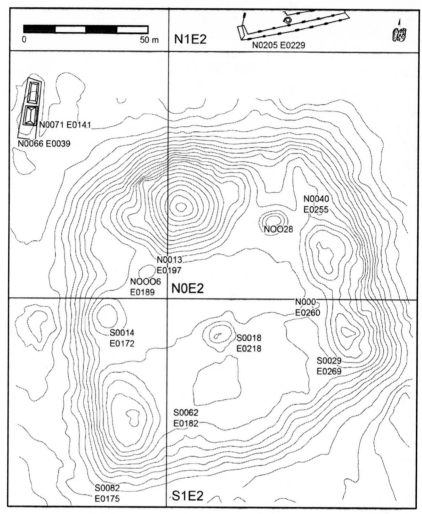

Figure 9.2. Topographic map of the central acropolis of Xocnaceh, at the northern base of the sierrita from Ticul or Puuc, Yucatan (courtesy of Tomas Gallareta Negron).

direction from its main acropolis, with a maximum distance of 700 m toward the south. The excavations of a series of stratigraphic test pits indicated that the construction of various residential structures dated within the Middle Preclassic period. Additionally, Puuc style "boot-cut stones" and distinctive sherds from the Cehpech ceramic horizon (see Smith 1971:144–169) were retrieved from most of the structures' surfaces, which suggests that a considerable sector of the residential zone was reoccupied for some time during the Late/Terminal Classic (ca. A.D. 550–1050) (Gallareta 2004; Gallareta and Ciau 2007).

More importantly, on top of the vast foundation (within the acropolis's plaza floor) a broad 2 × 4 m test pit was dug (Test pit: NO56EO49), which reached a depth of just over 7 m in the constructive nucleus. During the excavation, several layers of sealed stucco were uncovered before reaching the limestone bedrock. It was revealed that the grand foundation in Xocnaceh's acropolis is the result of two superimposed structures, the second of which has a greater volume. With the exception of intrusive offerings that consisted of the bottom part of a Postclassic Navula censer, a striated Yokat jar from the Cehpech horizon, two bowls from the Joventud group, and a vase from the Dzudzuquil group (the moment these offerings were deposited, three of the first stucco floors were breached), the ceramic sample obtained from the sequent layers of constructive fill corresponds to a repertoire that is similar to Early Nabanche materials from the Yucatecan plains. Additionally, in the materials that turned up, a considerable number of sherds shared various characteristics similar to those found in the Nabanche pottery pertaining to the contiguous Puuc-Chenes hill region to the south (described above). Moreover, the ceramics procured while retrieving materials from the initial clearing phase of the acropolis's foundation that has been consolidated, exhibits the same mix of northern Early Nabanche/Puuc-Chenes composition that corresponds to the same time period (Ceballos, personal observation obtained from the Xocnaceh collection; Gallareta 2004; Gallareta and Ciau 2007). None of this is surprising since Xocnaceh's location between the Puuc-Chenes hills region and the limestone plains in northwestern Yucatan's crook was undoubtedly a factor that led Xocnaceh to develop as strategic center linking the Maya communities that inhabited what is now the northeastern part of Campeche and northwestern Yucatan.

And so, the archaeological evidence obtained thus far leaves no doubt that the immense acropolis along with a considerable amount of the residential structures at Xocnaceh were constructed during the Middle Preclassic, and that the site had been virtually abandoned before the Late Preclassic period. After a prolonged hiatus, various residential structures were dismantled at Xocnaceh during the Late/Terminal Classic to make way for new constructions over their surfaces (Gallareta and Ciau 2007).

A portion of the bottom part of the eastern side was liberated revealing a vast foundation formed of three superimposed sections, each one consisting of a wall whose veneer is composed of rectangular stone blocks. Vestiges of an old stairway that leads to the superior part of the foundation were also found on this side, their lateral walls contained block-shaped veneers as well. Structures on top of the vast foundation also display stone block-shaped veneer walls.

Additionally, the rows of stone blocks from the walls of the three super-imposed sections of the vast foundation are each slightly recessed, forming pendent steps (Gallareta 2004; Gallareta and Ciau 2007). Both of Xocanceh's architectural features are of paramount importance, since they correspond to the same hewed-stone style and construction system as those employed in the outer walls of the structures from the relatively smaller acropolis in the contemporaneous site of Poxila.

Poxila is located 25 km southwest of the city of Mérida and 65 km northwest of Xocanceh (see map, Figure 9.1a). The site is located at a point in which the lower deciduous jungle that characterizes the semi-arid environment of Yucatan's northwestern corner becomes the dominant landscape. This pre-Hispanic settlement harbors an architectural nucleus surrounded by a series of structures and low-lying mounds distributed around a radius that extends just over 600 m (Figure 9.3a). The surface sherds obtained from mapped "residential" platforms suggest that most of them were initially occupied during the Middle Preclassic, and, just as in Xocanceh's case, these were reoccupied during the Late/Terminal Classic (ca. 550–1050 A.D.) after having been semi-abandoned for centuries.

At the heart of the settlement lies an impressive acropolis, which we have named Structure 1. Structure 1 consists of a wide platform that is 100 m long from east to west and 90 m long from north to south; its maximum height reaches 2.5 m above the calciferous flooring along the entire eastern perimeter; additionally, a vast-rectangular foundation was erected, known as Structure 1-a, with a north-south length of 80 m and an east-west width of 40 m, and an approximate height of 10 m. On its front, the foundation remains in a relatively good state of preservation, where the elongated exterior walls and the three superimposed constructions are concerned, as does the 17 m wide staircase that comes together at the center and grants access to the superior part of the third construction. As in the staircase on the eastern side of Xocnaceh's acropolis, both of the sidewalls of Poxila's 1-a staircase are flanked by a massive series of large, stepped rectangular blocks (it should be noted that the "blocks" that adorn the Poxila staircase are smaller and in a better state of preservation than those at Xocanceh).

At the center of the superior part of Structure 1-a, the semi-destroyed exterior walls of what would have been a fourth superior section of reduced dimensions are still present; these walls originally comprised the structure's zenith. After remaining in a state of ruin for various centuries, the superior

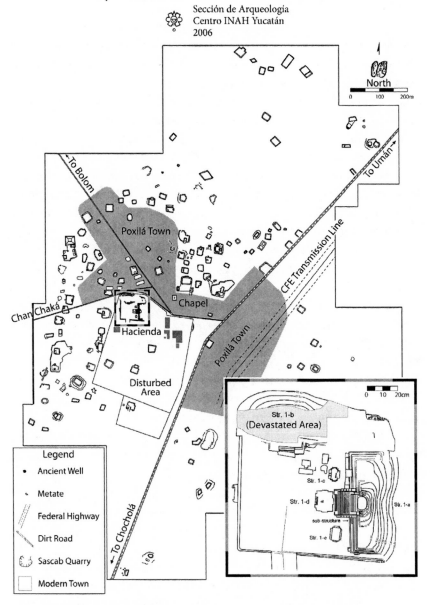

Figure 9.3. Map of the pre-Hispanic settlement of Poxila, municipality of Uman, Yucatan. Evidence indicates that the majority of the mapped structures were occupied in the Middle Preclassic; inset shows central acropolis of Poxila, municipality of Uman, Yucatan, indicating the area that was excavated during the 2003–2005 field seasons.

part of the Structure 1-a was dismantled and its construction material re-utilized to build an isolated 4 m high pyramid-shaped mound during the Late Classic which today sits atop the highest part of Structure 1-a (Figure 9.3b).

After removing the vegetation covering the western facade and the northern and southern sides of Structure 1-a's foundation, it was revealed that the central staircases' exterior walls and those of the other stairways were constructed with parallel-piped rectangular stone blocks identical to those used in the acropolis at Xocnaceh. Analogously, the rows of rocks distributed along the foundation's walls in Structure 1-a also show succes-sive recessing, which gives them all slightly sloped steps.

In the broader parts of Structure 1-a's base, remnants of an "earthy/brownish-yellow" stucco surface finish are still present. This allows us to suppose that the entirety of Structure 1-a at Poxila's acropolis was originally covered with an "earthy/brownish-yellow" colored plaster, which would have given the base the appearance of a "mountain of earth." It is possible that this alluded to the like-minded esoteric concept of an earthen pyramid found in the Olmec capital of La Venta, Tabasco, which was at the pinnacle of its splendor at the time.

With the exception of the pyramidal mound that was added during the Late Classic to the superior part of Structure 1-a and various stratigraphic test pits excavated within the base-pyramid, all of the ceramic evidence obtained from the construction fill verifies that the structures forming the Poxila acropolis date exclusively to the Middle Preclassic Early Nabanche horizon. Additionally, distinctive sherds that correspond to "Puuc-Chenes Nabanche" ceramics were also obtained from the primary contexts at Pox-ila, although in lesser numbers than those obtained at Xocnaceh. The lat-ter can be explained by the fact that both sites shared numerous affinities, and because Poxila held closer ties to its adjacent and contemporary Maya communities located in the northwestern plains of Yucatan than with those located much further along the south in the Puuc-Chenes hill region.

On the other hand, in a hollow situated over the inferior part of the southern side of the staircase in Structure 1-a, the rounded corners (south-west) of three constructions with stairs were found. This buried foundation reached a height of approximately 5 m; its construction is of an even ear-lier date and remains unexplored to this day. Uncovering a terminal Early Nabanche offering (which consisted of a vase from the Joventud Red group containing a tabular "green emerald" jade bead and a dial-disc lid made from a fragment of a Tipikal red-over-brushed type pot) deposited in the

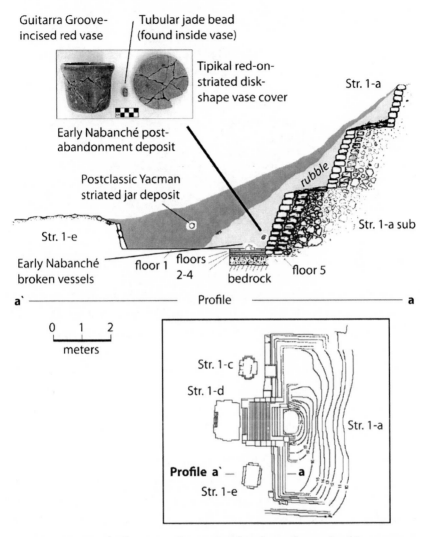

Figure 9.4. Context of Offerings 1 and 2, recovered on the southern side of Structure 1-a of the acropolis at Poxila.

debris that covered the vestiges of the first body on the southern side of Structure 1-a (Figure 9.4), allows us to assume that even before the Middle Preclassic period had concluded, the acropolis at Poxila had already succumb to abandonment (Robles 2004).

There are three additional low-lying platforms located in front of and on both sides of Structure 1-a's staircase, as well as the remains of a semi-destroyed mound situated at the extreme north of the platform. These constitute the remaining structures comprising Poxila's acropolis.

Figure 9.5. Itzamna deity masks on Structure 1-c on the acropolis at Poxila (*top*) and Structure IV at Becan (*bottom*).

The platform known as Structure 1-c, located on the northern side of the central staircase, is noteworthy since the vestiges of a stone mask with a robust nose and outlined rectangular eyes are attached to its southern side (Figure 9.5, top). It is likely that the mask was covered with stucco during ancient times; the mouth and jaw are noticeably absent and the rims of the nasal apertures mark the base's limit.

The "unfinished" shape of the mask at Poxila is analogous to the serpentine mask of *Itzamna* also known as "the monster of the earth," that adorns the step on the northern facade of the Late Classic Structure IV at Becan (Figure 9.5, bottom). The Middle Preclassic mask at Poxila is greater in size, not quite as refined and much older, but it seems to be the prototype for the Maya representation of the Classic *Itzamna* in Yucatan. In fact, today the vestiges of the Poxila mask constitute the oldest registered representation in Yucatan for a mythic creature from Maya cosmology; its attributes and esoteric symbolism differ from those of the widely diffused Olmec ideological system of that time.

The rest of the vast basal platform's surface located off the acropolis of Poxila is free of other constructions and forms an extensive open plaza that undoubtedly served as a space reserved for the realization of festivities and the contemporary ruling class's most important rituals.

Unquestionably, both Poxila and Xocnaceh operated as primary centers of political and economic power within their respective polities. Their contemporaneity, along with the fact that the acropolises of both sites share the same architectural style and identical ceramic repertoire, lead us to believe that both sites form part of the same larger cultural region. Moreover, the relatively smaller size of Poxila's acropolis suggests to us that, while during the Middle Preclassic its leader exerted complete control over its immediate territory, he may have been subordinate to the ruler of Xocnaceh, who was likely the paramount chief of the entire fertile region that lay along the northern base of the Puuc hill region.

Olmec Jades and Late Middle Preclassic Interregional Interaction

The excavations at Poxila recovered jade pendants in contexts that date within the Early Nabanche horizon. One of them is a small tubular jade bead with bi-conical perforations and the other is a small rectangular pectoral with rounded corners also known as a rectangular clam-shaped pendant with two apertures from which it can be hung. Based on the artistic quality as well as the shapes and green emerald and dark translucid green color of many of the jade pendants at Poxila, it appears many of them are similar to some of the "Olmec" shapes that originate from Chacsinkin, a town situated at the northern base of Ticul's small range, 50 km southeast of Xocnaceh and 106 km southeast of Poxila.

The opulent collection of 17 Olmec jade pendants from Chacsinkin was found haphazardly by contemporary inhabitants from the adjoining town when part of a pre-Hispanic mound's (of an unknown constructive period) exposed wall collapsed. Based on a comparative study that focused on both the shapes of the pendants and the iconography they display, E. Wyllys Andrews V, who studied the collection, postulated that the jade from Chacsinkin originally formed part of the widely diffused Middle Preclassic Olmec ideological system, whose chief presiding center at the time was La Venta in Tabasco. Thus, it is probable that jade was imported from Olmec territories (Andrews V 1986:11–29) (see Figure 9.6). Before this finding at Chacsinkin, there were only about 12 registered Middle Preclassic Olmec jade relics in northern Yucatan; these were found in later archaeological contexts, making it impossible to precisely identify when the materials were imported (Andrews V 1986:28–29).

In the particular case of Chacsinkin, Andrews V suggested it was logical to infer that the acquisition of Olmec jade probably occurred at some point during the Early Nabanche horizon, as it unquestionably corresponds to the second half of the Middle Preclassic, or rather the period of apogee for Olmec civilization on the Gulf Coast. This is primarily because when Andrews V was studying the ceramic collection of La Venta obtained by Drucker in 1942, he identified a considerable number of Early Nabanche

Figure 9.6. (*Upper*) Examples of the "jade" ornaments discovered in northern Yucatan, whose acquisition dates to the Middle Preclassic: (a) Part of the collection of "Olmec jades" from Chaksinkin; (b) pendants from Poxila; (c) ornaments from Tipikal; (d) recovered from pectoral Olmec San Gervasio, Cozumel. (*Lower*) Examples of "Olmec jades" from Costa Rica, CA: (e) National Museum of Costa Rica; (f) "chest-spoon" with incised design representing an Olmec mask with character; (g) "spoon chest" with Maya hieroglyphs encountered in Guanacaste. In particular, the pectorals from Yucatan that represent fluttering parrots, exhibit a singular formal and conceptual affinity with those from Costa Rica.

rims from bowls; these mainly belonged to the waxy "reddish-orange" Joventud group, while various sherds belonged to the Dzudzuquil group. Furthermore, while comparing Drucker's stratigraphic data, Andrews V realized that Early Nabanche sherds appear in the final part of La Venta's complex A (within contemporary terminology this is referred to as the

Late La Venta ceramic complex) (Andrews V 1986:34–49; see Rust 1992). This would imply that during the Middle Preclassic's final stage, Maya from northeastern Yucatan traveled with relative frequency to Olmec territories on the Gulf Coast, and returned not only with highly coveted Olmec jade jewelry and other important trade goods, but with grey obsidian blades, different sized ceremonial basalt "hand axes," and handmade basalt *metates* or grinding stones as well. Many fragments of these products, whose origins are notably foreign, have been found in Middle Preclassic contexts at excavations carried out in Xocnaceh and Poxila, as well as in numerous structures in Mérida's surrounding areas that were only recently explored (Gallareta 2004; Gallareta and Ciau 2007; Peniche May 2008c; Peraza et al. 2002; Robles 2004, 2005).

Additionally, a considerable number of bowl sherds were recovered from recent excavations in the Olmec site of San Andres, Tabasco, which is situated 9 km northeast of La Venta. These sherds (12% of the Middle Preclassic local ceramic collection) exhibit analogous base colors and surface finishes to those found in the Dzudzuquil (mottled chestnut-to-cream) and Joventud (red-orange) groups of the Early Nabanche tradition. These sherds were found in contexts associated with the Puente and Franco ceramic complexes that have been reliably dated with ^{14}C between 800/750 and 400/450 B.C. The ceramics indicate that pottery with Early Nabanche characteristics is more abundant during the earlier stage of the Franco ceramic complex between 750/650 and 550/450 B.C. (Von Nagy 2003; Von Nagy et al. 2002).

It is probable that pottery exhibiting Early Nabanche traits was also imported from sites as far away as the regional Olmec capital of Tres Zapotes, situated on the western slope of Los Tuxtlas range in south-central Veracruz (Figure 9.7). In a recent revision of the ceramic collections obtained from the Early Tres Zapotes complex retrieved by Drucker in the same site, Andrews V was able to reliably identify at least 12 sherds from the Dzudzuquil group (from the Majan red-over-chestnut and Tumben incised types), he also noticed the close similarity among types and shapes of culinary pottery with Chancenote Striated vessels, and, especially with the black-to-brown-reddish Brushed Unto-Tipikal from northern Yucatan (Andrews V 1986:42–43, note 4). The data mentioned above confirms the related idea that during the second half of the Middle Preclassic the Maya in the northwestern part of Yucatan maintained closer trade relations with the Zoque from the "Olmec Polity" of La Venta, Tabasco, than with their contemporary counterparts in the Peten region, with whom they seemingly

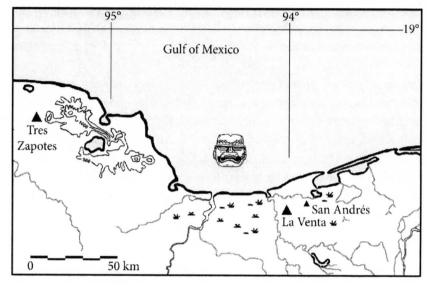

Figure 9.7. Map indicating the location of sites in the "Olmec territory" of the Gulf of Mexico where Early Nabanche ceramics from northwest Yucatan have been discovered.

held limited ties (Joesink-Mandeville 1977; See Andrews V 1986, 1990; Ball 1977:79).

Remarkably, even after half a century of arduous and extensive archaeological investigations, consisting of both site analysis and archaeological excavations in Middle Preclassic architectural contexts, we have not been able to identify a single "Olmec" sherd in Yucatan that originated from the Tabasco-Veracruz coast. Thus, everything that was previously mentioned strongly suggests that during the second half of the Middle Preclassic a predominant one-way long distance trade system was established (at least within our region of study) that ran from northwestern Yucatan to Olmec territories in the isthmus. This is why we suppose that the Yucatec-Maya from northwestern Yucatan were the prime navigators that regulated the Gulf's littoral trade at the time, granting them access to products and ideas that originated overseas, particularly in the Gulf coast of the Isthmus of Tehuantepec. To attain such domination of trade routes the Maya had various strategically placed outposts within the most important Olmec centers, and so their countrymen living in these enclaves would have been the users of the abundant ceramics that display Early Nabanche characteristics that have been found in these centers.

The confirmation of the temporal correlation between the period of the Olmec jades from Chacsinkin and the Early Nabanche ceramic horizon proposed by Andrews V became evident in recent salvage excavations in the site of Tipikal located 17 km northeast of Xocnaceh. In fact, during the exploration at Tipikal of Structure 6 which dated within the Late Classic, the vestiges of an interred substructure were uncovered; its constructive phase was dated within the Middle Preclassic period. This early edifice consists of a low-lying foundation over which a room (temple?) with an elliptical base, with wide walls and a thatch roof was constructed; it is still possible to identify the wooden posts' points of insertion in the stucco floor. Substructure 6's walls are made of parallelepiped stone blocks with shapes similar to those found in Xocnaceh's and Poxila's acropolis (Figure 9.8a). Based on the previously mentioned data and the site's location, it is likely that Tipikal was a third-ranked site that was incorporated into Xocnaceh's area of influence. Furthermore, inside the apsidal enclosure at Tipikal, an offering comprised of 10 vessels pertaining to the ceramic groups Joventud, Dzudzuquil, Ucu, and Saban (reclassified by the authors) from the Early Nabanche horizon was recovered from the stucco floor. Along with the vessels, four necklace beads and five jade pendants were recovered; their shapes are copies of the Olmec jades recovered in the neighboring "ruins" of Chacsinkin (Peraza et al. 2002:265, photo 17). The spoon-shaped pendant with a "parrot" profile recovered from Tipikal is virtually identical to the Olmec spoon-shaped pectorals that depict "parrots flapping their wings" found in Chacsinkin, Yucatan, and Guanacaste, Costa Rica (see Andrews V 1986).

Given its geographic location, we assume that early Maya leaders from the fertile region situated in the northern base of the Puuc hills were the ones that initially stressed the importance of Olmec jade as ritual paraphernalia of prime value. It is likely that this came about as a way to appropriate a symbolic means of proven authority that would sanction their acquired dominant role by prestigious association. This could have been an ideological measure to counteract their rivals' similar prerogatives, since they too meant to preside over pristine Maya political formation, which given the grandeur of the monument erected to their leaders was perhaps the most opulent that existed in the northern Yucatan peninsula in Middle Preclassic times.

Summary and Conclusions

And so, the most recent archaeological excavations that have been carried out in sites along the northern Yucatan Peninsula have revealed isolated Middle Preclassic stratigraphic contexts as well as new Early Nabanche

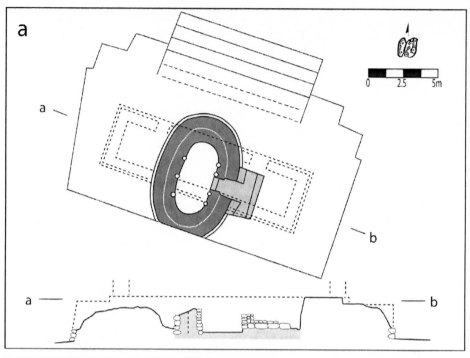

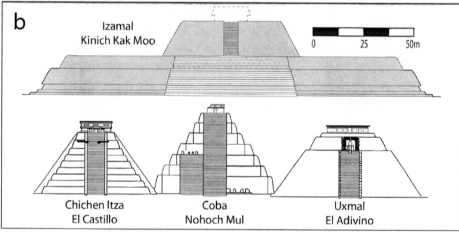

Figure 9.8. (a) Plan and section drawing of the apsidal enclosure (sub-structure 6) at Tipikal, Yucatan, whose construction goes back to the Middle Preclassic. Below, the northern part of the apsidal enclosure conserved after the conclusion of its exploration (courtesy of Carlos Peraza Lópe); (b) *above*, aerial view of Kinich Kak Moo at Izamal, the huge monument which began to be constructed in the megalithic style in the Late Preclassic (c. 400/300 B.C.–A.D. 250) and reached its height of splendor in the Early Classic (A.D. 250–550); *below*, an illustration of the magnitude of Kinich Kak Moo de Izamal, comparing it with the dimensions of the major structures of Chichen Itza, Coba and Uxmal from the subsequent Late/Terminal Classic Period (A.D. 550–1100).

collections. In light of these findings, we now have a more abundant and diverse representative sample that has allowed us to discern with greater clarity the distinctive ceramic components of the region as well as the formal and typological characteristics of primeval Maya ceramic traditions in the northern lowlands. Additionally, we now have new data that indicates, with the exception of Quintana Roo's eastern coast, Early Nabanche pottery quickly diffused throughout the entire northern part of the peninsula during the Middle Preclassic. We have been able to interpret these circumstances as a reflection of a rapid dispersion of the pioneering Maya-Yucatecan groups in the northern lowlands, or an accelerated population increase in the northern part of the state as a result of innovative agricultural techniques during the Middle Preclassic.

Nevertheless, a study is still underway to verify how regional variations and/or temporal modifications were related to variation in vessel shapes, decorative patterns, and paste composition within the Early Nabanche ceramic repertoire. It is equally important to note that we still need additional radiometric dates from isolated contexts that will grant us the greater chronological precision necessary for understanding the processes by which Early Nabanche ceramics diffused throughout the northern peninsula and the formation process of each complex pristine Maya society in Yucatan during the Middle Preclassic.

The origins of Early Nabanche ceramics are a complex matter. So far, sophisticated Early Nabanche ceramics have been the oldest samples obtained from every explored site; to further complicate matters, it appears this was not an in situ ceramic development (for an alternative view, see Andrews V et al. Chapter 4 this volume). In light of this, we assume that the pioneering Maya groups that established themselves in Yucatan during the Middle Preclassic also brought agriculture and previously developed ceramic techniques to the region that allowed them to produce "elegant" Early Nabanche pottery locally. And so, perhaps the most prominent question at hand is "Exactly who were the precursors from whom the Yucatec-Maya obtained advanced manufacturing techniques and the decorative patterns that adorn Early Nabanche vessels?" (Andrews V 1990; Rissolo et al. 2005), and more importantly, "How was it that without any prior existence of any sedentary-agricultural local communities in the area, the most remote Maya groups in northern Yucatan rapidly developed into competent complex societies during the Middle Preclassic?" This is particularly remarkable when one considers that at this exact moment other pristine sedentary Mesoamerican communities were still centuries away from the sociopolitical development that was necessary to reach this level of complexity. Of course, to unravel the mystery behind these burgeoning questions will take years/decades of further research.

The ongoing archaeological excavations in Yucatan have begun to change our previously held conceptions regarding the Middle Preclassic; where Maya archaeology is concerned, this remains the primeval stage in northern Yucatan. Everything seems to indicate that the Yucatec-Maya occupied northern Yucatan before 1000 B.C. Around this time Cholan-Maya groups, likely the bearers of Mamom ceramics, infiltrated the Mirador Basin in the Campeche-Guatemala Peten; after 800 B.C. their cultural predominance reached the "pre-Mamom" communities of Xe, Eb, Swasey, and Cunil, located in the southern lowlands (Andrews V 1990; Ball and Taschek 2000; Clark et al. 2000; Cheetham 2005; Forsyth and Hansen 2007; Hansen 2005).

Some of the pioneering Yucatec-Maya groups, especially those who settled in the Yucatecan plains that reach the northern part of the sierra Puuc, attained a far more complex political-cultural state than the traditionally depicted "modest village-type genesis." The existence of discrete cultural regions like Xocnaceh, with an established hierarchy among sites of at least three ranges, as well as the presence of powerful centers that harbor monumental architecture of a certain caliber, as is the case for Xocnaceh and Poxila, provide solid evidence that during the second part of the Middle Preclassic the earliest Maya to inhabit the northern part of Yucatan were able to establish relatively stable, or rather *emerging regional states* as centralized political-cultural entities. Their leaders exerted the necessary political control that enabled them to extract the sufficient economic resources and communal labor forces that are required to erect monumental constructions.

In the extra-regional landscape, the Maya centers that pertain to the first complex societies in northwestern Yucatan evolved while the powerful and prestigious Zoque-Olmec site of La Venta, located in the littoral Gulf of Mexico, and the site of Nakbe in the Campeche-Guatemala Peten developed as well. However, current evidence suggests that during this time the Yucatec-Maya held closer ties with the Olmecs on the Tabasco-Veracruz coast than with the Cholan-Maya in the southern lowlands.

After 400/350 B.C., that is, after the fall of La Venta, this initial stage began to give rise to another of much greater political and cultural complexity, in which the Maya world emerges as the only driving force of southeastern Mesoamerica (Clark et al. 2000). The ancient Olmec order perished, and although Nakbe continued to grow architecturally, it would soon be replaced by a new supra-regional seat of power known as El Mirador, which realized perhaps the most colossal of Maya constructions ever built in pre-Hispanic times. Other than the Mirador Basin, the southern Maya lowlands gave rise to a new era of prolific constructions whose size and complexity reached far greater feats than ever before, in places like Tikal, Uaxactun, and Rio Azul in the Guatemalan Peten, Calakmul, El Tigre in southern Campeche, etc. (Clark et al. 2000:480–484; Vargas 2001:98–105), these powerful centers would later reach other newly established sites such as Cerros in Belize's northern coast (Freidel 1986; Freidel Chapter 15 this volume).

The abandonment of the northwestern peninsula's pristine sites like Xocnaceh and Poxila resulted in their preserved state of ruin (which has facilitated archaeological explorations), this would later impel the establishment of other metropolitan sites (political centers) in the relatively distant regions of T'ho (Mérida), Izamal, and Ake, where each site's respective leaders would erect even greater monumental constructions that have been classified as megalithic architecture (Figure 9.8a). These new Yucatec-Maya powerful centers, along with their neighboring "Peten-like" rival cities of Oxkintok and Yaxuna, would be the dominant political-cultural forces in northern Yucatan peninsula during the Late Preclassic (400/300 B.C.–300 A.D.) and the Early Classic (300 A.D.–550 A.D.) periods.

10

The Preclassic Period

A View of Complexity in the Residential Settlement of Ek Balam

TARA BOND-FREEMAN

Traditional excavation strategies of the Maya lowlands have yielded Middle and Late Preclassic deposits that are useful for understanding the rise of complexity. At the Maya archaeological site of Ek Balam, located in northeastern Yucatan, Mexico, excavations from the area surrounding the monumental site center yielded Middle Preclassic deposits even though the largest occupation of the site dates to the Late Classic period which lies over the earlier occupation (Figure 10.1). Although the limits of this chapter do not permit a full discussion of the analytical strategies employed to study excavated material from Ek Balam, primarily from construction fill deposits (see Bond-Freeman 2007), the importance of using such data to better understand the rise of complexity in the Maya region is revealed. From such data the beginnings of a residential settlement pattern for the late Middle Preclassic period is presented as well as a brief discussion of the transition to the Late Preclassic period and information about the transition of village life during this ancient time at the site of Ek Balam. This study adds to the small corpus of information about the settlement during the Middle Preclassic for the northeastern part of the Yucatan peninsula (Bey 2006; Glover and Amador 2005; Johnstone 2005; Rissolo et al. 2005; Villamil 2009).

Project Overview

The Maya archaeological site of Ek Balam is located approximately 51 km northeast of Chichen Itza and 60 km northwest of Coba (Figure 10.1), in northeastern Yucatan. Ek Balam has an occupation that spans from the Middle Preclassic to the Colonial period (600 B.C.–A.D. 1600); however, it

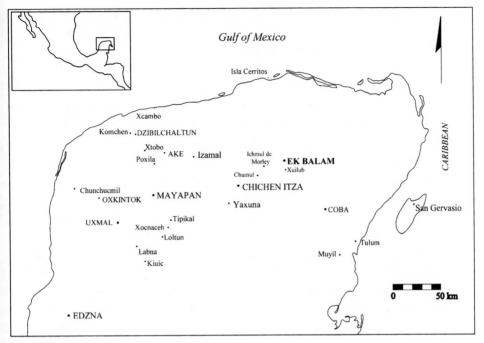

Figure 10.1. Map showing site of Ek Balam and other Maya archaeological sites in northern Yucatan.

is frequently recognized for its Late to Terminal Classic occupation (A.D. 600–1050). Excavations by the Instituto Nacional de Antropología e Historia (INAH) directed by Leticia Vargas de la Pena and Victor R. Castillo (1999; Vargas 2005), revealed an elaborate tomb dating to the Classic period located in a 31-m-high pyramid with remains of the Late Classic king Ukit Kan Le'k Tok'as well as ceramic vessels, jade pieces, obsidian blades and other regal items (Lacadena 2003, 2004; Schuster 2000).

Prior to and during the INAH excavations, research for the Ek Balam Project was conducted by William Ringle and George Bey from 1986 to 1999 (Ringle and Bey 1989, 1994, 1995, 1998) at Ek Balam and surrounding sites (Houck 2004; Smith 2000), which constituted some of the first archaeological explorations in northeastern Yucatan. The data in this chapter was collected by the Ek Balam Project.

The survey work conducted by the Ek Balam Project has revealed that the site covers over 12 km² of continuous settlement. Approximately 3.3 km² of this area has been mapped by the project (Ringle et al. 2004). This survey included 2.25 km² of the site, with an additional section extending eastward, associated with the exploration of the three longest *sacbeob*, or causeways (Ringle et al. 2004). A settlement survey was conducted by dividing areas around the walled site center into 500 m² quadrants, then cutting survey paths around the periphery and through the quadrant at 50 m intervals, creating a grid. Nearly 700 structures were mapped within the survey boundaries. Structures located in the survey paths were cleared and artifacts were systematically collected from the surface of most mounds (Bey et al. 1998). Selected mapped structures were then excavated in order to address project research goals. The later occupation at Ek Balam has left widespread structural ruins visible at the surface and distributed in a layout with much in common with other lowland Maya monumental centers.

The excavation strategy of the Ek Balam Project is noted for its innovative focus on the platforms surrounding the monumental center rather than focusing primarily on monumental architecture in the site core. A minimum of one and, depending on the investigation, up to fifty 2 × 2 m units or trenches were excavated into no less than 42 platforms, both residential and likely ceremonial platforms in later times, with the goal of sampling all aspects of the later construction history of the community around the center, with far less than usual concentration on the center itself. Consequently, many excavations were shallow and extensive rather than deep, however, a few key units, provided depths of up to 2.5 m; considered deep for Yucatan stratigraphy, and provided valuable data from the Preclassic period. One such test unit was excavated on Structure HT-12 that was approximately 2.5 m deep and provided an invaluable ceramic sequence for this research.

Three lines of evidence—natural stratigraphy and excavated levels in addition to the ceramic data—were used in this study to provide a more accurate understanding of the changes in the settlement pattern from the Middle Preclassic to the Late Preclassic periods. These data were also used to evaluate changes or increases in complexity.

The Middle Preclassic Balam Phase at Ek Balam

Balam Ceramic Groups and Types

In order to ascertain which of the excavated platforms contained late Middle Preclassic occupations, ceramics from the project were first analyzed in the field and then from a database created by William Ringle. The classification scheme used by the Ek Balam Project, and most other Maya archaeology projects, is the type: variety system. Late Middle Preclassic

(700–400/300 B.C.) deposits at Ek Balam were identified for the first time during the 1994 field season by myself. Markers for such deposits are ceramics of the Balam Complex, part of the Mamom sphere, as defined by the type: variety classification proposed by Andrews V (1988, 1989) at the site of Komchen. There, a substantial late Middle Preclassic pottery assemblage is also assigned to the Mamom sphere. Although the lowermost samples of the Ek Balam sequence resemble the Komchen Early Nabanche Complex in many details, they are not identical, so the label "Balam Complex" was adopted to define them (Bey et al. 1998). Balam ceramics occur below seven structures at Ek Balam as well as some surface collected material.

The Balam Complex at Ek Balam contains seven groups with 28 ceramic types (Bey et al. 1998), as summarized in Figure 10.2. Four ceramic groups (Achiotes, Dzudzuquil, Joventud Red, and Muxunal) are exclusive markers for the Balam Complex, while three others (Chunhinta Black, Sierra Red, and Saban) continue into the Late Preclassic Manab Complex, and possibly Sierra Red extending into the Early Classic, Alux Complex. Some of the type: varieties within ceramic groups are designated as v.n.s., which stands for variety not specified (Figure 10.2). These sherds are part of the particular ceramic group as types, but varieties are not assigned or not known for those sherds.

This study examined all the Preclassic ceramic material excavated by the Ek Balam Project. For a detailed discussion of the methods used in this analysis as well as information on the Early Classic period at the site see Bond-Freeman (2007).

Toward a Settlement Pattern

Bedrock or sterile *laja* was reached at 34 of the tested platform mounds in the vicinity of Ek Balam's monumental center (Figure 10.3). At just seven platforms (21%) did the excavations pass through Balam phase deposits before reaching bedrock. Most of the other 27 platforms were started during a later phase, and limited testing may have missed the Balam levels in a few others. Seven encounters with the Balam phase is of course too small a sample to reach any definitive conclusions about the original settlement pattern, but a few tentative observations can be made.

The two areas where all contiguous platforms were systematically tested (Figure 10.3) point to large spaces without a Middle Preclassic settlement. This in turn suggests a dispersed Balam phase settlement of low platforms spaced (with one exception) at least 100 m apart. There is no hint of a central area or cluster of platforms. If such a site concentration exists beneath

BALAM CERAMIC COMPLEX

GROUP

Achiotes	Chunhinta Black	Sierra Red	Dzudzuquil	Joventud Red	Saban (Chancenote)	Muxanal
Achiotes Unslipped: Achiotes	Ucu Black v.n.s.	Sierra Red: Laguna Verde Incised	Dzudzuquil Cream-to-Buff: Dzudzuquil	Joventud Red: Joventud	Chancenote Striated: Chancenote	Muxanal Red-On-Cream v.n.s.
Achiotes Unslipped v.n.s.	Nacolal Incised: Nacolal	Sierra Red: Sierra	Dzudzuquil v.n.s	Guitara Incised: Thin-Wall	Chancenote Striated: Chiquila	
	Nacolal Incised: Postslip-Incised	Sierra Red: V. Unidentified Bichrome	Kuche Incised: Kuche		Chancenote: v.n.s.	
	Uchben Incised Dichrome: Uchben	Sierra Red: Black-And-Red	Majan Red-And-Cream-To-Buff: Majan		Saban Unslipped v.n.s.	
	Dzocobel Red-on-Black: Dzocobel	Sierra: v.n.s	Tumben Incised: Tumben			
		Ciego Composite: Ciego	Bakxoc Black-And-Cream-To-Buff: v.n.s.			
			Canaima Incised Dichrome: Canaima			
			Petal Red-on-Black And-Cream-To-Buff: Incised			

v.n.s = variety not specified

Key

Ciego Composite: Ciego — Type — Variety

Figure 10.2. Diagram showing organization of the Balam Ceramic Complex.

the later monumental center, we have no way of knowing this due to the very limited testing there by the Ringle and Bey directed Ek Balam Project. There is one reference to a Middle Preclassic occupation by the INAH directed project (Vargas and Castillo 1999), but it is not stated that materials from this time period were found in the monumental center of Ek Balam. Additionally, six platforms had Balam phase sherds among their surface materials (Figure 10.3). If we assume that these platforms had earlier construction phases dating to the Balam phase, then we have founding structures in all quadrants surrounding the monumental center. The southeast quadrant appears to have less Balam phase occupation, however, this could be attributed to the limited surface collecting in this area of the site.

A settlement pattern begins to emerge when the data is examined more closely. The small sample of basal encounters with Balam phase material has revealed two pairs of Balam phase neighbors, labeled Pair A and Pair B in Figure 10.3, and a third in the southwest (Pair C) if we allow that surface finds reflect Balam deposits below. Pairs A and C have almost identical spacing—in each case the midpoints of the companion platforms are approximately 130 m apart. Mound B is the exception noted above, with platform midpoints just 50 m apart. It appears that spatial twinning of structures could be a feature of the Balam phase settlement pattern.

For now the Ek Balam Project investigations directed by Ringle and Bey have only a single surface sherd to indicate a Balam presence beneath the monumental center. Neither of the two excavations to bedrock in a very large platform, Structure GT-20 (see Figure 10.3) encountered any Balam phase ceramics at depth. The excavations at GT-20 did unearth later deposits with sherds that date to the end of the Late Preclassic into the Early Classic Period with several Chunhinta and Sierra Group sherds, but it lacks the other diagnostics, except the one surface find, for the late Middle Preclassic Balam Complex. This leaves open the possibility that other structures mapped in Figure 10.3 as non-Balam may yet prove to contain Balam material. Until further information is available about the Ek Balam site center, at present all other Balam deposits encountered by excavation and inferred from surface finds are set far back from Ek Balam's monumental center.

At first glance, this appears to reflect nothing more than sampling deficiency in and around the center itself, but a ca. 800 m diameter circle around the central mound (Figure 10.3, Structure GT-1) contains 12 excavations that reached bedrock with only one (8%) that encountered Balam phase deposits. Outside this circle, 20 reached bedrock and six (30%)

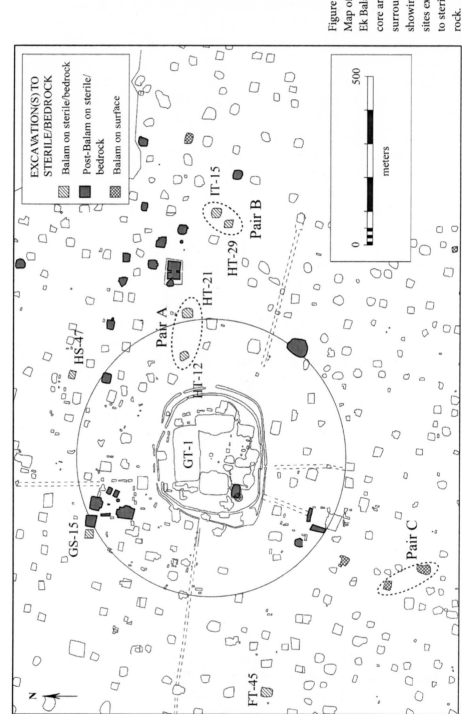

Figure 10.3. Map of the Ek Balam core area and surrounds, showing all sites excavated to sterile/bedrock.

encountered Balam levels. The current Ek Balam data suggests the Middle Preclassic founding structures were built around the site center rather than close to or within the monumental site center. Additional information from the monumental center investigations at the site or future excavations within this area would be necessary to further support this statement.

There is sparse evidence for settlement growth within the Balam phase, from the early to late Balam times. At Ek Balam, three out of seven Balam phase platforms were abandoned at or before the onset of the late Balam subphase (Figure 10.3). These were at Structures HT-21, HS-47, and IT-15. The platforms with continued occupation are HT-12, HT-29, and the westernmost FT-45. Another structure located near the site center, GS-15, has a high probability of containing Balam Complex deposits and is also included in this distribution analysis. However, details of the occupation are not currently available.

In summary, although observations on the Balam phase settlement pattern are somewhat limited by sample size, there are strong indications that initial settlement was one of dispersed, low platforms without any central location. Platforms and pairs of platforms were set a few hundred meters apart from each other. The settlement density appears to drop somewhat in the immediate vicinity of the later monumental compound at Ek Balam. The ceramic data suggests that there was a decline in construction with the onset of the late Balam subphase as many platforms appear to have been abandoned during this time period.

The Balam Phase Platforms

In spite of the very limited horizontal extent of excavations of Balam phase deposits, all available units and trenches appear to have excavated into low built platforms or terraces. Exposures are of three kinds. The most easily recognized are stucco floors and subfloors of densely packed rocks, stones, and *chich* over a rubble and earth fill (Figure 10.4; Type F exposures). In some cases there are stratified sequences of intact plaster floors, sometimes of cement-like hardness. Poor preservation was common, however, and the stucco in many of the cases had disintegrated into an indistinct line of fragments.

Also fairly straightforward to recognize are the excavations that have encountered a segment of a platform's stone retaining wall (Figure 10.4; Type W exposures). The base of the stacked rock may be surrounded by a packing of *mezcla* or and/or *chich*, and the walling itself is surrounded by rubble and earth fill.

The last kind of exposure is the most difficult to interpret because the pit has come down somewhere in the center of the platform (Figure 10.4; Type C) well away from its retaining wall and in some part where the surface was never plastered. Here the deposit is earth and rubble fill, with no obvious structural clues except perhaps a few bits of derived stucco incorporated as fill from elsewhere.

In none of these limited area, small exposures is it possible to speculate on the shape of the individual platform, let alone determine whether it was free-standing with a full surround of stone facing, or merely terrace fill backed up against a single retaining wall built on the bottom slopes of a rock dome.

Early Balam Platforms

Table 10.1 lists the details exposed in the 13 operations at nine sites that reached early Balam deposits above a sterile zone. Entries are synthesized from the Level Report Forms (LRFs), and platform exposure types appearing in the last column. More parts of the same platform are predictably exposed at sites with more test units.

Although all modest, the maximum thicknesses of these platform exposures fall into four tight groups (Figure 10.4, left). As exposed thickness has nothing to do with exposure type, this strongly hints at site-wide construction standards, perhaps involving stepped or staged platforms. Furthermore, when maximum thickness is mapped against exposure type (Figure 10.4, right), it emerges that Pairs A and B (Figure 10.3 and 10.4) display near-identical measurements: Pair B has 76 cm versus 39 cm while Pair A has 71 cm and 40 cm.

Returning to Table 10.1, the LRF records show that the thicker member of each pair, namely HT-12 and HT-29, is primarily associated with a fairly long list of non-ceramic items that collectively point to domestic trash mixed into the platform fill. A few possible artifacts from HT-12 may have had a public purpose, but this is not known definitively and the majority points to domestic use. Thus, it is reasonable to suggest that both were residential platforms based on the majority of the context of the trash. It should be noted in passing that all those in charge of excavations were instructed to make specific LRF entries on any non-ceramics artifacts encountered, so it is safe to assume that a blank LRF entry means extreme scarcity or total absence of such items. Where LRFs could not be consulted the midden column is marked "nd" (no data).

Table 10.1. Construction Details and Midden Exposed in Early Balam Phase Deposits.

Site (unit)	Spit Nos.	Max thickness cm	Midden	Walling	Flooring	Other	Exposure Type
HT-12(3)	8–9	40	chert flake, ground stone, shell, shell beads, charcoal			smashed vessel	C
HT-12(3)	10–13	71	charcoal, bone, shell, lithic debitage, re-touched chert flakes, pecked stone, shell beads		pieces of stucco	smashed vessels in base of lvl 12	C
HT-12(3A)	16–20	52	charcoal, shell, grindstones, lithic debitage, obsidian	line of 3 large stones in lvl.17	stucco floor in lvl 18 beneath stone line; lg. stone fill in lvl. 20. several pieces of stucco	smashed vessel in lvls. 19–20	F
HT-12(1)	6	26.5		stone wall foundation	rests on *laja*, with *mezcla*		W
HT-12(4)	3	13		stone wall foundation	*mezcla* surrounding base of wall		W
HT-21(7)	11–13	40			large fill stones and *chich* in NE. over sterile *chich*		C
HT-29(1)	5–11	76	charcoal, bone, shell, grindstone, shell beads in lvls. 10–8		large fill stones with *chich* throughout		C

(continued)

Table 10.1—*Continued*

Site (unit)	Spit Nos.	Max thickness cm	Midden	Walling	Flooring	Other	Exposure Type
HS-47(1)	10–12	51		unit truncates outer platform wall of large stones built on *laja*			W
FT-45(1A)	8A	21	bone fragment		three stucco floors, the first on *laja*, with *chich* filling between them		F
IT-15(1)	4–7	39	small rubber(?) ball		weathered stucco floor in lvl. 5; subfloor fill of rocks and *chich*, above 18–25 cm stack of destroyed stucco flooring over *laja*		F
IT-15(3)	6	21.5			*mezcla* on bedrock, covered by 18–19 cm of *chich* fill		C
GS-15(1)	4–5	22	nd		hard packed lens of pebbles in red matrix on rotted hardpan		C

Notes: W= stone walling

F= stucco floors

C= unplastered earth and rubble fill

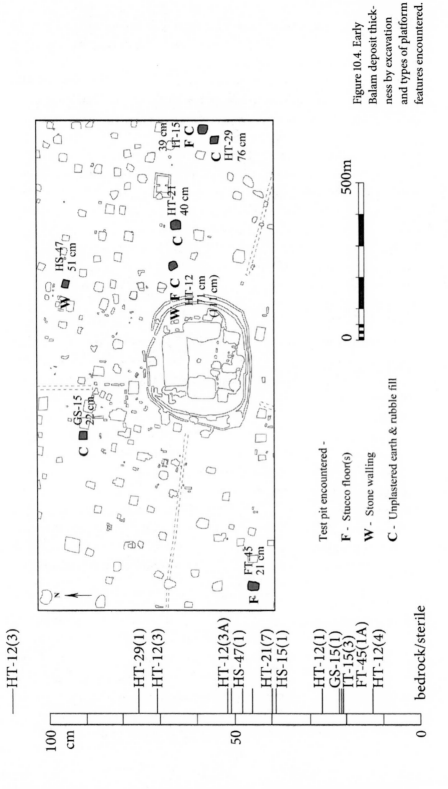

Figure 10.4. Early Balam deposit thickness by excavation and types of platform features encountered.

Test pit encountered -

F - Stucco floor(s)

W - Stone walling

C - Unplastered earth & rubble fill

If the highest platform of each pair supported a homestead and its adjacent midden, then the less elevated neighboring platform may have had a non-domestic function, possibly ceremonial. Although it will take another excavation project to determine whether or not the other thinner platforms encountered are ceremonial in function with taller residential neighbors, there is a possibility that separate platforms for ceremonial use occur early in the Maya archaeological record.

It appears that most early Balam platforms were not raised in single events, but grew in height by accumulation. The clearest evidence for this is the repeated plaster flooring. Where flooring is scarce or absent, the up-profile trends in pottery composition (see Bond-Freeman 2007), mixed with the earth and rubble fill, also point to gradual accumulation. If these fills came from off building episodes, the level-by-level composition of the ceramics in the fill should vary little, randomly, and with none of the percentage trends in the ceramics recovered repeatedly observed.

Late Balam Platforms

The residential platforms at HT-12 and HT-29 continued to accumulate through late Balam times. One of the excavated units on HT-12 had thicker accumulations than other early Balam excavated deposits on the platform. However, in the test unit on HT-12 with the early Balam deposits from domestic trash, the trash deposits persisted into the late Balam subphase (Table 10.2). Only a thin veneer of late Balam flooring was added to the other residential site at HT-29, but this was unplastered and there is no domestic trash associated with it. Elsewhere at Ek Balam, only the thin stack of early Balam floors in FT-45 continued to grow, doubling in thickness during this later subphase. Evidently the other sampled platforms ceased construction, but horizontal exposures are so small that we can only guess that any of them were abandoned during late Balam times. No new beginnings (late Balam on sterile/bedrock) were encountered at Ek Balam.

Early Balam Ceramics by Structure

The mix of early Balam, late Middle Preclassic ceramic groups at the six sampled structures for which there are data at Ek Balam is not uniform from location to location. To explore this variability, the early Balam levels at each site have been combined in Table 10.3, with their totals purged of all sherds identified as contaminants from overlying deposits (Bond-Freeman 2007). From this exercise it emerges that two locations are dominated by Chunhinta Black Group ceramics, namely at HT-12 and HT-29 (Figure

Table 10.2. Construction Details and Midden Exposed in Late Balam Phase Deposits.

Site (unit)	Level Nos.	Max thickness cm	Midden	Walling	Flooring	Other	Exposure Type
HT-12(3)	7	20			pieces of stucco		C
HT-12(3A)	15	14	charcoal, burnt bone, shell,		two heavy paving stones (*labrada*) with stucco fragments nearby		F
HT-12 (1)	3–5	31		wall of large stones with central boulder	*labrada*, piece of stucco floor over thick subfloor fill, *mezcla, chich*		W, F
HT-29(1)	4	11			*chich* throughout		C
FT-45(1A)	6–7	16	exotic stone		two stucco floors, each with *chich* subfloor		F
FT-45 (1B)	6–7	28			fragments of the upper stucco floor		F

Notes: W= stone walling

F= stucco floors

C= unplastered earth and rubble fill

Table 10.3. Early Balam–Merged Sherd Samples.

Site (unit)	Levels	Total	Purged	Final
HT-12(3)	8–9	124	14	110
HT-12(3)	10–13	148	1	147
HT-12(3A)	16–20	695	8	687
HT-12 (1)	6	17		17
HT-12(4)	3	26	6	20
HT-12 sum		*1010*	*29*	*981*
HT-21(7)	11–13	34	5	29
HT-29(1)	5–11	131	1	130
IT-15 (1)	4–7	30		30
IT-15 (3)	6	19		19
IT-15 sum		*49*		*49*
HS-47(1)	10–12	80	2	78
FT-45(1A)	8A	41		41
Combined		**1345**	**37**	**1308**

10.3). That these two happen to be the thicker, and likely residential companion of Pair A (HT-12) and of Pair B (HT-29) cannot be a coincidence (Figure 10.3). At the other four (thinner) platform accumulations, Sierra Red Group ceramics are clearly dominant over Chunhinta Black Group ceramics. At present the meaning of this association is obscure, but the possibility that Sierra Red could be associated with non-residential platforms is worthy of consideration.

Platform directionality and color preference for the paired platforms at Ek Balam merit further discussion. Both Structures HT-29 and HT-12 are associated with Chunhinta Black slipped ceramics and are the thicker Middle Preclassic deposits for the paired structures. These platforms are also located at the western side of each of the paired platforms. Structures HT-21 and IT-15 are associated with predominantly Sierra Red slipped ceramics, are thinner deposits, and located to the eastern side of each of the paired structures. The ancient Maya constructed their built environment with consideration of their cosmology and political order, which is mostly visible in the Classic and Postclassic periods (Ashmore and Sabloff 2002; Freidel et al. 1993). However, as mentioned previously, because of the depth of overburden at most Maya archaeological sites, understanding Preclassic period settlement plans, civic centers, and ceremonial functioning buildings is difficult. Building orientation is significant throughout ancient Maya civilization, with the east and west signifying the rising and setting of the sun (Ashmore and Sabloff 2002; Brown et al. 2011; Freidel et al. 1993).

Research in the Belize Valley (Ashmore and Sabloff 2002; Brown 2011) suggests that an east/west axial preference is found during the Preclassic Period, but shifts in the later times to a north-south orientation (Ashmore and Sabloff 2002). Red is a significant color among the ancient Maya (Freidel et al. 1993; Hammond 1991b) often associated with the east and the rising sun and it follows that the red-slipped dominated structures of the pairs at Ek Balam are to the eastern side, and the western side associated with the black slipped pottery and the setting sun. There are examples of the use of black and red-slipped pottery in other ceremonial contexts during the Preclassic period (Estrada-Belli et al. 2003). The association of the red-slipped and black-slipped ceramic preference for the paired structures is not currently known, but it is likely more than a coincidence for the color association and pairing of structures.

Of the other three ceramic groups, it can be noted that Achiotes is common throughout and is actually dominant at HS-47. Joventud is also found everywhere but invariably as a trivial component of the assemblage. Dzudzuquil is also a small component of each assemblage, but is notably absent from HS-47 and HT-21 (where the small sample could be to blame) and is little more than a trace at IT-15.

Late Balam Ceramics by Structure

These samples have been combined and intruder sherds removed in the same manner as for the early Balam Phase (Table 10.4; Bond-Freeman 2007). Three structures excavated contain late Balam ceramics at Ek Balam, HT-12, HT-29, and FT-45, all of which are relatively shallow deposits and are not uniform from site to site. HT-29 late Balam ceramics are dominated by Achiotes and Saban Unslipped sherds, which is a change from the early Balam deposits and may signal a change in platform function. FT-45 is dominated by Sierra, as is similar in the early Balam subphase, and does not indicate a change in platform function between the two subphases. HT-12 has more Sierra than Chunhinta, where it is the reverse in the early Balam. Differences in the samples of HT-12 may indicate a change in platform function, but the differences could also be attributed to chronology.

Implications for Complexity

In summary, ceramics from the seven available Balam phase platforms correlate unmistakably into two subphases—early and late Balam. There is no evidence for settlement growth from early to late Balam times. Three out

Table 10.4. Late Balam–Merged Sherd Samples.

Site (unit)	Levels	Total	Purged	Final
HT-12(3)	7	67	9	58
HT-12(3A)	15	74	4	70
HT-12 (1)	3–5	68	5	63
HT-12 sum		*209*	*18*	*191*
HT-29(1)	4	21	2	19
FT-45(1A)	6–7	14		14
FT-45 (1B)	6–7	87	1	86
FT-45 sum		*101*	*1*	*100*
Combined		**331**	**21**	**310**

of the seven platforms were abandoned at or before the onset of the late Balam subphase. None of the three platforms with continued occupation persisted for many levels.

Of great interest is that the mix of early Balam ceramic types in the thicker platforms are similar—both are dominated by the Chunhinta Black Group. Remarkably their lower-in-height companion platforms have Sierra Red types clearly dominant over Chunhinta Black, as do the other two solitary lower platforms. The meaning of this association is of great interest, and the possibility that Sierra Red was more often associated with non-residential platforms needs to be considered. HT-12 and HT-29, the structures dominated by black-slipped Chunhinta Group ceramics, are on the west side of the pairs and lower platforms dominated by Sierra Red (HT-21 and IT-15) ceramics are located on the east side of the pairs. If one considers the Maya directional colors where black represents the west and red represents the east, then the use of specific types of ceramics appears to be intentional at Ek Balam in the Middle Preclassic Period.

Although evidence is limited, a possible trace of ritual activity lies in the base of HT-12, Unit 3A, where the trash and (dated) charcoal may point instead to a potential feasting location (e.g., Bray 2003; Brown 2003, Brown et al. Chapter 5 this volume; Dietler 1996; Hayden 1996; LeCount 2001; Mills 1999). Feasting may act as a way to foster social identity and hierarchies as well as negotiate power and identity. Spouted vessels were used for serving cacao, or chocolate, which is one of the foods that was used in feasting during the Late Classic period (LeCount 2001) and has been recently documented in Middle Preclassic contexts as well (Brown 2007; Powis et al. 2002). A large frontal portion of a Joventud Red spouted vessel was recovered at the bottom of HT-12 Unit 3 (Bey et al. 1998), further support-ing the possibility of this deposit being a feasting location. Enough of the vessel form was not preserved to definitively argue for feasting, although there are dishes and plates present in the deposit which also support this possibility.

The Middle Preclassic, Balam Phase in Wider Context

In addition to the Middle Preclassic deposits found at Ek Balam, survey work conducted by the project in the region around Ek Balam revealed two additional sites yielding this early pottery, Chumul which is 40 km southwest of Ek Balam (Bond-Freeman 2007; Smith 2000) and Xuilub, located 10.8 km south of Ek Balam (Bond-Freeman 2007; Houck 2004). After surface collected material yielded Middle Preclassic ceramics, a single test 1 × 1 m test unit was placed on Structure 9, a north-south oriented rubble mound, at Chumul. This test unit produced both early and late Balam phase ceramics (Bond-Freeman 2007). The archaeological explo-rations were more extensive at Xuilub. Structure 20, with three test units produced both early and late Balam ceramics, and Structure 40, with one unit producing late Balam ceramics (Bond-Freeman 2007). Based on the preliminary work at these two sites, it would be worthwhile for future ar-chaeological explorations to be conducted in order to better understand the extent of the Middle Preclassic occupation.

There are well known regional differences between Middle Preclassic ceramics from different parts of northern Yucatan (Andrews V 1988; Bey 2006; Glover and Stanton 2007). Through the generosity of colleagues, I have been able to inspect several collections (Komchen, Yaxuna, Ek Balam, Xuilub, Chumul, Kuiuc, and some from the Yalahau region) and am im-pressed by how much similarity they exhibit at the group level. From these observations, I have found Middle Preclassic ceramics are very well made, often hard pasted with brilliant slips and with some decorations. The as-semblages from Ek Balam share all these attributes with the others, and share all the same groups (Achiotes Unslipped, Dzudzuquil, Joventud Red, Chunhinta Black), but they differ from the rest in the specific frequencies of certain groups. There is also a rare tradeware present, Muxanal, that is found also at Komchen, Yaxuna, Xocnaceh, and other Puuc sites (Bey 2006).

Once identified, the close similarities with so many other sites have made the analysis of Balam sherd samples relatively straightforward. At this time, there is evidently no need to differentiate greatly between ceramic spheres. Similarities at the group level must signify a relation among all known Middle Preclassic Maya groups of the northern lowlands.

One notable exception, however, is the presence of Sierra Red in the Middle Preclassic at Ek Balam. This has long been regarded as a marker of the Late Preclassic, but it is without doubt present throughout the basal levels of Ek Balam and is reinforced by two matching radiocarbon dates of the Middle Preclassic age. Two charcoal samples were radiocarbon tested and date to the Middle Preclassic period. These remains were found in the bottom two levels, 20 and 19, of the deepest excavation unit (Unit 3A) on HT-12 (Bond-Freeman 2007). The sample from Level 20 produced an uncalibrated date of 2460 ± 40 B.P. (Beta-228530) and a 2-sigma calibrated date of 770–410 B.C. The second sample from Level 19 produced an uncalibrated date of 2450 ± 40 B.P. (Beta-228529) and a 2-sigma calibrated date of 760–400 B.C. The Level 20 sample produced three calibrated intercepts with two dating to 720 B.C. and 700 B.C. and the third to 540 B.C. The Level 19 sample produced a single calibrated intercept of 530 B.C. The two samples have two almost identical intercepts; the estimated age of the samples is around 550 B.C. Thus, the Sierra Red Group has a longer production history than may have been realized. This pattern may also be present in the Belize River valley at the site of Blackman Eddy (Brown 2003; Shelton 2008). Other ceramic groups excavated from Levels 20 and 19 and are associated with the radiocarbon dated material include Achiotes, Joventud Red, Dzudzuquil, and Chunhinta Black.

Finally, it should be noted that the Ek Balam data recovered nothing of the architectural innovations as some of the other northern Yucatan sites to the west, such as Xocnaceh and Poxila (Gallareta and Ringle 2004; Bey 2006). Because of the extensive excavations at the site of Ek Balam, primarily outside the monumental center, with no significant architecture recovered associated with the Middle Preclassic deposits suggest the possibility of larger Middle Preclassic Period centers in northeastern Yucatan.

The Late Preclassic Manab Phase at Ek Balam

Although a full discussion of the residential pattern in the Late Preclassic Period at Ek Balam is not possible due to space limitations of this chapter, a few comments can be made about the transition from the late Middle Preclassic Balam phase to the beginning of the Late Preclassic Manab phase at the site. The same procedures for analyzing data from the Middle Preclassic period were also used for the Late Preclassic and the transitional periods into the Early Classic so that temporal boundaries could be ascertained for the site of Ek Balam (Bond-Freeman 2007).

Sherd samples ascribed to the Late Preclassic Manab phase were recovered from deposits covering four of the Balam phase structures discussed previously. Another five structures yielded Manab sherds in their basal deposits (Figure 10.5). Several of these ceramic sequences provide detailed insights into the transition from late Middle Preclassic to the Late Preclassic period.

The Manab Ceramic Complex

The Manab Complex ceramic assemblage (Figure 10.6) at Ek Balam contains eight ceramic groups. The three bichrome ceramic groups (Huachinango, Dzilam Verde, and lesser amounts of Carolina) are markers for the Manab Complex, while three others (Chunhinta Black, Sierra Red, and Saban) begin in the underlying Balam Complex and continue into the Manab phase, although in different percentages (Bond-Freeman 2007). The ceramic record at Structure HT-12 displays strong continuities between the end of the late Balam and the start of the Manab phase. Apart from a pair of newcomers (Huachinango and Carolina Bichrome Group ceramics), and a couple of disappearances (Achiotes and Joventud Red Group ceramics) the rest of the late Balam ceramic repertoire continues on unaltered into the Manab Late Preclassic at Ek Balam. The proportions of surviving types shift at the Balam/Manab boundary, hinting at limited reorganization of pottery production, acquisition, and consumption.

Cultural-Historical Reconstructions for the Manab Phase

For the Manab phase at Ek Balam the impression is given of a gradual drift to some sort of new order, rather than a radical upheaval in the fabric of village life at Ek Balam. However, this scenario cannot be corroborated as there are gaps with either the late Balam missing (Structures HT-21, IT-15, HS-47) or the Manab missing (Structures HT-29, FT-45) from the sequence.

There is some urgency about this, as the distribution map in Figure 10.5 plainly shows a radical dislocation in village layout at the start of (or perhaps during) Manab times. Besides the rather obvious nucleation, there is an emphatic shift to the east of what would later become the ceremonial

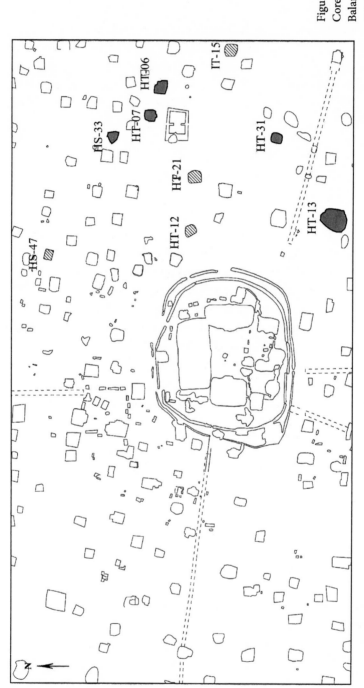

Figure 10.5. Core area of Ek Balam, showing structures where excavations encountered Manab Phase deposits.

HS-47

HS-33

HT-06

HT-07

HT-21

HT-12

HT-15

HT-31

HT-13

N

0

500

meters

▨ Manab on Balam Phase deposits

■ Manab on bedrock

MANAB CERAMIC COMPLEX GROUP

Saban (Chancenote)	Chunhinta Black	Sierra Red	Dzudzuquil	Dzilam	Huachinango	Carolina
Chancenote Striated: *Chancenote*	Ucu Black v.n.s.	Sierra Red: *Laguna Verde Incised*	Dzudzuquil Cream-to Buff: *Dzudzuquil*	Dzilam Verde: *Dzilam*	Huachinago Incised: *Huachinango*	Carolina Bichrome: *Carolina*
Chancenote Striated: *Chiquila*	Nacolal Incised: *Nacolal*	Sierra Red: *Sierra*	Dzudzuquil v.n.s	Dzilam Verde: v.n.s.	Huachinango: v.n.s.	Carolina: v.n.s.
Chancenote: v.n.s.	Dzocobel Red-on-Black: *Dzocobel*	Sierra: v.n.s	Tumben Incised: *Tumben*			
Saban Unslipped v.n.s.						

Xanaba

Xanaba Red: *Xanaba*

Xanaba Red: v.n.s.

Key

Dzilam Verde: ⟩ Type
Dzilam — Variety

v.n.s = variety not specified

Figure 10.6. Diagram showing organization of the Manab Ceramic Complex.

center. Three formerly abandoned early Balam platforms were reoccupied, and five new ones were established on bedrock. Only Structure HT-12 shows any sign of settlement continuity.

Based on the data available for the research, with the onset of the Manab phase, the western platforms were evidently abandoned as the village nucleated in the eastern half of its former distribution. There, four previously founded platforms either continued in occupation or came back into use, and another five new ones were founded on bedrock close by the others. The Balam pattern of platform pairing (residential with non-residential) is no longer present in the Late Preclassic period.

Why these things should have happened at a time when ceramic production, use, and disposal patterns were also undergoing change remains unclear. While it is reasonable to guess that the nucleation may have been for defense or maybe gathering of elite power, this is only speculation. At least it presents a testable hypothesis open to future field research.

In addition to the apparent eastern nucleation of the occupation in the Manab phase, based on a triaxal analysis of the identified ceramics (see Bond-Freeman 2007), there is also evidence of neighboring residential platforms sharing common pottery consumption in the Ek Balam village, based on sharing a preference for Chancenote Group ceramics, Sierra Red Group ceramics, and one with "eclectic" tastes for ceramics, but still favoring Sierra Red Group ceramics. Throughout the Manab phase each of the platform/households maintained its preferred ceramic system. Also, there are no signs of a social hierarchy with larger and smaller platforms, and no signs of deliberate raising of platform levels. They seem to have accumulated gradually with remarkably similar fill thicknesses added to all of them. The single raising up of the new, southernmost HT-13 to twice the normal height seems to have come to nothing in the end, as this platform was abandoned by the close of the Manab period (for further discussion see Bond-Freeman 2007).

Other sites surveyed during the Ek Balam regional project revealed Late Preclassic period ceramics. Both Xiulub and Chumul continue to be occupied during the Late Preclassic period, although nothing of their expansion is known.

Conclusions

In summary, the settlement pattern study on the Preclassic period at Ek Balam is from a site-wide settlement study that focuses outside the monumental center. The settlement data presented are consequently obtained mostly from residential trash and construction fill deposits, in sharp contrast to many other Maya ceramic studies that emphasize the ceramic histories on monumental centers. Conducting detailed analysis of all ceramics recovered during excavations and understanding the context in which they were derived is essential when examining archaeological artifacts, especially those from trash deposits. Since three lines of evidence, natural stratigraphy, excavated levels, in addition to the ceramic data, were used in the study a more accurate understanding of the changes in the settlement pattern from the Middle Preclassic to the Late Preclassic as well as increasing complexity were able to be evaluated.

For the Middle Preclassic Balam phase at Ek Balam, the ceramic assemblage is similar to others in the northern Maya lowlands. The current data suggests a dispersed settlement pattern during this time period with hints at a site-wide construction standard. Also of interest is that the archaeological data suggests paired structures, some of which are associated with red slipped and black slipped ceramics.

The data analyzed from the Late Preclassic period, Manab phase at Ek Balam suggests a limited reorganization of the pottery productions and consumption at the site. There is a gradual shift in the settlement pattern that occurs at the site with a possible nucleation to the eastern side. Also, there is no evidence of paired structures or ceramic preferences for the Manab phase structures.

11

At the Foot of the Hills

Early Monumentality at Xocnaceh, Yucatan, Mexico

TOMÁS GALLARETA NEGRÓN

The origin and rise of Maya civilization, as well as its relations with other Mesoamerican societies during the Preclassic period, remains a rapidly shifting field of research. Archaeological studies in the southern Maya lowlands and more recently, in the northern plains and the hill country of Yucatan, have documented population centers with Middle Preclassic, Mamom-affiliated ceramics and monumental architectural remains, as well as modest settlements with ballcourts (Anderson 2010, 2011; Anderson et al. Chapter 8 this volume; Andrews and Robles 2004, Andrews and Robles Chapter 2 this volume). The antiquity of Yucatecan sites has been estimated according to the ceramic sequence of Komchen, a largely Preclassic site on the northern plains, where Mamom-Early Nabanche deposits are dated to the last half of the Middle Preclassic period, between 800 and 400/300 B.C. (Andrews V 1988, 1990; Andrews V et al. Chapter 4 this volume). The number of settlements of different ranks where Early Nabanche ceramics have been recovered has multiplied across practically the entire peninsula, along the coast as well as deep in the interior. Together they provide the basis for new ideas concerning the size and complexity reached by Yucatecan Maya communities during the first millennium B.C. In fact, as the knowledge of early ceramics has increased, specialists have been able to distinguish regional variations leading to a variety of explanations for their distribution and antiquity, implying that social inequality was the result of local circumstances and not necessarily the result of external contacts (Robles and Ceballos Chapter 9 this volume).

This contribution is about Xocnaceh, an early Yucatecan site with monumental architecture dating to the Middle Preclassic period. The ruins of Xocnaceh are found on the southern edge of the northern plains of

Yucatan, at the foot of the escarpment known as the Puuc Ridge, close to the central section of the road Ticul-Oxkutzcab (Figure 11.1a). A program of excavations at the acropolis, the main architectural complex of the site, has identified building episodes and artifacts dating from the Middle Preclassic period (800–300 B.C.). All of the structures forming this main complex rest on a trapezoidal basal platform whose surviving volume exceeds 100,000 m³. This platform preserves evidence of several building stages and renovations, visible as the superposition of floors and retaining walls, facilitating the identification of synchronic contexts. This contribution will focus initially on the evidence for identifying the construction stages and the associated artifacts useful for dating these contexts and for inferring commercial contacts outside the region. Evidence for developing the sequence was obtained through vertical excavations on the basal platform and by horizontal explorations of the architectural remains partially exposed on the east side and at the southwest corner.

The remains of the ancient settlement of Xocnaceh were in a very poor state of preservation in the late 1970s, when they were first recorded during creation of the Archaeological Atlas of Yucatan (Garza and Kurjack 1980). For the Atlas archaeologists, the presence of veneer stone and the highly visible Puuc slate wares resulted in the identification of Xocnaceh as a minor Terminal Classic site. The dimensions and layout of the main structure of the site, the acropolis, became better known after mapping the complex and its surrounding area by the present project. The contour lines outline a basal platform measuring 130–140 m along its main axes, and rising an average of 7.5 m above ground level. On top of the elevated platform, several mounds define a large plaza with a small platform at its center (S0018 E0218). The main structure lies on the north side, a triadic pyramid facing toward the plaza and with an elevation of 21 m above ground level (Figure 11.1b). The southern edge of the acropolis preserves no remains of formal structures. Exploratory excavations showed that this side of the basal platform was heavily damaged, obscuring the positive identification of formal architecture in this area. On the east side, a stairway made with large stones leads to a structure of perishable materials built on top of a basal platform. This section is preserved, although large segments of the retaining walls were totally dismantled. Several walls remain standing however, defining the southwest corner of the basal platform. Small sections of retaining walls are preserved in few places mainly in the northeast wall and along the west side of the basal platform. A good number of pottery fragments recovered on the surface of the elevated plaza were initially identified by Fernando

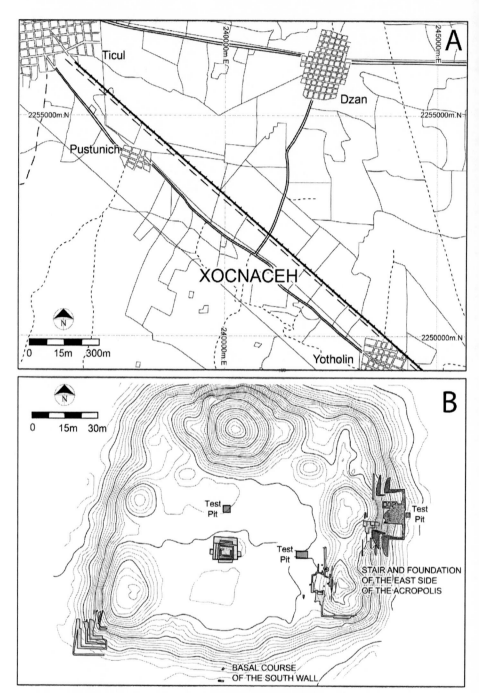

Figure 11.1. (a) Location of Xocnaceh (After INEGI's map Ticul F16C72); (b) map of the acropolis showing the location of structures and excavations.

Robles Castellanos as similar to Middle Preclassic types found in the site of Komchen.

The Exploration of the Acropolis

A program of vertical excavations followed the initial explorations. The main operation, Pozo N056 E049 (according to the acropolis grid), was located on the central-north section of the plaza in front of Structure N0013 E0197 and north of the central Structure S0018 E0218 (following the site's grid). This deep excavation recovered very important information about the building sequence and chronology. Another excavation on the east side of the plaza (Pozo N046 E066) confirmed the sequence, increased the ceramic sample related to the final building stage of the basal platform, and revealed the existence of a substructure above the oldest floor of what it seems was a basal platform-sub.

Information concerning the sequence of walls retaining the basal platform was obtained by means of excavations on the east side, done with the intention of stabilizing partially exposed sections of the retaining walls and the stairway leading up to the elevated plaza. This sequence of walls was confirmed at the southwest corner of the basal platform. A test pit located on the east side of the basal platform (Pit N0055 E0090), at the foot of the stairway, provided artifacts and exposed floors useful for determining the relative chronology of the building sequence.

Pit N0056 E0049, Center-North of the Acropolis Plaza

This vertical excavation revealed evidence for two main building stages of the basal platform, the result of the superposition of two large platforms, each of which was associated with a series of sequential floors. The earliest basal platform rises 2 m and its upper layers consist of six levels of very thick and compact stucco floors (P-6 to P-11). These floors were built one of top of the other, suggesting a number of renovations that increased the height of the original platform to a final height of 2.5 m at the time Floor P-6, the upper and last one of this group, was laid down. Platform fill consists of dry-laid boulders, mostly of large size, but also includes some medium and small stones. This first basal platform was built on top of a 15 cm *sascab* layer (Level C-XVI), leveling the natural surface; this suggests that a plaza existed before the acropolis was built. The 18 sherds recovered from Levels X–XV were all Mamom-like ceramic types. Two stone boxes were found built on top of Floor P-6, with some bone fragments inside.

We think these boxes were buried immediately after they were constructed by the fill below the Floor P-5, the earliest one of a series of floors of the second and last basal platform. Under the intact Floor P-6 was a circular opening, probably a posthole, extending from Floor P-7 down into the fill above Floor P-11. Under Floor P-8 and partially intruding into Floors P-9 and P-10 was a bowl of the Middle Preclassic type Joventud Red and a polished biface of green stone, the latter penetrating Floor P-11 (Figure 11.5). Under Floor P-10 (Layer C-XIV) and below Floor P-11 (Layer C-XV) sherds related to the Dzudzuquil and Joventud Red groups were recovered.

In a next building stage, about 3.5 m of fill was added above Floor P-6, reaching a final height of about 6 m above ground level. This stage is associated to a second group of floors (Floors P-1 to P-5, Levels C-II to C-IX). These stucco floors are also thick and hard, and rest on stone fill similar to that previously described for the first basal platform. Floors P-2, P-3, and P-4 were found partially broken in the southern section of the excavated area.

About 70% of the ceramics from above the final floor were identified as Late-Terminal Classic Cehpech slatewares. The remaining sherds are types related to the ceramic spheres Mamom (10%) and Chicanel (20%). Below Floors P-1 and P-2 a larger proportion of early ceramics were recovered, but also included an admixture of Late Classic Cehpech sphere fragments, including three sherds of Say pre-slate under Floor P-1. Under Floor P-3 four fragments of unslipped Achiote ceramics were the only ceramics recovered. Under Floor P-4, the lot included 133 Mamom-related sherds and eight from the Sierra group. From Floor P-5 down, only Mamom ceramics were recovered. This sample of 44 sherds contains examples of ceramic groups as Dzudzuquil cream-brownish-bayo, Joventud reds and oranges, and black Chunhinta ceramics, besides striated types of the Achiotes Group. In Level C-XVI, under the *sascab* layer, as well as under Layer C-XVII, three fragments similar to Dzudzuquil ceramics were recovered.

Pit N046 E066, East Side of the Acropolis Plaza

Excavations on the east side of the plaza confirmed the same building sequence and floor renovations described above for the central-north exploration. As in the previous pit, some of the ceramics recovered in contexts above Floor P-1 include sherds of Terminal Classic Muna Slate and Chum Unslipped vessels. Also identified were earlier types associated with the Late Chicanel sphere, such as Xanaba Red, Polvero Black and Tipikal pre-slip striated red. Except for two variegated sherds from the Tamanche

Group below Floor P-5, the remaining 99% of ceramics from below Floors P-2 through P-6 belonged principally to the Achiotes, Chunhinta, Joventud, and Dzudzuquil groups.

In addition, excavations revealed remains of formal architecture built on top of the basal platform-sub. These remains consist of a retaining wall running east-west, probably the edge of a platform contemporaneous with the earliest floor (Floor P-11), although this structure continued in use during the following floor renovations (Floors P-6 to P-10). A charcoal sample found in a layer (XOC 80251) close to this structure, below the sealed floor (P-6), suggests that the two last floor renovations of the first acropolis occurred about 400 B.C. (Beta-364482). The retaining wall, with a stepped profile, was built with rectangular stones of medium-to-large size, faced on their frontal side with a few chinking stones between them. They were set in such a way that each row was recessed about 10 cm with respect to the immediately lower row. Six in situ courses were exposed. The building technique and finish of the retaining wall of this early substructure is similar to the outer retaining wall found in the east, south, and west sides of the basal platform of the acropolis.

Pit N055 E090, at the Foot of the East Stairway of the Acropolis

The excavation of Pit N055 E090, on the east side of the acropolis at the foot of its access stairway, revealed the presence of two stucco floors above the bedrock. The upper floor covered part of the first step of the stairway. Early Nabanche sherds recovered below the floor were mixed with sherds from the Late Nabanche Flor, Tamanche, and Sierra groups. The second floor was laid down when the stairway was built, and its fill contained only ceramics from the Early Nabanche Achiotes, Dzudzuquil, Pital, Chunhinta, and Joventud groups, suggesting a Middle Preclassic date for the stairway.

Superposition of Retention Walls in the Basal Platform of the Acropolis

During the mapping of the acropolis, the partially exposed south lateral wall of a stairway was discovered on the east side, leading to Structure N0000 E0260. The flight of steps was fashioned from large carved limestone slabs; they probably had not been looted because of their weight and the solidity of the wall. Excavations in the area of the stairway showed the superposition of two retention walls. Despite their spatial and temporal proximity, each presented distinguishing features in form, composition, and construction methods.

The most ancient walls rose about 5 m above ground level. It is likely

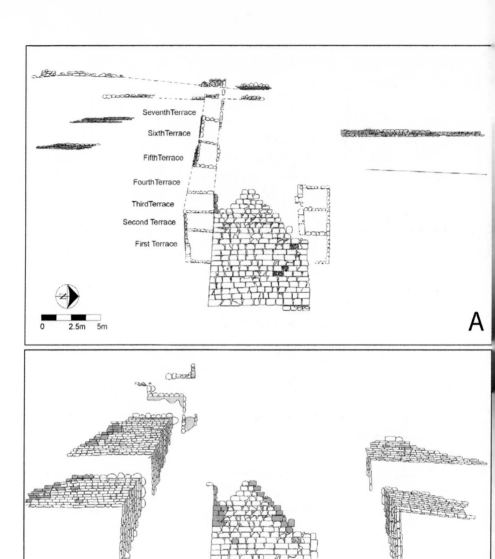

Seventh Terrace

Sixth Terrace

Fifth Terrace

Fourth Terrace

Third Terrace

Second Terrace

First Terrace

0   2.5m   5m

A

0   2.5m   5m

B

Figure 11.2. (a) Plan of the "stepped balustrade" in the south side of the east stairway; (b) plan of the second phase of the basal platform of the acropolis, when the east stairway became inset between the stepped walls that covered the "stepped balustrade" and the flat walls of the previous phase.

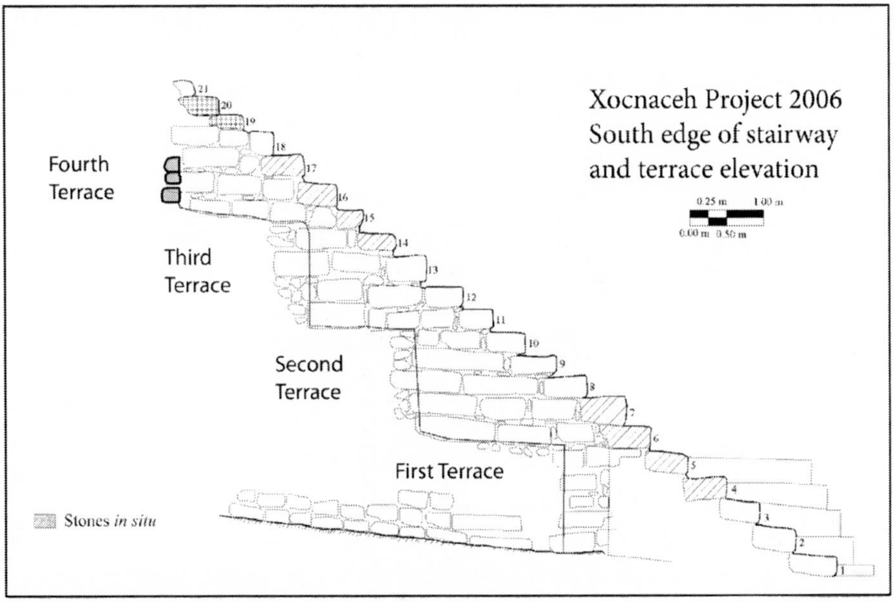

Figure 11.3. South end of the east stairway showing the profile of the four lower terraces of the "stepped balustrade."

that this section of the basal platform consisted of seven stepped tiers, as well as a flight of stairs a little more than 8 m in width, partially outset from the retention walls. On the south side, adjacent to the stairway, a series of seven outset vertical stepped bodies or "stepped balustrade" were identified (Figures 11.2a and 11.3) (although we have positively identified only four of these on the north side, everything indicates they were symmetrically placed). The retention walls and the "stepped balustrade" were fashioned from medium-sized, roughly faced rectangular block-shaped stones, with chinking between them. These walls were smooth, slightly inclined, and were totally covered with a stucco finish 3–4 cm thick. The access stairway also was built with faced stones, but much larger in size (ranging from 58–122 cm in length and from 22–32 cm in height). The treads of the stairs were approximately 40–50 cm in width. This first phase is related to the oldest floor at the foot of the stairway and possibly with the first of the upper floors of the acropolis summit (Floor P-5), since the stairway and the retaining walls which still survive are clearly higher than Floor P-6 of the acropolis. In the second building phase (Figure 11.2b), both sides of the stairway, as well as the retaining walls of the original basal platform, were covered with a new retaining wall that rises the entire height of the basal platform, giving it a monumental look. The sides of the east stairway now

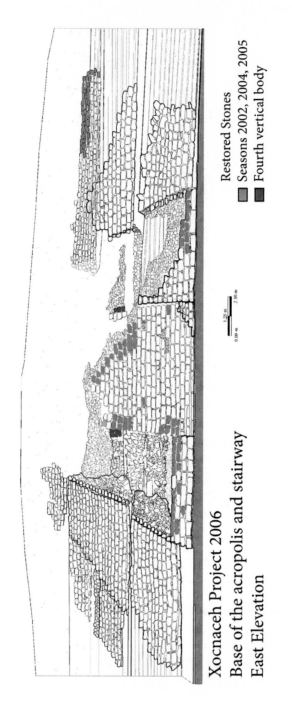

Xocnaceh Project 2006
Base of the acropolis and stairway
East Elevation

Restored Stones
Seasons 2002, 2004, 2005
Fourth vertical body

0.00 m   1.25 m   2.50 m

Figure 11.4. East side of the acropolis showing the stairway and the retaining walls of the last two building phases.

consisted of stepped courses of blocks forming two talud-like tiers, the uppermost being slightly inset from the lower by a narrow landing (Figure 11.4). This same new facade covered the east and south sides, although on the section we explored on the west side, the first retaining wall had been dismantled and reused as fill. The east stairway was in use during both building phases, partially outset during the early one, and then inset between the walls covering the "stepped balustrade." The new retaining walls of the basal platform were elaborated with large rectangular stone blocks, faced in the front and set without mortar. As we mentioned before, this second retaining wall is related to the latest floor of the two found at the foot of the stairway.

Although in a poor state of preservation, it was possible to identify the same sequence of retaining walls and floors on both sides of the southwest corner of the basal platform as we had on the east side (Figure 11.5). The remains of the retaining wall belonging to the second building phase were better preserved on the northern section of the west side, where up to six rows of stones were found in situ. Three rows of the first sloping tier of the basal platform were also preserved in situ along the eastern section of the south side. The total length of the wall and the location of the southwest corner of the basal platform were calculated by extending the well-preserved sections. The north-south retaining wall of the earliest platform was totally dismantled when the second phase wall was built. An exploratory trench in the central section of the south side of the basal platform revealed four large aligned stones (Figure 11.6). Extension of the bearing of the wall on the south side of the southwest corner suggests that there may have been another formal access to the upper platform plaza in this south side of the acropolis (See Figure 11.1b).

Form and Chronology of the Acropolis

Excavations revealed the basal platform resulted from two main building phases. The oldest exclusively contains Early Nabanche material affiliated with Mamom pottery, which at Komchen, Yucatan, has been dated to the second half of the Middle Preclassic period (800/700–400/300 B.C.). Although the fill of this platform was only a little over 2 m in depth, the actual height of the platform was somewhat greater because it had been built over a natural rise with an estimated height of more than a meter. We do not have an exact idea of the total extension of this first construction stage, because all of its retaining walls have not yet been located. However, based

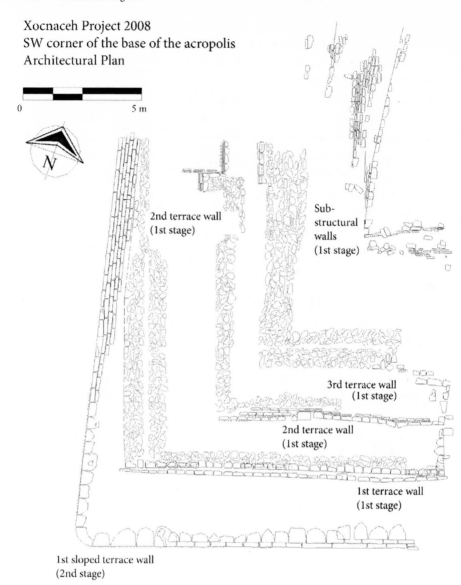

Xocnaceh Project 2008
SW corner of the base of the acropolis
Architectural Plan

0   5 m

N

2nd terrace wall
(1st stage)

Sub-
structural
walls
(1st stage)

3rd terrace wall
(1st stage)

2nd terrace wall
(1st stage)

1st terrace wall
(1st stage)

1st sloped terrace wall
(2nd stage)

Figure 11.5. Plan of the southwest corner of the basal platform of the acropolis.

on the floors of this first structure, identified on the north, east, and west sides of the elevated plaza, it is possible to calculate a minimum size of 64 m east-west by 20 m north-south. The substructure with stair-like walls found in the east excavation, on top of the first floor of the first basal platform, is preserved to a height of over a meter. It remained in use and was unaffected

Figure 11.6. Remains of the first and second steps of the south stairway of the acropolis.

by later plaza floor until it was partially dismantled and covered by almost 4 m of dry fill on average during the second major building stage.

The next basal platform of the complex was considerably higher and wider than the previous one. The volume of fill invested in this new construction is estimated at over 100,000 m³, considering that both axes measure over 140 m. The initial height of the second-stage acropolis platform was over 6 m above the *sascab*-leveled base over which the first one had been built and 2 m higher if the calculation is based upon the oldest floor found at the foot of the stairway. Given that practically all the ceramic material identified under the sets of floors of these two great platforms is Mamom affiliated, it seems clear that the resources invested and power involved in its construction were employed during the second half of the Middle Preclassic period. Mixed deposits with a minimum number of Late Preclassic ceramics indicate that floor renovations and all the constructions explored on top of the elevated plaza were built between the final years of the Middle Preclassic and the transition to the Late Preclassic. Some sections of the upper floors were not totally sealed, so possibly some intrusions may have occurred. The next and last occupation during Preclassic times is marked by the presence of surface ceramics equivalent to the Late Nabanche and Xculul complexes of Komchen.

There are radiometric dates relevant for dating the two main building phases of the acropolis. The East Pit, N046 E066, exposed a substructure built over the earliest plaza during its final building stage; a charcoal sample found in a layer (XOC 80251) close to this structure, below a sealed floor, suggests that the two last floor renovations of the first acropolis occurred about 400 B.C. (Beta-364482). The other charcoal sample was recovered in the lower levels of the West Pit N046 E034 (XOC 80263; not discussed in the text); this deep context indicates that construction started before 700 B.C. (Beta-364481) (Figure 11.1b). In summary, both dates support those based on ceramic data. The earliest building stages of the acropolis range from before 700 to after 400 B.C.; so the construction of the main and last building phase started after this last date, at the end of the Middle Preclassic.

The last construction on the acropolis plaza, during the Late/Terminal Classic, consisted of a low rectangular mound (S0018 E0218) built on Floor 1 and over an existing Preclassic structure. Cehpech ceramics are abundant on top of the last floor, including some preslate types evidencing a reoccupation at the beginning of the Late Classic, especially since no pottery from the Early Classic has been identified.

The retaining walls in talud still preserved from the first basal platform of the second building stage rise between seven to eight meters over ground level on the east side of the acropolis. The seven outset vertical stepped tiers were part of the design of this initial phase of the building climax during the Middle Preclassic. The stairway leads directly to Structure N000 E0260, built on top of a basal platform that probably supported a building with stone walls and a perishable roof. This structure, apparently late in the sequence, implies the existence of a stairway descending to the interior of the elevated plaza.

The southwest corner of the basal platform had an angle less than 90 degrees, suggesting that in its final stage the basal platform had a trapezoidal form with the west side being longer than the east. From the bearing of walls still in situ, it can be concluded that the other three corners were totally dismantled. The total area enclosed by the hypothetical corners implies that the volume of the great platform during its last stage could have exceeded 150,000 m³. Although we can assume that Floor 5 was related with the first retaining wall and phase of the second basal platform, the stepped wall of the second phase cannot as yet be associated with a particular floor. However, similarities in form and building technique of this retaining wall with the exposed wall of the substructure in the east pit, suggest that not much time elapsed between construction of the retaining walls of the great platform. This stepped profile and construction system has not been previously identified in Yucatan, but other examples are now known from sites such as San Francisco de Ticul and San Mateo Oxkutzcab. Poxila presents a combination of both types of walls: the main structure has "stepped buttress" similar to the walls of the first phase, but the retention walls present a stepped profile similar to the wall of the second phase.

Summarizing, the excavations have yielded contexts with ceramics indicating that monumental architecture in Xocnaceh dates from the Middle Preclassic. The last phase of the acropolis, that is the renovation of the acropolis by means of a retaining wall with a stepped profile, was done during the final centuries of this time period. Evidence recovered suggests that the last architectural stages of the acropolis diminished in scale and then ceased during the transition to, or very early during, the Late Preclassic, although occupation could have lasted until the transition to the Early Classic. Four structures were built on the upper floors of the acropolis, but the striking absence of ceramics with bichrome-incised decoration and, in general, of ceramic groups belonging to the northern Cochuah-Puuc sphere, suggests that a hiatus existed in the occupation of the site during the Early Classic period. Occupation then resumed at the beginning of the Late Classic when sherds of the Say group and slate wares of the Cehpech Puuc ceramic sphere are found.

The Geography of Xocnaceh

Access to water sources and the quality of nearby cultivable soils are two factors to consider in analyzing the locations of human settlements chiefly dependent on an agrarian economy. In Yucatan, the oldest and most productive soils are located in areas where access to the aquifer is restricted due to the great depth of the water table, whereas in areas where water is abundant or near the surface, the soils are young and of low fertility. As is well known, the control of salt production and access to local coastlines, as well as access to and distribution of imported commodities, provided economic alternatives to those groups on the northern plain settled within a short distance of the coast, in areas of low agricultural productivity, but with permanent access to the aquifer. Cities such as Dzibilchaltun, Chichen Itza, Ek Balam, and Coba were also founded in areas with permanent bodies of water such as cenotes or lakes. Less well known is that the fringe along the foot of the Sierrita de Ticul maximizes both access to water and to productive soils. The quality of soils eroded from the north face of the Puuc escarpment, coupled with a permanent supply of water from rock-hewn wells, has allowed moderately large communities to flourish at the base of this important physiographic feature, such as modern Maxcanu, Muna Ticul, Oxkutzcab, and Tekax.

The location of Xocnaceh in this strip of high agricultural potential enabled its leaders to organize agriculture production so as to obtain the surplus needed to support this grand construction program during the second half of the Middle Preclassic. The proximity of the Puuc escarpment also aided the procurement of building stone for its public structures. Similarly, the large but badly preserved platforms of San Francisco de Ticul and Akil, also located along this strip, probably also date to the Preclassic rather than the Late Terminal Classic period. Just as with Xocnaceh, their leaders must have had the power to integrate settlements, recruit the labor necessary, and to extract some of the surplus agricultural production for investment in these monumental works. Xocnaceh's strategic location also permitted its inhabitants access to the south slope of the Puuc escarpment where there were ample valleys with deep soils, and although no permanent water was available, inhabitants could take advantage of deep caves, dolines, and medium-sized ponds that accumulated water during the rainy season. The information recovered recently during fine-grained reconnaissance and vertical excavations at sites in the Bolonchen District of the Puuc, such as Labna, Paso del Macho, Kiuic, and Huntichmul, indicates that the supposed absence of Preclassic occupation in the Puuc was an assumption based upon an inadequate sample that did not appear to be linked to the lack of permanent sources of water on the surface. It has sometimes been argued that a sophisticated system of water storage was necessary to guarantee a permanent occupation in the Puuc, but the investment in formal stone architecture leaves little doubt that Paso del Macho and Kiuic were occupied, if not for the entire year, at least for long periods of time. As is well known, no Preclassic water storage feature has as yet been identified in the Puuc. A key question for future research will therefore be how agriculturalists of the Preclassic were able to assure their water supply since early settlements were by then sufficiently numerous to suggest a continuous occupation of the Puuc region, from the close of the Middle Preclassic onward.

The geographic location of Xocnaceh proved advantageous to explore the relations between the Puuc Preclassic centers, including Paso del Macho, Kiuic, Huntichmul, and Labna, and contemporary sites of the northern plains such as Poxila, Tzeme, and Komchen. Although the details of these relations are still unknown, similarities of architecture as well as site layouts are present from the Middle Preclassic onward, while non-ceramic artifacts such as shell and imported stone suggest some degree of interaction among them. The coexistence of sites with architectural complexes like those of Xocnaceh, Paso del Macho, and Kiuic, as well as other agrarian communities of minor rank such as we find at Labna and Huntichmul suggest a significant level of population as well as a regional hierarchy of sites in the greater Puuc region. In addition, the fact that during this time we also find more than 100 sites of various ranks in the northwest and north of Yucatan, in regions of especially low agricultural potential (although with some potential for irrigation at the household level), could indicate that by the closing centuries of the Middle Preclassic the northern peninsula had reached a high enough population density that even areas of less favorability were being intensively settled.

It is still somewhat premature to judge whether Xocnaceh was the capital of a large chiefdom, a proto-state, or an archaic state during the final centuries of the Middle Preclassic. It seems evident, however, that the volume and quality of its architecture indicates the management of a large labor force beyond the local level, as well as some specialized labor. It is also worth noting that the first large-scale architectural projects in Yucatan follow the widespread pattern of constructing monumental platforms. Instead of pyramidal temples or funerary monuments, these early structures were designed to accommodate large numbers of people, at least on special occasions. These great complexes with large open spaces suggest that social differences had as yet to harden sufficiently for restricting social interaction. It may also have been a social configuration that ultimately could not be sustained in the face of the emergence of communities with a more defined social hierarchy during the Late Preclassic period.

12

El Achiotal

An Interior Frontier Center in Northwestern Peten, Guatemala

MARY JANE ACUÑA

Introduction

Research at the site of El Achiotal began in 2009 with the goal of studying questions about regional politics and interactions during the Preclassic period (1200 B.C.–A.D. 300) in the southern Maya lowlands, with particular emphasis on the northwestern region of Peten, Guatemala. The site became quite significant because it was the first primarily Preclassic center to undergo archaeological investigation in this region. Geographically, El Achiotal's location in an ecotone between the central karstic uplands (more commonly known as the Mirador Basin) and the western wetlands characterizes it as an interior frontier site in the periphery of the Mirador region (Acuña 2013). The small center was built on a leveled ridge surrounded by seasonally inundated *bajos* on the western margin of the central karstic uplands of northern Peten. It was here that overland transport along formal causeways across *bajos* of the Mirador area and then on dry land trails westward from such large sites as El Tintal would have given way to rainy season canoe transport across seasonally inundated *bajos* draining into the tributary streams of the San Pedro Mártir River.

My investigations from 2009 through 2011 revealed that El Achiotal's principal temple locality, Structure 5C-01, was imbued with royal symbolism more commonly associated with large lowland centers of the period. However, several characteristics at the site, including the unique style of its mural paintings, settlement layout and organization, location, and early chronology, suggested a distinct variation from known Late Preclassic lowland Maya centers. While exhibiting many unique qualities and archaeological variables, El Achiotal certainly developed within the Late Preclassic geopolitical context of the broader lowland region, and through its iconographic expressions on monumental architecture demonstrated its knowledge of a widespread political ideology. Additionally, the population at El Achiotal was also familiar with the more ancient Olmec ideology that dates as early as the Middle Preclassic period. Although the investigations at El Achiotal continue, in this chapter I summarize the archaeological and iconographic evidence from Structure 5C-01 that indicate that rulership was established at the small center of El Achiotal in the Late Preclassic period. I argue that variables such as geographic location and control over knowledge provided Late Preclassic centers with leverage to negotiate their status and power within the broader regional geopolitics, thus challenging conventional models used to understand early political authority and its organization over the landscape.

The State of Affairs in the Preclassic Maya Lowlands

The absence of a widespread corpus of hieroglyphic inscriptions in the Preclassic period makes the study of the political geography of that early era substantially more challenging than during the later Classic period. Today, scholars of the Preclassic Maya have come a long way in the study and understanding of the early civilization since the benchmark seminar on origins of Maya civilization decades ago (Adams 1977; see Brown and Bey Chapter 1 this volume). Throughout the 20th century the discipline of anthropology also went through many paradigmatic changes that affected the explanatory models used for developing interpretations on early complex sociopolitical and economical organizations. Alongside these theoretical changes and to this day, archaeology has unearthed heaps of new data on the Preclassic Maya since the early discoveries at Uaxactun, Tikal, Ceibal, Altar de Sacrificios, and El Mirador in Guatemala, and the New River valley sites in Belize (Coe 1982, 1990; Hammond 1985; Hammond, ed. 1991; Matheny 1980; Pendergast 1981; Ricketson and Ricketson 1937; Smith 1950; Valdés 1986; Valdés et al. 1999; Willey 1973, 1982; Willey et al. 1975). With access to new and improved data, archaeologists have focused a great deal of their attention on the origin and development of early lowland Maya society, and thus have provided new avenues for understanding the origins of political authority. With the advantage of increased data, some scholars have now embraced a multi-variable approach that emphasizes inter-regional interaction as a catalyst for increased complexity throughout Mesoamerica as a whole, which included sociopolitical hierarchy and political leadership, control over resources and their movement over the landscape, control over esoteric knowledge, conspicuous consumption, control over labor, and the ability to establish and promote a religious ideology (Algaze 1993; Crumley 1976; Demarest 1992a; Drennan 1984; Freidel 1981; Marcus 1993; Rosenswig 2010; Scarborough and Clark 2007; Spencer and Redmond 2004). Interaction and exchange gave way to sharing and administration of knowledge, which led to the ability of some individuals to learn to control information and use it to garner power (Rosenswig 2010). Knowledge moved across the landscape in various ways, including via symbolic systems and religious ideologies (Brown et al. Chapter 5 this volume; Freidel 1981; Rosenswig 2010), in bundles and gifts (Stuart 2006), messengers, traders, diplomatic visits, and migrations. In tandem with the institutionalization of political authority through the manipulation of a religious ideology into state power was the need to develop a functional political economy that would guarantee access to goods over long distances (Drennan 1984; Freidel et al. 2002; Freidel and Reilly 2010; Rathje 1971).

The power of the state was institutionalized in part through the codification of religion into a symbolic system (Freidel 1981:190), registered in portable items, sculpture, site layouts, architecture, and mural paintings, among other forms. The display of knowledge in this way was at the same time a demonstration of wealth, which contributed directly to social inequality and status ranking (Acuña 2013). Wealth and status were critical in strengthening the integration of the political ideology with the economy, as they were characteristics associated with access to luxury items and knowledge of the symbolic vocabulary, as well as to the ability to store wealth in order to access food and goods through exchange networks (Freidel et al. 2002; Freidel and Reilly 2010).

Insofar as the political organization of the period in the southern lowlands, sites in the central karstic uplands, like Nakbe and El Mirador, contained evidence as early as the Middle Preclassic period for political authority as displayed through status differentiation, complex and monumental architecture, and evidence for long-distance trade (Clark and Hansen 2001:15; Hansen 1992a, 1998, 2001). Although not the only sites in the Maya lowlands to exhibit such traits, Nakbe and El Mirador were proposed as the earliest seats of state-level power in this region (Hansen 1998). El Mirador appears to have consolidated a more concrete system of governance some time in the fifth century B.C. These changes occurred around the same time that the Olmec site of La Venta in the Gulf Coast was declining. The relationship between Olman and the Maya lowlands during the final years of the Middle Preclassic remains a matter of intense interest and debate (Clark and Hansen 2001; Freidel and Reilly 2010; Freidel et al. n.d.), but during their heyday, the Olmec population experienced a time of abundance that favored long-distance exchange networks reaching into the Maya lowlands (Fields and Reents-Budet 2005a).

As sites flourished throughout the Maya lowlands during the Middle and Late Preclassic periods trade networks in all directions were strengthened, sharing knowledge and establishing cultural canons (Coe 1977a; Freidel 1979; Freidel et al. n.d.; Sharer and Traxler 2006:170, 180). It is through this process that scholars propose the Maya assimilated certain aspects of Olmec ideology, such as ascribing divine power to kings (Fields 1989; Fields and Reents-Budet 2005b; Guernsey 2006b; Reilly 1991).

The sophisticated symbolic expressions of Olmec ideology were displayed in monumental sculpture and art, and are referred to as the "Olmec style," as they appear throughout Mesoamerica. The primary themes represent cosmological concepts associated with rulership and authority, ritual, and religion (Clark and Pye 2006; Fields 1989, 1991; Freidel 1990; Guthrie et al. 1996; Pool 2007; Reilly 1989, 1996, 2005; Taube 1995, 1996). Olmec ideology was represented graphically with a fairly consistent repertoire of symbols and elements, which makes them recognizable outside of the Olman region. Olmec iconography is strongly associated with the natural and supernatural worlds, rulership, religion, and ritual. The connection between human life cycles and those of the natural world became broad Mesoamerican ideological themes that emphasized agricultural fertility, and focused on the rituals and beliefs around maize (Freidel and Reilly 2010; Joralemon 1971; Taube 1995, 1996). For the Olmec, and later the Maya, a ruler's divinity and power had its foundation through the maize cult. Rulers impersonated the Maize God to become agents of fertility and guarantee the well-being of the population (Fields 1991; Freidel et al. 1993; Reilly 1989; Taube 1996, 2004a). Graphically, one of the most significant ways of representing this concept was with a motif known as the trilobulate diadem jewel (Taube 1996), identified as the semantic equivalent of *ajaw* (Fields 1989), and nicknamed the Jester God (Schele 1974). This motif became the earliest symbol of Maya rulership.

In the Middle Preclassic, divine kingship may be present in the southern Maya lowlands (Estrada-Belli 2006), but the mechanisms by which that adoption occurred and its chronology remain obscure. The Late Preclassic, however, witnessed the flourishing of kingship, materialized in sophisticated artistic programs in murals, sculpted masks, carved stelae, and settlement organization. Yet, like the earlier period, what remains unresolved is how kings came into power during the Preclassic period, or what levels of rulership existed across the landscape and how they related to one another. There is no evidence to support the existence of the system based on paternal dynastic lineage prior to A.D. 90, when it was launched by Yax Ehb Xook of Tikal (Martin and Grube 2008). There is also no evidence for that system to have become widespread, especially not north of Tikal. Regardless of how, we do have sufficient evidence to suggest that contrary to earlier interpretations, Preclassic kings and rulers were not only concerned with mythology and religion, but were also greatly involved in politics and economics, which brings us back to the convergence of ideology and economy discussed earlier.

Life in the Preclassic period was expensive. Beyond basic subsistence, increased complexity required the acquisition of goods and materials from near and distant places to meet the expectations of the political and ceremonial festivities (Wells and Davis-Salazar 2007). Control over trade networks required spreading power over greater distances to secure continued access to goods, but it also meant the development of increased inequality at both the polity and social levels. The region of northern Peten, Guatemala, appears to have had limited sustainable resources, yet archaeological evidence supports the proposition that the power and influence of El Mirador spread far and wide (Reese-Taylor and Walker 2002). Given the apparent lack of navigable rivers, sites in the central karstic uplands relied almost exclusively on human porters to successfully transport the necessary subsistence and luxury goods in and out of the region.

The political landscape of the southern Maya lowlands is envisioned as a core of major sites, like El Mirador and El Tintal, located primarily on the central karstic uplands, surrounded by a periphery with numerous centers of various sizes and scales of monumentality. The wide distribution of local and non-local material culture and symbolic systems favors interaction as a principal component of the economy. The nature of the relationship between sites is still an ongoing subject of investigation, but it is increasingly apparent that interaction was not unilineal or top-down. The legacy of cultural evolutionary perspectives pertaining to societal development from simple to complex has led us to assume that, for the most part, size and monumentality of Maya centers are a direct reflection of hierarchical ranking between sites. Growing archaeological evidence favors a more symbiotic view of transactions among communities of various levels of authority, not necessarily dependent on their hierarchical ranking based on proximity to a core, but more likely correlated to their geographical position on important communication routes and control over resources (Freidel 1979; Masson 2002; Rathje 1971).

Furthermore, given the broad stylistic uniformity of the Chicanel ceramic sphere, it is assumed by scholars that Late Preclassic sites paralleled ceramic homogenization in other features and adhered to a particular pattern dictated by a dominant and shared ideology (Hansen 1998:76). Reese-Taylor and Walker (2002), writing from the vantage point of Cerros in Belize in particular and the eastern lowlands in general, argue that the homogeneity of characteristic features throughout the Late Preclassic was a direct result of efforts by El Mirador's rulers to control trade routes to its east. The link between El Mirador and the sites believed to fall under its influence is attested by similarities in artistic and architectural styles, site and settlement orientation, and the presence of particular architectural complexes such as the E-Group. For the most part, however, I would argue these traits are primarily indications of a shared ideology and religion codified into a complex system of symbols (Freidel 1981; Hansen 1998), promoting the notion of an integrated political system. Archaeological investigations have revealed that there is a greater diversity of Preclassic centers than previously thought, as a consequence of location and control over knowledge and resources.

The Western Frontier

In addition to considering the political organization of the Maya lowlands based on archaeological traits and variables that are used for ranking sites on a hierarchical scale, I think it is critical to incorporate geographical location as another variable to the equation. A particular feature of the landscape that characterizes the so-called core of the southern Maya lowlands is the natural boundary created by the karstic escarpment defining the eastern and southern limits of the upland region. On the western side, the escarpment is not as well defined, but it nonetheless marks the division between the western wetlands and the upland region. Geographically, this is an interior frontier zone, and is thus differentiated from a cultural frontier. It is where seasonal canoe transportation of materials transitioned to foot porters.

Frontier sites are elemental for studying interregional economic interactions (Green and Perlman 1985; Lightfoot and Martinez 1995; Rothman

2001). Examples from the northern Yucatan, such as Xtobo, indicate that frontier sites are often anomalous with respect to sites located in the core areas. Xtobo is a small moderate center with archaeological indicators of complexity in the Middle Preclassic, including settlement layout and architectural features, such as pyramids, causeways, and a ballcourt (Anderson 2010; Anderson et al. Chapter 8 this volume). The relevance here is the precocious presence of the rubber ball game. Rubber balls as offerings are present in El Manatí lagoon in the Gulf Coast heartland of the Olmec civilization at 1600 B.C. radiocarbon years (Hosler et al. 1999). Therefore, it is possible that the game was adopted in this Maya frontier zone of northwestern Yucatan as part of a trade network with sites in the Gulf Coast (Anderson 2010; Sharer and Traxler 2006). Another frontier site example is Ceibal, located on the Pasion River in southwestern Peten, where recent research demonstrates that during the Middle Preclassic Ceibal was expressing styles generally associated with Olmec sites, earlier than evidence known from core centers in the Maya lowlands (Inomata et al. 2013; Inomata et al. 2010).

Frontier regions west of the core plateau (traditionally termed the Mirador Basin) remain largely unknown. The archaeological site of El Achiotal is geographically peripheral to plateau core centers by its location in an ecotone. An ecotone is a boundary between ecosystems, for example between wetlands and uplands, and these transition zones are extremely important buffers (Holland et al. 1990). In this case, the ecotone is the transitional area between *bajos* and river systems in northwestern Peten and the elevated karstic plateau extending eastward. This geographical and natural boundary is similar to regions that Rathje called "buffer zones," where important polities would be established for the exchange of goods (Rathje 1972). Furthermore, the extensive water system spreading westward from El Achiotal would have facilitated the transportation of bulk goods and commodities by canoe in and out of the core region (Freidel et al. 2015).

El Achiotal

As noted, El Achiotal is a small southern lowland Maya site located between the northwestern Peten wetlands and the central Peten karstic uplands. The site is located atop a karst ridge, approximately 40 m elevated from the surrounding *bajos* (Figure 12.1). During the rainy season when these *bajos* flood, the ridge is transformed into a seasonal island. Preliminary studies of the regional topography and hydrology support the hypothesis of a

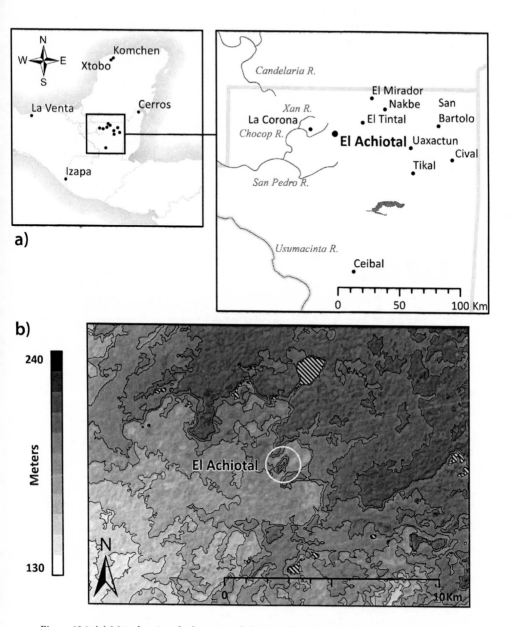

Figure 12.1. (a) Map showing the location of El Achiotal in the Maya lowlands; (b) topographic map of immediate area around the site; note location of the ridge just west of the central karstic uplands (maps by C. R. Chiriboga).

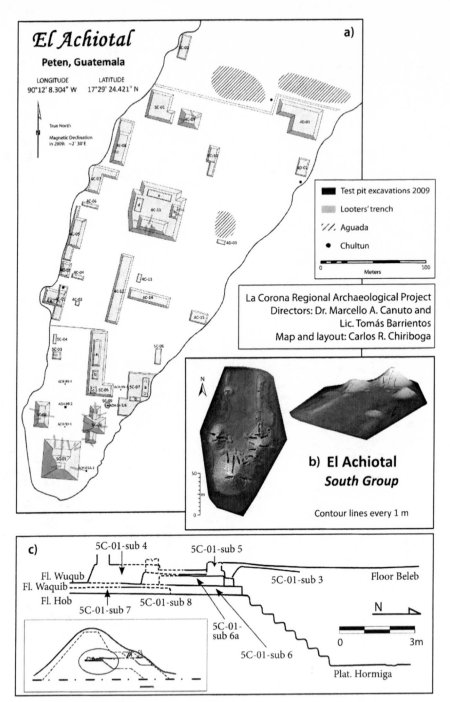

Figure 12.2. (a) Schematic map of El Achiotal. Structure 5C-01 is the southernmost and tallest building at the site; (b) topographic map of the South Group, with Str. 5C-01; (c) cross-section of Str. 5C-01 with enlarged architectural sequence that pertains to discussion (maps by C. R. Chiriboga; drawing by M. J. Acuña).

westward seasonal, navigable route through the San Juan Watershed toward the San Pedro Mártir River (Freidel et al. 2015). In addition to the networking routes known to link Central Peten with the rest of Mesoamerica through the northern lowlands, the New River valley in Belize, the Maya highlands, and southeastern Mesoamerica in general, there is now favorable evidence in support of an additional route to supply the central core centers. El Achiotal's location at the juncture of wetland to dry land characterizes it as a way station or port city (Acuña 2013; Freidel et al. 2015).

The ridge measures 700 m long by 200 m wide, and visible settlement is constrained to the southern half, while the northern area remains primarily flat. The site contains a total of 28 mounds arranged around two primary elongated plazas, with other patio groups of irregular size and form (Figure 12.2a). It seems likely that the shape of the narrow ridge determined to a certain extent the layout of the site, as one can appreciate the series of structures built along the western edge of the ridge paralleling a line of buildings along the center, and framing the two long plazas. So far, the earlier settlement appears to be on the southern tip of the ridge, the South Group, which follows a general orientation of ca. 4.5 degrees east of north. If the ridge shape did not dictate the earlier settlement, it certainly determined how the site expanded. The North Group was built along a ca. 14.5 degrees east of north orientation, following the general alignment of the ridge.

Unlike many of its known contemporaries, El Achiotal lacks the architectural and stylistic elements that commonly characterize Preclassic lowland Maya sites, or at the very least those believed to fall under the influence of El Mirador (cf. Hansen 1998; Reese-Taylor and Walker 2002). Instead, the settlement's dominant orientation is north-south, not east-west; it does not have a readily identifiable E-Group; and its Preclassic iconographic repertoire is unique in style.

Complexity in the Making

From 2009 to 2011, my research focused on the largest pyramid at the site, Structure 5C-01. The building is located at the southernmost tip of the ridge and it dominates the South Group by rising 17 m above plaza level (Acuña 2013; Acuña and Chiriboga 2010) (Figure 12.2b-c). As is the case at most archaeological sites, this building was severely damaged by looters' trenches and tunnels that penetrated deep into the core of the mound. These illegal excavations exposed a long sequence of early architecture, including a Late

Preclassic building that was decorated with stylistically unique murals on its exterior corners and lateral walls.

A detailed recording of the stratigraphic sequence exposed inside the looters' tunnels and archaeological excavations produced a long sequence of construction activity, likely beginning in the late Middle Preclassic. This long sequence of construction episodes began with compact earthen platforms, which subsequently transitioned to masonry buildings and the use of thick plaster floors. The foundations of Structure 5C-01 were built using *bajo* muck, consistent with construction techniques identified at contemporary sites in the region (Hansen 1998; Inomata et al. 2013). The small amount of pottery discovered in the earlier stratigraphic layers corresponds to the transitional period from the Middle to the Late Preclassic, and reveals that the early population was also familiar with the regional ceramic tradition, namely the Chicanel Horizon.

Atop the solid foundation, the first raised construction included primarily earthen mounds. With the available evidence at hand at the moment, it is impossible to discern the size and layout of these early buildings. About 5 to 6 m above that early construction is the surface of a large two-tiered masonry platform, Structure 5C-01-sub 8, with a staircase descending on its north side to the plaza (Figure 12.2c). This platform was evidently the first formal masonry construction, finished with a thick (about 6–7 cm) plaster floor and staircase. Although I was unable to define the platform's dimensions, its monumentality is evident by the subsequent construction of other buildings on the summit forming a patio group. Excavations exposed definite evidence of the eastern Structure, 5C-01-sub 8a that was a two-tiered building that faced west, and a smaller platform labeled Structure 5C-01-sub 8b that was slightly less than a meter in height on the northeast corner of the summit. Based on this organization and ancient Maya architectural symmetry, I proposed that there was likely also a building on the western and, perhaps, southern sides of the platform in keeping with Preclassic triadic architectural patterns (Acuña 2013). It was also evident that Structure 5C-01-sub 8 was built atop a larger basal platform, but it is still unclear whether they were part of the same building effort. The next series of identifiable construction events took place seemingly rapidly based on their stratigraphic placement; however, the chronological correspondence is unclear. First, the level of the platform summit was raised one step higher (Structure 5C-01-sub 7), but without reaching the edge of the staircase, which remained the same. A similar, new remodeling event took place a few inches above (Structure 5C-01-sub 6), only this time extending the surface as far as the staircase and thus adding one more step. Subsequently, Structure 5C-01-sub 6a, a small platform of approximately 3 m in width, was constructed at the top of the staircase and added yet another step. This new building was a small raised platform at the top of the stairs along the central axis, which I interpreted as a space intentionally elevating activity performed by a ruler or high-ranking leader (Acuña 2013). The monumentality of Structure 5C-01-sub 8 already suggested the presence of complex sociopolitical institutions at the site, but Structure 5C-01-sub 6a is for now the earliest evidence of public performance. I believe the next two construction phases lend support to this interpretation.

The patio above the platform soon became difficult to view from the plaza level, as a new building, Structure 5C-01-sub 5, replaced the small platform described earlier. This new, northern building was a true threshold structure. It was a small rectangular masonry building measuring 4.90 m on an east-west axis and 2.70 m on a north-south axis, with a doorway on both the north and south sides. Its position at the top edge of the staircase, providing access into the now restricted patio atop, was similar to that of Structure H-sub 10 at Uaxactun's Group H. Although much of Structure 5C-01-sub 5 was destroyed during the next remodeling episode, some painted decoration on the back (south) wall and the northwest doorjamb survived. The partial decoration on the doorjamb is quite geometrical in style, but the pattern is reminiscent of textiles, or early representations of scaffolding, both of which are symbolically associated with early kingship (Freidel and Reilly 2010; Freidel et al. n.d.; Guernsey 2006a). For now, this was the earliest aesthetic representation of a symbolic vocabulary that was integrated into an architectural program in the sequence. As such, it is the first formal evidence supporting increased political and ideological complexity at the site.

Subsequently, this early threshold building was superseded by the construction of a larger building, Structure 5C-01-sub 4 in the sequence. This later building was a modification of the earlier one. Remodeling involved raising the interior floor level, extending the building south making the north-south axis 4.80 m, and widening the new addition in the back 0.40 m in comparison to the front. Structure 5C-01-sub 4 was essentially a temple-style building with the only entrance located on the north, at the top of the staircase. In addition to the low basal platform, the main structure had masonry walls rising well above 1.50 m, based on the highest surviving portion exposed in one of the tunnels. The *talud* section of the platform was painted light red and framed with a band of darker red. The walls of

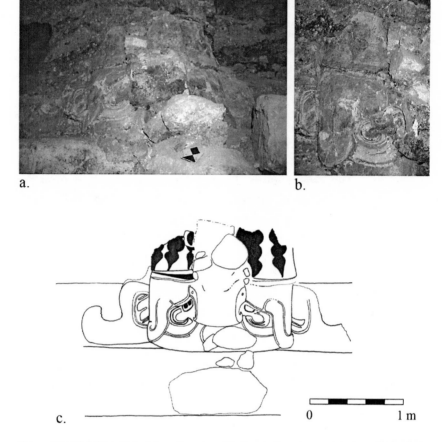

Figure 12.3. El Achiotal Mask 1 on Structure 5C-01-sub 4's staircase: (a) view of the whole mask; (b) close-up of west side of face; and (c) front view drawing (photos and drawing by M. J. Acuña).

the temple were coated in a light cream plaster. What characterized this building was the elaborate, stylistically unique set of murals that decorated the exterior walls. The symbolic vocabulary expressed in the murals points more definitively toward the presence of a political institution at El Achiotal in the Late Preclassic period. In addition to the murals, this building donned a modeled stucco mask located on the central axis of the main staircase, just outside the temple doorway. The upper surface of the mask would have created a doorway-level salient space, perhaps for ritual activity and performance. It is possible that the mask was used as a performance space for a ruler at El Achiotal, much in the same way as Classic period rulers were portrayed standing on images that represented their performance locations (Stuart and Houston 1994). The staircase mask at El Achiotal is considerably smaller than other contemporary masks from lowland Maya Late Preclassic sites (Brown and Garber 2005; Freidel 2005; Hansen 1992a). It measures only 0.70 m in height by 1.30 m wide (Figure 12.3a-b), and its location directly on the stairs is a unique departure from the typical Late Preclassic placement on platform walls flanking central staircases (Estrada-Belli 2006, 2008; Freidel 2005; Hansen 1992a).

Tunnel excavations along the exterior west wall of Structure 5C-01-sub 4, and along the base of Structure 5C-01-sub 8's north wall, which was still in use during the occupation of the temple above, revealed three ash lenses located on the associated floor surfaces. Carbon samples from each one were analyzed using Accelerated Mass Spectrometry, and combined produced a range of calibrated dates from 50 B.C. through A.D. 250, or the Late to Terminal Preclassic period (Acuña 2013:334). The facade of Structure 5C-01-sub 8, which supported the previously described sequence, was decorated with panels or masks flanking the central staircase that accessed the temple above (Structure 5C-01-sub 4). However, tunnel excavations exposed only sections of the armature of a mask on the west side of the staircase.

Trenches and tunnels on the front of Structure 5C-01 exposed features of additional construction episodes that covered the sequence described thus far. Structure 5C-01-sub 4 was buried no later than some time in the Terminal Preclassic period (ca. A.D. 200–250) based on the radiocarbon date range. The subsequent construction phases are not as clearly defined, but it is worth noting that they increased substantially in scale and monumentality. The penultimate phase, Structure 5C-01-sub 2, was decorated with large, mainstream modeled stucco masks flanking the central staircase. Toward the end of the Preclassic period, therefore, the main temple locus at El Achiotal experienced major changes, beginning with the enormous effort to cover and cancel the earlier sequence. There is also evidence for the intentional effacing and destruction of some iconographic programs that identified that earlier period, or recalled a particular ideological affiliation. The new construction was comparatively greater in size, it enlarged the footprint of the basal platform, and it also slightly shifted the orientation and central axis of the building. These alterations in art and architecture reflected changes in political and ideological spheres as well, likely in response to events occurring at a regional level.

The Iconography of Political and Economic Power at El Achiotal

Along with monumentality in architecture, the Preclassic Maya made statements of power by decorating important buildings with artistic programs whose content was primarily concerned with concepts of religion and ideology (Demarest 1992a; Estrada-Belli 2006; Freidel 1981, 1985). Much of the symbolic content included imagery associated with rulership, deities, creation myths, and cosmology, and served as a mechanism to unify the population into an organized system socially, politically, and economically (Freidel and Reilly 2010; Miller 2001:60). Combined, the monumental architecture and artistic programs served as propaganda and statements of sacred power. In comparison to large, visible sculpted decorations on building facades, buildings were also painted on their exterior or interior walls. Paintings were likely more restricted in access, and understood only by those with control over esoteric knowledge.

Excavations revealed a total of eight mural paintings that decorated Structure 5C-01-sub 4. These were located on all four corners, the middle of the lateral and back walls and the northeast doorjamb (presumably there was a ninth mural on the northwest doorjamb, but it was not excavated). All the murals shared a similarity in composition and style, painted in red using a resist style. Compositionally, all murals have a central panel that is comprised of stacked iconographic elements, framed by vertically positioned J-scroll-and-bracket motifs that are also stacked. While the framing motifs are the same in all the murals, the central panel is unique to each one. Intentional destruction, as well as subsequent construction activity, demolished much of the walls and therefore the murals. Most were left with about 20 cm of painted surface from the base up, just enough to appreciate that they shared the same compositional pattern. Murals 1, 2, and 4 are the best preserved, with as much as 1.40 m of painted surface for the former (Figure 12.4).

The first to be discovered, Mural 1 was located on the middle section of the lateral east wall of Structure 5C-01-sub 4. The central panel contains the representation of stacked elements, including from top to bottom: a head or mask in profile that faces south; a knot and bundle; three leaf-shaped elements that hang from the bundle; and, at the base a profile version of a J-scroll-and-bracket. I previously identified this composition as a bundle mask, likely an ancestor bundle mask (Acuña 2010, 2011, 2013), conceptually similar to contemporaneous examples from Tikal and San Bartolo. The example from Tikal consists of the fuschite mask found in Burial 85,

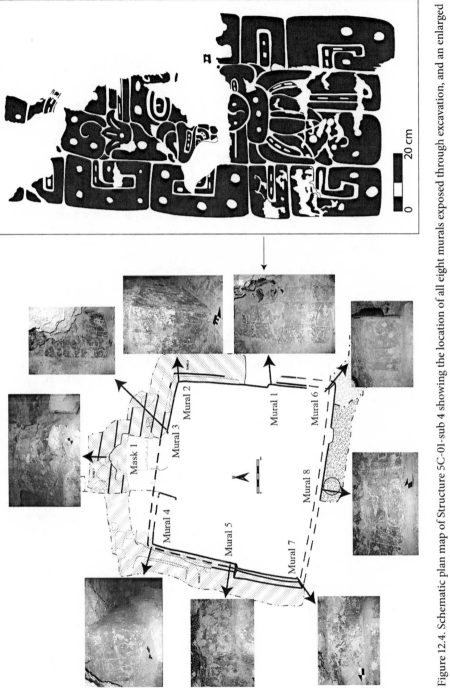

Figure 12.4. Schematic plan map of Structure 5C-01-sub 4 showing the location of all eight murals exposed through excavation, and an enlarged drawing of Mural 1 (photos and drawings by M. J. Acuña; photos are not at scale).

and the one from San Bartolo is a sacred bundle painted on the west wall of the Pinturas Sub-1A building (Figure 12.5b) (Coe 1965b:21; Saturno et al. 2005:8–9). Like these other examples, the bundle mask at El Achiotal's Mural 1 wears the trilobulate diadem jewel of kingship (Fields 1991). The concept of bundles with heads/masks is found in a variety of media, such as sculpture and decorated pottery, throughout Preclassic Mesoamerica and particularly Olmec sites (Reilly 2006a). The mask in Mural 1 shares a certain affinity with the scene of an open bundle incised on a vessel that is thought to come from the area of Chalcatzingo in the Mexican state of Morelos, dated to 1150–800 B.C. (Figure 12.5a) (Guthrie et al. 1996:288; Reilly 2006a). The similarity between these two examples suggests the concept of masks on bundles can be dated back at least to the Middle Preclassic in the Olmec region. In fact, the concept may be linked to the Olmec practice of illustrating rulers seated on top of large sculpted bundles such as La Venta Monument 77 (Reilly 2006a:17). Reilly (2006a:17–18) makes a connection between these styles of sacred bundle representations with the maize cult, which legitimized rulers' divinity. The trefoil jewel bears directly on this cult, as through its association with the Olmec maize cult it symbolized Maya royalty and authority (Fields 1991:167–168). Maya bundling representations such as this one were likely borrowed foreign concepts that were then adapted to the prevalent local ideology. The fact that the building is decorated with this symbolism suggests Structure 5C-01-sub 4 was important in the institutionalization of rulership at El Achiotal.

Other elements on the mural at El Achiotal can be undoubtedly identified as pertaining to the lowland Maya Preclassic iconographic corpus: the U-shape brow, the foliage hanging from the bundle, the crown jewel style, and the scrolls. The number of elements identified as Maya exceeds that of Olmec ones, however, the combination of these elements in the presentation of the mural's concept makes this artistic program unique. The bundle knot is a standard Maya knot, and can frequently be seen on ear-flares, wrists and ankles, belt assemblages, and other representations often associated with bundling. On Mural 1, three leaves hang from the bundle, reminiscent of the common representation of three celts, as found on the examples from Nakbe Stela 1 (Hansen and Guenter 2005:61), the Leiden Plaque (Florescano 2005:17), and on murals in the Pinturas building at San Bartolo (Saturno et al. 2005). The J-scroll-and-bracket just below the leaves is represented in profile, like the mask. A common element in Maya iconography of the Late Preclassic, the J-scroll-and-bracket is found often dangling from ear-flares or appended to belt assemblages, among other

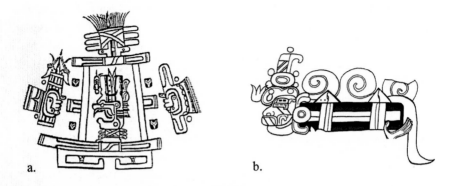

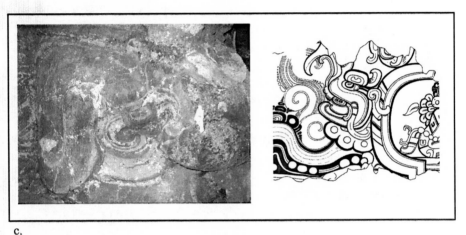

Figure 12.5. (a) Depiction of an open bundle incised on the Chalcatzingo vase (drawing by F. K. Reilly, after Reilly 2006a: 6); (b) drawing of a ritual bundle with mask, North Wall in Pinturas Sub-1A at San Bartolo (drawing by H. Hurst, after Saturno et al. 2005: Figure 30a); (c) comparison of mask features with the turtle from the San Bartolo west wall mural (photograph by M. J. Acuña; drawing by H. Hurst, after Saturno et al. 2009: 125) (images not at scale).

examples. In fact, Late Preclassic belt assemblages are composed of a similar set of stacked elements as those painted on Mural 1.

At El Achiotal, the entire composition is framed by vertically positioned J-scroll-and-bracket motifs. In her discussion on bound monuments, Julia Guernsey (2006a) proposed that the J-scroll-and-bracket motif represented patterns of cloth. The appearance of this motive on architecture further led Guernsey (2006a:33–34) to propose that, like monuments, buildings could also be bound into power—at least symbolically. Given that all the murals painted on Structure 5C-01-sub 4 are framed by vertically positioned

J-scroll-and-brackets, these elements are not only bundling the contents of each panel, but the entire set are symbolically "bundling" the building (Acuña 2013).

The mask discovered on the staircase axis breaks from the Preclassic Maya lowland traditional location pattern of flanking the staircase. The polychromatic palette used on the mask contrasts with the monochromatic murals. Like the murals, however, the mask represents a conflation of symbolism and meaning, and while individual elements are well known in the iconographic corpus of the Late Preclassic period, its composition is unique. The mask is a representation of a zoomorphic being characterized by a down-hooked nose, tear-shaped or squinted eyes, double incurved scroll mouth with molar, exterior mouth scrolls, scrolled earflares decorated with U-elements, and a headband decorated with droplets. Some features of the staircase mask at El Achiotal are comparable to elements used on the Principal Bird Deity, in particular the breath scrolls, as well as to features of the turtle painted on the west wall of the San Bartolo Pinturas's building (Saturno 2009:125) (Figure 12.5c). In a more detailed description of the mask (Acuña 2013:292–302), I pointed out that the droplets were representations of liquid or substances. With that in mind, I further compared the mask to other Late Preclassic representations of effigy censers and cylinder stands, in which substances were burned. Effigy censer stands were a long-standing tradition in the Maya lowlands, and the Late Classic Altar 4 from El Cayo (Taube 2009:Figure 12) depicts an effigy censer decorated with droplets very similar to those painted on the headband of the mask at El Achiotal. It is possible that the decoration on the headband symbolically represented substance residue of activity that took place on its surface. Perhaps, the architectural arrangement of Structure 5C-01-sub 4 is a physical antecedent to a scene incised on a Classic period vessel that depicts a mask built into the upper steps of a temple, on which rests an effigy censer burning something (see Taube 1998:Figure 13a). The scene on this vessel also includes a large bundle with a mask placed on top of a bench on the interior of the temple. The iconographic similarities of the Late Classic vessel scene with the evidence on Structure 5C-01-sub 4 are further suggestive of its identification as a bundle house.

Structure 5C-01-sub 4 as a Bundle House

Based on the iconographic representation of bundles painted on the walls of the exterior of Structure 5C-01-sub 4, I proposed the building was a bundle house (Acuña 2011, 2013). In addition to symbolizing a sacred ideology, it might have actually been used as a place for bundling items and ancestors, or bringing bundles for ritual and economic purposes. The iconography of Mural 1 represents the insignia of rulership with the use of the trefoil jewel, and it also references ancestry through the symbolic display of a bundle mask. The archaeological and iconographic equivalents were discovered in Tikal Burial 85 (Coe 1965b:21), and on the north wall of San Bartolo Pinturas's building where two individuals are carrying the bundles (Saturno et al. 2005:8–9) (Figure 12.5b). Structure 5C-01-sub 4 encapsulated all symbolism of rulership at the site and was a statement of the religiously sanctified, politically and economically successful power of its rulers (Acuña 2013:357).

Another example of an important Preclassic building associated with ancestral veneration is Holmul Building B, dated to 350 B.C., in northeastern Peten (Estrada-Belli 2008, 2009). This building was decorated with impressive stucco masks flanking the staircase (Figure 12.6). These consist of sacred mountains with open-mouthed jaguars out of which emerge the image of an old person or deity (Estrada-Belli 2008). This person or deity is wearing a mouth mask covered with an early symbol for *ajaw* with an extruded eyeball. Although stylistically different, an example of a mouth mask directly related to *ajaw* is found on a jadeite seated figure dated to the Early Classic period (see Fields and Reents-Budet 2005b:Plate 25). Mouth masks are commonly associated with bundles, as the examples from San Bartolo illustrate (Saturno et al. 2005:38–40), and they are a common feature in the iconography overall. At San Bartolo, the mouth masks portray mirrors like those in God C variants (Saturno et al. 2005:40). The association of bundles with mouth masks increase the possibility that Holmul Building B, like El Achiotal's Structure 5C-01-sub 4 is a bundle house. Strengthening the reference to ancestor bundling in Building B is the representation of a skull and crossed long bones flanking the image of the jaguar *witz*. The ancient Maya practiced tomb reentry, often to remove crania and long bones used to create bundles in order to commune with the ancestors, as a way to legitimize power (Brown et al. Chapter 5 this volume; McAnany 1995; Navarro Farr et al. 2008; Storey 2004).

The act of bundling has been traced throughout ancient Mesoamerica and extensive iconographic studies have revealed its use in assertions of authority and lineage (Guernsey and Reilly 2006:vii). Symbolic representations of bundles, such as the mural at El Achiotal and the mask at Holmul, are visual justifications of the authority enjoyed by the rulers in power. At the same time, they are evidence of rituals related to legitimization of

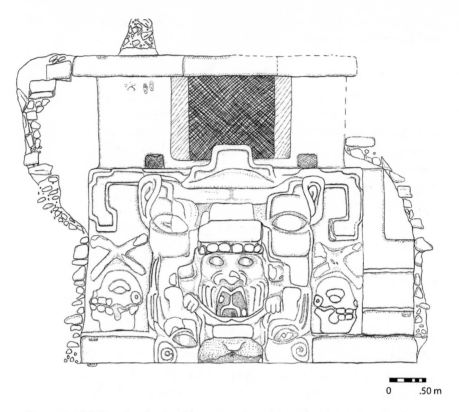

0   .50 m

Figure 12.6. Mask on façade of Building B, 1st phase, at Holmul (drawing by Nina Neivens de Estrada, courtesy of Holmul Archaeological Project).

power and authority (Guernsey and Reilly 2006). At El Achiotal, Mural 1 may represent the ritual bundle that validated the establishment of ruler-ship at the site, or perhaps it indicates that Structure 5C-01-sub 4 was a sacred space where acts of bundling took place. The bundle painted on Mural 2, not described in this chapter, contains symbolism of power, life, breath, and supernatural essence, all iconographic elements that also index the materiality of jade. These items represent preciosities stored in bundles, objects that were used to accrue sacred power (Schele and Miller 1986). As such, they also symbolize and convey notions of wealth and concepts of value. Thus, the entire composition of murals that symbolically bundled Structure 5C-01-sub 4 marked it as the most sacred space in the city, not only for ritual performances that sanctified political authority, but because bundles were also associated with economic functions as well (Olivier 2006; Reents-Budet 2006; Stuart 2006). The evidence indicates that at El

Achiotal, and elsewhere, the significance of sacred, ideological concepts was intertwined with pragmatic political economical structures as a means to ensure political authority.

Final Remarks

The archaeological and iconographic evidence from Structure 5C-01-sub 4 suggest that El Achiotal had established rulership in the Late Preclassic. The rulers were responsible for the development of the center and commissioning sacred spaces that legitimized their authority. The symbolic vocabulary present at El Achiotal indicates that the rulers were knowledgeable of the widespread ideology that was being institutionalized in the southern Maya lowlands. They were also literate in a more ancient symbolic vocabulary that represented the institution of kingship developed by the Middle Preclassic at La Venta and other centers in Mexico.

The importance of El Achiotal in the western frontier zone of the central karstic uplands relies on its strategic position on a route connecting the larger cities with the San Pedro Mártir River, via the San Juan River Watershed. Transportation of large quantities of bulk and prestige goods was likely easier using canoe transportation, so it is no surprise that many peripheral sites are located along major rivers or along the coast. However, several of the central karstic upland major sites could not be reached by water and relied on foot porters to move products inland. Transportation of bulk items by pedestrian porters has been seen as negative evidence for subsistence-based interregional interaction, arguing in favor of it being restricted to prestige items (Marcus 1983:19–20; Masson 2002). Positive evidence for the existence of wide exchange networks within the region is the widespread use of the Chicanel ceramic sphere in the Late Preclassic period. Rivers and seas were not the only aquatic navigation routes. Freidel et al. (2015) argue that wetland routes were one way of reaching sites not located on rivers or other major communication corridors, at least seasonally. Seasonal canoe transportation of bulk goods was likely an option through most of northwestern—and perhaps northern—Peten, and a way of circumnavigating the difficult and limiting capacity of foot porters. The closest known Preclassic site east of El Achiotal is El Tintal, located 24.4 km in a straight line and well within a day's walk. El Tintal is connected to El Mirador by a large causeway, which clearly facilitated mobility in a southwesterly direction toward the riverine communication networks.

Small sites like El Achiotal, on the margins of the core area, played important roles in broader regional geopolitics. The level of complexity exhibited at El Achiotal in the Late Preclassic calls for a re-evaluation of the archaeological variables we use to understand political authority on the hierarchical spectrum. Combined, the ruler's specialized knowledge of the symbolic vocabulary and the strategic location of El Achiotal provided the leverage to negotiate and assert status in relation to larger sites in the core. Within the broader geopolitical interaction sphere, different sites specialized in different knowledge, such as those with E-Groups that served a different function (Brown et al. Chapter 5 this volume; Doyle 2012; Estrada-Belli 2006, 2011). Site size, therefore, does not determine importance, but in the hierarchical spectrum of knowledge, each site played a key role in the increased complexity of political institutions.

13

Changing Stages

Royal Legitimacy and the Architectural Development of the Pinturas Complex at San Bartolo, Guatemala

WILLIAM SATURNO, FRANCO D. ROSSI, AND BORIS BELTRÁN

Introduction

In discussing the tenets of ancient Maya architecture and its relation to political ideology, various buildings and building arrangements have been explored in depth—from the Preclassic circular structures of northwestern Belize (Hansen 1998; Hendon 2000) to the twin pyramid complexes of Tikal (Jones 1969). However, of the multiple architectural forms constructed by the ancient Maya, perhaps the three most widely recognized are the ballcourt, E-Group, and triadic complex. Great strides have been made in evaluating the various functions and meanings of these architectural layouts—both as singular complexes as well as in relation to one another—but the inherent difficulty in deriving meaning from silent architectural remains continues to detract from our understanding of the diverse cultural and political values embedded within these complexes. This chapter seeks to add to the current debate, pulling from excavations at the site of San Bartolo where the remains of all three architectural assemblages, ballcourt, E-Group, and triadic complex, have been found within the Las Pinturas complex, marking a developmental sequence that highlights both significant changes and continuities in ceremonial expression during the last four centuries of the Preclassic period. The inclusion of a ceremonial ballcourt as part of a Late Preclassic E-Group explicitly informs our understandings of the conceptual underpinnings of this widespread architectural form and its previously attested association with E-Groups. More importantly, the overlaying of these three assemblages, one atop the other, is strongly suggestive of evolving notions of "center" and legitimacy during the Middle to Late Preclassic transition, as well as the connection between these notions and the codification of institutionalized kingship.

Architectural Sketch of San Bartolo

San Bartolo is a medium-sized Preclassic site located in the currently uninhabited northeastern region of the Department of Peten, Guatemala (Figure 13.1a). The site covers an area of approximately 1 km^2 and is comprised of more than 130 stone structures organized around four principal architectural groups. At the far west lies the Jabali complex, a group in which one of the earliest Maya royal burials (ca. 100 B.C.) was discovered in 2006 (Saturno 2006). Moving eastward, we arrive at the largest of the four groups, called Las Ventanas for the tall pyramid (Structure 20) on the north side of the main plaza. A small ballcourt sits at the northeast edge of this plaza and a large administrative palace (Structure 60, or Tigrillo) dominates its western side. This group also contains a large number of residential mounds. The Las Ventanas group demonstrates the deepest chronological evidence for occupation (600 B.C.), forming the administrative center of San Bartolo's Preclassic population, as well as the locus of subsequent Late Classic reoccupation and elaboration (Runggaldier 2009).

About 500 m east of Las Ventanas lies Las Pinturas, the most extensively investigated group at the site, and the place in which the Preclassic Maya murals were discovered in 2001. Standing more than 26 m in height, Structure I is the main building in a Late Preclassic triadic group, facing westward and constructed in at least eight architectural phases that stretch back to the late Middle Preclassic period (Escobedo 2002). It rises along with three other structures from a 75 m × 90 m platform, roughly 5 m high (Escobar and Runggaldier 2002). The three other mounds, Structures III, IV, and V, are situated on the south, west, and north edges of the platform respectively. Structures II and V stand at 5 m tall and, along with Structure I, comprise the final phase of the triadic group. The open end of this group was eventually closed off by Structure IV.

The final group, known as Saraguates, lies on the eastern edge of the settlement and constitutes the largest architectural complex at the site (Figure 13.1a). Arranged in a kind of reverse E-Group layout, Saraguates looks west over the sprawl of San Bartolo in architectural reaffirmation of the site's intentional east-west alignment—a commonly acknowledged feature of Preclassic lowland settlements (Ashmore and Sabloff 2002:203).

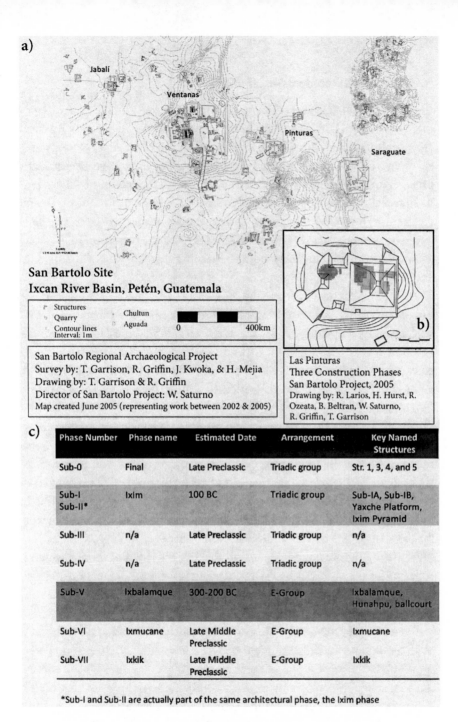

a)

Jabalí

Ventanas

Pinturas

Saraguate

San Bartolo Site
Ixcan River Basin, Petén, Guatemala

| Structures |
| Quarry | Chultun |
| Contour lines Interval: 1m | Aguada |

0 ———— 400km

b)

San Bartolo Regional Archaeological Project
Survey by: T. Garrison, R. Griffin, J. Kwoka, & H. Mejia
Drawing by: T. Garrison & R. Griffin
Director of San Bartolo Project: W. Saturno
Map created June 2005 (representing work between 2002 & 2005)

Las Pinturas
Three Construction Phases
San Bartolo Project, 2005
Drawing by: R. Larios, H. Hurst, R.
Ozeata, B. Beltran, W. Saturno,
R. Griffin, T. Garrison

c)

Phase Number	Phase name	Estimated Date	Arrangement	Key Named Structures
Sub-0	Final	Late Preclassic	Triadic group	Str. 1, 3, 4, and 5
Sub-I Sub-II*	Ixim	100 BC	Triadic group	Sub-IA, Sub-IB, Yaxche Platform, Ixim Pyramid
Sub-III	n/a	Late Preclassic	Triadic group	n/a
Sub-IV	n/a	Late Preclassic	Triadic group	n/a
Sub-V	Ixbalamque	300-200 BC	E-Group	Ixbalamque, Hunahpu, ballcourt
Sub-VI	Ixmucane	Late Middle Preclassic	E-Group	Ixmucane
Sub-VII	Ixkik	Late Middle Preclassic	E-Group	Ixkik

*Sub-I and Sub-II are actually part of the same architectural phase, the Ixim phase

Figure 13.1. (a) Map of San Bartolo (mapped by T. Garrison, R. Griffin, J. Kwoka, and H. Mejía); (b) plan of Pinturas complex with Sub-I and Sub-V highlighted (mapped by R. Larios, H. Hurst, R. Ozaeta, B. Beltrán, W. Saturno, R. Griffin, T. Garrison); (c) chart of architectural phases of Pinturas.

Architectural Antecedents at Pinturas

Initial archaeological investigations at Pinturas were focused on uncovering, documenting, and conserving the remarkably preserved Late Preclassic mural program. These early murals adorn the interior walls of a small structure (Sub 1A) built off the back (east face) of the buried penultimate phase (Ixim phase[1]) of Structure I (Saturno 2009; Saturno et al. 2005). For its first few hundred years of use, Pinturas existed as an E-Group. Recent excavations revealed its earliest three manifestations (Ixkik, Ixmucane, and Ixbalamque) to be E-Group complexes, with the transition to a triadic group not occurring until sometime between 250 and 100 B.C. (Figure 13.1b and 13.1c).

As an architectural feature, the "E-Group" was first defined at Uaxactun. It consisted of a decorated radial pyramid at the west (Structure E-VII sub) centrally aligned toward a low, range structure at the east. The overall complex was aligned east to west, and the range structure contained three elevated points (Structures E-I, E-II, E-III), at the north, at the south, and along the center-line (Blom 1924; Ricketson 1928; Ricketson and Ricketson 1937). Frans Blom (1924) first suggested its astronomical significance, deducing that the western pyramid functioned as a viewpoint for observing the sun's rise at the equinoxes and solstices. However, reconstructed alignments are generally too imprecise to denote true calendrical function. A general "subjectivity" in alignments and even form of E-Groups suggest a more commemorative value to such complexes, which although very much linked with sun watching, would not have necessarily served as the means for calculating solstice and equinox events. Instead, such groups seem to reflect less a rigidly precise means of tracking the sun and more a general concern for the sun's place at particularly important moments during the year (Aimers 1995; Aveni and Hartung 1989; Aveni et al. 2003:174; Hansen 1998; Laporte and Fialko 1990).

Beginning in 2006, excavations at Pinturas focused on exploring Sub V or the Ixbalamque phase, dated between 300 and 200 B.C.[2] and corresponding to the most recent of the three E-Group complexes buried within the Pinturas platform (Saturno et al. 2006). Exploration into this phase began from the east, exposing the group's range structure, also called Ixbalamque, for which the phase received its name. This structure runs 26 m × 12 m and stands roughly 2 m from the plaza floor. It is broken into three sections (characteristically corresponding to the sun's positions at the solstices and equinoxes) and has three staircases—two built into the east side

a)

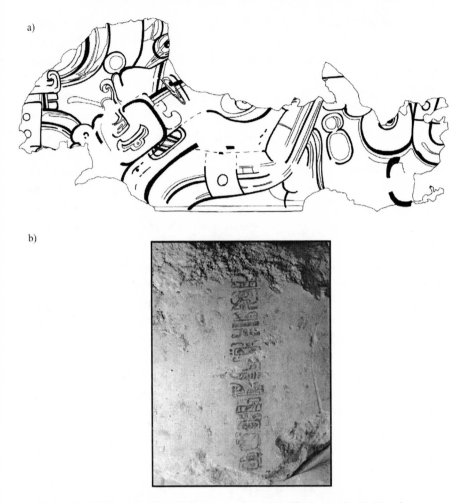

b)

Figure 13.2. (a) Maize God from Ixbalamque doorjamb (illustration by H. Hurst);
(b) early painted hieroglyphic block from Sub-5 (photograph by B. Beltrán).

and one central stairway on the west side. The entire structure is covered
in well-preserved white stucco. It consists of three sloping *talud* terraces
with an additional platform elevating the central section slightly above the
northern and southern extremities (Beltrán 2006). Only the foundations
remain of the three superstructures it once supported, though excavations
reveal that the central of the three rooms was decorated with polychrome
murals. Its painted doorjamb depicting the Maya Maize God (Figure 13.2a)
was found in 2005 (Saturno et al. 2006; Taube et al. 2010:10). A stone block
from the dismantled wall of the same room was also found (Figure 13.2b).
This block bears early painted hieroglyphs, one of which reads *ajaw* ("lord,"

"noble" or "ruler"), attesting not only to the Preclassic presence of a Maya writing system, but also to the royal title that would come to define the Classic period (Saturno et al. 2006). Though a search for the radial pyramid of the E-Group was initiated during the 2006 season, it was not discovered despite tunneling some 18 m west of the Ixbalamque range structure. However, the team did encounter a small, enigmatic structure standing 1.25 m tall, extending 2.25 m deep, and running the entire width of the excavation tunnel. This was temporarily termed an "altar."

It was not until the 2008 season that further excavations revealed this "altar" as the east bank of a miniature ballcourt built off of the eastern stairway of the E-Group radial pyramid (called Hunahpu) (Figure 13.3a). The ballcourt incorporates this stairway and the slope of Hunahpu into its west bank, and its thickly plastered surface is in an excellent state of preservation, mostly white with large sections painted red. The Hunahpu ballcourt alley runs north-south, measures 6 m × 1.8 m and stands at 1.25 m tall, too small for actual competition. The entirety of the ballcourt structure measures roughly 6 m × 6.3 m. An offering of human finger and rib bones, a jade axe fragment and a large Sierra Red sherd was found on the alley floor, marking the termination of the structure and the onset of Sub IV's construction episode (Beltrán 2008). In addition to the offering, a ballcourt marker was also discovered on the alley floor elegantly rendered in red paint (Figure 13.3b). The marker assumes the typical circular shape, and though the details are rather eroded, its interior image is still discernible as two figures facing an inverted U contained within a circle at the center (Beltrán 2008; Hurst 2009).

Excavations revealed matching sets of stucco masks flanking each of the four stairways on Hunahpu, identical in placement to the masks of the famed Uaxactun E-VII substructure and strikingly reminiscent in form. Eight additional narrow stairways, two per side, run from the plaza floor to the top of the masks and are located between each mask and its corresponding corner of the pyramid. The Hunahpu masks consist of an anthropomorphic face emerging from the sloped *talud*, and rest atop a stylized serpent. Although the amount of sculptural detail lost varies among them, on the whole, the Hunahpu masks look to be more similar to one another than do the masks decorating the E-VII sub.[3] Yet they still share basic iconographic elements with the Uaxactun masks: the swirled designs around the earflares, the forehead plaque, the elaborate (often "flame") eyebrows, and the fangs at each corner of the mouth (MacLellan 2009:36). However, the Hunahpu masks possess a rather protuberant nose/snout in contrast to

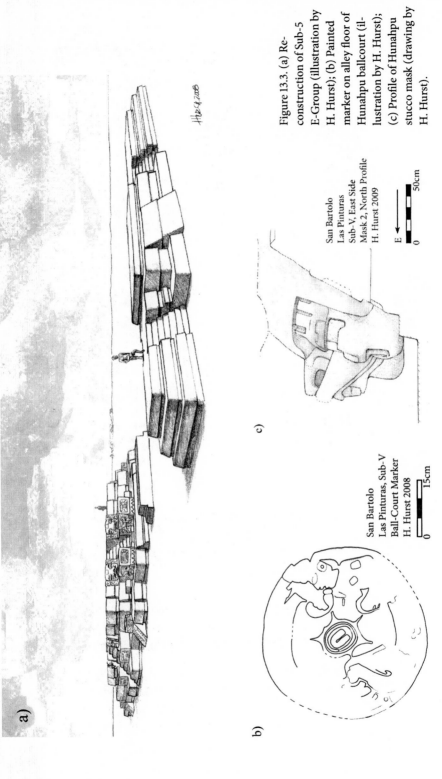

Figure 13.3. (a) Reconstruction of Sub-5 E-Group (illustration by H. Hurst); (b) Painted marker on alley floor of Hunahpu ballcourt (illustration by H. Hurst); (c) Profile of Hunahpu stucco mask (drawing by H. Hurst).

San Bartolo
Las Pinturas
Sub-V, East Side
Mask 2, North Profile
H. Hurst 2009

E

0   50cm

San Bartolo
Las Pinturas, Sub-V
Ball-Court Marker
H. Hurst 2008

0   15cm

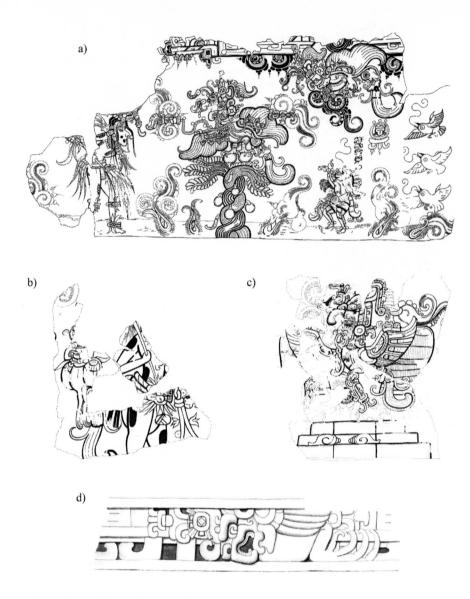

Figure 13.4. (a) West wall mural of Sub-1A portraying Principal Bird Deity descending from the sky and onto one of the four directional world trees (illustration by H. Hurst); (b) south wall scene with slain Principal Bird Deity dangling from Hun Ajaw's back (illustration by H. Hurst); (c) fragments from the East Wall of Sub-1A showing descending Principal Bird Deity, Itzamnaah's face visible with the bird mask (illustration by H. Hurst); (d) exterior frieze of Sub 1A depicting Principal Bird Deity (illustration by H. Hurst).

the E-VII sub masks. In addition to the masks, two stairless balustrades, adorned with descending skeletal serpents, extend out on both the north and south sides of Hunahpu.

The serpent component of the Hunahpu balustrade decoration extends out from the base of each mask *talud* nearly 2.5 m, leaving considerable space for elaborate feather swirls and the double-pronged fang visible in profile (Figure 13.3c). The front of this serpent depicts a rectangular frame containing a geometrically abstract form overlaying the center of an "X," perhaps in reference to the mask-serpent composite's origins in the sky. The feathers on both the serpent balustrades and the connected anthropo-morphic masks further support these origins, revealing the avian-serpent nature of the portrayed composites, a characteristic of both Preclassic and Classic period depictions of the Principal Bird Deity (PBD) (Bardawil 1976; Guernsey 2006b:102–108; Taube et al. 2010:29–46). This avian form of the aged deity Itzamnaah features prominently in the iconography of the later Ixim (Sub I) phase of the Pinturas complex—as both a narrative focus on the east and west wall murals of Sub 1A (Figure 13.4a, 13.4c) as well as the subject of that same building's decorative exterior frieze (Figure 13.4d) (Saturno 2009; Taube et al. 2010). In their analysis of the west wall, Karl Taube et al. (2010:33) write, "It appears that during the Late Preclassic pe-riod, the Principal Bird Deity was a strongly solar being, perhaps even a particular aspect of the sun." Given its regular depiction as "descending" in artistic representations of the time, perhaps that "aspect" was in fact the setting sun. The placement of the Hunahpu masks on the radial pyramid marking the sun's descent certainly supports this interpretation.

Paired with the Maize God doorjamb and the early painted "*ajaw*" glyph, the PBD masks demonstrate a striking continuity in the thematic content of public art at Pinturas between the Ixbalamque (Sub V) and Ixim (Sub I) phases, despite the dramatic alterations in architectural layout and monumentality. Besides its impressive artistic program, the Ixbalamque E-Group is unique in its attached radial pyramid ballcourt; yet rather than challenging existing theories, these findings at San Bartolo actually serve to firmly support many current hypotheses linking E-Groups to ballcourts.

E-Groups and Ballcourts

To examine the significance of these conjoined structures as they appear in San Bartolo, the existing literature on the recurring symbolic links be-tween E-Groups and ballcourts provides crucial context. An overwhelming

majority of support for these linkages is rooted in a mix of astronomical associations, iconographically derived evidence, and literary inference. Together, these demonstrate strong parallels bridging the underlying
meanings encoded within each architectural assemblage—concerned with
ballgame play and sacrifice (specifically by decapitation), agricultural renewal, cyclical time, and movement (specifically the descent[4]) of the sun
(Aimers and Rice 2006; Cohodas 1975, 1980, 1991; Miller and Houston 1987;
Reents-Budet 1994:269; Schele and Miller 1986:241–253). Aimers and Rice
(2006:89) conducted a study seeking to architecturally support these associations, tabulating the relationship between ballcourts and E-Group plazas
at 40 different Maya cities, and proposing the possibility of "a Maya ritual
complex involving competition in ballcourts, sacrifice on E-Group stairways, and burial in nearby plazas." However, their work reveals a rather
weak correlation between the two assemblages, with only 10 sites touting
ballcourts attached to E-Group plazas.[5]

A stronger link emerges between the ballgame and stairways. Nearly
every known example of ballgame scenes in Classic period Maya art
show game play against stairways, not in ballcourts, and many such artistic portrayals are actually set within stairways or in explicit relation to
them[6] (Miller and Houston 1987). This evidence leads Stephen Houston
(1998:357) to argue a Classic Maya conflation in the active roles of these
two distinct sets of buildings, explaining that, "two related sequences of
events—ball playing and the subsequent torture, mutilation, and decapitation of captives—have been merged, along with the architectural setting
appropriate to these activities."

It is in light of these long-argued connections that recent findings at San
Bartolo become important, providing the first known, explicitly architectural, link between E-Group complexes (specifically the radial pyramid)
and ballcourts. The Ixbalamque E-Group at San Bartolo unites the underlying meanings of ballcourt, E-Group, and stairway imagery of the Classic
period within a single Preclassic architectural complex. It reveals an early
and unequivocally ceremonial manifestation of the Maya ballcourt. The
court itself is too small to have supported play, raising questions regarding
the rationales of those who initiated its construction.

Evidence for a "Mesoamerican ballgame" stretches back at least to the
late Early Preclassic[7] with evidence of 14 rubber balls from the site of El
Manatí—attesting both to the game's early existence and ritual importance (Ortiz and Carmen Rodríguez 1999, 2000). Formalized ballcourt

architecture exists throughout Mesoamerica, occurring earliest in Chiapas during the Middle Preclassic (Agrinier 1991). The game itself was likely played long before the dates supplied by archaeological evidence (Miller and Houston 1987:47). However, its architectural adoption at San Bartolo is unmistakably ritualistic, supporting arguments which favor the ceremonial underpinnings of the game within Classic Maya royal culture over the game play itself. In their analysis of text and image concerning Classic period ballgame depictions, Mary Miller and Stephen Houston remark (1987:55):

> The image that most frequently accompanies the textual statement of ballgame is the play on stairs. That image holds a relationship to the ballgame like that of display to capture: as resonant qualities, text and image amplify and reinforce one another. At the same time, emphasis is given to the event on the stairs as if to imply the most important part of the ritual.

In other words, it was often not the game itself, but the ritual consequence of the game that was most important to the Maya. Miller and Houston continue with a discussion about how sacrifice was enfolded into the event, perhaps most vividly represented on the Yaxchilan hieroglyphic stairs VI and VII from Structure 33—depicting bound captives tumbling down the stairs as balls, descending painfully toward death. The pivotal importance of spectacle and theatricality to Classic Maya society—involving fire and censers, elaborate costume, music, dance, sacrifice, and so forth—has been discussed at length and supplemented by considerable material evidence (Houston 2006; Inomata 2006a, 2006b; Inomata et al. 2002; Schele and Miller 1986; Widmer 2009). Should one adopt a similar vision for such events at San Bartolo and pair it with Classic period ballgame imagery, the scene becomes luridly dramatic—an elaborately costumed *ajaw* standing atop Hunahpu before a vast audience occupying the E-Group plaza. Sacrificial offerings would have been made amidst smoke and music; some likely sent cascading down the eastern stairway. The effect from the plaza must have truly been impressive when these descending offerings would visually disappear behind a 1.25-m high bank as they struck the ballcourt alley floor, theatrically conveying a descent into the underworld to the audience. It is a ballcourt which serves as the entrance and exit to *Xibalba* in the *Popol Vuh* (Tedlock 1996). As such, it is no coincidence that a ballcourt in profile so strikingly resembles the cleft in the earth from which the Maize God is often depicted emerging in Classic Maya ceramic and stela scenes. The role of the ceremonial ballcourt at Hunahpu would have aligned with and reinforced these underworld associations.

Beyond speculating about the possible layered meanings that these rituals held, the Hunahpu ballcourt is significant for its specific location within the Ixbalamque E-Group. Architecturally bounding the horizons, an E-Group naturally emphasizes the centrality of its plaza. Built off the eastern stair of Hunahpu, the ballcourt lies between the eastern range structure and the radial pyramid of the E-Group, at the conceptual center of an architectural microcosm. In addition, the ballcourt's physical connection to Hunahpu is meaningful in that it becomes part of the very structure marking the descent of the sun. The ballgame has been argued as linked to the sun's descent into the underworld (Cohodas 1991; Pasztory 1972, 1978:130). The Hunahpu ballcourt's placement supports these assertions, located at the foot of a stairway flanked by matching masks depicting the solar PBD. The painted doorjamb fragment depicting the Maize God in the eastern Ixbalamque range structure offers an intriguing counterpoint to Hunahpu's descent imagery, coinciding with common portrayals of the PBD descending and the Maize God rising, reborn, like the eastern sun each morning. Though the Maize God also descends as part of his narrative, the focal point of his mythology is the moment of rebirth, his reentry into the earthly plain. Narratives concerned with the PBD invariably deal with his descent, clearly the thematic focus of his mythology. Despite the presence of this Maize God imagery within the group, the attachment of the ballcourt to the Hunahpu radial pyramid and not to the Ixbalamque range structure is telling. It suggests an initial primacy in the solar, descent-oriented, PBD narrative associations of the ballgame over later agricultural links to the Maize God's rebirth.

The Triadic Shift

The transition from E-Group to triadic group marks the largest single-phase construction event in the Pinturas architectural sequence. Drawing context from other architectural examples in the Maya world, this section explores the significance of this structural overlay. At Pinturas, there is a marked shift from the third architectural phase (Ixbalamque), in which the complex was an eastward facing E-Group, to the fourth phase, in which that E-Group was buried within a large platform. This platform constituted the base of a westward-facing triadic complex—a configuration which then persisted for the subsequent architectural reincarnations of the group. Besides the altered architectural layout of the Pinturas group itself, the relation of the complex to the rest of the site also changed. Formerly having been oriented toward the rising sun, the E-Group was supplanted by a complex facing west toward the site center (Ventanas group), suggesting a stronger integration of this architectural group with the official seat of local power.

At Pinturas, the most extensively investigated of these triadic group manifestations corresponds to the Ixim phase. The Ixim triadic group is the third of its kind since the reconfiguration from the Ixbalamque E-Group, and comprises the sixth and penultimate architectural phase of Pinturas. Ixim shares its layout with the final phase of the complex (as explained earlier), only smaller in mass and with an additional two structures (Sub 1A and Sub 1B) built off the east end of the complex platform (called the Yaxche platform).[8] In one of these two small structures (Sub 1A) lie the Preclassic murals, the details of which are thoroughly explained elsewhere (*see* Saturno 2009; Saturno et al. 2005; Taube et al. 2010). The Yaxche platform rose 7 m from the ancient plaza floor, with an earlier version of the final phase of Structure I (called the Ixim pyramid) rising as the main pyramid of the group. Excavations by Edwin Román revealed the Ixim pyramid to have been adorned with twin stucco masks, flanking the central, western facade stairway (unfortunately these are too eroded to accurately identify). In addition, this pyramid was topped with a six-room building, its exterior adorned with paintings and its interior littered with masterfully painted stucco fragments (Hurst et al. 2008; Román 2005, 2008). Initial analysis of these fragments shows that they contain familiar themes to the then-contemporaneous murals below in Sub 1A. However, although analogous content is reflected in a similar artistic hand, a greater investment of time and care went into creating the Ixim temple murals (Hurst 2009)—underscoring the greater importance of their "closed" location to those within a more accessible Sub 1A. Given the extensive archaeological work conducted, the Ixim phase serves as a vital tool for illuminating the conceptual underpinnings that motivated the change from E-Group to triadic complex at Late Preclassic Pinturas.

Richard Hansen (1992b:55–56) refers to triadic groups as stylized descendents of E-Groups. However, pulling from work at Tikal, Juan Pedro Laporte (1995) highlights a core difference between E-Groups and triadic groups. Laporte argues that triadic groups architecturally expressed royal power in contradistinction to E-Groups, which communicated messages less royal and more cosmically ideological—strongly demonstrating divergent meanings at the core of these assemblages.

Supplementing these arguments, William Folan et al. (2001) discuss Calakmul's behemoth, triadic Structure II, and its smaller version across the plaza, Structure III. These two triadic complexes are both identified as administrative palace structures. Structure II functioned as the more public administrative center while Structure III, an imitation of the earlier Structure II palace, acted as a more private elite compound in the Late Classic. David Kelley (1965) helped show that the triadic Temple of the Cross Group at Palenque was connected to the local triad of patron deities initially identified two years prior (Berlin 1963). This feature at Palenque has been expanded upon by recent epigraphic studies in which the texts of these three structures suggest them to be distinct *wahyib*, a sort of godhouse, each pertaining to a specific Palenque triad deity (Stuart 1998:399–400). Such patron deity triads (also dyads and other similar groupings) occur frequently at Classic Maya sites often as localized manifestations of more widespread deities. Such patron deities, "form special relationships with human *beings at particular sites and actively participate in contemporary human affairs while in return* receiving active ritual veneration" (Baron 2013:178–179). They are often said to have been "owned" by the local *ajaw*, and places like the Cross Group at Palenque emphasize a conceptual overlap between kings, local deities, and triadic groups (Houston and Stuart 1996:294–295; Stuart 2005).

The originally triadic, north acropolis at Tikal was *expressly* associated with the institution of kingship, as evidenced through its role as a Late Preclassic and Classic period royal necropolis (Laporte 1995). For Laporte, the triadic group is neither elite residence nor godhouse. Instead, his discussion suggests a meaning somewhere in between the two: a palace for the revered and divine royal ancestors—an intriguing and meaningful bridge between rulers and local deities. In all three examples, however, the palace, the *wahyib*, or the royal necropolis, the association is undeniably royal (implying a certain restricted accessibility) and local, as opposed to widely accessible and cosmically focused. The palace privately houses the rulership, the *wahyib* privately houses the local gods with whom the rulership intimately associates itself,[9] and the royal necropolis privately houses the deceased ancestors of the rulership. David Freidel et al. (1993:140–141) compare the layout of triadic complexes at Uaxactun to that of the three-stone hearth as it occurs in Classic period iconography. Taube (1998) expands upon their initial identification by underscoring the ubiquity and deep temporal roots of this three-stone iconographic motif, and demonstrating its inseparable ties to rulership and notions of centrality—the triadic group conceptually emerging as a kind of monumental hearth for the glorified royal household, ancestry, or local trinity.

A context at Cival supplies a pivotal corollary to the findings at San Bartolo, serving as one of the only other known examples in which a triadic group directly overlays an E-Group. Cival is a Preclassic center in the northeast of Peten district, Guatemala. Its ceremonial core was founded in a ritual caching event that took place at roughly 600 B.C. (Estrada-Belli 2006). Smashed *ollas* and maize-associated greenstone artifacts constitute the cache, which was found adjacent to the eastern range structure of an early E-Group.[10] However, the most important component of the work at Cival as it pertains to the current discussion relates to the triadic group that superseded the E-Group shortly after 300 B.C. (Estrada-Belli 2006:64)— the only other currently known example so strongly paralleling what we see at Pinturas. Unlike San Bartolo, this Cival complex does not engulf the E-Group within its platform, but instead assumes the primary ritual role by sheer means of its monumentality, blocking out the eastern sun. Estrada-Belli (2006:64) explains this shift as having "effectively removed the temples from the plaza and from public access, separating ritual actors from ritual observers."

Like Cival in the Late Preclassic, ceremonial access at the San Bartolo Pinturas group changes from a less restricted, ground level, E-Group plaza to an elevated and architecturally "closed" space, immediately hinting at the seeds of a more pronounced hierarchy (MacLellan 2009). The site center becomes the orientation guideline for the architectural group, not the sky—a feature Pinturas shares with the Jabali and Saraguates groups at San Bartolo, which also face inward toward the Ventanas group and the Preclassic palace (Runggaldier 2009; Saturno 2009).

Additional support can be gleaned from the north and west walls of the San Bartolo murals, also part of the Ixim triadic phase. In one of the painted narratives, a Maya hero claims a four-cornered, civilized space from a dangerous wild, represented by a great solar bird looming ominously atop a tree at each of the four conceptual world corners (Saturno 2009). The bird is eventually killed, shown dangling from the hero's back on the south wall (Figure 13.4b), depicting the triumph of a proto-*hun ajaw*, literally "first lord," over the unruly wild (Saturno 2009; Taube et al. 2010). In another narrative, the Maize God is the focus, portraying his descent to the watery underworld, resurrection, and eventual coronation as *ajaw* (Figure 13.5a). A scene to the immediate right shows a likely historical figure ascending the scaffold to be crowned ruler, a glaring parallel to the Maize God's own denouement (Figure 13.5b) (Saturno 2009; Saturno et al. 2005; Taube et al. 2010). This same historical figure is shown elsewhere as born of a gourd alongside four other babies who are clearly less important (see ballgame headgear; Figure 13.5c). The gourd is the very object depicted in two other narrative scenes: on the east wall where it sits between two divine beings and is identified as the blood of humanity; and on the north wall where this gourd is then carried by the Maize God toward a woman in a cave at the base of "Flower Mountain," a kind of primordial paradise and ancestral emergence/descent point in various Mesoamerican tales (Figure 13.5d) (Saturno et al. 2005; Taube 2004a). Together these various painted narratives portray the *ajaw* not only as of divine origin and intimately linked with the Maize God, but also demonstrate the role of such leaders in overcoming the powers of nature—as we see in the west wall sacrifice sequence that features *Hun Ajaw* and the bird. All of this served to naturalize kingly authority. There is a sense that the scene of lordly legitimation shown in the Pinturas murals is also mirrored in the architectural overlay of the building it lies within, as the triadic group (oriented toward the central plaza and palace) is established directly on top of the E-Group once oriented directly to nature as its mediator, rather than to the *ajaw*. In other words, through both the murals and the structure in which they are embedded, the Pinturas complex became physically and metaphorically aligned with the royal court.

During the Classic period, rulers were wholly conflated with deities in portraiture as were the hovering ancestral figures looking down upon them. Gods were often stated as owned by kings (Houston and Stuart 1996; McAnany 1995). Texts celebrated ancestral bloodlines with deep chronologies, as well as the lives and deeds of site rulers (Houston 1993; Martin and Grube 1995, 2008; Proskouriakoff 1960, 1963, 1964). Presaging these monumental, artistic metaphors legitimizing kingly rule, the Preclassic Pinturas architectural shift and coeval Maize God/ruler conflation clearly materialized the political ideologies which these later artistic metaphors came to represent.

Returning to the question of the shift from E-Group to triadic complex, we see a foundational difference in the underlying meanings of these two distinct architectural assemblages, strongly suggestive of broader changes in society as reflected in this ceremonial space. In the Late Preclassic, the widely accessible ceremonial E-Group space demarcated a cosmic "center,"

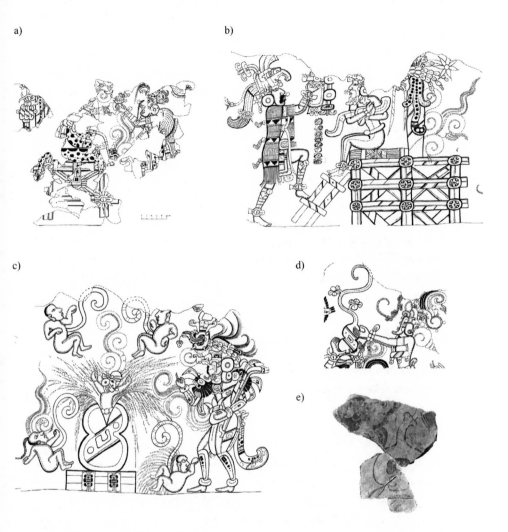

Figure 13.5. (*Upper*) Parallel coronations on the west wall of Sub-1A (illustrations by H. Hurst): (a) coronation scene of the Maize God and; (b) coronation scene of *ajaw*. (*Lower*) Sub 1A North wall mural; (c) future king's birth from the gourd (illustration by H. Hurst); (d) Maize God and "Flower Mountain," carrying the gourd from which the king is born (illustration by H. Hurst); (e) east wall fragments showing "blood man gourd?" (image by W. Saturno).

both aligning with and celebrating the solar and agricultural cycle with public art that declared the king's place within that cycle. These features were supplanted by a restrictively high and closed triadic platform, oriented toward the official site center and royal palace. Besides its thoroughly documented associations with royal court culture, the triadic complex contains extensive murals publically tying the ruler to the Maize God, the emergence myth, and the creation of a four-cornered civilized space.

Patricia McAnany (2008, 2010:158–176) highlights the various means employed by Classic period elites to distance themselves from commoners through features that become intimately associated with royalty: head shape, dental inlays, body smell, diet, and life expectancy, not to mention manifold names and titles linking royals to celestial powers. She argues that all these features serve to underscore and maintain social distance between elites and commoners. At San Bartolo, the change in the Late Preclassic from an E-Group to a triadic complex monumentally illustrates the social distancing that is part and parcel to establishing political legitimacy and institutionalized hierarchy.

Concluding Discussion: Architecture and Concepts of Center

Stephen Houston (2006:139) remarks, "Civic spectacle, theatrical 'mummery,' and ritual were as close here (Maya region) as any Balinese theater state, not least because of the need for competitive displays of wealth, sacrality, and gestures of generosity to courtiers." Notions of the king's social and political role as "the exemplary center within the exemplary center" (Geertz 1980:130) are especially resonant with regard to ancient Maya culture (Saturno 2009; Schele and Miller 1986), causing many scholars to liken the *ajaw* and his court to a glorified household embodying this center (McAnany and Plank 2001). Geertz (1980:130) provides further insight stating, "the ritual life of the court, and in fact the life of the court generally, is thus paradigmatic, not merely reflective, of social order. What it is reflective of . . . is supernatural order." As monumental stages for theatrically conveying this supernatural order (Inomata and Coben 2006:17), E-Groups, triadic groups, and ballcourts alike become "material representations of an elite ideology underpinning legitimacy, wealth, and power" (Rice 2007:153). These buildings themselves comprised an integral part of the evolving stagecraft behind a Maya theater-state.

Taking ideology as being "as much the material means to communicate and manipulate ideas as it is the ideas themselves" (DeMarrais et al.

1996:16), the murals of San Bartolo demonstrate a strong desire of early Maya rulers, the patrons of the arts, to portray themselves within certain mythologically familiar terms to the general populace. As such, they became the heirs to those responsible for bringing the world out of chaos and into settled, agricultural order, centering a kingdom amidst a chaotic and unruly world (Saturno 2009:131).

The architecture at San Bartolo further underscores this very technique of legitimation. There is a strong sense that the Ixbalamque E-Group structure served as a monumental stage for early rulers to theatrically convey their role in the supernatural order—perhaps in striking reminiscence to what is depicted in the mural room, since it is precisely within the subsequent Ixim triadic complex that the murals illustrating this mythological conflation occur. In other words, the murals might have served to publically immortalize the kingly performances of such narratives as they occurred within the E-Group—a community reminder, alongside the monumental triadic complex, of the underpinnings of royal legitimacy. The San Bartolo murals and other such imagery of the Late Preclassic testify to novel projections of the royal bloodline's divine roots and key role in not only carving out civilization, but in maintaining it. The shift at Pinturas from a celestially commemorative E-Group to a primarily state-aligned triadic group persists in its demarcation of center, but the "rebranding" of a former celestial stage as a royally domestic, monumental hearth implies a certain political success on the part of San Bartolo rulers in entering the perceived supernatural order. It is an architectural change indicative of evolving understandings in the role of *ajaw* in both elite and common Maya society, as the ruler became less an intermediary with divine forces and more a divine force in and of himself to which nature was subject.

Patricia McAnany (2010:158–159) states, "the most powerful and enduring forces of hierarchizing are those that naturalize difference so that it is beyond dispute and something to be tacitly accepted." The unique sequence of architectural assemblages at San Bartolo opens interesting avenues for exploring these forces, as they monumentally reflect successive stages in the codification of institutionalized kingship and the naturalization of social hierarchies. Analyzing the shifts in monumental ceremonial stages, suggestive glimpses emerge of the evolving social, ideological, and political roles occupied by Preclassic Maya rulers. The inclusion of the ceremonial ballcourt as part of the Ixbalamque E-Group corroborates the widespread assertions interrelating these two architectural forms, while simultaneously illuminating certain conceptual underpinnings that link them in later iconography and architecture. Large-scale investment in the Ixbalamque E-Group complex, alongside the construction of the Tigrillo palace in the central Ventanas group suggest a dual role for early rulers in northeast Peten, as both politically powerful in the affairs of the nascent state while supplicant to the divine and cyclical forces of nature. Overlying the Ixbalamque E-Group with the triadic group ultimately shows a transformation in the type of ritual commemoration taking place at Pinturas, shifting from a fundamental emphasis on these natural forces to instead foreground the preeminence of local royalty. The shift at Pinturas, from E-Group to triadic complex, thus characterizes an architectural expression of nascent institutions of kingship that would come to define the politics of the Classic period.

Notes

1. The Ixim phase is actually comprised of Sub I and Sub II phases, which were initially numbered as separate but actually existed at the same time.

2. Five charcoal samples from sealed contexts in each of the three architectural strata, Sub VI, Sub V, and Sub IV, were dated using an Accelerator Mass Spectrometry (AMS) radiocarbon dating method. The first came from within the floor of the Sub VI platform and provided a maximum uncalibrated radiocarbon date of 2260 ± 40 B.P. [400 to 200 B.C.; 2σ (95% probability) calibrated range]. The second sample came from the floor of Sub V (Ixbalamque), which completely covered over Sub IV, and dates its construction to 2200 ± 60 B.P. uncalibrated [390 to 80 B.C.; 2σ (95% probability) calibrated range]. The final three samples come from the construction fill of Sub VI, which completely encapsulated Sub V (Ixbalamque). These samples produced the following dates: 2260 ± 40 B.P uncalibrated [400 to 200 B.C.; 2σ (95% probability) calibrated range], 2180 ± 40 B.P. uncalibrated [370 to 100 B.C.; 2σ (95% probability) calibrated range], and 2150 ± 40 B.P. uncalibrated [360 to 60 B.C.; 2σ (95% probability) calibrated range]. For full discussion see Saturno et al. 2006.

3. At E-VII sub, each of the eight anthropomorphic masks flanking the four stairways are slightly different, though they share the same basic iconographic template (Ricketson and Ricketson 1937).

4. Cohodas (1991) draws a contrast between the Maya primary association of the setting sun with ballgames and Mexican associations incorporating both the rising and setting sun.

5. The Proyecto San Bartolo/Xultun has been unable to confirm one of the cited examples of an "attached" E-Group ballcourt, mentioned as lying within the Classic period center of Xultun.

6. Stelae 5 and 7 at Seibal flank the stairway of Structure A-10, the eastern range structure of an E-Group (see Aimers and Rice 2006:89).

7. The artifacts of El Manatí were deposited over a period of 600 years from 1600 to 1000 B.C. (Ortiz and Rodríguez 2000:75)

8. Sub 1A runs north-south and was built right up against the Yaxche platform, facing

east. Sub 1B is to the immediate north of Sub 1A. It runs east-west and was built facing southward with its west end up against the Yaxche platform. A third structure probably existed to the immediate south of Sub 1A that also ran east-west, but faced north; however, this building was likely razed in constructing the final phase of Pinturas.

9. See Houston and Stuart 1996

10. At this ritual event, a *quincunx* cache (cache 4) of smashed jars atop Olmec style jades and greenstone pebbles was deposited in a complex, multi-tiered cruciform pit, dug at the axial center line of a subsequently constructed late Middle Preclassic E-Group (Bauer 2005; Estrada-Belli 2006:59–60).

14

Naranjo, Guatemala, a Middle Preclassic Site in the Central Highlands of Guatemala

BARBARA ARROYO

Archaeology of the central valley of Guatemala is not well known. Some studies have been done, which include surveys (Sanders and Murdy 1982; Shook 1952) and salvage excavations (De León and Valdes 2002). The most important site of the Middle Preclassic period was Kaminaljuyu, and it is poorly understood in this critical era, which is characterized by the development of social complexity at various sites in the Maya zone in particular and Mesoamerica in general. This work presents information recovered from salvage excavations at the site of Naranjo, located on the outskirts of Guatemala City, and its relationship with the neighboring site of Kaminaljuyu, as well as other sites in the zone (Figure 14.1). Here, I will address the ritual practices at Naranjo in the central highlands of Guatemala and the relationship of ritual practices at Kaminaljuyu and its neighbors during the Middle Preclassic (800–400 B.C.). I will use the findings of the Naranjo investigations as a reference point, focusing on ritual practices that involved landscape and sacred geography, the use of monuments, and dedication rites for constructions. I will then present the case of a "re-visit" of individuals to Naranjo during the Late Classic period as a specific and focused ritual, reflecting the importance of this location through time and its potential role as a pilgrimage center.

The archaeological site of Naranjo is located on the northern edge of the Guatemala Valley, surrounded by large ravines on its north, west, and east sides. It is 3 km from Kaminaljuyu (Figure 14.1), and its principal occupation occurred during the Middle Preclassic period, between 800 and 400 B.C., at which point the site was abandoned and was not visited again until the Late Classic (around A.D. 600), when a specific ritual activity took place that did not represent a permanent occupation. Investigation

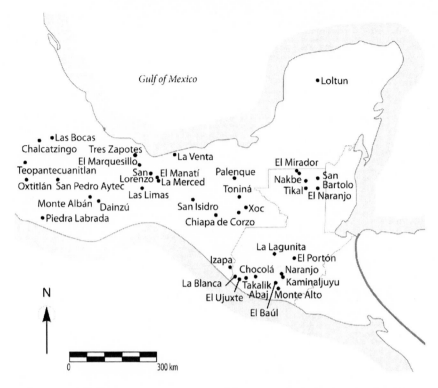

Figure 14.1. Map of region showing location of Naranjo and other sites mentioned in the text.

at Naranjo began as part of a salvage project due to the construction of a housing complex at the site. The opportunity to explore a site of this era in the central highlands was unique; work included excavations in the site's central sector, survey, and testing of the site's periphery (Arroyo 2006, 2010), leading to an understanding of the central architectural and sacred arrangement of the site, as well as its residential area.

Background

Naranjo was visited for the first time with archaeological ends in mind by Caroline Salvin, an artist who had illustrated botanical works for her husband. She painted several watercolors of the landscape, and among these she drew a mound located within Hacienda Naranjo, noting that it had been excavated. Her diary offers the following entry for Saturday, July 12, 1873: "At 8 o'clock we left for Naranjo to see the mounds with Mr. Corgett, the Duke [here she is referring to the owner of the farm, the Duke of

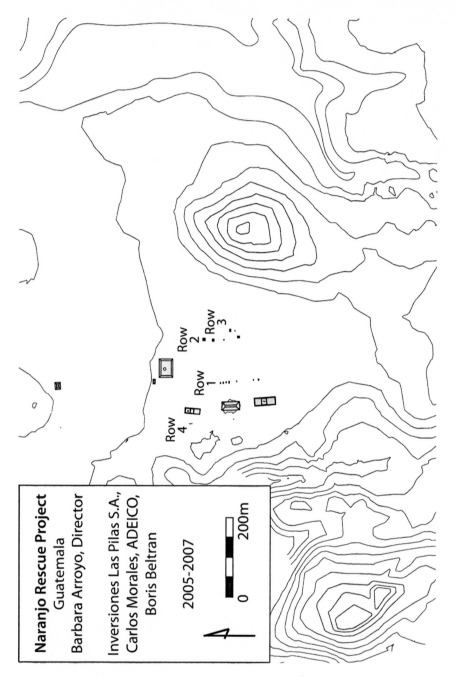

Figure 14.2. Map of Naranjo.

Aycinena], Don Chico, myself, the Duchess, and Mrs. Everall. Very agreeable . . . was the ride, very pretty" (Salvin 2000:138). Later, on Thursday, October 12th of that same year, she notes, "we went to open a mound at El Naranjo. We found a black jar and a bowl with a colored design; we also found a skeleton on the edge of the mound, it seems to have been interred in a vertical position . . . I made a drawing of it" (Salvin 2000:186). It is important to note that during the investigations of the recent Naranjo Project, we did not find burials, and so the excavation referred to by Salvin was done at the neighboring site of Pelikan, as identified by Shook (1952), a site which was also located on the property of Hacienda Naranjo but was destroyed prior to our investigations.

Muybridge subsequently visited the site and took a pair of photographs of the plaza with its monuments in their original position and a detail of Monument 1 (Burns 1986). Later, in 1876, G. Williamson (1877), who was the U.S. Ambassador to Central America and a fan of archaeology, visited the site. In Williamson's description, he includes references to the stone monuments placed in three rows, oriented north-to-south, some of which had been removed to other parts of the hacienda. Williamson drew a map that served as the initial reference for the Naranjo Project and was of great use in locating monuments (Figure 14.3). During his visit, he observed that "three rows of stones are still found standing on the surface" (Williamson 1877:419). Unfortunately, our excavations only uncovered Row 1 of the original placement. In addition, Williamson did not report a fourth row found by the Naranjo Project, which was located outside of the Central Plaza.

During the 20th century, Villacorta (1927) published a brief report of the site, based on Williamson's observations and a personal visit to the farm during which he took photographs of the plain monuments of the second row still located in their original placement. Edwin M. Shook visited the site on various occasions between 1940 and 1950 as part of his work with the Carnegie Institution of Washington, D.C., and the Kaminaljuyu Project. Shook did a sketch map (Figure 14.4) and contacted residents at the farm, who gave him a collection of Middle Preclassic figurines, leading him to suggest this date for the site's occupation. It was not until 2005 that the first formal archaeological work took place (Figure 14.2) with urbanization projects in the area.

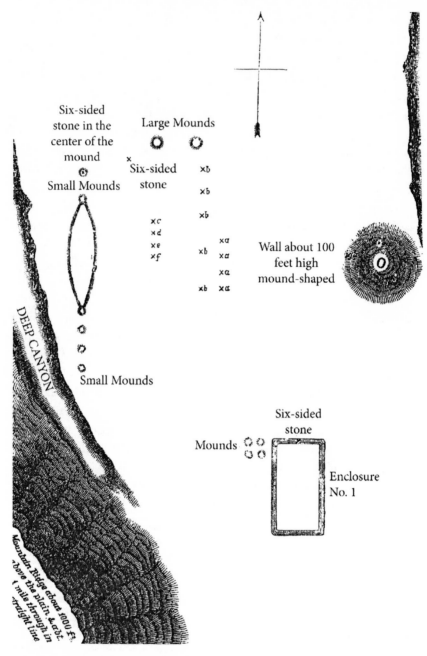

Figure 14.3. Naranjo first map (drawn by Williamson).

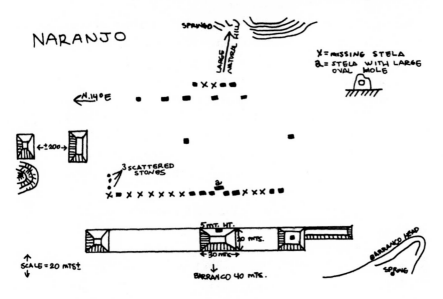

Figure 14.4. Naranjo map (drawn by Edwin M. Shook).

The Middle Preclassic Period in the Central Valley

Shook had documented the greatest number of settlements as part of his work for the Carnegie Institution. He reported a series of sites around Naranjo, specifically Cruz to the east, Bran and Guacamaya to the west, Betania to the south, and to the southeast, Aycinena, Rodeo, Cruz de Cotió, and Ross (Figure 14.1) (Shook 1952). According to his dating, the site of Bran could have had a relationship with Naranjo, as well as Cruz de Cotió (Figure 14.1). The majority of these places have already disappeared under modern constructions. It is important to highlight that the survey undertaken by Shook documented the presence of settlements with plain monuments, a practice also seen at Naranjo, and also likely dates the site of Rosario-Naranjo (also known as Tulam Tzu) as one of the principal neighbors of Naranjo, located only 1 km to the southwest. As part of real estate development since the 1980s, there have been various salvage projects in that area (Escobar and Alvarado 2004; Jacobo 1992; Ponciano and Foncea 1988), which have documented the site dimensions of Rosario-Naranjo and indicated that it was also an important Middle Preclassic site; it consists of five mounds and various plain monuments. A short distance to the east is the site of Trinidad (Velásquez 2005), on a property of the same name, today known as Parque La Democracia, which also had Middle Preclassic occupation and was possibly an extension of Kaminaljuyu.

The other great site of the period was Kaminaljuyu, which has suffered greatly due to the constant expansion of Guatemala City. From work by the Carnegie Institution and Shook and Popenoe de Hatch, we have an Early to Middle Preclassic chronology for the central highlands, defined by the ceramic phases: Arévalo (1200–1000 B.C.), Las Charcas (1000–750 B.C.), and Providencia (750–400 B.C.) (Shook and Popenoe de Hatch 1999). Later, Pennsylvania State University also undertook excavations, as well as studies of the settlement of Kaminaljuyu and its surroundings (Michels 1979), broadening our understanding of the site. Nonetheless, the majority of the data comes from salvage projects that offer only brief reports, hence reconstructing the Middle Preclassic landscape is complicated.

According to previous work, it seems that the largest occupation of the era is found around the Miraflores Lake (Popenoe de Hatch 2002:279). Multiple references mention Middle Preclassic ceramics, demonstrating its extent is much greater than previously thought. Kidder (1961) refers to finding a number of bell-shaped middens dating to the Las Charcas phase on the edge of what is today the Roosevelt Hospital (and were originally Mounds A and B of Kaminaljuyu), as well as Finca Las Charcas located in what is now Zone 11 of the city. This area had a dense Middle Preclassic occupation, and many artifacts were recovered by the Carnegie Institution in the 1940s and 1950s. This occupation goes well beyond the Kaminaljuyu illustrated by Navarrete and Luján (1986), who mention the presence of two Las Charcas mounds in what is today Zone 14. In addition, Navarrete and others found Middle Preclassic ceramics in the cemetery of Zone 3 (Navarrete and Luján 1986).

Beyond the central valley, there are a series of reports of occupation contemporaneous with Las Charcas. Piedra Parada, San José Pinula, and Canchón, near Fraijanes, are some of the sites reported by Shook with dense occupation in the Middle Preclassic (Figure 14.1). Some of these places have been excavated (De Leon and Valdés 2002), documenting significant populations in addition to complex sociopolitical organization. The sites of Santa Isabel in Fraijanes, Cieneguilla in San José Pinula, and Virginia, located on the road to Santa Elena Barillas (Shook 1952) also had plain monuments. The presence of plain monuments at Middle Preclassic sites is only one of the features shared among these places; they also demonstrate a certain similarity in spatial arrangement and cultural practices. The majority of these sites are geographically located on hills and mountains—another way in which these central region sites are related to what is also seen at Naranjo, as we will see later.

Description of Naranjo

The site consists of five structures aligned north-to-south, integrating a natural hill or *cerro* that measures more than 33 m in height on its east side and encloses a large plaza (Figure 14.2). The principal mound, located within the alignment to the west of the *cerro*, measures 6 m in height. As part of the large plaza, platforms are found to the south and the north, both aligned on a north-south axis and oriented 21 degrees east of north. The central sector has another mound, Mound 2, that encloses the plaza on the north side and Mound 3 is found 200 m to the north on the edge of a ravine. The site is surrounded by ravines on the north and west sides, both of which contain natural springs with small permanent streams; also, Naranjo Lagoon is located a short 2 km from the site, demonstrating that the presence and availability of abundant water was important for this settlement. In addition, the presence of the hill defining the east side of the site was likely one of the principal natural elements for establishing the site in this location, similar to the pattern seen for Chalcatzingo in Morelos (Grove 1989), Teopantecuanitlan in Guerrero (Martínez Donjuan 1994), and Las Bocas in Puebla.

The three rows of monuments in the plaza were located between the structures and the limestone *cerro*, with a fourth row placed in front of Mound 1 and the North Platform at the edge of the ravine. The South Platform consists of a natural elevation that was slightly modified for use during the Las Charcas phase (800–600 B.C.). Mound 1 shows constructions during Las Charcas and Providencia (600–400 B.C.), while those of Mound 2 and the North Platform were constructed during the Providencia phase at the end of the Middle Preclassic. Mound 3 dates to Providencia and follows the same construction patterns as that of North Platform and Mound 2.

The function of the structures in the site's center was undoubtedly ceremonial. Mound 1 is oriented 91 degrees toward the natural hill to the east and defines an area with the first row of monuments, creating a small plaza. This orientation suggests an equinox alignment as reported by Aveni and collaborators on the earliest E-Groups in the Maya area (Aveni et al. 2003). Carved clay stairs are found on the east side of Mound 1, which supports the idea that the principal use was on that side toward the first line of monuments.

North Platform

The North Platform was constructed during the Providencia phase, initiated by a dedicatory event, which included abundant ceramic sherds, ash, burned clay, and animal bones. The event may represent a banquet culminating in the construction. The remains of ash and burned clay suggest fires accompanied this episode.

After the dedication, box-like structures of clay were built, a common construction technique during that era, to place fills that elevated the surface of this structure some 90 cm. Over this, they placed a clay floor that was exposed in some places. Later, during the Middle Preclassic, more fill was placed over this floor, creating the last surface used.

Associated with this last floor were a series of significant features. Toward the northern side of the platform was a hearth containing the remains of burned columnar basalt and other small stones. A little to the east was an alignment of 13 stones and Stela 21, composed of columnar basalt. A few meters to the south was Monument 16, another columnar basalt located in a straight line with Stela 21 (Figure 14.5). All of these monuments were placed during the Middle Preclassic period; however, they were re-visited and re-used during the Late Classic. Also found with the monuments were 18 Amatle type ceramic vessels (vases, plates, bowls, and censers), a Late Classic ceramic type, a burned clay cruciform feature, and 13 pebbles, among which seven were identified as quartz.

It is possible that the erection of plain monuments is related to some calendrical event, and the northern area may have shared this connotation. The placement of the 13 stones could relate to the 13 months of the Tzolkin calendar. The Late Classic re-use could be interpreted as a commemoration of the location and its importance in the calendrical cycle.

What seem to be the remains of a sweat bath or *temascal* were uncovered east of the North Platform. This consisted of a circular stone feature, which incorporated various recycled monument fragments. Within the feature were stones of lesser size, apparently subjected to heat. Again, this would support the hypothesis of a *temascal*, since the stones would have been heated by fire, with water subsequently thrown on them, creating steam within the interior of the structure. This *temascal* dates to the Late Classic and would have been related to the re-use of the North Platform in that period.

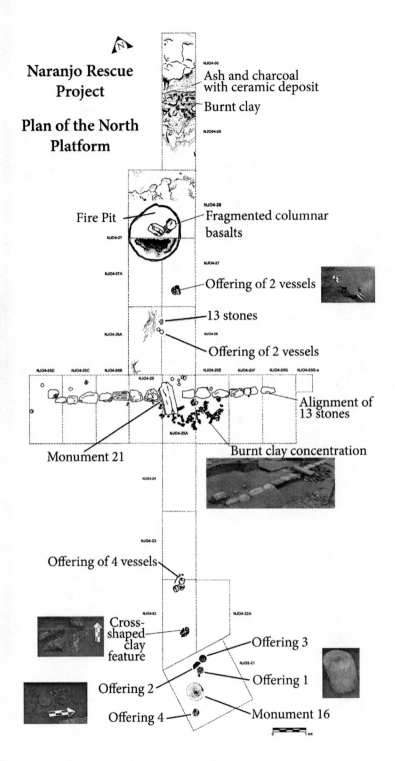

Figure 14.5. Illustration of offerings on North Platform.

Figure 14.6. Excavation of South Platform.

South Platform

The South Platform was a natural elevation accommodated for Prehispanic uses. In contrast to the majority of the principal structures at the site, this area was utilized only during the beginning of the Middle Preclassic, in the Las Charcas phase. There was no formal construction, as with the North Platform or the much larger mounds. Here, the Prehispanic inhabitants took advantage of high ground to conduct ritual activities. There are floors only in some areas of the platform, and there were no postholes or hearths from the Middle Preclassic. Nonetheless, the southwestern and northeastern corners had small holes carved into sterile soil, filled with dense ceramic and obsidian refuse (Figure 14.6). These holes are similar to the bell-shaped pits found at contemporary sites, although they were not as large.

The South Platform was used during the Las Charcas phase. Shook and Popenoe de Hatch (1999) had recovered sherds that they defined as Arévalo phase; however, there was no stratigraphic deposit of this earlier material under that of the Las Charcas phase to confirm the sequence. The findings from Naranjo, and other contemporary sites, suggest that Arévalo ceramics could be an early facet of the Las Charcas phase.

A radiocarbon date from this Charcas deposit in the South Platform came back with a date between 790 and 420 B.C. This date is later than the defined chronology for the Las Charcas period, but other results for understanding the absolute chronology are still pending.

Also in this area were numerous figurine fragments, as well as partial vessels, presenting the cosmology of the ancient inhabitants of Naranjo. The figurines primarily depict female individuals, with a few males (some with beards), animals, and others. The figurines correspond to Middle Preclassic markers and are diagnostic for this phase (Figure 14.7).

Among the deposits in the corners of the platform were ceramics that present important conceptions of the Prehispanic world at Naranjo. A plate with the image of an early deity is of great interest (Figure 14.8). The deity appears to correspond to an image indentified by David Stuart as G1 of Palenque (personal communication, 2005). G1 is one of the gods of the Palenque triad. Schele referred to G1, G2, and G3 not only as Palenque gods (Schele and Freidel 1990) but also noted that G1 and G3 are gods commonly represented in even earlier public images created during the Late Preclassic period. This portrait of G1 is found on a Middle Preclassic sherd indicating that the Maya highlands were part of a very wide interaction sphere since early times. It is relevant to highlight some facts about G1. He is the

Figure 14.7. Naranjo figurine heads.

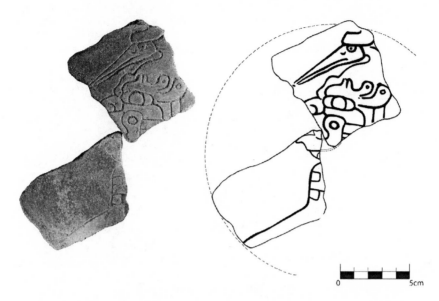

Figure 14.8. Red-on-buff ceramic fragment including depiction of potential G1 deity.

primogenitor of the Triad. He has a human aspect and is distinguished from his brothers by his *Spondylus* shell earspool, his square eye, and the fish barbles seen on his cheek. He also has an aquatic bird in his headdress. All of these characteristics suggest the origin of this god is a place with abundant water. Stuart refers to G1 as an ancestor of oceans (Stuart 2005). The presence of the shell earspool, fish scales, and the aquatic bird in the headdress suggest that G1 could be a coastal ancestor, from a place where fish, shell, and aquatic birds are abundant. It should be remembered that it is the Pacific Coast where the oldest sedentary human occupation has been documented in the region, as well as the earliest writing. Still, Cuevas and Bernal (2009) have recently referred to the mythical sea and paleoenvironmental studies of Palenque to explain the features of G1. Considering that G1 is a Classic period deity, an alternative interpretation to this figure is an individual that has an aquatic bird on his headdress and "Olmec style" features such as his mouth and arm decoration.

In addition to this sherd, a bowl fragment with what can be interpreted as an Olmec dragon or an Olmec style image was found (Figure 14.9). Clearly, Naranjo was a participant within a large Mesoamerican interaction sphere in the Middle Preclassic period. This ceramic type presents a series of special designs suggesting a particular function or transmission of a particular message. At Naranjo, there are many examples of this ceramic

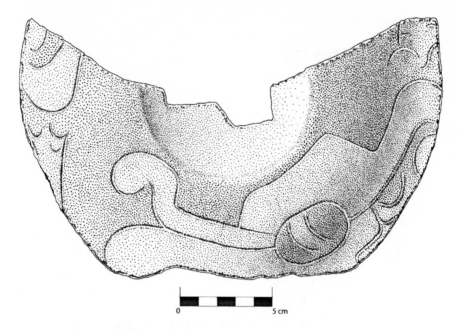

0   5 cm

Figure 14.9. Red-on-buff ceramics with dragon representation.

type, but at other Middle Preclassic sites of the valley, there are hardly any. One notes that the bowls of this ceramic type have worn bases indicating continuous use; however, the elaborate designs on the surface are only seen on the bottom of the vessel with the orifice facing down. This suggests the vessels had a special dual function: acting as a receptacle for food, while also serving as a lid or for communicating a message through the designs.

Mound 2

Mound 2 is located on the northeastern edge of the site center and was constructed toward the end of the Middle Preclassic, during the Providencia phase, making it contemporaneous with the North Platform and Mound 3. Like Mound 3, Mound 2 had a dedicatory event prior to its construction. Four construction episodes were identified, all dating between 700 and 400 B.C. No steps were identified, as at Mound 1, perhaps because the structure may have had a ramp for access.

Mound 3

Mound 3 is located 243 m north of Mound 2 on the edge of a ravine. This mound may have served as the entrance to the site on its northern border. Excavations documented three construction episodes, with a dedicatory deposit similar to that of the North Platform and Mound 2. Notably, the construction date is contemporaneous with those structures of the Providencia phase at the end of the Middle Preclassic.

The Central Plaza and Monuments

In the Central Plaza are three rows of monuments containing at least 17 monuments with a fourth found on the edge of a ravine for a total of 22 monuments (Figure 14.2). All four rows have the same orientation of 21 degrees east of north, although only Row 1 was found in its original placement. The first row consists of seven plain monuments and three altars associated with the South Platform and Mound 1 (Figure 14.10). The monuments are all made of basalt, giving them a similar appearance with the stelae, all of whose surfaces were polished. The plain altars are associated to Monuments 4 and 3 and are placed to the west of the plain monuments in front of the South Platform. A calibrated radiocarbon date recovered from the floor where Monument 3 was found with its corresponding altar dated this practice between 800 and 750 B.C. Excavations in Row 1 indicated it was placed during the Las Charcas phase.

The second row of monuments was 100 m east of the first and consisted of five monuments. These were large basalt and andesite blocks, one of which (Monument 27) presented evidence of having been carved. A calibrated radiocarbon date places the erection of this row between 790 and 500 B.C.; the carbon for the date was recovered between the wedges used to support the monument.

The third row was found 14 m to the east of Row 2 and directly west of the stone hill (Figure 14.9). This line consisted of three plain stelae of columnar basalt, one of which reached 2.50 m in height. Both Rows 2 and 3 were pulled down in modern times, and I am assuming that they followed the same orientation as the other rows, based on Shook's notes during his visit in the 1940s (Shook 1952).

A fourth row of monuments was discovered to the west of Mound 1 and the North Platform (Figure 14.9). This row consists of four monuments, but only one, Monument 17, was found in its original location by the Naranjo

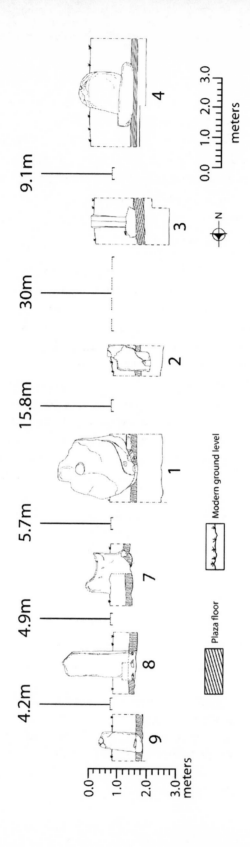

Figure 14.10. Illustration of line 1 of Naranjo Monuments (illustration by K. Pereira, Proyecto de Rescate Naranjo).

Project. The other three monuments were recovered accidentally when modern drains were being excavated. When the crew made the find, the location was documented, securely placing the row in an orientation 21 degrees east of north, like the others. It is possible that the monuments were integrated into the sacred landscape to convert them into markers left by the ancestors. Some of them were found in contexts without constructions, and therefore the monuments themselves had to have had their own significance. There has been much debate on the meaning of plain monuments. Some have proposed that they were painted, stuccoed, or covered in cloth (Guernsey 2006b; Stuart 2010). Notably, no traces of paint have been identified. Stuart has proposed recently that plain monuments or stelae had a cosmological ritual importance more complex than previously attributed to them; the monuments had multiple meanings based on the material substance of the stone and animated characteristics assigned to them. He suggests that the stone itself was a powerful substance, a permanent material of the earth, which withstood and transcended time, recalling other worlds and spatial categories. In short, the Maya and other Mesoamerican groups saw the stelae and altars as natural substances of the earth and its interior. These stone monuments were part of collective rituals, as they had both soul and animated spirit (Stuart 2010). It is possible that the Naranjo monuments represented important calendrical episodes where a monument was erected at each initiation or termination of a cycle. In this celebration, groups of individuals linked themselves to the location as a center of power that, in turn, could also function as a pilgrimage place.

The sources for the stone of the monuments have not been identified, although there are rocks with similar characteristics to those of Row 2 located approximately 1 km from the site. Columnar basalt is a specific formation whose closest known source is located in Palín, some 25 km south of the site.

In addition to the site center, other plain monuments were discovered associated with the springs, as was the case of Monument 19 on the edge of the ravine in the northern sector of the site, and another five in the southeastern sector. To date, Naranjo has the greatest number of monuments in the central highlands.

The Settlement Pattern

In addition to the central sector, the testpit program indicated a dense population inhabited the outskirts of the site. In particular, there was a

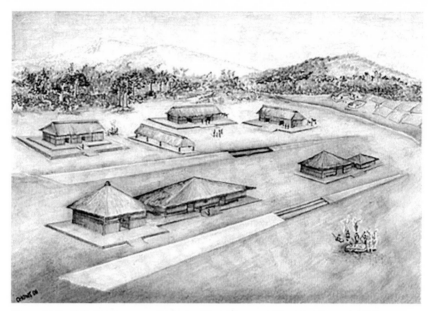

Figure 14.11. Artistic reconstruction of residential area at Naranjo (drawn by Edgar Arévalo, Proyecto de Rescate Naranjo).

preference for living in flat areas near natural elevations. These flat areas were completely unnoticeable, and as such, have been named "invisible structures"; they consist of clay floors, sometimes burned, with roofs of perishable material (Figure 14.11). Sometimes the walls were elaborated with wattle-and-daub, for which we find thousands of fragments in excavations. In a few places we can see the shape of the structures, noting that some of them are oval. All of the residential areas had easy access to water due to the presence of the nearby springs.

Landscape and Sacred Geography

The landscape offers an essential framework for archaeology, as a context that unites disparate human acts. Such a framework accommodates collective and individual ritual activities. The center of Naranjo was the scene of collective ritual practices where the landscape was a key element. In addition to the spatial arrangement of the site center already described, to the west of the site, some 2 km, is the Cerro Naranjo, which forms part of the greater landscape; besides integrating the physical site arrangement, it also creates a scene that represented the world and society of Naranjo in that era. Structures were built and accommodated between the space of the two hills, constructing a large plaza between the hill to the east and the central group. This required immense labor to level the ground surface and required two major construction episodes with fills, which were documented by deep stratigraphic excavations. This would have involved the control of a great many individuals needed to transport and erect the plain monuments in the central sector of the site. In comparison, areas of neighboring Kaminaljuyu also had a geographic composition constructed with various architectural groups tied to the Agua Volcano, the Cerro Naranjo, and other key topographic elements around the valley. Equally, the nearby site of Rosario-Naranjo also involved sacred geography as part of the landscape that validated its location.

The Springs

Along with the hills and structures at the site, the springs were also integrated into the spatial arrangement. Water was a key element for early societies and the concept of water that gushed up from the earth would have been favored for particular ritual practices. Currently, the springs are dry and there is little water even in the rainy season; however, the importance of these places and the practice of ritual that accompanied them can be seen along the edge of the ravine in the residential sector directly north of the site. Here, a plain stela of columnar basalt was uncovered and measured 2.5 m in height. The placement of this monument at the edge of a spring favors the interpretation of a ritual associated with water.

The rituals associated with water are not only seen near the natural springs but also recreated within the site's central sector. Monument 1, the only one moved .50 m from the rest in the row, had an associated artificial pool just to the east of it. This is the monument with the hole in the center seemingly indicating that at some moment water passed through it. The pool is small (around 2 m wide by 2 m long), but its importance lies in its association with the monument and the fact that it lies in the central part of the plaza. Similar practices have been documented for Cerro de las Mesas in Veracruz and Mirador and Izapa in Chiapas (Guernsey 2006b), probably recreating a sacred landscape within the very center of the site. The water emerging near Monument 1 at Naranjo could have had special significance according to its original location and the construction of the pool to the east could represent the re-creation of this landscape.

Water was a vital element for societies in addition to forming part of many rituals. For traditional societies, water erodes, washes away, purifies, and regenerates. Eliade (1982) has proposed that water constitutes one of the manifestations of the sacred, essential in archaic cultures.

Constructions and Public Rituals

Construction was accompanied by a series of rituals. This activity involved many individuals since once the structure was dedicated, people were needed to carry in the fills and elevate the ground surface to a desired level. Whoever would have participated in construction activity also would have likely been part of the dedicatory ritual, which may have required the observance of certain rules of abstinence and fasting, as do contemporary dedication ceremonies for special constructions.

Both the North Platform, as well as Mounds 2 and 3, had dedicatory events previous to their construction. These events are documented by traces of burning and hearths in place prior to construction, in addition to animal remains, possibly reflecting the consumption or offering of them. Once the dedicatory event was completed, which in some cases date to the latter half of the Middle Preclassic, construction was begun using clay blocks to build up the surface and elevate it to the desired height. The dense quantity of ceramics, consisting principally of plates and bowls associated with the dedicatory event of burning and consuming animal offerings, suggests the participation of many people, therefore I assume the ritual was public and integrated the population to involve them in the great effort of building the primary structures (see Brown et al. Chapter 5 this volume for a comparison).

Large-scale hearths also point toward the celebration of rituals involving many people. These hearths were perhaps used to cook food that was consumed at the dedicatory events. Similar examples have been documented by Popenoe de Hatch (1997) at Kaminaljuyu-San Jorge, where she identified the presence of seeds from avocado, plum, beans, zapote, and anona. Near Mound B at Kaminaljuyu, Kidder identified what may have been a pit for barbecuing, with similar characteristics to those seen at Naranjo (Kidder 1961). Food preparation on a grand scale supports the idea of public celebrations. These celebrations also may have been part of pilgrimages commemorating particular cycles at the site.

The northwest and southwest corners of the South Platform had in their deepest levels bell-shaped middens with deposits of ceramics, obsidian, and figurines dug into sterile soil (Figure 14.7). Some investigators (Marroquin 2006) have assigned particular functions to these pits, indicating that they could have served as deposits for water, grains, or other items. The irregular form and diverse sizes documented at Naranjo, however, suggest that these were strictly deposits of ceremonial garbage placed as part of the activities associated with the platform. It is possible that the enormous number of ceramic sherds found here represents an activity similar to the ethnographic ritual calendar of the *Guajxaquip Bats* celebration of Totonicapán (Goubaud 1964). This ceremony occurs at the beginning of the 260-day calendar, a time of purifying the spirit and offering thanks for the benefits received during the year. This celebration occurs at dawn in a place located 1 km from Momostenango, where various altars are found consisting of rises of 1 to 3 m in height, composed of the remains of clay vessels that, over time, have formed a solid mass of debris. Goubaud observed that families or groups of individuals arrived at the altars and deposited on one side sherds they had brought with them to offer. The ritual lasts until dusk, and then the ceremony is moved to the top of a *cerro* to the west of the altars. There, all kinds of food and drink are consumed, and candles and incense are lit, with everyone spending the night before similar altars to those already described which are continuously burning incense. The two subsequent days of the *Guajxaquip Bats* ceremony are also dedicated to the divinity of the earth, and almost everyone remains in Momostenango. This day has been referred to as the most important of the indigenous ritual calendar.

Curiously, no whole vessels are offered, only fragments, perhaps from a desire to multiply good omens with many pieces. The dating of the South Platform corresponds to the Las Charcas phase, between 800 and 600 B.C. It is possible that the placement of the monuments, and the offerings in the corners of the platform, form part of the same public calendrical ritual. It has been suggested that women could have played an integral role in this ritual, given the significant quantity of female figurines in these deposits in contrast to their presence in residential contexts (Linares 2009). In addition, the diversity of physical features depicted on the figurines (Figure 14.7) suggests they represent different ethnic groups participating in the ceremonies. Some of them are related to examples from the south coast and some even from the Gulf Coast of Mexico (Linares 2009).

The ceramic examples found as part of these deposits include many fragments of red-on-buff bowls, a generally rare and special ceramic type of the Las Charcas phase in the Guatemala Valley. In addition, as mentioned previously, they have special characteristics in which many unique designs are illustrated and likely formed part of the meaning of the ritual.

The Late Classic Revisit

Extensive investigations at Naranjo allow us to document that the site was occupied from 800 to 400 B.C., when it was suddenly abandoned. Very few Late Preclassic sherds were recovered suggesting a complete absence of subsequent occupation. This fact contrasts with the neighboring site of Kaminaljuyu, which saw its great apogee at the end of the Late Preclassic. Undoubtedly, Naranjo was the first ceremonial center of the central highlands, the scene of important public rituals that endured in the oral tradition and historical memory, when it was revisited in A.D. 600 (Paiz 2007). This re-visit consisted of the ritual use of the North Platform, accompanied by the construction and use of a *temascal* built from the fragments of broken monuments, and the short occupation on the east side of the South Platform. Equally, some of the monuments may have been offerings during the Late Classic. Nonetheless, this revisit probably corresponded to a single cycle and did not last long, given the evidence of very focused activity.

On the North Platform various offerings were found, aligned along the north-south orientation of Monuments 21 and 16. Excavations discovered Late Classic Amatle type vessels, among them were pans, vases, small plates, and a bowl with a basket handle. In addition, a cruciform-shaped burned feature was uncovered, as well as 13 pebbles, seven of which were quartz. All of these artifacts were linked to the 13 stones placed in Preclassic times at the base of the hearth containing fragments of plain columnar basalt monuments (Figure 14.5). This action suggests a termination ritual for these monuments burned to complete the final cycle and pass on to another life. Symbolic and ritual behavior has the power to transform material and conceptual structures, therefore through this revisit and detailed ritual activity, the Late Classic visitors "made it their own" or again gave life, at least temporarily, to the millennial Naranjo. Possibly these ritual activities were a symbolic renewal of objects and space.

Perhaps Late Classic activities in the central highlands were widely scattered, and it is possible the visitors were from the nearby site of Pelikan, located only 1 km southeast of Naranjo. Unfortunately, there is little to say about that site since it was destroyed in modern times, although Shook's (1952) survey identified it as Late Classic.

Final Considerations

The lack of burials and the ephemeral domestic constructions leads one to believe that Naranjo may have been a space utilized for pilgrimages during the Middle Preclassic. The continuity seen in the Late Classic revisit of the site would support this interpretation. Studies by Turner (1967) in traditional African communities indicate that pilgrimages occur in places that have been considered sacred by different cultures and peoples. These places locate the intersection of two or more lines or axes of energy that may be reflected in the confluence of two or more rivers. The geographic location of Naranjo is characterized by a small plain between *cerros* and ravines (Figure 14.2). The presence of the *cerros* on the east and west sides mark and define the territory of the place. The ravines surrounding the site would have been difficult barriers to cross, since they are extremely deep and it requires particular effort to gain access to the locale. The Naranjo and Molino Rivers surround and converge on the northeast sector of the site, placing Naranjo in a unique location (Figure 14.1).

To understand the explanation of Naranjo as pilgrimage center one must review some important themes. Whoever participated in the pilgrimage to visit the sacred place where a series of rituals would have taken place would have reached a liminal state. In this state new modes of being are tested, new combinations of symbols are accepted or rejected. The essence of ritual is its multi-dimensionality (Turner 1977). Liminality allows reflection and the realization of a critique, idealization, or creation of a state of equality and camaraderie occurring within the context of exchange among individuals who represent different social groups. In this experience, one reaches what Turner describes as *"communitas,"* a community spirit, the feeling of social equality and collective solidarity. The notion of *communitas* is characteristic of a group experiencing a liminal state (Tuner 1977).

Generally, the liminal phenomenon tends to be collective, tied to cycles and calendrical rhythms, or better when a crisis occurs in social processes, whether they be for internal reasons, external adaptations, or unexpected catastrophes (e.g., earthquakes, invasions, epidemics). The liminal phenomenon has an intellectual and emotional significance for all members of the community and is typically found in traditional societies.

With this in mind, one could argue that Naranjo represented such a liminal space. Here, particular cycles were commemorated and communitarian efforts brought the monuments and erected them to geographically mark the location and critical cycles, such as the initiation of the solar year, and so on. The placement of the monuments would have been accompanied by particular rituals in the site center, as is seen in the corners of the South Platform and the dedication of some of the other structures, including the North Platform and Mound 2. In addition, as occurs in liminal spaces, there would likely have been a transcultural zone where many cultural and social groups would have been present. There, liminal spaces are the scenes of cultural interactions using images, symbols, architecture, designs, ideology, powers, and so on, incorporating more than one identity.

Examining the cultural material recovered from the Naranjo excavations, one observes a confluence of social groups at the site. Clay figurines, which in some way represent portraits of the actors of that era, show a physical diversity that would reflect the presence of different groups who came to this location to interact. Some ceramics also exhibit a diversity of styles related to groups from the south coast who also could have participated in these activities. Another shared practice with the south coast sites is the erection of plain monuments, which, in turn, seems related to the Achiguate ceramic tradition described by Popenoe de Hatch (1999), based on her research in the region.

A pilgrimage to Naranjo would have allowed Middle Preclassic society to highlight cohesion between the sites of the region. For example, it is possible that groups from Piedra Parada, Santa Isabel, Virginia, and elsewhere on the outskirts of the valley could have participated in pilgrimages to Naranjo. At the same time, people from places further away, such as the Baja Verapaz and the south coast, also may have visited. The unity of the broader society was reinforced beyond differences and tensions that were smoothed out along the road toward the pilgrimage place. The sharing of food, walking time, and so on, would have promoted a sense of community and the moment of *communitas* described by Turner (1977). During pilgrimages relationships would be established, as everyone participated in the same conditions, instead of highlighting the differences between roles and statuses.

It could be that the structures that appear on the outskirts of Naranjo represent neighborhoods of people in co-habitation during the Middle Preclassic. Potentially, the presence of the Majadas phase, sometimes mixed with deposits of Las Charcas and Providencia, could represent these groups and not a chronological stage. While the settlement patterns and some cultural practices were shared, the ceramics incorporated particular types, like Zinc Orange, demonstrating a distinct ethnic affiliation (and not necessarily a chronological distinction as proposed by Shook and Popenoe de Hatch

[1999]). Additionally, the materials of the Majadas phase are not identified at all in Middle Preclassic sites in the valley, which supports a link between these materials and a particular cultural group.

The presence of different ethnic groups may be demonstrated in the inventory of clay figurines representing a diversity of physical features (Linares 2009). On the other hand, the sculptural tradition would also represent differences between groups. Popenoe de Hatch (1997) has identified the presence of three ceramic traditions for the Middle Preclassic: Ocosito, Naranjo, and Achiguate. While the Naranjo ceramic tradition has been identified at La Blanca as the principal site of San Marcos of the south coast, it does not have many similarities with the site of Naranjo in the central highlands in spite of being contemporaries. La Blanca has sculpture fragments but no plain monuments, as is the case with some sites within the neighboring Achiguate tradition to the east. Bove has also observed this pattern in a study of plain stelae distribution throughout the south coast (Bove 2002, 2011). In the case of the Achiguate tradition, the site of El Bálsamo was the most important center of the Escuintla region, sharing a series of ceramic styles, plain stelae, as well as a spatial layout similar to Naranjo.

Naranjo was abandoned around 400 B.C. If Naranjo was a pilgrimage site, whatever made it important and attractive in the Middle Preclassic ended when power was centralized in Kaminaljuyu, which dominated the local population in the Late Preclassic. Some have proposed that the control exercised by Kaminaljuyu over the El Chayal obsidian source and the production of prismatic blades could have played a critical role in the growth of the site as center of power. Perhaps Kaminaljuyu subjugated the population to utilize the labor required for great hydraulic works associated with the Miraflores Lake and the agricultural demands to sustain a population that had grown toward the end of the Middle Preclassic and early Late Preclassic. The abandonment of Naranjo reflects a drastic change in the organization of society, and it is not until the Late Classic when the site was revisited for ritual purposes, potentially for commemorating some particular cyclical event. If Naranjo was a pilgrimage center in the Middle Preclassic, the revisit in the Late Classic was a re-commemoration of a location which had been maintained in oral tradition in the valley for 900 years afterward.

Undoubtedly, Naranjo is a critical place in the development of social complexity that dominated the Maya highlands during the Middle Preclassic. Its role as a ceremonial center of importance is indisputable and the continuing investigations will improve our understanding of the site. What is lacking is deeper insight into the connection of Naranjo with other settlements in the Maya region and beyond, but for now, this brief summary offers information on the importance this settlement had in the first steps of social complexity in the central highlands of Guatemala.

Acknowledgments

This project was possible thanks to the generous support of a FAMSI emergency grant to Barbara Arroyo and a research grant to Karen Pereira. John Clark and the New World Archaeological Foundation also offered financial support for this project. I appreciate comments and editorial support given by Mary Pye.

15

Maya and the Idea of Empire

DAVID FREIDEL

Encountering the Maya Idea of Empire

El Perú, ancient Waka' in northwestern Peten, Guatemala, was the royal capital of an ancient dynasty. El Perú Stela 28, a badly worn, eroded, and distressed monument that can be stylistically dated to around A.D. 600. (Guenter 2005), declares the anonymous king to be the 24th successor in the dynasty. Calculating average reigns, this would place the Wak dynasty founder in the second century A.D. in the same general time range as the Tikal founder, Yax Ehb Xook (Freidel 2008; Martin and Grube 2008). El Perú-Waka' straddled a crossroads and was repeatedly attacked in antiquity, but through luck and the earnest effort of late inhabitants of the community to unearth and recollect the remains of these carvings, vital history remains preserved in the aggregate. The kings of the Wak dynasty were strategic allies or vassals to regionally dominant kings during two episodes of regional war in the southern lowlands, in the Early Classic and in the Late Classic periods. Scribes of El Perú-Waka' and scribes from other royal capitals wrote down what was, in effect, a collaborative history, and these texts show that this kingdom interacted intensely with others, particularly Tikal and Calakmul, the major contenders for regional power in the Late Classic period (Martin and Grube 2008; Sharer and Traxler 2006). It is through this collective history that one can discern the idea of empire in the Classic period.

The Waka' city center covers about 1 km^2 and it is on top of a 100 m escarpment. The settlement pattern features a large hillside temple acropolis in the east (Marken 2015). The western section of the city is a dense arrangement of plazas, temples, palaces, and homes, while the eastern section features hilltop residential complexes and the temple acropolis. Research since 2003 has revealed a history spanning more than a millennium based on ceramic chronology, radiocarbon dating, and text dates (Eppich 2012; Escobedo and Freidel 2007).

Stanley Guenter, epigrapher for both our project (Guenter 2005) and the El Mirador Project (Hansen and Guenter 2005) has identified a number of rulers from the more than 25 kings in a dynasty spanning more than four centuries. The most important of these are K'inich Bahlam I and K'inich Bahlam II. K'inich Bahlam I was vassal to Kaloomte' or supreme warrior, Sihyaj K'ahk', conqueror of Tikal in January of 378 A.D. El Perú Stela 16 has a posthumous portrait of this man who established a hegemony called the New Order by Simon Martin and Nikolai Grube (2008; see also Martin and Grube 1995). Sihyaj K'ahk' may have come from Teotihuacan to conquer Tikal according to David Stuart (2000) and other epigraphers. To be sure this general proposition remains controversial in Maya archaeology (Braswell 2003) but here I am operating on the premise that there was such a historical personage and regional overarching political order.

K'inich Bahlam II was vassal to the Kaanul king Yuknoom Ch'een the Great who consolidated power over most of Peten during the seventh century. The capital of the Kaanul in the seventh century was the city of Calakmul in Campeche Mexico (Stuart 2012). Several experts (see Hansen and Guenter 2005; Martin 1997), myself included, believe that the original seat of the Kaanul regime was the Preclassic city of El Mirador in north central Peten. I propose that the Kaanul lords of El Mirador established the first political regional hegemony in the Maya lowlands, the original idea of empire. But before I pursue the idea of empire, I need to review the idea of Maya kingship.

The Idea of Maya Kingship in Space and Time

When Linda Schele and I proposed (1988a) that the Maya institution of kingship originated in the Preclassic period it was still a controversial notion, indeed the epigraphic identification and contextualization of Classic kingship was less than two decades old (Lounsbury 1973). Kingship was revealed in the process of the phonetically based decipherment advanced by Schele, Mathews, Lounsbury, Kelly, and Greene Robertson in the mini-conferences at Dumbarton Oaks organized by Elizabeth Benson. Ed Shook, William Coe (1965a), and their colleagues in the Tikal project knew that the entombed individuals that they discovered in the early North Acropolis were surely high elite presaging the kings of the Classic period. Their existence manifested a complex and sophisticated society in the lowlands preceding the Classic apogee of Tikal. Gordon Willey (1984) reflecting on the efforts of the School of American Research Advanced Seminar on the Origins of Maya Civilization (see Brown and Bey Chapter 1 this volume) and also on the discoveries at Cerros (Cerro Maya), Cuello, and El Mirador presciently posited the existence of two "construction crests" in Maya civilization, in the Late Preclassic and the Late Classic. In this chapter I will propose that this pattern coincides with the florescence of regional imperial hegemonies in the lowlands. But that idea of empire must build on the idea of kingship.

Schele and I in *A Forest of Kings* contemplated this matter of the origins of Maya kingship, and we said the following in our endnotes: "Eventually, further discoveries in the interior may push the origins of the institution of ahau (sic) back into the Middle Preclassic period. Even were this to be the case, however, ethnographic analogy with other areas of the tropical world, such as Central Africa, shows that small complex societies can coexist with large tribal societies for centuries without the tribal societies developing into states. The empirical record of the Late Preclassic still suggests that the institution of kingship coalesced and dominated lowland society in a rapid transformation during the last two centuries BC" (Schele and Freidel 1990:422).

This notion of an archipelago of more complex societies in a sea of people content to live with less elite imposition is now current in the work of Takeshi Inomata and his colleagues (Inomata et al. 2013) contemplating the origins of early Middle Preclassic sedentary communities in the lowlands relying on staple maize subsistence. It was a notion I advanced in a paper honoring Gordon Willey and Berg Wartenstein in 1980 dubbed, tongue-in-cheek, "Political Systems in Lowland Yucatan" (Freidel 1983). Teaching Edmund Leach's classic monograph on the Kachin and Shan of Burma to Harvard undergraduates as an anthropology tutor, I had absorbed the lesson that social landscapes outside the industrialized West are, and have been in the past, usually composed of many quite distinct and dynamically engaged political organizations. I proposed in my paper that when Cerros, now called Cerro Maya, had collapsed at the end of the Late Preclassic its people no doubt survived. Some may have migrated to other complex centers, but others may have reorganized as simpler societies. I said "The thesis of this brief and speculative discussion is that the hierarchical organization we see in Maya settlement patterns masks the movement over time of consolidating and dissolving polities. This dynamism not only recurred at periodic intervals, but was also a constant factor of the Maya social consciousness" (Freidel 1983:385–386).

Arthur Demarest (1992b) later articulated this notion of populations aggregating at centers and then disaggregating away from centers in his application of the galactic polity model proposed for Southeast Asian states by Stanley Tambiah (2013). Basic to this model is what Tambiah terms a quinary conception of cosmology and geography, or four quadrant points surrounding a center, in East Asian cultures and he is in good company (Wheatley 1971). Tambiah is, however, quite adamantly of the view that such a model is not an essential manifestation of some archaic mentality or that it is statically enduring. He does observe significantly that this notion of four outer points and a center operates as an ordering principle pervasively, from the humblest household to the state. Arthur Demarest in his application of the galactic polity model was well aware of this quincunx conception in Maya cultures as documented ethnohistorically, ethnographically, and as inferred in the Precolumbian material record. Linda Schele and I reviewed the Maya literature on this "centering" principle in *Maya Cosmos* and agree that it is discernable over the long term (Freidel et al. 1993:231-256).

In a paper presented in 1989, Joyce Marcus (1993) used this idea of societies aggregating and disaggregating in organization in her dynamic model of the archaic state with special reference to the lowland Maya. This effort built upon her dissertation research on lowland Maya regional states (Marcus 1973, 1976) in which she discerned four major capitals at the apogee of Late Classic Maya civilization, Calakmul, Tikal, Palenque and Copan, potentially manifesting a quadripartite version of the quinary principle. Certainly an eighth-century Copan king, Waxaklahun Ubah K'awiil, listed these royal capitals in a cosmological text on one of his stelae (Marcus 1973; Schele and Mathews 1998). In my 1983 paper I referenced these efforts by Marcus as support for the existence of such a common quadripartite conceptual and spatial model in the Maya world facilitating political aggregation.

After an enthusiastic reception of her presentation at the Dumbarton Oaks conference on the eighth-century Maya, Marcus organized a School of American Research Advanced Seminar on the Archaic State. In that setting she applied the dynamic model to several cases in the Old and New Worlds (Feinman and Marcus 1998; Marcus 1998). In her 1998 Archaic State paper Marcus also critiqued a model of Maya regional state organization first circulated by Simon Martin and Nikolai Grube in 1994 and then published in 1995 in *Archaeology* magazine (Martin and Grube 1994, 1995). Martin and Grube based their model on an epigraphic analysis of Classic Maya texts. In *A Forest of Kings* Schele and I (1990:165-215), in our own effort to provide a regional synthesis of Classic period political and military dynamics anchored in epigraphy and archaeology, deciphered a relationship as "in the land of." Martin and Grube convincingly demonstrated that this relationship was closer to "by the command of" or "under the aegis of." A second decipherment of "possessed lord or king" reinforced the pattern. Their "superstate" model thus rests on substantive decipherments of superordinate and subordinate relationships declared between rulers, with the reasonable presumption that these rulers spoke for their polities, now generally agreed to be kingdoms (Martin and Grube 2008).

While it is true that Marcus, as she claims, had hypothesized hierarchical relationships between kingdoms in her dissertation, she did so epigraphically, based simply on the patterns of mentioning rulers at other kingdoms (Emblem Glyphs) (Berlin 1958) and on a prescient deduction of hypergamous royal marriages from some well-preserved monuments, including especially El Perú Stela 34. Her study was carried out during the early seventies before the phonetic decipherment of Maya texts was truly in place (cf. Benson 1973) as it was by the early nineties. In the SAR *Archaic States* chapter critique, Marcus also inferred that archaic empire is by necessity territorial, embracing contiguous subordinate polities within its administration. In some famous archaic empires that had contiguous territories, like that of the Akkadians, the emperor ruled hegemonically through local conquered lords called *ensi*.

Adam Smith (2003:135), in the context of a broad review of archaeological models of political landscapes, critiqued the application of static central place geographic models in the Maya lowlands (e.g., Marcus 1973, 1993; Mathews 1992). He wrote approvingly of the model proposed by Martin and Grube (1995, 2008), which he correctly identified as dynamic because of the transient nature of Classic period historical affiliations, alliances, and subordinations. Smith challenged Maya archaeologists to investigate how these relationships might manifest through what he calls memorialization, emulation, and authorization, and these are productive suggestions.

What Simon Martin and Nikolai Grube outlined, and continue to pursue (e.g., Grube 2005; Martin 2005), was a model of hegemonic overlordship, with the specific nature of the power and influence of such overlords left largely open to future investigation. I am of the view that lowland Maya political economic institutions, from the Preclassic through the Postclassic, had in common an integrating network of trade routes provisioning market places (Masson and Freidel 2013, 2014). In general terms command of the routes, maintained through war and diplomacy, pragmatically reinforced the power of superordinate rulers over vassals. The trend in the field is toward the identification of marketplaces and marketing as long-term institutional arrangements linking polities in the lowlands (Hirth and Pillsbury 2013; King 2015).

All of these researchers agree that a major feature of the social and political dynamic in question is dissolution of large regional states into smaller entities. This consensus is of course anchored into the acknowledged area-wide social chaos of the ninth century A.D. (Demarest et al. 2004). In the Maya case the idea of kingship institutionalized in the late Middle Preclassic period survived, with modifications, the ups and downs of regional consolidation into what I would now term empires, comparable to some empires elsewhere in the ancient world (e.g., Tambiah 2013), and into alliances that stood counterpoised to empires. At the core of my own early treatment of the dynamic model was the notion that there were always variations in social complexity in the lowland Maya world from the advent of the first sedentary societies through the rise and fall of the regional states. This is certainly also evident in Tambiah's study of Southeast Asian societies and in Arthur Demarest's application of the model.

But what are the different roles and statuses of rulers in the context of large hegemonic states and smaller vassal states, and how do even smaller political entities, provinces, and independent alliances of towns figure into the mix? I addressed this with reference to Postclassic political geography in Yucatan, well synthesized by Ralph Roys (1957), and Marcus (1993) did the same in her studies. There was such variety in early sixteenth-century Yucatan, and apparently the relationships between these differing kinds of polity were indeed dynamic and contested. As I underscored in my effort, the names could be the same and the roles and statuses different in the instances of participants in hegemonies and independent or autonomous polities. Marcus in her critique of the "superstate" model pointed out that there were few variable statuses denoted with specific titles in Classic Maya politics of the kind that might reveal the existence of hierarchy.

While the challenges to discerning hierarchy are real, progress in the decipherment even in the eighties included David Stuart's identification of a distinct second rank category of king below *ajaw* called *sahal*. His breakthrough pointed to the prospect that the Classic texts contain information regarding the ranking of statuses within governments. This is now a burgeoning field of inquiry in Maya studies (for example, Golden and Scherer 2014; Jackson 2013; Rossi et al. 2015). The institutions of kingship and the royal court surely evolved over the more than a millennium and a half of Preclassic and Classic Maya civilization (see Giron-Ábrego 2012, 2013; Saturno et al. 2006 for a second to third century B.C. inscription with the term *ajaw* at San Bartolo). Based on robust epigraphic, iconographic, and archaeological information in the Early Classic, evidently only kings and their immediate family members were *ajaw* (Freidel and Suhler 1999a), but it is clear that some people carried the *ajaw* title or wore the insignia of *ajaw* in Late Classic Maya polities who were not in fact high kings or were vassals to overlords (Ringle et al. 1998). These individuals shared this important status with high kings. *K'uhul Ajaw*, people qualified as holy or sacred, ruled as high lords, and it was the discovery of this attribution (Mathews 1985) that inspired the idea of Maya divine kingship from the eighties forward.

Preclassic Maya divine kingship must have emerged from existing institutions fostering the concentration of political, religious and economic power in the hands of leaders. Kent Reilly and I (Freidel and Reilly 2010) argue that this developmental trajectory involved political economic dynamics surrounding the adoption of agrarian lifeways and staple maize in the southeastern Mesoamerican lowlands. In our scheme divine kings were, as in Southeast Asia, the pivots of the quinary model, exemplary interlocutors with the gods, charged with supernatural abilities, and ultimate arbiters of the pragmatic policies of states maintaining security and prosperity. No doubt kingship manifested in variable ways in material symbol systems and ceremonial features during the course of the Middle to Late Preclassic, and this is particularly evident in central Belize (see Brown et al. Chapter 5 this volume); but just as certainly the mature, canonical, and pervasive royal symbolism of the Late Preclassic period (Estrada-Belli 2011) displays some decisive derivations from Middle Preclassic Olmec antecedents (Fields 1989; Freidel 2008; Reilly 2006b; Taube et al. 2010).

The West Wall mural of the Pinturas building at San Bartolo (Saturno 2009; Saturno et al. Chapter 13 this volume; Taube et al. 2010) reveals a uniquely explicit depiction of the rites of lowland Maya rulership in the early Late Preclassic period. The cycle of death, resurrection, and rebirth of the Maize God surely alludes to the human cycle of generational succession in ways that endure throughout Maya history (Carlsen and Prechtel 1991). This affirms the fundamental armature of kinship and descent on which Maya rulership must have been constructed (McAnany 1995). At the same time, I believe that the adjacent North Wall scene in the Pinturas building depicts the sacrifice of infants by a god impersonator and the resurrection of a ruler from a great gourd. I take this performer to be a human being and not a god because he does not have the face of the Maize God. This is by no means a certainty, as other participants in the North Wall pageant are also humanform, especially the women, and quite possibly deities. Still, this resurrecting fellow wears a mouth sash that is the same as found on two youths bearing royal bundles of dead kings, a status conveyed by their mortuary masks. I propose that the North Wall scene thus combines divinities and human beings in one ritual sequence representing royal death and resurrection.

The transformation of a human being through sacrifice of surrogates and ritual resurrection was in my view the vital feature of the status of Maya divine king (Freidel 2008). In the perspective of many of my colleagues, such a person must inherit the privilege and opportunity to die and be resurrected through descent. Certainly the succession of divine kings is dynastic in many ancient civilizations, but just as certainly in some instances divine kings were also subject to complex processes of selection, election, and vetting by councils of sages, patriarchs, matriarchs, priests, nobles, and other factions (Brisch 2008). This latter process has the advantage of sometimes mediating potential disputes between rival claimants. I now believe that the Preclassic Maya, and several other peoples of ancient Mesoamerica, elected kings in this way, regarded the rites of transformation of a person into a divine king as decisive, and the direct kinship pedigree of the individual as complementary. Removing kinship as the core institutional framework for recruiting kings means having some productive alternative institutional means for doing so. Nanette M. Pyne (1976) contemplated the idea of sodalities in Formative Oaxaca, but we have not looked at what are called traditional "power associations" in Africa (see Gagliardi 2015) in the Maya area much beyond Barbara Price's (1974:462) effort to explore Precolumbian analogies to the cargo hierarchies of the Colonial and Republican eras: "What is most needed from ethnographers is a broader comparative picture of institutions from a range of peasant-organized societies which do the work of the Mesoamerican *cargo* system." Schele and I (1988a) conjectured that the Preclassic Maya must have had such institutions in order to naturalize burgeoning social inequality. But those of us who think this might be a productive avenue of inquiry have our work cut out for us.

In a way this departure from kin-based rulers is finessing the archaeological data on Maya Preclassic kingship, which is decisively lacking in bodies and is relatively rich in cached cenotaphic insignia celebrating the institution per se (Freidel 2008). But it is also a way to acknowledge, and begin to account for, a fundamental pattern in Classic Maya data: there are no Early Classic dynasties in the northern lowlands. To be sure there are Early Classic Kaanul kings in inscriptions at Dzibanche, El Resbalon, and Pol Box (Esparza Olguin and Perez Guitierrez 2009; Grube 2005; Martin 2005) and they are referenced as hegemons at some other sites like Yo'okop (Nygard and Wren 2011; Shaw 2015). But in these rare inscriptions there are no references to dynastic founders, to successions in the line of founders, or even to kin relations, beyond Mam, grandfather or ancestor, between successors and predecessors. These epigraphic ties are all characteristic features of southern lowland dynastic texts already in the fifth century, retrospectively projected into the fourth century in some cases. There is evidence of a dynasty founded by King Ukit Kan L'ek Tok' in A.D. 770 at Ek Balam and lasting a century or so (Grube et al. 2003), but this effort is the exception that proves the rule: northerners knew about dynasty but they did not practice it. I propose that the Kaanul kings of the Preclassic period left a lasting legacy among their most loyal constituencies in the central and northern lowlands: a divine kingship institutionalized around the careful vetting of councils and transformation rituals, a kingship which no one could claim outright by simple kin succession from the prior king.

This is a kind of kingship in which the institution itself lends divinity to the ruler, who, to be successful, must indeed be the kind of charismatic leader postulated by Tambiah and Demarest. But a divine king by election and transformation must also be supported by other kings, and by their collective capacity to insure security and prosperity. As outlined in the ensuing discussion I think that the political economic obligations of Preclassic Maya kingship strongly reinforced such collective effort, particularly risk-reducing marketplace distribution of food and other vital commodities. I think it also encouraged the establishment of regional hegemonic hierarchies, courts in coordination, facilitating effective administration of common political economic objectives. Still, this is indeed a relatively fragile institutionalized rulership compared to dynasty. The northern lowland record has some great individual kings who commissioned some grand buildings, but it does not have evidence of any sustained long traditions of rulers in succession. The kind of periodic dissolution of realms into constituent parts contemplated by Marcus, Demarest, Tambiah, and me is more readily apparent in the northern lowlands. And in the central lowlands the Late Classic rulers appear to have been content with exquisitely designed mansions rather than royal capitals.

Finally, although the Olmec portrayed individual rulers, there is no evidence of dynasty in Olmec material symbol-systems or archaeology. There is iconographic evidence of collectivities, consortiums of Olmec rulers as portrayed on thrones and also in the famous Cache 4 of La Venta. So I think that Olmec divine kingship was quite likely also non-dynastic and founded in the transformation of elected or selected individuals into rulers embodying supernatural powers.

Maya Kingship and the Kaanul Empire

As referenced earlier, the Maya adopted important features of their institution of divine kingship from the neighboring Olmec in the Middle Preclassic period (Fields 1989; Fields and Reents-Budet 2005b; Freidel 2008; Freidel et al. 1993; Guernsey 2006b; Reilly 1991). The Olmec Maize God was the template for Middle Preclassic kingship at La Venta in Tabasco. Later Maya kings used Olmec style heirloom jewels, like the Dumbarton Oaks Pectoral (Coe 1966). The relationship between the Olmec civilization and the origins of Maya civilization has been controversial (see Clark and Hansen 2001). In my view the cult of maize is a key to unraveling this relationship (Stanton and Freidel 2003). Along with Kent Reilly (Freidel and Reilly 2010), I have proposed that the Middle Preclassic societies of Mesoamerica committed to maize as a staple commodity in the context of a regional currency-based market economy that insured the circulation of this hard-to-store food. Marilyn Masson and I (2012, 2013) have pursued the theoretical and methodological challenges to identifying the continuation of such a regional economy in the ensuing Classic period.

I began studying Preclassic trade in the Maya lowlands at the site of Cerros in Belize (Freidel 1979, 1981). Structure 5C-2nd at Cerros revealed monumental masks that I now identify, based on the work of Karl Taube (1996), as the Maize God and Principal Bird Deity, avatar of the creator god Itzamnaaj. In Cache 1 on Structure 5C at Cerros we also found Late Preclassic royal jewels depicting the Maize God inspired by Olmec style Middle Preclassic prototypes (Garber 1983).

Building on the models proposed by William Rathje in the 1970s but with different commodities, my colleagues Kent Reilly, Marilyn Masson, and I have been working to understand the shift in the political center of gravity from La Venta to El Mirador during the Middle to Late Preclassic transition. Key commodities linked to staple maize include mineral salt as a dietary supplement, high quality lime for making *nixtamal*, as pointed out to me by Carlos Chiriboga (personal communication, 2011; Freidel et al. 2015), and jade, serpentine, and cacao as currencies. Geographically, all of these commodities are found in Maya country rather than in the Olmec heartland (see Taube 2004b). The massive city center of El Mirador is on high ground surrounded by seasonal swampland (Hansen 1998). It is linked to satellite cities by broad roads that include stone causeways across low ground (Hansen 1991). This system of inter-site causeways is remarkable not only for being early, but as a distinctive cultural feature of the northern Maya lowland societies (Kurjack and Andrews V 1976; Kurjack and Garza 1981).

During the Classic period regional survey and exploration over nearly a century has revealed that southern lowland kingdoms established intrasite causeway systems but evidently did not build intersite causeways such as reported from the northern lowlands. One of the Mirador region causeways links El Mirador to the city of Nakbe. Richard Hansen's research there indicates that it was a city already in the Middle Preclassic period (Hansen 1991). Hansen thinks Nakbe is the predecessor to El Mirador as a regional political capital. However, while it is the case that Nakbe evidently declines in the Late Preclassic period, we have still only a limited grasp of the chronology of El Mirador in the Preclassic. In light of the ambient presence of Middle Preclassic occupations to the south and north of El Mirador, it is quite possible in my view that it was already a great city in the Middle Preclassic. Moreover, there are other cities, like Yaxnohcah to the north of El Mirador, that have major buildings in the Middle Preclassic (Reese-Taylor 2014, 2017; Reese-Taylor, personal communication, 2012).

The cities of the Mirador area are built on the Central Karstic Plateau, and they have easily quarried sources of excellent limestone for masonry and plaster. As discussed above, Carlos Chiriboga, who is surveying sites to the west of El Mirador, thinks this area may have been a major source for the high quality lime needed to make hominy, *nixtamal*. Lime is extracted from many sources, but it is clear from the thick plaster on buildings and plazas at El Mirador that the craftspeople of this city had abundant quantities of it (E. Hansen 2000; Hansen et al. Chapter 7 this volume). Chiriboga thinks this may have been a major export commodity of the Mirador state. Richard Hansen thinks that plaster-making figured into the decline of El Mirador toward the close of the Preclassic era, as it caused widespread deforestation, local climate change, and agricultural collapse (Hansen et al. 2002). As previously discussed, Joyce Marcus (1993) proposed that Maya archaic states were dynamic, showing significant ups and downs. Adapting

Marcus's scheme to the archaeological and historical evidence in hand, I see three episodes of regional hegemony or empire. The first is the Mirador state in the Middle to Late Preclassic; the second is the New Order of the Early Classic led by Tikal; and the third is the empire of the resurgent Late Classic Kaanul regime seated at Calakmul.

In this historical scheme the Kaanul kings at Calakmul sponsored one variant of the remarkable Codex style of vase painting. Richard Hansen (2002) has also identified Codex-style vase painting in looters trenches at the site of Nakbe and elsewhere in the vicinity of El Mirador, and he argues that the meaning of these vases resonates with memories of the original Mirador state. Simon Martin (1997, but see Martin 2017 for a new interpretation of the list as Early Classic) proposed that king lists on Codex-style vases registered not Late Classic Kaanul kings, but legendary Preclassic predecessors. I have proposed (2000, 2008) that the words for snake, sky, and four, all variants of Kaan, have a sacred connection to another cluster of words pronounced k'an, meaning yellow, precious, and cordage, referencing umbilicus cords. In this way, the Kaan emblem is linked to the birthplace of the Maize god.

Stanley Guenter is the epigrapher of the El Mirador Project as well as the El Perú-Waka' Project. In recent public lectures he supports Martin's argument, noting that the dates for Late Classic Kaan king Yich'aak K'ahk' are not the same as the date given for this Kaan king on Codex-style king lists. Further, the name Yuknoom Ch'een is used by an Early Classic king at Dzibanche before its seventh century use by Yuknoom Ch'een the Great of Calakmul (Martin and Grube 2008:108). Guenter and Hansen (Hansen and Guenter 2005) point to other evidence that the Kaanul homeland was in the Mirador region in the form of an elaborate bas-relief in a lime quarry at the Early Classic site of La Muerta, an eastern satellite of El Mirador. This relief includes a Kaan Emblem Glyph or royal epithet and Guenter suggests this is the earliest documented such Emblem Glyph. In the same article Hansen and Guenter note a Preclassic stela found at El Mirador depicts a floating deified ancestor Guenter identifies as one of the legendary kings of the state. In addition, the Late Preclassic facade on Structure 34 at El Mirador has jaguar paw ear flares that Guenter identifies again with the name Yich'aak K'ahk' or Fiery Paw. Again, I have proposed that the words for snake and yellow or precious are linked and that the Mirador area was sacred to all the lowland Maya as the birthplace of the Maize God, the source for the legitimacy of the idea of empire.

Kathryn Reese-Taylor and Debra Walker (2002) have proposed that the

Kaan kingdom hegemony, declared to be Kaanul (snake land) on a text at La Corona (Stuart 2012) extended to the east coast at Cerros in Belize, and I believe that it extended well into the northern lowlands to include Yaxuna in Yucatan. Reese-Taylor and Walker are now working at the site of Yaxnohcah, some 27 km north of El Mirador in Mexico. The massive size and layout of this Middle to Late Preclassic civic center (Sprajc and Suarez Aguilar 2003) makes it a clear candidate for a city on a route linking the interior northern lowlands to the Mirador area. Their work to date at this site (Reese-Taylor, personal communication, 2012), originally mapped by Ivan Sprajc and his Mexican colleagues, suggests that the major architecture dates to the Middle Preclassic period. If this holds up, Yaxnohcah was substantially larger than Nakbe, Hansen's candidate for original capital in the Mirador state.

Returning to the site of Cerros in Belize, the original project there (followed by the project directed by Debra Selsor Walker) documented the site as predominantly Late Preclassic with continued modest Classic period occupation. The site is presently on Corozal Bay, but it is clear that the shoreline has been receding and it is quite possible that the center was originally on a protected shore of the New River just before it debouched into the bay. We argue (see Robertson and Freidel 1986) that Cerros was a port of trade linking the coastal canoe traffic with the interior by way of the New River. Walker and Reese-Taylor (2002) propose on the basis of ceramic analyses that Cerros was a salient of the Mirador regional state, and I agree with this assessment. In addition to the ceramic links and evidence for regional interaction (Freidel 1979) the dramatically sudden transformation of Cerros from a fishing village into a ceremonial center with very sophisticated polychrome painted modeled architecture makes best sense if it was transformed into a royal capital through incorporation into a regional hegemonic empire governed from the city of El Mirador. Already in my co-authored book with Linda Schele (1990), *A Forest of Kings*, I wrote a vignette in which royal insignia jewels (Cache 1) were brought from outside to crown the king of Cerros.

One of the intriguing features of the Cerros research was the absence of any evidence of royal burials in the civic-religious architecture. We did excavate in plausible locations for such interments based on Classic period patterns in the Maya lowlands. The absence of evidence found in discovery is not evidence for the absence of a proposed pattern; nevertheless, it is the case that the only unequivocal Preclassic royal tomb in lowland Maya civic-religious architecture is Burial 85 at Tikal (Coe 1965a). Recent reported discoveries of royal insignia in Preclassic burials at San Bartolo (Pellecer Alecio 2006; Saturno 2006) and Holtun (Tomasic and Bozarth 2011) were not in civic-religious public architecture. Clearly this is a frontier in our knowledge, and the recent discovery of unequivocally royal Preclassic interments in monumental architecture at Chiapa de Corzo southwest of the Maya region suggests that there may be royal tombs out there somewhere. Intensive tunneling searching for tombs in monumental buildings at El Mirador has not yielded results to date, although Richard Hansen has reported a looted Preclassic tomb chamber from the site of Wakna in the Mirador region (Hansen 1993).

What we did find at Cerros was a rich cache of Late Preclassic ritual vessels including a big bucket containing the remains of a bundle. The content of the bundle included carefully arranged greenstone royal insignia jewels, along with small mirrors and *Spondylus* shells. I have interpreted Cache 1 as a cenotaph symbolizing a king (Freidel et al. 1993), but I now think that it is actually symbolizing kingship rather than any individual king. This is an important distinction in my view. Royal insignia jewels have been found widely in scientifically documented Late Preclassic contexts by archaeologists researching lowland Maya sites (Freidel 1991) and recently, as elaborated below, in Middle Preclassic contexts as well. But the combination of human remains, masonry tomb chamber, royal insignia and monumental architecture found in the Classic period remains an elusive one in Preclassic lowland Maya archaeology. The contrast between the remarkable concentrations of Preclassic interments at the nearby site of K'axob (McAnany 1995, 2004) and the absence of royal burials at Cerros and Lamanai (Pendergast 1981) in the same era seems more than coincidence to me. I think that despite the obvious connection between kinship and kingship in the southern lowland Classic record, and despite earlier evolutionary schemes (Freidel and Schele 1988b), that Preclassic kingship may have evolved more directly out of shamanic orders than out of lineage patriarchies and matriarchies. This is an idea I will continue to explore in the rest of this brief and programmatic overview. But now I will turn to my second major research project and its implications for lowland Maya empires.

Yaxuna is in north central Yucatan just south of Chichen Itza. Research reported by Brainerd (1958) suggested that the massive central acropolis there dated to the Preclassic period, and on that basis I initiated a decade of research at the site (1986–1996) (see Stanton et al. 2010). I was particularly interested in the institution of Preclassic kingship and whether it was present in the northern lowlands as in Belize. By the 1990s I was convinced that

Yaxuna was a political and economic salient of the Mirador State in the Pre-classic period. One feature in common between Yaxuna and the Preclassic sites in the Mirador region is major acropolis construction. The original construction of Structure 5F-1, 125 m × 95 m at the base and 24 m in eleva-tion at the highest promontory, appears to be Preclassic. A test excavation on the eastern summit (Structure 5F-3) of this acropolis dated the bulk of its construction to the Late Preclassic period (Stanton et al. 2010:82). Other excavations by the first Selz Foundation Yaxuna Project documented the existence of major Middle Preclassic construction and strong ceramic style links to Peten (see Stanton and Ardren 2005).

The second Yaxuna Project is discovering more Middle Preclassic con-struction (Stanton, personal communication, 2012). Like Yaxuna (Stanton and Freidel 2005), Yaxnohcah has a north-south axis defined by intrasite stone causeways and the scale and plan of their centers is comparable, but both sites also have east-west oriented E-Groups like Middle Preclassic Na-kbe and other sites in Peten. Travis Stanton, co-director of the new Selz Foundation Yaxuna Project, and I have suggested that the east-west axis of Yaxuna is anchored in the east by a triad of small performance platforms representing the three stars of the creation hearth where the Maize god is resurrected in the sky. He will have to test this proposition eventually through excavation to see if the third platform is actually there, but there are certainly two such platforms, and they have subterranean corridors, central sanctuaries, and stairways leading to their summits via trapdoors (Freidel and Suhler 1999b). We propose that these are effigy turtles like the cosmic turtles that give birth to the Maize god in depictions from the San Bartolo murals to Late Classic Codex plates.

Charles Suhler discovered a foundation cache under the sanctuary of one of these platforms (Stanton et al. 2010; Suhler 1996). The cache bucket contained a limestone effigy hearthstone, and underneath that a greenstone celt nested into a greenstone mirror. These are Olmec style Middle Forma-tive royal regalia and symbolic versions of them are displayed on crowns. The cache bucket from Structure 6E-53 is a late Middle Preclassic-early Late Preclassic masterpiece. A radiocarbon date from a sample sealed into the floor of Structure 6E-120 is fifth century B.C., again late Middle Preclas-sic (Freidel et al., n.d.). Returning to the consideration of Preclassic caches of royal insignia, I think this example is comparable to that of Cache 1 at Cerros.

At the site of Chacsinkin to the south of Yaxuna local people discov-ered a Middle Preclassic cache of royal regalia redeposited in a Late Classic platform. E. Wyllys Andrews V (1986) suggested that this cache registered trade relations between the Gulf Coast Olmec and the lowland Maya in Middle Preclassic times. I would go further and suggest that it registers a trade route running from the north coast to El Mirador in a late Middle Preclassic hegemony it ruled. Monolithic block masonry construction is a hallmark of Late Preclassic El Mirador. Jennifer Mathews and Ruben Maldonado have reported on a Late Preclassic to Early Classic interaction sphere in the northern lowlands characterized by such monolithic block masonry (Mathews and Maldonado Cardenas 2006).

The Mirador state dramatically declined with the political collapse of El Mirador toward the end of the Late Preclassic period, probably in the second century A.D. Based on an analysis of Codex-style vessels and other texts, Stanley Guenter hypothesizes that the last historical king of El Mirador, the Chi-Altar place, was Foliated Ajaw, who acceded in 112 A.D. and then later in his career fled Mirador and established kingship at Copan in Honduras. Only further research at El Mirador can test this bold idea. However, as the history of the collapse of El Mirador unfolds, it is clear that the power vacuum following it ushered in the rise of Tikal and eventually the New Order of the Early Classic period. The earliest evidence we have relevant to the rise of Tikal is archaeological and comes primarily from the North Acropolis excavations (Coe 1965a). The University of Pennsylvania project discovered a Late Preclassic phase of the acropolis that featured the only intact royal tombs dating from this period in Peten to date. The main tomb, Burial 85, was discovered underneath a small scaffold platform in the plaza area fronting the main pyramid of this early acropolis. Postholes on this platform show it sustained a perishable superstructure, as did one of the performance platforms at Yaxuna, Structure 5E-120. William Saturno's (2009) research at San Bartolo clearly documented key aspects of Late Preclassic royal accession ritual, including the death of the Maize God, his incubation in the cosmic turtle, his rebirth, and the accession of a divine king on a scaffold in commemoration of his resurrection.

I suggested in a presentation at UCLA in 1996 on stratigraphic and iconographic grounds that that the king in Burial 85 under this scaffold platform is likely the founder of the Tikal dynasty, Yax Ehb Xook. Martin and Grube (2008) agree with this identification. But I now propose that Yax Ehb Xook did not just found the Tikal Dynasty, but much more importantly that he founded the very principal of patrilineal succession which is the hallmark of Classic period divine kingship in the southern lowlands. I think that this king was a rebel asserting independence from the Mirador Empire and from its domination of political succession in the Maya lowlands. Guenter notes that a late Tikal inscription identifies Yax Ehb Xook as a Chi-Altar K'awiil, that is, as a vassal of the Mirador state. I would agree that he started out that way. It is in his burial that his rebellion is revealed. A key clue to the royal status of the Burial 85 king is his fuchsite bundle mask that replaces his skull, taken as a relic and evidently displayed by a succession of Tikal kings during the Classic period (Guenter, personal communication, 2010). This mask is decisively non-Olmec in style and bears a remarkable resemblance to the foundation cache mask discovered by Saburo Sugiyama and his Mexican colleagues under the Pyramid of the Sun at Teotihuacan (Instituto Nacional de Antropología e Historia, Mexico 2011).

One reason I think that the Tikal founder was historically decisive in the establishment of kin-based succession, true dynasty, is that successor kings at Tikal are obsessively focused on their relationship to him from the earliest Classic period stela there. Sihyaj Chan K'awiil II on Stela 31 is the *bakel way*, spirit companion of the bone, the dynastic founder. I propose that this principle of patrilineal succession was broadly adopted in the southern lowlands, but not the northern lowlands because the kings of Tikal were ethnically and linguistically southern Chol speakers in contrast to the Yucatec-speaking northern lowlanders. The idea that Yucatec speakers occupied the northern lowlands at the beginning of the Classic period, while the southern lowlands were occupied by Cholan language speakers, is controversial; but it does enjoy support among some epigraphers and linguists. And the fact of the geographic distribution of Emblem Glyph using dynasties in the southern lowlands and not in the northern lowlands is incontrovertible.

Returning to the first part of this paper, this hypothesis challenges the view, held by me (Freidel and Schele 1988b) and many others, that the principle of divine kingship developed structurally out of lineage and kinship systems in which patriarchs, matriarchs, and kin ancestors were venerated (McAnany 1995). Again, I now think that the principle of divine kingship evolved out of existing institutions of spiritual adepts capable of engaging supernatural power, what Schele and I termed shamans following E. Z. Vogt's (1966) discussion of modern Tzotzil Maya practice in Zinacantan, Mexico. Long contemplation of Maya divine kingship in the Preclassic era has led me to the conclusion that the evidence for its derivation from kin-based patriarchy is not very substantial (Freidel 2008), whether or not it had such basis in other areas of Mesoamerica. But more important than the paucity of emergent chiefly incipient kings in elite residential contexts is their virtual absence in the form of buried remains from lowland Maya

Preclassic civic-religious contexts as mentioned earlier. This is a surprising and unnerving conclusion for me, running counter to most current arguments concerning the advent of lowland Maya divine kingship, including many of my own. But the record is beginning to get sufficiently robust to suggest that in contrast to some other adjacent areas in Mesoamerica, the Preclassic lowland Maya are not interring royal ancestors in public buildings or immediately proximate spaces. Instead they generally are interring cenotaphic insignia of royal office, a practice emphasizing the office and not the human being holding it in a way commensurate with means of recruitment other than kinship such as ritual initiation.

So in my view the historical significance of Yax Ehb Xook is paralleled by the archaeological significance of Burial 85. This was the focal point of the North Acropolis, which in turn was the primary dynastic shrine complex in the city. The Preclassic Acropolis attracted the attention of enemies, commensurate with the rebel status I propose for King Yax Ehb Xook, and its buildings were thoroughly desecrated and burnt soon after the establishment of the scaffold accession place over the sacred bundle of the founder. Dramatically, the threshold building of the Acropolis was particularly incinerated. The entire surface of the Maize God images flanking it was blackened and crazed with heat cracks. This was not the product of reverential incense smoke, but rather of heaped flammable materials and bonfires. The immediately ensuing construction phases of the North Acropolis register repeated violent destruction events involving burning, pitting, and the problematic deposit of smashed and broken preciosities. Finally, there is the prominent entombment of an individual in what should have been a royal location without any burial furniture. These stratigraphic layers also include healing and rebuilding events.

Some clues to these events may be found in retrospective history. For example, the early history on Tikal Stela 31 describes a Kaloomte' Foliated Jaguar. The title Kaloomte', supreme warrior, was first attributed to the conqueror Sihyaj K'ahk' on Stela 15 at El Perú-Waka', and was not used by an historical Maya king until the early sixth century. Its use on Stela 31 presages the narrative entry into Tikal of Kaloomte' Sihyaj K'ahk' in 378 A.D., and it suggests that Tikal experienced an earlier conquest. Intriguingly, as Guenter notes Foliated Jaguar is also associated with the Chi-Altar place, El Mirador. These clues are sparse, but I think the pattern unfolding here is of a rebel Tikal experiencing repeated attack and conquest by partisans of the Snake kings of the Mirador state, even as its capital is collapsing as its royal court is moving northwards into safer and more peaceful territory.

I think that the attacks on Tikal abated with the accession of King Sihyaj Chan K'awiil I at the beginning of the fourth century. The Proyecto Nacional Tikal discovered archaeologically that this is when the first substantial evidence of Teotihuacan presence registers in the Lost World Pyramid Complex to the southwest of the North Acropolis. I hypothesize that this king allied with southern neighbors in the mountains and on the Pacific Slopes, and with Teotihuacan lords heavily invested in that southern region. His successor was a woman, Unen Bahlam, a ruling queen in the dynastic succession who may have been married to a Teotihuacan Lord. Some epigraphers now question her identification as female, declaring that the title is that of a deity. However, one inscription names her as Tikal ruler and gives a title that is only known to have been applied to human rulers in that dynasty. King Muwaan Jol followed Unen Bahlam; a likely usurper whom I would suggest registers another imposition by the partisans of the Kaanul kings. His son Chak Tok Ich'aak I follows him to the throne, only to be overthrown by Sihyaj K'ahk'. Less than a year later, Sihyaj K'ahk' installed a new king Yax Nuun Ahiin I, who is depicted as a Teotihuacan warrior and whose father is Spearthrower Owl, a foreign king whom David Stuart postulates was king of Teotihuacan.

As mentioned before, David Stuart (2000) sees Sihyaj K'ahk' as a Teotihuacan warrior marching from Teotihuacan to impose hegemony on the lowland Maya. His first recorded stop was at El Perú-Waka', and this is one of the reasons for my current research interest there. Early Classic stelae, broken and dumped in the later Classic, were collected as fragments and redeposited in Terminal Classic contexts at El Perú-Waka'. The pattern of their distribution suggests that these last occupants of the city were recalling the glory of the New Order era, and focusing particular attention on Structure M13-1, the main temple complex of the city center with an *adosada* frontal platform shrine on its main stairway. A basal stela fragment of El Perú Stela 9 dragged to the base of this building depicts a fire mountain, K'ahk' Witz, that has the Maya Sun God emerging from one of the snakes in its mouth. A fine line inscription next to the leg of this late fifth to early sixth century ruler mentions a Wite' Naah (Guenter 2005). As research at Copan has demonstrated, the cult of the Maya Sun God, K'inich Ajaw, was integrated into the cult of the Wite' Naah introduced by Sihyaj K'ahk'.

There are only two real *adosada* frontal platform shrine pyramids in the Maya lowlands; one is Early Classic in date, the other Late Classic in its final form and both are at El Perú-Waka'. Olivia Navarro Farr and her colleagues

Griselda Perez, Damaris Menedez, and Juan Carlos Perez have initiated architectural investigations into the Structure M13-1 stairway shrine complex. They have not determined if seventh century A.D. Structure M13-1 Sub. 2 is an *adosada*, but it might be given its relation to the main pyramid to the east of it. There is a Sub 3 building yet to be investigated that should date to the New Order era of the fifth century. William Fash and his colleagues have suggested that the original Wite' Naah fire shrine is the *adosada* shrine on the Pyramid of the Sun at Teotihuacan. Their arguments are based on the iconography of sculpture discovered in the ruin of this shrine, and I think these are productive. Michelle Rich has already substantially investigated the second *adosada* shrine at El Perú-Waka,' Structure O14-04 (Rich et al. 2006, 2007). In contrast to M13-1, this pyramid is on top of the temple acropolis hill to the east of the main center. The plan of the main pyramid is apsidal and so far we have only found typical Maya apron molding design in preserved masonry. Excavation in the *adosada* platform revealed two Early Classic funerary offerings, one of a mature woman in a cist burial and another of two young women in a small masonry tomb. The elderly woman had a water jar with her, later a symbol of Chak Chel, the cosmic midwife. The two women in their twenties were buried in a tableau macabre, a signature of sacrificial offerings at Teotihuacan that comes into fashion during the New Order in the Maya lowlands, with the lower woman face down and the upper woman face up directly on top of her. The lower woman was about five months pregnant.

The offerings with the young women are fine vessels painted with royal symbolism. Bioarchaeologist Jennifer Piehl, who helped to excavate and study the remains, noted that the young women were exceptionally healthy and lacking any dental caries, suggesting a very elite diet. She thinks these were sacrificed royalty, and looking at the vessels I agree. The vessels in these burials date from the late fourth century, and while they do not evince Teotihuacan style, Michelle Rich did discover two Teotihuacan-style stucco effigy heads in the final debris of the *adosada* shrine. The best preserved of these heads is larger than life, and the individual wears the tight goggles and buccal mask seen on the portrait of Sihyaj K'ahk' on Stela 16.

In the course of his career Sihyaj K'ahk' placed in power kings at Tikal, El Perú-Waka,' Uaxactun, and Bejucal-El Zotz, and he seems to have had a hand in establishing new regimes at Rio Azul and Copan. The list will likely continue to grow as we know more about other Early Classic dynasties, and as Martin and Grube cogently observe there is a blossoming of Emblem Glyph using dynasties in the lowlands during the New Order era.

Significantly, while Sihyaj K'ahk' is explicitly the overlord of the Tikal king and implicitly the overlord of these others, he himself did not formally rule any lowland Maya kingdom. Federico Fahsen and Juan Antonio Valdés (Valdés and Fahsen 1995) reasonably speculate that he was eventually buried in Group A at Uaxactun, but he is neither portrayed as king there nor listed as one. In this king-making role, I see a clear parallel to the Preclassic Kaanul kings of the Mirador state, whom I think were also king-makers electing rulers from high elite families in the kingdoms within their hegemony. Certainly Guenter is compiling evidence that early Maya kings, and even some later ones, journeyed to the Chi-Altar place to receive legitimate insignia of rule in a way strikingly analogous to the journey Stuart sees the fifth century founder of dynasty at Copan making to Teotihuacan.

The idea of a Kaanul kingdom heartland in the north receives some support by archaeological patterns that show New Order partisans not only pressing north in Peten but also efforts to encircle Kan territory in Yucatan. A New Order faction staging out of Oxkintok in the west conquered Yaxuna (Freidel and Suhler 1998; Suhler and Freidel 1998). A stucco-decorated palace in the south of the city is ritually destroyed at the end of the fourth century (Stanton et al. 2010:97–108), and in the North Acropolis the conquerors created an elaborate tableau macabre with the bodies of sacrificed royalty. First they desecrated the existing shrine on top of Structure 6F-4, then they rebuilt the front of the structure to have a palace at the base and a performance space on the roof, with a special tomb chamber in it. Then they performed an elaborate sacrifice, carefully arranging the bodies inside the tomb. A stela portrait of the conqueror was evidently placed on the stairway, depicting him as a Teotihuacan warrior. This stela was subsequently defaced and dumped on the northern side of the building.

The small tomb chamber contained the remains of 11 men, women, and children, 10 of them arranged around the body of a male victim. The remains of a burnt king were at the south end (Tiesler et al 2017). The royal jewels of the family were cached inside the destroyed summit temple in a black painted jar from Oxkintok. They included the collar beads, ear and hair flares and diadem jewels—some Preclassic heirlooms. On top of this set the conqueror placed a special new jewel, an owl diadem, a Teotihuacan-style jewel such as adorned the crown of Spearthrower Owl lofted by his descendant Sihyaj K'ahk' at Tikal on Stela 31. In the adjacent pyramid, Structure 6F-3, the conqueror reentered a slightly earlier royal tomb, probably the predecessor of the king he sacrificed. He removed the three royal jewels from the head and jammed one of them into the end of a manatee bone from a three-legged sacrificial altar, the ceramic binding of which was still intact. He took a second of the jewels and threw it into the white earth he used to refill the antechamber, and placed the third one in construction fill next to a subsurface corridor he built in the overlying pyramid. In this way he laid a path linking this king to his new underworld performance place. That predecessor king was buried in majesty with a deer antler drumstick as a headdress. I proposed that this identified him as wearing deer antler as Chijchan, the Deer Snake spirit companion of the Kan kings. If this hypothesis is on the right track, it reinforces the notion that this conquest was carried out by New Order kings to take over a strategic Kaanul center. In the early sixth century the Kaanul or Snake dynasty kings had started to succeed in their push back against the New Order kings. King Tun K'ab Hiix established a foothold at La Corona in northwestern Peten and Naranjo in eastern Peten (Martin 2008). Eventually King Sky Witness conquered Tikal in A.D. 562 with the aid of the king of Caracol in Belize, Y'ajaw Te' K'inich (Martin 2005).

In my view of the Early and Middle Classic Tikal dynasty, partisans of the Kaanul kings repeatedly contested with the successors of Yax Ehb Xook. This enduring struggle between Kaanul Kings and the rebel alliance led by Tikal witnessed the rise of the last regional conqueror of the Classic era, the Kaanul king Yuknoom Ch'een the Great. Born in A.D. 600, Yuknoom Ch'een over a lifetime of 86 years and a career of half a century managed to bring the Peten again under the sway of the Kaanul regime. A key part of his successful strategy was to establish a royal road from his capital at Calakmul in Campeche 250 km south to Cancuen on the upper reaches of the Pasion River in southern Peten. To secure that road as a means of launching conquest, Yuknoom Ch'een created loyal vassals at Waka' and other strategic royal capitals long the route. He drew on the prestige of the earlier conqueror Sihyaj K'ahk' when he installed a Wak dynasty king named K'inich Bahlam II and married him to a Kaanul princess. A looted slate royal belt celt (Just 2007) portrays K'inich Bahlam II and its obverse provides his birth date and childhood names. We know as a result that El Perú Stela I dedicated in A.D. 657 celebrates the completion of his first k'atun of life and his overlord's first k'atun of rule. Stela 1 was set in front of the *adosada* shrine on the temple mountain.

A royal tomb placed in a pit cut through the shrine platform at about this time, Burial 39, was discovered by Michelle Rich (Rich 2011; Rich et al. 2010; Rich and Freidel n.d.) and appears to be the tomb of K'inich Bahlam II's immediate predecessor—probably his father. The interred is laid in majesty within an elaborate array of furniture preparing him for resurrection. This suggests that his demise was peaceful and that he was a vassal to the Kaanul kings who had controlled this area for a century or more from the time of Tun K'ab Hiix. There are four different royal names on painted vessels in this tomb, one of which is likely that of the king. I think the individual was male, despite equivocal skeletal material, because at the feet of the deceased was this funeral tableau in figurines. The deceased king is portrayed as a kneeling penitent Maize God being prayed over by a deer spirit. The witnessing people include a king and queen. The ritualists performing include a singing old monkey woman shaman and a trumpet-wielding dwarf with a deer headdress.

The temporal placement of this funeral ceramically and other ways to the mid-seventh century, the erection of Stela 1 by a young K'inich Bahlam II in that same time window, and the vassal status of K'inich Bahlam II to Yuknoom Ch'een the Great all lead me to hypothesize that the king presiding over the funeral is the Snake emperor himself. Like Sihyaj K'ahk' before him, he was launching his conquest from Waka', and like Sihyaj K'ahk he soon marched on Tikal, conquering that city in A.D. 657. On the middle of the deceased king was a special jade jewel depicting a Maize God king as a sacrifice, severed in half in a ritual specifically fashionable in the time of the entrada of Sihyaj K'ahk'. On top of that jewel was a plate decorated with the head of Gl, the watery sun according to David Stuart, the eastern sun of resurrection and the return of the rains to nourish planted seeds of maize. Offerings included a Middle Preclassic Olmec style heirloom figurine of serpentine, a material found in the southern foothills. The figure is of a dancing youthful Maize God wearing the death mask of his previous body, the Olmec era death shark. In the Classic period the shark transports the sun from dawn to dusk, and with the rains, the Maize God from death to resurrection. The faint and worn incised design on the figurine depicts snake cords flowing from the nostrils of the boy, K'aan/Kan, the birthplace of maize, and the three peaks of the cosmic hearth. This heirloom could have been made at Middle Preclassic El Mirador and carried by untold generations of Snake kings in their bundles of authority, as it is in a bundle here in Burial 39.

Adjacent to the bundle holding this figure was a giant deer cowrie. Again, I propose that the Chijchan Deer Snake spirit of the Snake dynasty took the guise of a deer cowrie. The deer spirit in the figurine funeral is not the companion of Wak rulers but of Snake rulers. The dwarf conjuring this spirit wears a male horned deer head, referencing the Snake emperor. The emperor wears a royal jewel that is a water snake, the returning rains that presage resurrection. If the presiding king is Yuknoom Ch'een the Great, I think that the presiding queen is his daughter Lady K'abel. She stands between her father and the deceased king gesturing toward him with a bundle in her left hand. She wears a Maize God head as her royal jewel, a direct allusion to the deceased as a resurrecting Maize God. It is she who actually brings about this miracle because the deer spirit healing the penitent king of death is a hornless female. In the final tableau, the kneeling king wears in his hair the red earth of the planted fields, droplet jade jewels of rain, and a small sprout coming out of the top of his head. The Snake emperor and his daughter have ushered in a new era of wealth and prosperity for Waka', as they promise to bring to all Peten the glory of the first empire. Yuknoom Ch'een aspired to be emperor to all the lowland Maya, and on this dedication vessel portraying him as the embodiment of the day ajaw, he declares himself the Chi-Altar lord of the Preclassic Mirador State, and also the lord of the Wite' Naah of the rebel kings of the southern New Order. His vision of a united Maya world would soon falter after his death, but the Maya world would not forget and the idea of empire and its legends would inspire later efforts.

Acknowledgements

Thanks to M. Kathryn Brown and George Bey III for inviting me to participate in the volume and present this argument for Preclassic Maya kingship. I also wish to thank to William Fash for the chance to present this idea at Harvard in 2012 in the Gordon R. Willey lecture. I am indebted to my students and colleagues of the Cerros, Yaxuna, and El Perú-Waka' Projects for the rewarding research partly reported here and their inspiration and guidance in thinking about this subject. Finally, I am especially grateful to Jerry Glick for his support of the El Perú-Waka' Project.

16

Conclusion

Charting the Pathways to Complexity in the Maya Lowlands

M. KATHRYN BROWN AND GEORGE J. BEY III

There have been many important Preclassic discoveries over the past three decades that have significantly changed our understanding of the early Maya. The authors of the chapters in this volume highlight many of these recent discoveries, with the common goal of understanding the pathways to complexity of the ancient Maya. In this concluding chapter, we draw their findings together to highlight the diachronic, social, and political changes that occurred in the Middle Preclassic, and how these culminated in the institutionalized social hierarchies that emerged during the Late Preclassic, which laid the foundation for the divine kingdoms of the Classic period.

When preparing this chapter, we were particularly struck by the very significant fact that the Middle Preclassic period spans as much if not more time than the entire Classic period. Although the Middle Preclassic traditionally has been understudied, this important period witnessed dramatic change and development in the nature of early Maya society. In fact, it represents a contrast with the Early and Late Classic periods, when relatively little changed regarding the social and political structure of the society. Yet the Classic period has been emphasized in Maya studies because of the impressive monumental architecture, art, and inscriptions of this period, coupled with the rich and fine-grained data available.

While in no way downplaying its importance, we do not consider the developments of the Classic period to represent the type of radical social transformations that took place in the Preclassic. Instead, we see Classic period social and ideological developments as the natural outgrowth of those of the Preclassic. Of course, new ways of legitimization were grafted upon the evolving social and political structures, but the most significant shifts in social order occurred in the Preclassic period, especially the late

Middle Preclassic. And while the Classic Maya faced challenges of severe population pressure, environmental degradation, and escalating warfare, some of these same pressures may have impacted the Late Preclassic Maya, albeit perhaps on a lesser scale.

We asked our contributors to think about social changes during the Preclassic in terms of three major periods, early Middle Preclassic (1000 B.C.–700/600 B.C.), late Middle Preclassic (700/600 B.C.–300 B.C.), and Late Preclassic (300 B.C.–A.D. 300). Often the Middle Preclassic is a generic catch-all for developments that occurred before the Late Preclassic, but in our opinion, this 700-year-long period from 1000 to 300 B.C.—a span of some 30 generations—is the most dynamic period of Maya history. Maya society saw the emergence of a hierarchical social structure, shifts in ideology to naturalize and support the newly established social order, creation of social mechanisms that reenforced hierarchies and institutionalization of the beliefs and practices that legitimized those hierarchies. We, admittedly, focus most of our discussion on this complex period of Lowland Maya history.

In the introduction to this volume, we examined how our understanding of the rise of complexity in the Maya lowlands has changed over the past three decades by discussing the "problems for consideration" that were identified as significant by the participants in the *Origins of Civilization in the Maya Lowlands* (Adams and Culbert 1977:22). These provide an important benchmark for measuring how far we have come in addressing the rise of Maya civilization. At the same time, a perusal of the list of those problems reveals just how much the study of the rise of Maya complexity has changed since 1977. Some questions deemed important in 1977 now seem almost irrelevant, such as the role of the Protoclassic period. Conversely, questions that we today consider central, such as the role of ideology and ritual in the rise of complexity, were barely considered 40 years ago. As Gordon Willey pointed out in his 1977 summary contribution of the *Origins* volume, "No one offered a formal model to explicate the role of ideology in the growth of Maya civilization, but it is difficult to look at the monuments and remains of this civilization without believing that this role must have been an important one" (Willey 1977:416). Slightly over a decade later, Freidel and Schele (1988a:549) argued that an "empirical difficulty with investigating the origins of the Late Preclassic institution of *ahaw* is the paucity of antecedent evidence pertaining to ideology because of the simplicity and ambiguity of the material symbol systems prior to the Late Preclassic transformation." Since the *Origins* volume, mostly spearheaded by Marxist approaches to archaeology, scholars have broadened their views on this topic and the role of ideology and ritual has moved to the forefront of early Maya studies (see Demarest 1992a, 1992b). As Brown et al. (Chapter 5 this volume) state, "understanding early rituals is crucial for understanding the rise of complexity, as it serves as the point of articulation between religion and the rise of complexity and sheds light on the utilization and manipulation of religious ideology by emerging elites to ensure the acceptance of new social conventions that ultimately support a hierarchical social system." This shift in the study of the Preclassic period can be attributed both to archaeological discoveries that have produced new empirical data pertaining to ancient Maya ideology, such as the San Bartolo murals, the stone monuments at Naranjo in the Guatemala Valley, early E-Group architectural assemblages, the numerous late Middle Preclassic ballcourts in northwest Yucatan, as well as the introduction of theoretical paradigms that have led us to new approaches to interpreting archaeological data. Several of the chapters in this volume address ritual and ideology in the Preclassic and add to the growing data on this important aspect of the ancient Maya.

One of the primary questions in the 1977 *Origins* volume that still remains an enduring issue is the origins of the first agricultural villagers in the lowlands. What was the source of the people who settled the Maya lowlands, and how did they come to arrive there? It was assumed that the lowland region was colonized by one or more migrations. The uncovering of the "cultural statuses of the original population" was a primary focus of research (Adams and Culbert 1977:22). We begin here as several of the chapters in the volume address these issues. We follow this with a discussion of the contributions within this volume and themes that are evident related to the rise of complexity, specifically charting the similarities and differences between regions in regards to ceramics, craft specialization, ritual, and architecture. Finally, we conclude with a new list of problems for consideration that we hope will challenge scholars to dig deeper into the archaeological record of the Preclassic Maya.

Preceramic Populations

Many scholars still argue today that the Maya lowlands were settled via migration of outside groups, although a growing number have come to believe that Preclassic Maya society developed out of an earlier lowland Archaic or Preceramic population of hunter-gatherer-horticulturalists. Still others see the distinction of local development versus in-migration as overly simplistic, and favor some combination of the two extremes, involving immigrants settling among and interacting with previous populations. As Sullivan et al. (Chapter 3 this volume) point out, "Scholarly debate between models of indigenous development and immigration has been unresolved due to lack of stratigraphic continuity between the Preceramic period (3500–1200 B.C.) and the Early Preclassic period (1200–900 B.C.)." As our knowledge of the Preceramic and Preclassic periods has increased, we are now able to actually address detailed questions using empirical data, look for patterns of continuity and discontinuity between these two periods, and examine the developmental process on a more regional scale. As we do so, the data reveal different trajectories in the diverse regions of the large spatial area we call the Maya lowlands suggesting that both migration and in situ development may have played a role.

Recent finds in the Belize River valley, such as the shallow cave site of Actun Halal, provide some interesting new data pertaining to the Archaic period (Lohse 2010). Lohse (2007) has documented both maize and cotton pollen from Preceramic levels at Actun Halal, indicating early horticulture in the region. As Sullivan et al. (Chapter 3 this volume) point out, the cave site continued to be utilized during the Middle Preclassic, possibly indicating that the knowledge of this special place was transferred.

Another potential Preceramic occupation was located at the site of Xunantunich. Brown et al. (2011) report a buried paleosol with a notable absence of ceramics and numerous highly patinated flakes directly underlying an early Middle Preclassic occupation layer, suggesting continuity of use at this location. Also of importance, Lohse et al. (2006) suggest that many of the lithic tool forms seen in the Preceramic are also found in the Middle Preclassic suggesting some continuity in the lithic assemblages.

Although more data is necessary to shed light on the relationships between the populations of the Preceramic period and the earliest settled ceramic-producing villages in the Belize valley, scholars working in the region have explored models of indigenous development (Awe 1992). Sullivan et al. (Chapter 3 this volume) provide a similar argument as they suggest current data point toward an "in situ development, albeit with influences that were derived from interaction beyond the regional level." Estrada-Belli (2011:38) suggests that the "spatial correlation and continuity between the earliest stone tools and the later ceramics suggest a cultural and ethnic continuity between the pre-Ceramic and Ceramic inhabitants of the coastal Lowlands." While the data remain far from clear, we currently cannot rule out an indigenous development from Archaic hunter-gatherer-horticulturalists in some regions of the Maya lowlands, specifically the Belize River valley.

A different picture is seen in the northern Maya lowlands. Andrews and Robles (Chapter 2 this volume) summarize the Paleo-American, Archaic, and Preceramic data amassed to date in the northern Maya lowlands. They note that—unlike in Belize, where a well-defined Archaic occupation is beginning to emerge—the evidence in the northern lowlands is much more fragmentary. In fact, the data presently available does not allow us to create a chronological framework for the Archaic/Preceramic period. Documenting Preceramic sites is challenging and our current sample from across the lowlands is clearly an underrepresentation of the earliest occupants. Exciting new data are emerging in the north as this book goes to press, where skeletal remains from the underwater caverns of Hoyo Negro in Quintana Roo dated to 12,000 B.P. have provided DNA evidence suggesting these early inhabitants were associated genetically with later Native American populations (Chatters et al. 2014).

Despite progress in the study of the Preceramic period in the Maya lowlands, there is much work that remains to be done and we think this important transition period should be a priority for future research.

Early Middle Preclassic: Earliest Settled Villages and Pre-Mamom Populations (ca. 1000 B.C. to 700/600 B.C.)

The early Middle Preclassic period from approximately 1000 B.C. to 700/600 B.C. exhibits some of the most fundamental changes in Maya culture history. Additionally, regional chronologies are beginning to emerge as a growing number of scholars investigate this dynamic early period. For the purposes of this chapter, we define the early Middle Preclassic as the period prior to the widespread Mamom ceramic sphere, that is, pre-Mamom. Several of the contributions in this volume add to our knowledge of this understudied time period and are discussed in the section below. Although Maya scholars are making great progress toward filling in the gaps, the early Middle Preclassic remains one of the "muddiest points" in Maya culture history and deserves intensive further study.

Moving from the Preceramic to the earliest settled villages in the Maya lowlands, we begin to see a slightly clearer picture, albeit still somewhat unfocused. Most scholars agree that settled, ceramic-producing communities were present by ca. 1000 B.C. (or slightly earlier) in several regions of the Maya lowlands. The archaeological signature for these earliest villages is more robust due to the presence of pre-Mamom ceramic material. Pre-Mamom ceramic complexes have been documented across the lowlands, including Ah Pam (Rice 1979), Bolay (Valdez 1987), Cunil and Kanocha (Awe 1992; Garber, Brown, Awe, and Hartman 2004), early facet Jenney Creek (Gifford 1976), Eb (Culbert 1977; Laporte and Fialko 1995), Ek (Andrews V et al. Chapter 4 this volume), Real Xe (Willey 1970), Swasey (Kosakowsky 1987), and Xe (Adams 1971).

Sullivan et al. (Chapter 3 this volume) present new data related to this early time period (ca. 1100/1000–900 B.C.). Both the Cunil (Awe 1992) and Kanocha (Brown 2003; Garber, Brown, Awe, and Hartman 2004) ceramic assemblages exhibit decorated serving vessels with incised pan-Mesoamerican motifs and symbols. This indicates that the earliest settled villagers in the Belize River valley were tied into a pan-Mesoamerican ideological interaction sphere (Garber and Awe 2009). Brown (2007) suggests that these serving vessels may have been produced for display during feasting activities by aspiring elites. This coupled with exotic items such as jade, obsidian, and marine shell from Cunil and Kanocha occupation layers suggests the possible beginnings of emerging inequality at this time (Sullivan et al. Chapter 3 this volume).

Although clear evidence of public or ceremonial architecture has not yet been discovered dating to the Cunil phase (1100/1000 B.C.–900 B.C.) in the Belize River valley, red paint adhering to daub fragments found at Cahal Pech does suggest some architectural decoration was present. Cunil inhabitants initially constructed low platforms made of clay and tamped marl; however, lime plaster was introduced by the end of the phase. The Kanocha phase from the nearby site of Blackman Eddy dates to the same time period (Brown et al. Chapter 5 this volume) and provides comparable architectural data with the presence of low apsidal platforms associated with a double chambered chultun (Brown 2003; Garber, Brown, Awe, and Hartman 2004).

Pre-Mamom ceramics have been found in sizable quantities beneath the E-Group plaza at Cival and beneath Group H at Holmul (Estrada-Belli 2011), suggesting the presence of settled villages in these locations. The incised motifs on these early ceramics are similar to motifs seen on Cunil and Kanocha serving vessels with the addition of the woven-mat, crossed-bands, and U-shaped motifs. Estrada-Belli (2011:43) suggests that "the motifs depicted on pre-Mamom ceramics at various sites in the Maya lowlands are consistent with rituals of evocation of sky deities, rain gods and the birth of the maize god" and are related to the Maya creation story.

The earliest documented ceremonial architecture in the Maya lowlands is located at the site of Ceibal, Guatemala. Pre-Mamom occupation was first documented at the site by Harvard University (Sabloff 1975). Recent work by Inomata and his team revealed an E-Group complex dating to ca. 1000 B.C. (Inomata et al. 2013). Relatively modest in size, the earliest version of the Ceibal E-Group was constructed by cutting and shaping bedrock. Several ritual offerings of greenstone were found beneath the E-Group plaza. Inomata et al. (2013:468) argue that this ceremonial space "served as the primary stage of communal ritual throughout the Middle Preclassic period." The Ceibal E-Group was modified and enlarged throughout the early Middle Period suggesting that this sacred space continued to be a place of communal ritual.

Slightly later in the early Middle Preclassic, beginning around 800 B.C., we see an increase in the investment in architecture in some areas of the Maya lowlands, albeit relatively small in scale. We begin to see the spread of E-Groups into different regions in the Maya lowlands by at least 800 B.C., such as the Central Karstic Uplands at the site of Yaxnohcah (Reese-Taylor 2017), the Peten at the site of Cival (Estrada-Belli 2011), and in the Belize River valley at Xunantunich (Brown 2017; Brown et al. Chapter 5 this volume). The spread of E-Group architectural arrangements suggests the importance of this form of ritual architectural assemblage in the founding of early communities in the Maya lowlands beginning in the early Middle Preclassic. Ritual offerings in E-Group plazas are also suggestive of a specialized ceremonial complex that emphasizes the cosmos and ideological ties to the Maize God. Long-distance trade of exotic materials such as jade, marine shell, and obsidian increases during the later portion of the early Middle Preclassic and continues through the Classic period. Additionally, there is evidence of specialized craft production of marine shell ornaments in the Belize River valley beginning around 800 B.C. (Hohmann et al. Chapter 6 this volume; see also Cochran 2009; Keller 2012).

The Belize River valley provides a rich database from several sites dating to the latter portion of the early Middle Preclassic time period as is detailed in Brown et al. (Chapter 5 this volume). After the Cunil phase (ca. 800 B.C.), we see an expansion of settlement in the Belize River valley with sites filling in the bottomland and upload zones between the rivers, suggesting a gradual increase in population throughout the early Middle Preclassic

(Brown et al. Chapter 5 this volume). The Cunil ceramics develop into the more widespread early facet Jenney Creek ceramic tradition defined originally by Gifford (1976). The pre-Mamom early facet Jenney Creek phase exhibits several developments including the evidence for public and ceremonial architecture beginning around 800 B.C., or slightly later. Research at Blackman Eddy documented a series of non-domestic rectangular platforms that may have been used for communal activities such as feasting (Brown and Garber 2008). At the nearby site of Cahal Pech, an early Middle Preclassic rectangular platform (dating prior to 600 B.C.) was encountered buried beneath Plaza B. This small platform had offerings in the corners (Garber and Awe 2008) suggesting an elaboration of ritual activity at this time.

Early occupation has also been documented in the Peten region of Guatemala. Hansen et al. (Chapter 7 this volume) suggest that the Mirador Basin was first occupied around 1000 B.C., during the early Ox phase. The earliest architectural constructions at Nakbe mirror that of the Cunil and early facet Jenney Creek phases in the Belize River valley with small perishable structures built directly on bedrock or on packed clay floors. In addition, Hansen (1998) has documented low residential platforms with retaining walls dating slightly later to the end of the early Ox phase, suggesting a slight increase in labor investment. The ceramics of the early Ox phase consist of restricted-rim vessels and *tecomates*, as well as serving bowls with pre-slip and post-slip incised rims (Hansen 2005). Figurines were also found from the earliest levels at Nakbe.

The construction of formal stone platforms begins around 800 B.C. in the Mirador region (Hansen et al. Chapter 7 this volume). These early platforms reached an approximate height of 2 m and were covered with crude lime plaster. Hansen et al. (Chapter 7 this volume) argue that evidence for "embryonic leadership and status hierarchy is available, as suggested by the importation and distribution of exotic goods, variations in residence size and structural sophistication, and the introduction of the symbols that in later Maya society were representative of rank and status of patron elite."

Roughly modified marine shell beads were common in early deposits in the Mirador region and may have been imported from the Belize River valley (see discussion below and Hohman et al. Chapter 6 this volume). These early Middle Preclassic marine shell ornaments may represent an important status or economic indicator (Hansen et al. Chapter 7 this volume). It is important to note that three-pronged Jester images on figurines and examples of the *pop* or woven mat motif have been encountered in early Middle Preclassic deposits from this region. This leads Hansen et al. (Chapter 7 this volume) to suggest "that the iconography of rulership, evident in Olmec societies, was also present in the contemporaneous Maya societies prior to 600 B.C." Although these symbols represent institutionalized rulership in later periods within the Maya lowlands, we emphasize a bit of caution when projecting symbolic meaning back several centuries. Therefore, we take a more conservative viewpoint and suggest that these symbols may reflect emerging social and political hierarchies in the early Middle Preclassic that were transformed into symbols of rulership over several centuries.

Thanks to recent discoveries in the northern lowlands, we now have a refined chronological framework for the early Middle Preclassic. Until recently, the earliest ceramic-using villages in that region were thought to date to the late Middle Preclassic (the Early Nabanche phase). Andrews V et al. (Chapter 4 this volume) demonstrate that the Ek ceramic complex (now considered to be pre-Mamom) dates to the early Middle Preclassic, thus predating the Early Nabanche complex. This new discovery pushes back the established timeline for settled, ceramic producing populations in the north, making the chronological trajectory more in-line with central and southern regions of the Maya lowlands. Furthermore, recent identification by William Ringle of Ek levels at the Puuc sites of Yaxhom and Lakin, as well as the recovery of Ek material at other sites in the region (mentioned in Andrews V et al. Chapter 4 this volume) indicate this early Middle Preclassic occupation was widespread at least in the northwest part of the northern peninsula.

In a point of comparison to the central/southern lowlands discussed above, it is important to note that at Komchen, Andrews argues that Ek-phase inhabitants were responsible for the construction of two small ceremonial buildings at ca. 800 B.C. These two buildings were Structure 24G1 which measured 1.2 to 1.4 m high and Structure 23F1 which was .6 m in height. Both structures are sizable for this early time period. Andrews sees Komchen consisting of a formal plaza flanked by these structures by the early Middle Preclassic. These pre-Mamom structures may represent the earliest ceremonial buildings in the northern Maya lowlands suggesting an established early population in the region.

The appearance of an Ek complex predating the Early Nabanche also provides a distinct and less complex cultural phase than that associated with the monumental architecture and dense occupations of this later ceramic complex, further reducing the abruptness of this transition. Additional radiocarbon dates from primary Ek and Early Nabanche contexts, however, are necessary to flesh out a more refined chronology of this important period in the northern Maya lowlands and shed light on key social transformations.

In the northern Maya lowlands despite the new evidence for a somewhat widespread pre-Mamom occupation (see Robles and Ceballos Chapter 9 this volume for an alternative view), there is little archaeological evidence that can be specifically associated with the early Middle Preclassic. Although it undoubtedly exists, a lack of dated contexts by absolute methods makes it difficult to assign architecture to this earlier half of the Middle Preclassic. The utilitarian bowls and jars known as Chancenote Striated and Achiotes Unslipped appear in the pre-Mamom period and continue into the Early Nabanche time period. This suggests important continuities in the occupations of these two time periods with many communities founded in the early Middle Preclassic. The problem is the lack of chronological control that allows communities to be subdivided into early and late Middle Preclassic facets. At Xocnaceh, a new calibrated ^{14}C date of 780 cal. B.C. is associated with a pounded *sascab* plaza floor, though there is no evidence of associated architecture, and at the Kiuic, the first .75 m high platform which was at least 14 m × 14 m also had a pounded *sascab* floor possibly suggesting that it dates to the early Middle Preclassic. Recently, just meters north of this Kiuic platform, at the base of the site's main pyramid, a second small structure was encountered directly on bedrock. It may or may not be associated with the initial larger Kiuic platform but did produce two ^{14}C dates. Unfortunately both samples have wide 2-sigma ranges (760–410 and 750–405 B.C.) meaning the structure can only be dated to sometime during the early or late Middle Preclassic (with the latter most likely).

The newly discovered pre-Mamom occupation in the northern Maya lowlands is significant and changes our understanding of the early landscape of the Maya lowlands. Because of this, we emphasize the need for more focused investigations that target potential pre-Mamom occupation in the north coupled with comparative ceramic analysis of pre-Mamom ceramic assemblages across the lowlands in order to enhance our understanding of this important period in Maya history.

This volume is dedicated primarily to new data related to the development of lowland Maya civilization, however, the important ritual center of Naranjo in the Guatemala highlands provides an important regional comparative example. The parallels of development are intriguing and deserve further consideration. Although recent chronological revision of Preclassic Kaminaljuyu by Inomata et al. (2014) may have implications for the timing of certain social processes in the region, evidence from Naranjo indicates some connections to the lowlands by the Middle Preclassic. The Las Charcas period at Naranjo in the Guatemala Valley provides some possible evidence of an early Middle Preclassic occupation in the Guatemala highlands, at a time when there was undoubtedly increasing interaction with the Maya lowlands. Although the Charcas material is dated at between 790 and 420 B.C., suggesting it may date predominately to the late Middle Preclassic, Arroyo notes that unlike other Middle Preclassic sites in the valley, there are significant amounts of highly decorated pottery which appear to have affinities to pre-Mamom. For example, she highlights two decorated pottery fragments that suggest connections with Maya and Olmec ideology. One is a beautiful post-slip incised depiction of a deity interpreted as a version of G1 of the Palenque Triad and the second is argued to represent an Olmec-style dragon. The highland Maya site of Naranjo was apparently part of a larger interaction sphere, connected to the Maya/Olmec world during the early Middle Preclassic. We discuss this important ritual site in more detail below and examine some of the interesting connections between the lowland and highland pathways to complexity.

Late Middle Preclassic 700/600 B.C. to 300 B.C.

As we were writing this chapter, it became very clear to us that scholars working in different regions of the Maya lowlands had diverse ideas about the chronology related to the Mamom ceramic tradition. In fact, some scholars push the start date for the Mamom sphere back to 1000 B.C. (see Ceballos and Robles 2012; Robles and Ceballos Chapter 9 this volume), while others favor a more traditional chronological start date of 600 B.C. We prefer to take a more conservative stance on this issue and suggest that the late Middle Preclassic begins sometime between 700 and 600 B.C., allowing for a 100-year transition period for the spread of the Mamom ceramic sphere across the lowlands. Although not all the contributors to this volume agree with us on this chronological framework, we feel that the current archaeological data from across the lowlands does indeed support the Mamom ceramic tradition beginning sometime between 700 and 600 B.C. With that said, we urge scholars to refine this framework with absolute dates from primary contexts when possible. It is evident that in order to understand and track the timing of important social and political developments, we need to rely primarily on absolute dates and reduce our reliance on ceramic data for chronology. The late Middle Preclassic Mamom ceramic tradition, like other ceramic traditions in the Maya lowlands, was relatively conservative and exhibited only modest changes over a 400-year period, thus presenting challenges for fine-grained chronological assessments. We hope that an emphasis on the use of absolute dating methods will bring forth a more defined chronology for this dynamic period.

With the spread of the Mamom ceramic tradition, we see a striking increase in population and markers of complexity across the Maya lowlands. Sites become larger and more numerous, and therefore allow for a better understanding of this period. In fact, over the past few decades, our knowledge of the late Middle Preclassic has increased significantly, especially from the core region of the Maya lowlands. Impressive published datasets from across the lowlands have provided a foundation for understanding the development of complexity during the late Middle Preclassic. These sites, just to name a few, include Komchen and Yaxuna in Mexico, Ceibal, Tikal, Uaxactun, Cival, and Nakbe in Guatemala, and a number of sites in Belize including Cuello, Colha, K'axob, Cahal Pech, Blackman Eddy, Pacbitun, and Chan. Of course, the list of late Middle Preclassic sites goes on, but we want to illustrate the amount of data that has been amassed for this dynamic period. The late Middle Preclassic, a period of three to four centuries, is a time when we see some of the most dramatic shifts in Maya society including a significant increase in long-distance trade, investment in monumental architectural construction, and the establishment of a hierarchical social order supported by an elaborate symbol system. Although we see the underpinnings of complexity in the early Middle Preclassic period, it is during the late Middle Preclassic, especially toward the end of this period (ca. 400/300 B.C.) that social, economic, and political complexity is manifested in the archaeological record.

Researchers focusing on this period have documented truly monumental construction efforts often in the form of large flat-topped platforms throughout the Maya lowlands (see Reese-Taylor 2017 for examples for Yaxnocah). Pyramidal structures make their appearance for the first time during this period and early carved and uncarved stone monuments are found at a handful of lowland sites. The use of plaster and stucco becomes commonplace during the late Middle Preclassic. Additionally, site hierarchies emerge during this period (see Anderson et al. Chapter 8 this volume). Several contributions to this volume have added to our knowledge of this important time in Maya prehistory and we highlight these new data below.

Turning our attention again to the Belize River valley, Brown et al. (Chapter 5 this volume) present data that illustrates the evolution of ceremonial architecture in the Middle Preclassic. As discussed briefly above, beginning in the early Middle Preclassic, low, rectangular, plastered platforms found at Blackman Eddy have been suggested to be venues for communal rituals such as feasting. These platforms increase in size and elaboration through the late Middle Preclassic. The introduction of architectural decoration in the form of mask facades is seen by the end of this period and there is an emphasis on height, culminating in the introduction of the pyramid form of architecture. Additionally, researchers at Blackman Eddy have found evidence that suggests that warfare in the form of raiding was present at least by the late Middle Preclassic as seen through the destruction and burning of a ceremonial platform (Brown and Garber 2003). We imagine that with more focused excavations of buildings dating to this period (and earlier), further evidence of warfare events, such as that seen at Blackman Eddy, will come to light.

Of special interest, several of the late Middle Preclassic platform construction phases at Blackman Eddy (dating to approximately 600 B.C. or slightly later) were associated with dense deposits of fauna remains and smashed ceramic vessels, interpreted as ritual feasting debris. Several of the ceramic vessels were intentionally halved and quartered leading Brown (2007:17) to suggest that the ritual splitting of vessels "may be related to the notion of partitioning the universe."

An increase in long-distance trade is evident with larger quantities of exotic materials found at sites within the late Middle Preclassic. We also see an increase in craft production. For example, at the site of Pacbitun in the Belize River valley, Hohmann et al. (Chapter 6 this volume) have documented marine shell production beginning in the early Middle Preclassic period within household contexts. The earliest assemblage is dominated by irregular beads; however, by the late Middle Preclassic, disk beads are more common indicating a shift in preference of bead form. Marine shell is widespread within the Belize River valley during the late Middle Preclassic period indicating the importance of this long-distance trade item. Although marine shell ornaments may have functioned as prestige and wealth items due to their exotic nature, there is evidence that this raw material also had significant symbolic importance. As both Brown et al. (Chapter 5 this volume) and Hohmann et al. (Chapter 6 this volume) point out, worked and un-worked marine shell items are commonly found in ritual deposits such as caches, burials, and feasting debris during the Middle Preclassic.

The marine shell assemblage study at Pacbitun provides a significant contribution to our understanding of early craft specialization in the Maya lowlands. While the evidence from Pacbitun and other sites in the Belize River valley indicate that marine shell production was substantial, Hohmann et al. (Chapter 6 this volume) argue that the current evidence from Pacbitun suggests that "production activities at Pacbitun were undertaken by a small, kin-based group organized at the household level." It is interesting to note that Hansen et al. (Chapter 7 this volume) document the presence of predominately finished marine-shell ornaments in the Peten region during the Middle Preclassic, suggesting that they were crafted and imported to Peten from a nearby region, possibly the Belize River valley. This indicates that at least some marine shell production in the Belize River valley may have been for export (Hohmann et al. Chapter 6 this volume).

The marine shell production data from Pacbitun is intriguing and complements the data for late Middle Preclassic ritual activities found at the nearby sites of Blackman Eddy and Cahal Pech. Hohmann et al. (Chapter 6 this volume) suggest that marine shell ornaments may have been used "in exchanges and competitive displays designed to build power and prestige and establish and maintain alliances at the intra- and inter-community levels." Models for the establishment of social hierarchies by Clark and Blake (1994) and Hayden (1998) suggest that certain motivated individuals would engage in competitive displays, gift-giving activities, and hosting feasts in order to acquire prestige within the community. The emphasis on working exotic raw material such as marine shell, does have implications for competitive displays of wealth. This coupled with the evidence for feasting activities found at Blackman Eddy is compelling (see Brown et al. Chapter 5 this volume).

In the Mirador region at the sites of El Mirador, Xulnal, and Nakbe, Hansen et al. (Chapter 5 this volume) note that between 600–400 B.C. pyramids were constructed, some as tall at 28 m. Additionally, E-Groups are present during this period suggesting that this early form of ceremonial architecture had spread throughout much of the central Maya lowlands by the late Middle Preclassic, if not earlier. Furthermore, there is a consistent pattern of utilization of large limestone blocks within monumental constructions seen in both the Mirador Basin and the Belize River valley. Hansen et al. (Chapter 7 this volume) document an increase in agricultural intensification indicating a dramatic increase in population. Furthermore, Hansen et al. (Chapter 7 this volume) argue that the major cultural innovations seen during this period "were fueled by a differential access to wealth, organized exploitation of natural resources, implementation of systematic, intensive agriculture, and an increasing focus on labor intensification and specialist production systems." They suggest that these major transformations led to the consolidation of political and economic power within the hands of "emerging administrative elite."

The most radical shift in our understanding of the late Middle Preclassic comes from new evidence from the northern Maya lowlands. Prior to the late 1990s, except for the sites of Komchen and Dzibilchaltun, there was very little evidence for this time period; however, since that time there has been an explosion of data that are leading to a major rethinking of the role of the northern lowlands in the evolution of Maya society and the nature of the northern Maya. These new data are powerfully highlighted in this volume, with work from Ek Balam, Poxila, Xocnaceh, and northwestern Yucatan in general.

Work at Ek Balam and the surrounding region show the existence of a widespread late Middle Preclassic occupation by at least 550 B.C. (Bond-Freeman Chapter 10 this volume). It is argued that during this time paired residential/ceremonial platforms were constructed in several areas of the site, although there was no indication of major construction in what was to become the Classic Period site center. These paired platforms have not been reported elsewhere and may represent a regional variation in social organization associated with the northeastern portion of the peninsula.

The results presented in Anderson et al. (Chapter 8 this volume) significantly change our understanding of the nature of late Middle Preclassic society in the northern lowlands, particularly in the northwestern region. Until recently, only eight sites were identified in the Proyecto Costa Maya study area. Current research, however, has identified over 140 Preclassic sites, with the majority dating to the late Middle Preclassic. Some 1,500 structures were mapped as part of an intensive survey in the related Proyecto Salvamento Arqueologico Ciudad Caucel. Many of these were noted to have had late Middle Preclassic and Late Preclassic construction phases.

Anderson and his colleagues see initial populations entering the area around 1000 B.C. with rapid population growth in the late Middle Preclassic. They argue for the development of a three-tiered settlement system that included hamlets, towns with modest public architecture, and then large sites (including Xtobo, Komchen, and Xama Susula). They have identified 25 ballcourts which appear to date to the late Middle Preclassic. Many are associated with towns, but others are also found at larger sites like Xtobo. In fact, much of the site of Xtobo appears to date to the late Middle Preclassic to Late Preclassic transition. Additionally, these recent investigations have identified a relatively large late Middle Preclassic platform at Xama Susula. Both Xtobo and Xama Susula, like Komchen, are characterized by the existence of *sacbeob*. Anderson et al. (Chapter 8 this volume) suggests that all three of these major sites in the northwest area (Xtobo, Komchen, and Xama Susula) emerge as significant centers in the late Middle Preclassic and reach their peak in the Late Preclassic. Additionally, it appears that Komchen becomes the primary regional center by the middle of the Late Preclassic. It is interesting to note that the use of ballcourts declines at this time.

In addition to the change in our understanding of the intensity and variety of late Middle Preclassic occupation as evidenced by Ek Balam and the northwestern projects, equally dramatic has been the new evidence of massive construction programs during the late Middle Preclassic in the area bordering the Puuc region as well as in the Puuc itself. These examples of monumental architecture, taking the form of huge stone-faced acropolises with superstructures that possibly include triadic groups, are associated with Early Nabanche ceramics (late Middle Preclassic). For example, a carbon sample from within the main acropolis at Xocnaceh, associated with a platform with a large cut stone superstructure has produced a calibrated ^{14}C date with a tight 2-sigma range of 400–380 B.C. This carbon sample was associated with a late floor of this substructure suggesting that it was built perhaps as early as 500 B.C. Additionally, this platform supported an 8-m high acropolis, which was also associated with Early Nabanche pottery suggesting that it dated to at least the end of the late Middle Preclassic (ca. 350–300 B.C.).

Xocnaceh, Poxila, Yaxhom, Lakin each exhibit enormous late Middle Preclassic acropolises, with massive stairways and superstructures. These structures are characterized by the use of megalith cut stone blocks. As mentioned above, it is interesting to note that a shift to the use of large cut limestone blocks is a pattern seen in the Peten and Belize River valley, suggesting that this might be a hallmark of the late Middle Preclassic across the lowlands. In the case of Xocnaceh, Yaxhom, and perhaps Lakin, the giant acropolises support what appears to be early triadic complexes. Data collected to date strongly suggest a late Middle Preclassic date for these platforms as they are associated with Early Nabanche ceramics (Gallareta Chapter 11 this volume; Robles and Cabellos Chapter 9 this volume; Ringle et al. 2014). As Gallareta (Chapter 11 this volume) points out, these early constructions were "designed to accommodate large numbers of people, at least on special occasions," suggesting that the monumental platforms were not solely centered on certain important individuals. And, although we are only beginning to shed light on the society that produced these impressive structures we do know they were connected to a larger world that included the acquisition of obsidian, jade and greenstone, and basalt.

One other site that should probably be placed in this category is Xcoch, located in the northwestern Puuc region (Smyth et al. 2014). Here a number of large structures with stonework similar to Xocnaceh and the other major late Middle Preclassic centers have been defined. Evidence suggests that the construction of these monumental buildings began in the late Middle Preclassic. Other late Middle Preclassic sites are known in the Puuc including Kiuic, Escalero al Cielo, Labna, Huntichmul; however, none of these are associated with massive architectural assemblages possibly suggesting that like the northwestern settlement system, we are looking at a tiered system of occupation along the base and over most of the Puuc.

The site of Naranjo, located only 3 km from Kaminaljuyu, provides an excellent comparative example of late Middle Preclassic Maya society in the Guatemalan highlands, located at the crucial link between the Maya lowlands and the Pacific coast. Consisting of several plazas and platforms supporting perishable structures, Naranjo is not impressive for its monumental architecture. What is striking about the site and its late Middle Preclassic (Providencia phase) occupation is the site's location, probable function, and the rows of stone monuments found there. Arroyo (Chapter 14 this volume) argues that Naranjo most likely served as a regional pilgrimage or ritual center located in a special landscape at the base of a sacred hill. As she notes in her contribution to this volume, "Naranjo is a critical place in the development of social complexity that dominated the Maya highlands during the Middle Preclassic. . . . What is lacking is deeper insight into the connection of Naranjo with other settlements in the Maya region and beyond." This is a significant point that emphasizes the need for a fuller understanding of the relationship between the highlands and the lowlands.

We now turn to the Late Preclassic, a time period that is much clearer and has been the focus of decades of research resulting in numerous publications. In this conclusion, we highlight the contributions by our volume participants to this impressive Late Preclassic database and touch upon some of the general trends that, from our perspective, are important to recap here.

By the Late Preclassic, the evidence points toward the institution of kingship being firmly in place. This period boasts of several architectural hallmarks, including triadic complexes, pyramid structures decorated with elaborate stucco facades, widespread ballcourts, and the continued elaboration of E-Group complexes. The Mamom ceramic tradition develops into the trademark ceramic tradition of the Late Preclassic time period, Chicanel. As several of the chapters in this volume have shown, many of the Late Preclassic hallmarks have their origin in the early and late Middle Preclassic, however, they become widespread during the Late Preclassic. In the lowlands, carved stone monuments appear with more frequency during this period, as seen in the Mirador Region and the Belize River valley. It is also during the Late Preclassic that we begin to see an increase in burials, both primary and secondary, within ceremonial structures such as E-Groups and other important ritual pyramids suggesting that ancestor veneration played an important part of the lowland Maya cultural tradition (for a thoughtful synthesis, see Estrada-Belli 2011). Brown et al. (Chapter 5 this volume) argue that ancestor veneration, beginning in the Middle Preclassic, was an important strategy for the legitimacy of power and wealth during later periods. They present data from the Belize River valley of early burials that were reentered and from which bones were removed for ritual reburial at key ritual locations within Late Preclassic ceremonial contexts.

The site of San Bartolo has received much scholarly attention for the recent discovery of its elaborately painted Late Preclassic murals. The murals provide us with incredible data pertaining to Preclassic ideology illustrating on a grand scale themes from the Maya creation story; however, placing the murals into the larger context of the site furthers our understanding of the nature of Late Preclassic complexity. The contribution by Saturno et al. in this volume highlights the architectural data from the site of San Bartolo and illustrates the importance of examining changes in ceremonial spaces in a diachronic fashion. As Saturno et al. (Chapter 13 this volume) illustrate in their chapter, the three most widely recognized architectural forms constructed by the ancient Maya are the ballcourt, E-Group assemblage, and triadic complex. Moreover, as discussed above, these architectural forms originate in the Middle Preclassic and represent some of the earliest ceremonial architecture in the Maya lowlands. Although a clear understanding of the origins and subsequent spread of these architectural forms remains an important topic of study, we are beginning to see patterns emerge from collective data across the lowlands indicating regional distinctions. However, by the Late Preclassic, these important architectural canons are widespread and project symbolic messages related to the emerging institution of kingship.

The chapter by Saturno et al. examines the archaeological data from San Bartolo pertaining to these three architectural forms and adds significantly to our knowledge. They detail a sequence of ceremonial buildings that is suggestive of important transformations occurring during the Middle to Late Preclassic transition. One of the important finds at San Bartolo pertaining to these architectural complexes is a Late Preclassic miniature ballcourt attached to the western radial pyramid within the Pinturas Group. Although ballcourts are not commonly found within E-Groups, Saturno et al. argue that this is not inconsistent with the ceremonial function of the E-Group and, in fact, it symbolically complements it. The ballcourt was constructed on the eastern side of the western radial pyramid of the E-Group. The ballgame is often linked to the setting sun and therefore is appropriately placed on the west side of an architectural complex that celebrates the annual cycles of the sun. Saturno et al. link the architectural arrangement of the E-Group at San Bartolo with the rising of the Maize God in the east and setting of the Principal Bird Deity in the west. Their interpretation of the symbolism within the architecture is thought provoking and illustrates the importance of exposing and thoroughly documenting early architectural phases. Furthermore, they document a shift in the use of the Pinturas Group. The E-Group is covered over by a large western-facing platform that supported a triadic complex. They argue that this shift changed the focus of Pinturas from a generally accessible space, the E-Group, to a restrictive and elevated triadic platform space. This shift also re-oriented this ceremonial space toward the site center and royal palace emphasizing the power and authority of the king. Saturno et al. (Chapter 13 this volume) argue that "the change in the Late Preclassic from an E-Group to a triadic complex monumentally illustrates the social distancing that is part and parcel to establishing political legitimacy and institutionalized hierarchy."

This example from the Peten illustrates how ancient Maya elites in the Late Preclassic built upon the ideological foundations set in the Middle Preclassic and elaborated on these concepts to legitimize and support the newly established institution of kingship. Of course, the massive center of El Mirador with numerous triadic groups exemplifies this on a grand scale (see Hansen et al. Chapter 7 this volume).

As Acuña (Chapter 12 this volume) suggests, the frontier site of El Achiotal provides an interesting contrast to El Mirador and neighboring sites. El Achiotal was occupied predominately from the Middle Preclassic through the Early Classic (ca. 800 B.C.–A.D. 550). Although located on the edge of the Mirador region, El Achiotal differed from many Preclassic lowland Maya sites as the site plan emphasized a north-south orientation as opposed to the more common east-west orientation. North-south site-plans are common in the Chiapas and Olmec regions during the Preclassic (Clark and Hansen 2001). Additionally, El Achiotal lacked an E-Group. The site plan and lack of an identifiable E-Group complex, coupled with the fact that the site's artistic style emphasized elements from both Olmec and Maya art, is intriguing (see Acuña Chapter 12 this volume). The chapter by Acuña illustrates how divine kingship was sanctioned and legitimized through the elaborate iconographic program displayed at the site. El Achiotal provides a rare opportunity to examine the interregional interactions that occurred during the Preclassic and how these were manifested in both constructed sacred space and iconography of a site located on the frontier. Of course, further work in this region is necessary to gain a better understanding of the connection between El Achiotal and sites in the Mirador region such as the large Preclassic center of Tintal.

Turning to the northern Maya lowlands, there seem to be some interesting differences between this region and the southern lowlands during the Late Preclassic. The massive construction projects that are typical of the Late Preclassic in the central and southern lowlands do not seem to be reflected in the archaeological record of the north. Yet, very few excavations in the northern Maya lowlands have not produced some evidence of Late Preclassic occupation. Local versions of the Late Nabanche ceramic complex (Chicanel) are found throughout the northern peninsula and there is significant continuity in the Early and Late Nabanche ceramics with little evidence of any major disjunction in the ceramic tradition or the economic system. This point has recently been emphasized by Ceballos and Robles (2012). What is much less understood is the nature of Late Preclassic society in many of these regions and the relationship of the Late Preclassic Maya to their Middle Preclassic ancestors in the northern lowlands.

In the northwest corner of the peninsula the work of Robles, Andrews, and Anderson indicates that settlement peaked in the late Middle Preclassic, including most sites with ballcourts. The site of Xtobo, seen by Anderson et al. (Chapter 8 this volume) as the main competitor of Komchen during the late Middle Preclassic, continues to be occupied in the Late Preclassic, although Komchen becomes the largest center in the northwest during this time. During the Late Preclassic, Komchen, appears to be the most prominent site in Yucatan. Late Preclassic occupation is relatively widespread throughout the region, including what was to become the major Classic center of Dzibilchaltun.

In the Puuc region, the major construction episodes of monumental architecture were primarily associated with the late Middle Preclassic as discussed above. For example, at Xocnaceh the main acropolis was almost exclusively associated with the late Middle Preclassic with only minor architectural renovations associated with the Late Preclassic. The monumental acropolis at Poxila discussed by Robles and Ceballos (Chapter 9 this volume) also dates exclusively to the late Middle Preclassic. Recent work by William Ringle in the Puuc's Yaxhom Valley, not far from Xocnaceh, has also defined massive monumental constructions dated to the late Middle Preclassic and Early Classic, but the evidence for Late Preclassic construction is unclear at this point (Ringle et al. 2014). Although it appears that the Late Preclassic occupation was relatively large, the evidence for architectural construction and renovation is minimal. Only one construction phase of the main platform at Kiuic can be definitively assigned to the Late Preclassic. These data are intriguing and may suggest a de-emphasis on monumental construction.

In the eastern peninsula of the northern Maya lowlands, Ek Balam, Coba, and Yaxuna exhibit some growth during the Late Preclassic. Bond-Freeman (Chapter 10 this volume) notes a shift in the layout of Late Preclassic Ek Balam with greater nucleation to an area east of what was to become the site's Classic period ceremonial center. Bond-Freeman (Chapter 10 this volume), however, does not identify evidence to suggest an increase in social hierarchy in the Late Preclassic community at Ek Balam.

Some of our best evidence for the elaboration and investment of ceremonial architecture in the Late Preclassic in the northern Maya lowlands comes from the site of Yaxuna. Stanton (2012) identifies a Late Preclassic E-Group suggesting that at least by this period, E-Group assemblages had spread to a handful of sites in the northern Maya lowlands. Freidel and Suhler (1998) identified two Preclassic "performance" platforms with subterranean passageways and a staircase leading to the platform summit via trapdoors. Based on ceramics and a ^{14}C date, these structures date to the late Middle Preclassic to Late Preclassic transition. These features, along with the presence of ceramics that look to be from the south/central lowlands may indicate that Yaxuna was serving as a major node in an inland trade route linking the northern and southern lowlands by the Late Preclassic.

The triadic architectural arrangements that are typical in the central and southern lowlands during the Late Preclassic are uncommon in the north, indicating that the architectural symbols of divine kingship may manifest themselves differently in the two regions. Although, as we mentioned above, Xocnaceh, Yaxhom, and perhaps Lakin may represent examples of late Middle Preclassic triadic architectural arrangements, possibly suggesting an earlier tradition of this architectural form in the north, further research is necessary to confirm this (see Reese-Taylor 2017 for an example from Yaxnohcah in the Central Karstic Uplands region). A more thorough study of Late Preclassic ceremonial architecture in the north is necessary in order to shed light on the symbolic differences between the different regions of the Maya lowlands. In spite of this, current data suggests that the northern Maya lowlands did not exhibit the same surge of architectural development and elaboration that occurred in the central and southern lowlands, such as seen at El Mirador and neighboring sites.

We do want to point out that there are more data pertaining to the Early Classic in the northern Maya lowlands. Evidence suggests that northern lowlands witnessed impressive growth during the Early Classic with the development of a number of new megalithic centers (see Mathews and Maldonado Cardenas 2006), including such major centers as Ake, Acanceh, Nohoch Cep, and Izamal. Their Late Preclassic roots are unfortunately poorly understood though they must exist and await future research. The pattern that stands out is evidence for shifts in population and occupation throughout the northern Maya lowlands highlighted by the decline of many of the major monumental centers in the Puuc region at the end of the late Middle Preclassic and the rise of new megalithic centers in the Early Classic. Although Late Preclassic Maya occupation in the north was widespread, as seen from the ceramic data, we know surprisingly little about the specifics of this period in the north, albeit with a few exceptions such as the sites of Komchen and Yaxuna. We emphasize the need for long-term research projects in this region to tackle this important time period. Nevertheless, we feel confident that we are on the threshold of a more widespread culture-historical synthesis based on empirical data from across the lowlands.

Moving to a more general picture of the Late Preclassic period, one of the chapters in this volume conceives the developments in the Late

Preclassic to be foundational in the ideology of later Classic period political concepts. Taking the long view, David Freidel (Chapter 15 this volume)
presents exciting and provocative ideas on the development of kingship in
the Preclassic. As far back as 1990 he and Linda Schele have made a case for
the existence of kingship in the Late Preclassic. They argued that a cache
from Cerros contained royal insignia that they felt symbolized the presence of a king. More recently, he suggests that this royal insignia actually
symbolized kingship as opposed to an individual king. The difference is
important as Freidel argues "that in contrast to some other adjacent areas in
Mesoamerica the Preclassic lowland Maya are not interring royal ancestors
in public buildings or immediately proximate spaces. Instead they generally are interring cenotaphic insignia of royal office, a practice emphasizing
the office and not the human being holding it in a way commensurate with
means of recruitment other than kinship such as ritual initiation."

This fits into a larger discussion that focuses on the role of the Mirador
area in the rise of social complexity in the Maya lowlands. Freidel presents
an argument in his chapter proposing that "the Mirador area was sacred
to all the lowland Maya as the birthplace of the Maize God, the source for
the legitimacy of the idea of empire." He argues that the arrival of the office
of kingship at Cerros and the community's sudden transformation into an
important ceremonial center is the result of incorporation in the "regional
hegemonic empire" governed by the city of El Mirador in the Late Preclassic. Freidel argues that divine kingship comes to the Maya in the Mirador
area (Nakbe, Yaxnohcah, El Mirador) via the Olmec along with the cult of
maize. He further argues that maize production is one of the key elements
contributing to rise of social complexity in the late Middle Preclassic to
Late Preclassic transition, along with lime production and the development of a regional currency-based market economy (Freidel Chapter 15
this volume). He proposes that Preclassic kings and the idea of empire at
El Mirador serve as the cultural and later legendary basis for the evolution
of the later Kan Kingdom, spreading the idea of kingship in the southern
Maya lowlands in the Late Preclassic.

Freidel is not arguing so much that El Mirador was the capital of an
empire, but rather that El Mirador evolved as a special place in the Maya
lowlands—a place quite different and undoubtedly more complex than any
other sociopolitical entity in the late Middle to Late Preclassic period. In his
case, it was additionally a place where a shamanistic-based kingship (anchored by a large-scale economic production and distribution system and
highly developed maize mythology) first emerged in the Maya lowlands

and spread throughout other parts of the southern lowlands (he differentiates what took place in the northern lowlands). His contribution to this volume is thought-provoking and challenges us to think in new and different ways about the magnitude and impact of lowland Maya Preclassic developments. Undoubtedly, the Classic Maya state has its roots firmly planted by the Late Preclassic.

Pathways to Complexity in the Maya Lowlands: New Ideas and Problems for Consideration

Together, the research presented in this volume presents an enhanced understanding of the evolution of Maya society. It highlights the complexity of the Maya adaptation and degree of change that took place over the 700 years (or longer) of the Middle Preclassic, a time period as long as the entire Classic Period. It recalibrates our understanding of the timing and nature of the origins of settled village life in the Maya lowlands as well as the pathways to complexity that led to the appearance of kingship and the state in the Preclassic. It reflects a major step forward in our consideration of the relations between elites, economy, politics, and ideology during the Preclassic as well as presents a range of thought on the level of cultural complexity reached by the late Middle Preclassic, with some archaeologists now arguing for the appearance of the state by the end of this time period. If nothing else, this volume has established the central role of the Middle Preclassic in understanding the nature of Late Preclassic and Classic Maya society.

The development of Maya civilization did not occur in a vacuum, but rather, was a process that included interactions between people from different regions and environmental zones, including regions that were once considered "peripheral" (Sharer and Traxler 2006:178). As Sharer and Traxler (2006:178) state, "these so-called peripheries—including Yucatan to the north and the highland and coastal zone from Chiapas to El Salvador and Honduras to the south—played crucial roles in the evolution of Maya civilization." We agree with this statement and feel that this volume contributes a more balanced view of the Maya lowlands with the presentation of various contributions from the northern and southern lowlands and a chapter from the highlands. Although our understanding of the pathways to complexity in the Maya lowlands has dramatically increased over the past four decades, we see some gaps in our knowledge and important research areas that need to be addressed by Maya scholars.

While our understanding of the Preceramic period has increased considerably, we still do not have a clear understanding of the origins of the earliest settled villages. Although some scholars are proposing in situ development models as alternatives to the more traditional model of migration, we feel that more data are necessary to elucidate patterns of continuity or discontinuity in the archaeological record. We hope that this becomes a sustained focus by researchers in the Maya lowlands.

Another important problem for consideration is the timing of the establishment of pre-Mamom populations in different regions of the Maya lowlands and the connection between these early populations. Pre-Mamom pottery traditions are now seen across the lowlands, including the northern lowland region and possibly into the highlands (as seen from the highland site of Naranjo). A shared symbol system is evident throughout the Maya lowlands, connecting these early ceramic-producing communities with other regions of Mesoamerica. We greatly need a refined chronology for this important period in Maya history. One issue that we see is that Maya scholars rely heavily on ceramic analysis for chronological assessment. As we emphasized above, we believe this is problematic and we urge scholars to use absolute dating methods to refine ceramic chronologies and date specific features. Of course, we caution that context is crucial and that dates should come from solid, primary contexts when possible. With more intensive penetrating excavations, we feel that our understanding of pre-Mamom settlement and interaction spheres will be greatly enhanced.

Although there is still much to learn about this early time period, we suggest that key elements in the emergence of Maya complexity are found by the early Middle Preclassic across the lowlands. Several of the contributors of this volume (including Brown et al., Hansen et al., and Freidel) emphasize the role of religion in this process. Thus, a better understanding of the nature of pre-Mamom ritual and religion, and how the ideological system shifted and conformed to support an emergent elite is necessary. Future studies that emphasize both pre-Mamom household and community ritual activities will help shed light on these issues.

By the late Middle Preclassic, we see the development of monumental stone architecture in the form of large platforms, and in some cases, acropolises and pyramids. We also see the emergence of regional settlement hierarchies and the widespread use of ritual architecture such as ballcourts in the northern lowlands and E-Groups in the southern/central regions. While our knowledge of this period (ca. 700/600–300 B.C.) is rapidly growing, we emphasize a need for a refined chronology based on absolute dates. The timing of important developments, such as the erection of truly monumental platforms and pyramids, needs to be confirmed so that we can directly compare these data across the lowlands. Another problem for consideration is the distribution of certain types of ceremonial features such as ballcourts and E-Groups. Our current data are suggestive of regional distinctions that might reflect larger differences in religious practices between the northern and central/southern lowlands.

These new data are especially important in light of the recent chronological revision in the Maya highland region centering on the site of Kaminaljuyu. Based on the reevaluation of radiocarbon dates through Bayesian statistics combined with ceramic cross-dating, Inomata et al. (2014) argue that the chronological sequence of Kaminaljuyu should be revised by 300 years or so. Although there is still ongoing debate pertaining to the new chronology that they propose, we find their argument compelling and more in line with the chronological sequence of the Maya lowlands, especially in light of the ceramic cross-dating. We bring this up here as their proposed chronology for Kaminaluyu may have implications for the sudden expansion we see during the late Middle Preclassic in the northern lowlands and elsewhere in the lowlands. Inomata et al. (2014) argue that the Kaminaljuyu region experienced a rapid decline around 400 B.C., not coincidently at around the same time as the collapse of the Olmec center of La Venta and numerous sites in the Grijalva region of Chiapas (Clark and Hansen 2001). It is around this same time (the end of the late Middle Preclassic), we see a dramatic increase in monumental architecture in the northern lowlands. Although more empirical data are necessary at this point to understand these major social and political transformations across both the highlands and lowlands, the new data from the northern lowlands are intriguing in light of the proposed revisions to highland chronology, and the "significant political disruption at around 400 B.C." proposed by Inomata et al. (2014:402).

The late Middle Preclassic is a crucial period in Maya history and many of the underpinnings of a state system are emerging or are present by this time. Moreover, with the increasing evidence for the development and widespread use of ritual architecture (E-Groups and ballcourts), an increase in ritual activity such as offerings, feasting, and ancestor veneration, as well as a documented increase in long-distance exchange of exotic items (shell, obsidian, and greenstone), it is not surprising that a number of authors in this volume argue for the rise of rulers or a ruling group with recognized legitimacy at least by the end of the late Middle Preclassic (the Middle to

Late Preclassic transition). In fact, some of the contributors to this volume suggest that by the latter part of the late Middle Preclassic, we see emerging regional states in the northern lowlands (see Robles and Ceballos Chapter 9 this volume). While Robles and Ceballos (and others) make compelling arguments, we feel that more data are necessary to flesh out the nature of late Middle Preclassic Maya society. Nevertheless, we think that all the contributors in this volume would agree that there is a mounting body of evidence that demonstrates a rapid increase in complexity across the lowlands during this dynamic period and that this complexity is both supported by and legitimized through an elaborate ideological system that by this time emphasizes the maize cult.

Maya scholars have a much-enhanced understanding of the Late Preclassic period. With widespread settlement across the lowlands by this period, archaeologists have amassed an astonishing amount of data (archaeological, iconographic, and epigraphic) pertaining to Late Preclassic society. The polity centered at El Mirador is the best example of a potential regional state in the Late Preclassic (see Hansen et al. Chapter 7 this volume), and we would argue that the evidence for this is substantial. As Hansen and his team have demonstrated, the monumentality present at El Mirador is unprecedented in the Maya lowlands. Freidel presents a novel and compelling argument that El Mirador served as the foundation for the institution of kingship (the maker of kings) in places such as Cerros, a process of legitimization we see utilized throughout the Classic period by Maya polities. So powerful was El Mirador in the Late Preclassic world, Freidel thinks it served as the idea of empire to the Classic period Maya, the legendary place where the concept of a king-led Maize God state had its inception and first flowering, providing a model for all later polities. He emphasizes social memory in this process.

It is apparent that social memory played an important role in the legitimization process within the newly formed institution of kingship during the Late Preclassic, as we see from sites such as San Bartolo (Saturno et al. Chapter 13 this volume). In fact, many of our contributors feel that social memory and ancestor veneration are two key mechanisms that elites employed to reinforce their social position. These strategies can be seen through careful investigation as is documented in the chapters in this volume. It is during the Late Preclassic that these strategies become clearly visible, especially embedded in the visual displays of monumental architecture. Yet there appears to be something very different happening in the northern Maya lowlands during the Late Preclassic. While the Peten region and areas to the south are exploding with construction efforts and expanding settlement during the Late Preclassic, there is little evidence for a comparable boom in the north. In fact, there seems to be a decreased emphasis on monumental construction efforts. We feel that this is another problem for consideration for future scholars to tackle. We need a clearer understanding of the nature of Late Preclassic society in the north in order to understand how this region was impacted (or not) by the rapid consolidation of power and authority at El Mirador in the Mirador region.

While the Late Preclassic period may have been a time of slowed construction efforts in the north, it is during this period that we see definitive evidence for the institution of kingship in other regions of the Maya lowlands. We do want to emphasize that many of the authors in this volume see the Late Preclassic as not the beginning of the rise of kingship and the state but as the end product of a set of pathways that began several centuries earlier.

It is our hope that this edited volume has contributed to our understanding of these pathways to complexity. From our current vantage point, we see the evidence from the early Middle Preclassic onward as reflecting a pathway toward complexity based on the development of social hierarchies in which communities practiced a set of behaviors (competitive displays, gift-giving, and feasts) embedded in the maize cult that led to certain individuals or groups acquiring prestige within the community. The Maya were moving along a set of pathways leading to increased social inequality since the early Middle Preclassic, with the network of evolution accelerating throughout the late Middle Preclassic, culminating in the rise of kingship, elites, and a complex ideological and political system that legitimized it by the late Middle Preclassic to Late Preclassic transition. We anticipate that this volume will stimulate new questions and lead to further Preclassic discoveries that, in turn, will refine our current knowledge. We look forward to the unearthing of new data and ideas, and encourage scholars to dig deeper into the Maya past.

REFERENCES

Abbott, Robert T.
1974   *American Seashells: The Marine Mollusca of the Atlantic and Pacific Coasts of North America*. Van Nostrand Reinhold, New York.

Abrams, Elliot M.
1984   Replicative Experimentation at Copan, Honduras: Implications for Ancient Economic Specialization. *Journal of New World Archaeology* 6: 39–48.
1987   Economic Specialization and Construction Personnel in Classic Period Copan, Honduras. *American Antiquity* 52: 485–499.
1994   *How the Maya Built their World: Energetics and Ancient Architecture*. University of Texas Press, Austin.
1995   A Model of Fluctuating Labor Value and the Establishment of State Power: An Application to the Prehispanic Maya. *Latin American Antiquity* 6: 196–213.
1996   The Evolution of Plaster Production and the Growth of the Copan Maya State. *Arqueología Mesoamericana, Homenaje a William P. Sanders*. Instituto Nacional de Antropología y Historia, Mexico.

Abrams, Elliott M., and Thomas W. Bolland
1999   Architectural Energetics, Ancient Monuments, and Operations Management. *Journal of Archaeological Method and Theory* 6: 263–291.

Acuña, Mary J.
2010   *Monitoring the Development of Early Kingship at a Preclassic (800 BCE–200 CE) Maya Frontier Royal Center in Northwestern Petén, Guatemala*. National Science Foundation, Doctoral Dissertation Improvement Grant.
2011   Excavaciones en la Estructura 5C-01 de El Achiotal. In *Proyecto Arqueológico La Corona, informe final, temporada 2010*, edited by Tomás Barrientos, Marcello Canuto, and Mary J. Acuña, pp. 47–81. Report submitted to the Instituto de Antropología e Historia, Guatemala.
2013   Art, Ideology, and Politics at El Achiotal: A Late Preclassic Frontier Site in Northwestern Petén, Guatemala. Unpublished Ph.D. dissertation, Department of Anthropology, Washington University in St. Louis.

Acuña, Mary J., and C. Chiriboga
2010   Investigación Arqueológica en el sitio El Achiotal. In *Proyecto Arqueológico La Corona, informe final, temporada 2009*, edited by Marcello Canuto and Tomás Barrientos, pp. 201–245. Report submitted to the Instituto de Antropología e Historia, Guatemala.

Adams, Richard E. W. (editor)
1977   *The Origins of Maya Civilization*. University of New Mexico Press, Albuquerque.

Adams, Richard E. W.

1971   *The Ceramics of Altar de Sacrificios*. Papers of the Peabody Museum of Archaeology and Ethnology, Vol. 63, No. 1. Harvard University, Cambridge.

1980   Swamp, Canals, and the Locations of Ancient Maya Cities. *Antiquity* 54: 206–214.

Adams, Richard E. W., and T. Patrick Culbert

1977   The Origins of Civilization in the Maya Lowlands. In *The Origins of Maya Civilization*, edited by Richard E. W. Adams, pp. 3–24. University of New Mexico Press, Albuquerque.

Agrinier, Pierre

1975   *Mounds 9 and 10 at Mirador, Chiapas, Mexico*. Papers of the New World Archaeological Foundation, No. 39. Brigham Young University, Provo.

1991   Ballcourts of Southern Chiapas, Mexico. In *The Mesoamerican Ballgame*, edited by Vernon L. Scarborough and David R. Wilcox, pp. 175–194. University of Arizona Press, Tucson.

Aimers, James J.

1992   *A Third Season of Excavations at the Zotz Group, Cahal Pech*. Manuscript on file in the Department of Anthropology, Trent University, Peterborough.

1995   An Hermeneutic Analysis of the Maya E-Group Complex. Unpublished Master's thesis, Department of Anthropology, Trent University, Peterborough.

Aimers, James J., and Prudence M. Rice

2006   Astronomy, Ritual, and the Interpretation of Maya "E-Group" Architectural Assemblages. *Ancient Mesoamerica* 17: 79–96.

Alcina Franch, José, Andrés Ciudad Ruiz, and Josefa Iglesias Ponce de León

1980   "Temazcal" en Mesoamérica: evolución, forma y función. *Revista Española de Antropología Americana* 10: 93–132.

Algaze, Guillermo

1993   Expansionary Dynamics of Some Early Pristine States. *American Anthropologist* 95: 304–333.

Alvarez, Ticul

1983   Restos de mamíferos recientes y pleistocénicos procedentes de las Grutas de Loltún, Yucatán, México. In *Restos de moluscos y mamíferos cuaternarios procedentes de Loltún, Yucatán*, edited by Ticul Alvarez and Oscar J. Polaco, pp. 7–35. Cuaderno de Trabajo 26, Departamento de Prehistoria, Instituto Nacional de Antropología e Historia, Mexico.

Anderson, David S.

2003   El asentamiento preclásico en la región noroeste de Yucatán. In *Proyecto Costa Maya: Reconocimiento arqueológico en el noroeste de Yucatán. Reporte interino, temporada 2002: Reconocimiento arqueológico de la esquina noroeste de la península de Yucatán y primeras aproximaciónes a los temas de investigación*, edited by Fernando Robles Castellanos and Anthony P. Andrews, pp. 46–61. Report submitted to the Instituto Nacional de Antropología e Historia, Mexico.

2005   Preclassic Settlement Patterns in Northwest Yucatán. *Mono y Conejo* 3: 13–22.

2009   Xtobo, Yucatán, México, and the Emergent Preclassic of the Northern Maya

Lowlands. Paper presented at the 74th Annual Meeting of the Society for American Archaeology, Atlanta.

2010   Xtobo, Yucatán, México: The Study of a Preclassic Maya Community. Unpublished Ph.D. dissertation, Department of Anthropology, Tulane University, New Orleans.

2011   Xtobo, Yucatan, Mexico, and the Emergent Preclassic of the Northern Maya Lowlands. *Ancient Mesoamerica* 22: 301–322.

2012   The Origins of the Mesoamerican Ballgame: A New Perspective from the Northern Maya Lowlands. In *The Ancient Maya of Mexico: Reinterpreting the Past of the Northern Maya Lowlands*, edited by Geoffrey E. Braswell, pp. 43–64. Equinox Publishing, London.

Anderson, David S., Anthony P. Andrews, and Fernando Robles Castellanos

2004   The Preclassic in Northwest Yucatán. Paper presented at the 103rd Annual Meeting of the American Anthopological Association, Atlanta.

Andrews, Anthony P., and Fernando Robles Castellanos

2004   An Archaeological Survey of Northwest Yucatan, Mexico. *Mexicon* 26: 7–14.

2008   *Proyectos Costa Maya and Ciudad Caucel: Archaeological Survey of Northwestern Yucatan: Ceramic and Lithic Analysis.* Report submitted to the Foundation for the Advancement of Mesoamerican Studies, Inc. Electronic document, http://www.famsi.org/reports/07034/, accessed August 25, 2017.

Andrews, E. Wyllys IV

1965 (1975)   Progress Report on the 1960–1964 Field Seasons, National Geographic Society-Tulane University Dzibilchaltun Program. In *Archaeological Investigations on the Yucatan Peninsula*, pp. 23–67. Middle American Research Institute Publication 31. Tulane University, New Orleans.

1973   Archaeology and Prehistory in the Northern Maya Lowlands. In *Handbook of Middle American Indians*, Vol. 2, *Archaeology of Southern Mesoamerica*, edited by Gordon R. Willey, pp. 288–330. University of Texas Press, Austin.

Andrews, E Wyllys IV, and E. Wyllys Andrews V

1980   *Excavations at Dzibilchaltun, Yucatan, Mexico.* Middle American Research Institute Publication 48. Tulane University, New Orleans.

Andrews, E. Wyllys V

1981   Dzibilchaltun. In *Supplement to the Handbook of Middle American Indians, Vol. 1: Archaeology,* edited by Victoria R. Bricker and Jeremy A. Sabloff, pp. 313–341. University of Texas Press, Austin.

1986   Olmec Jades from Chacsinkin, Yucatan, and Maya Ceramics from La Venta, Tabasco. In *Research and Reflections in Archaeology and History: Essays in Honor of Doris Stone*, edited by E. Wyllys Andrews V, pp. 11–49. Middle American Research Institute Publication 57. Tulane University, New Orleans.

1988   Ceramic Units from Komchen, Yucatan, Mexico. *Cerámica de Cultura Maya et al.* 15: 51–64.

1989   Komchen Ceramic Type Descriptions. Manuscript on file at the Middle American Research Institute, Tulane University, New Orleans.

1990   The Early Ceramic History of the Lowland Maya. In *Vision and Revision in*

Maya Studies, edited by Flora S. Clancy and Peter D. Harrison, pp. 1–19. University of New Mexico Press, Albuquerque.

2005 Review of *The Ancient Maya of the Belize Valley: Half a Century of Archaeological Research*, edited by James F. Garber. *Journal of Field Archaeology* 30: 353–357.

Andrews E. Wyllys V, and Anthony P. Andrews

2001 Northern Maya Lowlands. In *The Oxford Encyclopedia of Mesoamerican Cultures: The Civilizations of Mexico and Central America*, Vol. 2, edited by David Carrasco, pp. 378–385. Oxford University Press, Oxford.

Andrews, E. Wyllys V, and George J. Bey III

2011 The Earliest Ceramics of the Northern Maya Lowlands. Paper presented at the 8th Annual Tulane Maya Symposium, New Orleans.

Andrews, E. Wyllys V, George J. Bey III, and Christopher Gunn

2008 Rethinking the Early Ceramic History of the Northern Maya Lowlands: New Evidence and Interpretations. Paper presented at the 73rd Annual Meeting of the Society for American Archaeology, Vancouver.

Andrews, E. Wyllys V, Noberto Gonzalez Crespo, and William M. Ringle

1980 Map of the Ruins of Komchen, Yucatan, Mexico. Document on file at the Middle American Research Institute, Tulane University, New Orleans.

Andrews, E. Wyllys V, and William M. Ringle

1992 Los mayas tempranos en Yucatán: Investigaciones arqueológicas en Komchén. *Mayab*, Special Publication No. 8, pp. 5–17. Sociedad Española de Estudios Mayas, Universidad Complutense, Madrid.

Andrews, E. Wyllys V, William M. Ringle, Philip J. Barnes, Alfredo Barrera Rubio, and Tomás Gallareta Negrón

1984 Komchen, An Early Maya Community in Northwest Yucatan. In *Investigaciones recientes en el área maya* 1: 73–92. XVII Mesa Redonda of the Sociedad Mexicana de Antropología, San Cristóbal de las Casas, Chiapas, Mexico.

Aoyama, Kazuo

1995 Microwear Analysis in the Southeast Maya Lowlands: Two Case Studies at Copan, Honduras. *Latin American Antiquity* 6: 129–144.

Arendt, Carmen, Rhanju Song, and Paul F. Healy

1996 The 1995 Excavations in Plaza C, Pacbitun, Belize: A Middle Preclassic Burial and a Late Classic Stela. In *Belize Valley Preclassic Maya Project: Report of the 1995 Field Season*, edited by Paul F. Healy and Jaime J. Awe, pp. 128–138. Occasional Papers in Anthropology, No. 12. Trent University, Peterborough.

Arnold, Jeanne E.

1991 Transformation of a Regional Economy: Sociopolitical Evolution and the Production of Valuables in Southern California. *Antiquity* 65: 953–962.

1995 Transportation Innovation and Social Complexity among Maritime Hunter-Gatherer Societies. *American Anthropologist* 97: 733–747.

Arnold, Jeanne E., and Annabel Ford

1980 A Statistical Examination of Settlement Patterns at Tikal, Guatemala. *American Antiquity* 45: 713–726.

Arnold, Jeanne E., and Ann Munns
1994   Independent or Attached Specialization: The Organization of Shell Bead Pro-
            duction in California. *Journal of Field Archaeology* 21: 473–489.
Arroyo, Bárbara (editor)
2006   *Informe final del Proyecto Arqueológico de Rescate Naranjo.* Report submitted
            to the Instituto de Antropología e Historia, Guatemala.
2010   *Entre cerros, cafetales y urbanismo en el Valle de Guatemala: Proyecto de Res-
            cate Naranjo.* Academia de Geografía e Historia de Guatemala, Special Pub-
            lication No. 47, Guatemala.
Arroyo, Bárbara, Hector Neff, Deborah Pearsall, John Jones, and Dorothy Freidel
2002   Ultimos resultados del proyecto sobre el medio ambiente en la costa del Pací-
            fico. In *XV Simposio de investigaciones arqueológicas en Guatemala*, edited by
            Juan Pedro Laporte, Héctor L. Escobedo, and Bárbara Arroyo, pp. 415–24.
            Museo Nacional de Arqueología y Etnología, Ministerio de Cultura y Deport-
            es, Instituto de Antropología e Historia, and Asociación Tikal, Guatemala
            City.
Ascher, Robert
1961   Experimental Archaeology. *American Anthropologist* 63: 793–816.
Ashmore, Wendy, and Jeremy A. Sabloff
2002   Spatial Orders in Maya Civic Plans. *Latin American Antiquity* 13: 201–215.
Aveni, Anthony, and Horst Hartung
1989   Uaxactun, Guatemala, Group E and Similar Assemblages: An Archaeoastro-
            nomical Reconsideration. In *World Archaeoastronomy*, edited by Anthony
            Aveni, pp. 441–461. Cambridge University Press, Cambridge.
Aveni, Anthony, Anne Dowd, and Benjamin Vining
2003   Maya Calendar Reform? Evidence from Orientations of Specialized Architec-
            tural Assemblages. *Latin American Antiquity* 14: 159–178.
Awe, Jaime J.
1992   Dawn in the Land between the Rivers: Formative Occupation at Cahal Pech,
            Belize and Its Implications for Preclassic Development in the Maya Lowlands.
            Unpublished Ph.D. dissertation, Institute of Archaeology, University of Lon-
            don.
2013   Journey on the Cahal Pech Time Machine: An Archaeological Reconstruc-
            tion of the Dynastic Sequence at a Belize Valley Polity. *Research Reports in
            Belizean Archaeology* 10: 33–50.
n.d.   Archaeological Evidence for the Preclassic Origins of the Maya Creation
            Story and the Resurrection of the Maize God at Cahal Pech, Belize. To be
            published in: Popol Vuh: The Ancient Maya Creation Myth in Literature, Ico-
            nography, Epigraphy, Ethnohistory & Archaeology, edited by Holley Moyes
            and Allen Christensen.
Awe, Jaime J., Cassandra Bill, Mark Campbell, and David Cheetham
1990   Early Middle Formative Occupation in the Central Maya Lowlands: Recent
            Evidence from Cahal Pech, Belize. In *Papers from the Institute of Archaeology*,
            No. 1, pp. 1–5. University College London.

Awe, Jaime J., Nikolai Grube, and David Cheetham

2009 Cahal Pech Stela 9: A Preclassic Monument from the Belize Valley. *Research Reports in Belizean Archaeology* 6: 179–190.

Balcarcel, Beatriz, Stephanie Schrodt, Richard D. Hansen, and Gustavo Martinez

2010 El ultimo suspiro ceramico del Preclásico Tardio en la zona Cultural Mirador. In *XXIII Simposio de Investigaciones Arqueológicas en Guatemala*, edited by Bárbara Arroyo, Adriana Linares Palma, Lorena Paiz Aragón, pp. 1125–1140. Museo Nacional de Arqueología y Etnología, Ministerio de Cultura y Deportes, Instituto de Antropología e Historia, and Asociación Tikal, Guatemala City.

Ball, Joseph W.

1977 The Rise of the Northern Maya Chiefdoms: A Socioprocessual Analysis. In *The Origins of Maya Civilization*, edited by Richard E. W. Adams, pp. 101–132. University of New Mexico Press, Albuquerque.

1977–1979 A Descriptive Inventory and Preliminary Typology of the Formative Ceramics of Dzibilchaltún (the Mirador Group, Komchen, and the Xculul Group) from the Tulane University Excavations of 1960 to 1965. Typescript on file at the Middle American Research Institute, Tulane University, New Orleans.

1993 Pottery, Potters, Palaces, and Polities: Some Socioeconomic and Political Implications of Late Classic Maya Ceramic Industries. In *Lowland Maya Civilization in the Eighth Century A.D.*, edited by Jeremy A. Sabloff and John S. Henderson, pp. 243–272. Dumbarton Oaks Research Library and Collection, Washington, D.C.

2001 Maya Lowlands: North. In *Archaeology of Ancient Mexico and Central America*, edited by Susan T. Evans and David L. Webster, pp. 433–441. Garland Publishing, Inc., New York.

Ball, Joseph W., and Jennifer T. Taschek

2000 Pioneering the Belize Valley in the Early Middle Preclassic: Ceramics, Settlement, Interaction, and Culture History at a Maya-Zoque Interface. Paper presented at the 65th Annual Meeting, Society of American Archaeology, Philadelphia.

2003 Reconsidering the Belize Valley Preclassic: A Case for Multiethnic Interactions in the Development of a Regional Culture Tradition. *Ancient Mesoamerica* 14: 179–217.

2007 "Mixed Deposits," "Composite Complexes," or "Hybrid Assemblages?" A Fresh Reexamination of Middle Preclassic (Formative) Ceramics and Ceramic Assemblages from the Northern Maya Lowlands. In *Archaeology, Art, and Ethnogenesis in Mesoamerican Prehistory: Papers in Honor of Gareth W. Lowe*, edited by Lynneth S. Lowe and Mary E. Pye, pp. 173–191. Papers of the New World Archaeological Foundation, No. 68. Brigham Young University, Provo.

Barba, Luis A., and José Luis Córdova Frunz

1999 Estudios energéticos de la producción de cal en tiempos teotihuacanos y sus implicaciones. *Latin American Antiquity* 10: 168–179.

Bardawil, Lawrence
1976   The Principal Bird Deity in Maya Art: An Iconographic Study of Form and
            Meaning. In *The Art, Iconography, and Dynastic History of Palenque, part III*,
            edited by Merle Green Robertson, pp. 195–209. Precolumbian Art Research,
            Robert Louis Stevenson School, Pebble Beach.

Baron, Joanne P.
2013   Patrons of La Corona: Deities and Power in a Classic Maya Community. Un-
            published Ph.D. dissertation, Department of Anthropology, University of
            Pennsylvania, Philadelphia.

Barrales Rodríguez, Dehmian
2002   *Informe cerámico preliminar. Proyecto Acanceh 1999–2000*. Report submitted
            to the Instituto Nacional de Antropología e Historia, Mexico.

Barrera Rubio, Alfredo
1999   Avances y perspectivas de la arqueología Yucateca. *Investigadores de la Cul-
            tura Maya* 7(1): 156–167.

Baudez, Claude-Francois
1994   *Maya Sculpture of Copan: The Iconography*. University of Oklahoma Press, Norman.

Bauer, Jeremy R.
2005   Between Heaven and Earth: The Cival Cache and the Creation of the Meso-
            american Cosmos. In *Lords of Creation: The Origins of Sacred Maya Kingship*,
            edited by Virginia M. Fields and Dorie Reents-Budet, pp. 28–29. Scala, London.

Beltrán, Boris
2006   SB-1A: Excavaciones en la Estructura Ixbalamque (Pinturas Sub 6), San Bar-
            tolo, Petén. In *Proyecto Regional Arqueológico San Bartolo: Informe prelimi-
            nar No. 5, segunda temporada 2006*, edited by Mónica Urquizú and William
            Saturno, pp. 59–78. Report submitted to the Instituto de Antropología e His-
            toria, Guatemala.

2008   Excavaciones de la tercera etapa constructiva del complejo arquitectónico
            Las Pinturas (Pinturas Sub-6). In *Proyecto Regional Arqueológico San Bartolo:
            Informe preliminar No. 7, septima temporada 2008*, edited by Mónica Urquizú
            and William Saturno, pp. 42–60. Report submitted to the Instituto de Antro-
            pología e Historia, Guatemala.

Benson, Elizabeth P. (editor)
1973   *Mesoamerican Writing Systems*. Dumbarton Oaks Research Library and Col-
            lection, Washington, D.C.

Benson, Elizabeth P.
1981   *The Olmec and Their Neighbors: Essays in Memory of Matthew W. Stirling*.
            Dumbarton Oaks Research Library and Collection, Washington, D.C.

Berlin, Heinrich
1940   Relaciones precolombinas entre Cuba y Yucatán. *Revista Mexicana de Estu-
            dios Antropológicos* 4(1–2): 141–160.

1958   El glifo "emblem" en las inscripciones mayas. *Journal de la Societe des Ameri-
            canistes* 47: 111–119.

1963   The Palenque Triad. *Journal de la Societe des Americanistes* 52: 91–99.

Bey, George J. III

2006   Changing Archaeological Perspective on the Northern Maya Lowlands. In *Lifeways in the Northern Maya Lowlands: New Approaches to Archaeology in the Yucatan Peninsula*, edited by Jennifer P. Mathews and Bethany Morrison, pp. 13–40. University of Arizona Press, Tuscon.

Bey, George J. III, Tara M. Bond, William M. Ringle, Craig A. Hanson, Charles W. Houck, and Carlos Peraza Lope

1998   The Ceramic Chronology of Ek Balam, Yucatan, Mexico. *Ancient Mesoamerica* 9: 101–120.

Bey, George J. III, Evan Parker, Jiyan Gu, Timothy Ward, Tomás Gallareta Negrón, E. Wyllys Andrews V, and Amanda Strickland.

2012   An ICP-MS Analysis of Early Maya Pottery from the Northern Maya Lowlands. Paper presented at the 77th Annual Meeting of the Society for American Archaeology, Memphis.

Blake, Michael, Brian S. Chisholm, John E. Clark, and Karen Mudar

1992   Non-Agricultural Staples and Agricultural Supplements: Early Formative Subsistence in the Soconusco, Mexico. In *Transitions to Agriculture*, edited by Anne B. Gerbauer and T. Douglas Price, pp. 133–151. Monographs in World Archaeology, No. 4. Prehistory Press, Madison.

Blake, Michael, Brian S. Chisholm, John E. Clark, Barbara Voorhies, and Michael W. Love

1992   Prehistoric Subsistence in the Soconusco Region. *Current Anthropology* 33: 83–94.

Blake, Michael, John E. Clark, Barbara Voorhies, George H. Michaels, Michael W. Love, Mary E. Pye, Arthur A. Demarest, and Barbara Arroyo

1995   Radiocarbon Chronology for the Late Archaic and Formative Periods on the Pacific Coast of Southeastern Mesoamerica. *Ancient Mesoamerica* 6: 161–183.

Bleed, Peter

1991   Operations Research and Archaeology. *American Antiquity* 56: 19–35.

Blitz, John H.

1993   Big Pots for Big Shots: Feasting and Storage in a Mississippian Community. *American Antiquity* 58: 80–96.

Blom, Frans

1924   Report on the Preliminary Work at Uaxactun, Guatemala. *Carnegie Institution of Washington Yearbook* 23: 217–219.

1932   The Maya Ball-game *Pok-ta-pok* (Called *Tlachtli* by the Aztec). In *Middle American Papers*, edited by Frans Blom and Maurice R. Ries, pp. 486–527. Middle American Research Institute Publication 4. Tulane University, New Orleans.

Bond-Freeman, Tara

2007   The Maya Preclassic Ceramic Sequence at the Site of Ek Balam, Yucatan, Mexico. Unpublished Ph.D. dissertation, Department of Anthropology, Southern Methodist University, Dallas.

Boserup, Ester

1965   *The Conditions of Agricultural Growth*. Aldine, Chicago.

Boucher, Sylviane, and Yoly Palomo

2005   Cerámica del preclásico medio y tardío en depósitos sellados del sitio Tzubil, Yucatán. *Temas Antropológicos* 27 (1–2): 153–188.

Bove, Frederick

2002   The People with No Name: Rulership, Ethnic Identity, and the Transformation of Late-Terminal Formative Societies in Pacific Guatemala. Paper presented at the 101st Annual Meeting of the American Anthropological Association, New Orleans.

2011   The People with No Name: Some Observations about the Plain Stelae of Pacific Guatemala, El Salvador, and Chiapas with Respect to Issues of Ethnicity and Rulership. In *The Southern Maya in the Late Preclassic: The Rise and Fall of Early Mesoamerican Civilization*, edited Michael Love and Jonathan Kaplan, pp. 77–114, University Press of Colorado, Boulder.

Bozarth, Steven

2007   Phytolith Analysis at Blackman Eddy, Belize. Manuscript on file at the University of Texas at San Antonio.

Bozarth, Steven, and Richard D. Hansen

1998   Estudios paleo-botanicos de Nakbe: Evidencias de ambiente y cultivos en el Preclásico. Paper presented at the XII Simposio de investigaciones arqueológicas en Guatemala, Guatemala City.

Brainerd, George W.

1951   Early Ceramic Horizons in Yucatan. In *The Civilization of Ancient America*, edited by Sol Tax, pp. 72–78. Selected Papers of the XXIXth International Congress of Americanists, Vol. 1. University of Chicago Press, Chicago.

1958   *The Archaeological Ceramics of Yucatan*. University of California, Anthropological Records Vol. 19. Berkley and Los Angeles.

Braswell, Geoffrey (editor)

2003   *The Maya and Teotihuacan: Reinterpreting Early Classic Interaction*. University of Texas Press, Austin.

Bray, Tamara

2003   The Commensal Politics of Early States and Empires. In *The Archaeology and Politics of Food and Feasting in Early States and Empires*, edited by Tamara Bray, pp. 1–16. Kluwer Academic/Plenum Publishers, New York.

Bray, Warwick

1978a   An Eighteenth-Century Reference to a Fluted Point from Guatemala. *American Antiquity* 43: 457–460.

1978b   Civilizing the Aztecs. In *The Evolution of Social Systems*, edited by Jonathan Freidman and Michael J. Rowlands, pp. 373–400. University of Pittsburgh Press, Pittsburgh.

1980   Fluted points in Mesoamerica and the Isthmus: A Reply to Rovner. *American Antiquity* 45: 168–170.

Brisch, Nicole (editor)

2008   *Divine Kingship in the Ancient World and Beyond*. Oriental Institute Seminars, No. 4. The Oriental Institute of the University of Chicago, Chicago.

Bronson, Bennet

1966   Roots and the Subsistence of the Ancient Maya. *Southwestern Journal of Anthropology* 22: 251–279.

Brown, M. Kathryn

2003   Emerging Complexity in the Maya Lowlands: A View from Blackman Eddy, Belize. Unpublished Ph.D. dissertation, Department of Anthropology, Southern Methodist University, Dallas.

2007   *Ritual Ceramic Use in the Early and Middle Preclassic at the sites of Cahal Pech and Blackman Eddy, Belize, CA.* Report submitted to the Foundation for the Advancement of Mesoamerican Studies, Inc. Electronic document, http://www.famsi.org/reports/02066/02066Brown01.pdf, accessed August 25, 2017.

2008   Establishing Hierarchies in the Belize River Valley. *Research Reports in Belizean Archaeology* 5: 175–183.

2011   Postclassic Veneration at Xunantunich, Belize. *Mexicon* 33: 126–131.

2012   A Modern Maya Ritual at Xunantunich and Its Implications for Ancient Maya Ritual Behavior. *Research Reports in Belizean Archaeology* 9: 195–205.

2013   Missing Persons: The Role of Ancestors in the Rise of Complexity. *Research Reports in Belizean Archaeology* 10: 57–64.

2017   E Groups and Ancestors: The Sunrise of Complexity at Xunantunich, Belize. In *Early Maya E Group, Solar Calendars, and the Role of Astronomy in the Rise of Lowland Urbanism,* edited by David A. Freidel, Arlen F. Chase, Anne S. Dowd, and Jerry Murdock, pp. 386–411. University Press of Florida, Gainesville.

Brown, M. Kathryn, and James F. Garber

2003   Evidence of Middle Preclassic Conflict: A View from Blackman Eddy, Belize. In *Ancient Mesoamerican Warfare,* edited by M. Kathryn Brown and Travis W. Stanton, pp. 91–108. AltaMira Press, Walnut Creek.

2005   Preclassic Architecture, Ritual, and the Emergence of Cultural Complexity: A Diachronic Perspective from Belize Valley. In *Lords of Creation: The Origins of Sacred Maya Kingship,* edited by Virginia M. Fields, Dorie Reents-Budet, and Ricardo Agurcia Fasquelle, pp. 47–51. Scala, London.

2008   Establishing and Re-using Sacred Space: A Diachronic Perspective from Blackman Eddy, Belize. In *Ruins of the Past: The Use and Perception of Abandoned Structures in the Maya Lowlands,* edited by Travis W. Stanton and Aline Magnoni, pp. 147–170. University Press of Colorado, Boulder.

Brown, M. Kathryn, Jennifer Cochran, Leah McCurdy, and David Mixter

2011   Preceramic to Postclassic: A Brief Synthesis of the Occupation History of Group E, Xunantunich. *Research Reports in Belizean Archaeology* 8: 209–219.

M. Kathryn Brown, Jason Yaeger, and Bernadette Cap

2016   A Tale of Two Cities: LiDAR Survey and New Discoveries at Xunantunich. *Research Reports in Belizean Archaeology* 13: 51–60.

Brown, Kenneth L.

1980   A Brief Report on Paleoindian-Archaic Occupation in the Quiche Basin, Guatemala. *American Antiquity* 45: 313–324.

Brumfiel, Elizabeth M.

1983   Aztec State Making: Ecology, Structure, and the Origins of State. *American Anthropologist* 85: 261–284.

1994   Factional Competition and Political Development in the New World: An Introduction. In *Factional Competition and Political Development in the New*

World, edited by Elizabeth M. Brumfiel and John M. Fox, pp. 3–13. Cambridge University Press, Cambridge.

Brumfiel, Elizabeth M., and Timothy K. Earle

1987   Specialization, Exchange, and Complex Societies: An Introduction. In *Specialization, Exchange, and Complex Societies,* edited by Elizabeth M. Brumfiel and Timothy K. Earle, pp. 1–9. Cambridge University Press, Cambridge.

Bullen, Ripley P., and William W. Plowden

1963a   Preceramic Archaic Sites in the Highlands of Honduras. *American Antiquity* 28: 382–386.

1963b   Preceramic Archaic Sites in the Central Highlands of Honduras. *XXXV Congreso Internacional de Americanistas, Mexico, 1962. Actas y Memorias. Anales de Antropología* 1: 563–564.

Burns, E. Bradford

1986   *Edward Muybridge in Guatemala, 1875: The Photography as Social Recorder.* University of California Press, Berkeley and Los Angeles.

Buttles, Palma J.

1992   Small Finds in Context: The Preclassic Artifacts of Colha, Belize. Unpublished Master's thesis, Department of Anthropology, University of Texas, Austin.

2002   Material and Meaning: A Contextual Examination of Select Portable Material Culture from Colha, Belize. Unpublished Ph.D. dissertation, Department of Anthropology, University of Texas, Austin.

Callaghan, Michael

2005   Ceramica del Proyecto Arqueolagico Holmul, muestras de 2004 y 2005. In *Investigaciones arqueolagicas en la region de Holmul, Peten, Guatemala. Informe preliminar de la temporada 2005,* edited by Francisco Estrada-Belli, pp. 225–328. Report submitted to the Instituto de Antropoligía e Historia, Guatemala.

Callaghan, Michael G., and Nina Neivens de Estrada

2016   *The Ceramic Sequence of the Holmul Region, Guatemala.* Anthropological Papers of the University of Arizona, No. 77. The University Press of Arizona, Tucson.

Callaghan, Richard T.

2003   Comments on the Mainland Origins of the Preceramic Cultures of the Greater Antilles. *Latin American Antiquity* 14: 323–338.

Campbell, Lyle, and Terrense Kaufman

1976   A Linguistic Look at the Olmec. *American Antiquity* 41: 80–89.

Campbell-Trithart, Melissa J.

1990   Ancient Maya Settlement at Pacbitun, Belize. Unpublished Master's thesis, Department of Anthropology, Trent University, Peterborough.

Carlsen, Robert, and Martin Prechtel

1991   The Flowering of the Dead: An Interpretation of Highland Maya Culture. *Man* 26: 23–42.

Carlson, Lisabeth A.

1993   Strings of Command: Manufacture and Utilization of Shell Beads among the Taino Indians of the West Indies. Unpublished Master's thesis, Department of Anthropology, University of Florida, Gainesville.

Carneiro, Robert L.

1973   Slash-and-Burn Cultivation among the Kuikuru and Its Implications for Cultural Development in the Amazon Basin. In *Peoples and Cultures of Native South America*, edited by Daniel R. Gross, pp. 98–123. Doubleday/The Natural History Press, New York.

1981   The Chiefdom: Precursor of the State. In *The Transition to Statehood in the New World*, edited by Grant D. Jones and Robert R. Kautz, pp. 37–79. Cambridge University Press, Cambridge.

Castellanos, Jeanette E., and Antonia E. Foias

2017   The Earliest Maya Farmers of Petén: New Evidence from Buenavista-Nuevo San José, Central Petén Lakes Region, Guatemala. *Journal of Anthropology*. Electronic document, https//doi.org/10.1155/2017-8109137, accessed August 25, 2017.

Ceballos Gallareta, Teresa

2004   Informe preliminar del estudio de la cerámica preclásica del sitio arqueológico de Ek Balam, Yucatán. In *The 2004 report of Leticia Vargas de la Peña, Directora del Proyecto Ek Balam*. Report submitted to the Instituto Nacional de Antropología e Historia, Mexico.

2005a   *Informe del análisis preliminar de la cerámica del sitio arqueológico 16Qd (7) 152, Fracc. "Villa Magna del Sur" en la Col. Serapio Rendón del Municipio de Mérida.* Report submitted to the Instituto Nacional de Antropología e Historia, Mexico.

2005b   Informe preliminar del estudio de la cerámica del tramo carretero Kancab-Kantemó, Yucatán. In *The 2005 project report of Tomás Gallareta Negrón, Director del proyecto de Salvamento Arqueológico*. Report submitted to the Instituto Nacional de Antropología e Historia, Mexico.

2008a   Informe preliminar del estudio de la cerámica del sitio arqueológico Uitziná Yucatán. In *The 2008 project report of Thelma Sierra Sosa and Agustín Peña Castillo, Co-directores del Proyecto de Prospección Arqueológica del Sitio Uitziná*. Report submitted to the Instituto Nacional de Antropología e Historia, Mexico.

2008b   Informe preliminar del estudio de la cerámica del sitio arqueológico El Ramonal, Yucatán. In *The 2008 project report of Thelma Sierra Sosa and Agustín Peña Castillo, Co-directores del Proyecto de Prospección Arqueológica del Sitio El Ramonal*. Report submitted to the Instituto Nacional de Antropología e Historia, Mexico.

2008c   Informe preliminar del estudio de la cerámica del tramo carretero Catmís-Tigre Grande, Yucatán. In *The 2008 project report of Thelma Sierra Sosa and Agustín Peña Castillo, Co-directores del Proyecto de Salvamento Arqueológico "Tramo carretero Catmís-Tigre Grande."* Report submitted to the Instituto Nacional de Antropología e Historia, Mexico.

2009a   Informe preliminar del estudio de la cerámica del tramo carretero San Diego Buenavista-Pocoboch, Yucatán. In *The 2009 project report of Thelma Sierra Sosa and Agustín Peña Castillo, Co-directores del Proyecto de Salvamento Arqueológico "Tramo carretero San Diego Buenavista-Pocoboch."* Report submitted to the Instituto Nacional de Antropología e Historia, Mexico.

2009b   Informe preliminar del estudio de la cerámica del tramo carretero Muna-Tekax, Yucatán. In *The 2009 project report of Tomás Gallareta Negrón, Director del Proyecto de Salvamento Arqueológico "Tramo carretero Muna-Tekax."* Report submitted to the Instituto Nacional de Antropología e Historia, Mexico.

Ceballos Gallareta, Teresa, and Socorro Jiménez Álvarez
2000   La esfera cerámica Cochuah-Chikin (c. 300–600 dC) de las comarcas prehispánicas de T'Hó (Mérida) e Izamal. *Ichcanzihó* 5 (July/September): 8–9.

Ceballos Gallareta, Teresa, and Fernando Robles Castellanos
2012   Las etapas más tempranas de la alfarería maya en el noroeste de la península de Yucatán. *Ancient Mesoamerica* 23: 403–419.

Ceballos Gallareta, Teresa, Fernando Robles Castellanos, and Nereyda Quiñones Loria
2008   La secuencia cerámica preliminar de los sitios de la reserva territorial de Caucel, municipio de Mérida. In *Informe del proyecto salvamento arqueológico en áreas de crecimiento urbano de la ciudad de Mérida, Yucatán, etapa Ciudad Caucel (2004–2006),* edited by Fernando Robles Castellanos and Joseph Ligorred Perramon. Report submitted to the Instituto Nacional de Antropología e Historia, Mexico.

Ceja Tenorio, Jorge Fausto
1985   *Paso de la Amada: An Early Preclassic Site in the Soconusco, Chiapas, Mexico.* Papers of the New World Archaeological Foundation, No. 49. Brigham Young University, Provo.

Chagnon, Napoleon A.
1968   *Yanomamö: The Fierce People.* Holt, Rinehart and Wintson, New York.

Chase, Arlen F., and Diane Z. Chase
1995   External Impetus, Internal Synthesis, and Standardization: E-Group Assemblages and the Crystallization of Classic Maya Society in the Southern Lowlands. In *The Emergence of Maya Civilization: The Transition from the Preclassic to the Early Classic,* edited by Nikolai Grube, pp. 87–101. Acta Mesoamericana 8. Verlag Anton Saurwein, Markt Schwaben.

Chase, Diane Z., and Arlen F. Chase
1992   *Mesoamerican Elites: An Archaeological Assessment.* University of Oklahoma Press, Norman.

Chatters, James C., Douglass J. Kennett, Yemane Asmerom, Brian M. Kemp, Victor Polyak, Alberto Nava Blank, Patricia A. Beddows, Eduard Reinhardt, Joaquin Arroyo Cabrales, Deborah A. Bolnick, Ripan S. Malhi, Brendan J. Culleton, Pilar Luna Erreguerena, Dominique Rissolo, Shanti Morell-Hart, Thomas W. Stafford Jr.
2014   Late Pleistocene Human Skeleton and mtDNA Link Paleoamericans and Modern Native Americans. *Science* 434: 750–754.

Cheetham, David
1995   Excavations of Structure B-4, Cahal Pech, Belize. In *Belize Valley Preclassic Maya Project: Report of the 1995 Field Season,* edited by Paul F. Healy and Jaime J. Awe, pp. 18–44. Occasional Papers in Anthropology, No. 10. Trent University, Peterborough.
1996   Reconstruction of the Preclassic Period Site Core of Cahal Pech, Belize. In *Belize Valley Preclassic Maya Project: Report of the 1995 Field Season,* edited by

Paul F. Healy and Jaime J. Awe, pp. 1–33. Occasional Papers in Anthropology, No. 12. Trent University, Peterborough.

1998   Interregional Interactions, Symbol Emulation, and the Emergence of Socio-Political Inequality in the Central Maya Lowlands. Unpublished Master's thesis, Department of Anthropology and Sociology, University of British Columbia, Vancouver.

2005   Cunil: A Pre-Mamom Horizon in the Southern Maya Lowlands. In *New Perspectives on Formative Mesoamerican Cultures*, edited by Terry G. Powis, pp. 27–38. BAR International Series 1377. British Archaeological Reports, Oxford.

Cheetham, David, and Jaime J. Awe

1996   The Early Formative Cunil Ceramic Complex at Cahal Pech, Belize. Paper presented at the 64th Annual Meeting of the Society for American Archaeology, New Orleans.

2002   The Cunil Ceramic Complex, Cahal Pech, Belize. Manuscript on file in the Department of Anthropology, Trent University, Peterborough.

Cheetham, David, Donald W. Forsyth, and John E. Clark

2003   La cerámica Pre-Mamom de la cuenca del Río Belice y del centro de Petén: Las correspondencias y sus implicaciones. In *XVI Simposio de investigaciones arqueológicas en Guatemala*, edited by Juan Pedro Laporte, Bárbara Arroyo, Héctor L. Escobedo, and Héctor E. Mejía, pp. 615–634. Museo Nacional de Arqueología e Etnología, Ministerio de Cultura y Deportes, Instituto de Antropología e Historia, and Asociación Tikal, Guatemala City.

Claessen, Henri J. M., and Peter Skalník (editors)

1981   *The Study of the State.* Mouton, The Hague.

Clark, John E.

1988   *The Lithic Artifacts of La Libertad, Chiapas, Mexico: An Economic Perspective.* Papers of the New World Archaeological Foundation, No. 52. Brigham Young University, Provo.

1991   Modern Lacandon Lithic Technology and Blade Workshop. In *Maya Stone Tools: Selected Papers from the Second Maya Lithic Conference*, edited by Thomas R. Hester and Harry J. Shafer, pp. 251–266. Monographs in World Archaeology, No. 1. Prehistory Press, Madison.

1994a   Antecedentes de la cultura olmeca. In *Los olmecas en Mesoamérica*, edited by John E. Clark, pp. 31–41. Citibank, Mexico.

1994b   The Development of Early Formative Rank Societies in the Soconusco, Chiapas, Mexico. Unpublished Ph.D. dissertation, Department of Anthropology, University of Michigan, Ann Arbor.

2001   Mesoamerica's First Kings. Paper delivered at the Maya Meetings held at the University of Texas, Austin.

Clark, John E., and Michael Blake

1994   The Power of Prestige: Competitive Generosity and the Emergence of Rank Societies in Lowland Mesoamerica. In *Factional Competition and Political Development in the New World*, edited by Elizabeth M. Brumfiel and John W. Fox, pp. 17–30. Cambridge University Press, Cambridge.

Clark, John E., and David Cheetham
2002   Mesomerica's Tribal Foundations. In *The Archaeology of Tribal Societies*, edited by William A. Parkinson, pp. 278–339. International Monographs in Prehistory, Ann Arbor.

Clark, John E., and Dennis Gosser
1995   Reinventing Mesoamerica's First Pottery. In *The Emergence of Pottery: Technology and Innovation in Ancient Societies*, edited by William K. Barnet and John W. Hoopes, pp. 209–221. Smithsonian Institution Press, Washington, D.C.

Clark, John E., and Richard D. Hansen
2001   The Architecture of Early Kingship: Comparative Perspectives on the Origins of the Maya Royal Court. In *Royal Courts of the Ancient Maya, Volume 2: Data and Case Studies*, edited by Takeshi Inomata and Stephen D. Houston, pp. 1–45. Westview Press, Boulder.

Clark, John E., Richard D. Hansen, and Tomás Pérez Suárez
2000   La zona maya en el Preclásico. In *Historia Antigua de México*, Vol. 1, edited by Linda Manzanilla and Leonardo López Luján, pp. 436–510. Instituto Nacional de Antropología e Historia, Instituto de Investigaciones Arqueológicas, and Universidad Nacional Autónoma de México, Mexico.

Clark, John E., and Mary E. Pye
2006   The Pacific Coast and the Olmec Question. In *Olmec Art and Archaeology in Mesoamerica*, edited by John E. Clark and Mary E. Pye, pp. 217–251. Yale University Press, New Haven.

Cobos, Raphael
1994   Preliminary Report on the Archaeological Mollusca and Shell Ornaments of Caracol, Belize. In *Studies in the Archaeology of Caracol, Belize*, edited by Diane Z. Chase and Arlen F. Chase, pp. 139–147. Pre-columbian Art Research Institute, San Francisco.

Cochran, Jennifer Lynn
2009   A Diachronic Perspective of Marine Shell Use from Structure B1 at Blackman Eddy, Belize. Unpublished Master's thesis, Department of Anthropology, The University of Texas, Arlington.

Coe, Michael D.
1960   A Fluted Point from Highland Guatemala. *American Antiquity* 25: 412–413.

1966   *An Early Stone Pectoral from Southeastern Mexico*. Studies in Precolumbian Archaeology, No. 1. Dumbarton Oaks Research Library and Collection, Washington, D.C.

1977a   Olmec and Maya: A Study in Relationships. In *The Origins of Maya Civilization*, edited by Richard E. W. Adams, pp. 183–196. University of New Mexico Press, Albuquerque.

1977b   Supernatural Patrons of Maya Scribes and Artists. In *Social Process in Maya Prehistory*, edited by Norman Hammond, pp. 327–347. Academic Press, London.

1978   *Lords of the Underworld: Masterpieces of Classic Maya Ceramics*. Princeton University Press, Princeton.

Coe, Michael D., and Richard A. Diehl

1980   *In the Land of the Olmec. Volume 1. The Archaeology of San Lorenzo Tenochti-tlán.* University of Texas Press, Austin.

Coe, William R.

1957   A Distinctive Artifact Common to Haiti and Central America. *American Antiquity* 22: 280–282.

1965a   Tikal, Guatemala, and Emergent Maya Civilization. *Science* 147: 1401–1419

1965b   Tikal: Ten Years of Study of a Maya Ruin in the Lowlands of Guatemala. *Expedition* 8: 5–56.

1982   *Introduction to the Archaeology of Tikal, Guatemala.* University Museum Monograph. University of Pennsylvania, Philadelphia.

1990   *Excavations in the Great Plaza, North Terrace and North Acropolis of Tikal.* Tikal Report No. 14, Volume II. University Museum Monograph 61. The University Museum, University of Pennsylvania, Philadelphia.

Cohodas, Marvin

1975   The Symbolism and Ritual Function of the Middle Classic Ball Game in Mesoamerica. *American Indian Quarterly* 11: 99–130.

1980   Radial Pyramids and Radial Associated Assemblages of the Central Maya Area. *Journal of the Society of Architectural Historians* 39: 208–223.

1991   Ballgame Imagery of the Maya Lowlands: History and Iconography. In *The Mesoamerican Ballgame*, edited by Vernon L. Scarborough and David R. Wilcox, pp. 251–288. University of Arizona Press, Tuscon.

Coke, James, Eugene C. Perry, and Austin Long

1991   Sea-level Curve. *Nature* 353: 25.

Connor, Judith G.

1975   Ceramics and Artifacts. In *A Study of the Changing Precolombian Commercial Systems*, edited by Jeremy Sabloff and William Rathje, pp. 114–135. Monographs of the Peabody Museum of Archaeology and Ethnology, No. 3. Harvard University, Cambridge, MA.

Crumley, Carole L.

1976   Toward a Locational Definition of State Systems of Settlement. *American Anthropologist* 78: 59–73.

Cruz Alvarado, Wilberth Antonio

2010   Distribución y cronología cerámica de sitios arqueológicos del centro-sur de Yucatán. Unpublished Licenciatura thesis, Department of Anthropological Sciences, Universidad Autónoma de Yucatán, Merida.

Cuevas García, Martha, and Guillermo Bernal Romero

2009   El mar en la creación primordial en Palenque a partir de información iconográfica, epigráfica y arqueológica. Paper presented at XXIII Simposio de investigaciones arqueológicas en Guatemala, Guatemala City.

Culbert, T. Patrick

1977   Early Maya Development at Tikal, Guatemala. In *The Origins of Maya Civilization*, edited by Richard E. W. Adams, pp 27-44. University of New Mexico Press, Alburquerque.

1993   *The Ceramics of Tikal: Vessels from the Burials, Caches and Problematical De-*

posits. Tikal Report No. 25, Part A. University Museum Monograph 81. University Museum, University of Pennsylvania, Philadelphia.

2003   The Ceramics of Tikal. In *Tikal: Dynasties, Foreigners, & Affairs of State*, edited by Jeremy A. Sabloff, pp. 47–81. School of American Research, Santa Fe.

Cyphers Guillén, Ann

1994   San Lorenzo Tenochtitlan. In *Los Olmecas en Mesoamerica*, edited by John E. Clark, pp. 42–67. Equilibrista, Mexico.

1996   Reconstructing Olmec Life at San Lorenzo. In *Olmec Art of Ancient Mexico*, edited by Elizabeth P. Benson, Beatriz de la Fuente, and Marcia Castro-Leal, pp. 60–71. National Gallery of Art, Washington, D.C.

Dahlin, Bruce E.

1984   A Colossus in Guatemala: The Preclassic Maya City of El Mirador. *Archaeology* 37(5): 18–25.

Dalton, George

1977   Aboriginal Economies in Stateless Societies. In *Exchange Systems in Prehistory*, edited by Timothy K. Earle and Jonathon E. Ericson, pp. 191–212. Academic Press, New York.

Dalton, Rex

2005   Skeleton Keys. *Nature* 433: 454–456.

De León, Francisco, and Juan Antonio Valdés

2002   Excavaciones en piedra parada: Más información sobre el Preclásico Medio del Altiplano Central de Guatemala. In *Incidents of Archaeology in Central America and Yucatan, Essays in Honor of Edwin M. Shook,* edited by Michael Love, Marion Popenoe de Hatch, and Héctor L. Escobedo, pp. 375–398. University Press of America, New York.

Deal, Michael

1985   Household Pottery Disposal in the Maya Highlands: An Ethnoarchaeological Interpretation. *Journal of Anthropological Archaeology* 4: 243–291.

Demarest, Arthur A.

1984   La cerámica de El Mirador: Resultados preliminaries y análisis en curso. *Mesoamerica* 7: 53–92.

1989   The Olmec and the Rise of Civilization in Eastern Mesoamerica. In *Regional Perspectives on the Olmec,* edited by Robert J. Sharer and David C. Grove, pp. 303–344. Cambridge University Press, Cambridge.

1992a   Archaeology, Ideology, and the Pre-Columbian Cultural Evolution: The Search for an Approach. In *Ideology and Pre-Columbian Civilizations*, edited by Arthur A. Demarest and Geoffrey Conrad, pp. 1–13. School of American Research Press, Santa Fe.

1992b   Ideology in Ancient Maya Cultural Evolution: The Dynamics of Galactic Polities. In *Ideology and Pre-Columbian Civilizations,* edited by Arthur A. Demarest and Geoffrey Conrad, pp. 135–157. School of American Research Press, Santa Fe.

Demarest, Arthur A., and Goeffrey Conrad (editors)

1992   *Ideology and Pre-Columbian Civilizations.* School of American Research Press, Santa Fe.

Demarest, Arthur A., Prudence M. Rice, and Don S. Rice (editors)
2004   *The Terminal Classic in the Maya Lowlands, Collapse, Transition, and Trans-formation.* University Press of Colorado, Boulder.

DeMarrais, Elizabeth L., Jaime L. Castillo, and Timothy K. Earle
1996   Ideology, Materialization, and Power Strategies. *Current Anthropology* 37: 15–31.

Dietler, Michael
1996   Feasts and Commensal Politics in the Political Economy: Food, Power, and Status in Prehistoric Europe. In *Food and the Status Quest: An Interdisciplinary Perspective*, edited by Polly Wiessner and Wulf Schiefenhovel, pp. 87–126. Berghahn Books, Providence.

Dietler, Michael, and Brian Hayden
2001   Digesting the Feast—Good to Eat, Good to Drink, Good to Think: An Introduction. In *Feasts: Archaeological and Ethnographic Perspectives on Food, Politics, and Power*, edited by Michael Dietler and Brian Hayden, pp. 1–20. Smithsonian Institution Press, Washington, D.C.

Douglas, Mary
1958   Raffia Cloth Distributions in the Lele Economy. *Africa* 28: 109–122.

Doyle, James A.
2012   Regroup on "E-Groups": Monumentality and Early Centers in the Middle Preclassic Maya Lowlands. *Latin American Antiquity* 23: 355–379.

Dreiss, Meredith L.
1982   An Initial Description of Shell Artifacts from Colha, Belize. In *Archaeology at Colha, Belize: The 1981 Interim Report*, edited by Thomas R. Hester, Harry J. Shafer, and Jack D. Eaton, pp. 208–224. Center for Archaeological Research, University of Texas, San Antonio.
1994   The Shell Artifacts of Colha: The 1983 Season. In *Continuing Archaeology at Colha, Belize*, edited by Thomas R. Hester, Harry J. Shafer, and Jack D. Eaton, pp. 181–197. Studies in Archaeology 16. Texas Archeological Research Laboratory, University of Texas, Austin.

Drennan, Richard D.
1976   Religion and Social Evolution in Formative Mesoamerica. In *The Early Meso-american Village*, edited by Kent V. Flannery, pp. 345–368. Academic Press, New York.
1984   Long-Distance Movement of Goods in the Mesoamerican Formative and Classic. *American Antiquity* 49: 27–43.

Drucker, Philip
1946   Preliminary Notes on an Archaeological Survey of the Chiapas Coast. *Middle American Research Records* 1: 151–169. Middle American Research Institute Publication 15. Tulane University, New Orleans.
1951   *The Northern and Central Nootkans Tribes.* Bureau of American Ethnology Bulletin 144. Smithsonian Institution Press, Washington, D.C.
1952   *La Venta, Tabasco: A Study of Olmec Ceramics and Art.* Bureau of American Ethnology Bulletin 153. Smithsonian Institution, Washington, D.C.

Dunning, Nicholas P., Sheryl Luzzadder-Beach, Timothy Beach, John G. Jones, Vernon
Scarborough, and T. Patrick Culbert
2002   Arising from the Bajos: The Evolution of a Neotropical Landscape and the
           Rise of Maya Civilization. *Annals of the Association of American Geographers*
           92: 267–283.

Earle, Timothy
1982   The Ecology and Politics of Primitive Valuables. In *Culture and Ecology:*
           Eclectic Perspectives, edited by John G. Kennedy and Robert B. Edgerton, pp.
           65–85. Special Publication, No. 15. American Anthropological Association,
           Washington, D.C.

Eaton, Jack D.
1974   Shell Celts from Coastal Yucatán, Mexico. *Texas Archaeological Society Bul-*
           letin 45: 197–208.
1978   Archaeological Survey of the Yucatan-Campeche Coast. In *Studies in the Ar-*
           chaeology of Coastal Yucatan and Campeche, Mexico, edited by Jennifer S.
           H. Brown and E. Wyllys Andrews V, pp. 1–67. Middle American Research
           Institute Publication 46. Tulane University, New Orleans.

Ebert, Claire E.
2017   Preclassic Maya Social Complexity and Origins of Inequality at Cahal Belize.
           Unpublished Ph.D. dissertation, Department of Anthropology, Pennsylvania
           State University, State College.

Ebert, Claire E., Kenneth G. Hirth, Casana Popp, Daniel Pierce, Michael Glascock, Sarah
B. McClure, Jaime J. Awe, and Douglas J. Kennett
n.d.   Maya Household Economies and the Origins of Inequality in the Preclassic
           Belize River Valley. Submitted to *Journal of Anthropological Archaeology*.

Ebert, Claire E., Nancy Peniche May, Brendan Culleton, Jaime J. Awe, and Douglas J.
Kennett
2017   A Regional Response to Drought During the Formation and Decline of Pre-
           classic Maya Societies. *Quaternary Science Reviews* 173: 211–235.

Echeverría, Susana, Dalia Paz, and Ángel Góngora
2011   Ocupación en Komchen durante el Clásico Tardío. Paper presented at the III
           Congreso Internacional de Cultura Maya, Merida, Mexico.

Ek, Jerald D.
2013   Patrones de asentamiento y cronología cerámica del período Formativo en
           la cuenca del Río Champotón, Campeche. In *La Costa de Campeche en los*
           tiempos prehispánicos: Una visión 50 años despues, edited by Rafael Cobos
           Palma, pp. 235–256. Universidad Nacional Autónoma de México, Mexico.
2015   Resilience in the Midst of Collapse: A Regional Case Study of Socio-Ecolog-
           ical Dynamics in the Río Champotón Drainage, Campeche, Mexico. Unpub-
           lished Ph.D. dissertation, Department of Anthropology, State University of
           New York, Albany.

Ekholm, Susan
1972   *Power and Prestige: The Rise and Fall of the Congo Kingdom*. Skriv Service,
           Uppsala, Sweden.
1977   External Exchange and the Transformation of Central African Social Systems.

In *The Evolution of Social Systems*, edited by Jonathan Friedman and Michael J. Rowlands, pp. 115–136. University of Pittsburgh Press, Pittsburgh.

Eliade, Mircea
1982   *A History of Religious Ideas, Vol. 2, From Gautama Buddha to the Triumph of Christianity*. University of Chicago Press, Chicago.

Elson, Christina
2011   Diving Ice Age Mexico. *Archaeology* 64(3): 46–49.

Emery, Kitty, and Kazuo Aoyama
2007   Bone, Shell and Lithic Evidence for Crafting in Elite Maya Households at Aguateca, Guatemala. *Ancient Mesoamerica* 18: 69–89.

Engerrand, Jorge
1912   La huella más antigua quizá del hombre en la península de Yucatán. Estudio de la industria de Concepción (Campeche). *Reseña de la segunda sesión, XVII Congreso Internacional de Americanstas* (Mexico, 1910), pp. 89–100. Mexico.

Engerrand, Jorge, and Federico Urbina
1909   Nota preliminar sobre un yacimiento prehistórico ubicado en Concepción (Estado de Campeche) acompañado de un respumen en francés. *Boletín de la Sociedad Geológica Mexicana* 6: 79–87.

Eppich, Keith
2012   Lineage and State at El Perú-Waka': Ceramic and Architectural Perspectives on the Classic Maya Social Dynamic. Unpublished Ph.D. dissertation, Department of Anthropology, Southern Methodist University, Dallas.

Erasmus, Charles
1965   Monument Building: Some Field Experiments. *Southwestern Journal of Anthropology* 21: 277–301.

Escobar, Luisa, and Carlos Alvarado
2004   *Proyecto de Rescate arqueológico Rosario-Naranjo*. Report submitted to Dirección General del Patrimonio Cultural y Natural de Guatemala, Guatemala.

Escobar, Luisa, and Astrid Runggaldier
2002   SB 1B: Excavaciones en la parte posterior de la pirámide de Las Pinturas. In *Proyecto Regional Arqueológico San Bartolo: Informe preliminar No. 1, primera temporada 2002*, edited by Monica Urquizú and William Saturno, pp. 12–13. Report submitted to the Instituto de Antropología e Historia, Guatemala.

Escobedo, Héctor
2002   SB-1: Excavaciones en la pirámide de Las Pinturas. In *Proyecto Regional Arqueológico San Bartolo: Informe preliminar No. 1, primera temporada 2002*, edited by Monica Urquizú and William Saturno, pp. 42–46. Report submitted to the Instituto de Antropología e Historia, Guatemala.

Escobedo, Héctor L., and David A. Freidel (editors)
2007   *Proyecto Arqueológico El Perú-Waka': Informe No. 4, temporada 2006*. Universidad Metodista del Sur, Dallas. Report submitted to the Direccion General del Patrimonio Cultural y Natural de Guatemala.

Esparza Olguin, Octavio Q., and Vania E. Perez Guitierrez
2009   Archaeological and Epigraphic Studies in Pol Box, Quintana Roo. *The PARI Journal* 9(3): 1–16.

Estrada-Belli, Francisco

2006   Lightning Sky, Rain, and the Maize God: The Ideology of Preclassic Maya
            Rulers at Cival, Peten, Guatemala. *Ancient Mesoamerica* 17: 57–78.

2008   *Investigaciones arqueológicas en la región de Holmul, Petén: Holmul, Cival, La
            Sufricaya y K'o.* Report submitted to the Foundation for the Advancement
            of Mesoamerican Studies, Inc. Electronic document, http://www.famsi.org/
            reports/07028es/, accessed August 25, 2017.

2009   *Investigaciones arqueológicas en la región de Holmul, Petén: Holmul y Hamon-
            tun. Informe preliminar de la temporada 2009.* Report submitted to the Insti-
            tuto de Antropología e Historia, Guatemala.

2011   *The First Maya Civilization: Ritual and Power before the Classic Period.* Rout-
            ledge, New York.

Estrada-Belli, Francisco, Jeremy Bauer, Molly Morgan, and Angel Chavez

2003   Symbols of Early Maya kingship at Cival, Peten, Guatemala. Electronic docu-
            ment, http://www.antiquity.ac.uk/projgall/estrada_belli298/, accessed August
            25, 2017.

Fash, William L.

1991   *Scribes, Warriors and Kings: The City of Copán and the Ancient Maya.* Thames
            and Hudson, New York.

1998   Dynastic Architectural Programs: Intention and Design in Classic Maya
            Buildings at Copan and Other Sites. In *Function and Meaning in Classic Maya
            Architecture,* edited by Stephen D. Houston, pp. 223–270. Dumbarton Oaks
            Research Library and Collection, Washington, D.C.

Fauvet-Berthelot, Marie-France

1980   Taille de l'Obsidienne et Fabrication de la Chaux: Deux Exemples de'Activite
            Specialisee a Cauinal. In *Cahiers de la R. C. P 500 2. Rabinal et la Vallée Moy-
            enne du Rio Chixoy, Baja Verapaz, Guatemala.* Centre National de la Recher-
            che Scientifique, Institut d'Ethnologie, Paris.

Fedick, Scott L.

1994   Ancient Maya Agricultural Terracing in the Upper Belize River Area: Com-
            puter-aided Modeling and the Results of Initial Field Investigations. *Ancient
            Mesoamerica* 5: 107–127.

Feinman, Gary M.

1999   Rethinking our Assumptions: Economic Specialization at the Household
            Scale in Ancient Ejutla, Oaxaca, Mexico. In *Pottery and People: A Dynamic
            Interaction,* edited by James M. Skibo and Gary M. Feinman, pp. 81–98. Uni-
            versity of Utah Press, Salt Lake City.

Feinman, Gary M., and Joyce Marcus (editors)

1998   *Archaic States.* School of American Research Press, Santa Fe.

Feinman, Gary M., and Linda M. Nichols

2000   High-Intensity Household-Scale Production in Ancient Mesoamerica: A
            Perspective from Ejutla, Oaxaca. In *Cultural Evolution: Contemporary View-
            points,* edited by Gary M. Feinman and Linda Manzanilla, pp. 119–142. Klu-
            wer Academic/Plenum Publishers, New York.

Feldman, L. H.

2001   Nakbe Shell Species. Unpublished manuscript on file with the Foundation for
            Anthropological Research and Environmental Studies, Idaho.

Ferguson, Jocelyn

1995   Jewels among the Thorns: An Examination of the Modified Shell Artifacts
            from Zubin, Cayo District, Belize. In *Belize Valley Archaeological Recon-*
            naissance Project: Progress Report of the 1994 Field Season, edited by Gyles
            Iannone and James M. Conlon, pp. 152–171. Institute of Archaeology, Lon-
            don.

Ferguson, Jocelyn, Tina Christensen, and Sonya Schwake

1996   The Eastern Ballcourt, Cahal Pech, Belize: 1995 Excavations. In *Trent Univer-*
            sity Occasional Papers in Anthropology: Report of the 1995 Field Season, edited
            by Paul F. Healy and Jaime J. Awe, pp. 34–58. Occasional Papers in Anthro-
            pology, No. 12. Trent University, Peterborough.

Fields, Virginia M.

1989   Origins of Divine Kingship among the Lowland Classic Maya. Unpublished
            Ph.D. dissertation, Department of Anthropology, University of Texas, Austin.

1991   The Iconographic Heritage of the Maya Jester God. In *Sixth Palenque Round*
            Table, 1986, edited by Virginia M. Fields, pp. 167–174. University of Oklahoma
            Press, Norman.

Fields, Virginia M., and Dorie Reents-Budet

2005a   Introduction: The First Sacred Kings of Mesoamerica. In *Lords of Creation:*
            The Origins of Sacred Maya Kingship, edited by Virginia M. Fields and Dorie
            Reents-Budet, pp. 21–26. Scala, London.

2005b   *Lords of Creation: The Origins of Sacred Maya Kingship*. Scala, London.

Filoy Nadal, Laura

2001   Rubber and Rubber Balls in Mesoamerica. In *The Sport of Life and Death: The*
            Mesoamerican Ballgame, edited by E. Michael Whittington, pp. 21–31. Thames
            and Hudson, London.

Flannery, Kent V.

1972   The Cultural Evolution of Civilization. *Annual Review of Ecology and System-*
            atics 3: 399–426.

1976   Research Strategy and Formative Mesoamerica. In *The Early Mesoamerican*
            Village, edited by Kent V. Flannery, pp. 1–12. Academic Press, New York.

1999   Process and Agency in Early State Formation. *Cambridge Archaeological Jour-*
            nal 9: 3–21.

Flannery, Kent V., and Joyce Marcus

1994   *Early Formative Pottery of the Valley of Oaxaca, Mexico*. Memoirs of the Mu-
            seum of Anthropology, University of Michigan, No. 27. Ann Arbor.

Flannery, Kent V., and Marcus C. Winter

1976   Analyzing Household Activities. In *The Early Mesoamerican Village*, edited by
            Kent V. Flannery, pp. 34–47. Academic Press, New York.

Florescano, Enrique

2005   Preface. In *Lords of Creation: The Origins of Sacred Maya Kingship*, edited by
            Virginia M. Fields and Dorie Reents-Budet, pp. 17–19. Scala, London.

Folan, William J., Joel D. Gunn, and María del Rosario Domínguez Carrasco
2001   Triadic Temples, Central Plazas and Dynastic Palaces: A Diachronic Analysis
            of the Royal Court Complex. In *Royal Courts of the Ancient Maya, Volume 2:
            Data and Case Studies*, edited by Takeshi Inomata and Stephen D. Houston,
            pp. 223–265. Westview Press, Oxford.
Folan, William J., and Silverio Gallegos Osuna
1992   Uso prehispanico del suelo. In *Programa de Manejo Reserva de la Biosfera
            Calakmul, Campeche*, edited by William J. Folan, José Manuel Garcia Ortega,
            and María Consuelo Sánchez González, pp. 85–88. Centro de Investigacio-
            nes Historicas y Sociales, Universidad Autónoma de Campeche, Campeche,
            Mexico.
1996   El uso del suelo del sitio arqueológico de Calakmul, Campeche. *Yum Kaax*
            2(3): 7–8. Boletin de Información Ecológica de la Universidad Autónoma de
            Campeche, Campeche, Mexico.
Forsyth, Donald W.
1983   *Investigations at Edzna, Campeche, Mexico. Vol. 2. Ceramics*. Papers of The
            New World Archaeological Foundation, No. 46. Brigham Young University,
            Provo.
1989   *The Ceramics of El Mirador, Peten, Guatemala*. Papers of the New World Ar-
            chaeological Foundation, No. 63. Brigham Young University, Provo.
1992   Un estudio comparativo de la cerámica temprana de Nakbe. In *IV Simposio de
            arqueología Guatemalteca*, edited by Juan Pedro Laporte, Hector L. Escobedo,
            Sandra V. de Brady, pp. 45–56. Museo Nacional de Arqueología y Etnología,
            Ministerio de Cultura y Deportes, Instituto de Antropología e Historia, and
            Asociación Tikal, Guatemala City.
1993a   La ceramica arqueologica de Nakbe y El Mirador, Petén. In *III Simposio de
            arqueología Guatemalteca*, edited by Juan Pedro Laporte, Héctor L. Escobedo,
            Sandra V. de Brady, pp. 111–140. Museo Nacional de Arqueología y Etnología,
            Ministerio de Cultura y Deportes, Instituto de Antropología e Historia, and
            Asociación Tikal, Guatemala City.
1993b   The Ceramic Sequence at Nakbe, Guatemala. *Ancient Mesoamerica* 4: 31–53.
Forsyth, Donald W., and Richard D. Hansen
2007   La cerámica de la cuenca del Mirador. Paper presented at the VII Congreso
            Internacional de Mayistas. Origenes, memoria y lealtad de los pueblos ma-
            yas. Centro de Estudios Mayas, Universidad Nacional Autónoma de México,
            Merida.
Foster, George M.
1942   *A Primitive Mexican Economy*. Monographs of the American Ethnological
            Society. J. J. Augustin, New York.
Freidel, David A.
1979   Culture Areas and Interaction Spheres: Contrasting Approaches to the Emer-
            gence of Civilization in the Maya Lowlands. *American Antiquity* 44: 36–54.
1981   Civilization as a State of Mind: The Cultural Evolution of the Lowland Maya.
            In *The Transition to Statehood in the New World*, edited by Grant D. Jones and
            Robert Kautz, pp. 188–227. Cambridge University Press, Cambridge.

1983   Political Systems in Lowland Yucatan: Dynamics and Structure in Maya Settlement. In *Prehistoric Settlement Patterns: Essays in Honor of Gordon R. Willey*, edited by Evon Z. Vogt and Richard M. Leventhal, pp. 375–386. University of New Mexico Press, Albuquerque.

1985   Polychrome Facades of the Lowland Maya Preclassic. In *Painted Architecture and Polychrome Monumental Sculpture in Mesoamerica*, edited by Elizabeth H. Boone, pp. 5–30. Dumbarton Oaks Research Library and Collection, Washington, D.C.

1986   The Monumental Architecture. In *Archaeology at Cerros, Belice, Central America, Vol. I: An Interim Report*, edited by Robin A. Robertson and David A. Freidel, pp. 1–22. Southern Methodist University Press, Dallas.

1991   The Jester God: The Beginning and End of a Maya Royal Symbol. In *Vision and Revision in Maya Studies*, edited by Flora Clancy and Peter D. Harrison, pp. 67–78. University of New Mexico Press, Albuquerque.

1992   The Trees of Life: *Ahua* as Idea and Artifact in Classic Lowland Maya Civilization. In *Ideology and Pre-Columbian Civilizations*, edited by Arthur A. Demarest and Geoffrey Conrad, pp. 115–134. School of American Research Press, Santa Fe.

2000   Mystery of the Maya Façade. *Archaeology* 53(5): 24–28.

2005   The Creation Mountains: Structure 5C–2nd and Late Preclassic Kingship. In *Lords of Creation: The Origins of Sacred Maya Kingship*, edited by Virginia M. Fields and Dorie Reents-Budet. Scala, London.

2008   Maya Divine Kingship. In *Religion and Power: Divine Kingship in the Ancient World and Beyond*, edited by Nicole Brisch, pp. 191–206. Oriental Institute Seminars Number 4. The Oriental Institute of the University of Chicago, Chicago.

Freidel, David A., Carlos R. Chiriboga, and Mary Jane Acuña
2015   Inland Ports in Northwestern Petén, Guatemala: A Preliminary Assessment. Paper resented at the 80th Annual Meeting of the Society for American Archaeology, San Francisco.

Freidel, David A., and Maynard B. Cliff
1978   Energy Investment in Late Postclassic Maya Masonry Religious Structures. In *Papers on the Economy and Architecture of the Ancient Maya*, edited by Raymond V. Sidrys, pp. 184–208. University of California, Los Angeles.

Freidel, David A., Kathryn Reese-Taylor, and David Mora-Marín
2002   The Origins of Maya Civilization: The Old Shell Game, Commodity, Treasure, and Kingship. In *Ancient Maya Political Economies*, edited by Marilyn A. Masson and David A. Freidel, pp. 41–86. AltaMira, New York.

Freidel, David A., and F. Kent Reilly III
2010   The Flesh of God: Cosmology, Food, and the Origins of Political Power in Southeastern Mesoamerica. In *Pre-Columbian Foodways: Interdisciplinary Approaches to Food, Culture, and Markets in Mesoamerica*, edited by John E. Staller and Michael D. Carrasco. Springer, New York.

Freidel, David A., and Linda Schele
1988a   Kingship in the Late Preclassic Maya Lowlands: The Instruments and Places of Ritual Power. *American Anthropologist* 90: 547–567.

1988b   Symbol and Power: A History of the Lowland Maya Cosmogram. In *Maya Iconography*, edited by Elizabeth P. Benson and Gillett Griffin, pp. 44–93. Princeton University Press, Princeton.

Freidel, David A., Linda Schele, and Joy Parker

1993   *Maya Cosmos: Three Thousand Years on the Shaman's Path*. William Morrow, New York.

Freidel, David A., and Charles K. Suhler

1998   Visiones serpentinas y laberintos mayas. *Arqueología Mexicana* 6(34): 28–37.

1999a   Crown of Creation, The Development of the Maya Royal Diadems in the Late Prelassic and Early Classic Periods. In *The Emergence of Lowland Maya Civilization, The Transition from the Preclassic to the Early Classic*, edited by Nikolai Grube, pp. 137–150. Acta Mesoamericana, Vol. 8. Verlag Anton Saurwein, Markt Schwaben.

1999b   The Path of Life: Towards a Functional Analysis of Ancient Maya Architecture. In *Mesoamerican Architecture as a Cultural Symbol*, edited by Jeff K. Kowalski, pp. 250–275. Oxford University Press, Oxford.

David A. Freidel, Charles K. Suhler, George J. Bey III, F. Kent Reilly III, Travis W. Stanton, Tara Bond-Freeman, and Fernando Robles Castellanos

n.d.   Early Royal Accession Platforms at Yaxuna, Yucatán, Mexico: Possible Evidence of Direct Olmec-Maya Political Interaction. Manuscript prepared for *The Coming of Kings: A Reflection on the Early Periods in Maya Area*, edited by M. Kathryn Brown and Travis W. Stanton. University Press of Colorado, Boulder.

Freiwald, Carolyn

2008   Preliminary Report on the Faunal Analysis from the 2002 Operation 20i Problematic Deposit. Manuscript on file at the University of Texas at San Antonio.

Gagliardi, Susan E.

2015   *Sefundo Unbound: Dynamics of Art and Identity in West Africa*. Cleveland Museum of Art, Cleveland.

Gallareta Negrón, Tomás (editor)

2003   *Investigaciones arqueológicas y restauración arquitectónica en Labná, Yucatán, México. La temporada de campo 2002*. Report submitted to the Instituto Nacional de Antropología e Historia, Mexico.

2004   *Proyecto Xocnacéh. Informe de actividades y resultados alcanzados hasta mayo de 2004*. Report submitted to the Instituto Nacional de Antropología e Historia, Mexico.

2005   *Proyecto Arqueológico Xocnaceh. Segunda temporada de campo*. Report submitted to the Instituto Nacional de Antropología e Historia, Mexico.

Gallareta Negrón, Tomás, George J. Bey III, and William M. Ringle

2003   *Investigaciones arqueológicas en las ruinas de Kiuic y la zona Labná-Kiuic, distrito de Bolonchén, Yucatán, México*. Report submitted to the Instituto Nacional de Antropología e Historia, Mexico.

Gallareta Negrón, Tomás, and Rossana May Ciau
2007   *Proyecto Arqueológico Xocnaceh, tercera temporada de campo.* Report submitted to the Instituto Nacional de Antropología e Historia, Mexico.

Gallareta Negrón, Tomás, and William M. Ringle
2004   The Earliest Occupation of the Puuc Region, Yucatan, Mexico: New Perspectives from Xocnaceh and Paso del Macho. Paper presented at the 103rd Annual Meeting of the American Anthropological Association, Atlanta.

Gallareta Negrón, Tomás, William M. Ringle, Rossana May Ciau, Juluieta Ramos Pacheco, and Ramón Carrillo Sánchez
2005   Evidencias de ocupación durante el período Preclásico en el Puuc: Xocnacéh y Paso del Macho. Paper presented at the Segundo Congreso Internacional de Cultural Maya, Mérida.

Gann, Thomas W. F.
1925   *Mystery Cities: Exploration and Adventure in Lubaantun.* Duckworth, London.

Garber, James F.
1983   Patterns of Jade Consumption and Disposal at Cerros, Northern Belize. *American Antiquity* 48: 800–807.
1989   *Archaeology at Cerros, Belize, Central America: Volume 2, The Artifacts.* David A. Freidel, series editor. Southern Methodist University Press, Dallas.

Garber, James F., and Jaime J. Awe
2008   Middle Formative Architecture and Ritual at Cahal Pech. *Research Reports in Belizean Archaeology* 4: 185–190.
2009   A Terminal Early Formative Symbol System in the Maya Lowlands: The Iconography of the Cunil Phase (1100–900 BC) at Cahal Pech. *Research Reports in Belizean Archaeology* 6: 151–159.

Garber, James F., M. Kathryn Brown, Jaime J. Awe, and Christopher J. Hartman
2004   Middle Formative Prehistory of the Central Belize Valley: An Examination of the Architecture, Material Culture, and Sociopolitical Change at Blackman Eddy. In *The Ancient Maya of the Belize Valley: Half a Century of Archaeological Research*, edited by James F. Garber, pp. 25–47. University Press of Florida, Gainesville.

Garber, James F., M. Kathryn Brown, W. David Driver, David M. Glassman, Christopher J. Hartman, F. Kent Reilly III, and Lauren A. Sullivan
2004   Archaeological Investigations at Blackman Eddy. In *The Ancient Maya of the Belize Valley: Half a Century of Archaeological Research*, edited by James F. Garber, pp. 48–69. University Press of Florida, Gainesville.

Garber, James F., Jennifer Cochran, and Jaime J. Awe
2005   Excavations in Plaza B at Cahal Pech: The 2004 Field Season. In *The Belize Valley Archaeological Project: Results of the 1997 Field Season*, edited by James F. Garber, pp. 4–41. Report submitted to the Belize Institute of Archaeology, Belmopan.

García-Bárcena, Joaquín
1979   *Una punta acanalada de la Cueva de los Grifos, Ocozocuautla, Chiapas.* Cuadernos de Trabajo, No. 17. Departamento de Prehistoria, Instituto Nacional de Antropología e Historia, Mexico.

1982 *El precerámico de Aguacatenango, Chiapas, México.* Colección Científica, No. 110. Instituto Nacional de Antropología e Historia, Mexico.

García-Bárcena, Joaquín, and Diana Santamaría Estevéz
1982 *La cueva de Santa Marta, Ocozocuautla, Chiapas. Estratigrafía, cronología y cerámica.* Colección Científica, No. 3. Instituto Nacional de Antropología e Historia, Mexico.

García-Bárcena, Joaquín, Diana Santamaría Estevéz, Ticul Alvarez, Manuel Reyes Cortés, and Fernando Sánchez Martínez
1976 *Excavaciones en el Abrigo de Santa Marta, Chiapas. (1974).* Informes, No. I. Departamento de Prehistoria, Instituto Nacional de Antropología e Historia, Mexico.

Garza Tarazona de González, Silvia, and Edward B. Kurjack
1980 *Atlas arqueológico del estado de Yucatán.* Instituto Nacional de Antropología e Historia, Mexico.

Geertz, Clifford
1980 *Negara: The Theatre State in Nineteenth-Century Bali.* Princeton University Press, Princeton.

Gifford, James C.
1976 *Prehistoric Pottery Analysis and the Ceramics of Barton Ramie in the Belize Valley.* Memoirs of the Peabody Museum of Archaeology and Ethnology, Vol. 18. Harvard University, Cambridge.

Giron-Abrego, Mario
2012 An Early Example of the Logogram TZUTZ at San Bartolo. *Wayeb Notes*, No. 42. Electronic document, http://www.wayeb.org/notes/wayeb_notes0042.pdf, accessed August 25, 2017.
2013 A Late Preclassic Distance Number. *PARI* 13(4): 8–12.
2015 On a Preclassic Long-Lipped Glyphic Profile. Electronic document, http://www.mesoweb.com/articles/giron-abrego/Giron-Abrego2015.pdf, accessed August 25, 2017.

Glover, Jeffrey, and Fabio Esteban Amador II
2005 Recent Research in the Yalahau Region: Methodological Concerns and Preliminary Results of a Regional Survey. In *Quintana Roo Archaeology*, edited by Justine Shaw and Jennifer P. Mathews, pp. 51–65. University of Arizona Press, Tuscon.

Glover, Jeffrey, and Travis W. Stanton
2007 The Long Road to the Classic: Assessing the Role of Preclassic Traditions in the Formation of Early Classic Yucatec Cultures. Paper presented at the 72nd Annual Meeting of the Society for American Archaeology, Austin.

Golden, Charles, and Andrew K. Scherer
2014 Territory, Trust, Growth and Collapse in Classic Maya Kingdoms. *Current Anthropology* 54: 397–435.

González, Silvia, David Huddart, and Matthew Bennett
2006 Valsequillo Pleistocene Archaeology and Dating: Ongoing Controversy in Central Mexico. *World Archaeology* 38: 611–627.

González Crespo, Norberto

2000   Henry Mercer. In *Arqueología, historia y antropología: In memoriam, José Luis Lorenzo Bautista,* edited by Jaime Litvak King and Lorena Mirambell, pp. 79–83. Colección Científica, No. 415. Instituto Nacional de Antropología e Historia, Mexico.

González González, Arturo H., Carmen Rojas Sandoval, Octavio del Río Lara, and Pilar Luna Erreguerena

2003   Submerged Prehistoric Caves in Quintana Roo, Mexico: Study of the Early Inhabitants through Underwater Archaeology. Paper presented at the Fifth World Archaeological Conference, Washington, D.C.

González González, Arturo H., and Carmen Rojas Sandoval

2004   Evidencias de poblamiento temprano en la Península de Yucatán localizadas en cuevas sumergidas de Quintana Roo, México. Paper presented at the II Simposio Internacional del Hombre Temprano en América. Museo Nacional de Antropología, Mexico.

González González, Arturo H., Carmen Rojas Sandoval, Alejandro Terrazas Mata, Martha Benavente Sanvicente, Wolfgang Stinnesbeck, Jeronimo Avilés Olguin, Magdalena de los Ríos, and Eugenio Acevez

2008   The Arrival of Humans on the Yucatan Peninsula: Evidence from Submerged Caves in the State of Quintana Roo, Mexico. *Current Research in the Pleistocene* 25: 1–24.

González González, Arturo H., Carmen Rojas Sandoval, Eugenio Acevez Núñez, Jerónimo Avilés Olguín, Santiago Analco Ramírez, Octavio del Río Lara, Pilar Luna Erreguerena, Adriana Velázquez Morlet, Wolfgang Stinnesbeck, Alejandro Terrazas Mata, and Martha Benavente Sanvicente

2008   Evidence of Early Inhabitants of Submerged Caves in Yucatan, Mexico. In *Underwater and Maritime Archaeology in Latin America and the Caribbean,* edited by Margaret E. Leshikar-Denton and Pilar Luna Erreguerena, pp. 127–142. Left Coast Press, Walnut Creek.

González Lauck, Rebecca B.

2000   La zona del Golfo en el Preclásico: La etapa olmeca. In *Historia Antigua de México,* Vol. 1, edited by Linda Manzanilla and Leonardo López Luján, pp. 363–406. Instituto Nacional de Antropología e Historia, Instituto de Investigaciones Arqueológicas, and Universidad Nacional Autónoma de México, Mexico.

González Licón, Ernesto

1986   *Los mayas de la Gruta de Loltún, Yucatán, a través de sus materiales arqueológicos.* Colección Científica, No. 149. Instituto Nacional de Antropología e Historia, Mexico.

Goubaud Carrera, Antonio

1964   *Indigenismo en Guatemala.* Seminario de Integración Social, Publication 14. José de Pineda Ibarra, general editor. Ministerio de Educación, Guatemala.

Graham, Ian

1967   *Archaeological Explorations in El Peten, Guatemala.* Middle American Research Institute Publication 33. Tulane University, New Orleans.

Green, Stanton W., and Stephen M. Perlman
1985   Frontiers, Boundaries, and Open Social Systems. In *The Archaeology of Fron-
            tiers and Boundaries*, edited by Stanton W. Green and Stephen M. Perlman,
            pp. 3–13. Academic Press, New York.
Griffith, Cameron, Reiko Ishihara, and Sarah Jack
2002   Report on the 3rd Year of Archaeological Investigations in Actun Halal. In
            The Western Belize Regional Cave Project: A Report of the 2001 Field Season,
            edited by Jaime J. Awe, pp. 27–50. Occasional Paper, No. 5. University of New
            Hampshire Department of Anthropology, Durham.
Grove, David C.
1981   The Formative Period and the Evolution of Complex Culture. In *Supplement
            of the Handbook of Middle American Indians. Volume 1: Archaeology*, edited
            by Victoria R. Bricker and Jeremy A. Sabloff, pp. 373–391. University of Texas
            Press, Austin.
1989   Chalcatzingo and its Olmec Connection. In *Regional Perspectives on the Ol-
            mec*, edited by Robert J. Sharer and David C. Grove, pp. 122–147. Cambridge
            University Press, Cambridge.
1997   Olmec Archaeology: A Half Century of Research and Its Accomplishments.
            Journal of World Prehistory 11: 51–101.
2000   La zona del Altiplano central en el Preclásico. *Historia Antigua de México*,
            Vol. 1, edited by Linda Manzanilla and Leonardo López Luján, pp. 363–406.
            Instituto Nacional de Antropología e Historia, Instituto de Investigaciones
            Archqueologicas, and Universidad Nacional Autónoma de México, Mexico.
Grove, David C., and Ann Cyphers Guillén
1987   The Excavations. In *Ancient Chalcatzingo*, edited by David C. Grove, pp. 21–
            55. University of Texas Press, Austin.
Grube, Nikolai
2005   Toponyms, Emblem Glyphs, and the Political Geography of Southern
            Campeche. *Anthropological Notebooks* 11: 89–102.
Grube, Nikolai, Alfonso Lacadena, and Simon Martin
2003   *Notebook for the XXVIIth Maya Hieroglyphic Forum at Texas, Chichen Itza
            and Ek Balam: Terminal Classic Inscriptions from Yucatan*. University of Tex-
            as, Department of Art and Art History, Austin.
Gruhn, Ruth, and Allan L. Bryan
1976   An Archaeological Survey of the Chichicastenango Area of Highland Guate-
            mala. *Cerámica de Cultura Maya* 9: 75–119.
1977   Los Tapiales: A Paleo-American Campsite in the Guatemala Highlands. *Pro-
            ceedings of the American Philosophical Society* 121: 235–273.
Guderjan, Thomas H., and James F. Garber
1995   *Maya Maritime Trade, Settlement, and Populations on Ambergris Caye, Belize*.
            Labyrinthos, Lancaster.
Guenter, Stanley P.
2005   Informe Preliminar de la Epigrafia de El Perú. In *Proyecto Arqueologico El
            Perú-Waka' Informe No. 2, temporada 2004*, edited by Héctor L. Escobedo and

David A. Freidel, pp. 364–399. Report submitted to the Instituto de Antropología e Historia, Guatemala.

Guernsey, Julia

2006a   Late Formative Period Antecedents for Ritually Bound Monuments. In *Sacred Bundles*, edited by Julia Guernsey and F. Kent Reilly III, pp. 22–39. Boundary End Archaeology Research Center, Barnardsville.

2006b   *Ritual and Power in Stone: The Performance of Rulership in Mesoamerican Izapan Style Art*. University of Texas Press, Austin.

Guernsey, Julia, and F. Kent Reilly III

2006   Introduction. In *Sacred Bundles: Ritual Acts of Wrapping and Binding in Mesoamerica*, edited by Julia Guernsey and F. Kent Reilly III, pp. v–xviii. Boundary End Archaeological Research Center, Barnardsville.

Guthrie, Jill and Elizabeth P. Benson (editors)

1996   *The Olmec World: Ritual and Rulership*. The Art Museum, Princeton University, Princeton.

Haines, Helen R.

1997   Continuing Excavations of Preclassic Deposits at Structure 9. In *The Blue Creek Project: Working Papers from the 1996 Field Season*, edited by W. David Driver, Heather L. Clagett, and Helen R. Haines, pp. 19–24. Manuscript on file with the Maya Research Program, St. Mary's University, San Antonio.

Hammond, Norman (editor)

1991   *Cuello: An Early Maya Community in Belize*. Cambridge University Press, Cambridge.

Hammond, Norman

1985   *Nohmul, A Prehistoric Maya Community in Belize: Excavations, 1973–1983*. BAR International Series 250. British Archaeological Reports, Oxford.

1986   New Light on the Most Ancient Maya. *Man* 21: 399–413.

1991a   Ceramic, Bone, Shell, and Ground Stone Artifacts. In *Cuello: An Early Maya Community in Belize*, edited by Norman Hammond, pp. 176–191. Cambridge University Press, Cambridge.

1991b   Precious Stone of Grace. *Natural History* 100(8): 8.

1999   The Genesis of Hierarchy: Mortuary and Offertory Ritual in the Pre-Classic at Cuello, Belize. In *Social Patterns in Pre-Classic Mesoamerica*, edited by David C. Grove and Rosemary A. Joyce, pp. 49–66. Dumbarton Oaks Research Library and Collection, Washington, D.C.

Hammond, Norman, and Jeremy R. Bauer

2001   Preclassic Maya Sweatbath at Cuello, Belize. *Antiquity* 75: 683–684.

Hammond, Norman, Duncan Pring, Richard Wilk, Sara Donaghey, Frank P. Saul, Elizabeth Wing, Arlene V. Miller, and Lawrence R. Feldman

1979   The Earliest Lowland Maya? Definition of the Swasey Phase. *American Antiquity* 44: 117–135.

Hanks, William F.

1990   *Referential Practice: Language and Lived Space among the Maya*. University of Chicago Press, Chicago.

Hansen, Eric F.
2000   Ancient Maya Burnt Lime Technology: Cultural Implications of Techno-
            logical Styles. Unpublished Ph.D. dissertation, Department of Anthropology,
            University of California, Los Angeles.
Hansen, Eric F., Richard D. Hansen, and Michele F. Derrick
1995   Los análisis de los estucos y pinturas arquitectónicas de Nakbe: Resultados
            preliminares de los estudios de los métodos y materiales de producción. In
            VIII Simposio de investigaciones arqueológicas en Guatemala, edited by Juan
            Pedro Laporte, and Hector L. Escobedo, pp. 543–560. Museo Nacional de Ar-
            queología y Etnología, Ministerio de Cultura y Deportes, Instituto de Antro-
            pología e Historia, and Asociación Tikal, Guatemala City.
Hansen, Eric F., Carlos Rodriguez-Navarro, and Richard D. Hansen
1997   Incipient Maya Burnt-Lime Technology: Characterization and Chronologi-
            cal Variations in Preclassic Plaster, Stucco, and Mortar at Nakbe, Guatemala.
            In Materials Issues in Art and Archaeology V, edited by Pamela B. Vandiver,
            James R. Druzik, John F. Merkel, and John Stewart, pp. 207–216. Materials
            Research Society, Vol. 462, Pittsburgh.
Hansen, Eric F., Arie Wallert, and Michele R. Derrick
1997   An Organic Colorant Used in Painted Ancient Maya Architectural Sculpture
            at Nakbe, Peten, Guatemala. In Materials Issues in Art and Archaeology V,
            edited by Pamela B. Vandiver, James R. Druzik, John F. Merkel, and John
            Stewart, pp. 287–300. Materials Research Society, Vol. 462, Pittsburgh.
Hansen, Richard D.
1984   Excavations on Structure 34 and the Tigre Area, El Mirador, Peten, Guate-
            mala: A New Look at the Preclassic Lowland Maya. Unpublished Master's
            thesis, Department of Anthropology, Brigham Young University, Provo.
1990   Excavations in the Tigre Complex, El Mirador, Petén, Guatemala. Papers of the
            New World Archaeological Foundation, No. 62. Brigham Young University,
            Provo.
1991   Road to Nakbe. Natural History 5(1): 8–14.
1992a   The Archaeology of Ideology: A Study of Maya Preclassic Architectural
            Sculpture at Nakbe, Peten, Guatemala. Unpublished Ph.D. dissertation, De-
            partment of Anthropology, University of California, Los Angeles.
1992b   El proceso cultural de Nakbe y el area del Petén Nor-Central: Las epocas
            tempranas. In V Simposio de investigaciones arqueológicas en Guatemala, ed-
            ited by Juan Pedro Laporte, Héctor L. Escobedo, and Sandra V. de Brady, pp.
            81–96. Museo Nacional de Arqueología y Etnología, Ministerio de Cultura y
            Deportes, Instituto de Antropología e Historia, and Asociación Tikal, Guate-
            mala City.
1992c   Proyecto regional de investigaciones arqueológicas del norte de Petén, Gua-
            temala: Temporada 1990. In IV Simposio de arqueología Guatemalteca, edited
            Juan Pedro Laporte, Héctor L. Escobedo, and Sandra V. de Brady, pp. 1–36.
            Museo Nacional de Arqueología y Etnología, Ministerio de Cultura y Deport-
            es, Instituto de Antropología e Historia, and Asociación Tikal, Guatemala
            City.

1993 Investigaciones arqueologicas en el sitio Nakbe: Los estudios recientes. In *IV Simposio de arqueología Guatemalteca*, edited Juan Pedro Laporte, Héctor L. Escobedo, and Sandra V. de Brady, pp. 115–122. Museo Nacional de Arqueología y Etnología, Ministerio de Cultura y Deportes, Instituto de Antropología e Historia, and Asociación Tikal, Guatemala City.

1994 Investigaciones arqueológicas en Petén, Guatemala: Una mirada diacrónica de los orígines Mayas. In *Campeche Maya Colonial: 450 aniversario de la fundación de Campeche, Mexico*, edited by William J. Folan, pp. 14–54. Universidad Autónoma del Sureste, Campeche, Mexico.

1995 *Early Environmental Impact: The Ecological Consequences of Incipient Maya Settlement*. Report submitted to the National Geographic Society, Washington, D.C.

1998 Continuity and Disjunction: Preclassic Antecedents of Classic Maya Architecture. In *Function and Meaning in Classic Maya Architecture*, edited by Stephen D. Houston, pp. 49–122. Dumbarton Oaks Research Library and Collection, Washington, D.C.

2000 Arquitectura e ideología de los antiguos mayas. In *Memoria de la Segunda Mesa Redonda de Palenque*, edited by Silvia Trejo, pp. 73–108. Consejo Nacional para la Cultura y las Artes and Instituto Nacional de Antropología e Historia, Mexico.

2001 The First Cities: The Beginnings of Urbanization and State Formation in the Maya Lowlands. In *Maya: Divine Kings of the Rain Forest*, edited by Nikolai Grube, pp. 50–65. Konemann Press, Cologne.

2002 Plundering the Peten. In *Secrets of the Maya*, edited by Peter D. Young, pp. 151–153. Hatherligh Press, London.

2005 Perspectives on Olmec-Maya Interaction in the Middle Formative Period. In *New Perspectives on Formative Mesoamerican Cultures*, edited by Terry G. Powis, pp. 51–72. BAR International Series 1377. British Archaeological Reports, Oxford.

2009 Mirador Basin 2008. A Report on the 2008 Field Season. Report on file with the Foundation for Anthropological Research and Environmental Studies, Idaho.

2012a Kingship in the Cradle of Maya Civilization: The Mirador Basin. In *Fanning the Sacred Flame: Mesoamerican Studies in Honor of H. B. Nicholson*, edited by Matthew A. Boxt and Brian D. Dillon, pp. 139–172. University of Colorado Press, Boulder.

2012b The Beginning of the End: Conspicuous Consumption and Environmental Impact of the Preclassic Lowland Maya. In *An Archaeological Legacy: Papers in Honor of Ray T. Matheny*, edited by Joel Janetski, Deanne Gurr, and Glenna Nielson-Grimm, pp. 243–291. Brigham Young University Press, Provo.

2016 Cultural and Environmental Components of the First Maya States: A Perspective from the Central and Southern Maya Lowlands. In *The Origins of Maya States*, edited by Robert J. Sharer and Loa Traxler, pp. 329–416. University of Pennsylvania Press, Philadelphia.

Hansen, Richard D., Beatriz Balcarcel, Edgar Suyuc, Hector E. Mejia, Enrique Hernandez, Gendry Valle, Stanley P. Guenter, and Shannon Novak

2006 Investigaciones arqueológicas en el sitio Tintal, Petén. In *XIX Simposio de investigaciones arqueológicas en Guatemala*, edited by Juan Pedro Laporte, Bárbara Arroyo, Héctor E. Mejia, pp. 683–694. Museo Nacional de Arqueología y Etnología, Ministerio de Cultura y Deportes, Instituto de Antropología e Historia, and Asociación Tikal, Guatemala City.

Hansen, Richard D., and Steven Bozarth, John Jacob, David Wahl, and Thomas Schreiner
2002   Climatic and Environmental Variability in the Rise of Maya Civilization: A Preliminary Perspective from Northern Peten. *Ancient Mesoamerica* 13: 273–296.

Hansen, Richard D., and Donald W. Forsyth
1987   Late Preclassic Development of Unslipped Pottery in the Maya Lowlands: The Evidence from El Mirador. In *Maya Ceramics: Papers of the 1985 Maya Ceramic Conference*, edited by Prudence M. Rice and Robert J. Sharer, pp. 439–468. BAR International Series 345. British Archaeological Reports, Oxford.

Hansen, Richard D., and Stanley P. Guenter
2005   Early Social Complexity and Kingship in the Mirador Basin. In *Lords of Creation: The Origins of Sacred Maya Kingship*, edited by Virginia M. Fields and Dorie Reents-Budet, pp. 60–61. Scala, London.

Hansen, Richard D., Wayne K. Howell, and Stanley P. Guenter
2008   Forgotten Structures, Haunted Houses, and Occupied Hearts: Ancient Perspectives and Contemporary Interpretations of Abandoned Sites and Buildings in the Mirador Basin, Guatemala. In *Ruins of the Past: The Use and Perception of Abandoned Structures in the Maya Lowlands*, edited by Travis W. Stanton and Aline Magnoni, pp. 25–64. University Press of Colorado, Boulder.

Hansen, Richard D., Edgar Suyuc-Ley, and Beatriz Balcarcel
2004   *Investigación, conservación y desarrollo en El Mirador, Petén, Guatemala: Informe final de la temporada 2003.* Report submitted to the Instituto de Antropología e Historia, Guatemala.

Harrison, Peter D.
2001   Thrones and Throne Structures in the Central Acropolis of Tikal as an Expression of the Royal Court. In *Royal Courts of the Ancient Maya, Vol. 2: Data and Case Studies*, edited by Takeshi Inomata and Stephen D. Houston, pp. 74–101. Westview Press, Boulder.

Harrison, Peter D., and Bruce L. Turner (editors)
1978   *Pre-Hispanic Maya Agriculture.* University of New Mexico Press, Albuquerque.

Hather, Jon G., and Norman Hammond
1994   Ancient Maya Subsistence Diversity: Root and Tuber Remains from Cuello, Belize. *Antiquity* 68: 330–335.

Hatt, Robert F., Harvey I. Fischer, Dave A. Langeberbartel, and Geroge W. Brainerd
1953   *Faunal and Archaeological Researches in Yucatan Caves.* Cranbrook Institute of Science, Bulletin No. 33, Bloomfield Hills, Michigan.

Hayden, Brian
1980   A Fluted Point from the Guatemalan Highlands. *Current Anthropology* 21: 702.

1995   Pathways to Power: Principles for Creating Social Inequality. In *Foundations of Social Inequality*, edited by T. Douglas Price and Gary Feinman, pp. 15–85. Plenum Publishers, New York.

1996   Feasting in Prehistoric and Traditional Societies. In *Food and the Status Quest: An Interdisciplinary Perspective*, edited by Polly Wiessner and Wulf Schiefenhovel, pp. 127–148. Berghahn Books, Providence.

1998   Practical and Prestige Technologies: The Evolution of Material Systems. *Journal of Archaeological Method and Theory* 5: 1–55.

2001   Fabulous Feasts: A Prolegomenon to the Importance of Feasting. In *Feasts: Archaeological and Ethnographic Perspectives on Food, Politics, and Power*, edited by Michael Dietler and Brian Hayden, pp. 23–64. Smithsonian Institution Press, Washington D.C.

Hayden, Brian, and Aubrey Cannon
1983   Where the Garbage Goes: Refuse Disposal in the Maya Highlands. *Journal of Anthropological Archaeology* 2: 117–163.

Healy, Paul F.
1984   The Archaeology of Honduras. In *The Archaeology of Lower Central America*, edited by Frederick W. Lange and Doris Z. Stone, pp. 113–161. University of New Mexico Press, Albuquerque.

1988   Music of the Maya. *Archaeology* 41(1): 24–31.

1990a   Excavations at Pacbitun, Belize: Preliminary Report on the 1986 and 1987 Investigations. *Journal of Field Archaeology* 17: 247–262.

1990b   An Early Classic Maya Monument at Pacbitun. *Mexicon* 12: 109–110.

1992   Ancient Maya Ballcourt at Pacbitun, Belize. *Ancient Mesoamerica* 3: 229–293.

1999   Radiocarbon Dates from Pacbitun, Belize: Results from the 1995 Field Season. In *Trent University Occasional Papers in Anthropology*, edited by Paul F. Healy, pp. 69–82. Occasional Papers in Anthropology, No. 13. Trent University, Peterborough.

Healy, Paul F., and Jaime J. Awe (editors)
1995   *Belize Valley Preclassic Maya Project: Report on the 1994 Field Season*. Occasional Papers in Anthropology, No. 10. Trent University, Peterborough.

1996   *Belize Valley Preclassic Maya Project: Report on the 1995 Field Season*. Occasional Papers in Anthropology, No. 12. Trent University, Peterborough.

Healy, Paul F., Jaime J. Awe, Gyles Iannone, and Cassandra Bill
1995   Pacbitun (Belize), and Ancient Maya Use of Slate. *Antiquity* 69: 337–348.

Healy, Paul F., David Cheetham, Terry G. Powis, and Jaime J. Awe
2004   Cahal Pech: The Middle Formative Period. In *The Ancient Maya of the Belize Valley: Half a Century of Archaeological Research*, edited by James F. Garber, pp. 103–124. University Press of Florida, Gainesville.

Healy, Paul F., Kitty Emery, and Lori Wright
1990   Ancient and Modern Maya Exploitation of the Jute Snail (*Pachychilus*). *Latin American Antiquity* 1: 170–183.

Healy, Paul F., Christopher G. B. Helmke, Jaime J. Awe, and Kay S. Sunahara
2007   Survey, Settlement, and Population History at the Ancient Maya Site of Pacbitun, Belize. *Journal of Field Archaeology* 32: 17–39.

Healy, Paul F., Bobbi Hohmann, and Terry G. Powis

2004 The Ancient Maya Center of Pacbitun: 900 B.C. to A.D. 900. In *The Ancient Maya of the Belize Valley: Half a Century of Archaeological Research*, edited by James F. Garber, pp. 207–227. University Press of Florida, Gainesville.

Healy, Paul F., John D. H. Lambert, J. T. Arnason, and Richard J. Hebda

1983 Caracol, Belize: Evidence of Ancient Maya Agricultural Terraces. *Journal of Field Archaeology* 10: 397–410.

Helms, Mary W.

1979 *Ancient Panama: Chiefs in Search of Power*. University of Texas Press, Austin.

1992 Long-Distance Contacts, Elite Aspirations, and the Age of Discovery in Cosmological Context. In *Resources, Power, and Interregional Interaction*, edited by Edward M. Schortman and Patricia A. Urban, pp. 157–174. Plenum Press, New York.

1993 *Craft and the Kingly Ideal: Art, Trade, and Power*. University of Texas Press, Austin.

Henderson, John S.

1997 *The World of the Ancient Maya*. 2nd ed. Cornell University Press, Ithaca.

Hendon, Julia A.

1989 Elite Household Organization at Copan, Honduras: Analysis of Activity Distribution in the Sepulturas Zone. In *Households and Communities: Proceedings of the Twenty-first Annual Conference of the Archaeological Association of the University of Calgary*, edited by Scott MacEachern, David J. W. Archer, and Richard D. Garvin, pp. 371–380. University of Calgary, Alberta.

1999 The Pre-Classic Maya Compound as the Focus of Social Identity. In *Social Patterns in Pre-Classic Mesoamerica*, edited by David C. Grove and Rosemary A. Joyce, pp. 97–125. Dumbarton Oaks Research Library and Collection, Washington, D.C.

2000 Round Structures, Household Identity and Public Performance in Preclassic Maya Society. *Latin American Antiquity* 11: 299–301.

Hernández Hernández, Concepción

2004 *Informe parcial del salvamento arqueológico del sitio 16Qd(7)152 de la Col. Serapio Rendón. Temporada 2003-2004.* Report submitted to the Instituto Nacional de Antropología e Historia, Mexico.

2005 La cerámica del periodo Preclásico tardío (300 a.C.–350 d.C.) en el norte de la península de Yucatán. In *La producción alfarera en el México antiguo, Volumen I*, edited by Beatriz L. Merino Carrión and Ángel García Cook, pp. 753–779. Archaeology Series, No. 484. Instituto Nacional de Antropología e Historia, Mexico.

Hernández Hernández, Concepción, and Teresa Ceballos Gallareta

2006 Los complejos cerámicos del sitio arqueológico Serapio Rendón 16 Qd (7) 152, en el Municipio de Mérida, Yucatán. *Los Investigadores de la Cultura Maya* 14(1): 227–240.

Hester, Thomas R.

1982 The Maya Lithic Sequence in Northern Belize. In *Archaeology at Colha, Belize. The 1981 Interim Report*, edited by Thomas R. Hester, Harry J. Shafer, and Jack D. Eaton, pp. 39–59. Center for Archaeological Research, University of Texas at San Antonio.

Hester, Thomas R., Thomas C. Kelly, and Giancarlo Ligabue

1981   *A Fluted Paleo-American Projectile Point from Belize, Central America.* Colha Project Working Paper # 1, Center for Archaeological Research, San Antonio.

Hester, Thomas R., Harry J. Shafer, Thomas C. Kelly, and Giancarlo Ligabue

1982   Observations on the Patination Process and the Context of Antiquity: A Fluted Point from Belize, Central America. *Lithic Technology* 11(2): 29–34.

Hester, Thomas R., Harry B. Iceland, Dale B. Hudler, and Harry J. Shafer

1996   The Colha Preceramic Project: Preliminary Results from the 1993–1995 Field Seasons. *Mexicon* 18: 45–50.

Hill, Warren D., Michael Blake, and John E. Clark

1998   Ball Court Design Dates Back 3,400 Years. *Nature* 392: 878–879.

Hill, Warren D., and John E. Clark

2001   Sports, Gambling, and Government: America's First Social Compact? *American Anthropologist* 103: 331–345.

Hirth, Kenneth G.

1992   Interregional Exchange as Elite Behavior. In *Mesoamerican Elites: An Archaeological Assessment*, edited by Diane Z. Chase and Arlen F. Chase, pp. 18–29. University of Oklahoma Press, Norman.

Hirth, Kenneth G., and Joanne Pillsbury (editors)

2013   *Merchants, Markets, and Exchange in the Pre-Columbian World.* Dumbarton Oaks Research Library and Collection, Washington D.C.

Hodges, Glenn

2014   Most Complete Ice Age Skeleton Helps Solve Mystery of First Americans. *National Geographic Explorer Connect.* Electronic document, http://news.nationalgeographic.com/news/2014/05/140515-skeleton-ice-age-mexico-cave-hoyo-negro-archaeology, accessed August 25, 2017.

2015   First Americans. *National Geographic* 227(1): 124–137.

Hohmann, Bobbi M.

2002   Preclassic Maya Shell Ornament Production in the Belize Valley, Belize. Unpublished Ph.D. dissertation, Department of Anthropology, University of New Mexico, Albuquerque.

Hohmann, Bobbi M., and Terry G. Powis

1996   Excavations at Pacbitun, Belize: Archaeological Investigations of the Middle Preclassic Occupation in Plaza B. In *Belize Valley Preclassic Maya Project: Report of the 1995 Field Season*, edited by Paul F. Healy and Jaime J. Awe, pp. 98–127. Occasional Papers in Anthropology, No. 12. Trent University, Peterborough.

1999   The 1996 Excavations of Plaza B at Pacbitun, Belize. In *Belize Valley Preclassic Maya Project: Progress Report on the 1996 and 1997 Field Seasons*, edited by Paul F. Healy, pp. 1–18. Occasional Papers in Anthropology, No. 13. Trent University, Peterborough.

Hohmann, Bobbi M., Terry G. Powis, and Carmen Arendt

1999   The 1997 Investigations at Pacbitun, Belize. In *Belize Valley Preclassic Maya Project: Report of the 1995 Field Season*, edited by Paul F. Healy, pp. 19–30. Occasional Papers in Anthropology, No. 12. Trent University, Peterborough.

Hohmann, Bobbi M., Andrew Vaughn, and Terry G. Powis
2009   Investigating Middle Preclassic Specialized Shell Bead and Lithic Production at Pacbitun, Belize. Paper presented at the 74th Annual Meeting of the Society for American Archaeology, Atlanta.

Holland, Marjorie, Dennis Whigham, and Brij Gopal
1990   The Characteristics of Wetland Ecotones. In *The Ecology and Management of Aquatic-Terrestrial Ecotones*, edited by Henri Decamps and Robert J. Naiman, pp. 171–198. The Parthenon Publishing Group, Carnforth.

Hoopes, John W.
1991   The Isthmian Alternative: Reconstructing Patterns of Social Organization in Formative Costa Rica. In *The Formation of Complex Society in Southeastern Mesoamerica*, edited by William R. Fowler Jr., pp. 171–192. CRC Press, Boca Raton.

Hopkins, Joseph W. III
1968   Prehispanic Agricultural Terraces in Mexico. Unpublished Master's thesis, Department of Anthropology, University of Chicago.

Horn, Sherman W.
2015   The Web of Complexity: Socioeconomic Networks in the Middle Preclassic Belize Valley. Unpublished Ph.D. dissertation, Department of Anthropology, Tulane University, New Orleans.

Hosler, Dorothy, Sandra L. Burkett, and Michael J. Tarkanian
1999   Prehistoric Polymers: Rubber Processing in Ancient Mesoamerica. *Science* 284: 1988–1991.

Houck, Charles
2004   The Rural Survey of Ek Balam, Yucatan, Mexico. Unpublished Ph.D. dissertation, Department of Anthropology, Tulane University, New Orleans.

Houston, Stephen D.
1993   *Hieroglyphs and History at Dos Pilas: Dynastic Politics of the Classic Maya.* University of Texas Press, Austin.
1998   Classic Maya Depiction of the Built Environment. In *Function and Meaning in Classic Maya Architecture*, edited by Stephen D. Houston, pp. 333–372. Dumbarton Oaks Research Library and Collection, Washington, D.C.
2006   Impersonation, Dance, and the Problem of Spectacle among the Classic Maya. In *Archaeology of Performance: Theaters of Power, Community, and Politics*, edited by Takeshi Inomata and Lawrence S. Coben, pp. 135–155. AltaMira Press, Walnut Creek.

Houston, Stephen D., and David Stuart
1996   Of Gods, Glyphs, and Kings: Divinity and Rulership among the Classic Maya. *Antiquity* 70: 289–312.

Howell, Wayne K., and Denise R. Evans Copeland
1989   *Excavations at El Mirador, Petén, Guatemala: The Danta and Monos Complexes.* Papers of the New World Archaeological Foundation, Nos. 60 and 61. Brigham Young University, Provo.

Hurst, Heather
2009   Murals and the Ancient Maya Artist: A Study of Art Production in the Guate-

malan lowlands. Unpublished Ph.D. dissertation, Department of Anthropology, Yale University, New Haven.

Hurst, Heather, Jessica Craig, William Saturno, Francisco Estrada-Belli, Boris Beltrán, and Edwin Román

2008 Tesoro o basura: Un estudio sobre la terminación de murales de San Bartolo, Cival y La Sufricaya, Petén. In *XXI Simposio de investigaciones arqueológicas en Guatemala, 2007*, edited by Juan Pedro Laporte, Bárbara Arroyo, and Héctor E. Mejía, pp. 253–262. Museo Nacional de Arqueología y Etnología, Ministerio de Cultura y Deportes, Instituto de Antropología e Historia, and Asociación Tikal, Guatemala City.

Hutson, Scott R.

2012 "All That Is Solid . . .": Sacbes, Settlement and Semiotics at Tzacauil, Yucatan. *Ancient Mesoamerica* 23: 297–311.

Iannone, Gyles

1996 Problems in the Study of Ancient Maya Settlement and Social Organization: Insights from the "Minor Center" of Zubin, Cayo District, Belize. Unpublished Ph.D. dissertation, Institute of Archaeology, University of London.

Iannone, Gyles, and David F. Lee

1996 The Preclassic Period Chipped Stone Assemblage from Cahal Pech, Belize: A Preliminary Comparative Analysis. Paper presented at the 61st Annual Meeting of the Society for American Archaeology, New Orleans.

Iceland, Harry B.

1997 The Preceramic Origins of the Maya: The Results of the Colha Preceramic Project in Northern Belize. Unpublished Ph.D. dissertation, Department of Anthropology, University of Texas, Austin.

2005 The Preceramic to Early Middle Formative Transition in Northern Belize: Evidence for the Ethnic Identity of the Preceramic Inhabitants. In *New Perspectives on Formative Mesoamerican Cultures*, edited by Terry G. Powis, pp. 15–26. BAR International Series 1377. British Archaeological Reports, Oxford.

Inomata, Takeshi

2001a The Power and Ideology of Artistic Creation: Elite Craft Specialists in Classic Maya Society. *Current Anthropology* 42: 321–349.

2006a Politics and Theatricality in Mayan Society. In *Archaeology of Performance: Theaters of Power, Community, and Politics*, edited by Takeshi Inomata and Lawrence S. Coben, pp. 187–221. AltaMira Press, Walnut Creek.

2006b Plazas, Performers, and Spectators: Political Theaters of the Classic Maya. *Current Anthropology* 47: 805–842.

2007 Knowledge and Belief in Artistic Production by Classic Maya Elites. In *Rethinking Craft Specialization in Complex Societies: Archaeological Analyses of the Social Meaning of Production*, edited by Zachary X. Hruby and Rowan K. Flad, pp. 129–142. American Anthropological Association, Virginia.

2011 La secuencia cerámica de Ceibal. In *Informe del Proyecto Arqueológico Ceibal-Petexbatun: La temporada de 2011*, edited by Victor Castillo Aguilar and Takeshi Inomata, pp. 157–167. Report submitted to the Instituto de Antropología e Historia, Guatemala.

Inomata, Takeshi, and Lawrence S. Coben
2006   Overture: An Invitation to the Archaeological Theater. In *Archaeology of Performance: Theaters of Power, Community, and Politics*, edited by Takeshi Inomata and Lawrence S. Coben, pp. 11–44. AltaMira Press, Walnut Creek.

Inomata, Takeshi, Jessica MacLellan, Daniela Triadan, Jessica Munson, Melissa Burham, Kazuo Aoyama, Hiroo Nasu, Flory Pinzon, and Hitoshi Yonenobu
2015   Development of Sedentary Communities in the Maya Lowlands: Coexisting Mobile Groups and Public Ceremonies at Ceibal, Guatemala. *PNAS* 112: 4268–4273.

Inomata, Takeshi, Raúl Ortiz, Barbara Arroyo, and Eugenia J. Robinson
2014   Chronological Revision of Preclassic Kaminaljuyú, Guatemala: Implications for Social Processes in the Southern Maya Area. *Latin American Antiquity* 25: 377–408.

Inomata, Takeshi, Daniela Triadan, Kazuo Aoyama, Victor Castillo, and Hitoshi Yonenobu
2013   Early Ceremonial Constructions at Ceibal, Guatemala, and the Origins of Lowland Maya Civilization. *Science* 340: 467–471.

Inomata, Takeshi, Daniela Triadan, Erick Ponciano, Estela Pinto, Richard E. Terry, and Markus Eberl
2002   Domestic and Political Lives of Classic Maya Elites: The Excavation of Rapidly Abandoned Structures at Aguateca, Guatemala. *Latin American Antiquity* 13: 305–330.

Inomata, Takeshi, Daniela Triadan, and Otto R. Román
2010   Desarrollo de las comunidades preclásicas e interacciones entre las tierras bajas y el área Olmeca. In *XXIII Simposio de investigaciones arqueológicas en Guatemala*, edited by Bárbara Arroyo, Adriana Linares Palma, and Lorena Paiz Aragón, pp. 53–66. Museo Nacional de Arqueología y Etnología, Ministerio de Cultura y Deportes, Instituto de Antropología e Historia, and Asociación Tikal, Guatemala City.

Instituto Nacional de Antropología e Historia, Mexico
2011   Foundational offering of the Pyramid of the Sun found in Teotihuacan. Electronic document, http://inah.gob.mx/es/boletines/1746-hallan-ofrenda-originaria-de-piramide-del-sol, accessed August 25, 2017.

2014   Encuentran en Hoyo Negro nuevas posibilidades para estudiar el orígen del hombre americano. Electronic document, http://www.inah.gob.mx/en/boletines/1830-encuentran-en-hoyo-negro-nuevas-posibilidades-para-estudiar-el-origen-del-hombre-americano, accessed August 25, 2017.

Isaza Aizpurua, Ilean I.
1997   Shell Working and Social Differentiation at the Formative Maya Village of K'axob. Unpublished Master's thesis, Department of Anthropology, Boston University, Boston.

Isaza Aizpurua, Ilean I., and Patricia M. McAnany
1999   Adornment and Identity: Shell Ornaments from Formative K'axob. *Ancient Mesoamerica* 10: 117–127.

Jackson, Sarah
2013   *Politics of the Maya Court: Hierarchy and Change in the Late Classic Period.* University of Oklahoma Press, Norman.

Jacob, John

1994   Evidencias para cambio ambiental en Nakbe, Guatemala. In *VII Simposio arqueológico de Guatemala*, edited by Juan Pedro Laporte, Héctor L. Escobedo, and Sandra V. de Brady, pp. 275–280. Museo Nacional de Arqueología y Etnología, Ministerio de Cultura y Deportes, Instituto de Antropología e Historia, and Asociación Tikal, Guatemala City.

Jacobo, Álvaro

1992   *Proyecto de Rescate Arqueológico Tulam Tzu. Final Report*. Report submitted to the Instituto de Antropología e Historia, Guatemala.

Joesink-Mandeville, LeRoy V.

1970   The Comparative Cultural Stratigraphy of Formative Complexes in the Maya Area: A Reappraisal in Light of New Evidence from Dzibilchaltun, Yucatan. Unpublished Ph.D. dissertation, Department of Anthropology, Tulane University, New Orleans.

1977   Olmec-Maya Relationships: A Correlation of Linguistical Evidence with Archeological Ceramics. *Journal of New World Archaeology* 2: 30–39.

Johnson, Frederick, and Richard S. MacNeish

1972   Chronometric Dating. In *The Prehistory of the Tehuacan Valley, Volume 4, Chronology and Irrigation*, edited by Frederick Johnson, pp. 3–55. University of Texas Press, Austin.

Johnstone, Dave

2001   The Ceramics of Yaxuna. Unpublished Ph.D. dissertation, Department of Anthropology, Southern Methodist University, Dallas.

2005   The Ceramic Placement of Yo'okop: Chronological and Regional Considerations. In *Quintana Roo Archaeology*, edited by Justine Shaw and Jennifer P. Mathews, pp. 158–165. University of Arizona Press, Tucson.

Jones, Christopher

1969   *The Twin-Pyramid Group Pattern, a Classic Maya Architectural Assemblage at Tikal, Guatemala*. University of Pennsylvania Museum of Archaeology and Anthropology, Philadelphia.

Jones, Christopher, and Linton Satterthwaite

1982   *The Monuments and Inscriptions of Tikal: The Carved Monuments*. Tikal Report No. 33. University Museum Monograph 44. The University Museum, University of Pennsylvania, Philadelphia.

Jones, John G.

1994a   Pollen Evidence for Early Settlement and Agriculture in Northern Belize. *Palynology* 18: 205–211.

1994b   Wetland Agricultural Fields in Cobweb Swamp. Paper presented at the 59th Annual Meeting of the Society for American Archaeology, Anaheim.

Jones, John G., and Barbara Voorhies

2004   Human and Plant Interaction. In *Coastal Collectors of the Holocene: The Chantuto People of Southwestern Mexico*, edited by Barbara Voorhies, pp. 300–343. University Press of Florida, Gainesville.

Joralemon, Peter D.
1971   *A Study of Olmec Iconography*. Studies in Pre-Columbian Art and Archaeology 7. Dumbarton Oaks Research Library and Collection, Washington, D.C.

Joyce, Rosemary A., and David C. Grove (editors)
1999   *Social Patterns in Pre-Classic Mesoamerica*. Dumbarton Oaks Research Library and Collection, Washington, D.C.

Joyce, Rosemary A., and John S. Henderson
2001   Beginnings of Village Life in Eastern Mesoamerica. *Latin American Antiquity* 12: 5–24.

Just, Bryan R.
2007   An Incised Slate Belt Plaque at the Princeton University Art Museum. *Mexicon* 29: 62–64.

Justeson, John S., and Peter Mathews
1983   The Seating of the *Tun*: Further Evidence Concerning a Late Preclassic Lowland Maya Stela Cult. *American Antiquity* 48: 586–593.

Kaplan, David
1963   Men, Monuments, and Political Systems. *Southwestern Journal of Anthropology* 19: 397–409.

Katz, Solomon H., Mary L. Hediger, and Linda A. Vallery
1974   Traditional Maize Processing Techniques in the New World. *Science* 1984: 765–773.

Kaufman, Terrence
1976   Archaeological and Linguistic Correlation in Mayaland and Associated Areas in Meso-America. *World Archaeology* 8: 101–118.

Keegan, William F.
2000   West Indian Archaeology: Ceramic Age. *Journal of Archaeological Research* 8: 135–167.

Keller, Angela H.
2008   The Chan Shell Collection: Creating Community with Shell. Paper presented at the 73rd Annual Meeting of the Society for American Archaeology, Vancouver.
2012   Creating Community with Shell. In *Chan: An Ancient Maya Farming Community*, edited by Cynthia Robin, pp. 253–270. University Press of Florida, Gainsville.

Kelley, David H.
1965   Birth of the Gods at Palenque. In *Estudios de Cultura Maya* 5: 93–134.

Kelly, Thomas C.
1993   Preceramic Projectile-Point Typology in Belize. *Ancient Mesoamerica* 4: 205–227.

Kennett, Douglas J., Barbara Voorhies, and Dean Martorana
2006   An Ecological Model for the Origin of Maize-Based Food Production on the Pacific Coast of Southern Mexico. In *Behavioral Ecology and the Transition to Agriculture*, edited by Douglas J. Kennett and Bruce Winterhalder, pp. 103–136. University of California Press, Berkeley.

Kerr, Justin (editor)

1992   *The Maya Vase Book: A Corpus of Rollout Photographs of Maya Vases*, Vol. 3. Kerr Associates, New York.

Kidder, Alfred V.

1947   *The Artifacts of Uaxactun, Guatemala.* Carnegie Institution of Washington Publication 576. Carnegie Institution of Washington, Washington, D.C.

1961   Archaeological Investigations at Kaminaljuyu, Guatemala. *Proceedings of the American Philosophical Society* 105: 559–570.

King, Eleanor M. (editor)

2015   *The Ancient Maya Marketplace: The Archaeology of Transient Space.* University of Arizona Press, Tucson.

Kirch, Patrick Vinton

1984   *The Evolution of Polynesian Chiefdoms.* Cambridge University Press, Cambridge.

Konieczna Z., Bárbara

1981   Estudio del material lítico procedente de la Gruta de Loltún, Yucatán. *Revista Mexicana de Estudios Antropológicos* 27(2): 193–204.

Kosakowsky, Laura J.

1987   *Preclassic Maya Pottery at Cuello, Belize.* Anthropological Papers of the University of Arizona, No. 47. University of Arizona Press, Tucson.

Kosakowsky, Laura J., and Duncan C. Pring

1998   The Ceramics of Cuello, Belize: A New Evaluation. *Ancient Mesoamerica* 9: 55–66.

Kunselman, Raymond

2000   Yacimiento Mesoamericano de obsidiana: Estudios de utilización, conexiones y contactos en Nakbe. In *Investigaciones arqueológicas y ecológicas en la cuenca Mirador, 1998: Informe de la temporada de campo,* edited by Richard D. Hansen and Judith Valle, pp. 630–644. Report submitted to the Proyecto Regional de Investigaciones Arqueológicas del Norte del Peten, Guatemala.

Kurjack, Edward B.

1974   *Prehistoric Lowland Maya Community and Social Organization: A Case Study at Dzibilchaltun, Yucatan, Mexico.* Middle American Research Institute Publication 38. Tulane University, New Orleans.

Kurjack, Edward B., and E. Wyllys Andrews V

1976   Early Boundary Maintenance in Northwest Yucatan, Mexico. *American Antiquity* 41: 318–325.

Kurjack, Edward B., and Sylvia Garza Tarazona de Gonzalez

1981   Pre-Columbian Community Form and Distribution in the Northern Maya Area. In *Lowland Maya Settlement Patterns,* edited by Wendy Ashmore, pp. 287–310. University of New Mexico Press, Albuquerque.

Lacadena, Alfonso

2003   *Notebook for the XXVIIth Maya Hieroglyphic Forum at Texas.* University of Texas, Austin.

2004   *The Glyphic Corpus from Ek' Balam, Yucatán, México.* Report submitted to the Foundation for the Advancement of Mesoamerican Studies, Inc. Electronic document, http://www.famsi.org/reports/01057/index.html, accessed August 25, 2017.

Laporte, Juan Pedro

1995   Preclásico a Clásico en Tikal: Proceso de transformación en el Mudo Perdido. In *The Emergence of Lowland Maya Civilization: The Transition from the Preclassic to the Early Classic*, edited by Nikolai Grube, pp. 17–35. Acta Mesoamericana 8, Verlag Anton Saurwein.

Laporte, Juan Pedro, and Vilma Fialko

1990   New Perspectives on Old Problems: Dynastic References for the Early Classic at Tikal. In *Vision and Revision in Maya Studies*, edited by Flora S. Clancy and Peter D. Harrison, pp. 33–66. University of New Mexico Press, Albuquerque.

1995   Un reencuentro con Mundo Perdido, Tikal, Guatemala. *Ancient Mesoamerica* 6: 41–94.

Laporte, Juan Pedro, and Juan Antonio Valdés

1993   *Tikal y Uaxactun en el Preclásico*. Instituto de Investigaciones Antropológicas, Universidad Nacional Autónoma de México, Mexico.

LeCount, Lisa J.

1996   Pottery and Power: Feasting, Gifting, and Displaying Wealth among the Late and Terminal Classic Lowland Maya. Unpublished Ph.D. dissertation, Department of Anthropology, University of California, Los Angeles.

1999   Polychrome Pottery and Political Strategies in Late and Terminal Classic Lowland Maya Society. *Latin American Antiquity* 10: 239–259.

2001   Like Water for Chocolate: Feasting and Political Ritual among the Late Classic Maya at Xunantunich, Belize. *American Anthropologist* 103: 935–953.

LeCount, Lisa J., and Jason Yaeger (editors)

2010   *Classic Maya Provincial Politics: Xunantunich and Its Hinterlands*. University of Arizona Press, Tuscon.

Lee, David F.

1996   Nohoch Na (The Big House): The 1995 Excavations at the Cas Pek Group, Cahal Pech, Belize. In *Belize Valley Preclassic Maya Project: Report on the 1995 Field Season*, edited by Paul F. Healy and Jaime J. Awe, pp. 77–97. Occasional Papers in Anthropology, No. 12. Trent University, Peterborough.

Lee, David F., and Jaime J. Awe

1995   Middle Preclassic Architecture, Burials, and Craft Specialization: Report on the 1994 Investigations at the Cas Pek Group, Cahal Pech, Belize. In *Belize Valley Preclassic Maya Project: Report on the 1994 Field Season*, edited by Paul F. Healy and Jaime J. Awe, pp. 95–115. Occasional Papers in Anthropology, No. 10. Trent University, Peterborough.

Lesure, Richard G.

1998   Vessel Form and Function in an Early Formative Ceramic Assemblage from Coastal Mexico. *Journal of Field Archaeology* 25: 19–36.

Leyden, Barbara W.

2002   Pollen Evidence for Climatic Variability and Cultural Disturbance in the Maya Lowlands. *Ancient Mesoamerica* 13: 85–101.

Lightfoot, Kent G., and Antoinette Martinez
1995   Frontiers and Boundaries in Archaeological Perspective. *Annual Review of Anthropology* 24: 471–492.

Ligorred Perramón, Joseph
2007–2008   T´Hó, una ciudad maya antigua bajo una ciudad maya moderna, Mérida. *Arqueología* 14: 137–172.

Linares, Adriana María
2009   Las figurillas como representación femenina relevante en áreas ceremoniales de la sociedad preclásica media de Naranjo, Guatemala. Unpublished Licenciatura thesis, School of History, Universidad de San Carlos de Guatemala, Guatemala.

Littman, Edwin R.
1960   Ancient Mesoamerican Mortars, Plasters, and Stuccos: The Use of Bark Extracts in Lime Plasters. *American Antiquity* 25: 593–597.

Lockwood, C. C.
1989   *The Yucatán Peninsula.* Louisiana State University Press, Baton Rouge.

Lohse, Jon C.
2007   *In Search of the Preceramic: 2006 Season Invesitgations at Actun Halal, Belize.* Report submitted to the Foundation for the Advancement of Mesoamerican Studies, Electronic document, http://www.famsi.org/reports/06019/06019 Lohse01.pdf, accessed August 25, 2017.
2010   Archaic Origins of the Lowland Maya. *Latin American Antiquity* 21: 312–352.

Lohse, Jon C., Jaime J. Awe, Cameron Griffith, Robert M. Rosenswig, and Fred Valdez Jr.
2006   Preceramic Occupations in Belize: Updating the Paleoindian and Archaic Record. *Latin American Antiquity* 17: 209–226.

Longyear, John M.
1948   A Sub-Pottery Deposit at Copan, Honduras. *American Antiquity* 13: 248–249.

Lopez, Francisco, Sheryl Carcuz, and Giovanni Gonzalez
2007   La Danta: Excavaciones en el primer basamento de la Estructura 2A8–2. In *Informe final, temporada 2007: Investigación y conservación en los sitios arqueológicos de la zona cultural y natural Mirador,* edited by Nora M. Lopez, pp. 432–444. Report submitted to the the Instituto de Antropología e Historia, Guatemala.

Lorenzo, José Luis
1955   Los concheros de la costa de Chiapas. *Anales del Instituto Nacional de Antropología e Historia* 7: 41–50.
1961   Un buril de la cultura precerámica de Teopisca, Chiapas. In *Homenaje a Pablo Martínez del Rio en el XXV aniversario de la primera edición de "Los Orígenes Americanos,"* edited by Pablo Martinez del Rio, pp. 75–90. Instituto Nacional de Antropología e Historia, Mexico.
1977   *Un conjunto lítico de Teopisca, Chiapas.* Informes, No. 4. Departamento de Prehistoria, Instituto Nacional de Antropología e Historia, Mexico.

Lounsbury, Floyd
1973   On the Derivation and Reading of the "Ben-Ich" Prefix. In *Mesoamerican Writing Systems,* edited by Elizabeth P. Benson, pp. 99–143. Dumbarton Oaks Research Library and Collection, Washington, D.C.

Love, Michael W.

2002   *Early Complex Society in Pacific Guatemala: Settlements and Chronology of the Río Naranjo, Guatemala*. Papers of the New World Archaeological Foundation, No. 66. Brigham Young University, Provo.

Lowe, Gareth W.

1975   *The Early Preclassic Barra Phase of Altamira, Chiapas: A Review with New Data*. Papers of the New World Archaeological Foundation, No. 38. Brigham Young University, Provo.

1977   The Mixe-Zoque as Competing Neighbors of the Early Lowland Maya. In *The Origins of Maya Civilization*, edited by Richard E. W. Adams, pp. 197–248. University of New Mexico Press, Albuquerque.

1989   The Heartland Olmec: Evolution of Material Culture. In *Regional Perspectives on the Olmec*, edited by Robert J. Sharer and David C. Grove, pp. 33–67. Cambridge University Press, Cambridge.

McAnany, Patricia A. (editor)

2004   *K'axob: Ritual, Work and Family in an Ancient Maya Village*. University of California, Cotsen Institute of Archaeology, Los Angeles.

McAnany, Patricia A.

1995   *Living with the Ancestors: Kinship and Kingship in Ancient Maya Society*. University of Texas Press, Austin.

2008   Shaping Social Difference: Political and Ritual Economy of Classic Maya Royal Courts. In *Dimensions of Ritual Economy, Research in Economic Anthropology*, Vol. 27, edited by E. Christian Wells and Patricia A. McAnany, pp. 219–247. Emerald Group Publishing Limited, Bingley.

2010   *Ancestral Maya Economies in Archaeological Perspective*. Cambridge University Press, Cambridge.

McAnany, Patricia A., and Shannon Plank

2001   Perspectives on Actors, Gender Roles, and Architecture at Classic Maya Courts and Household. In *Royal Courts of the Ancient Maya Volume 1: Theory, Comparison and Synthesis*, edited by Takeshi Inomata and Stephen D. Houston, pp. 84–129. Westview Press, Oxford.

McDonald, Andrew J.

1983   *Tzutzuculi: A Middle-Preclassic Site on the Pacific Coast of Chiapas, Mexico*. Papers of the New World Archaeological Foundation, No. 47. Brigham Young University, Provo.

McKillop, Heather

1994   Ancient Maya Tree Cropping: A Viable Subsistence Adaptation for the Island Maya. *Ancient Mesoamerica* 5: 129–140.

MacLellan, Jessica

2009   Change and Continuity in the Preclassic Architecture of the Las Pinturas Group San Bartolo, Petén, Guatemala. Unpublished Undergraduate Senior Thesis, Department of Archaeology, Boston University, Boston.

MacNeish, Richard S.

1981   *Second Annual Report of the Belize Archaic Archaeological Reconnaissance*. Phillips Academy, R. S. Peabody Foundation for Archaeology, Andover.

1982 *Third Annual Report of the Belize Archaic Archaeological Reconnaissance*. Phillips Academy, R. S. Peabody Foundation for Archaeology, Andover.

MacNeish, Richard S., and Antoinette Nelken-Turner

1983 *Final Annual Report of the Belize Archaic Archaeological Reconnaissance*. Center for Archaeological Studies, Boston University, Boston.

MacNeish, Richard S., and Frederick A. Peterson

1962 *The Santa Marta Rock Shelter, Ocozocuautla, Chiapas, Mexico*. Papers of the New World Archaeological Foundation, No. 14. Brigham Young University, Provo.

MacNeish, Richard S., Jeffrey K. Wilkerson, and Antoinette Nelken-Turner

1980 *First Annual Report of the Belize Archaic Archaeological Reconnaissance*. Phillips Academy, R. S. Peabody Foundation for Archaeology, Andover.

Magaloni, Diana I.

1996 Materiales y técnicas de la pintura mural Maya. Unpublished Ph.D. dissertation, Universidad Nacional Autónoma de México, Mexico City.

Maldonado Cárdenas, Rubén, and Susana Echeverría Castillo

2004 El sitio preclásico Quintas del Mayab, un lugar periférico de Dzibilchaltún. *Los Investigadores de la Cultura Maya* 12(1): 268–277. Universidad Autónoma de Campeche, Mexico.

Malinowski, Bronislaw

1961 (1922) *Argonauts of the Western Pacific*. E. P. Dutton, New York.

Marcus, Joyce

1973 Territorial Organization of the Lowland Classic Maya. *Science* 180: 911–916.

1976 *Emblem and State in the Classic Maya Lowlands: An Epigraphic Approach to Territorial Organization*. Dumbarton Oaks Research Library and Collection, Washington, D.C.

1983 Lowland Maya Archaeology at the Crossroads. *American Antiquity* 48: 454–488.

1993 Ancient Maya Political Organization. In *Lowland Maya Civilization in the Eighth Century A.D.*, edited by Jeremy A. Sabloff and John S. Henderson, pp. 111–184. Dumbarton Oaks Research Library and Collection, Washington, D.C.

1998 The Peaks and Valleys of Ancient States: An Extension of the Dynamic Model. In *Archaic States*, edited by Gary M. Feinman and Joyce Marcus, pp. 59–94. School of American Research Press, Santa Fe.

Marcus, Joyce, and Kent V. Flannery

1996 *Zapotec Civilization: How Urban Society Evolved in Mexico's Oaxaca Valley*. Thames and Hudson, London.

2004 The Coevolution of Ritual and Society: New C14 Dates from Ancient Mexico. *PNAS* 101: 18257–18261.

Marken, Damien B.

2015 Conceptualizing the Spatial Dimensions of Classic Maya States: Polity and Urbanism at El Perú-Waka,' Petén. In *Classic Maya Polities of the Southern Lowlands: Integration, Interation, and Dissolution*, edited by Damien B. Marken and James L. Fitzsimmons, pp. 123–166. University of Colorado Press, Boulder.

Marroquín, Luz Midilia
2006   Los botellones en el Valle Central de Guatemala: Rasgos y contextos. Unpublished Licenciatura thesis, School of History, Universidad de San Carlos de Guatemala, Guatemala.

Martin, Simon
1997   The Painted King List: A Commentary on Codex-Style Dynastic Vases. In *The Maya Vase Book: A Corpse of Rollout Photographs of Maya Vases*, Vol. 5, edited by Justin Kerr, pp. 846–867. Kerr Associates, New York.

2005   Caracol Altar 21 Revisited: More Data on Double Bird and Tikal's Wars of the Mid-Sixth Century. *The PARI Journal* 6(1): 1–9.

2008   Wives and Daughters on the Dallas Altar. Electronic document, http://www.mesoweb.com/articles/martin/Wives&Daughters.pdf, accessed August 25, 2017.

2017   Secrets of the Painted King List: Recovering the Early History of the Snake Dynasty. Electronic document, https://decipherment.wordpress.com/2017/05/05/secrets-of-the-painted-king-list-recovering-the-early-history-of-the-snake-dynasty/, accessed August 25, 2017.

Martin, Simon, and Nikolai Grube
1994   Evidence for Macro-Political Organization amongst the Classic Maya Lowland States. *Mesoweb*. Electronic document, http://www.mesoweb.com/articles/martin/Macro-Politics.pdf, accessed August 25, 2017.

1995   Maya Superstates. *Archaeology* 48(6): 41–46.

2008   *Chronicle of Maya Kings and Queens*, 2nd ed. Thames and Hudson, New York.

Martínez Donjuan, Guadalupe
1994   Los olmecas en el estado de Guerrero. In *Los Olmecas en Mesoamérica*, edited by John E. Clark, pp. 143–165. Citibank, Mexico.

1995   Teopantecuanitlán: Sitio Olmeca en Guerrero. *Arqueología Mexicana* 2(12): 58–62.

Martinez Hildalgo, Gustavo, and Richard D. Hansen
1993   Excavaciones en el Complejo 59, Grupo 66, y el Grupo 18, Nakbe, Peten. In *III Simposio de arqueología Guatemalteca*, edited by Juan Pedro Laporte, Héctor L. Escobedo, Sandra V. de Brady, pp. 73–86. Museo Nacional de Arqueología y Etnología, Ministerio de Cultura y Deportes, Instituto de Antropología e Historia, and Asociación Tikal, Guatemala City.

Martinez Hildalgo, Gustavo, Richard D. Hansen, John Jacob, and Wayne K. Howell
1999   Nuevas evidencias de los sistemas de cultivo del Preclásico en la cuenca Mirador. In *XII Simposio de investigaciones arqueológicas en Guatemala*, edited by Juan Pedro Laporte, Héctor L. Escobedo, Ana C. de Suasnavar, pp. 327–336. Museo Nacional de Arqueología y Etnología, Ministerio de Cultura y Deportes, Instituto de Antropología e Historia, and Asociación Tikal, Guatemala City.

Mason, J. Alden
1960   *Mound 12, Chiapa de Corzo, Chiapas, Mexico*. Papers of the New World Archaeological Foundation, No. 99. Brigham Young University, Provo.

Masson, Marilyn A.
2002   Introduction. In *Ancient Maya Political Economies*, edited by Marilyn A. Masson and David A. Freidel, pp. 1–30. AltaMira Press, Walnut Creek.

Masson, Marilyn A., and David A. Freidel
2012   An Argument for Classic Maya Era Maya Market Exchange. *Journal of Anthropological Archaeology* 31: 455–484.
2013   Wide Open Spaces: A Long View of the Importance of Maya Market Exchange. In *Merchants, Markets, and Exchange in the Pre-Columbian World*, edited by Kenneth G. Hirth and Joanne Pillsbury, pp. 201–228. Dumbarton Oaks Research Library and Collection, Washington, D.C.

Mata Amado, Guillermo, and Richard D. Hansen
1992   El diente incrustado temprano de Nakbe. In *V Simposio de investigaciones arqueologicas en Guatemala*, edited by Juan Pedro Laporte, Héctor L. Escobedo, Sandra V. de Brady, pp. 115–118. Museo Nacional de Arqueología y Etnología, Ministerio de Cultura y Deportes, Instituto de Antropología e Historia, and Asociación Tikal, Guatemala City.

Matheny, Ray T. (editor)
1980   *El Mirador, Petén, Guatemala: An Interim Report*. Papers of the New World Archaeological Foundation, No. 45. Brigham Young University, Provo.

Matheny, Ray T.
1986   Investigations at El Mirador, Peten, Guatemala. *National Geographic Research* 2: 332–353.
1987   Early States in the Maya Lowlands during the Late Pre-Classic Period: Edzna and El Mirador. In *City States of the Maya: Art and Architecture*, edited by Elizabeth P. Benson, pp. 1–44. Rocky Mountain Institute for Pre-Columbian Studies, Denver.

Matheny, Ray T., Deanne L. Gurr, Donald W. Forsyth, and F. Richard Hauck
1980   *Investigations at Edzná, Campeche, Mexico, Volume 1, Part 2: Maps*. Papers of the New World Archaeological Foundation, No. 46. Brigham Young University, Provo.

Matheny, Ray T., Richard D. Hansen, and Deanne L. Gurr
1980   Preliminary Field Report, El Mirador, 1979 Season. In *Project El Mirador, Peten, Guatemala: An Interim Report*, edited by Ray T. Matheny, pp. 1–23. Papers of the New World Archaeological Foundation, No. 45. Brigham Young University, Provo.

Mathews, Jennifer P.
1995   The Box Ni Group of Naranjal, and Early Architecture of the Central Maya Lowlands. In *The View from Yalahau: 1993 Archaeological Investigations in Northern Quintana Roo, Mexico*, edited by Scott L. Fedick and Karl A. Taube, pp. 79–87. Latin American Studies Program, Field Report Series, No. 2. University of California, Riverside.

Mathews, Jennifer P., and Ruben Maldonado Cardenas
2006   Late Formative and Early Classic Interaction Spheres Reflected in the Megalithic Style. In *Lifeways in the Northern Maya Lowlands: New Approaches to Archaeology in the Yucatan Peninsula*, edited by Jennifer P. Mathews and Bethany A. Morrison, pp. 95–118. University of Arizona Press, Tucson.

Mathews, Peter

1985 Maya Early Classic Monuments and Inscriptions. In *A Consideration of the Early Classic Period in the Maya Lowlands*, edited by Gordon R. Willey and Peter Mathews, pp. 5–54. Institute for Mesoamerican Studies, State University of New York at Albany.

1992 Classic Maya Emblem Glyphs. In *Classic Maya Political History: Hieroglyphic and Archaeological Evidence*, edited by T. Patrick Culbert, pp. 19–29. Cambridge University Press, Cambridge.

Medina Castillo, Edgar René

2003 Los juegos de pelota de la región noroeste de Yucatán. In *Proyecto Costa Maya: Reconocimiento arqueológico en el noroeste de Yucatán. Reporte interino, temporada 2002: Reconocimiento arqueológico de la esquina noroeste de la península de Yucatán y primeras aproximaciones a los temas de investigación*, edited by Fernando Robles Castellanos and Anthony P. Andrews, pp. 62–87. Report submitted to the Instituto Nacional de Antropología e Historia, Mexico.

2005 El juego de pelota del Preclásico Medio en el noroeste de Yucatán, México. Unpublished Licenciatura thesis, Department of Anthropology, Universidad Autónoma de Yucatán, Merida.

Medina Castillo, Edgar, and Crorey Lawton

2002 El juego de pelota: Nuevos hallazgos en el noroeste de Yucatán. In *Los investigadores de la cultura Maya* 10(2): 278–285.

Medina Chemor, Alfredo (editor)

2008 *Cenotes: Huellas de agua y luz en la selva.* Pixel Press, Cancún.

Meillassoux, Claude

1978 The Economy in Agricultural Self-Sustaining Societies: A Preliminary Analysis. In *Relations of Production: Marxist Approaches to Economic Anthropology*, edited by David J. Seddon, pp. 127–157. Frank Cass, London.

Mercer, Henry C.

1896 (1975) *The Hill-Caves of Yucatan.* 2nd ed. University of Oklahoma Press, Norman.

Michaels, George H., and Barbara Voorhies

1992 Los recolectores costeros del período Arcaico Tardío en el sur de Mesoamérica: La gente de Chantuto visitada de nuevo. In *Memorias del Primer Congreso Internacional de Mayistas*, edited by Mercedes de la Garza, pp. 247–291. Universidad Nacional Autónoma de México, Mexico.

Michelet, Dominique, Carlos Morales-Aguilar, Julien Sion y Philippe Nondedeo (editors)

2013 *Proyecto Peten-Norte Naachtun 2010–2014: Informe de la tercera temporada de campo 2012.* Report submitted to the Instituto de Antropología e Historia, Guatemala.

Michels, Joseph W.

1979 *The Kaminaljuyu Chiefdom.* Pennsylvania State University Press, College Station.

Miller, Arlene V.

1976 Artifact or Fiction: The Lithic Objects from Richmond Hill, Belize. In *Maya Lithic Studies: Papers from the 1976 Belize Field Symposium*, edited by Thomas

R. Hester and Norman Hammond, pp. 119–135. Center for Archaeological Research, University of Texas at San Antonio.

Miller, Mary Ellen

1986   *The Murals of Bonampak*. Princeton University Press, Princeton.

2001   *The Art of Mesoamerica: From Olmec to Aztec*. 3rd ed. Thames and Hudson, London.

Miller, Mary Ellen, and Stephen D. Houston

1987   The Classic Maya Ballgame and Its Architectural Setting: A Study of Relations between Text and Image. *RES: Anthropology and Aesthetics* 14: 46–65.

Mills, Barbara

1999   Ceramics and the Social Contexts of Food Consumption in the Northern Southwest. In *Pottery and People: A Dynamic Interaction*, edited by James Skibo and Gary Feinman, pp. 99–114. University of Utah Press, Salt Lake City.

Moholy-Nagy, Hattula

1963   Shells and Other Marine Material from Tikal, Guatemala. *Estudios de Cultura Maya* 3: 65–68.

1978   The Utilization of *Pomacea* Snails at Tikal, Guatemala. *American Antiquity* 43: 65–73.

1985   The Social and Ceremonial Uses of Marine Molluscs at Tikal. In *Prehistoric Lowland Maya Environment and Subsistence Economy*, edited by Mary D. Pohl, pp. 147–158. Papers of the Peabody Museum of Archaeology and Ethnology, Vol. 77. Harvard University, Cambridge.

1989   Formed Shell Beads from Tikal, Guatemala. In *Proceedings of the 1986 Shell Bead Conference: Selected Papers*, edited by Charles F. Hayes III and Lynn Ceci, pp. 139–156. Research Records, No. 20. Rochester Museum and Science Center, Rochester.

1994   Tikal Material Culture: Artifacts and Social Structure at a Classic Lowland Maya City. Unpublished Ph.D. dissertation, Department of Anthropology, University of Michigan, Ann Arbor.

1997   Middens, Construction Fill, and Offerings: Evidence for the Organization of Classic Period Craft Production at Tikal, Guatemala. *Journal of Field Archaeology* 24: 293–313.

Moholy-Nagy, Hattula, and Fred W. Nelson

1990   New Data on Sources of Obsidian Artifacts from Tikal. *Ancient Mesoamerica*: 71–80.

Morales-Guos, Paulino Israel, and Maria Laura Velasquez-Fergusson

2006   Excavaciones en la Estructura 3A8-1. In *Investigacion y conservación en los sitios arqueologicos El Mirador, La Muerta, Wakna, El Porvenir, El Guiro, La Iglesia, La Sarteneja, Chib Che' y La Ceibita: Informe final de la temporada 2005*, edited by Edgar Suyuc-Ley and Richard D. Hansen, pp. 418–492. Report submitted to the Instituto de Antropología e Historia, Guatemala.

Morley, Sylvanus G.

1943   Archaeological Investigations of the Carnegie Institution of Washington in the Maya Area of Middle America, during the Past Twenty-Eight Years. *Proceedings of the American Philosophical Society* 86: 205–219.

Morris, Ann A.
1931   *Digging in Yucatan*. Doubleday, New York.
Mulleried, Federico
1928   Sobre los artefactos de piedra de la parte central y occidental del Petén, Guatemala, su forma, y su probable edad. *Revista Mexicana de Estudios Históricos* 2: 71–101.
Navarrete, Carlos, and Luis Luján Muñoz
1986   *El Gran Montículo de la Culebra en el Valle de Guatemala*. Universidad Nacional Autónoma de México, Mexico, and Academia de Geografía e Historia de Guatemala, Guatemala.
Navarro Farr, Olivia, David A. Freidel, and Ana L. Arroyave
2008   Manipulating Memory in the Wake of the Dynastic Decline al El Perú-Waka': Termination Deposits at Abandoned Structure M13–1. In *Ruins of the Past: The Use and Perception of Abandoned Structures in the Maya Lowlands*, edited by Travis W. Stanton and Aline Magnoni, pp. 113–145. University of Colorado Press, Boulder.
Neff, Hector, Bárbara Arroyo, John G. Jones, and Deborah Pearsall
2003   ¿Dónde están los asentamientos arcaicos en la costa sur de Guatemala? In *XVI Simposio de investigaciones arqueológicas en Guatemala, 2002*, edited by Juan Pedro Laporte, Bárbara Arroyo, Héctor L. Escobedo, and Héctor E. Mejía, pp. 833–844. Museo Nacional de Arqueología y Etnología, Ministerio de Cultura y Deportes, Instituto de Antropología e Historia, and Asociación Tikal, Guatemala City.
Neff, Hector, Deborah M. Pearsall, John G. Jones, Barbara Arroyo, Shawn K. Collins, and Dorothy Freidel
2006   Early Maya Adaptive Patterns: Mid–Late Holocene Paleoenvironmental Evidence from Pacific Guatemala. *Latin American Antiquity* 17: 287–315.
Neff, Hector, Deborah M. Pearsall, John G. Jones, Barbara Arroyo, and Dorothy Freidel
2006   Climate Change and Population History in the Pacific Lowlands of Southern Mesoamerica. *Quaternary Research* 65: 390–400.
Neivens de Estrada, Niña
2010   Early Lowland Maya Ceramics: Material from Holmul, Peten, Guatemala. Paper presented at the 75th Annual Meeting of the Society for American Archaeology, St. Louis.
Nelken-Turner, Antoinette
1987   Belize: Tiempos y espacios. *America Indígena* 47(1): 23–31.
1993   De la percepción de un Belice muy antiguo. In *Belice: Sus fronteras y destino*, edited by Francesca Gargallo and Adalberto Santana, pp. 13–29. Universidad Nacional Autónoma de México, Mexico.
Nelson, Fred W.
1985   Summary of the Results of Analysis of Obsidian Artifacts from the Maya Lowlands. *Scanning Electron Microscopy* 1985: 631–649.
Novotny, Anna
2012   The Chan Community: A Biorarchaeolgical Perspective. In *Chan: An Ancient Maya Farming Community*, edited by Cynthia Robin, pp. 231–251. University Press of Florida, Gainesville.

Nygard, Travis, and Linnea Wren
2011 The Ritual Space of Yo'okop's Queen Chaak Kab: Inscriptions, Sculpture, and Architecture of a Lesser-Known Maya City. In *It's Good to Be King: The Archaeology of Power and Authority. Proceedings of the 41st (2008) Annual Chacmool Archaeological Conference*, edited by Shawn Morton and Don Butler, pp. 95–106. University of Calgary, Chacmool Archaeological Association, Calgary.

Olivier, Guilhem
2006 The Sacred Bundles and the Coronation of the Aztec King in Mexico-Tenochtitlan. In *Sacred Bundles: Ritual Acts of Wrapping and Binding in Mesoamerica*, edited by Julia Guernsey and F. Kent Reilly III, pp. 199–225. Boundary End Archaeological Research Center, Barnardsville.

Ordoñez-Fajardo, Anaite, and Edgar Suyuc-Ley
2006 Escalinata de acceso de la primera plataforma hacia la segunda del complejo arquitectónico La Danta, El Mirador: Operación 402Q y 402 N. In *Investigaciones en el sitio arqueológico El Mirador, Petén, Guatemala*, edited by Nora Lopez, pp. 178–203. Report submitted to the Instituto de Antropología e Historia, Guatemala.

Ortiz Butrón, Agustín
2005 El temazcal arqueológico. *Arqueología Mexicana* 13(74):52–53.

Ortiz, Ponciano, and María del Carmen Rodríguez
1992 Las ofrendas de El Manatí y su posible asociación con el juego de pelota: Un yugo a destiempo. In *El juego de pelota en Mesoamérica: Raíces y supervivencia*, edited by María T. Uriarte. Colección América Nuestra, No. 39. Siglo Veintiuno Editores, Mexico.

1999 Olmec Ritual Behavior at El Manatí: A Sacred Space. In *Social Patterns in Pre-Classic Mesoamerica*, edited by David C. Grove and Rosemary A. Joyce, pp. 225–254. Dumbarton Oaks Research Library and Collection, Washington, D.C.

2000 The Sacred Hill of El Manatí: A Preliminary Discussion of the Site's Ritual Paraphernalia. In *Olmec Art and Archaeology in Mesoamerica, Studies in the History of Art*, Vol. 58, edited by John E. Clark and Mary E. Pye, pp. 74–93. Yale University Press, New Haven.

Paiz, Lorena
2007 El Clásico Tardío en el sitio Naranjo, Departamento de Guatemala. Unpublished *Licenciatura* thesis, Deparment of Social Sciences, Universidad del Valle de Guatemala, Guatemala.

Pasztory, Esther
1972 The Historical and Religious Significance of the Middle Classic Ballgame. In *Religión en Mesoamerica, XII Mesa Redonda of Sociedad Mexicana de Antropología*, edited by Jaime Lituak King and Noemi Castillo Tejero, pp. 441–455. Universidad de los Americas, Mexico City.

1978 Artistic Traditions of the Middle Classic Period. In *Middle Classic Mesoamerica A.D. 400–700*, edited by Esther Pasztory, pp. 108–142. Columbia University Press, New York.

Peacock, David P. S.
1982 *Pottery in the Roman World: An Ethnoarchaeological Approach.* Longman, London.

Pellecer Alecio, Monica
2006 El Grupo Jabalí: Un complejo arquitectónico de patrón tríadico en San Bartolo, Petén. In *XIX Simposio de investigaciones arqueológicas en Guatemala, 2005,* edited by Juan Pedro Laporte, Bárabara Arroyo, and Héctor Mejia, pp. 1018–1030. Museo Nacional de Arqueología y Etnología, Ministerio de Cultura y Deportes, Instituto de Antropología e Historia, and Asociación Tikal, Guatemala City.

Pendergast, David
1979 *Excavations at Altun Ha, Belize, 1964–1970,* Vol. 1. Royal Ontario Museum Publications in Archaeology, Toronto.
1981 Lamanai, Belize: Summary of Excavation Results, 1974–1980. *Journal of Field Archaeology* 8: 29–53.

Peniche May, Nancy
2008a Industria molida y pulida: Los artefactos de piedras ígneas y metamórficas. In *Informe del proyecto salvamento arqueológico en áreas de crecimiento urbano de la ciudad de Mérida, Yucatán, etapa Ciudad Caucel (2004–2006),* edited by Fernando Robles Castellanos and Josep Ligorred Perramon. Report submitted to the Instituto Nacional de Antropología e Historia, Mexico.
2008b La obsidiana de la esquina noroeste de Yucatán. In *Informe del proyecto salvamento arqueológico en áreas de crecimiento urbano de la ciudad de Mérida, Yucatán, etapa Ciudad Caucel (2004–2006),* edited by Fernando Robles Castellanos and Josep Ligorred Perramon. Report submitted to the Instituto Nacional de Antropología e Historia, Mexico.
2008c La industria lítica: Análisis formal y temporal. In *Informe del proyecto salvamento arqueológico en áreas de crecimiento urbano de la ciudad de Mérida, Yucatán, etapa Ciudad Caucel (2004–2006),* edited by Fernando Robles Castellanos and Josep Ligorred Perramón, pp. 3378–3464. Report submitted to the Instituto Nacional de Antropología e Historia, Mexico.
2009 El caso de Xaman Susulá: Un sitio Preclásico en el norte de Yucatán. Paper presented at the 74th Society for American Archaeology Annual Meeting, Atlanta.
2010 The Architecture of Power and Sociopolitical Complexity in Northwestern Yucatan during the Preclassic Period. Unpublished Master's thesis, Department of Anthropology, University of California, San Diego.
2016 Building Power: Political Dynamics in Cahal Pech, Belize during the Middle Preclassic. Unpublished Ph.D. dissertation, Department of Anthropology, University of California, San Diego.

Peniche May, Nancy, Mónica E. Rodríguez Pérez, and Teresa Ceballos Gallareta
2009 La funcion de un edificio del periodo Preclásico: La estructura 1714 de Xaman Susulá. *Los Investigadores de la Cultura Maya* 17(2): 253–264.

Peraza Lope, Carlos, Pedro Delgado Ku, and Bárbara Escamilla Ojeda
2002 Intervenciones en un edificio del preclásico medio en Tipikal, Yucatán. *Los Investigadores de la Cultura Maya* 10(1): 263–276.

Pereira, Karen

2008   Plain, but not Simple: Monuments at Naranjo, Guatemala. Unpublished Master's thesis, Department of Anthropology, University of Florida, Gainesville.

Pires-Ferreira, Jane W.

1976   Shell and Iron-Ore Mirror Exchange in Formative Mesoamerica, with Comments on Other Commodities. In *The Early Mesoamerican Village*, edited by Kent V. Flannery, pp. 311–328. Academic Press, New York.

1978   Shell Exchange Networks in Formative Mesoamerica. In *Cultural Continuity in Mesoamerica*, edited by David L. Browman, pp. 79–100. Mouton Publishers, Paris.

Pitcavage, Megan R.

2009   Investigacion del muro defensivo y acceso a la calzada La Danta en El Mirador 2008: Operaciones 130-A-F. In *Investigaciones multidisciplinarias en El Mirador: Informe final de la temporada 2008, Vol. 1 & II*, edited by Héctor E. Mejia, Richard D. Hansen, and Edgar Suyuc-Ley, pp. 613–620. Report submitted to the Instituto de Antropología e Historia, Guatemala.

Pohl, Mary D.

1983   Maya Ritual Faunas: Vertebrate Remains from Burials, Caches, Caves, and Cenotes in the Maya Lowlands. In *Civilization in the Ancient Americas: Essays in Honor of Gordon R. Willey*, edited by Richard M. Leventhal and Alan L. Kolata, pp. 55-103. University of New Mexico Press, Alburquerque.

1990   Summary and Proposals for Future Research. In *Ancient Maya Wetland Agriculture: Excavations on Albion Island, Northern Belize*, edited by Mary D. Pohl, pp. 397–439. Westview Press, Boulder.

Pohl, Mary D., Kevin O. Pope, John G. Jones, John S. Jacob, Dolores R. Piperno, Susan D. France, David L. Lentz, John A. Gifford, Marie E. Danforth, and Kathryn Josserand

1996   Early Agriculture in the Maya Lowlands. *Latin American Antiquity* 7: 355–372.

Polaco, Oscar J.

1983   Restos de moluscos recientes y pleistocénicos procedentes de Loltún, Yucatán, México. In *Restos de moluscos y mamíferos cuaternarios procedentes de Loltún, Yucatán*, edited by Ticul Alvarez y Oscar J. Polaco, pp. 37–41. Cuaderno de Trabajo, No. 26. Departamento de Prehistoria, Instituto Nacional de Antropología e Historia, Mexico.

Ponciano, Erick, and Carolina Foncea

1988   *Reporte Final de Investigaciones Arqueológicas y Rescate Montículo D-III-10, Kaminaljuyu, Guatemala*. Report submitted to the Instituto de Antropología e Historia, Guatemala.

Pool, Christopher A.

2007   *Olmec Archaeology and Early Mesoamerica*. Cambridge University Press, Cambridge.

Pope, Kevin O., Mary D. Pohl, John G. Jones, David L. Lentz, Christopher von Nagy, Francisco J. Vega, and Ivry R. Quitmyer
2001   Origin and Environmental Setting of Ancient Agriculture in the Lowlands of Mesoamerica. *Science* 292: 1370–1373.

Popenoe de Hatch, Marion
1997   *Kaminaljuyu/San Jorge. Evidencia arqueológica de la actividad económica en el Valle de Guatemala, 300 a.C. a 300 d.C.* Universidad del Valle de Guatemala, Guatemala.
1999   La agricultura Precolombina en el altiplano de Guatemala y la vitalidad Maya. *Estudios Sociales* 59: 231–238.
2002   New Perspectives on Kaminaljuyu, Guatemala: Regional Interaction During the Preclassic and Classic Periods. In *Incidents of Archaeology in Central America and Yucatan, Essays in Honor of Edwin M. Shook,* edited by Michael Love, Marion Popenoe de Hatch, and Héctor L. Escobedo, pp. 277–296. University Press of America, Lanham.

Potter, Dan R.
1991   A Descriptive Taxonomy of Middle Preclassic Chert Tools at Colha, Belize. In *Maya Stone Tools: Selected Papers from the Second Maya Lithic Conference,* edited by Thomas R. Hester and Harry J. Shafer, pp. 21–30. Monographs in World Archaeology, No. 1. Prehistory Press, Madison.

Powis, Terry G. (editor)
1995   *New Perspectives on Formative Mesoamerican Cultures.* BAR International Series 1377. British Archaeological Reports, Oxford.

Powis, Terry G.
1996   Excavations of Middle Preclassic Period Round Structures at the Tolok Group, Cahal Pech, Belize. Unpublished Master's thesis, Department of Anthropology, Trent University, Peterborough.
2004   Ancient Lowland Maya Utilization of Freshwater Pearly Mussels (*Nephronais* spp.). In *Maya Zooarchaeology: New Directions in Method and Theory,* edited by Kitty Emery, pp. 125–140. Cotsen Institute of Archaeology, Monograph 51. University of California, Los Angeles.
2009   *Pacbitun Preclassic Project: Report of the 2008 Field Season.* Report submitted to the Belize Institute of Archaelogy, Belmopan.
2010   *Pacbitun Preclassic Project: Progress Report of the 2009 Field Season.* Report submitted to the Belize Institute of Archaelogy, Belmopan.

Powis, Terry G., Paul F. Healy, and Bobbi M. Hohmann
2009   An Investigation of Middle Preclassic Structures at Pacbitun, Belize. *Research Reports in Belizean Archaeology* 6: 169–178.

Powis, Terry G., Norbert Stanchly, Christine White, Paul F. Healy, Jaime J. Awe, and Fred Longstaffe
1999   A Reconstruction of Middle Preclassic Maya Subsistence Economy at Cahal Pech, Belize. *Antiquity* 73: 1–13.

Powis, Terry G., Fred Valdez Jr., Thomas R. Hester, W. Jeffrey Hurst, and Stanley M. Tarka Jr.
2002   Spouted Vessels and Cacao Use Among the Preclassic Maya. *Latin American Antiquity* 13: 85–106.

Price, Barbara

1974   The Burden of Cargo: Ethnographical Models and Archaeological Inference. In *Mesoamerican Archaeology: New Approaches*, edited by Norman Hammond, pp. 445–465. University of Texas Press, Austin.

1984   Competition, Productive Intensification, and Ranked Society: Speculations from Evolutionary Theory. In *Warfare, Culture, and Environment*, edited by R. Brian Ferguson, pp. 209–240. Academic Press, New York.

Pring, Duncan C.

1977   The Preclassic Ceramics of Northern Belize. Unpublished Ph.D. dissertation, Department of Anthropology, University of London.

Proskouriakoff, Tatiana

1960   Historical Implications of a Pattern of Dates at Piedras Negras, Guatemala. *American Antiquity* 25: 454–475.

1962   The Artifacts of Mayapan. In *Mayapan, Yucatán, Mexico*, edited by Harry E. D. Pollack, Ralph L. Roys, Tatiana Proskouriakoff, and A. Ledyard Smith. Carnegie Institution of Washington, Publication 619. Carnegie Institution of Washington, Washington, D.C.

1963   Historical Data in the Inscriptions of Yaxchilan, Part 1. *Estudios de Cultura Maya* 3: 149–167.

1964   Historical Data in the Inscriptions of Yaxchilan, Part 2. *Estudios de Cultura Maya* 4: 177–201.

Prufer, Keith M., Mark Robinson, and Douglas J. Kennett

2017   New Evidence for Early Humans in Belize. Paper presented at the 15th Annual Belize Archaeology Symposium, San Ingracio, Belize.

Puleston, Dennis

1975   Richmond Hill: A Probable Early Man Site in the Maya Lowlands. *Actas del XLI Congreso Internacional de Americanistas* (Mexico 1974) 1: 522–33.

1976   Pre-Maya Hunters in Belize. *National Studies* 3(2): 8–23. [Reprinted in *Recent Archaeology in Belize*, edited by Richard S. Buhler, pp. 24–39. Belize Institute for Social Research and Action, Occasional Publications, No. 3.]

1977   The Art and Archaeology of Hydraulic Agriculture in the Maya Lowlands. In *Social Process in Maya Prehistory*, edited by Norman Hammond, pp. 449–467. Academic Press, New York.

1978   Terracing, Raised Fields, and Tree-Cropping in the Maya Lowlands: A New Perspective on the Geography of Power. In *Pre-Hispanic Maya Agriculture*, edited by Peter D. Harrison and Bruce L. Turner, pp. 225–245. University of New Mexico Press, Albuquerque.

Pyne, Nanette M.

1976   The Fire-Serpent and Were-Jaguar in Formative Oaxaca: A Contingency Table Analysis. In *The Earliest Mesoamerican Village*, edited by Kent V. Flannery, pp. 272–282. Academic Press, New York.

Rathje, William L.

1971   The Origins and Development of Lowland Classic Maya Civilization. *American Antiquity* 36: 275–285.

1972   Praise the Gods and Pass the Metates: A Hypothesis of the Development of Lowland Rainforest Civilizations in Mesoamerica. In *Contemporary Archaeology*, edited by Mark P. Leone, pp. 29–36. Southern Illinois University Press, Carbondale.

Ray, Clayton E.
1957   Pre-Columbian Horses from Yucatán. *Journal of Mammology* 38: 278.

Reents-Budet, Dorie
1994   *Painting the Maya Universe: Royal Ceramics of the Classic Period.* Duke University Press, Durham.
2006   Power Material in Ancient Mesoamerica: The Roles of Cloth Among the Classic Maya. In *Sacred Bundles: Ritual Acts of Wrapping and Binding in Mesoamerica*, edited by Julia Guernsey and F. Kent Reilly III, pp. 105–126. Boundary End Archaeological Research Center, Barnardsville.

Reents-Budet, Dorie, Ronald L. Bishop, Jennifer T. Taschek, and Joseph W. Ball.
2000   Out of the Palace Dumps: Ceramic Production and Use at Buenavista del Cayo. *Ancient Mesoamerica* 11: 99–121.

Reese-Taylor, Kathryn
2014   Yaxnohcah. Electronic document, http://people.ucalgary.ca/~kreeseta/research/yaxnohcah.html, accessed August 25, 2017.
2017   Founding Landscapes in the Central Karstic Uplands. In *Maya E Groups: Calendars, Astronomy, and Urbanism in the Early Lowlands*, edited by David A. Freidel, Arlen F. Chase, Anne S. Dowd, and Jerry Murdock, pp. 480–616. University Press of Florida, Tallahassee.

Reese-Taylor, Kathryn, and Debra Selsor Walker
2002   The Passage of the Late Preclassic into the Early Classic. In *Ancient Maya Political Economies,* edited by Marilyn A. Masson and David A. Freidel, pp. 87–122. Altamira Press, Walnut Creek.

Rehder, Harald A.
1981   *The Audubon Society Field Guide to North American Seashells.* Chanticleer Press, New York.

Reilly, F. Kent III
1989   The Shaman in Transformation Pose: A Study of the Theme of Rulership in Olmec Art. *Record of the Art Museum, Princeton University* 48(2): 4–21.
1991   Olmec Iconographic Influences on the Symbols of Maya Rulership: An Examination of Possible Sources. In *Sixth Palenque Round Table*, 1986, edited by Merle G. Robertson and Virginia M. Fields, pp. 151–166. University of Oklahoma Press, Norman.
1996   Art, Ritual, and Rulership in the Olmec World. In *The Olmec World: Ritual and Rulership*, edited by Jill Guthrie and Elizabeth P. Benson, pp. 27–45. The Art Museum, Princeton University, Princeton.
2005   Olmec Ideological, Ritual, and Symbolic Contributions to the Institution of Classic Maya Kingship. In *Lords of Creation: The Origins of Sacred Maya Kingship*, edited by Virginia M. Fields and Dorie Reents-Budet, pp. 30–36. Scala, London.
2006a   Middle Formative Origins of the Mesoamerican Ritual Act of Bundling. In *Sacred Bundles: Ritual Acts of Wrapping and Binding in Mesoamerica*, edited by Julia Guernsey and F. Kent Reilly III, pp. 1–21. Boundary End Archaeological Research Center, Barnardsville.

2006b Olmec Origins of Classic Maya Symbols of Rulership. In *Lords of Creation: The Origin of Divine Kingship amongst the Classic Maya*, edited by Virginia M. Fields and Dorie Reents-Budet, pp. 30–36. Scala, London.

Renfrew, Colin

1973 Monuments, Mobilization, and Social Organization in Neolithic Wessex. In *The Explanation of Cultural Change: Models in Prehistory*, edited by Colin Renfrew, pp. 539–558. University of Pittsburgh Press, Pittsburgh.

2008 The City through Time and Space: Transformations of Centrality. In *The Ancient City: New Perspectives on Urbanism in the Old and New World*, edited by Joyce Marcus and Jeremy A. Sabloff, pp. 29–52. School for Advanced Research Press, Santa Fe.

Rice, Don S.

1976 Middle Preclassic Settlement in the Central Maya Lowlands. *Journal of Field Archaeology* 3: 425–445.

Rice, Prudence M.

1979 Ceramic and Nonceramic Artifacts of Lakes Yaxha-Sacnab, El Peten, Guatemala. Part 1. The Ceramics. Section A, Introduction and the Middle Preclassic Ceramics of Yaxha-Sacnab, Guatemala. *Cerámica de Cultura Maya et al.* 10: 1–36.

1984 Obsidian Procurement in the Central Peten Lakes Region, Guatemala. *Journal of Field Archaeology* 11: 181–194.

1999 On the Origins of Pottery. *Journal of Archaeological Method and Theory* 6: 1–54.

2007 *Maya Calendar Origins: Monuments, Mythistory, and the Materialization of Time*. University of Texas Press, Austin.

2015 Middle Preclassic Interregional Interaction and the Maya Lowlands. *Journal of Archaeological Research* 23: 1–47.

Rich, Michelle E.

2011 Ritual, Royalty, and Classic Period Politics: The Archaeology of the Mirador Group at El Perú-Waka,' Petén, Guatemala. Unpublished Ph.D. dissertation, Department of Anthropology, Southern Methodist University, Dallas.

Rich, Michelle E., and David A. Freidel

n.d. The El Perú-Waka' Burial 39 Figurine Scene: The Importance of Archaeological Context and Potential of a Gendered Approach. In *Figurillas mesoamericanas: Contextos, representaciones y usos. Una mirada caleidoscópica*. Autonomous University of Yucatan, Mexico

Rich, Michelle E., David A. Freidel, F. Kent Reilly III, and Keith Eppich

2010 An Olmec-Style Figurine from El Perú-Waka,' Petén, Guatemala: A Preliminary Report. *Mexicon* 17: 115–122.

Rich, Michelle E., Varinia Matute, and Jennifer Piehl

2007 WK-11: Excavaciones en la Estructura O14-4. In *Proyecto Arqueológico El Perú-Waka': Informe No. 4, temporada 2006*, edited by Héctor L. Escobedo and David A. Freidel, pp. 217–257. Report submitted to the Instituto de Antropología e Historia, Guatemala.

Rich, Michelle E., Jennifer Piehl, and Varinia Matute

2006 WK-11A: Continuación de las excavaciones en el Complejo Mirador, Estructura O14-4. In *Proyecto Arqueológico El Perú-Waka': Informe No. 3, tempo-*

rada 2005, edited by Héctor L. Escobedo and David A. Freidel, pp. 225–274. Report submitted to the Instituto de Antropología e Historia, Guatemala.

Richie, Clarence J.
1990 Ancient Maya Settlement and Environment of the Eastern Zone of Pacbitun, Belize. Unpublished Master's thesis, Department of Anthropology, Trent University, Peterborough.

Ricketson, Oliver G. Jr.
1928 Astronomical Observatories in the Maya Area. *Geographical Review* 18: 215–225.

Ricketson, Oliver G. Jr. and Edith B. Ricketson
1937 *Uaxactun, Guatemala Group E: 1926–1931.* Carnegie Institution of Washington Publication 477. Carnegie Institution of Washington, Washington D.C.

Ringle, William M.
1985 The Settlement Patterns of Komchen, Yucatan, Mexico. Unpublished Ph.D. dissertation, Department of Anthropology, Tulane University, New Orleans.
1999 Pre-Classic Cityscapes: Ritual Politics among the Early Lowland Maya. In *Social Patterns in Pre-Classic Mesoamerica,* edited by David C. Grove and Rosemary A. Joyce, pp. 183–224. Dumbarton Oaks Research Library and Collection, Washington, D.C.

Ringle, William M., and E. Wyllys Andrews V
1988 Formative Residences at Komchen, Yucatan, Mexico. In *Household and Community in the Mesoamerican Past,* edited by Richard Wilk and Wendy Ashmore, pp. 171–197. University of New Mexico Press, Albuquerque.
1990 The Demography of Komchen, An Early Maya Town in Northern Yucatan. In *Precolumbian Population History in the Maya Lowlands,* edited by T. Patrick Culbert and Don S. Rice, pp. 215–243. University of New Mexico Press, Albuquerque.

Ringle, William M., and George J. Bey III
1989 *Preliminary Report on the Ruins of Ek Balam, Yucatan, Mexico: 1987 Field Season.* Report submitted to Instituto Nacional de Antropología e Historia, Mexico.
1994 *Report on the 1992 Field Season of the Proyect Ek Balam.* Report submitted to the Instituto Nacional de Antropología e Historia, Mexico.
1995 *Proyecto Ek Balam: Preliminary Report on the 1994 Field Season.* Report submitted to the Instituto Nacional de Antropología e Historia, Mexico.
1998 *Report on the 1995 Field Season of the Proyecto Ek Balam.* Report submitted to the Instituto Nacional de Antropología e Historia, Mexico.

Ringle, William, George J. Bey III, Tara Bond-Freeman, Craig Hanson, Charles Houck, and J. Gregory Smith
2004 The Decline of the East: The Classic to Postclassic Transition at Ek Balam, Yucatan. In *The Terminal Classic in the Maya Lowlands: Collapse, Transition, and Transformation,* edited by Arthur A. Demarest, Prudence M. Rice, and Don S. Rice, pp. 588–633. University of Colorado Press, Boulder.

Ringle, William M., George J. Bey III, and Tomás Gallareta Negrón
2014 Preclassic Monumentality in the Eastern Puuc Hill, Yucatan, Mexico. Paper presented at the 79th Annual Meeting of the Society for American Archaeology, Austin.

Ringle, William M., Tomás Gallareta Negrón, and George J. Bey III
1998   The Return of Queztalcoatl. *Ancient Mesoamerica* 9: 183–232.

Rissolo, Dominique, José Manuel Ochoa Rodríguez, and Joseph W. Ball
2005   A Reassessment of the Middle Preclassic in Northern Quintana Roo. In *Quintana Roo Archaeology,* edited by Justine M. Shaw and Jennifer P. Mathews, pp. 66–76. University of Arizona Press, Tucson.

Robertson, Robin A., and David A. Freidel (editors)
1986   *Archaeology at Cerros, Belize, Central America, Volume 1, An Interim Report.* Southern Methodist University, Dallas.

Robichaux, Hugh R.
1998   Excavations at the Upper Plaza. In *The 1997 Season of the Chan Chich Archaeological Project,* edited by Brett A. Houk, pp. 31–52. Papers of the Chan Chich Archaeological Project, No. 3. Center for Maya Studies, San Antonio.

Robin, Cynthia
1989   Preclassic Maya Burials at Cuello, Belize. BAR International Series 480. British Archaeological Reports, Oxford.

2000   Toward an Archaeology of Everyday Life: Maya Farmers of Chan Noohol and Dos Chombitos Cik'in, Belize. Unpublished Ph.D. dissertation, Department of Anthropology, University of Pennsylvania, Philadelphia.

Robin, Cynthia, and Norman Hammond
1991   Burial Practices. In *Cuello: An Early Maya Community in Belize,* edited by Norman Hammond, pp. 204–225. Cambridge University Press, Cambridge.

Robin, Cynthia, James Meierhoff, Caleb Kestle, Chelsea Blackmore, Laura J. Josakowsky, and Anna C. Novotny
2012   Ritual in a Farming Community. In *Chan: An Ancient Maya Farming Community,* edited by Cynthia Robin, pp. 113–132. University Press of Florida, Gainesville.

Robicsek, Francis, and Donald M. Hales
1981   *The Maya Book of the Dead: The Ceramic Codex; The Corpus of Codex Style Ceramics of the Late Classic Period.* University of Virginia Art Museum, Charlottesville.

Robles Castellanos, Fernando
1990   *La secuencia ceramica de la region de Coba, Quintana Roo.* Instituto Nacional de Antropología e Historia, Mexico.

1997   Tipología de la cerámica de la Gruta Loltún, Yucatán, que se encuentra en el Museo Peabody de la Universidad de Harvard. In *Homenaje al profesor César A. Sáenz,* edited by Ángel García Cook, Alba G. Mastache, Leona Merino, and Sonia Rivero Torres, pp. 251–317. Instituto Nacional de Antropología e Historia, Mexico.

2004   *Proyecto Arqueológico Poxilá, municipio de Umán, Yucatán (Temporada de campo 2003).* Report submitted to the Instituto Nacional de Antropología e Historia, Mexico.

2005   *Proyecto Arqueológico Poxilá, municipio de Umán, Yucatán (Temporada de campo 2004).* Report submitted to the Instituto Nacional de Antropología e Historia, Mexico.

Robles Castellanos, Fernando, and Anthony P. Andrews

2000 *Proyecto Costa Maya: Reporte interino, temporada 2000: Reconocimiento arqueológico de la esquina noroeste de la peninsula de Yucatán.* Report submitted to the Instituto Nacional de Antropología e Historia, Mexico.

2001 *Proyecto Costa Maya: Reporte interino, temporada 2001: Reconocimiento arqueológico de la esquina noroeste de la peninsula de Yucatán.* Report submitted to the Instituto Nacional de Antropología e Historia, Mexico.

2003 *Proyecto Costa Maya: Reporte interino, temporada 2002: Reconocimiento arqueológico de la esquina noroeste de la peninsula de Yucatán.* Report submitted to the Instituto Nacional de Antropología e Historia, Mexico.

Robles Castellanos, Fernando, Angeles Cantero Aguilar, and Antonio Benavides Rosales

2006 *Proyecto Arqueológico Poxilá, municipio Umán, Yucatán, temporada de campo 2005.* Report submitted to the Instituto Nacional de Antropología e Historia, Mexico.

Robles Castellanos, Fernando, and Teresa Ceballos Gallareta

2003 La cronoligía cerámica preliminar del noroeste de la península de Yucatán. In *Proyecto Costa Maya: Reporte interino, temporada 2002: Reconocimiento arqueológico de la esquina noroeste de la peninsula de Yucatán,* edited by Fernando Robles Castellanos and Anthony P. Andrews, pp. 38–45. Report submitted to the Instituto Nacional de Antropología e Historia, Mexico.

Robles Castellanos, Fernando, and Josep Ligorred Perramon (editors)

2008 *Informe del proyecto salvamento arqueológico en áreas de crecimiento urbano de la ciudad de Mérida, Yucatán, etapa Ciudad Caucel (2004–2006).* Report submitted to the Instituto Nacional de Antropología e Historia, Mexico.

Román, Edwin

2005 Excavaciones en la penúltima versión de la pirámide de Las Pinturas: Plataforma Yaxche y Estructura Ixim. In *Proyecto Regional Arqueológico San Bartolo: Informe preliminar No. 4, cuarta temporada 2005,* edited by Mónica Urquizú and William Saturno, pp. 34–58. Report submitted to the Instituto de Antropología e Historia, Guatemala.

2008 Excavaciones en la Estructura Ixim. In *Proyecto Regional Arqueológico San Bartolo: Informe preliminar No. 7, séptima temporada 2008,* edited by Mónica Urquizú and William Saturno, pp. 34–58. Report submitted to the Instituto de Antropología e Historia, Guatemala.

Rosenswig, Robert M.

2001 Preceramic Evidence from Northern Belize and Caye Coco. In *The Belize Postclassic Project 2000: Investigations at Caye Coco and the Shore Settlements of Progresso Lagoon,* edited by Robert M. Rosenswig and Marilyn A. Masson, pp. 87–93. Institute of Mesoamerican Studies Occasional Publication, No. 6. The State University of New York, Albany.

2004 The Late Archaic Occupation of Northern Belize: New Archaeological Excavation Data. *Research Reports in Belizean Archaeology* 1: 267–277.

2010 *The Beginning of Mesoamerican Civilization: Inter-Regional Interaction and the Olmec.* Cambridge University Press, Cambridge.

Rosenswig, Robert M., and Marilyn A. Masson
2001   Seven New Preceramic Sites Documented in Northern Belize. *Mexicon* 23: 138–140.
Rosenswig, Robert M., Amber M. VanDerwarker, Brendan J. Culleton, Douglas J. Kennett
2015   Is It Agriculture Yet? Intensified Maize-use at 1000 cal BC in the Soconosco and Mesoamerica. *Journal of Anthropological Archaeology* 40: 89–108.
Rossi, Franco, William A. Saturno, and Heather Hurst
2015   Maya Codex Book Production and the Politics of Expertise: Archaeology of a Classic Period Household at Xultun, Guatemala. *American Anthropology* 117: 116–132.
Rothman, Mitchell S.
2001   The Local and the Regional: An Introduction. In *Uruk Mesopotamia and Its Neighbors*, edited by Mitchell S. Rothman. School of American Research Press, Santa Fe.
Rovner, Irwin
1980   Comment on Bray's "An Eighteenth Century Reference to a Fluted Point from Guatemala." *American Antiquity* 45: 165–167.
Rovner, Irwin, and Suzanne M. Lewenstein
1997   *Maya Stone Tools of Dzibilchaltún, Yucatán, and Becán and Chicanná, Campeche*. Middle American Research Institute Publication 65. Tulane University, New Orleans.
Roys, Lawrence, and Edwin M. Shook
1966   *Preliminary Report on the Ruins of Aké, Yucatan*. Memoirs of the Society for American Anthropology, No. 20. Society for American Anthropology, Salt Lake City.
Roys, Ralph L.
1957   *The Political Geography of the Yucatan Maya*. Carnegie Institution of Washington Publication 613. Carnegie Institution of Washington, Washington D.C.
Rue, David
1989   Archaic Middle American Agriculture and Settlement: Recent Pollen Data from Honduras. *Journal of Field Archaeology* 16: 177–184.
Ruiz de Alcarcon, Hernando
1984   *Treatise on the Heathen Superstitions that Today Live among the Indians Native to this New Spain, 1629*. Translated and edited by J. Richard Andrews and Ross Hassig. University of Oklahoma Press, Norman.
Runggaldier, Astrid
2009   Memory and Materiality in Monumental Architecture: Construction and Reuse of a Late Preclassic Maya Palace at San Bartolo, Guatemala. Unpublished Ph.D. dissertation, Department of Archaeology, Boston University, Boston.
Ruppert, Karl, and John H. Denison Jr.
1943   *Archaeological Reconnaissance in Campeche, Quintana Roo, and Petén*. Carnegie Institution of Washington Publication 543. Carnegie Institution of Washington, Washington, D.C.
Rust, William F. III
1992   New Ceremonial and Settlement Evidence at La Venta, and Its Relation to

Preclassic Maya Cultures. In *New Theories on the Ancient Maya*, edited by Elin C. Danien and Robert J. Sharer, pp. 123–129. University Museum Monograph 77. The University Museum, University of Pennsylvania, Philadelphia.

Rust, William F., and Barbara W. Leyden
1994   Evidence of Maize Use at Early and Middle Preclassic La Venta Olmec Sites. In *Corn and Culture in the Prehistoric New World*, edited by Sissel Johannessen and Christine A. Hastorf, pp. 181–202. Westview Press, Boulder.

Rust, William F., and Robert J. Sharer
1988   Olmec Settlement Data from La Venta, Tabasco, Mexico. *Science* 242: 102–104.

Sabloff, Jeremy
1975   Ceramics. In *Excavations at Seibal, Department of Peten, Guatemala*. Memoirs of the Peabody Museum of Archaeology and Ethnology, Vol. 13, No. 2. Harvard University, Cambridge.

Sahlins, Marshall
1972   *Stone Age Economics*. Aldine, New York.

Salvin, Carolyn
2000   *Un paraíso: Diarios Guatemaltecos, 1873–1874/A Pocket Eden: Guatemalan Journals, 1873–1874*. Plumsock Mesoamerican Studies, South Woodstock.

Sanders, William T.
1960   Prehistoric Ceramics and Settlement Patterns in Quintana Roo, Mexico. *Contributions to American Anthropology and History*, Vol. 12, No. 60: 155–264. Carnegie Institution of Washington, Washington, D.C.

Sanders, William T., and Carson Murdy
1982   Cultural Evolution and Ecological Succession in the Valley of Guatemala: 1500 B.C.–A.D. 1524. In *Maya Subsistence. Studies in Memory of Dennis E. Puleston*, edited by Kent V. Flannery, pp. 19–63. Academic Press, New York.

Sanders, William T., and David Webster
1988   The Mesoamerican Urban Tradition. *American Anthropologist* 90: 521–546.

Saraydar, Stephen, and Izumi Shimada
1971   A Quantitative Comparison of Efficiency between a Stone Axe and a Steel Axe. *American Antiquity* 36: 216–217.
1973   Experimental Archaeology: A New Outlook. *American Antiquity* 38: 344–350.

Saturno, William A.
2006   The Dawn of Maya Gods and Kings. *National Geographic* 1: 69–77.
2009   Centering the Kingdom, Centering the King: Maya Creation and Legitimization at San Bartolo. In *The Art of Urbanism: How Mesoamerican Kingdoms Represented Themselves in Architecture and Imagery*, edited by William L. Fash and Leonardo López Luján, pp. 111–134. Dumbarton Oaks Research Library and Collection, Washington, D.C.

Saturno, William A., David Stuart, and Boris Beltrán
2006   Early Maya Writing at San Bartolo, Guatemala. *Science* 311: 1281–1283.

Saturno, William A., Karl A. Taube, David Stuart, and Heather Hurst
2005   *The Murals of San Bartolo, El Peten, Guatemala. Part 1: The North Wall*. Ancient America, Vol. 7, Center for Ancient American Studies, Barnardsville.

Saxe, Arthur A., and Henry T. Wright
1966 Terracing in the Maya Mountains of British Honduras: A Test Excavation at Cubetas Viejas. Paper presented at the 31st Annual Meeting of the Society for American Archaeology, Reno.

Scarborough, Vernon L., and John E. Clark
2007 Introduction. In *The Political Economy of Ancient Mesoamerica: Transformations during the Formative and Classic Periods*, edited by Vernon L. Scarborough and John E. Clark, pp. 1–10. University of New Mexico Press, Albuquerque.

Scarborough, Vernon L., Robert P. Connolly, and Steven P. Ross.
1994 The Pre-Hispanic Maya Reservoir System at Kinal, Peten, Guatemala. *Ancient Mesoamerica* 5: 97–106.

Scarborough, Vernon L., and David R. Wilcox (editors)
1991 *The Mesoamerican Ballgame.* University of Arizona Press, Tucson.

Scheffler, Timothy E.
2001 Research Report on the Proyecto Cueva El Gigante–2000, La Paz, Honduras. *Mexicon* 23: 115–123.

Schele, Linda
1974 Observations on the Cross Motif at Palenque. In *Primera Mesa Redonda de Palenque Part I*, edited by Merle G. Robertson, pp. 41–62. Pre-Columbian Art Research, Pebble Beach.

Schele, Linda, and David A. Freidel
1990 *A Forest of Kings: The Untold Story of the Ancient Maya.* William Morrow, New York.

Schele, Linda, and Peter Mathews
1998 *The Code of Kings: The Language of Seven Sacred Maya Temples and Tombs.* Scribner, New York.

Schele, Linda, and Mary Ellen Miller
1986 *The Blood of Kings: Dynasty and Ritual in Maya Art.* George Braziller, New York.

Schellhas, Paul
1904 *Representation of Deities of the Maya Manuscripts.* Papers of the Peabody Museum of American Archaeology and Ethnology, Vol. 4, No. 1. Harvard University, Cambridge.

Schieber de Lavarreda, Christa
1994 A Middle Preclassic Clay Ball Court at Abaj Takalik, Guatemala. *Mexicon* 16: 77–84.

Schmidt, Peter J.
1988 La entrada del hombre en la península de Yucatán. In *Orígenes del Hombre Americano*, edited by Alba González Jácome, pp. 245–261. Secretaría de Educación Pública, Mexico.

Schreiner, Thomas
1992 Possible Sources of Red Sandstone Used for Tintal Stela 01.00: Progress Re-

port. Manuscript on file with Foundation for Anthropological Research and Environmental Studies, Rupert, Idaho.

1998 Fabricación de la cal en Mesoamerica: Implicaciones para el Preclásico Maya. Paper presented at the XII Simposio de investigaciones arqueologicas en Guatemala, Guatemala City.

2000a Maya Use of Vegetal and Mineral Additives to Architectural Lime Products. Paper presented at the 32nd Archaeometry International Symposium, Mexico City.

2000b Social and Environmental Impacts of Mesoamerican Lime Burning. *Estudios del Cuaternario* 20(3): 170.

2000c Fabricación de cal en Mesoamerica: Implicaciones para los Mayas Preclásicos de Nakbe, Peten. In *Investigaciones arqueológicas y ecológicas en la cuenca Mirador, 1998: Informe de la temporada de campo*, edited by Richard D. Hansen and Judith Valle, pp. 645–669. Report submitted to the Instituto de Antropología e Historia, Guatemala.

2001 Fabricación de cal en Mesoamerica: Implicaciones para los Mayas del Preclásico en Nakbe, Peten. In *XIV Simposio de investigaciones arqueologicas en Guatemala*, edited by Juan Pedro Laporte, Ana C. de Suasnavar, and Bárbara Arroyo, pp. 405–418. Museo Nacional de Arqueología y Etnología, Ministerio de Cultura y Deportes, Instituto de Antropología e Historia, and Asociación Tikal, Guatemala City.

2002 Traditional Maya Lime Production: Environmental and Cultural Implications of a Native American Technology. Unpublished Ph.D. dissertation, Department of Architecture, University of California, Berkeley.

2003 Aspectos rituales de la producción de cal en Mesoamérica: Evidencias y perspectivas de las tierras bajas Mayas. In *XVI Simposio de investigaciones arqueológicas en Guatemala*, edited by Juan Pedro Laporte, Bárbara Arroyo, Héctor L. Escobedo, Héctor E Mejía, pp. 487–494. Museo Nacional de Arqueología y Etnología, Ministerio de Cultura y Deportes, Instituto de Antropología e Historia, and Asociación Tikal, Guatemala City.

2007 Traditional Lime Production in the Maya Lowlands. Paper presented at the 72nd Annual Meeting of the Society for American Archaeology, Austin.

Schuster, Angela

2000 Tomb of King of Snake Gourd. *Archaeology Magazine* 53(3): 18.

Schwake, Sonya

1996 Ancestors among the Thorns: The Burials of Zubin, Cayo District, Belize. In *Social Archaeology Research Program: Progress Report of the Second (1996) Season*, edited by Gyles Iannone, pp. 84–105. Trent University, Peterborough.

Service, Elman

1962 *Primitive Social Organization: An Evolutionary Perspective*. Random House, New York.

1975   *Origins of the State and Civilization: The Process of Cultural Evolution.* W. W.
            Norton, New York.

Shafer, Harry J., and Thomas R. Hester
1983   Ancient Maya Chert Workshops in Northern Belize, Central America. *American Antiquity* 48: 519–543.

Sharer, Robert J.
1978   Pottery. In *The Prehistory of Chalchuapa, El Salvador, Vol. 3, Pottery and Conclusions*, edited by Robert J. Sharer, pp. 1–203. University Museum, University of Pennsylvania Press, Philadelphia.

Sharer, Robert J., and James C. Gifford
1970   Preclassic Ceramics from Chalchuapa, El Salvador, and Their Relationships with the Maya Lowlands. *American Antiquity* 35: 441–462.

Sharer, Robert J., and David C. Grove
1989   *Regional Perspectives on the Olmec.* Cambridge University, Cambridge.

Sharer, Robert J., and Loa P. Traxler
2006   *The Ancient Maya.* 6th ed. Stanford University Press, Palo Alto.

Shaw, Justine M. (editor)
2002   Informe final del Proyecto Arqueológico Yo´okop, temporada del 2002: Excavaciones y continuación del mapeo. Report on file at the College of the Redwoods, Eureka, CA.

Shaw, Justine M.
2015   *The Maya of the Cochuah Region: Archaeological and Ethnographic Perspectives.* University of New Mexico Press, Albuquerque.

Shelton, Rebecca
2008   A Contextual Analysis of a Preclassic Problematic Deposits at Blackman Eddy, Belize. Unpublished Master's thesis, Department of Anthropology, University of Texas, Arlington.

Sholes, Frances V., and Dave Warren
1965   The Olmec Region at Spanish Contact. In *Handbook of Middle American Indians, Vol. 3: Archaeology of Southern Mesoamerica,* edited by Gordon R. Willey, pp. 776–787. University of Texas Press, Austin.

Shook, Edwin M.
1951   The Present Status of Research on the Preclassic Horizons in Guatemala. In *The Civilizations of Ancient America. Selected Papers of the XXIX International Congress of Americanists,* edited by Sol Tax, pp. 93–100. University of Chicago Press, Chicago.
1952   Lugares arqueológicos en el Altiplano Meridional Central de Guatemala. *Antropología e Historia de Guatemala* 4(2): 3–40.
1955   Yucatan and Chiapas. *Carnegie Institution of Washington Yearbook* 54: 289–295.

Shook, Edwin M., and Marion Popenoe de Hatch
1999   Las tierras altas central: Periodos Preclásico y Clásico. In *Historia General de Guatemala,* Vol. 1, edited by Marion Popneoe de Hatch and Jorge Lujan, pp. 289–318. Fundación para la Cultura y el Desarrollo, Guatemala.

Sidrys, Raymond V.
1976   Mesoamerica: An Archaeological Analysis of a Low-Energy Civilization.
            Unpublished Ph.D. dissertation, Department of Anthropology, University of
            California, Los Angeles.
1978   Megalithic Architecture and Sculpture of the Ancient Maya. In *Papers on the
            Economy and Architecture of the Ancient Maya*, edited by Raymond V. Sidrys,
            pp. 155–183. Institute of Archaeology, Monograph 8. University of California,
            Los Angeles.

Sierra Sosa, Thelma, and Leticia Vargas de la Peña
1995   Investigaciones arqueológicas en el trazo de la supercarretera Mérida-Can-
            cún. Paper presented at the Congreso Interno del Centro Yucatán of the In-
            stituto Nacional de Antropología e Historia, Mérida.

Smailes, Richard L.
2011   Building Chan Chan: A Project Management Perspective. *Latin American
            Antiquity* 22: 37–63.

Smith, A. Ledyard
1950   *Uaxactun, Guatemala: Excavations of 1931–1937*. Carnegie Institution of
            Washington Publication 588. Carnegie Institution of Washington, Washing-
            ton, D.C.

Smith, Adam T.
2003   *The Political Landscape: Constellations of Authority in Early Complex Polities*.
            University of California Press, Berkeley.

Smith, J. Gregory
2000   The Chichen Itza-Ek Balam Transect Project: An Intersite Perspective on the
            Political Organization of the Ancient Maya. Unpublished Ph.D. disstertation,
            Department of Anthropology, University of Pittsburgh.

Smith, Robert E.
1955   *Ceramic Sequence at Uaxactun, Guatemala, Vol. 2*. Middle American Re-
            search Institute Publication 20. Tulane University, New Orleans.
1971   *The Pottery of Mayapan: Including Studies of Ceramic Material from Uxmal,
            Kabah, and Chichen Itza*. Papers of the Peabody Museum of Archaeology and
            Ethnology, Vol. 66. Harvard University, Cambridge.

Smyth, Michael P., and David Ortegón Zapata
2008   A Preclassic Center in the Puuc Region: A Report on Xcoch, Yucatan, Mexico.
            Mexicon 30: 63–68.

Smyth, Michael P., David Ortegón Zapata, Nicholas P. Dunning, and Eric Weaver
2014   Settlement Dynamics, Climate Change, and Human Response at Xcoch in the
            Puuc, Region of Yucatán, Mexico. In *The Archaeology of Yucatán: New Direc-
            tions and Data*, edited by Travis W. Stanton, pp. 45–64. Archaeopress, Oxford.

Song, Rhanju
1995   Bones and Bowls of the Preclassic Maya: Preliminary Report on the Human
            Skeletal Remains from Cahal Pech, Belize and the Implications for Mortuary
            Behavior. In *Belize Valley Preclassic Maya Project: Report on the 1994 Field
            Season*, edited by Paul F. Healy and Jaime J. Awe, pp. 173–197. Occasional
            Papers in Anthropology, No. 10. Trent University, Peterborough.

Spencer, Charles S.
1979   Irrigation, Administration, and Society in Formative Tehuacan Valley. In *Prehistoric Social, Political, and Economic Development in the Area of the Tehuacan Valley*, edited by Robert D. Drennan, pp. 13–109. University of Michigan Museum, Ann Arbor.
1993   Human Agency, Biased Transmission, and the Cultural Evolution of Chiefly Authority. *Journal of Anthropological Archaeology* 9: 1–30.

Spencer, Charles S., and Elsa Redmond
2004   Primary State Formation in Mesoamerica. *Annual Review of Anthropology* 33: 173–199.

Spinden, Herbert J.
1957   *Maya Art and Civilization*. Falcon's Wing Press, Colorado.

Sprajc, Ivan, and Vicente Suarez Aguilar
2003   Reconocimiento arqueologico en el sureste del Estado de Campeche, Mexico: Temporada 1998. In *Cuarto Congreso Internacional de Mayistas: Memoria: 2 al 8 agosto de 1998*, edited by Mario H. Ruz, pp. 492–505. Universidad Nacional Autónoma de México, Mexico.

Stanchly, Norbert
1995   Preclassic Period Maya Faunal Utilization at Cahal Pech, Belize: Preliminary Analysis of the Animal Remains from the 1994 Field Season. In *Belize Valley Preclassic Maya Project: Report on the 1994 Field Season*, edited by Paul F. Healy and Jaime J. Awe, pp. 124–149. Occasional Papers in Anthropology, No. 10. Trent University, Peterborough.

Stanish, Charles
2004   The Evolution of Chiefdoms: An Economic Anthropological Model. In *Archaeological Perspectives on Political Economies*, edited by Gary M. Feinman and Linda M. Nicholas, pp. 7–24. University of Utah Press, Salt Lake City.

Stanton, Travis W.
2012   The Rise of Formative Period Complex Societies in the Northern Maya Lowlands. In *Oxford Handbook of Mesoamerican Archaeology*, edited by Deborah L. Nichols and Christopher A. Pool, pp. 268–282. Oxford University Press, Oxford.

Stanton, Travis W., and Traci Ardren
2005   The Middle Formative of Yucatan in Context: The View from Yaxuna. *Ancient Mesoamerica* 16: 213–228.

Stanton, Travis W., and David A. Freidel
2003   Ideological Lock-In and the Dynamics of Formative Religions in Mesoamerica. *Mayab* 16: 5–14.
2005   Placing the Centre, Centring the Place: The Influence of Formative Sacbeob in Classic Site Design at Yaxuná, Yucatán. *Cambridge Archaeological Journal* 15: 225–249.

Stanton, Travis W., David A. Freidel, Charles K. Suhler, Traci Ardren, James N. Ambrosino, Justine M. Shaw, and Sharon Bennett
2010   *Archaeological Investigations Yaxuná, 1986–1996: Results of the Selz Foundation Yaxuna Project*. Archaeopress, Oxford.

Stanton, Travis W., and Tomás Gallareta Negrón.
2002   *Proyecto Xocnacéh. 1ª Temporada de Campo.* Report submitted to the Instituto
           Nacional de Antropología e Historia, Mexico.

Stark, Barbara
2007   Out of Olmec. In *The Political Economy of Ancient Mesoamerica: Transformations
           during the Formative and Classic Periods*, edited by Vernon L. Scarborough and
           John E. Clark, pp. 47–64. University of New Mexico Press, Albuquerque.

Stemp, W. James, and Jaime J. Awe
2013   Possible Variation in Late Archaic Period Bifaces in Belize: New Finds from
           the Cayo District of Western Belize. *Lithic Technology* 38: 17–31.

Stemp, W. James, Jaime J. Awe, and Christophe G. B. Helmke
2016   A Possible Paleoindian/Early Archaic Point from Ladyville, Belize, Central
           America. *PaleoAmerica* 2: 70–73.

Stemp, W. James, Jaime J. Awe, Keith M. Prufer, and Christophe G. B. Helmke
2016   Design and Function of Lowe and Sawmill Points from the Preceramic Period
           of Belize. *Latin American Antiquity* 27: 279–299.

Stocker, Terry, Sarah Meltzoff, and Steve Armsey
1980   Crocodillians and Olmecs: Further Interpretations in Formative Period
           Iconograpy. *American Antiquity* 45: 740–758.

Storey, Rebecca
2004   Ancestors: Bioarchaeology of the Human Remains of K'axob. In *K'axob:
           Ritual, Work, and Family in an Ancient Maya Village*, edited by Patricia A.
           McAnany, pp. 109–138. The Cotsen Institute of Archaeology, University of
           California, Los Angeles.

Strelow, Duane, and Lisa LeCount
2001   Regional Interaction in the Formative Southern Maya Lowlands: Evidence of
           Olmecoid Stylistic Motifs in a Cunil Ceramic Assemblage from Xunantunich,
           Belize. Poster presented at the 66th Annual Meeting of the Society for Ameri-
           can Archaeology, New Orleans.

Stross, Fred H., Frank Asaro, Helen V. Michel, and Ruth Gruhn
1977   Sources of Some Obsidian Flakes from a Paleo-American Site in Guatemala.
           American Antiquity 42: 114–118.

Stuart, Anthony J., Pavel A. Kosintsev, Thomas F. G. Higham, and Adrain M. Lister
2004   Pleistocene to Holocene Extinction Dynamics in Giant Deer and Wooly
           Mammoth. *Nature* 431: 684–689.

Stuart, David
1998   "The Fire Enters His House": Architecture and Ritual in Classic Maya Texts.
           In *Function and Meaning in Classic Maya Architecture*, edited by Stephen D.
           Houston, pp. 373–425. Dumbarton Oaks Research Library and Collection,
           Washington, D.C.

2000   The Arrival of Strangers: Teotihuacan and Tollan in Classic Maya History.
           In *Mesoamerica's Classic Heritage: From Teotihuacan to the Aztecs*, edited by
           David Carrasco, Lindsay Jones, and Scott Sessions, pp. 565–613. University of
           Colorado Press, Boulder.

2005   *The Inscriptions from Temple XIX at Palenque: A Commentary.* The Pre-

Columbian Art Research Institute Research Library and Collection, San Francisco.

2006 Jade and Chocolate: Bundles of Wealth in Classic Maya Economics and Ritual. In *Sacred Bundles: Ritual Acts of Wrapping and Binding in Mesoamerica*, edited by Julia Guernsey and F. Kent Reilly III, pp. 127–144. Boundary End Archaeological Research Center, Barnardsville.

2010 Shining Stones: Observations on the Ritual Meaning of Early Maya Stelae. In *The Place of Sculpture in Mesoamerica's Preclassic Transition: Context, Use, and Meaning*, edited by Julia Guernsey, John E. Clark, and Barbara Arroyo. Dumbarton Oaks Research Library and Collection, Washington, D.C.

2012 Notes on a New Text from La Corona. *Maya Decipherment*. Electronic document, http://decipherment.wordpress.com/2012/06/30/notes-on-a-new-text-from-la-corona/, accessed August 25, 2017.

Stuart, David, and Stephen D. Houson

1994 *Classic Maya Place Names*. Studies in Pre-Columbian Art and Archaeology, No. 33. Dumbarton Oaks Research Library and Collection, Washington, D.C.

Stuiver, Minze, and Paula J. Reimer

1993 Extended ^{14}C Database and Revised CALIB 3.0 ^{14}C Age Calibration Program. *Radiocarbon* 35: 215–230.

Suhler, Charles K.

1996 Excavations at the North Acropolis, Yaxuna, Yucatan, Mexico. Unpublished Ph.D. dissertation, Department of Anthropology, Southern Methodist University, Dallas.

Suhler, Charles K., Traci Ardren, and David Johnstone

1998 The Chronology of Yaxuna: Evidence from Excavation and Ceramics. *Ancient Mesoamerica* 9: 176–182.

Suhler, Charles K., and David A. Freidel

1998 Life and Death in a Maya War Zone. *Archaeology* 51(3): 28–34.

Sullivan, Lauren A., and Jaime J. Awe

2013 Establishing the Cunil Ceramic Complex at Cahal Pech, Belize. In *Ancient Maya Pottery: Classification, Analysis, and Interpretation*, edited by James J. Aimers, pp. 107–120. University Press of Florida, Gainesville.

Sullivan, Lauren A., Jaime J. Awe, and M. Kathryn Brown

2009 Refining the Cunil Ceramic Complex at Cahal Pech Belize. *Research Reports in Belizean Archaeology* 6: 161–168.

Sunahara, Kay S.

1995 Ancient Maya Settlement: The Western Zone of Pacbitun, Belize. Unpublished Master's thesis, Department of Anthropology, Trent University, Peterborough.

Sunahara, Kay S., and Jaime J. Awe

1994 A Slice Through Time: 1993 Investigations at the Cas Pek Group, Cahal Pech. In *Belize Valley Archaeological Reconnaissance Project: Progress Report of the Sixth Field Season*, edited by Jaime J. Awe, pp. 193–210. Institute of Archaeology, University of London.

Suyuc-Ley, Edgar, Ana Luisa Arriola, and Enrique Hernandez
2006   Excavaciones en el Grupo La Pava, Complejo Danta, Operacion 402. In *In-vestigacion y conservación en los sitios arqueologicos El Mirador, La Muerta, Wakna, El Porvenir, El Guiro, La Iglesia, La Sarteneja, Chib Che' y La Ceibita: Informe final de la temporada 2005*, edited by Edgar Suyuc-Ley and Richard D. Hansen, pp. 493–522. Report submitted to the Instituto de Antropología e Historia, Guatemala.

Taladoire, Eric
1981   *Les terrains de jeu de balle (Mésoamérique et Sud-ouest des Etats-Unis)*. Etudes Mesoamericaines, Vol. 2, No. 4. Mission Archeologique et Ethnologique Française au Mexique, Mexico.
2003   Could We Speak of the Super Bowl at Flushing Meadows?: La Pelota Mixteca, a Third Pre-Hispanic Ballgame, and Its Possible Architectural Context. *Ancient Mesoamerica* 14: 319–342.

Taladoire, Eric, and Benoit Colsenet
1991   "Bois Ton Sang, Beaumanoir": The Political and Conflictual Aspects of the Ballgame in the Northern Chiapas Area. In *The Mesoamerican Ballgame*, edited by Vernon L. Scarborough and David R. Wilcox, pp. 161–174. University of Arizona Press, Tucson.

Tambiah, Stanley J.
2013   The Galactic Polity in Southeast Asia. *Journal of Ethnographic Theory* 3: 503–534.

Taschek, Jennifer T.
1994   *The Artifacts of Dzibilchaltun, Yucatan, Mexico: Shell, Polished Stone, Bone, Wood, and Ceramics*. Middle American Research Institute Publication 50. Tulane University, New Orleans.

Taube, Karl A.
1995   The Rainmakers: The Olmec and Their Contribution to Mesoamerican Belief and Ritual. In *The Olmec World: Ritual and Rulership*, edited by Jill Guthrie and and Elizabeth P. Benson, pp. 83–103. The Art Museum, Princeton University, Princeton.
1996   The Olmec Maize God: The Face of Corn in Formative Mesoamerica. *RES: Anthropology and Aesthetics* 29/30: 39–81.
1998   The Jade Hearth: Centrality, Rulership, and the Classic Maya Temple. In *Function and Meaning in Classic Maya Architecture*, edited by Stephen D. Houston, pp. 437–478. Dumbarton Oaks Research Library and Collection, Washington, D.C.
2004a   Flower Mountain: Concepts of Life, Beauty, and Paradise among the Classic Maya. *RES: Anthropology and Aesthetics* 45: 69–98.
2004b   *Olmec Art at Dumbarton Oaks*. Dumbarton Oaks Research Library and Collection, Washington, D.C.
2009   The Womb of the World: The Cuauhxicalli and Other Offering Bowls of Ancient and Contemporary Mesoamerica. *Maya Archaeology* 1: 86–106.

Taube, Karl A., William A. Saturno, David Stuart, and Heather Hurst
2010   *The Murals of San Bartolo, El Petén, Guatemala. Part 2: The West Wall*. Ancient America, Vol. 10. Center for Ancient American Studies, Barnardsville.

Taylor, Michael Ray
2000   *Caves: Exploring Hidden Realms.* National Geographic Society, Washington, D.C.

Tec Pool, Fátima del Rosario
2004   Análisis arqueológico de la estructura CA-13 del Grupo Ah Canal, de Oxkintok, Yucatán, México. Unpublished Licenciatura thesis, Department of Anthropology, Universidad Autónoma de Yucatán, Merida.

Tedlock, Dennis
1985   *Popul Vuh: The Mayan Book of the Dawn of Life.* Simon & Schuster, New York.
1996   *Popol Vuh: The Definitive Edition of the Mayan Book of the Dawn of Life and Glories of Gods and Kings.* 2nd ed. Simon & Schuster, New York.

Thompson, J. Eric S.
1950   *Maya Hieroglyphic Writing: An Introduction.* University of Oklahoma Press, Norman.

Tiesler, Vera, Andrea Cucina, Travis W. Stanton, and David A. Freidel
2017   *Before Kukulcán: Bioarchaeology of Maya Life, Death, and Identity at Classic Period Yaxuná.* University of Arizona Press, Tuscon.

Titmus, Gene L., and James C. Woods
1996a   Un estudio arqueológico y experimental de las canteras antiguas de Nakbe, Petén, Guatemala. Paper presented at the X Simposio de investigaciones arqueologicas en Guatemala. Museo Nacional de Arqueología y Etnología, Guatemala City.
1996b   Las antiguas canteras de piedra caliza en Nakbe, Petén, Guatemala. Manuscript on file with the Foundation for Anthropological Research & Environmental Studies, Rupert, Idaho.
2000   Un estudio arqueologico y experimental de las canteras antiguas de Nakbe, Petén, Guatemala. In *Investigaciones arqueologicas y ecológicas en la cuenca Mirador, 1998: Informe de la temporada de campo,* edited by Richard D. Hansen and Judith Valle, pp. 266–296. Report submitted to the Instituto de Antropología e Historia, Guatemala.

Tomasic, Johnand Steven Bozarth
2011   New Data from a Preclassic Tomb at K'o, Guatemala. Paper presented at the 76th Annual Meeting of the Society for American Archaeology, Sacramento.

Tozzer, Alfred M.
1941   *Landa's Relacion de las Cosas de Yucatan.* Papers of the Peabody Museum of American Archaeology and Ethnology, Vol. 17. Harvard University, Cambridge.

Turner, Bruce L. II
1974   Prehistoric Intensive Agriculture in the Mayan Lowlands. *Science* 185: 118–124.
1978   Prehispanic Terracing in the Central Maya Lowlands: Problems of Agricultural Intensification. In *Maya Archaeology and Ethnohistory,* edited by Norman Hammond and Gordon R. Willey, pp. 103–115. University of Texas Press, Austin.

Turner, Bruce L., II, and Peter D. Harrison
1983   *Pulltrouser Swamp: Ancient Maya Habitat, Agriculture, and Settlement in Northern Belize.* University of Texas Press, Austin.

Turner, Victor
1967   *The Forest of Symbols.* Cornell University Press, Ithaca, New York.
1977   Symbols in African Ritual. In *Symbolic Anthropology: A Reader in the Study of Symbols and Meanings,* edited by Janet L. Dolgin, David S. Kemnitzer, and David M. Schneider, pp. 183–194. Columbia University Press, New York.

Uriarte, María Teresa (editor)
1992   *El juego de pelota en Mesoamérica: Raíces y supervivencia.* Siglo Veintiuno Editores, Mexico.

Uriarte Torres, Alejandro J.
2011   Estrategias políticas y organización espacial durante el Formativo en Ciudad Caucel, Yucatán. Unpublished Master's thesis, Department of Anthropology, Colegio de Michoacán, Mexico.

Uriarte Torres, Alejandro J., and Román Mier Aragón
2004   El sitio 16Qd(4): 49 y el desarrollo cultural de los asentamientos menores en el noroeste de Yucatán. *Los Investigadores de la Cultura Maya* 12(2): 332–347.

Valdés, Juan Antonio
1986   Uaxactún: Recientes investigaciones. *Mexicon* 8: 125–128.

Valdés, Juan Antonio, and Federico Fahsen
1995   The Reigning Dynasty of Uaxactun during the Early Classic: The Rulers and the Ruled. *Ancient Mesoamerica* 6: 197–291.

Valdés, Juan Antonio, Frederico Fahsen, and Héctor L. Escobedo
1999   *Reyes, tumbas y palacios: La historia dinástica de Uaxactún.* Centro de Estudios Mayas, Universidad Nacional Autónoma de México, Mexico.

Valdez, Fred Jr.
1987   *The Prehistoric Ceramics of Colha, Northern Belize.* Unpublished Ph.D. dissertation, Department of Anthropology, Harvard University, Cambridge.

Valdez, Fred Jr., Laura J. Kosakowsky, Lauren A. Sullivan, and Duncan Pring
2008   The Earliest Ceramics of Belize: A Comparative Analysis. Paper presented at the 73rd Annual Meeting of the Society for American Archaeology, Vancouver.

Van Bussel, Gerard W., Paul L. F. van Dongen, and Ted J. J. Leyenaar (editors)
1991   *The Mesoamerican Ballgame: Papers Presented at the International Colloquium 'The Mesoamerican Ballgame 2000 BC–AD 2000.'* Rijksmuseum voor Volkenkunde, Leiden.

Van der Leeuw, Sander
1977   Towards a Study of the Economics of Pottery Making. In *Ex Horreo,* edited by B. L. van Beek, R. W. Brant, and Willy Gruenman van Watteringe, pp. 68–76. Albert Egges van Giffen Instituut voor Prae-en Protohistorie, University of Amsterdam, Amsterdam.

Vargas, Ernesto
2001   Itzamkanac y Acalan. Tiempos de crisis anticipando el futuro. Unpublished Ph.D. dissertation, Instituto de Investigaciones Arqueológicas, Universidad Nacional Autónoma de México, Mexico.

Vargas de la Pena, Leticia

2005   Hallazgos recientes en Ek' Balam. *Arqueologia Mexicana* 13(76): 56–63.

Vargas de la Pena, Leticia, and Victor R. Castillo Borges

1999   Ek' Balam: Ciudad que empieza a revelar sus secretos. *Arqueologia Mexicana* 7(37): 24–31.

Vaughn, Hague H., Edward S. Deevey, and S. E. Garrett-Jones

1985   Pollen Stratigraphy of Two Cores from the Petén Lake District, with an Appendix on Two Deep Water Cores. In *Prehistoric Lowland Maya Environment and Subsistence Economy,* edited by Mary D. Pohl, pp. 73–89. Harvard University Press, Cambridge.

Velásquez, Juan Luis

1993a   Excavaciones en la Estructura 31 de Nakbe, Peten. In *III Simposio de arqueología Guatemalteca,* edited by Juan Pedro Laporte, Héctor L. Escobedo, Sandra V. de Brady, pp. 87–98. Museo Nacional de Arqueología y Etnología, Ministerio de Cultura y Deportes, Instituto de Antropología e Historia, and Asociación Tikal, Guatemala City.

1993b   Aspectos Constructivos durante el Preclásico en Nakbe y su Cerámica Asociada. In *VI Simposio de Investigaciones Arqueológicas en Guatemala, 1992,* edited by Juan Pedro Laporte, Hector L. Escobedo, Sandra V. de Brady, pp. 123–130. Museo Nacional de Arqueología y Etnología, Ministerio de Cultura y Deportes, Instituto de Antropología e Historia, Asociación Tikal, Guatemala City.

2005   *Proyecto Arqueológico La Trinidad.* Report submitted to the Instituto de Antropología e Historia, Guatemala.

Velázquez Valadéz, Ricardo

1980   Recent Discoveries in the Caves of Loltún, Yucatan, Mexico. *Mexicon* 2: 53–55.

1981   Etapas de funcionalidad de las Grutas de Loltún. In *Memoria del Congreso Interno 1979,* pp. 139–144. Centro Regional del Sureste, Instituto Nacional de Antropología e Historia, Mexico.

Vesilind, Priit J.

2003   Watery Graves of the Maya. *National Geographic* 204(4): 82–101.

Villacorta, Carlos A.

1927   Versitigos de un edificio arcaico, Miraflores, Kaminaljuyu. *Anales de la Sociedad de Geografía e Historia de Guatemala* 4: 51–64.

Villamil, Laura

2009   *Ancient Maya Cityscapes: Insights from Lagartera and Margarita, Quintana Roo, Mexico.* BAR International Series 1955. British Archaeological Reports, Oxford.

Vogt, Evon Z.

1964   Some Implications of Zinacantan Social Structure for the Study of the Ancient Maya. In *XXXV Congreso Internacional de Americanistas* 1: 307–319.

1966   H'iloletik: The Organization and Function of Shamanism in Zinacantan. In *Summa antropologica en Homenaje a Roberto J. Weitlander,* edited by Antonio

Pompa y Pompa, pp. 359–369. Instituto Nacional de Antropología e Historia, Mexico.

von Nagy, Christopher L.

2003   Of Meandering Rivers and Shifting Towns: Landscape Evolution and Community within the Grijalva Delta. Unpublished Ph.D. dissertation, Department of Anthropology, Tulane University, New Orleans.

von Nagy, Christopher L., Mary D. Pohl, and Kevin O. Pope

2002   Ceramic Chronology of the La Venta Olmec Polity: The View from San Andrés, Tabasco. Paper presented at the 67th Annual Meeting of the Society for American Archaeology, Denver.

Voorhies, Barbara

1975   Los conchales de la Zona Chantuto, Chiapas, Mexico. In *13th Mesa Redonda de la Sociedad Mexicana de Antropología*, pp. 1–10. Sociedad Mexicana de Antropología, Mexico.

1976   *The Chantuto People: An Archaic Period Society of the Chiapas Littoral, Mexico*. Papers of the New World Archaeological Foundation, No. 41. Brigham Young University, Provo.

2002   A Middle Archaic Archaeological Site on the West Coast of Mexico. *Latin American Antiquity* 13: 179–200.

2004   *Coastal Collectors of the Holocene. The Chantuto People of Southwestern Mexico*. University Press of Florida, Gainesville.

Voorhies, Barbara, George H. Michaels, and George M. Riser

1991   An Ancient Shrimp Fishery in South Coastal Mexico. *National Geographic Research* 7(1): 20–35.

Voorhies, Barbara, Douglas J. Kennett, John G. Jones, and Thomas A. Wake

2002   A Middle Archaic Archaeological Site of the West Coast of Mexico. *Latin American Antiquity* 13: 179–200.

Wahl, David

2005   Climate Change and Human Impacts in the Southern Maya Lowlands: A Paleoecological Perspective from the Northern Peten, Guatemala. Unpublished Ph.D. dissertation, Deptartment of Geography, University of California, Berkeley.

Wahl, David, Thomas Schreiner, and Roger Byrne

2005   La secuencia paleo-ambiental de la cuenca Mirador en Petén. In *XVIII Simposio de investigaciones arqueológicas en Guatemala*, edited by Juan Pedro Laporte, Barbara Arroyo, Hector E. Mejia, pp. 53–58. Museo Nacional de Arqueología y Etnología, Ministerio de Cultura y Deportes, Instituto de Antropología e Historia, and Asociación Tikal, Guatemala City.

Wahl, David, Roger Byrne, Thomas Schreiner, and Richard Hansen

2006   Holocene Vegetation Change in the Northern Peten and Its Implications for Maya Prehistory. *Quaternary Research* 65: 380–389.

Wahl, David, Thomas Schreiner, Roger Byrne, and Richard Hansen

2007   A Paleoecological Record from a Maya Reservoir in the North Peten. *Latin American Antiquity* 18: 212–222.

Wason, Paul K.

1994   *The Archaeology of Rank*. Cambridge University Press, Cambridge.

Webb, Clarence H.

1977   *The Poverty Point Culture*. Geoscience and Man, Vol. 17. School of Geoscience, Lousiana State University, Baton Rouge.

Webster, David

1976   *Defensive Earthworks at Becan, Campeche, Mexico*. Middle American Research Institute Publication 41. Tulane University, New Orleans.

1992   Maya Elites: The Perspective from Copán. In *Mesoamerican Elites: An Archaeological Assessment*, edited by Diane Z. Chase and Arlen F. Chase, pp. 135–156. University of Oklahoma Press, Norman.

Webster, Gary S.

1990   Labor Control and Emergent Stratification in Prehistoric Europe. *Current Anthropology* 31: 185–197.

Weigand, Phil C.

1991   The Western Mesoamerican Tlachco: A Two-Thousand-Year Perspective. In *The Mesoamerican Ballgame*, edited by Vernon L. Scarborough and David R. Wilcox, pp. 73–86. University of Arizona Press, Tucson.

Wells, E. Christian, and Karla L. Davis-Salazar (editors)

2007   *Mesoamerican Ritual Economy: Archaeological and Ethnological Perspectives*. University of Colorado Press, Boulder.

Whalen, Michael E., and Paul E. Minnis

1996   Ball Courts and Political Centralization in the Casas Grandes Region. *American Antiquity* 6: 732–746.

Wheatley, Paul

1971   *The Pivot of the Four Quarters: An Enquiry into the Origins and Character of the Ancient Chinese City*. Aldine, Chicago.

White, Christine D., Fred Longstaffe, and Rhanju Song

1996   Preclassic Maya Diet at Cahal Pech, Belize: The Isotopic Evidence. Paper presented at the 61st Annual Meeting of the Society for American Archaeology, New Orleans.

Whittington, E. Michael (editor)

2001   *The Sport of Life and Death: The Mesoamerican Ballgame*. Thames and Hudson, London.

Widmer, Randolph J.

2009   Elite Household Multicrafting Specialization at 9N8, Patio H, Copan. In *Housework: Specialization, Risk and Domestic Craft Production in Mesoamerica, Archaeological Papers of the American Anthropological Association, Vol. 19*, edited by Kenneth G. Hirth, pp. 174–204. American Anthropological Association, Washington, D.C.

Wier, Stuart Kirkland

1996   Insight from Geometry and Physics into the Construction of Egyptian Old Kingdom Pyramids. *Cambridge Archaeological Journal* 6: 150–163.

Wilkerson, S. Jeffrey K.

1985   Observations on the Archaic Period of the Caribbean Coast: A Summary of the 1980 Belize Archaeological Reconnaissance Project. In *Fourth Palenque Round Table, 1980*. Vol. 4, edited by Merle G. Robertson and Elizabeth P. Benson, pp. 277–280. Pre-Columbian Art Research Institute, San Francisco.

Willey, Gordon R. (editor)

1982   *Excavations at Seibal, Department of Peten, Guatemala*. Memoirs of the Peabody Museum of Archaeology and Ethnology, Vol. 15. Harvard University, Cambridge.

Willey, Gordon R.

1970   Type Descriptions of the Ceramics of the Real E Complex, Seibal, Peten, Guatemala. In *Monographs and Papers in Maya Archaeology*, edited by William R. Bullard Jr., pp. 313–355. Papers of the Peabody Museum of Archaeology and Ethnology, Vol. 61. Harvard University, Cambridge.

1972   *The Artifacts of Altar de Sacrificios*. Papers of the Peabody Museum of Archaeology and Ethnology, Vol. 62, No. 1. Harvard University, Cambridge.

1973   *The Altar de Sacrificios Excavations: General Summary and Conclusions*. Papers of the Peabody Museum of Archaeology and Ethnology, Vol. 64, No. 3.

1977   The Rise of Maya Civilization: A Summary View. In *The Origins of Maya Civilization*, edited by Richard E. W. Adams, pp. 383–423. University of New Mexico Press, Albuquerque.

1978   *Artifacts. Excavations at Seibal, Department of Peten, Guatemala*. Memoirs of the Peabody Museum, Vol. 14, No. 1. Harvard University, Cambridge.

1984   Changing Conceptions of Lowland Maya Culture History. *Journal of Anthropological Research* 40: 44–59.

Willey, Gordon R., William R. Bullard Jr., John B. Glass, and James C. Gifford

1965   *Prehistoric Maya Settlements in the Belize Valley*. Papers of the Peabody Museum of Archaeology and Ethnology, Vol. 54. Harvard University, Cambridge.

Willey, Gordon R., A. Ledyard Smith, Gair Tourtellot III, and Ian Graham

1975   Introduction: The Site and Its Setting. In *Excavations at Seibal, Department of Peten, Guatemala*. Memoirs of the Peabody Museum of Archaeology and Ethnology, Vol. 13, No. 1. Harvard University, Cambridge.

Williamson, George

1877   *Antiquities in Guatemala*. Smithsonian Institute, Washington, D.C.

Wilson, Samuel M., Harry B. Iceland, and Thomas R. Hester

1998   Preceramic Connections between Yucatán and the Caribbean. *Latin American Antiquity* 9: 342–352.

Woodbury, Richard B., and James A. Neely

1972   Water Control Systems of the Tehuacán Valley. In *Prehistory of the Tehuacan Valley: Chronology and Irrigation, Vol. 4*, edited by Frederick Johnson. University of Texas Press, Austin.

Woods, James C., and Gene L. Titmus

1994   Piedra en piedra: Perspectivas de la civilización Maya através de los estudios líticos. In *VII Simposio arqueológico de Guatemala*, edited by Juan Pedro Laporte, Héctor L. Escobedo, and Sandra V. de Brady, pp. 349–368. Museo Nacional de Arqueología y Etnología, Ministerio de Cultura y Deportes, Instituto de Antropología e Historia, and Asociación Tikal, Guatemala City.

1996   Stone on Stone: Perspectives of Maya Civilization from Lithic Studies. In

Eighth Palenque Round Table, 1993, edited by Merle G. Robertson, Martha J. Macri, and Jan McHargue, pp. 479–489. Pre-Columbian Art Research Institute, San Francisco.

Wright, Henry T.

1984   Prestate Political Formations. In *On the Evolution of Complex Societies: Essays in Honor of Harry Hoijer,* edited by Timothy K. Earle, pp. 43–77. Undena, Malibu.

Wyshak, Lillian W., Rainer Berger, John A. Graham, and Robert F. Heizer

1971   A Possible Ball Court at La Venta, Mexico. *Nature* 232: 650–651.

Xelhuantzi-López, María Susana

1986   *Estudio palinolinológico del perfil estratigráfico de la Unidad "El Toro," Grutas de Loltún, Yucatán.* Cuaderno de Trabajo 31, Departamento de Prehistoria, Instituto Nacional de Antropología e Historia, Mexico.

Xolocotzi, Efraín Hernandez, Eduardo Bello Baltazar, and Samuel Levy Tacher

1995   La milpa en Yucatán: Un sistema de producción agrícola tradicional. Colegio de Postgraduados, Instituto Nacional de Antropología e Historia, Mexico City.

Zeitlin, Robert N.

1984   A Summary Report on Three Seasons of Field Investigations into the Archaic Period Prehistory of Lowland Belize. *American Anthropologist* 86: 358–369.

CONTRIBUTORS

Mary Jane Acuña received a Licenciatura degree in archaeology from Universidad de San Carlos de Guatemala in 2005, a Master's degree in Latin American studies from the University of Texas at Austin in 2007, and a Ph.D. in anthropology from Washington University in St. Louis in 2013. Since 1998, she has been an active archaeologist in Guatemala at sites in the Motagua Valley and Peten, including El Peru-Waka,' La Corona, and El Achiotal. In 2014 she initiated and continues to direct the El Tintal Archaeological Project. Her research focuses on questions related to regional politics and interactions during the Preclassic period in the southern Maya lowlands.

David S. Anderson is an instructor of archaeology at Radford University. He completed his Ph.D. at Tulane University in 2010. His research focuses on the Preclassic site of Xtobo, the emergence of social complexity in the northern Maya lowlands, and the nature of the ballgame in the Preclassic period.

Anthony P. Andrews holds a Ph.D. from the University of Arizona and is a professor of anthropology at New College. He has published extensively on the Maya of the northern lowlands and is a preeminent scholar on the Postclassic and Historic periods. His monograph on the role of salt in Maya prehistory is considered a classic.

E. Wyllys Andrews V is Professor Emeritus of Anthropology at Tulane University, where he was director of the Middle American Research Institute and a professor in the Department of Anthropology from 1975 until 2009. He has conducted field research in the southeastern and southwestern United States, Mexico, Guatemala, El Salvador, and Honduras. His work at Komchen opened the way for the modern study of the rise of civilization in the northern Maya lowlands. He developed the ceramic typology which remains the standard for understanding the Preclassic period in northern Yucatan and also carried out extensive research on a Late Classic royal residence at the site of Copan.

Barbara Arroyo holds a Ph.D. from Vanderbilt University. Currently she is the coordinator from the Kaminaljuyu Archaeological Zone at the Instituto de Antropología e Historia in Guatemala. Her research has focused on the Preclassic in the Maya Highlands. She conducted research at the site of Naranjo, documenting early ritual behavior of the ancient Maya. Currently she has an active research program at Kaminaljuyu, Guatemala.

Jaime J. Awe received his Ph.D. from the University of London. He is currently an associate professor of anthropology at Northern Arizona University. His dissertation research documented the Preclassic Maya of Cahal Pech and was the foundation for future studies on the early Maya in the Belize valley. He has published numerous articles on Cahal Pech, Baking Pot, and the caves of Western Belize. He has also completed several documentaries. Currently, he is directing the Belize Valley Archaeological Reconnaissance Project.

Boris Beltrán is an archaeologist specializing in the ancient Maya and the archaeology of Precolumbian Guatemala and Honduras. He is also co-director of the San Bartolo/Xultun Regional Archaeological Project. A graduate of the University of San Carlos of Guatemala, his work draws from his investigations across a variety of sites including El Motagua Medio, El Zotz, El Tintal, and Río Amarillo. His research at San Bartolo has been especially integral to questions of the evolution of E-Group complexes and the origins of writing.

George J. Bey III holds a Ph.D. from Tulane University. He is currently a professor of anthropology at Millsaps College, Associate Dean of International Education, and Chisholm Foundation Chair in Arts and Sciences. His research has focused on the early Maya in the northern Maya lowlands. He has studied the ceramics of both Central Mexico and the northen Maya lowlands and co-directed a long-term project at Ek Balam. He is presently one of the co-directors of the Bolonchen Regional Archaeological Project where he has focused his efforts on studying the site Maya site of Kiuic.

Tara Bond-Freeman holds a Ph.D. from Southern Methodist University and is currently an independent scholar with a research focus on the Preclassic period in the northern Maya lowlands. In particular, she has studied ceramics from the northern Maya lowlands from the Preclassic to the Colonial periods from Ek Balam and many other sites in the region. In addition to working in the northern Maya lowlands, she has worked and analyzed ceramics from the historical period in the southeastern United States.

M. Kathryn Brown is the Lutcher Brown Endowed Associate Professor of Anthropology at the University of Texas at San Antonio. Her research focuses on the rise of complexity in the Maya lowlands and role of ritual and ceremonial architecture in the Preclassic period. She is currently the director of the Mopan Valley Preclassic Project and co-director of the Mopan Valley Archaeological Project.

She has focused her recent investigations at the site of Xunantunich, Belize. She is the coeditor of *Ancient Mesoamerican Warfare*.

Teresa Ceballos Gallareta is a senior archaeologist with Mexico's National Institute of Anthropology and History (INAH). She has carried out projects for the past 20 years at the sites of Xcambo and Ek Balam. She has also directed innumerable salvage projects in the area around Merida as well as in Campeche and Quintana Roo. She is an expert in the study of Maya ceramics and has published internationally on her research.

David Freidel holds a Ph.D. from Harvard University and is currently Professor of Anthropology at Washington University. He is directing a long-term research project at the ancient Maya city of El Perú, Waka' in northwestern Peten, Guatemala. He has numerous publications and is co-author of *Maya Cosmos*. His foundational research at the ancient Maya site of Cerros focused on the rise of complexity and the development of ancient Maya kingship.

Donald W. Forsyth holds a Ph.D. from the University of Pennsylvania and is currently Professor of Anthropology at Brigham Young University. He specializes in early ceramics in Mesoamerica and the rise of complexity.

Tomás Gallareta Negrón completed his Ph.D. at Tulane University and is a senior archaeologist for Mexico's National Institute of Anthropology and History (INAH). Recognized as an expert in settlement archaeology, he has also directed excavations at a number of major Maya centers. He is currently senior director of the Bolonchen Regional Archaeological Project (BRAP).

James F. Garber holds a Ph.D. from Southern Methodist University and is Professor of Anthropology at Texas State University. He was the Project Director of the Belize Valley Archaeology Project (BVAP) for over two decades focusing his research on the social and political landscape of the Belize valley. He directed excavations at the site of Blackman Eddy and Cahal Pech, documenting some of the earliest buildings found to date in the Maya lowlands.

Christopher M. Gunn specializes in ceramic analysis, and completed his Ph.D. at the University of Kentucky in 2015. His research interests include prehistoric economies, households, political economy, and archaeometry. A member of the Bolonchen Regional Archaeological Project, his research most recently explored the stability and change in household ceramic exchange systems during the Late and Terminal Classic periods of the Puuc site of Kiuic.

Richard D. Hansen holds a Ph.D. in archaeology from UCLA and is currently Adjunct Professor of Anthropology at the University of Utah. He is the founder and president of the Foundation for Anthropological Research and Environmental Studies (FARES). and is the director of the Mirador Basin Project, a large scale multidisciplinary project in northern Guatemala. He has authored hundreds of reports, book chapters, and articles as well as three books, including *Mirador: Research and Conservation in the Ancient Kaan Kingdom* (with Edgar Suyuc), and "The Cultural and Environmental Components of the First Maya States: A Perspective from the Central and Southern Maya Lowlands" (in *The Origins of Maya States*, edited by L.P. Traxler and R. J. Sharer). His research has identified some of the largest and earliest ancient Maya cities, and his work has contributed greatly to the understanding of the developmental history of Maya civilization.

Paul F. Healy holds a Ph.D. from Harvard University and is currently Professor Emeritus of anthropology at Trent University. He has numerous publications and has excavated sites in Mexico (Tehuacan Valley) and in Belize (Moho Cay, Caracol, Caledonia, Pacbitun, and Cahal Pech). His interests also include the archaeology of the Intermediate Area of Lower Central America, having worked in Honduras and Nicaragua and also in the Caribbean (Antigua and Trinidad).

Bobbi Hohmann holds a Ph.D. from the University of New Mexico. She is currently the Vice President of Programming and Collections, Curator, and Archaeologist at Fernbank Museum of Natural History. Her research has focused on craft production and marine shell ornaments in the Preclassic period. Her dissertation work at the Maya site of Pacbitun documented some of the earliest evidence for intensive craft production in the form of marine shell beads.

Terry G. Powis holds a Ph.D. from the University of Texas at Austin and is currently Associate Professor of Anthropology at Kennesaw State University. He is the director of the Pacbitun Regional Archaeology Project. He was editor of *New Perspectives on Formative Mesoamerican Cultures* BAR International Series.

Fernando Robles Castellanos holds a Ph.D. from Harvard University and is a senior archaeologist for Mexico's National Institute of Anthropology and History (INAH). He a leading scholar on Maya ceramics and the rise of social complexity in the northern Maya lowlands and is presently director of the Proyecto Costa Maya.

Franco D. Rossi is an archaeologist and epigrapher specializing in the Precolumbian Americas, with a focus on politics of literacy, art and architecture of Maya peoples. His research draws from work he conducted at the sites of Xultun and San Bartolo in Northeastern Guatemala as a part of the San Bartolo/Xultun Regional Archaeological Project. His current work investigates broader questions of how writing, expertise, and science education were managed in ever-evolving systems of ancient Mesoamerican statecraft.

William Saturno holds a Ph.D. from Harvard University. He is the director of the Proyecto San Bartolo Project. His recent discoveries of the oldest intact painted murals in the Maya lowlands has greatly broadened our understanding of Preclassic Maya iconography and ideology.

Thomas P. Schreiner earned his Ph.D. in anthropology from the University of California Berkeley in 2002. His research focuses on lime production among the ancient Maya. He is a member of the Mirador Basin Project.

Lauren A. Sullivan received her Ph.D. at the University of Texas at Austin. She is a Senior Lecturer II and the General Education Intermediate Seminar Coordinator at the University of Massachusetts at Boston. Her main research focus is on pottery in order to gain a better understanding of the establishment and collapse of social hierarchies and how these processes are expressed in the archaeological record. Lauren is the ceramicist for the Programme for Belize Archaeological Project where she conducts pottery analysis on a number of different sites in northwestern Belize. She has also analyzed pottery from a number of sites in the Belize River valley focusing on the Preclassic period.

Gene L. Titmus was a renowned scholar of lithic studies in Mesoamerica and North America. He was honored with the Don E. Crabtree award given by the Society for American Archaeology. He was a Research Associate for the Herrett Center for Arts and Science and was a member of the RAINPEG project in Guatemala.

James C. Woods received his Master's degree in anthropology from the Idaho State University and currently teaches at the College of Southern Idaho. His research focuses on ancient technologies, in particular lithics. He is a member of the Mirador Basin Project.

INDEX

Page numbers in *italics* refer to illustrations.

CPSIA information can be obtained
at www.ICGtesting.com
Printed in the USA
LVOW12*2140180218

566957LV00004B/6/P